KAYANERENKÓ:WA
THE GREAT LAW OF PEACE

KAYANERENKÓ:WA
THE GREAT LAW OF PEACE

Kayanesenh Paul Williams

UMP

UNIVERSITY OF MANITOBA PRESS

Kayanerenkó:wa: The Great Law of Peace
© Kayanesenh Paul Williams 2018

29 28 27 26 25   6 7 8 9 10

University of Manitoba Press
Winnipeg, Manitoba, Canada
Treaty 1 Territory
uofmpress.ca

For EU product safety concerns please contact Mare Norstrum Group
B.V., Mauritskade 21D, 1091 GC Amsterdam, The Netherlands,
gpsr@mare-norstrum.co.uk.

Cataloguing data available from Library and Archives Canada
ISBN 978-0-88755-821-4 (PAPER)
ISBN 978-0-88755-193-2 (CLOTH)
ISBN 978-0-88755-556-5 (PDF)
ISBN 978-0-88755-554-1 (EPUB)

Cover design by Kirk Warren
Cover art by Arnold Jacobs
Interior design by Karen Armstrong

All photographs of wampum in this book are reproduced
with Haudenosaunee permission.

Printed in Canada

This book has been published with the help of a grant from the
Federation for the Humanities and Social Sciences, through the Awards
to Scholarly Publications Program, using funds provided by the
Social Sciences and Humanities Research Council of Canada.

The University of Manitoba Press acknowledges the financial support for
its publication program provided by the Government of Canada through
the Canada Book Fund, the Canada Council for the Arts, the Manitoba
Department of Sport, Culture, and Heritage, the Manitoba Arts Council,
and the Manitoba Book Publishing Tax Credit.

Funded by the Government of Canada | Canadä

Contents

PART III Bringing the Great Peace 143

About Names

To name something or someone is an act of power. In Genesis, God gave Adam authority to name the animals. The naming confirmed dominion over them. European explorers all over the world renamed places, mountains, and waters after their own people, eclipsing original names and the peoples who gave them. The people who provided the information and inspiration for this book often had several names in the course of their lifetimes. For the Haudenosaunee, people's personal names have coexisted with their European names for more than three centuries. Today, it is common to refer to "real names" and "English names," using the former for some purposes and the latter for others.

To use only English names would disrespect people's identities. To use only their Haudenosaunee names would lead to confusion when it came time to cite their publications or quote from historical accounts of their deeds and words.

My solution has been to adopt the approach taken by the Haudenosaunee Documentation Committee for Haudenosaunee citizenship documents: that is, to place a person's Haudenosaunee name as that person's first name. This is consistent with the concept of the name being ón:kwe, first or original. The first reference in this text to any individual would follow this rule: Joagquisho Oren Lyons, for example.

Where a person has only a Haudenosaunee name or only a European name, there is no issue: Tekanissorens and Woodrow Wilson stand as they are.

Where an individual becomes a royá:ner, a Confederacy chief, I deliberately use his title, which replaces his original name. Thus, Hai:wes became Deskahe Steven Jacobs. Using both the English name and the title helps to distinguish individuals and at the same time to acknowledge the continuity of titles: there have also been Deskahe Levi General, Deskahe Alexander General, and Deskahe Harvey Longboat. When referring to people who are no longer living, I have not used the traditional suffix –*ken* after their names. It would have been correct, but it would have meant further confusing those unfamiliar with Haudenosaunee customs.

I had considered distinguishing between people who had been born Haudenosaunee and people who had received names through adoption. Since the law does not distinguish between them, I will not do so either. Warraghyhagey William Johnson and Dayodekane Seth Newhouse are named in the same way.

Treating Haudenosaunee names as "first names" provides a solution to the issue of citations in footnotes. When an individual is mentioned for the first time, I use his or her full name. Subsequent references to the individual will use only the surname, unless it is necessary to distinguish between several individuals with the same surname.

It's complicated. It's important. It's right. You'll get used to it.

Ohe'n:ton Karihwatékwen: Words Before All Else

The enduring legal systems of the world are the result of people bringing their minds together to foster order and peace. For the People of the Longhouse, the Haudenosaunee, giving thanks is the first step towards law and the beginning of any meeting of the people.[1] Words of thanksgiving, Kanonhweratonhsera, are spoken at the opening (and closing) of every council, whether internal or with other people or nations. Viewed through the lens of Kanonhweratonhsera, the world is an orderly place: every part of the natural world has been given instructions and responsibilities, and each continues to fulfill those instructions as well as it can. This gratitude reminds us, too, that we humans are no more important than the other living parts of the world. Kanonhweratonhsera is not a recitation of a hierarchy. It is not a prayer. Giving thanks as people gathered together is the beginning of being of one mind. As they come together, our minds are "bundled together" into one: entitewahwe'non:ni ne onkwa'nikonikon:ra.[2] Kanonhweratonhsera reminds us that order is the natural and intentional condition of creation, and that being of one good mind is the ideal condition of the people.

> The Great Power came from up in the sky, and now it is functioning,
> the Great Power that we accepted when we reached consensus.
> So now our house has become complete.
> Now, therefore, we shall give thanks, that is,
> we shall thank the Creator of the earth, that is,
> he who has planted all the kinds of weeds
> and all the varieties of shrubs
> and all the kinds of trees;
> and springs,
> flowing water, such as rivers
> and large bodies of water, such as lakes;
> and the sun that keeps moving by day,
> and by night the moon,
> and where the sky is, the stars, which no one is able to count;

---

1   In the 1862 Council at Cattaraugus, it is stated "when our forefathers finished the law they in the first place would return thanks." Parker 1916, 145.

2   The nations of the Haudenosaunee are also brought together into one family in the same way.

moreover, the way it is on earth in relation to which
no one is able to tell the extent to which it is to their benefit, that is,
the people who he created and who will continue to live on earth.
This, then, is the reason we thank him, the one with great power,
the one who is the Creator,
for that which will now move forward,
the Good Message and the Power and the Peace; the Great Law.[3]

---

3   Skaniatariio John Arthur Gibson 1912, 294–96. Ohe'n:ton karihwatékwen has been
translated as "the words that come before all else." The term is currently applied by many
Mohawks to the Opening, or Thanksgiving Address, which, indeed, is spoken before all
other business. Horatio Hale ([1883] 1989) uses Ohe'n:ton karihwatékwen to describe
the Three Bare Words spoken to visiting nations or delegations when they are met at the
woods' edge, before being allowed into the clearing surrounding the village. Those are
also words spoken to the visitors before all others—words of comfort and condolence.

KAYANERENKÓ:WA
THE GREAT LAW OF PEACE

Introduction

Several centuries ago, a new kind of law was born in the northeast of North America, or Turtle Island.[1] The Great Law of Peace—Kayanerenkó:wa[2]—is a message of peace, power, and righteousness. The message was carried, at first, by one inspired messenger. With immense courage, patience, and authority, he took his message of peace and law to five nations trapped in cycles of bloodshed and revenge. This Peacemaker found a way to break those bloody cycles, and to shape a legal system that would maintain peace for the future. The five nations are the Mohawk, Oneida, Onondaga, Cayuga, and Seneca, and once the law bound them together as one family in one structure, they began to call themselves Haudenosaunee, the People of the Longhouse.

In places shattered in the early twenty-first century by internal warfare, like Rwanda, Ethiopia, Northern Ireland, Congo, Syria, Afghanistan, and the Balkans, fostering harmony and stability for the future is at least as challenging as stopping the violence. If the causes of the bloodshed—the ill will, feelings, and factors that caused and promoted the wars—are still present, the cycles will start again as soon as the forces that restrain them leave.

The Peacemaker understood that, for peace to exist, people must not only be rational but must also accept that other people are capable of rationality, for

---

1   In the Haudenosaunee Creation story, the woman who fell from the Sky World spread the first land on the back of a sea turtle. Turtle Island can be North America, or it can be all the land in the world.

2   Hale ([1883] 1989, 33) wrote: "The name by which their constitution or organic law is known among them is *kayanerenh*, to which the epitaph *-kowa*, 'great,' is frequently added. This word, *kayanerenh*, is sometimes rendered 'law' or 'league,' but its proper meaning seems to be 'peace.' . . . Its root is *yanere*, signifying 'noble' or 'excellent', which yields, among many derivatives, *kayanere*, 'goodness', and *kayanerenh*, 'peace' or 'peacefulness.'" The concept of moral goodness pervades the law: it reappears in the word usually translated as "chiefs": one is called a *royaner*, from *ro*, "he is" *ianere*, "of goodness": that is, "a man of the Good." The Good Message of Peace, Power, and Righteousness, as we shall see, goes beyond "good is better than evil because it is nicer," and into the very nature of human beings. A deeper root is *-yan*, meaning "way" or "path," so that *iánere* would mean a proper or good way or path (which reverberates with Taoism). See Momaday 1997, 38: "I believe that her word *good* meant many things; for one thing it meant 'right' or 'appropriate.'" The prefix *ka-* indicates something that was made, generally by people, as distinct from something that exists naturally. In the end, it is a "great good way of being that was made." If, as Tehahenteh Frank Miller suggests, the root *ian* refers to the stride that, once it gains direction, becomes a path, then the root is in effect a way of walking or conducting oneself. It is a way of life or living—as opposed to the way of death and killing that it replaced.

rational minds will seek, create, and maintain peace. The story of the making of the Great Law is thus also about ways of restoring people to rationality. It charts a map for a healthy society, not just for healthy individuals.[3] The makers of the Great Law of Peace assumed that good-mindedness is a natural and proper state for human beings, and that a person, a family, or a nation taken to antisocial conduct by grief, anger, pain, or greed can be brought back to the right path.

With the ceremony of Condolence, the Peacemaker created a compassionate way to break the cycle, clear the people's minds, and allow them to "put away the bones and blood that cried for revenge."[4] It became sacred and honourable as well as logical to choose peace over war and to look to the future (and consider the welfare of future generations) instead of listening to the hurt and angry voices of the past. The Condolence opened the door to peace and harmony.

The Great Law also accomplished the necessary second step: it built the structure that maintained the peace. It realistically recognized that peace is never static or secure, but needs to be maintained, preserved, recovered, and spread. Peace is a process, not a state.[5]

The law was not made up completely of new ideas. It was deliberately designed for the people who embraced it. It includes many elements of the societies and governments that were already in place. Its symbols—the longhouse, the pine, the eagle—are things the people would have seen every day. For a people whose language is metaphoric, the law was a long set of metaphors. The new law was pragmatic. It kept, strengthened, and extrapolated what worked well. It discarded what was not working. It broadened useful concepts. It protected government and society against some of the people's unchangeable weaknesses and harmful tendencies. It created a democracy without the confrontations inherent in choosing leaders by voting. Some of its elements were profoundly new. It was indeed a message of peace, power, and righteousness.

If the Good Mind—Ka'nikonhrí:io—is a first element of the law, the next, pervasive one, woven throughout the law, is the idea of family. All the people are related.[6] They are kin, living within a single extended longhouse. As family, they cannot shed one another's blood, and they cannot make war on one

---

3   Skén:nen, "peace," includes the sense that health—of the body and the mind—is a vital element of peace, for a person without health will not be at peace, and a people without health will also be without peace.

4   Among the Cherokees, as well, the dead called out for revenge: "crying blood" would haunt relatives who let a death go unanswered. Sturm 2002, 32.

5   Haudenosaunee languages are said to be made of verbs rather than nouns. This promotes understanding that things like "peace," "fire," and "treaty" are ongoing processes rather than objects or isolable events.

6   The sense of family is not restricted to human beings. The Haudenosaunee call the Earth "our mother," the moon "our grandmother," the sun "our elder brother," and the animals and birds "our brothers and sisters," out of a sense of true kinship, and in recognition of the shared life force of all aspects of the world.

another. As family, as well, they bear an obligation to help one another. Tribal peoples all over the world carry this sense of family. It can engender a strong, aggressive sense of ethnic identity, leading to blood vengeance when provoked.[7] Instead, the Peacemaker transformed the nature of family, allowing it to break the bonds of blood and to generously embrace strangers, to take in outsiders by adoption and by welcome. The Great White Roots of the Tree of Peace not only spread the Great Law over the earth, fostering a landscape of peace: they also encouraged the people who were touched by them to become part of the family of peace.

The Great Law, despite its constant references to family terms, created a civic, not an ethnic, society.[8] "Family" meant support, responsibility, and mutual aid. If humanity follows a path from band to tribe to nation to nation-state,[9] one might say that most Indigenous (or tribal) peoples insist on family relationships as their identifiers, while most nations define themselves by bloodlines, without insisting on family relations between their citizens, and nation-states exhibit a spectrum from ethnic groups (like Serbs) to purely civic ones (like the United States). If it can be said that the Haudenosaunee moved from tribe to nation, it must also be said that, unlike other peoples in the world, they did away with the blood requirement while maintaining family as an essential element of society. Every Haudenosaunee citizen, according to traditional law, is so because he or she is a member of a family and a clan. Adoptees are brought into families and clans. Belonging to a family brings webs of reciprocal responsibility and relations—and a social support system. Within a family, people help one another.

---

7   Non-tribal peoples sometimes assert that tribalism has an inevitable primitive and violent streak (see, for example, Benjamin Barber's 1995 book, *Jihad vs. McWorld*). Yet tribal societies need not be violent, and need not be unsophisticated, nor is technology a prerequisite to intelligence.

8   In *Blood and Belonging*, Michael Ignatieff (1994) thoughtfully considered the nature and consequences of nationalism, including the difference between ethnic and civic nationalism.

9   In the first theoretical anthropological expression of this thinking, Ta-ya-dao-wu-kah Lewis Henry Morgan wrote *Ancient Society* in 1877. He divided the stages of human social and political development into savagery, barbarism, and civilization. More modern anthropologists have mostly abandoned this linear model. The idea that some forms of social and political organization are far superior to others led almost inevitably to the idea that superior peoples have the right to colonize inferior ones, and in the process to take their lands and resources. The evolutionary theory of anthropology has since been discredited, though it found a home in British colonialist law with the case of *Re Southern Rhodesia* in 1919, followed by Canadian courts' insistence that anyone claiming Aboriginal rights or title must show that they constituted, at the time of "first contact" with Europeans, an "organized society."

Another crucial aspect of the Great Law is its constant closeness to the natural world.[10] The obligation to help one another reflects how the Haudenosaunee see the natural world, as a balanced system that retains its balance through the efforts of all its components. The web and circle of life are maintained because each living thing is carrying out its own responsibilities. The natural world is a web of symbiotic relationships, of organisms that are partners, interdependent and mutually supportive.[11]

Furthermore, the law, like the longhouse that is one of its enduring symbols, requires maintenance. The maintenance is cooperative and collaborative: there is no room in this legal system for institutionalized opposition, or for adversarial relationships. While the principles behind its architecture remain constant, inevitably the processes and relationships that sustain it will evolve as society changes. There is a strong sense that the law and the peace are constantly being made, and are not ever going to be completed.

Also constant within the law is the idea of balance. There is balance between the authority of men and that of women. There is balance in council between the "Elder Brothers" and the "Younger Brothers." When sorrow affects people's minds, the Condolence restores balance. In constitutional terms, such a system could be said to contain "checks and balances," yet the Haudenosaunee would stress that the checks are less important than the balances. In this sense, balance can mean harmony, but it also evokes a sense of duality. In the natural world, examples of this duality abound: night and day; male and female; young and old; forest and meadow. The two sides of the longhouse, divided by the imaginary line down the middle of the building, reflect this, and so do many aspects of the law.[12]

---

10   Gonwaiannih Audrey Shenandoah (2006) pointed out that, in Haudenosaunee languages, "We have no word for nature." When the law was made, there was no other kind of world. Today, we need to distinguish between the "natural world" and the world of cities and cleared lands, mines and forestry, just as we distinguish between an acoustic and an electric guitar, or an analogue or digital clock. At one time, for everyone, there was only the "natural world."

11   Robert Venables (2010, 41) states that "since the Creator filled the world with symbiotic, equal souls who nevertheless carry out specific functions, the most logical premise upon which to base an organized human community was also communal."

12   Haudenosaunee names also contain frequent reference to "two-ness": Tekanawita; Tekarihoken; Tekanissorens; Tekahionhake; Thayendenega—all names of crucial or prominent people—contain *teka-*, the prefix meaning "two." Haudenosaunee names contain fewer references to other numbers, while English names rarely refer to numbers at all. Many common Haudenosaunee words begin with *ta-*, signifying two-ness.

Several times in any account of the making of the Kayanerenkó:wa, tasks are assigned to two men—rarely to a single one.[13] The great partners, the Peacemaker and Hiawatha, work together like the two sides, as well.

Since it draws part of its inspiration from the way the people understand the natural world and how it works, Haudenosaunee leaders often call the Great Law "Natural Law."[14] The inspiration from nature leads to an obligation: as a matter of responsibility, lawmakers must constantly consider the impact of their decisions on the natural world. This concern about the environment is not an aspect of most "modern" nation-state constitutions, and has only recently become a part of most administrative systems of government, now that climate change and the degradation of the global environment have made it urgent.

As people who lived and travelled by rivers, the Haudenosaunee understood that the world flows; that time and space both flow; and that relationships also flow. They sought constant relationships, ones that would remain true through change. Within that sense of flow, the Haudenosaunee see the people who are alive at any one time as simply part of a larger people, one that includes those who have gone before and those who will come after. The nature of Haudenosaunee names is a reminder of this: names belong to a clan family,[15] were carried by many other individuals in the past, and return to the clan to be carried by other people in the future. In the law, this sense of flow also places an express responsibility on lawmakers to consider the impact of their decisions

---

13 "Hayewatha sent two men to summon Tekanawita"; "Thereupon the chief chose two men to send"; "Now you two will depart to go and look for smoke" (all in twenty pages of Gibson 1899). Why send two? Several pragmatic reasons. A single messenger is vulnerable. He can get lonely. The two can share tasks. If something happens to one, the other carries on. Often, one is younger, and is learning along the way, by carrying out the task with a mentor or companion. Sometimes, the two represent different sides or factions in the community. Sometimes, they can corroborate what happened, where a single envoy might not be able to: it is useful to have a witness.

14 "There is one law which prevails over all law—and that's the universal law, the natural law. And it will prevail no matter what this government says, no matter what any government says. And we are all subject to it. Indians recognize this, so they base their law on the natural law. The natural law and the original Indian governments are intertwined and they rest on one another" (Joagquisho Oren Lyons 1982, v). This is not to be confused with the "natural law" discussions of Western ethicists and philosophers—whether there exists a *summum bonum,* a set of things that is always good (or, conversely, whether there are acts that are always wrong), as a matter of nature rather than man-made values. Haudenosaunee law does not distinguish between human beings and other parts of the natural world in its reference to "natural law." It is not a matter of good and bad, but rather of reflecting the way the world was created and operates naturally. We as humans can choose to live within its rules or to constantly defy them.

15 Actually, a person's name belongs to a family segment of a clan, an ohwátsi're, but that detail will be addressed later. The important principle, for the purpose of this introduction, is that even names remind people of their place in a flowing, organic social and temporal environment.

on the coming seven generations, the people downstream from us, whose faces we will never see.

Compatible with this sense of flow is a consciousness of cycles: the year consists of seasons that are repetitions of the seasons of the previous year, and the ceremonies are the same as those of the year before and the year coming. They are re-enactments of earlier cycles and events. In that sense, the Haudenosaunee understanding of the nature of time is not the same as European or Euro-American perspectives, which explain time as a line rather than a cycle, and "progress" along that line as part of a deliberate path[16] towards a utopian ideal.[17] Haudenosaunee history for the past four centuries can be understood not only in geopolitical and economic terms but also in terms of coping with the collisions between two very different views of humanity's purpose in the world.[18]

Today's oral and written versions of the narrative of the Great Law describe first how the Peacemaker brought this message to the people, and the challenges—physical, political, and spiritual—that he faced along the way. The story of how he brought the people together, and how he overcame and transformed obstacles, is a manual for the process of creating consensus (one-mindedness—ska'níkon:ra) as well as a series of demonstrations of the power of the Good Mind and Peace. The story inspires, for it is one of patience, thought, and strength.

Upon first reading or hearing the Great Law, one could easily conclude that the story of how the Peacemaker brought people and nations together is a pleasant legend, but not law. As a legend, it includes entertaining stories of the hero making a magical stone canoe; tricking a cannibal into changing his evil ways; surviving a great fall from a tree into raging waters; devising enchanting songs; and confronting monsters and evil wizards. These do not seem to be the stuff of law.[19] A North American lawyer looking for the Haudenosaunee constitution

---

16   There are many different ways of seeing time: for example, Maori tradition looks forward to the past, because it can be seen, while the future is still not revealed.

17   Sotsisowah John Mohawk (1999) began to address this fundamental difference in views in *Utopian Legacies,* seeking to explain the path of European destruction as a consequence of the thinking that a society that has a destination also acquires a sense of destiny, which in turn justifies the removal of other societies that stand in its way. Ronald Wright's *Short History of Progress* (2011) examines the consequences of utopian societies' ideologies and consumption.

18   Amber Meadow Adams has suggested that the principle of the Two Row Wampum can be found in the Creation Story: the victorious right-handed twin could have banished his brother far away, but instead says that, though they cannot live together, they should remain close because of their love for each other. So it is with the wampum between Haudenosaunee and Western society.

19   Mark Twain wrote: "You believe in a book that has talking animals, wizards, witches, demons, sticks turning into snakes, burning bushes, food falling from the sky, people walking on water, and all sorts of magical, absurd and primitive stories, and you say that we are the ones that need help?"

might conclude that the true lawmaking only began once the Peacemaker had gathered all the chiefs and clan mothers together in one place, and began to identify and create legislative authorities and structures. It would be easy to conclude this, but it would be wrong.

The Kayanerenkó:wa is all law. Every part of it is law.

The story of how the Peacemaker brought the people together is not just a story. Certainly it is full of metaphors and lessons, but the story also contains many of the fundamental concepts and principles of the law. All great messages are taught by metaphor. Jesus, in his "Good Message" (which is what "Gospel" means in Middle English), resorted to "parables." Buddha told stories (and, as the Acoma Pueblo scholar Simon Ortiz said: "There are no truths, only stories"). Centuries later, history and metaphor become mixed. The message remains constant. Metaphor—the ability of human beings to think bridges between different concepts—is essential to visualizing any legal system.

The meta-narrative of the Great Law provides the tone and spirit: the determination that the bloodshed must stop, and will stop. It also delivers the vital threshold of the law: the ceremony of Condolence, an act of caring, compassion, and respect that has no duplicate in any other legal system. The Condolence is a tool to stop the killing, open the path of peace, and raise up the minds of the people. It prepares them to accept the message of peace, power, and righteousness. It stands for a crucial concept: that before it can accept peace, a mind must be healed, and must be working properly and rationally. And another: that "peace" is a combination of factors, including health (mental and physical), for a person whose mind or body are in pain will be distracted from peace. And another: there is no mind so bad that it cannot be changed and healed by the right approach and the right power. This is not mere legend. It is the foundation of a distinct approach to law.[20] And another: for a government of good minds to work, they must help one another, not oppose one another. People must recognize their fundamental kinship, their common humanity.

The story of the making of the Great Law follows deliberate paths, temporally and geographically but also thoughtfully. The Peacemaker delivers his

---

20   It is the foundation of the Haudenosaunee approach to criminal law, for example. People do bad things because their minds cause them to do so. If they demonstrate that their mind has been made good again—usually by a sincere repentance—then there is no need to continue to punish them. For reconciliation, though, there must be both repentance and forgiveness:

> The Iroquois myths . . . make no promise about a future world. They are concerned completely with the foundations of a civil society, based on universal principles, natural law, and divine intervention, as a means of overcoming death. Not death in the abstract, but deaths of Iroquois caused by other Iroquois, deaths created by a fatal cycle of mourning and revenge. The myths define political, civil society as a means to comfort mourners and cleanse the mind of vengeance. (Vecsey 1988, 95)

message first to individuals, then to communities, then to nations, and finally to the entire newly formed Confederacy. The themes of transformation and transcendence are constant: the Peacemaker is able to address what is dysfunctional, or not working properly, in individuals as well as in society, and to transform the power to injure into the responsibility to protect.[21]

In many encounters described in the making of the law, the Peacemaker is confronted by a dangerous, angry person or group of people. One aspect of his genius was to recognize that there was nevertheless a capacity for rationality in these people. He dealt with their humanity. He was able to transform them from forces of chaos into peacekeepers.

In a modern world where the best minds can find no way to stop the killing in its "hot spots," the Kayanerenkó:wa stands as an example of one people's way to end the violence and embrace peace. Of course, there have been other ways: Hobbes maintained that men form commonwealths (states) with the aim of "getting themselves out from that miserable condition of warre . . . of every man against every man,"[22] which he saw as humanity's natural condition.[23] Nations, however, are as effective and efficient in pursuing war against others as they are in preventing internal strife. The League of Nations[24] emerged from "the war to end all wars," the First World War, and was unsuccessful in preventing a Second World War. Today's United Nations is intended to prevent aggression. Each of these leagues, in its statement of principles, recalls the Peacemaker's desire that the Great Peace should spread, as the white roots of the Tree of Peace would spread to the four directions. The inability of these leagues to achieve peace is often regarded as a failure of will, or a failure of true desire, on the part of the leaders of the nations for peace.

A good mind will seek peace, create peace, maintain peace, and do so by uniting with other good minds.

---

21   Part of the thinking behind judo, a Japanese way of self-defence as well as a sport, is to use an opponent's strength and momentum against him. "Let him have his way," a black-belt instructor once told me. The Peacemaker took this thinking a step further: he transformed the strength and power of his potential opponents (the Cannibal, Tsikonsaseh, Thadadaho, the warriors) into forces to create, maintain, and protect the peace. He did not allow them to attack him, and therefore never had to use his abilities to cause injury.

22   Hobbes (1651) 1997, 67–70.

23   Is war a natural inclination for human beings? See Fry (2006), Wrangham (1997), and LeBlanc and Register (2003).

24   There is a persistent legend that Woodrow Wilson, who had been a history professor at Princeton (his doctoral dissertation had addressed "Congressional Government"), commissioned research at the end of World War I into the nature and structure of the Haudenosaunee, as an example of a league of peace, and that he used that research in his promotion of the League of Nations. When Deskahe Levi General went to Geneva in 1924, he did so expecting a favourable reception from a league that he saw was a reflection, in its goals and ideals, of the principles of the Haudenosaunee.

The second part of the Kayanerenkó:wa is more technical and more constitutional.[25] Chiefs—rotiyanershon—are appointed, and given specific responsibilities. Procedures are set in place to maintain checks and balances among the nations of the League. Decision-making processes are firmed up, including ways to avoid and resolve disputes. The law provides for continuity, not transition. The distinct roles of men and women are set out. The rights of nations are clarified. The rights of foreigners, and the way the League will relate to foreign nations, are stated so that they will promote the spread of the Great Peace. The symbols of the law and the people are described. Provision is made for renewing commitments, for maintaining the law, and also for future changes consistent with the architecture of the longhouse, an architecture symbolizing the functional principles of the law.

It is this second part, the structural part, that is said to have inspired (or influenced) the Constitution of the United States of America,[26] a confederation of putatively equal partners, joining together voluntarily to form a government replete with checks and balances and mutual respect. Certainly at the Albany Conference in 1754, Tekarihoken Hendrick Peters[27] encouraged the colonies to form a confederation.[28] Some Haudenosaunee say that, in imitating the Great Law, the United States did so poorly, for their constitution neglects some of the most important aspects: peace, the Good Mind, obligations to the natural

---

25   Fenton (1998, 215–33) referred to the second part as "the by-laws of the League." Perhaps, like most of the U.S. constitution, it consists of "by-laws."

26   In 1976, the U.S. Senate passed a resolution "to recognize the contribution of the Iroquois Confederacy of Nations to the development of the United States Constitution and to reaffirm the continuing government-to-government relationship between Indian tribes and the United States established in the Constitution. Whereas the original framers of the Constitution, including most notably, George Washington and Benjamin Franklin, are known to have greatly admired the concepts, principles and governmental practices of the Six Nations of the Iroquois Confederacy; and Whereas the Confederation of the original Thirteen Colonies into one republic was explicitly modeled upon the Iroquois Confederacy as were many of the democratic principles which were incorporated into the Constitution itself. . . . Now therefore, be it resolved . . . that the Congress, on the occasion of the two hundredth anniversary of the signing of the United States Constitution, acknowledges the historical debt which this Republic of the United States of America owes to the Iroquois Confederacy and other Indian nations for their demonstration of enlightened, democratic principles of government and their example of a free association of independent Indian nations." (S. Con. Res. 76: S. Hrg. 100-610).

27   At that time, the holder of the Mohawk Turtle Clan title was the man also known as Theyanoguin, King Hendrick, and Henry Peters. It has been suggested that there were actually two men known as "Hendrick," since the man who met Queen Anne in 1710 already appears middle-aged (and was named Teyoninhokarawen, and held a Wolf Clan title). The man who was Warraghihagey William Johnson's elderly mentor died at the Battle of Lake George in 1755, forty-five years later (see Hinderaker 2011).

28   Shannon (2000, 8) maintained that his work "proves conclusively that no evidence exists of an Iroquois influence in the drafting of the Albany Plan of Union," and his work purports to "disprove the Iroquois Influence Thesis."

world, the importance of families, obligations to future generations, spirituality, respect for women (and, until the 1920s, women's part in government).
Nevertheless, the influence of one powerful confederate system on the formation of the constitution of the other has been acknowledged, and is undeniable.
Only the extent of that influence has become the subject of bitter debate among
academics.[29]

The Haudenosaunee constitution and the constitution of the United States
share another feature that is not the result of the influence of the former upon
the latter, and seldom receives comment. Because both were created by a small
group of people during a short, dramatic period (a "constitutional moment")
that has become invested with a degree of sacredness over time, and both can be
read (despite United States amendments and Haudenosaunee additions to the
rafters of the longhouse) as the product of the minds of the "founding fathers"
and as a fixed canon, the result, in legal and social terms, has been what some
British commentators have called "ancestor worship"—an inability or unwillingness to evolve.[30] This manifests itself in U.S. courts' tendency to seek the
intentions of the framers of the Constitution (the "Founding Fathers") in cases
two centuries later, and in Haudenosaunee Condolence ceremonies wistfully
referring to the acts of "my grandsires" as the days of greatness.[31]

The Kayanerenkó:wa establishes a democracy. It creates a system of government in which each person participates and has an effective place and voice. It
does not meet the criteria of late twentieth-century participatory democracies,
in which all people are theoretically absolutely equal and governments are selected in periodic elections. It answers some basic questions quite differently. It
does not assume absolute equality, and instead assigns responsibility as well as
authority according to ability,[32] assuming that each person has different gifts[33] to
be fulfilled. It avoids elections, because elections divide the people into factions

---

29   See, e.g., Johansen 1982 and 1998.

30   Bogdanor 2009.

31   This "ancestor worship" is not isolated. For example, Wahhabi Muslim belief maintains
      that the great days, those to be emulated, were those immediately after the Prophet's
      time, so that the customs and dress of those days are to be maintained.

32   If this is a meritocracy, then why are the chiefs' titles hereditary, ask some commentators.
      There are two answers to this. The first is that all a person inherits is the possibility of be-
      ing chosen as his family's representative, while the fundamental principle is still that the
      best person among those eligible should be chosen. The second is that where there are
      individuals of great merit who are not eligible for a family title, the institution of Pine
      Tree Chiefs permits adding them to the council as respected and protected advisers.

33   This is a word that, in its frequent use by Haudenosaunee, means something subtly
      different from its usual English meaning. It refers to natural talents or attributes that
      have been given by the Creator to an individual. Thus, the purpose of a Haudenosaunee
      education is said to be the identification and fulfillment of that person's gifts.

and parties,[34] whereas the law seeks one-mindedness and unity. It also avoids elections because they tend to install governments whose horizon of thought and vision is the next election, whereas the Kayanerenkó:wa admonishes decision makers to cast their minds to the welfare of the coming generations.

Recognition of gifts also extends to the nations: the law creates an asymmetric confederation, in which each nation has specific authority and obligations. In Haudenosaunee legal thinking, authority and responsibility are inseparable.[35] Only the Senecas can bring into council issues coming from the west, but they, as doorkeepers, are also charged with protecting that entrance to Haudenosaunee territory. The Onondagas, as firekeepers, both maintain and protect the central council and its continued functions.[36] In the United States and Canada, each state or province has identical and equal powers within the constitution.[37] If the Great Law's principles were to be applied, perhaps modern Québec would become the official steward of the French language; British Columbia might be the guardian of the forests; New York could protect its nation's finances; Washington could become the preserver of salmon fisheries. Each authority is balanced by a matching responsibility, which requires a degree of unselfishness. Morgan explained that "the tribe was neither weakened nor impaired by the confederate compact. Each was in vigorous life within its appropriate sphere."[38] Venables takes this description several steps further: "The Woods are the equal responsibility of the Confederacy as a whole and, in their different locales, the responsibility of one of the five founding nations. Because there is no ultimate sovereign power, these simultaneous and equal responsibilities have no real parallel in Western law, including Western property law. These simultaneous

---

34 The Haudenosaunee would agree with the maxim that democracy must consist of more than two wolves and a sheep voting on what is for dinner.

35 This is also true in other legal cultures. Giving meaning to the fiduciary relationship between the Crown and Aboriginal peoples, Chief Justice Dickson in *Guerin* explained that Crown authority must be reconciled with Crown responsibility—an early manifestation of the constitutional goal of reconciliation.

36 As an Onondaga spokesman explained to the British at Fort George on 3 August 1826 on behalf of the Six Nations:
  Brother: It is natural for us to wish to preserve our ancient customs and to walk in the paths of our forefathers ... We consider each nation alike respectable and although we are the firekeepers and appointed to speak for the whole, yet we do not consider ourselves any better than the rest in point of power and respectability. (Library and Archives Canada, Portfolio of Upper Canada, 1826, 214; cited in the Reply of Great Britain, *Cayuga Arbitration*, Vol. II)

37 This is not quite so: while each state has an equal number of senators, the states have different numbers of members of the electoral college, which actually elects the president, who appoints the administration.

38 Morgan 1871, 132.

and equal responsibilities are also what make the Confederacy a unique and delicate balance of equal responsibilities among its confederate parts."[39]

Where the Kayanerenkó:wa differs from modern Euro-American law, there are reasons for the differences. Some of those differences are the result of a different approach to law. Some are a reflection of their times and technologies. Others flow from the nature of the people themselves, for this legal system reflects the people for whom it was created. Some aspects of the law are exportable, universal, as the Peacemaker said that the Great White Roots of the Tree of Peace ought to spread over the world. Other aspects of the law make sense mainly in a Haudenosaunee context. For example, peoples who have no clan system would find no usefulness in that complex interweaving of relationships, or would have to invent their own.[40]

Nevertheless, the Great Law of Peace is intrinsically valuable. Sotsistowah John Mohawk, the pre-eminent Haudenosaunee thinker of the twentieth century, wrote: "The political thought of the Haudenosaunee deserves to be judged on its own merits, not as an artifact of the past. We should investigate it today, question it, expand on it, learn from it just as we would from any doctrine of political thought. It will stand against that kind of scrutiny."[41]

There have been several efforts to reduce the Kayanerenkó:wa to writing. The first were by the Haudenosaunee themselves, as part of an effort to agree on processes, as well as to show that the governments created by the Great Law are respectable, consistent, complex, and legal. Some of these were simply an attempt to describe the system to outsiders, or to protect that system against those who claimed the Haudenosaunee had no law. Others were internal exercises in standardization. There was little written analysis. More recent writing about the Great Law has been, for the most part, by academics. In a demonstration of their own compartmentalization, each of the writers has come from a particular perspective. Anthropologist-ethnohistorians,[42] linguists,[43] and political

---

39 Venables 2010, 36.

40 Obversely, the destruction of clans is a tool for assimilation. Among Central Asian peoples, uncles and aunts are important parts of a person's family constellation, part of the clan system. The twentieth-century Han Chinese population-control policy of one child per family would, over time, mean that there would be no uncles or aunts. England's eighteenth-century efforts to break the cohesion of Scottish clans are another example.

41 Mohawk 1989, 218.

42 Morgan concluded that kinship was the basis of the law. His greatest treatise as the first anthropologist was on the nature of kinship, not only among the Haudenosaunee, but as an aspect of human societies. William Fenton's 1998 *The Great Law and the Longhouse* lies somewhere between history and anthropology.

43 Kanuhsyuniké:ha (Gibson 1912), as set out by Hanni Woodbury and Shagohendehta Reg Henry, is to a great extent a linguistic exercise. The Onondaga text has a word-for-word English translation, with grammatical notations under it, and a more flowing, tighter English translation appears at the bottom of the page.

scientists[44] have each adopted anthropological, ethnohistorical, linguistic, or political approaches to the Kayanerenkó:wa.

Strangely—considering what is being analyzed and written about is, on its face, a legal system—there has been almost no *legal* writing about it. This is all the more curious since many of the people who were involved in its description, recording, and publication were lawyers, by profession or training. Morgan, Parker, Hale: the early recorders of the Great Law were lawyers. This is no coincidence.

Ta-ya-dao-wuk-kah Lewis Henry Morgan[45] was a practising lawyer in western New York State in the mid-1800s. His companion on his path into the Great Law and into Haudenosaunee society was Hasanonda—later Donehogowa—Ely S. Parker, a Tonawanda Seneca teenager Morgan had met in an Albany bookstore. Morgan has been called "the first anthropologist": his work on the kinship system of the Haudenosaunee was truly seminal for the science of understanding human societies. Morgan was also intrigued by the Great Law. He created a semi-secret white society that imitated its structures.[46] As both lawyer and adopted Seneca, he joined the fight for the preservation of Seneca land at Tonawanda. He came close to functioning within the circle of the law, but he also retained a sense of European superiority.[47] However, there are some indications that Morgan considered his *League of the Hau-de-no-sau-nee* as both an imperfect work and his final Iroquois effort, a way of getting the people out of his system.[48] It has been suggested that the academic, speculative parts of the book are Morgan's ruminations on "man's ascent to civilization," while the more informative and factual parts are in a style different enough that it is most likely that they are actually Donehogowa Ely Parker's writing.

---

44   Taiaiake Gerald Alfred's *Peace, Power and Righteousness* (1999) is a Kahnawake Mohawk's setting of the Kayanerenkó:wa in the context of 1990s political thought and speech.

45   Morgan was adopted by the Hawk Clan of the Tonawanda Senecas on October 31, 1846, and given the name Ta-ya-dao-wuk-kah, *One lying across* (Beauchamp [1907] 1975, 406, described by Donehogowah Ely Parker). "One lying across" might allude to a person who lies between the canoe and the sailing ship, between the nations and their cultures, or the name may simply have been one that belonged to the Hawk Clan.

46   Upstate New York in the mid-1800s was the birthplace of many of the college fraternities that came to dominate American campus social scenes.

47   It is possible that Morgan decided not to treat the Great Law as a complete, complex legal system because to do so would not accord with his theories of the evolution of human societies. As a people who had no domesticated animals or iron, the Haudenosaunee, by his reckoning, were somewhere between Lower and Middle Barbarism, well short of the "progress" and civilization required for a sophisticated legal system. See Morgan 1877.

48   Morgan wrote of the *League of the Iroquois*: "My principal object in writing this work, which exhibits abundant evidence of hasty execution, was to free myself of the subject. . . . I laid aside the Indian subject to devote time to my profession." White 1957, 262.

Parker himself qualified to become a lawyer in New York State. Either he chose not to present himself to the bar, because that would require him to seek U.S. citizenship, or he was refused admission to the bar because he was not a citizen, or not white.[49] During the Civil War, as a Confederacy chief, he needed a special dispensation from his nation to be allowed to join the U.S. Army, where he became adjutant to his friend, Ulysses S. Grant. Later, when Grant became president, Parker was appointed commissioner of Indian Affairs. Long before that, though, he had become Donehogowa,[50] one of the fifty rotiyanershon, or Lords[51] of the Confederacy.

A third recorder of parts of the Great Law, Horatio Hale (1817–96), was also a lawyer (in Clinton, Ontario) by the time he became deeply involved with the Haudenosaunee, publishing two transcripts of the entire Condolence ceremony in his *Iroquois Book of Rites.*[52] Hale had been a member of the United States Exploring Expedition when he was twenty-one; he never ceased from exploration. He may have been what is now called an anthropologist or ethnologist—but his initial fascination was with the people and their law.

My own path, half a lifetime long, has been marked by stages.

At first, with the confidence of youth and the brashness of law school, I accepted intellectually that the Great Law represented a unique constitutional structure, with a powerful legend accompanying its creation. I was quite prepared to argue in court that the Iroquois Confederacy had an organized society,

---

49   The modern Seneca explanation is that he did not want to become a U.S. citizen, as that would require him to lose his Haudenosaunee citizenship. Different biographies offer different reasons. Armstrong (1978, 41) affirms that he was refused admission by the courts because he could not become an American citizen. Brown (1970, 179) asserts that Parker was told that "only White male citizens could be admitted to law practice in New York. No Indians need apply." Largent says that when Parker's patron, William P. Angel, of Ellicotville, "fell out of favor with the ruling Democratic Party ... Parker was declared ineligible for the bar because he was not an American citizen" (Largent 1996). Arthur C. Parker wrote that a Supreme Court decision had ruled that "only a male white man and a citizen" could be admitted to the bar (1919, 79).

50   How would a Confederacy chief, committed to the Great Peace, justify participating in a war? His title is one of the two that is of both a peace chief and a war chief. The United States was an ally, and its cause, to Parker, was just. See Armstrong 1978 and Hauptman 1995. Nevertheless, by joining a foreign army, and later by joining the U.S. government, it could be said that he had effectively stepped outside the circle of the law, and strictly speaking the "horns" of his office as royá:ner would have fallen from him, or been removed. While it might be said that, by acting in an administrative capacity rather than on the front lines, he had avoided taking part in war, Parker never made that argument. Whether promoting, managing, or fighting it, war is war, the antithesis of peace: that is the lesson to be drawn from Tsikonsaseh.

51   "Lord" appears to have been used as an appropriate translation because British members of the House of Lords also have continuity in titles and are supposed to have nobility of thought as well as pedigree.

52   Hale (1883) 1989. See also Hale 1882.

a sophisticated constitution, and a detailed system of landholding.[53] In the 1970s, that was all Canadian law required Indigenous societies to prove, in order to hold rights and to have Aboriginal title to land.[54] I had also read enough of the history books, treaties, and treaty conferences to see that the Confederacy had dealt with the French, the Dutch, the British, and the United States as equals, as partners or enemies, to be respected or challenged as political circumstances required. There were patterns and principles to the treaties. The people I associated with—at Oneida, at the Grand River Territory, and then throughout Haudenosaunee communities—were convinced of the power of the Great Law as a way of life, and of the sovereignty of the Confederacy. In 1980, my master's thesis in law concentrated on the Covenant Chain relationship between the Iroquois Confederacy and the British Crown, and on how that relationship was reflected in the history of several distinct issues: criminal jurisdiction, border-crossing rights, land rights, and political rights. For more than two centuries, representatives of the British Crown had understood, adopted, and used Iroquois law and metaphor in treaty relations, creating a well-defined relationship within the Iroquois legal system. At the time, I sought to find parallels in the law of nations, suggesting that the treaty relationship met the definitions of a protectorate relationship in modern international law.

By 1990, my perspective had matured and deepened. I understood, as the Maoris had in Aotearoa, that it is important to retain the original names for things, because English translations are never exact and often misleading. To me, the Iroquois Confederacy became the Haudenosaunee; the chiefs became rotiyanershon; and the Great Law became the Kayanerenkó:wa. By 1990, I had also been personally transformed: I was now Kayanesenh of the Wolf Clan of the Onondaga Nation, and my wife and children Mohawks of the Turtle Clan. I attended ceremonies and Condolences and councils as an insider. Seeing things from within the circle gave me a fundamentally new perspective on the law.

The events of 1990 were tumultuous and traumatic. In the early part of the summer, an internal war in Akwesasne showed how bad things must have been before the coming of the law: the sorrow and anger in that community were deep and bloody.[55] Mohawks had killed one another. There was blood on their hands. Twenty-five years later, many of the wounds remain unhealed. For me, 1990 culminated in desperate, principled, ultimately doomed autumn negotiations with Canada and Quebec as the Canadian Army encircled defiant warriors in

---

53 In the Union of Ontario Indians' intervention in *Isaac v. Davey*, [1977] 2 SCR 897.

54 *Hamlet of Baker Lake v. The Queen* (1980), 107 DLR (3rd) 513. In contrast, anthropological consensus had moved on, concluding that the "organized society" standard was ethnocentric, obsolete, and unhelpful (Bell and Asch 1997).

55 *People of the Pines*, by Geoffrey York and Loreen Pindera (1991), is as good a history of that year as any yet written.

Kanehsatake and laid siege to Kahnawake. All this caused me a great deal of soul-searching. Could we, as the Haudenosaunee negotiators, have done anything differently and remained true to the law? How much does law determine behaviour, and how much pragmatic flexibility does it allow? The warriors: were they something new, or just a modern face to an ancient challenge? How much of the original Longhouse still exists, in reality or in people's minds—or dreams?

The Confederacy lives first and foremost in people's minds. It is a constant re-enactment of the way of the Peacemaker.[56] It is as real as people are prepared to believe it is. For some, it is a shining ideal in the distance, unattainable and largely irrelevant. For others, it is something to *live*. Those who lived the Confederacy in 1990, the ones I worked with, convinced me that the dream is real.

After 1990, with Tehatkarine (Arihote) Curtis Nelson and Kanatiio Allen Gabriel, I put together what has been called Kahswénhtha, the Haudenosaunee treaty study for the Canadian Royal Commission on Aboriginal Peoples. The message of that study can be summarized in four points. First: the Haudenosaunee are a people of law, with a respectable legal system of their own. Second: the British, in their dealings with Indigenous nations, accepted and worked effectively within that legal system for the first two centuries of their presence on this continent. Third: there is a continuum of treaty relations between the Crown and the Haudenosaunee. It resembles a river flowing through time rather than a succession of events. It is based on relationships more than on details, and on principles more than on politics. It is based in the concepts and thinking of the Great Law of Peace. Fourth: the more recent history of that treaty relationship reveals a record of neglect, ignorance, and bad faith on the part of the Crown.

Twenty more years passed. With new tools, I continued to turn over the Kayanerenkó:wa in my mind. The publication of the most complete version, recited by Skaniatariio John Arthur Gibson, and access to other, unpublished versions by Dayodekane Seth Newhouse, Deyonwe'ton Jake Thomas, and J.N.B. Hewitt helped me see patterns where before I had seen mostly details. Long conversations with Sotsisowah John Mohawk, Deskahe Harvey Longboat, Kaientaronkwen Ernie Benedict, Hayadaha Rick Hill, Roronhiakewen Dan Longboat, and Amber Meadow Adams continued to point me towards principles and patterns. Moving out of Toronto, to the Six Nations Grand River Territory, helped change my outlook, legally, culturally, and socially. I could see and sense the natural world every day. The forest literally began to replace the trees, and I watched the river's flow every day. Where I had been learning *what*

---

56   It is said that some of the ceremonies in the Longhouse are both re-enactments of events in the Creation Story and reflections of simultaneous ceremonies in the Sky World. As above, so below. We repeat the actions and principles of the Peacemaker as part of a commitment that the Great Peace shall continue.

the law provided, I was now seeking to learn *why* it did so. The tone of my law practice had shifted from adversarial to conciliatory, and from seeking to win to seeking mutual benefit. There were successful, precedent-setting negotiations. I had not realized the extent to which the Great Law had influenced my approach to cases and courts. I began to recognize that one could practise the principles of that law in a pragmatic, principled, and effective way. In 2007, we negotiated a series of agreements with the City of Hamilton about the Red Hill Valley Parkway, using those principles in exciting, effective, contemporary ways.[57] In 2009, I taught a course in Haudenosaunee law at the University of Toronto, and discussions with the students helped temper the thinking in this book. A series of repatriations from museums, of wampum and haduwi medicine masks, left nothing behind but good will and friendships. In 2016, Sakom Hugh Akagi, Kanatiio Allen Gabriel, and I arranged a reaffirmation of Peskotomuhkati (Passamaquoddy) treaty relations with the Crown. The ways of the law have tempered many of my negotiations with the Crown on behalf of Indigenous peoples. Anishinaabe and Peskotomuhkati people also find those ways compatible with their own principles.

Canada's laws about Indigenous peoples had also evolved. The 2015 report of the Truth and Reconciliation Commission of Canada usefully distinguished between "Indigenous law," the legal systems of Indigenous nations, and "Aboriginal law," the laws of Canada about Indigenous peoples. It was Aboriginal law that was evolving quickly. In 1985, for the first time in over a century, the Supreme Court of Canada in the *Guerin* case clarified that the Crown bore a fiduciary, trust-like obligation in dealing with the lands of Indigenous peoples—a duty enforceable in courts of law. It also acknowledged that principles of law emanating from medieval England might not find counterparts in Indigenous North America. In 1990, the *Sparrow* decision showed that the protection of Aboriginal rights in the 1982 Constitution Act was not simply an "empty box." At the end of 1997, the Supreme Court overturned a woefully ignorant judgement by the Chief Judge of British Columbia to craft its *Delgam'uukw*[58] decision. For the first time, that court spoke of Indigenous "nations" and of respecting their "laws" and "legal systems."[59] By the turn of the

---

57 The agreements reflected Haudenosaunee drafting as well as thinking. Thus, a clause stated "we are human beings, and as such, are likely to make mistakes. When we find we have omitted or misstated something, we will bring our minds together to amend our agreement."

58 *Delgam'uukw v. Attorney General of British Columbia*, [1997] 3 SCR 1010: "Aboriginal title originates in part from pre-existing stems of aboriginal law. . . . The common law should develop to recognize aboriginal rights (and title, where necessary) as they were recognized by either *de facto* practice or by the aboriginal system of governance."

59 In *Delgam'uukw*, "Aboriginal nations" are mentioned at paragraph 84; at paragraph 114, the court states that "[there is] a second source for aboriginal title—the relationship between common law and pre-existing systems of aboriginal law."

century, though, with the *Donald Marshall* and *Michael Mitchell (Kanentakeron)* decisions, Canadian courts began to recede from forceful recognition of the rights of Indigenous nations. New limits and new obstacles to broad recognition of rights were being born. Generosity in allowing evidence into Canadian courts masked the way the courts had moved the goalposts. Only "established" Aboriginal title carried the same weight as actual land ownership, and the Tsilhqot'in people had spent twenty years and $30 million to gain their limited victory—over part of their territory, an area where there were virtually no people but Tsilhqot'ins—in 2014. Aboriginal peoples had to show their occupation and use of the land, but also prove that it met the principles of exclusivity,[60] and was not "incompatible with Canadian sovereignty."[61] Recognition of the laws of Indigenous nations faded into a vague, less respectful requirement of taking "the Aboriginal perspective" into account. In *Delgam'uukw,* the Supreme Court of Canada explained that Aboriginal title had to be determined as of the date of the assertion of British Crown sovereignty, because the Crown and Indigenous land law systems would have to coexist and be reconciled. In *Marshall* and *Bernard,* the Supreme Court used the term "European sovereignty," possibly to include the French regime, moving towards a racially based, doctrine-of-discovery approach to Aboriginal title. In *Tsilhqot'in,* the court affirmed that it had meant British Crown sovereignty all along—only to refer to "European sovereignty" again a few pages later. In that case, as well, the Supreme Court of Canada tempered the broad range of possible justifications for taking Aboriginal rights and land with a new requirement: that the project had to further the constitutionally mandated goal of reconciliation.

---

60   *R. v. Marshall; R. v. Bernard,* [2005] 2 SCR 220. On the same day that the Supreme Court of Canada insisted that an Indigenous nation's Aboriginal title to land required continuous, exclusive occupation, a Canadian Armed Forces helicopter dropped the Minister of National Defence onto an island off Greenland for all of fifteen minutes—to assert Canada's rights there.

61   *Mitchell (Kanentakeron) v. Minister of National Revenue,* [2001] 1 SCR 911. The case involved Mohawks' rights to trade across the Canadian border with other Indigenous nations. At paragraph 62, the Supreme Court stated that "the doctrine of continuity . . . governed the absorption of aboriginal laws and customs into the new legal regime upon the assertion of Crown sovereignty over the region . . . this incorporation of local laws and customs into the common law was subject to an exception for those interests which were inconsistent with the sovereignty of the new regime." The Haudenosaunee held land collectively, not as individuals. Their practice, noted by the Jesuits in the seventeenth century, of placing armed sentinels along the paths leading into their territory was the kind of thing that nations do: not enough exclusivity, and you have no title; too much, and it is "incompatible with Canadian sovereignty."

The rest of the world was watching and changing, too. In Australia, the High Court[62] had actually stated that the idea that a light-skinned people, happening upon land owned by a dark-skinned people, could take over that land was racist and had no place in a late twentieth-century world. At least, there was no place unless the concept lay at the very backbone of a nation's legal system. In Hawai'i, the rights of the Kanaka Maoli, the Indigenous people, were coming under attack in ways that challenged concepts like blood quantum, culture, the sale of remaining Hawai'ian lands, and Indigenous survival itself.[63] Canada and the United States were the two last holdouts in ratifying the United Nations Declaration on the Rights of Indigenous Peoples.[64]

Canadian courts have admitted that racism has existed in the past (rejecting the *Syliboy*[65] judgement, for example) but have avoided confronting or abandoning it in the present.[66] In the late 1990s, they concluded that the "magic date" that determines a people's Aboriginal rights is the "date of first

---

62   *Mabo v. Queensland* (1992), 175 CLR 1 (Australian High Court). Eddie Mabo had been banished from Murray Island as a teenager and worked as a gardener in an Australian university. He died of cancer two months before the decision that recognized the Mer Islanders' rights to their land. Three years later, his body was returned to his homeland. He was buried as a chief.

63   *Rice v. Cayetano*, 528 US 495 (2000); *Doe v. Kamehameha Schools*, US Ct. of Appeals, 9th Circuit, 8921 (2005). But see Alani Apio's (2003) transcendent article, "New Hopes Arise for Ancestral Culture."

64   Canada's November 2010 endorsement of the Declaration rang particularly hollow: like Australia, it recognizes it as an "aspirational" declaration—but then Canada further asserted that the Declaration "is a non-legally binding document that does not reflect customary international law nor change Canadian laws." Canada's full acceptance of the Declaration in 2016 still placed it within the limits of the Canadian constitution. See http://www.cbc.ca/news/indigenous/canada-adopting-implementing-un-rights-declaration-1.3575272.

65   In *R. v. Syliboy*, [1929] 1 DLR 307, Ben Syliboy, the Grand Chief of the Mi'kmaq Nation, had been charged with trapping muskrats without a licence. Acting County Court Judge Campbell found that "the savages' rights of sovereignty even of ownership were never recognized. Nova Scotia had passed to Britain not by gift or purchase from or even by conquest of the Indians but by treaty with France, which had acquired it by priority of discovery and ancient possession, and the Indians passed with it." The Government of Canada continued to cite this decision as law well into the 1980s, basing its view that Aboriginal title had been "superseded by law," relying upon what the Supreme Court of Canada later called "the biases and prejudice of another era in our history. Such language is no longer acceptable in Canadian law." *Guerin v. The Queen*, [1985] 2 SCR 387 at 400.

66   The Donald Marshall Inquiry, the Aboriginal Justice Inquiry of Manitoba, and even the Royal Commission on Aboriginal Peoples concluded that the existing criminal justice system is rife with racism and unsuited to Indigenous people, and that a separate justice system ought to be created. None of the more fundamental recommendations of any of these commissions have been implemented.

contact with Europeans."[67] It does not matter that the contact may have been with a tiny number of Europeans,[68] or even that those Europeans merely shot at people and then ran away.[69] What is it about Europeans that makes them so magical that they affect other peoples' rights permanently, like a kind of reverse Midas touch? Why the first European? Why not the first African? Or Maya? Or Chinese? Racism is alive and well in the Canadian legal system: it just hides behind clouds of liberal language and legal sophistry.

Canadian courts have said that their understanding of Aboriginal title must be shaped by the legal systems of both Canada and the Indigenous people involved,[70] and their approach to implementing and respecting treaties must be shaped by the "Indian understanding" of those treaties.[71] In the United

---

67   The *Van der Peet* trilogy: *R. v. Van der Peet,* [1996] 2 SCR 546; *R. v. NTC Smokehouse,* [1996] 2 SCR 672; *R. v. Gladstone,* [1996] 2 SCR 723. More recently, the courts have acknowledged that what is involved is a period of a few decades before and after first contact, rather than a single moment in time. However, acknowledging that Métis Aboriginal rights could not have existed until at least nine months after "first contact," the Supreme Court of Canada decided that the "magic date" for Métis rights is when the Crown acquired practical control over the area—in some cases, nearly two centuries after "first contact" with Indians. *R. v. Powley,* [2003] 2 SCR 207. In 2016, the *Daniels* decision [*Daniels v. Canada (Indian Affairs and Northern Development)*], [2016] 1 SCR 99, declared the Métis to be "an aboriginal people of Canada." In 2015, the Truth and Reconciliation Commission of Canada recommended that the federal and provincial governments abandon any reliance on the doctrine of discovery.

68   In 1608, the year in which Mohawk rights were changed forever in Canadian law by contact with the French, there were six French families, totalling twenty-eight people, settled in New France. Twenty years later, there were seventy-six settlers. By 1640, there were still fewer than 300. Delage 1993, 243.

69   This "bullet to the head school of first contact" describes what the courts decided about Mohawk Aboriginal rights: the crucial moment was when Champlain and two of his French friends stepped into the open and, with dangerously overloaded arquebuses, shot three Mohawks dead in 1609 (*Mitchell, supra,* and *R. v. Adams,* [1996] 3 SCR 101).

70   *Delgam'uukw v. Attorney General of British Columbia.*

71   *Blueberry River Band v. The Queen,* [1995] 4 SCR 344. *R. v. Badger,* [1996] 1 SCR 771, para. 52: "The words in the treaty . . . must be interpreted in the sense that they would naturally have been understood by the Indians at the time of the signing." The term "the Indian understanding" is borrowed from the decisions of U.S. courts. This forms the basis of an "intention-based" approach that is used to override technicalities that might render a treaty or surrender void, in the name of respecting the intentions of the chiefs and principal men. Canadian law seeks a "reconciliation" of Aboriginal rights and title with Canadian laws and sovereignty, though generally this means seeking concessions from the Indigenous people rather than compatibility between the two legal systems.

States,[72] "land claims" vacillate between court and negotiated settlements, but the courts insist that "the Indian understanding" of the treaties is relevant and vital.[73] The time is ripe for texts in both Canada and the United States explaining the Haudenosaunee legal system, since it is the one within which the "Indian understanding" of many treaties exists. It is also the system that shaped the conduct and thinking of the representatives of the British Crown and of the United States of America in their treaties with many other Indigenous nations.

The treaties between the Haudenosaunee and the Crown and the United States do not exist in a vacuum. They live in a universe of Haudenosaunee law, a long series of international councils, governed by rules of process and interpretation, assisted by precedents in the Kayanerenkó:wa itself. The images, words, and even the sequences of words used in treaty councils are linked not only to all other treaty councils, but to their sources in the laws of the Confederacy. This is important not just historically but also legally: both U.S. and Canadian courts have stated unequivocally that "the words of the treaty must be construed

---

The use of the word "reconciliation" began with the Supreme Court's *Guerin* decision in 1984 ([1985] 2 SCR 335), in which the chief justice stated that Crown authority must be reconciled with Crown responsibility. From that point, one can trace an evolution of the word, ending with the court's statement in *Guerin* that Crown authority must be reconciled with Crown responsibility, and in *Mikisew* in 2005 ([2005] 3 SCR 388) that "the fundamental objective of the modern law of aboriginal and treaty rights is the reconciliation of aboriginal peoples and non-aboriginal peoples and their respective claims, interests and ambitions." What began with admonitions that indigenous legal systems ought to be reconciled *with* the common law has ended with the admonishment that they should reconcile themselves *to* it and its rule. Justice Binnie's explanation that the two watercraft symbolized by the Two Row Wampum had become a single Canadian wood, iron, and canvas ship of state depicts this "reconciliation" (*Mitchell* at para. 130).

72   There is a persistent tendency in U.S. law to begin any examination of history with the American Revolution. In fact, 200 years of British colonial history and law are direct antecedents of the United States, and the politicians who represented the federal and state governments in the late eighteenth century were often the same men who had represented the colonial governments before 1776.

73   This insistence is tempered by the courts' refusal to permit the introduction of contextual and historical evidence unless there is ambiguity in the treaty language: see *The People v. Neil Patterson Jr.*, New York Court of Appeals, 14 June 2005: "where the scope of a treaty right is unclear, we must look 'beyond the written words to the larger context that frames the [t]reaty, including "the history of the treaty, the negotiations, and the practical construction adopted by the parties"' (*Mille Lacs*, 526 U.S. at 196). Articles III and IV [of the Canandaigua Treaty], however, admit of no ambiguity. In contrast, the Supreme Court of Canada, in *R. v. Marshall*, [1999] 3 SCR 456, said that "extrinsic evidence of the historical and cultural context of a treaty may be received even absent any ambiguity on the face of the treaty" (Para. 10).

. . . in the sense in which they would naturally be understood by the Indians."[74] Actually, the transaction itself must be placed within its proper "Indian" legal context.

From the mid-seventeenth century to the mid-eighteenth century, the Haudenosaunee were a powerful military and political force in northeastern North America. The European colonists met with the Haudenosaunee in designated locations (council fire places),[75] and adhered to the forms and processes of Haudenosaunee councils. They did so for several reasons: because these processes were demanded by nations who were in a position to demand them; because they functioned on the basis of equality and respect, which often gave the Europeans power beyond their numbers; and because the processes were effective in accomplishing their goals. From 1755 to 1830, the British Imperial Indian Department was effectively controlled by the Johnson family, which maintained intimate ties with the Mohawks and was comfortable and familiar with Haudenosaunee processes and law. For nearly two centuries, the law that governed treaty making was Haudenosaunee law.

The legal system that gave rise to the process of treaty councils also lent its forms, vocabulary, metaphors, and rules to the agreements and relationships that emerged from the treaty councils. Mutual obligations in the Covenant Chain relationship between the Haudenosaunee and the Crown are reflections of the internal obligations between the nations of the Haudenosaunee. Dispute resolution mechanisms in the treaties, including the 1664 Fort Albany Treaty with the Crown and the 1794 Canandaigua Treaty with the United States, are borrowed from the mechanisms used among Haudenosaunee families, clans, and nations. To properly understand the treaties, in their historical and legal context, one must have some grasp of Haudenosaunee law. It is the legal environment, the ecosystem, in which the treaties live and breathe.

For the Haudenosaunee at this crucial time, there has been no law textbook. There are history books, but almost all of them have been written by foreigners. There are cases in the courts of the United States and Canada. None of them has seriously considered Haudenosaunee law. There are written versions of the

---

74   Justice Horace Gray, in *Jones v. Meehan,* 175 US 1 at 10–11 (1899), following *Worcester v. Georgia,* 6 Pet. (31 US) 515 at 552 (1832). The identical words appear in Lamer, C.J.'s decision in *R. v. Sioui,* [1990] 1 SCR 1025. There has been no judicial interpretation of the term "*naturally* understood." It may be taken to refer to the way the Indians would have understood the matters in their own laws—as *Delgam'uukw* suggests—or it may be the equivalent of interpreting the records according to their "clear and plain meaning," independent of "extrinsic" information.

75   The locations were pragmatically chosen: Albany at the confluence of the Mohawk and Hudson Rivers; Fort Stanwix at the portage between the Mohawk River and Lake Ontario; Niagara where Lake Ontario and Lake Erie meet; Detroit at the intersection of Lake Erie and Lake Huron.

laws,[76] but no modern Haudenosaunee law books. The written versions of the law are like the statutes in a law library. There is also a need for textbooks, jurisprudence, analysis, and journals. Otherwise, there is not enough for "law": there is only the meat chewed endlessly by anthropologists and historians, political scientists, ethnologists, and sociologists.

For a legal system based on thinking, there has been precious little written about the thought behind the laws.

The Haudenosaunee themselves are in danger of becoming immersed in arguments about the details of the various versions of the law, and missing the fundamental principles upon which the law is based.

This is a Haudenosaunee law book.

It is written in the humble knowledge that possibly nobody else is in the same position to do it now as I am: those who know more about the law itself lack the legal training, or the writing skills, or the time.

In humility, I begin with an apology, for I truly will not do as well as my elders would have, and my understanding is not as good as theirs. I miss my teachers, deeply and sadly. Much has been lost, and there is so much I have not learned, and may never learn. I can only do my best, and hope it is enough. For us, there is only the trying.

I would like to acknowledge the help of many people who guided my path. My brothers Roronhiakewen Dan Longboat, Kanakalût Roland Chrisjohn, Odatsehte Howard Elijah, Kanatiio Allen Gabriel, Tehennakarine Curtis Nelson, Hayadaha Rick Hill, and Sotsisowah John Mohawk, with whom long conversations always led to principles explained, are examples of how humans can be governed by the Kayanerenkó:wa today. My uncles, Kaientaronkwen Ernie Benedict, who taught me patience and perspective, and Tosawentsiadases Norm Jacobs, Tekaronianeken Jake Swamp, and Sakokwenonkwas Tom Porter, who taught me sweetness. My departed chiefs, Deskahe Harvey Longboat, Kanuhkitawi Bernie Parker, Donehogowa Hubert Buck, Coleman Powless, Deyonwe'ton Jake Thomas, and Orenrekowa Brian Skidders, who led and lived by example. So have Kawennokie Salli Benedict and Carol Jacobs.

Amber Meadow Adams has been more of an editor than any writer deserves. Her compassion, kindness, erudition, affection and thoughtfulness pervade the pages of this book as they have transformed my life.

And of course, my daughters, Kahsenneyohsta Lauren and Kahyoh'no Karenna continue to teach me, support me, encourage me, and, despite all my faults, love me.

All these people changed and raised up my mind.

Haii, Haii.

---

76 Faced with controversy over differing written versions of the law, the chiefs at Onondaga in the 1980s decided there was no single "official" version, nor would there ever be. This is the opposite of the reaction of the Grand River chiefs nearly a century before. To counter Newhouse's "inaccurate" version, they formed a committee to consolidate a correct one.

PART I

Context

Creation

. . . how she fell . . .

The Haudenosaunee Creation Story is as important to an understanding of the Kayanerenkó:wa as the Bible is important to an understanding of the laws of Canada and the United States.[1] The role of the Judeo-Christian tradition is more obvious in the United States, where money bears the motto "In God We Trust" and references to the Almighty exist within the constitution of the country itself.[2] It is equally present in Canadian law. The Constitution Act, 1982, begins: "Whereas Canada is founded upon principles that recognize the supremacy of God." Each Canadian coin bears the words "Elizabeth D.G. Regina," and the initials "D.G." remind us that she is Queen *dei gratia*, "by the grace of God"—that is, by divine right. The existence of the monarchy owes its principles to a tradition that is both Christian and Biblical. Canada's national anthem, in an increasingly secular society, still proclaims that *"il sait porter la croix."*[3] The traditions are not irrelevant to law: they illustrate some of the basic societal assumptions that lie at the foundations of the legal system, even as both countries insist that they maintain a separation between church and state.

Just as there are several versions of the Kayanerenkó:wa, there are several versions of the Creation story.[4] While some versions are inconsistent with others, and some contain internal contradictions, the fundamental principles are in most cases the same. The most complete recital of the Creation story was provided by Skaniatariio John Arthur Gibson, and transcribed by J.N.B. Hewitt

---

1   "The Bible contains legendary, historical and ethical contents. It is quite possible to consider them separately, and one doesn't have to accept the legends to get the ethics. Fundamentalists make a grave mistake to insist on the letter of the writings, because they drive away many who can't swallow the Adam-and-Eve bit" (Isaac Asimov 1994).

2   The Oath of Allegiance recited by schoolchildren every day refers to "one nation under God."

3   "Your arm knows how to carry the cross" is a direct reference to the Catholic missionary heritage of French Canada, carrying the cross to "heathen" tribes.

4   There are also several versions of the Biblical Genesis. See, e.g., Fox 2000.

at the end of the nineteenth century.[5] Sotsisowah John Mohawk's (2005) *Iroquois Creation Story* provides an edited version that reduces repetitiveness, updates the Victorian English, and seeks to remove Europeanizing elements.[6]

In the Haudenosaunee story of creation, a woman fell from the Sky World to earth. The earth was covered in water, and only water creatures were living there. The water birds, ducks and geese, saw the woman falling and slowed her descent. A great turtle allowed her to land on his back. She met with the animals and persuaded them that she needed soil.[7] The muskrat brought up a little soil for her,[8] and, dancing earth-wise (the direction of almost all Haudenosaunee ceremonies—counter-clockwise, like the Aeolian forces in the Northern Hemisphere), shuffling so that her feet never left the earth, she spread that soil all around Turtle Island, making the land habitable. She had grasped at the sides of the hole as she fell, and in her hands she carried the first seeds. She had been pregnant when she fell, and her daughter was born in the new land and grew quickly. They were still the only people in a cold, dark place, and they were always hungry. The daughter became pregnant in due course—but with no men around, Sky Woman was angry and suspicious. The daughter gave birth to twins. The left-handed twin, Tawiskaron (Flint), cut his way out of his mother's side, killing her. The right-handed twin, Nikarondase (Sapling), was born in the normal way.[9] The twins are symbols of the duality, reciprocity, or two-sidedness that permeates Haudenosaunee thinking and law.

---

5   Hewitt 1928. Hewitt worked for the Bureau of American Ethnology (his papers are in the Smithsonian Museum of Natural History today), but he was Tuscarora, spending a great deal of time with the chiefs at the Grand River. They thought highly enough of him that he was given the task of some of the speaking at the Condolence at Oneida in 1917.

6   Mohawk 2005a.

7   The meeting with the animals is itself a precursor of the structure of councils under the Great Law: it had two sides—Sky Woman on one side, and the animals on the other—and the exchange between them reflects the process followed in council. This meeting may also be a precursor of the division of things into male and female, for it appears all the animals in the council were male.

8   In this council, as in the councils of Haudenosaunee chiefs, the question asked was: "How can we help each other?" and the answer involved willing sacrifice for long-term benefits, for future generations. Muskrat died immediately after bringing the mud from the ocean depths.

9   Taharonhiawakon, which means "He holds up the heavens," is another of his names—probably more proper, but harder to read. He has also been called the Earth Grasper, a name that recalls the moment in the story when he takes a handful of earth and declares to his brother, "*I tell you this is alive!*" (Mohawk 2005a, i). Note the contrast between the names, animate and inanimate.

Later writers would suggest that there was a "Good Twin" and an "Evil Twin":[10] earlier versions are not nearly so simplistic. Nikarondase was good at creating things, and he made beautiful flowers, useful trees, graceful animals, while his twin made snakes and thorny bushes, inedible and poisonous creatures. Nikarondase made waters flow both ways; his brother installed falls and rapids and caused the rivers to flow in only one direction. What emerges from classic Haudenosaunee thinking about this, though, is not only that there are always two sides, but that there is also the need for balance. Without the thorns, the rose would be defenceless. Without the mosquitoes, the songbirds would lack food.[11] The twins may have created different-looking things, but the totality of their creation was harmonious. At a time of uncertainty and hunger, each twin made decisions to the best of his ability, and each might have been right. The right-handed twin created human beings—today he is addressed in gratitude as Shonkwaiatíson—"He Completed Our Bodies."[12] Where Tawiskaron made ultimately harmful creatures, Nikarondase found ways to transform them into useful parts of a harmonious whole. Mary Arquette explains: "It was not his nature to destroy things, even those created by his brother, the Left-Handed Twin. Instead, he found an important role for most of them and gave them special duties."[13]

Transforming or deflecting harmful forces into benevolence and benefit is typical of the strategies of the Peacemaker in forming Haudenosaunee government. That our Creator himself would have used the same principles in establishing the ecosystems of the land is both consistent and reassuring.[14]

---

10 The Biblical parallel may not be Christ and Satan but rather Cain and Abel: nothing in the book of Genesis suggests that the work of one brother was better than that of the other, yet God smiled on Abel's efforts, and Cain slew Abel. Some versions of the Bible infer that God turned against Cain because of the latter's negative attitude. The Jesuits in the 1600s pressed the parallels upon their converts.

11 Niwadenraah Henry Lickers, personal communication, 1989. Taharionwakon, in some cases, modified his brother's creations to cause them to fit more beneficially within the web of life.

12 It is said that Shonkwaiatíson blew three times into the mouth of the first human to give him life. The three-ness of those first breaths is repeated in the law: in the three warnings to a chief before he is removed; in the three invitations to another nation to join the peace; in the three sharp cries to drive bad spirits away at a sunrise thanksgiving; in the three sighs, *yo-ho-oh*, at the end of a dance in the ceremonies.

13 Iotenerahtatenion Mary Arquette, in Haudenosaunee Environmental Task Force 2001, 84.

14 Shonkwaiatishon means "He finished our bodies." That is, our Creator created us humans. He is by far not the only Creator: his twin brother made many things; from the grave of his mother grew tobacco, corn, potatoes, squash, and strawberries; his grandmother, Katsisayen, Sky Woman, danced the earth across the great Turtle's back; and many other forces brought their contributions to creation.

At one point, Tawiskaron challenged Nikarondase to a gambling game. The stakes were the very highest: would life continue? The game was the Peach Stone Bowl Game: six stones, white on one side and dark on the other, are tossed into the air, landing in the bowl. The side that gets all six the same colour first wins it all. The boys' grandmother, Katsisayen (Mature Flowers), better known today as Sky Woman, favoured Tawiskaron and sided with him. Nikarondase borrowed the heads of some chickadees and tossed them into the air. As they fell, turning, turning, all creation called out in support of that one throw, and the six heads all landed the same way. There would indeed be life.[15] Tawiskaron was sent away but not killed, and his influence over darkness and winter is still with us.[16] Today, in every longhouse at Midwinter, the two sides of the house play the same game, in commemoration of that great gamble.[17] It remains one of the four great sacred ceremonies of the Haudenosaunee.

This story reminds us that life on earth is not a sure thing. It is a matter of chance. It is a close thing, too. It could as easily not have been, or not have been as it is. "Modern" scientists have only recently come to the same conclusion: that when those primordial strands of DNA were twisting in some lukewarm pool millions of years ago, if the sun had passed behind the clouds or a nearby volcano had erupted or a stone had rolled into the puddle, life as we know it might not have existed. Carol Jacobs, a Cayuga Bear clan mother, told the United Nations:

> In one throw, supported by all the living forces of the natural world, our Creator won this bet. He won it all for us. He won it for all of us. We commemorate this each year in our Midwinter ceremonies.
>
> This is not just a quaint legend. It is a reminder that, as scientists now agree, life on earth is a result of chance, as well as of intent. Life on earth is a fragile matter. That magnificent gamble could have gone the other way: life could just as easily not have been at all.
>
> That is a reason for constantly giving thanks. We know very well how close life is to not being. The reminders are all around us.[18]

---

15   Mohawk 2005a, 50–51. The odds of getting all six the same colour are just over 1 percent.

16   In Haudenosaunee cosmology and legend, there is recognition that matter and energy are constants—that they are not destroyed, but only set aside or sent away. In the case of evil or negative forces, their influence is still present, and we must seek to avoid it. The victorious Taharionwakon does not kill his brother, nor does he exile him into oblivion. Instead, in a precursor to the Two Row Wampum, he states that while they cannot live together, nevertheless he wants to keep him near.

17   Blau 1967.

18   Carol Jacobs, July 18, 1995, in *Akwesasne Notes,* Fall 1995.

If life is a close thing, then we must care for it, acknowledge it, and be constantly grateful for it. The words that open and close each meeting of the people, ohe'n:ton karihwatékwen, the "words that come before all else," are words of gratitude for and to each part of the natural world. An attitude of modest gratitude—atenonhwaratonhtserakon—is pervasive.[19]

Gratitude is offered to the Creator for making the world a place that supports life, but in giving thanks, the Haudenosaunee also acknowledge the plants and animals that sacrifice their lives so that humans can survive. There are ceremonies to give thanks as each of the plants are harvested: maple, berries, beans, green corn, and white corn. Hunters greet the animals before hunting and thank each animal after it is taken. In thanking each part of the natural world, the Haudenosaunee are also thanking Creation itself.

Sostsisowah John Mohawk expanded on the traditional Haudenosaunee saying that we cannot see the Creator's face, a metaphoric reference to our inability to fully comprehend the complexity of the creative force of the universe:

> In the native tradition the Creator has a less specific personage, if it's even a personage at all. The Creator could be time or space or energy or all of those. The Creator could be everything there is. And the Creator could be our dream. But whatever it is, we don't know, so we ought to be humble about that. And we ought to be humble because we are really the tiniest little speck on a little star in a not-very-large galaxy, on the edge of other galaxies that may be among billions and billions of galaxies that we've never heard of and never will.[20]

Gratitude is perhaps an inadequate way of describing the thanksgiving. Wallace Chafe explained the inadequacy of English to match the Seneca thinking that goes with the words:

> The word "thanksgiving" seems no worse a choice than any other and has been used by most previous writers. When confronted with the Seneca words involved, some speakers balk at any attempt to give an English equivalent. Others translate, to some extent according to context, as *"thank, be grateful to or for, rejoice in, bless, greet."* The trouble is that the Seneca concept is broader than that expressed in any simple English term, and covers not only the conventionalized

---

19   A careful observer will notice that many Christian "prayers" consist of asking for things—our daily bread, forgiveness for our trespasses—while Haudenosaunee orations at the same place in gatherings are expressions of gratitude, not desire.

20   Mohawk 1996.

amenities of both thanksgiving and greeting, but also a more general
feeling of happiness over the existence of something or someone.[21]

The Haudenosaunee story of creation provides principles that shape and
affect many aspects of the law.[22] Fundamental beliefs find their way into constitutional and statutory provisions. The separation of church and state, a relatively
recent occurrence in Anglo-Saxon law in North America, is not a line drawn in
Haudenosaunee law. The cycle of ceremonies of gratitude is not at all the same
as a European organized church, though some anthropologists assert that they
have coalesced into a religion with "deacons" (the faithkeepers) and an organized
structure (the annual Six Nations meetings to recite the Karihwí:iyo, the Code
of Handsome Lake). By law, the rotiyanershon are responsible for helping to
maintain the Four Ceremonies.[23] They have no other religious functions. The
ceremonies, Sotsisowah John Mohawk explained, are at the heart of what it
means to be Haudenosaunee:

> Despite all the information which came to light about the existence
> of an Iroquois cosmology, anthropologists … generally failed to see
> a connection between the cosmology and the ceremonial life of the
> Iroquois. This is interesting because one of the major themes of the
> narrative pointedly answers a central question about Haudenosaunee
> identity. Who are we? We are the people who carry on the tradition
> of ceremonials of thanksgiving. Why do we do these ceremonials?
> Because we recognize our great good fortune as receivers of the gifts
> of the Giver of Life. The people who composed this narrative did

---

21   Chafe 1961, 6. The English transcription of a detailed Seneca Thanksgiving is Chafe's
     publication of Shogʌdzowa Corbett Sundown's words (9–16). Sotsisowah John Mohawk
     believed that the Thanksgiving, in its present form, was developed by the Tonawanda
     Senecas in the two or three decades after the death of Handsome Lake—that is, in the
     early years of the nineteenth century—and based on the invocation that would ac-
     company the burning of the white dog. However, he was not suggesting that either the
     attitude of gratitude or the words used were of recent invention. Gratitude permeates all
     the ceremonies. Thinking about structure and place is constant. It is just the particular
     wording that is a distillation of earlier ideas and has emerged from another set of dark
     times.

22   "Since the time of Creation the population of the Onkwehonwe were instructed. That's
     why we always go back to the time of Creation. We were always instructed from that
     time. Where did we come from? And what's our purpose in being here? And how did
     that tradition come about?" Deyonwe'ton Jake Thomas, in RCAP 1995, 631.

23   The Four Ceremonies are: Atonwa, the personal chant to honour the Creator;
     Kaientowá:nen, the bowl game, to give thanks for Creation; Ohstow'kówa, the Great
     Feather Dance, to celebrate life together; and Kanehó:ron, the Drum Dance, to thank
     the spirits. They arrived, temporally, between the Creation Story and the Great Law.
     They were brought to the Haudenosaunee by a fatherless man as a means of giving
     thanks together. For information on the Four Ceremonies, see Native North American
     Travelling College 2000, and also Mohawk 2005a, 90. There is also a Skaniatariio John
     Arthur Gibson version, 1900, collected by J.N.B. Hewitt, NAA MS 2181 (271 pages).

so to transmit that message to future generations. As long as there are Haudenosaunee people, the narrative tells us, they will perform the Great Gamble for Life. For as long as the Haudenosaunee exist, according to this tradition, they will remember this story.[24]

It is to questions about the meaning of existence that grand mythologies, sometimes called meta-narratives, turn their attention. Mythologies construct visions of the past which address the question about how the world came to be the way it is and, equally important, how we, as cultural beings in a certain culture, came to be the way we are.[25]

Such a story was not intended to be a secret among a few selected individuals. It was heard by all, the young and old, together, as a group experience. In the same way that everyone who participates in modern American culture has heard of the child who was born in a manger, everyone in ancient Iroquoia heard about the woman who fell from the sky.[26]

[The Creation story offers] an Haudenosaunee vision of humankind's role in the universe, and [calls] upon the bearers of the culture to join that vision, to act it out, to join in with a dream, and to form a society which reflects it.[27]

One fundamental principle that flows from the Creation story is the relationship between human beings and the natural world. The Book of Genesis gives human beings "dominion" over all parts of the natural world[28] and suggests that everything was created to serve the needs of humanity. More recent Christian thinkers have struggled to insert the concept of "stewardship" into these words.[29] While logic agrees with the approach, fundamentalists who see an obligation to develop and exploit wage theological war with environmentalists who feel a need to conserve. The Haudenosaunee Creation story places human beings

---

24   Mohawk 2005a, v.

25   Mohawk 2005a, ix.

26   Mohawk 2005a, viii

27   Mohawk 2005a, x.

28   Genesis 1: 26–28.

29   The eviction of Adam and Eve from the Garden, condemned thereafter to derive their sustenance by scraping the soil, living by the sweat of their brows, has been seen as the end of a hunter-gatherer world and the beginning of agriculture. The Haudenosaunee did not suffer a similar condemnation by their Creator. In the 2015 encyclical *Laudato Si'*, Pope Francis stated that Christians "must forcefully reject the notion that our being created in God's image and given dominion over the earth justifies absolute domination over other creatures. . . . Human life is grounded in three fundamental and closely intertwined relationships: with God, with our neighbour, and with the earth itself."

squarely in the midst of a natural world in which they form an integral part, and in which each part has been given responsibilities. Sotsisowah explained:

> The Haudenosaunee Creation Story, which we can assume predates the foundation of the League, is replete with symbols of a rational universe. In the Creation Story, the only creature with a potential for irrational thought is the human being. All the other creatures of Nature are natural, i.e. rational.
>
> Nature is depicted as a threatening and irrational aspect of existence in the West's cosmologies. The Haudenosaunee cosmology is quite different. It depicts the natural world as a rational existence[30] while admitting that human beings possess an imperfect understanding of it. The idea that human beings have an imperfect understanding of the rational nature of existence is something of a caution to Haudenosaunee in their dealings with nature. Conversely, the idea that the natural world is disorganized and irrational has served as something of a permission in the West and may be the single cultural aspect which best explains the differences between these two societies' relationships to Nature.[31]
>
> The reason it's so important to get people to cease fearing nature is that negative emotions invade one's ability to think clearly. People who are afraid of nature have much more difficulty defending it than people who are not. All of those negative emotions give you permission to enact violence on nature.[32]

---

30   The idea that the natural world is not only rational but also organized is reflected in the layered structure set out in the Thanksgiving Address. Modern Haudenosaunee insist that this is a specific way of looking at the world. For example, the Akwesasne science curriculum follows the structure of the Thanksgiving. The Haudenosaunee Environmental Task Force, in setting out a view of the natural world and the challenges it faces, also followed this structure (see Haudenosaunee Environmental Task Force 2001).

31   Mohawk 1989, 223. John Mohawk has suggested that the difference between Haudenosaunee (and other natural world) religions and Christianity is the difference between magic and miracles. Haudenosaunee ceremonies call upon the powers of the natural world for assistance: if the power is beyond human, Western observers tend to call this "magic." Haduwi, for example, the power behind the masked medicine societies, is in some ways a culmination of the forces of the natural world that we cannot control. Haudenosaunee medicine societies tend to be reflections of natural forces—the help of the Bears, the Otters, and the Buffalo, for example. Christianity, on the other hand, sees "miracles" as unnatural by definition. If a cure attributed to a saint's intervention can be shown to have been the result of a natural cause, it is no longer considered to be a miracle.

32   Mohawk 1996, 10.

The values and principles inherent in the Creation story remain close to the day-to-day thinking and conduct of traditional Haudenosaunee today. Neil Patterson confirms:

> From a Haudenosaunee perspective, there is a personal mandate from the Creation to protect Mother Earth and all that inhabit her. We should all begin to look at what personal changes we can make to reduce waste that our waters will eventually receive. . . . If there are doubts in the minds of our leaders about action like this on the Natural World, the answer is obvious. These past mistakes of history serve as a guideline for future generations: not only our grandchildren, but for the fish and everything that is in the Circle of Life. Our elders have learned from their elders these rules and guidelines.[33]

The Creation story establishes relationships—family relationships—between its characters in ways that resound through Haudenosaunee society. The earth, receiving the body of our Creator's mother, becomes our mother. The moon is our grandmother (because she was formed when Nikarondase (Thaharionwakon) placed his grandmother's head in the heavens after her death).[34] The animals and plants are our brothers and sisters. If the law is founded upon bringing disparate people into a single family, the Creation story sets the tone for doing so.

A second principle is the nature of good and evil. Christianity has wrestled with the issue of how an all-powerful God who is absolutely good could permit evil to exist and even to flourish. The Church answers: it is a mystery that we humans cannot fathom; we are told we must have faith. Haudenosaunee thinking recognizes that good and evil both exist, and have been here from the beginning. They *are*, and therefore the question is not why, but rather how to address them in our lives and societies, and how to find balance.[35] Evil will not go away: we must continue to recognize it, understand it, and guard against it.

---

33   Neil Patterson Jr., "The Fish," in Haudenosaunee Environmental Task Force 2001.

34   One can find the same reverence for family in Polynesian creation stories: that Maui used his grandmother's jawbone as the fishhook that brought the islands to the surface is an indicator of the affection and respect one must have for one's elder relatives.

35   In the Creation story, the right-handed twin banishes his brother, but does not kill him. Indeed, he says that he thinks one day his twin may win (however, it would probably be wrong to simplify their conflict into a match between good and evil, rather than a typical Haudenosaunee account of different ways to think about survival). When Thadadaho has the snakes combed from his hair, the serpents are not killed. They go somewhere else, and Thadadaho is given a staff with which to keep crawling things away from the council fire. The snakes continue to exist; the balance between "good force" and "bad force" remains.

A third principle is the relationship between the real and the spiritual, or what Wade Davis has called an "inner horizon."[36] In "scientific" societies, things exist if their physical presence is provable.[37] In most Indigenous societies, a thing that is dreamed also exists. The Haudenosaunee Creation story reflects a society that recognizes (as quantum theory suggests) that beings can move between our world and the spirit world, and that each world influences the other.[38]

There is another set of lessons in the Creation story, urgently relevant to people alive today. Sky Woman, the only person the story follows through her entire lifetime, is thrust into a dark, wet, cold world. She is pregnant and alone. She survives what can only be described as catastrophic environmental change: the loss of her entire world. She and her grandsons are hungry much of the time. The ways in which they coped—how they dealt with the issues of sharing, of adapting, of making decisions—are shapers and reflections of the kind of society the Haudenosaunee developed. The Creation story is old: the world its people faced has features of an ice age.[39]

There is always friction between those who say "we were created here" and those who say "you're just immigrants like everyone else—your ancestors came over the ice bridge across the Bering Sea less than 25,000 years ago." Those who support the "bridge" theory often use it to assert that Aboriginal title is only immigrant title; that nobody has a better claim to the land than anyone else; that human occupation of North America is not ancient.[40] From a scientific perspective, the same accusations could be levelled at the British, since human occupation of the British Isles is no older (humans crossed to England after the last ice age). In fact, *humans* as we know them have not been around that long

---

36 "They don't separate dreams from reality." Davis 1998, 36. Just as Aboriginal Australians assert that there was a Dreamtime before there was this age of the earth, so the Haudenosaunee Creation story takes place in a Dreamtime in which the animals are also spirits, and in which the formation of the world is happening at the same time as its first inhabitants are both already existing and taking shape.

37 A proposed Canada Health Protection Act, for example, would have required clinical testing by "science and objective observation." Haudenosaunee medicine, which sees a partnership between the patient, the healer, the plants, and the spirits that assist the healing, would have a difficult time providing scientific proof of its effectiveness.

38 A stream of court cases in Canada and the United States reduce Indigenous realities to mere "subjective beliefs," which results in a lack of protection for what has been argued as religious freedom: epitomized in the United States, *Navajo Nation v. United States Forestry Service*, 479 F.3d 1024 (9th Cir. 2007), reversed 535 F.3d 1058 (9th Cir. 2008); in Canada, *Ktunaxa Nation v. British Columbia (Forests, Lands and Natural Resource Operations)* 2017 SCC 54. Probably by no coincidence, both cases involve the protection of sacred mountain areas from ski resorts.

39 Amber Meadow Adams explores these issues in her 2014 dissertation, "Teyotsi'tsiahsonhatye: Medicine and Meaning in the Haudenosaunee Story of Life's Renewal," and has done so in our many conversations since.

40 Hayadaha Richard Hill says that these people ought to get their Berings straight.

compared to the age of the world. We are all very recent.[41] The Haudenosaunee do not believe (as the Bible seems to assume, in saying that we were made in God's image) that we are the ultimate beings in the world, the end of all evolution. Things change. Sotsisowah John Mohawk observed:

> Things flow from sources which have roots deeper than individual talents or society's gifts. They flow from nature, and the sacred beings who designed nature. If one embraces the initial premise, that human beings were extremely lucky that of all the places in the universe, they have a home just the right distance from a sun of just the right intensity, that there is enough water, grass, and enough of everything. From there, it's a small step to accept that whatever created all that is a force of unexcelled sacred dimensions and the will of that force is something people should try to cooperate with to perpetuate life. The way a group expresses its cooperation is through ceremonies which recreate the conditions present when people first came to consciousness of these things.
>
> Humankind's relationship to nature projected in this precolonial, pre-patriarchal, pre-modern story carries a fundamental and unchanging truth, but one which subsequent generations would need to relearn over and over. Humans exist in a context of nature, and not vice versa. Everything we have ever had, everything we have, everything we will ever have—our health, our good looks, our intelligence, everything—is a product not of our own merit but of all that which created our world. That which created our world is not society, but the power of the universe. Nature, which is the context of our existence, is sacred. A significant manifestation of nature, the regenerative power of life, is also sacred, and we who walk about on the earth are not without obligations to perpetuate this system, the "work" of the Giver of Life, in the greater scheme of things.[42]

Those who say "we were created here" may or may not be wrong in biological terms. For legal purposes, though, biological creation is irrelevant. It is enough to say "we were created here, *as a people*," in social and legal terms. The land has shaped its societies. Given half a chance, the land will shape the people who came to the Americas from Europe, from Asia, from Africa. Haudenosaunee society is "Indigenous," in legal terms. It exists nowhere else. The term carries two distinct legal meanings. One is that the people have a special connection to

---

41   Paul Ehrlich (2002, 98–99) states that modern humans emerged from Africa "within the past 100,000 years, starting perhaps 60,000–45,000 years ago, or even more recently, and replaced premodern populations."

42   Mohawk 2005a, xviii.

the land in which their society was formed (Gary Paul Nabhan calls Indigenous peoples "cultures of habitat," existing effectively only within the ecosystems in which they evolved).[43] The other is that they were here first, before all the waves of more recent immigrants—and as an Indigenous society, they have the rights that come from being first.[44]

The Land

As a people with a culture of habitat, the Haudenosaunee developed, over millennia, a sense of balance and comfort with the land around them. The homeland of the Haudenosaunee was not, as is sometimes assumed, a forbidding, untouched, and wild forest. Engelbrecht observed: "A commonly held image in need of revision is that eastern North America was covered by unbroken virgin forest before European settlement. Europeans coming from regions that had been clear-cut may have thought the environment untouched, but long human presence in the northeast had affected the distribution of plant and animal communities even before the establishment of Native American horticulture . . . the environment in which Native Americans lived is increasingly viewed as an environment that Native Americans altered, both consciously and unconsciously."[45]

Fire was a powerful tool. Deliberately set fires were a means of maintaining meadows, encouraging the natural progression from meadow to thicket to forest and back to meadow again, propagating certain trees and plants. Fire was sometimes used to drive game, but there was also an understanding of its long-term role in supporting hunting by maintaining diverse habitats and therefore biodiversity itself.[46] There were natural meadows and prairies, so that it was not necessary to carve new village sites out of dense forests. Parker, though, explained that "by burning off tracts in the forest large clearings were made suitable for fields and towns."[47] Warren Johnson, visiting his brother Sir William in 1760, noted Haudenosaunee restraint in using fire as a tool: "When clearing land, they Set fire to the Timber, & burn it to ashes, which they scatter

---

43　　Nabhan 1997.

44　　"When Europeans arrived in North America, Aboriginal peoples were already here, living in communities on the land, and participating in distinctive cultures, as they had done for centuries." *R. v. Van der Peet,* [1996] 2 SCR 507 at 538.

45　　Engelbrecht 2003, 9; Alfred Crosby 1986; and Charles Mann 2005.

46　　Engelbrecht 2003; see also Russell 1983.

47　　Parker 1968, 21.

about on the ground, they make Charcoal of Wood; they never clear more Land than Serves for their Own Use."[48]

The absence of many earthworms (introduced with European settlement in the seventeenth century) meant that the forest's understory was not mulched with the same intensity, and therefore it supported different plant life than it does today.[49] The Haudenosaunee deliberately encouraged some trees and plants: black walnut, for example, appears in areas of settlement, well north of its "normal" Carolinian range.[50] The forests around the villages, to the Haudenosaunee before (and after) the arrival of Europeans, were managed ecosystems, not a wild frontier. The idea of managed fields and forests blurs the sharp human/non-human line between the clearing and the woods.

Until recently, archaeologists believed that the knowledge of how to deliberately plant crops arrived in northeastern North America about ten centuries ago, spreading northward from Mexico. It is likely that knowledge of different plants came at different times, and that some knowledge was imported while other plants were domesticated locally.[51] Corn and beans came from the south a thousand years ago; squash and gourds (cucurbits) may have been bred locally a thousand years before that.[52] Sunflowers,[53] other fleshy flowers (chenopods and sumpweed), Jerusalem artichoke, and nut groves (hickory nuts, walnuts, acorns, chestnuts, and hazelnuts) may have been developed in the northeast and spread from there. The people also gathered fruit: plums and cherries, strawberries and raspberries, sumac and blackberries.

The cultivation of crops transformed the way of life of the peoples of the northeast of Turtle Island. Corn, beans, and squash became known as the Three Sisters, "our life supporters." Fields around the villages and towns of the Haudenosaunee might stretch for a mile or two in all directions.

What Gayle Fritz (drawing on Maxi'diwaic's commentary in *Buffalo Bird Woman's Garden*) said of Hidatsa women and the land could equally apply to

48   Johnson 1921, 13:195. The ashes scattered on the fields after Midwinter are known to be helpful in regenerating life in the spring.

49   Mann 2007. "In worm-free woodlands, leaf litter piles up in drifts on the forest floor. But when earthworms are introduced, they can do away with the litter in a few months. The problem is that northern trees and shrubs beneath the forest canopy depend on that litter for food. . . . These creatures literally changed the ground beneath the Indians' feet" (32–33).

50   Wykoff 1991, 13. There is also archaeological evidence of deliberate planting of pawpaw, bladder-nut shrub, hickory, and nut trees. Until the arrival of a devastating blight, up to one-quarter of the trees of the Carolinian forest were American chestnuts, which are now nearly extinct.

51   "The recognition of eastern North America as an independent center of plant domestication has been one of the most exciting archaeological revelations of the late twentieth century." Fritz 2002, 225.

52   Keener and Kuhns 1997.

53   Bodner 1999.

the Haudenosaunee: "The hoe and stick digging technique was labor inten-
sive, but the women loved their fields and pampered their crops, even singing
to them, and most of the work was appreciated for the comradeship, the
natural beauty, and the emotional satisfaction it afforded."[54] The earth, say the
Haudenosaunee, is a mother to all of us. We must treat her as we treat our own
mothers, with respect and gentleness: "The feeling of reverence toward the earth
itself is also to be found behind some of the lingering reluctance to adopt the
white man's agricultural equipment. The 'Old People' believe that since Mother
Earth nurtured her children, they should not tear at her breasts with ploughs,
but rather tickle them gently with a stick or hoe."[55]

The transformation from a society of hunter-gatherers to a society of garden-
ers (horticulturalists) took place gradually: "By A.D. 900, cucurbits, chenopod,
little barley and sunflower were being grown with maize in the West Branch
of the Susquehanna River basin. . . . In Europe, the time between A.D. 900
and A.D. 1200 is known as the Medieval Warm Period or neo-Atlantic climate
episode. It is suggested that a similar warm period in New York facilitated the
spread of farming."[56]

It meant the people could live together in larger, more permanent settlements. These larger settlements required more permanent and sophisticated
forms of government.

Not long after the growth of towns came the kinds of war that required
palisades, not just to keep wild animals out, but for protection against human
enemies.[57]

Physically, there were visible and conceptual boundaries in the minds of the
people (as every culture provides visible boundaries). They radiated outward
from the family's hearth or fire,[58] which itself was a circle of stones.[59] The next
boundary was the walls of the longhouse. Then came the walls of the town.
They represented security from danger: within those walls the land was under

---

54   Fritz 2000, 237; Wilson 1987.

55   Snyderman 1951, 17. See also Stiles 1905; Day 1953, 329–46.

56   Engelbrecht 2003, 24.

57   Not all towns were palisaded. Archaeological evidence suggests that there were large
      palisaded towns and smaller "satellite hamlets" some distance away, whose people could
      seek refuge in the towns in times of peril.

58   The root-word in Mohawk for "fire"—ó:tsire—is the same as the root-word for "family"
      —ohwátsi're.

59   In wampum belts, council fires (and therefore nations) are depicted sometimes as
      hexagons, sometimes as squares. Were the real fires of these shapes, or were the wam-
      pums using these shapes because of the restrictions of working with beads? Probably the
      latter: but not much attention has yet been paid by archaeologists to the shape of fires
      in Haudenosaunee longhouses. They have noticed a difference between deeper hearths
      (probably for cooking and roasting) and shallower, shifting ones (probably for warmth)
      (Englebrecht 2003, 77). The colder the weather, the closer the people slept to the fire.

almost complete human control. Outside the palisades, the fields and gardens were cleared by men and cultivated by women. The fields ran to the woods' edge. The woods, which could be seen in a circle around the town, were another clear boundary.

Between the settlements, and between the nations, there was a network of paths and trails, both by land and water.[60] People wishing to visit another settlement would travel along the wide paths of peace. The paths share another aspect with international relations: the more they are used, the plainer they are, and the smoother they become. Those wishing to do harm would move in swift silence through the woods. Those who came in peace would often come singing their peace songs[61] to announce themselves. A watchful town would

---

60   See, e.g., Toriwawakon Paul A.W. Wallace 1971, 2: "Most Indian paths were so well planned that, until the invention of the internal combustion engine, there was little occasion for any but minor changes in route."

61   In 1666, La Pause described a Haudenosaunee embassy to the French: "One of the more notable men walks at the head, and pronounces a long string of words which have been handed down to them by tradition, and which are repeated by the others after him. The ambassador who is to be the spokesman comes last of all, singing in a rather agreeable tone; he continues his song until he has entered his cabin; around which he walks five or six times, still singing; then he sits down. There the pledges of friendship are renewed, the presents are given to dispel fatigue; to wipe away tears; to remove scales from their eyes, so that they may easily see one another; and finally, to open their throats and give free passage to their voices." *Relation de l'Ambassade des Cinq Nations*, Archives Nationales, Paris, CIIA 2: 264 v.[1666]; RAPQ 1932-33-328. In May 1756, the British met with the Shawnees and Delawares. An observer wrote: "The Shawanese came over the River with the English Prisoners, beating a Drum & singing their Peace Song, agreeable to the Antient Custom of their Nation, which they continued 'till they entered the Council Room" (SWJP 11: 727). The Senecas recalled "dancing the peace dance" approaching other nations at a peace treaty at Detroit (Fenton 1953, 108). The Miamis met the French in 1667 as they "approached singing and dancing, bending their knees in turn almost to the ground" (La Potherie, in Blair 1911, 1:325–30); in 1710, the Haudenosaunee met Ottawas at Onondaga: the three Ottawa delegates were "singing the Song of Joy. They had long stone Pipes in their hands & under the Pipes hung Feathers as big as Eagles Wings. When they left off singing well we filled their Pipes & let them smoak, when They had done, They filled the Pipes for us to Smoak—this is the token of Friendship" (Wraxall [1754] 1915, 70). The calumet—the pipe with the hanging feathers—is the peace instrument of the western nations. In July 1751, Conrad Weiser described a Catawba peace delegation to the Haudenosaunee: "I went to meet them and Conducted them to their proper place they Came along Singing with their Collabashes dressed with feders in their hands, they Continued Singing for a while after they sat down" (du Simitière Collection, Yi 966, Ridgway Library, Library Company of Pennsylvania).

always have young men posted in the woods to guard against danger.[62] Visitors would stop at the edge of the woods, and wait to be greeted.[63] The narratives of the Kayanerenkó:wa describe several instances where individuals stop some distance from a community and light a fire, so that the smoke "pierces the sky."[64] This would give the people of the community a chance to investigate who the visitor is, and what is his business. In the story of the making of the law, the Peacemaker and Hiawatha consistently make fires near the woods' edge, and tell the men sent to meet them to go ahead and announce that they are coming, bringing a message.[65] In uncertain times, it is prudent to be announced, and to be invited.

The woods' edge is a place of visible transition, from the shadows of the forest to the soaring sky of the clearing[66] It is a dividing line between light and darkness.

If the people know the visitors are coming, they will light the fire and wait for their arrival to perform the greeting.

When he approached Hochelaga in 1534, Jacques Cartier described the broad path of peace to the town, and the greeting at the woods' edge that he and his men received:

> The City of Hochelaga is six miles from the riverside, and the road
> thither is as well-beaten and frequented as can be, leading through
> as fine a country as can be seen, full of fine oaks as any in France,
> the whole ground being strewn over with fine acorns. When we had

---

62   The watchers might be placed at some distance: "the Iroquois always have sentinels upon
      the routes of their enemies," noted the Jesuit Relation of 1623 (Thwaites 1901, 1:105).
      When singing was combined with joyous firing of muskets (or as an additional way of
      announcing one's coming), the safety factor could be reduced: William Johnson wrote
      of an incident at Niagara in which "a party of 30 Friend Indians who were coming in to
      joyn the rest I sent there, on passing an Outpost sang their Song and discharged their
      pieces as is always customary, but the Sergeant who commanded mistaking them for an
      Enemy fired upon them and dangerously wounded three of the Indians." SWJP 4: 451.
      The *feu de joie* is a worldwide practice. It can get dangerous, as when celebrants fire their
      AK-47s in the air at an Afghan wedding.

63   In modern Europe and North America, the boundaries are different, but some of the
      etiquette is the same. When you go to visit someone, you stop at the front door of the
      house. In some societies, you wait in the car in the driveway for a short time before go-
      ing to the door. Then you ring the bell, or knock on the door, and wait politely at this
      boundary between the house and the outside world.

64   "Piercing the sky" by making a smoky fire was a way of making one's presence known
      from a distance. However, the term also applies to the smoke from burning tobacco,
      which rises through the sky we can see, and into the Sky World, calling the attention of
      the Creator to what is being said or requested. In Gibson 1899, it is used as a synonym
      for travelling southward.

65   Gibson 1912, 70, 96–99.

66   Pollan 2008, 212, 215. Pollan asserts that the "trope of constriction and release resonates
      most powerfully in a culture raised on a deeply forested continent, in a place where the
      moment of coming into a clearing has had a special urgency and savor."

gone four or five miles we were met by one of the great lords of the
city, accompanied by a great many natives, who made us understand
by signs that we must stop at a place where they had made a large
fire, which we did accordingly. When we had rested there some time,
the chief made a long discourse in token of welcome and friendship,
showing a joyful countenance and every mark of goodwill.[67]

Nearly a century and a half later, another French visitor described a similar
experience at Onondaga. By now, the French knew how to announce themselves:

This is why he came two leagues to meet us, accompanied by four
or five others of the Ancients,[68] an honor which they are never accustomed to give to the other ambassadors, to meet whom they are
contented to go a little eighth of a league outside of the town. . ∴ . I
walked gravely between two rows of people, who give me a thousand
benedictions. . . . I kept making my cry of Ambassador while walking . . . then having returned in two words[69] my thanks for this good
welcome, I continued my journey and my cry.[70]

The woods' edge is like a front door. The host has less control over the
world beyond it, but a great deal of control within the house. With the visitor
standing and waiting at the front door, the host has time to get the house in
order and to decide how the visitor will be greeted. For the visitor, the front
door is also a place of decision: to stay or to leave. That decision becomes more
difficult once he is inside the house, with the door closed behind him. Being
welcomed in, he leaves behind him the safety of the woods, exchanging it for

---

67   Biggar 1924, cited in Hale (1883) 1989, 346. Hale recognized what Cartier could
     not have: that the French were being greeted by people familiar with the Woods' Edge
     Ceremony as part of international relations. If the town was six miles from the river, and
     the fire of greeting was four or five miles along Cartier's path, and the fields spread for a
     mile around the town—then the fire would have been at the woods' edge, or very close
     to it. See Bonaparte 2006; also Lightall 1899.

68   The word would more commonly be translated into English as "Elder" nowadays. In
     Haudenosaunee society, age requires respect, but not every old person is revered as a
     leader or knowledge-keeper.

69   Beauchamp ([1907] 1975) wrote that "the *two words* were short speeches emphasized
     with strings or belts." While "words" in Haudenosaunee metaphor are usually individual
     paragraphs or matters, it is equally likely that in the case of Father Le Moine, writing in
     French, "deux mots" would mean "briefly"—as in the famous speech in Corneille's *Le
     Cid*—"*A moi, Comte, deux mots.*" In Haudenosaunee languages, a word, a matter, and a
     piece of business can all be described by the same term: *oríhwa*.

70   Beauchamp (1907) 1975, 421, describing Father Le Moine's second visit to Onondaga
     in 1661.

the hospitality of the house, becoming a guest. Stepping past the woods' edge into the clearing is an act of trust.[71]

The visitors standing by the fire at the woods' edge are able to leave if they choose: they have not made the commitment to come in; they have not yet been assured of their safety.

If the triad described in the Covenant Chain relationship is respect, trust, and friendship, in that specific order, then the ceremony at the woods' edge fits comfortably into the sequence. Acknowledgment, greeting, sharing the words of comfort—all are acts of respect, visible, palpable acts that demonstrate esteem and welcome. They are mutual efforts to send the message of trust that will enable the host to truly welcome the guest, and the visitor to feel safe in entering the host's domain as a friend.

In 1645, when the Mohawk speaker Kiotsaeton spoke to the French and Hurons at Three Rivers, he conducted the preliminaries of the treaty making from a canoe. Possibly, since the Haudenosaunee had arrived by canoe, by the water paths, standing near the water's edge was the river equivalent of standing at the woods' edge. But the fact that he did not land, that he remained in the canoe, also sent a message: we are not sure of our welcome, and we do not yet have enough of a relationship, enough trust in you, to step onto the shore before being invited to do so.[72]

Today, the greeting at the woods' edge is preserved in the ceremony of Condolence: the clear-minded people stop their walk some distance from the longhouse of those who are grieving, and they wait to be approached and welcomed. They have come singing the peace songs, to announce themselves, and they stop to give their friends the opportunity to prepare themselves and to be satisfied that the delegation is indeed coming in peace.[73]

Present-day Haudenosaunee territories are an archipelago in ecological as well as cultural terms. They can be seen on satellite photographs and topographical maps as containing some of the last viable Carolinian forests in Ontario and Quebec, and among the last old-growth forest in New York (much of the landscape that is similar is in national, provincial, and state parks). Today, as in centuries past, the Haudenosaunee are people of clearings, not of cleared lands

---

71   The Senecas and Mohawks are the doorkeepers of the Longhouse: the Great Black Rafters at the doorway to Seneca country are perilous: true visitors are welcomed, while dangerous ones may be killed.

72   Two hundred years later, when the Mi'kmaq and Maliseet chiefs would visit Peskotomuhkati (Passamaquoddy) or Penobscot country to condole and raise up a chief, they, too, would wait in their canoes to be greeted at the water's edge.

73   The Maori *karanga* is remarkably similar to the woods' edge greeting in its spirit and its sequences. Peoples at the edge of war conduct deliberate, brave rituals together to accentuate both their desire for peace and their continuing capacity to defend themselves. Such meetings are often demonstrations of courage and spirit as well as friendship.

like their neighbours. The forests are deliberately preserved as places for hunting, for gathering food and medicines, and for spiritual comfort and strength.

Fenton maintained that the cultivated land belonged to the women,[74] while the woods were men's territory.[75] He wrote that this reflects the duality that men were mainly concerned with killing (animals, fish, enemies, and even the trees they would clear for the fields), while women were concerned with promoting life (the crops and the children). Men take life; women give life. This perspective misses the deeply collaborative nature of the division of labour in Haudenosaunee communities, but it acknowledges that the woods, more dangerous than the fields, were more often considered men's business.[76] Robert Venables writes of Haudenosaunee lands as "gendered landscapes," though he rejects any suggestion that Haudenosaunee society was imbalanced as a result of women's rights to land. Venables also recognizes that Haudenosaunee perceptions that the elements of the natural world are linked to and equal to humans result in a different attitude towards the world as a whole:

> Because the Haudenosaunee worldview is incorporative and seeks to balance what is perceived to be a world inhabited by spiritually equal beings, the Haudenosaunee worldview is still evident today in their spiritual perception of the non-Indians who now occupy so much of their homelands. . . .
>
> This is not to say, either in history or today, that the Haudenosaunee never made mistakes, for indeed they have and they still do. But when they make mistakes, they ask different questions and pose different solutions based on their worldview—a worldview, it must be stressed, that is what the Creator intended them to follow, and not simply a human invention.[77]

---

74   At the inquiry into George Klock's fraudulent purchase of Canajoharie Mohawk land, there was the following question and answer: "Being asked whether the Women were looked upon, as having any right in the Disposal of Lands, he answered: 'They are the truest Owners being the persons who labour on the Lands, and therefore are esteemed in that Light.'" SWJP 4:56. Taylor states that women decided the locations of the villages: Taylor 2006, 18; citing Wallace 1969, 29; Shoemaker 2010, 18–19. See also Goldenweiser 1915, 15:696–97.

75   Snow (1994, 39) notes the absence of "men's houses" in Haudenosaunee towns, and suggests that this was because the men were often away at trade, war or diplomacy, so "their domain was a lodge turned inside out." But why the assumption that a people would have gendered houses?

76   A network of wayfarers' huts and hunting shelters, a day's travel from the village, made life in the woods easier. It is said that there were also huts at the woods' edge, where the path of peace met the clearing, where the visitors could stay while they waited to be greeted.

77   Venables 2010, 28.

One source of this balanced view is the constant contrast between the forest and the clearing. The forest is also the "hunting grounds," a term that describes the major activity that takes place there, and one that took on additional legal significance as it became part of the vocabulary of dealings with European powers.[78]

As one moves away from one's town, one gradually moves into territory in which one has less and less control—through the territory of other settlements of one's own nation, and into the territory of other friendly nations where one remains a visitor, though the "Dish with One Spoon" provisions of the Kayanerenkó:wa allow one to hunt for food. Then one travels into the territory of less friendly or hostile nations. A journey moves one from being owner to guest to visitor to stranger.

The "deep dark forest," the woods beyond one's familiar territory, could be a place of danger and uncertainty. Light and darkness are important opposites in Haudenosaunee thought: day is our Creator's time, while night is said to belong to his brother (so councils are not held after sundown, when minds and bodies are tired); white wampum is the symbol of peace, as purple wampum is often associated with misfortune. The dark forest is a place of peril, populated not only by potential enemy humans but also by monsters: flying heads, stone giants, and serpents.

At the world's rim dwells Hadu'wi, a being our Creator encountered in the early days of the world. A powerful figure, Hadu'wi may symbolize all the elements of the natural world over which humans have no control. His alliance with us, arranged by the Creator, is invoked by the medicine society whose members wear the wooden masks bearing his image, and maintained by the tobacco burned for him. It is said that, in the deep woods, people can sometimes see him flitting between trees. The woods are a place of power, but it is not necessarily power that humans can command.

If the forest—and the paths through it—is one dominant aspect of the landscape of the Haudenosaunee, a second important feature is the river. The people lived by both rivers and lakes—the core of the Haudenosaunee homeland is the Finger Lakes area, where it is said that the Creator scraped his fingers along

---

78   In 1701, the Haudenosaunee placed the Ohio country and southwestern Ontario under
     British protection: the area was called the "Beaver Hunting Ground," in contrast to the
     "deer hunting ground" that lay south of Lake Ontario. Beaver hunting took place at a
     distance, and one returned home with pelts. Deer hunting meant bringing home the
     meat, unspoiled. In 1755, the British used the terms of the 1701 treaty as a recruit-
     ing tool—they announced that General Braddock had come to remove the French
     from their encroachments on Haudenosaunee hunting grounds. In 1763, the Royal
     Proclamation reserved all the lands west of the Appalachians and the Quebec boundary
     to the "Nations or Tribes of Indians with Whom We are Connected, or Who live under
     Our Protection" as their "Hunting Grounds." Later literature and countless films refer to
     the afterlife as "the Happy Hunting Grounds."

the land, creating today's waters. The St. Lawrence, Susquehanna, Hudson, Mohawk, and Genesee Rivers were also crucial, as were the many smaller streams and creeks. The rivers, because they are flowing paths of communication, are a recurring metaphor in the thinking of the people and the law.

The Elder Brothers—the Mohawks and Senecas—sometimes refer to the Younger Brothers—the Oneidas and Cayugas—as "you who are downstream from us." Geographically, this makes no sense. On the Mohawk River, the Oneidas are west, and upstream, from the Mohawks. To the west, the rivers flow north–south, and the Cayugas, in their homeland on Cayuga Lake, were not downstream from the Senecas on any river. But when one juxtaposes this affectionate term with its alternatives, "younger brothers" and "offspring," one understands that the river in the Kayanerenkó:wa is not geographic and literal: it is a river of time.[79] Like fire, a river is a process, not an event.

Understanding a river in temporal terms comes naturally to people who see and use a river every day. When you stand on the shore, an object upstream from you now will soon be downstream. For the Haudenosaunee, three centuries ago, the rivers were highways, sources of water, food, and medicine, and a constant part of their landscape.

Rivers are also metaphors of life, constantly changing. "You can never step into the same river twice" is not geographic, but temporal.[80] The river that is placid and clear today may be overflowing its banks, muddy, and brown tomorrow. Like human life, rivers are affected by storms and high winds, drought, freezing and flood. It is their flowing nature, though, that finds its way into the Great Law, into the spirit of the law.

In the Creation story, the people's clans are revealed to them when they go for water at the river.[81] In the narrative part of the Great Law, many events take place by rivers or small lakes. The Cannibal lives by a river; so does Tsikonsaseh; so does Hiawatha in his hermit stage. The Peacemaker is tested by the Mohawks at Cohoes Falls on the Mohawk River. In the narrative, rivers are not important except as locators. In the substantive aspects of the law, the rivers become metaphors, vehicles for principles.

---

79   Tehahenteh Frank Miller asserts that in Haudenosaunee language as in Haudenosaunee thought, time and space are treated differently than in English, and their boundaries are blurred.

80   Heracleitus, the fifth-century BC Greek philosopher, actually wrote something more like: "The sum of things flows like a stream. . . . It is impossible to descend twice into the same river and it is impossible to touch a mortal substance twice in the same condition, but because of the impetuosity and speed of the changes, it is scattered and gathered together, it comes and goes."

81   Mohawk 2005a, 92–93. Unlike many other people's stories of creation, the Haudenosaunee story, very much located in the Carolinian biome in its description of plants and animals, does not name any specific places.

An underground river sweeps the weapons of war away once they have been buried under the Tree of Peace. In that metaphor, the Confederacy stays in one place, "on the bank," as it were, while the river becomes the agent of healing, change, and removal.[82]

The river is the symbol of travel through time and life. The words and ideas contained in wampum belts are intended to flow through time, so the wampums themselves are likened to that temporal river: kahswénhtha, "it flows." The river stands for the idea that the principles of the law, and the relationships they foster, can remain constant, even as the temporal, social, and political landscape changes. Another word for a wampum belt, kahionni, is interpreted as "the river formed by the hand of man."[83]

The term kahswénhtha is often applied, nowadays, to the Tekeni teyohá:te, the Two Row (or more properly "Two Path") Wampum. In that wampum, the canoe of the Haudenosaunee and the sailing ship of the Europeans are said to be travelling down the River of Life, side by side, neither interfering in the path of the other. They remain close to each other, bound by friendship, trust, and respect, but they also keep a respectful distance from each other. It is easy to see the flowing nature of the relationship and commitments in a wampum that uses the river itself as a symbol.[84] The constancy within change in the law has been extrapolated to a constant relationship within changing circumstances in international relations.

Every wampum belt, though, includes the symbolism of the temporal river, and is thus called kahswénhtha.[85] The Two Row is not the only wampum that flows. Every wampum that represents a relationship or a principle of law flows through time.

"Flowing through time" requires a second perspective. If the ship and the canoe are on the river together, they are moving through time at the same speed. Their relationship to each other, on the river, is constant, even as the river changes in relation to its banks and its bottom.

---

82   One might also find another parallel: in the Creation story, Sky Woman falls through a hole in the sky created by an uprooted tree, and she falls towards the waters below.

83   Parmenter 2013, 84, citing Cuoq 1882, 160. Parmenter suggests that the metaphor is due to the linear form of the belt and the way "its constituent shell beads resemble ripples and waves." He misses the way the principles embodied in wampum flow through time like a river, the most important aspect of how the wampum is used.

84   Perhaps, with the increasing pace of change, the Haudenosaunee have come to see themselves less as the people who met the newcomers on the river's banks, and more as a people in a fragile watercraft swept along on the current of the river of life, with its uncertainties and lack of control.

85   See, e.g., Morgan (1851) 1995, 3:53, the illustration of "Ga-sweh-ta Ote-ko-a or belt of wampum" (otkó:wa refers to the "Great Shell," the shell beads). The word also indicates a spine.

Flowing through time also means flowing downstream.[86] On a river, it means flowing with the current, not fighting against it.[87]

The nature and use of rivers lead to another powerful metaphor: on a river, going downstream, the most significant effort is not propulsion, but navigation. In the land of the Haudenosaunee, navigation meant avoiding rocks, falls, sunken logs, and fallen trees. The people were using light, quick, fragile canoes in fast-moving water. If the rivers were highways, it was important to keep them clear and safe.

Since the rivers were paths of communication, they—and the wampum belts that flowed—became part of symbolically keeping minds and paths open. Where the visitors to a council came on foot, both the greeting at the woods' edge and the opening of the council would refer to keeping the path open and free from brambles and weeds, and removing fallen trees. Where they came by water, the concern would be to keep the rivers open. When Kiostaeton spoke to the French and Algonquins in 1645, he spoke of calming waters and opening the paths, by water and by land:

> The fifth [wampum "present"] was given to clear the river, and to drive away the enemy's canoes, which might impede navigation. He made use of a thousand gestures, as if he had collected the waves and had caused a calm, from Quebec to the Iroquois country.
>
> The sixth was to smooth the rapids and waterfalls, or the strong currents, that occur in the river on which one must sail to reach their country. "I thought that I would perish," he said, "in those boiling waters. This is to appease them;" and with his hands and arms he smoothed and arrested the torrents.[88]
>
> The seventh was to produce a profound calm on the great Lake Saint Louys[89] that has to be crossed. "Here," he said, "is something to make it smooth as ice, to appease the winds, and to allay the anger of the

---

86 In the Creation story, it is said that the right-handed twin made the rivers flow both ways, for the convenience of people's travel, and then the left-handed twin caused them to flow only one way, and filled them with rapids and other obstacles. By smoothing the waters, Kiotsaeton was also re-enacting Teharionwakon's calming of the rivers. Re-enacting parts of the law and re-enacting parts of the story of creation are often the same thing.

87 When one gathers water for medicine, it is scooped with the current, not against it. One works with the forces of the natural world, not against them.

88 Haudenosaunee travellers and traders, and the voyageurs who took up the fur trade with them, would put down tobacco before entering difficult rapids or dangerous waters. When Arendt van Curler not only refused to do this at an island in Lake Champlain, but showed his backside to the sacred place, the Mohawks were not surprised that he drowned in a storm on that lake three days later.

89 Lake Ontario (the Beautiful Lake), also known as Cataraqui Lake.

waves." Then, after having by his gestures rendered the route easy, he tied a collar of porcelain beads on the arm of a Frenchman, and pulled him straight across the square, to show that our canoes could go to their country without any difficulty.

The eighth performed the whole journey that had to be made on land. You would have said that he felled trees; that he lopped off branches; that he pushed back the bushes; that he put earth in the deepest holes. "There," said he, "is the road, quite smooth and straight." He bent toward the ground, looking to see whether there were any more thorns or bushes, and whether there were any mounds over which one might stumble in walking. "It is all finished. We can see the smoke of our villages, from Quebec to the extremity of our country. All obstacles are removed."[90]

The Jesuit recorder of the 1645 council saw a pantomime of a literal removal of physical obstacles.[91] Kiotsaeton intended more: a metaphorical performance of the removal of obstacles to clear-minded communication. As his final statement after removing the obstacles suggests, seeing clearly is the beginning of understanding clearly.[92]

The river is a part of the metaphor in the law for open communication and clear thought. Equally important, though, it is a metaphor for the need for constancy of principle amid the certainty of change.

If the forest and the river are two important landscape metaphors, the sky is the third. Haudenosaunee territory is not mountainous. Much of it is low rolling hills. Human presence would be detected, not by sight of village clearings from a distance, but by the smoke of the fires rising to the sky. The narrative of the Great Law contains dozens of references to the smoke rising—sometimes the fire a person lights at the woods' edge to notify the people of the village of his presence; sometimes the stand for peace of villages unafraid to show themselves; sometimes the smoke of a fire of gratitude, of

---

90   Thwaites 1901, 27:96–98, in Jennings 1985, 137.

91   This was a very early council with the French, and sign language may have been deemed necessary to ensure understanding: in later councils, when there were reliable interpreters, some of the pantomime disappeared.

92   Recall that the first "word" of the Condolence, as well as the first "word" at the Woods' Edge, wipes away the tears so that the people can see clearly again.

tobacco-burning. In each case, the smoke links the earth and its people to the Sky World, a constant reminder of the lessons of the Creation story.[93]

A Haudenosaunee perspective on the relationship between the people and the land was explained to the Supreme Court of Canada in *Ktunaxa Nation v. British Columbia* in 2016:

> While it is dangerous to generalize about Indigenous laws, they seem to share a key difference from the common law. It is exemplified in the Haudenosaunee Creation story, when Taharonhiawakon picks up a clod of earth in his hands and says: "I tell you the Earth is ALIVE!" Compare this to the origins of Canadian property law: centuries ago, when an Englishman bought a parcel of land, the transaction was not complete until he went to the place, picked up a lump of its earth, and declared: "This is MINE!" Seisin is not far from seizure.
>
> For many Indigenous peoples, the assumption that one can "own" land is as repugnant as the idea that one can "own" other human beings (abandoned by the Crown only in 1833). The theory that open land is there for the taking, that there is a broad individual or corporate right to develop, is foreign to Indigenous legal systems in which humans hold stewardship of Earth, not dominion, and in which so many things are relatives.[94]

The people did not own the land in some of the ways that modern Western "civilization" considers ownership. They had no practice of individual land ownership, and they also did not believe that the whole territory belonged only to the people who happened to be alive at the time. Since the Haudenosaunee see themselves as part of a continuum, to the extent that the land belongs to anyone, it is the property of everyone—past, present, and future.

In his commentary on concepts of land ownership among the Iroquois, Snyderman wrote that:

> The belief that the land belonged not only to the present generation, but to all future generations was widely accepted. The present generation, it was believed, had no power to sell lands, for obviously the future generations could not express their wishes in council. The present generation acted as custodians of the land for the unborn;

---

93 If the sky is part of people's perception of what the world consists of, that explains why so many of the great Indigenous speeches (including those of Tecumseh) ask "Can you sell the sky? Can you sell the air? Then why do you think you can sell the land?" It took a few centuries before Euro-Americans concluded that it was possible to sell a legal part of the air, since that is what a condominium apartment partly consists of.

94 Factum of the Passamaquoddy Nation at Schoodic, *Ktunaxa Nation v. British Columbia*, heard 1 December 2016 (Paul Williams, Counsel).

they could only utilize the land during the period of their actual existence.[95] This attitude is clearly discerned in the now famous speech of Cornplanter, Halftown, and Big Tree in 1790. In one of the opening paragraphs they stated quite dramatically that: "We will not conceal from you that the Great God and not men, has preserved the Cornplant from the hands of his nation. For they ask continually, where is the land on which our children and their children after them are to lie down upon?" (Drake, S.G., 1834, p.96)[96]

The Haudenosaunee did not "own" land the way the Europeans did. They expressed their relationship to land more in terms of their belonging to, and sharing an identity with, a specific region. Traditionally, one does not say just where one is from, but rather "that kind of clay I am made of" (niwaki'taró:ten)—which means the same thing.[97] "Belonging," in several aspects of Haudenosaunee relations, is more important than "owning," and being made of the clay of a place is an expression of being part of it, just as identifying oneself as being Wolf Clan is not an expression of authority, but rather of belonging. One belongs to a family, to a clan, or to a medicine society in the sense that one bears privileges and protection as a result of the relationship, but also obligations. In the same way, and because the land is provident and protective, as we protect the land, we "belong" to the land more than it belongs to us. After all, it will be here long after our bodies have returned to it. Haudenosaunee views of relations with land are often expressed in terms of stewardship, a relationship between a person and a thing he or she is looking after. This is not dissimilar to the relationship between a person and a medicine mask: he or she looks after it as a custodian, a steward, but also as a companion of a thing that is alive, rather than as an owner. European societies and their laws did not have clear concepts and words to describe what they found in the Americas 500 years ago. Nor should one forget that, 500 years ago, the societies of western Europe often treated wives and children as a form of property, and did practise slavery. Land ownership was as often the result of recent conquest as

---

95   The idea that the people have only a usufruct in the land is consistent with the view of Euro-American law about the land rights of Indigenous peoples. The problem is that Euro-American societies do not consider that their governments or people have only a usufruct: they believe in ownership and the right to exploit and dispose, for all time. The idea that one has the use of a matter during one's lifetime, but that the thing will be used by future generations, is reflected in the way names are also passed on (see Thwaites 1901 27–28:96–98; Vachon 1992).

96   Snyderman 1951. "The land we live on, our fathers received from God, and they transmitted it to us, for our children, and we cannot part with it": Kayantwakon (Cornplanter) John O'Bail to Kanatakarias George Washington, 1 December 1790; Lowrie and Clarke 1832–34, 2:142.

97   Hill 2017, 5. When one considers that "Adam" means "Red Earth," the concept of Man made from the clay of the earth seems more universal.

of ancient intimacy. In European society, based increasingly on private property, many more things were typically individually owned than in Haudenosaunee society at the time. It is not unexpected that land should be considered fungible and often private in Euro-American society, and considered a relative, alive and to be cared for, in the view of the Haudenosaunee.

Nevertheless, there were aspects of the connection between the people and the land that would be taken by Europeans as indicators of land ownership. Along the paths into Haudenosaunee country, young men were sentinels against any invaders or intruders. Haudenosaunee law provides that the hunting grounds shall be shared between allied nations—the metaphor is that the land is like a dish with a single wooden spoon—so the Haudenosaunee would welcome guest hunters. But they would, in the most forceful terms, resist anyone seeking to take the land without their consent, or threaten the safety of their villages.

Since the women cultivated the fields, they had primary authority for making decisions about that land.[98] The earth, after all, is our mother, not some male entity.[99] Europeans, who for centuries had placed women in a subordinate position in which they rarely owned land, often found the authority of Haudenosaunee women difficult to accept. The Haudenosaunee had to explain the difference, often bluntly. Agwerondongwas, an Oneida royá:ner, stated: "Brothers! Our Ancestors considered it a great Transgression to reject the Counsels of their Women, particularly the female Governesses. Our Ancestors considered them the Mistresses of the Soil. Our Ancestors said who brings us forth, who cultivates our Land, who kindles our fires and boils our Pots, but the Women . . . they are the Life of the Nation."[100]

The fact that the responsibility for speaking with outsiders was a men's matter[101] made it even more complicated—since the Europeans generally assumed that those who spoke were also the decision makers. Lafitau wrote of the chiefs that "it seems that they serve only to represent and aid the women in the matters in which decorum does not permit the latter to appear or act."[102] Sometimes, though, the women had to speak for themselves, to take an exceptional step to make their position clear: "Your sisters, the women, have taken the same into great consideration, because that you and our sachems have said so much upon

---

98   "In them resides all the real authority: the lands, fields and all their harvest belong to them," wrote Lafitau in 1724 (1974, 69).

99   The ancient Greeks recognized Gaia, wife of Uranus, as the earth mother.

100 Agwerondongwas (Good Peter), Oneida royá:ner, to Governor Clinton of New York, cited in Viau 2000, 263.

101 Why was this the men's responsibility? Possibly because the initial meeting with strangers might involve physical threats, and the defence of the community was the responsibility of the men.

102 Lafitau (1724) 1974, 69. In this context, "decorum" really means protocol rather than etiquette.

it . . . [Y]ou ought to hear & listen to what we women shall speak, as well as the sachems, for we are the owners of the land & it is ours; for it is we that plant it, for our and their use. Hear us, therefore, for we speak of things that concern us & our children & you must not think hard of us while our men shall say more to you; for we have told them."[103]

Modern Western law concerning land separates its consideration between the right of a nation or nation-state over its territory (sovereignty or jurisdiction) and the nature of land ownership within that polity. Haudenosaunee law does the same thing. Where internally, notions of stewardship, women's rights, and the concern for future generations governed land rights, a different set of considerations determined whether the land was Haudenosaunee land or the land of other nations.

To complicate matters further, the frequent tension between the chiefs and the warriors sometimes strayed into land issues. As constant war increased the perceived power of the warriors, they would sometimes claim to have authority for the land, too: a speaker for the warriors told the British: "Now Brother I let you know that our Kings having nothing to do with our Lands; for we, the Warriors fought for the Lands and so the right belongs to us & we will take Care of them."[104]

Conquest? It is unclear whether there was a pre-Columbian idea of conquest, but certainly the Haudenosaunee understood the idea by 1701, when they made a "trust deed"[105] concerning the "Beaver Hunting Ground"[106]—the territory of southwestern Ontario "won by the sword" from the Wendat, Tiionontate, and Attiwandaronon. To the Haudenosaunee in the seventeenth century, though, conquest of territory meant a permanent military solution, not a temporary one: as the chiefs explained to the British on February 13, 1688:

---

103 Sakoyewatha (Red Jacket), speaking for the women on May 15, 1791. He also speaks for the women at the 1794 Canandaigua Treaty, "saying that it was they who made the men" and "that they had found themselves much distressed by being hemmed in," as part of a statement supporting the men's stated desire that the Erie Triangle be returned. Ganter 2006, 20, 62.

104 Gibson 1939, 5:284. The less visible part of this statement: these men may have fought for the land at the bidding of the women. There was direct communication between women and men, and it did not have to go through the rotiyanershon.

105 The document drafted by the British states that the Haudenosaunee gave up all right of ownership of the land, keeping only the right to hunt. The Haudenosaunee understanding of the transaction, as confirmed by Sir William Johnson in 1755 and through a series of interactions at the beginning of the Seven Years' War, was that the area was to remain Haudenosaunee land, but that it was being placed under British protection.

106 Close to the towns were the deer hunting grounds, from which one could bring home the meat before it spoiled. Beaver hunting grounds, from which one brought furs, were more distant.

The French can have no title to those places which they possesse, nay not to Cadarachqui and Mount Royall nor none of our lands toward the Ottawawas, Dionondadas, Twichtwis; for by what means can they pretend them, because they came to the Maquase country formerly and now laterly to the Sinnekes country and burnt some bark houses and cut down our corne—if that be a good title then we can claim all Canida, for we not only did soe, but subdued whole nations of Indians who liv'd there, and demolished there castles in so much, that now great oake trees grow where they were built, and afterwards we plyed the French home in the warr with them, that they were not able to go over a door to pisse.[107]

Newhouse asserts that the territory of an exterminated nation becomes territory of the Haudenosaunee by right of conquest, and that conquered nations have no voice in the council.[108]

When a nation joined the Confederacy, its land came with it;[109] its people became indistinguishable from the component nations, and the external boundaries of the Haudenosaunee were extended as a longhouse would be extended. The British opportunistically applied their own beliefs about "empire" to this, and asserted that, since the Haudenosaunee were their subjects and had an empire, it was, in effect, a British empire.[110] Prudently, they chose not to inform their Haudenosaunee brothers of this assertion.

---

107 NYCD, London Docs., 6:534. The last phrase was not just confusion about indoor plumbing: Haudenosaunee campaigns against New France included deliberate expeditions to take captives, and the French were apprehensive about venturing into the fields and woods alone, even as near to Montreal as Lachine. See Brandão 1997.

108 Parker (Newhouse and Cusick) 1916, 53. Newhouse's versions of the law, though, tend to be more draconian and aggressive than other versions, on a number of points. This leaves open the question of whether nations that have joined voluntarily rather than through conquest would have a voice in council. The Tuscaroras, for example, retain their seats "under the wing" of the Oneidas, even as they are called the sixth nation. Their voice in council is not required for a decision, but they are seldom denied the right to speak when they request it.

109 In 1793, Lieutenant Governor Simcoe wrote of the "Grounds between the Genesee & Buffalo Creek" that "the Senecas claim them, but Capt. Brant seems to think 'as they were conquered Lands that they belong to the Confederacy of the Six Nations.'" If they were indeed "conquered lands," the conquest had taken place more than 150 years earlier. Cruikshank 1923, 2:50.

110 Jennings 1990.

Concepts of land ownership evolved over time and with exposure to other cultures.[111] They also evolved as European settlement spread and nations that were allied with the Haudenosaunee were displaced westward. George Snyderman asserted that "land was given or loaned by the League or its members to alien people for their use during good behavior."[112]

Other nations were allowed to continue to use and occupy their lands, after being "subdued." The Seneca chiefs Kayantwakon (Cornplanter), Halftown, and Great Tree told President Washington: "Many nations inhabited this country; but they had no wisdom, and, therefore, they warred together. The Six Nations were powerful, and compelled them to peace; the lands, for a greater extent, were given up to them; but the nations which were not destroyed, all continued on those lands, and claimed the protection of the Six Nations, as their brothers and their fathers."[113]

The fundamental relationship between the people and the land supplies some of the principles of the law. The law tells the people that they are part of a continuum of people who all have and share land rights; their presence on the land is not "ownership" in the sense that they may do what they wish, but a kind of stewardship, both for their own future generations and for the other living things with which they share the land. Their work with the land also finds its way into the ceremonies of thanksgiving—as they help, acknowledge, and renew the land, so it returns the stuff of life to the people.

In Haudenosaunee law, ohwentsiá:ke, "on the earth," includes the soil, the rocks, the waters, and all the parts of the world.[114] This is different from Euro-American law, in which "land" can be separated from "nature" in order to be developed or exploited. In Euro-American law, it is possible not only to

---

111 By the eighteenth century, the Haudenosaunee also considered inheritance of land by na-
      tions. Sir William Johnson wrote to Governor Penn that "the Five Nations have desired
      that I shall acquaint you that as by the extinction of the Conestogas, the lands they pos-
      sessed revert to them their relations & next heirs, that they therefore expect to have the
      liberty of disposing of them, or that a proper consideration be made for them" (SWJP
      4:324). The Cayugas had adopted the remaining Conestogas (or Susquehannocks).

112 Snyderman 1951, 22. The best-documented example of this is the Susquehanna Valley,
      loaned to the Delawares. When the Delawares signed agreements selling parts of the
      valley to colonial governments, the Haudenosaunee reasserted their own ownership in
      blunt, angry terms.

113 Documents, Legislative and Executive, of the Congress of the United States, vol. 4,
      Washington, 1832. From written speech in Philadelphia in 1791. Thayendenega Joseph
      Brant suggested that "although the Five Nations have an equal right one with the other,
      the country having been obtained by their joint exertions in war with a powerful nation
      formerly living southward of Buffalo Creek called Eries, and another nation then living
      at Tioga Point, so that by our successes all the country between that and the Mississippi
      became joint property of the Five Nations" (Clark, cited in Murray 1931, 29).

114 "When Aboriginal people speak of the land they mean not only the ground that supports
      our feet: they also include waters, plants, animals, fish, birds, air, seasons—all the beings,
      elements and processes encompassed by the term 'biosphere.'" RCAP 1995, 631.

draw lines on the land as boundaries between individual properties, but also to "own" mathematically calculated shares of undivided land with other people (a "condominium"); to own the crops or fruit but not the land (a "usufruct"); to own the right to cross or use the land (an "easement"); to own land only during one's lifetime; and to subdivide the land into increasingly smaller parcels. To the Haudenosaunee, land "ownership" was communal, not individual: the community extends back through the ancestors and ahead to the coming faces. Perhaps this difference is fundamental to cultures—the holistic approach of the Haudenosaunee contrasts with the Euro-American ability to break things into distinct and independent parts.[115] In the same way, Euro-American science and medicine use the "scientific method," where Haudenosaunee healing sees an entire human in his environment, and tends to be more comfortable with what is now called an "ecosystem approach" to earth sciences and an "environmental" approach to medicine.

Communal landholding was the Haudenosaunee way before the arrival of the Europeans, but technological change brought a change in attitudes about land. Sotsisowah John Mohawk suggested that the advent of draft animals had the most impact: now one man with a horse could plow land that it had earlier taken twenty women to prepare. Horses and oxen transformed the way the people related to the land. Just as the fur trade was dying and the homelands were filling up with European settlers, the plow made it possible for Haudenosaunee men to become farmers, and for the single-family farm to become economically and socially viable. It is not difficult to understand the Karihwí:iyo, the Code of Skaniatariio (Handsome Lake) of the 1790s, as including a pragmatic effort to maintain the principles of traditional values in the face of this rapid societal change.[116] The Code explains that it is acceptable to have draft animals like the white people, but that one should not become too proud of them; that it is acceptable, too, to have single-family houses, but that they should be modest, painted simply in white.

Today, traditional Haudenosaunee values concerning land are evident in each of the communities, manifesting themselves in an "ownership" pattern that is a combination of private landholding and community values. The sense of shared stewardship, of responsibility to the land and the natural world and to future generations, is not formally visible to outsiders, but it remains real, more than vestigial, evident in a hundred ways.[117] Joagquisho Oren Lyons explained: "We are the indigenous people to this land. We are like a conscience. We are small, but not a minority. We are the landholders; we are the landkeepers; we

115　Byrne 2003.

116　Ferris (2006) discusses the relative longevity and constancy of societal principles as technological and other changes occur.

117　Hill 2017.

are not a minority. For our brothers are all the natural world, and by that we are far the majority."[118]

The Longhouse and the Village

There are precious few surviving contemporary depictions of a Haudenosaunee bark longhouse—so few that there is no consensus whether the roof was domed or peaked,[119] or how tall the longhouses actually were.[120] What is known with some precision is how long they were, and how wide, and what they were made of.[121] The framework was cedar poles, for cedar does not rot in the ground and grows straight and clean. The building's skin was massive elm bark, from trees large enough and old enough that the bark provided insulation from the weather and the cold. As compared to the habitations of other peoples, there were several defining characteristics of the Haudenosaunee longhouse.

The most fundamental building block of Haudenosaunee society was the fire. The hearth, within the longhouse, was not a single-family fire. There was a family on each side of the fire. This duality that people would see upon waking every day reflects the two-sidedness of every aspect of the law.

The longhouse contains many fires, and they are aligned. That straight line, running from the eastern to the western door, provides coherence to the way the families live, just as a string of wampum reflects the organization of what would otherwise be scattered beads.

The longhouse reflects the clan family of the women who live in it. As such, it is a constant reminder of the role of women in society and government, for the women of that house are sisters.

The longhouse is capable of being extended at either end. Archaeologists have concluded that perhaps one-third of excavated longhouses show evidence

---

118   Lyons 1981, 93.

119   That kanónhsa, the Mohawk word for the longhouse, looks to –nons, which is a root word denoting the dome of the top of a person's head (and the repository of his mind), suggests the rounded rather than peaked or sharp shape. The dome of the longhouse roof recalls the Sky Dome, the dome of the heavens.

120   The Haudenosaunee had really stopped living in bark longhouses by the early 1700s: the replacement buildings took advantage of sawed lumber, and kept many aspects of the original architecture. It may be that so few descriptions exist of early longhouses because the Norman and Breton explorers had themselves lived in *longères*, the elongated stone farmhouses of northeast France that would have resembled the bark longhouses in shape and size, and would therefore have seemed unremarkable.

121   Modern archaeology extrapolates the nature of historic and prehistoric longhouse villages by examining the locations of postholes, fire pits, holes for stockades, and the locations of middens and graves.

of having been extended during their lifetimes. The extendability of the longhouse became the metaphor for the flexibility and generosity of the law, designed to bring new people under its protection while remaining true to the original architecture.

Not only were the bark longhouses often extended during their lifetimes: those lifetimes were relatively short. In this age of steel and concrete, we tend to forget the limited lifespan of all the structures we are creating—most residential homes are designed to last about fifty years; most office buildings might last seventy-five. The bark longhouse tended to last a single generation.[122] Its structural integrity began to weaken at the same time as the soil of the fields was becoming tired, and at the same time as the distance to walk for firewood was becoming longer. There was a built-in signal: the walls of the longhouse needed to be propped up from the outside. The leaning poles against the walls were the sign that the men should begin to look for a new location for the town. The poles—outside the house, but needed to hold it up—became the diagonal lines on wampum belts given by other nations who wished to become allies while remaining outside the Confederacy.

People stopped living in bark longhouses 300 years ago. The spread of European technology was quick: Harmen van den Bogaert, the first Dutchman to visit Oneida and Onondaga settlements, found that iron nails and hinges had preceded him. The spread was from east to west—so that the Senecas, least exposed to the Europeans, were the last to give up the bark structures. By the mid-1700s, Mohawks were living in barn-like structures that echoed the internal layout of the bark longhouse, while incorporating European sawn lumber and post-and-beam construction. By the end of the eighteenth century, the Onondagas of Oswegatchie were living in log houses that were home to two families each, with a shared hearth that reflected the two-sided fire in the original longhouses. In Seneca country at the same time, some people were living in log houses—with a shared fireplace between two houses.

The palisaded village of the seventeenth century became the "castle" of the eighteenth century. Defensive designs intended to protect against men with bows and arrows gave way to the cannons of the Mohawk village of Scoharie by the latter half of that century. There were still outlying settlements that were not fortified and temporary habitations in the hunting grounds; extended use of large territories continued.

The advent of single-family farms scattered communities further during the nineteenth century. Teyawentathe Susan Hill has demonstrated that fundamental Haudenosaunee principles about the relationship between people and

---

122 The *Jesuit Relations* recorded Wendat longhouse villages moving nearly twice as frequently, though it is not clear whether this was because of needing fresh soil for the crops, or internal turmoil, or disease.

land remained consistent and relatively constant as technologies and settlement patterns evolved. The same principles are reflected in Haudenosaunee law.

The Haudenosaunee

Before the arrival of the Europeans in this part of the world, a man carrying a message of Peace, Power, and Righteousness brought together five nations that had been trapped in a cycle of violence and revenge. This message—also called Karihwí:iyo, the Good Message[123]—led to the five nations uniting in a league or confederacy, governed by law, bound by spirit and commitment.

Each of the original five nations carries responsibility within the structure of the League: the Mohawks and Senecas are doorkeepers, responsible for working with the nations approaching the Longhouse from the east and west. The Onondagas are firekeepers, carefully weighing and balancing decisions. The Oneidas and Cayugas have taken entire nations under their wings. The nations have different functions in the house, but as a chief explained in the 1600s, "we are all alike respectable." Equality does not require sameness.

The Confederacy is sometimes called "the Iroquois Confederacy." The word "Iroquois" is of uncertain origin—possibly a name used by the enemies of the Haudenosaunee.[124]

---

123 Though this term is more often used today for the "Code of Handsome Lake," the Good Message that was revealed to Skaniatariio in the 1790s, it also applies to the Great Law.

124 Bakker 1990, 89–93; see also Snow 1994, 2; Time-Life 1993, 25. These works suggest the word was originally the Basque *hilokoa*, "the killer people." Champlain used "Irocois" in 1603, and while "the name became standardized and universally known very early . . . the ultimate origin and meaning of the name are unknown" (Fenton 1978, 320). See Day 1968. It has been suggested that the name comes from a call-and-reply sequence of approval of words in council. It is also possible that the name is Huron and refers to the use of smoking tobacco (Hale [1883] 1989, 172).

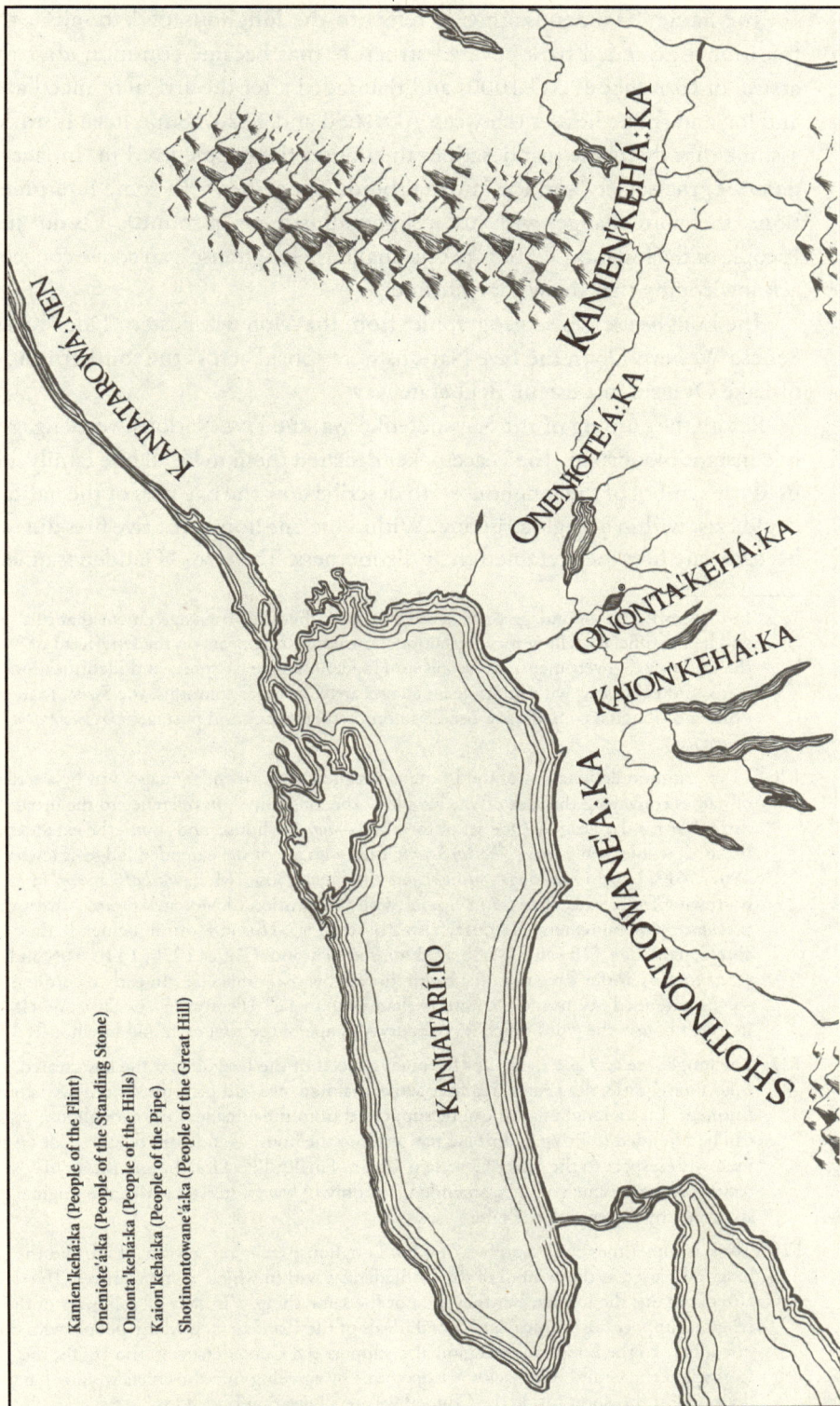

Kanien'kehá:ka (People of the Flint)
Oneniote'á:ka (People of the Standing Stone)
Ononta'kehá:ka (People of the Hills)
Kaion'kehá:ka (People of the Pipe)
Shotinontowane'á:ka (People of the Great Hill)

KANIATAROWA:NEN

KANIEN'KEHÁ:KA

ONENHOTE'A:KA

ONONTA'KEHÁ:KA

KAION'KEHÁ:KA

KANIATARÍ:IO

KANIATARONWANE'Á:KA

SHOTINONTOWANE'Á:KA

Map 1. Five Nations Territory, c. 1650. Courtesy of Kanien'kehàka Onkwawén:na Raotitióhkwa Language and Cultural Center.

The name "Haudenosaunee"[125] refers to the longhouse,[126] kanónhsa, the traditional extended bark-covered structure that became common after the arrival of corn (about AD 1000) and that faded after the arrival of metal axes and log and frame houses (between AD 1680 and 1720). Superficial histories assume that the name just describes the houses the people lived in. In fact, it describes the society and the law that binds it together.[127] In some interpretations (the word changes with just a slight adjustment in sound), it is not just "people of the longhouse," but "people making a longhouse": an active concept, acknowledging that the work continues.

The Longhouse is also geographic: from the Mohawk Eastern Door to the Seneca Western Door, the Five Nations were spread across the southern shore of Lake Ontario in a useful, deliberate way.

Before the coming of the Kayanerenkó:wa, the Five Nations were engaged in constant bloodshed. The Peacemaker declared them to be all one family. He used the symbol of the longhouse[128] to describe how the five fires of the nations could exist within a single structure. Within the one house, the five fires did not become one fire: they retained their distinctness. The term "Haudenosaunee"

---

125 In this work, the Onondaga word is used, because there has been agreement that this will be the official spelling for international purposes. It appears on the letterhead of the traditional governments, as well as on Haudenosaunee passports and identification cards. Other nations with multiple languages arrive at other solutions: the Swiss, that other multilingual confederacy, use Latin on their currency and postage: *Confoederatio Helvetica*.

126 "The common designation of the Iroquois League in their own languages was by a series of names conveying the idea of 'the people of the longhouse', in reference to the usual metaphor for the League. One set of forms has *–nonhs-* 'house' and *–yoni-* 'be extended, finished, whole, real'; Seneca *hotinohsyoni* 'they who are of the extended lodge' (Hewitt 1907c, 617, 620); Onondaga *hotinohsyoni* 'their real house,' Mohawk *hotinosyó:ni* (a borrowing from Seneca) or *rotinohsyó:ni* (with substitution of Mohawk prefix), Tuscarora *yekwanehsyeni* 'our extended house' (also a borrowing), Huron Hotinnonchiendi 'the completed lodge' (Thwaites 41:86) and hotinnonchiondi (Potier 1920, 154). A second set of forms has the same nominal root followed by *–oni-* 'make'. . . In early recordings *–yoni-* 'extended' seems more common than *–oni-*'make'" (Fenton 1981, 320). *Nohs* is indeed a house: the word describes the curved shape of the roof of an old longhouse.

127 The longhouse acts as a metaphor for many aspects of the League that the law created. Like a longhouse, the League requires active maintenance and periodically renewed commitment. Like a longhouse, it can be supported from the outside. Like a longhouse, it can be extended to bring additional nations into the house—and later the same idea was used with respect to the Silver Covenant Chain. Finally, like a longhouse, the architecture of the League could be amended, but only in ways consistent with the original structure, by "extending the rafters."

128 There is sometimes confusion between the Longhouse "religion" or way of life and the longhouse used as the symbol of the Confederacy, within which all are relatives. The latter contains the former, but they are not the same thing. Virtually all followers of the religion support the political and moral ideals of the Confederacy. Many people who do not adhere to the Longhouse religion also support the Confederacy: in the 1880s, the Council at the Grand River acknowledged this by agreeing that the chiefs would "hang their hats at the door: inside the Council we are all wearing buckskins."

is more of a description of the relationship between all the people than it is a reference to their housing.

The political system created by the Peacemaker continues to exist. It is actively maintained today by a rather small group of people within the fifteen Haudenosaunee communities (though it is supported by many more),[129] and it has been battered by high winds of change, war, and dispossession. Its survival—when so many other nations have been swept away by those winds—is remarkable in itself. Elements of the law that helped it work from the start have been the key to that survival.[130]

The Haudenosaunee are a people of law.

Today, the Haudenosaunee live in an archipelago from Kahnawake and Kanehsatake, near Montreal, in the east, to the Oklahoma Seneca and Cayuga communities in the west. "Archipelago" is a particularly appropriate word, for Haudenosaunee communities are islands in many ways. Linguistically they are islands—places where languages are spoken that are heard nowhere else (linguists call these endangered languages "isolates"). Culturally and ethnically they are islands, surrounded by a sea of people of different cultures and origins. Ecologically, they are also islands, and most of them are visible on satellite photographs and topographical maps as the last "green" areas for miles around. Like the life forms in island ecosystems, Haudenosaunee communities are home to skills, thought, ceremonies, and ways of viewing the world that are uniquely adapted to the land, and that have evolved over centuries of

---

129 John Mohawk said that there have always been two "cultures" among the Haudenosaunee. The first is the "village culture"—people who go about the daily business of building their houses, growing their food, attending the ceremonies, raising their families, and generally living their lives. The second culture is much smaller: it is the "Confederacy culture," made up of people in each community who maintain the ties between the communities, maintain the communications, attend the councils, assist in setting policies, and generally think about the nature of the law and the government it has created. The "Confederacy culture" has always been a small part of the people, and has only needed to be a small part of the people. This may be so in every society.

130 William Fenton maintained that the League and the Confederacy are different: that one is mainly spiritual and ritualistic, while the other is political and pragmatic. The Haudenosaunee disagree: they are both aspects of the same legal framework in action. Fenton (1998) also wrote that the maternal family is a physical reality, while the clan is a "legal fiction." The Haudenosaunee would say that both are equally real. By extending the clan-family relationship across the nations, the Peacemaker used law to enhance the people's likelihood of survival, by giving them one more level of relationships to bring them together.

challenge and experimentation. Like island life forms, too, they are vulnerable to introduced predators.[131]

There have never been very many Haudenosaunee. Archaeologists believe that the population of what is now upper New York State did not change much as a result of the shift from hunting, fishing, and gathering to a more agricultural society.[132] Instead, the people moved from living in small family-based camps to large, organized villages,[133] without a change in overall population. Dennis explained:

> What emerges from the archaeological reconstruction of later Owasco[134] life [about 1000 A.D.] is a picture of increasingly local-ized, complexly organized, isolated, defensive and parochial people. At the same time that Owasco villages grew in size and decreased in number, they became more completely self-sufficient, because of a greater emphasis on horticulture and a declining dependence on hunting and fishing, though these subsistence activities remained important. Trade declined; in pre-Owasco times exchange networks had connected Woodland bands with the elaborate cultures of the Ohio Valley, and perhaps beyond to Cahokia in mid-America. The nature and frequency of travel changed as Owasco people settled further from waterways and developed forest routes that kept them closer to home.[135]

> Like their descendants, Owasco people enjoyed abundance and pros-perity in the diversity of their subsistence, and there was plenty to go around. Nevertheless, they increasingly found themselves living in a

---

131 For a review of the thinking on island ecologies, see Quammen 1996; or the semi-nal work of E.O. Wilson on island biogeographies. For the bridge between thought about protection of biological and cultural diversity in a Haudenosaunee context, see Rohoronhiakewen Dan Longboat 2007.

132 While Snow (1994) has suggested that Haudenosaunee population was deliberately kept low so that their harvest of deer would not exceed a sustainable supply of hides for moc-casins, there is no historic or cultural evidence of such a policy.

133 Engelbrecht (2003, 89) argues that a village of about 2000 people would be the "upper limit": more people would strain local resources and increase the potential for internal conflict.

134 Archaeologists tend to name extinct or archaic peoples with the modern names of the places where they lived, or rather the places where significant archaeological evidence of them was found. "Owasco people," ancestors of the modern Haudenosaunee, were named after Owasco Lake, one of the Finger Lakes. The archaeologists would not know the language of the people, nor their name for themselves. There is no reason to doubt that "Owasco people" were the ancestors of modern Haudenosaunee, sharing basic cultural and genetic traits.

135 Dennis 1993, 48.

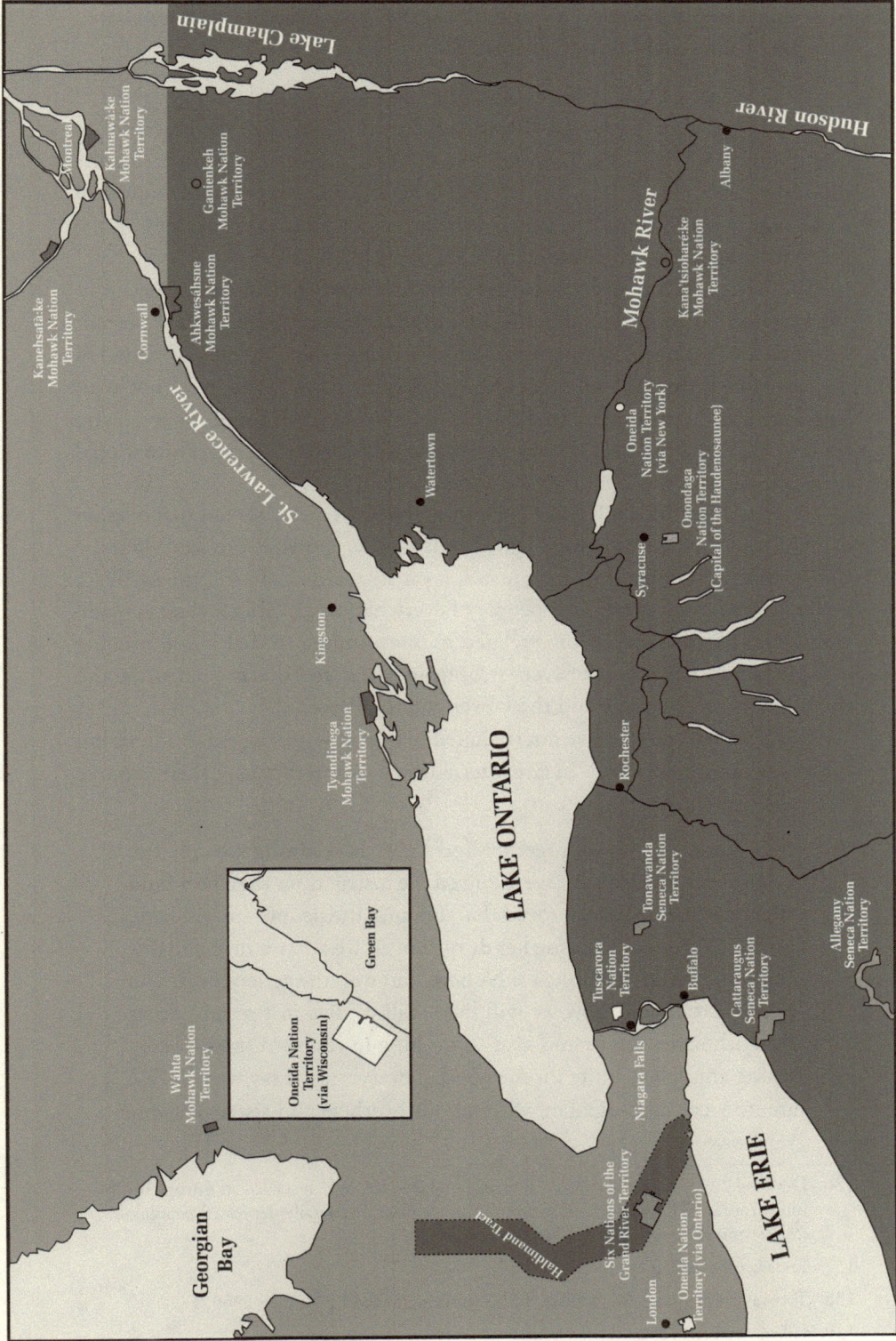

Map 2. Territories of the Haudenosaunee Confederacy. Courtesy of Kanien'kehá:ka Onkwawén:na Raotitióhkwa Language and Cultural Center.

landscape of violence, a world of fear that humans, not impersonal environmental forces, had created.[136]

These were the Dark Times of bloodshed and scalping and revenge-taking,[137] of fear and isolation. They were the times before the coming of the Peacemaker. The tradition of the Great Law of Peace does not explain the reasons for the bloodshed: it only affirms that it existed for so long that people could not recall how it had begun. The story of the arrival of peace concentrates on the peacemaking, not on the warmaking that preceded it.

The nature of a people and their culture shapes the nature of their law. Wallace asserted: "The legend [of the founding of the Confederacy] is important . . . both for the core of truth contained in it and for the influence it exerted in its elaborated form upon subsequent Iroquois history. . . . The legend itself, with its wisdom and its poetry, seized the imagination of the Iroquois people, who took to heart the message it conveyed and derived from it a sense of national mission: to make the Tree of Peace *prevail*."[138]

"A sense of national mission"? Certainly. The Peacemaker set out that mission explicitly, in the clearest terms: "The law is now as young as the day when the sun is rising and lights the earth; just as it causes warmth all over the earth for all the people, we will help the people of every nation . . . This is what you will work at: everyone shall become related to one another, so that it will become a single family, consisting of every people on earth; and this is what will unite them, the Good Message and the Power and the Peace."[139]

The Haudenosaunee have not hesitated to take that message of brotherhood to the nations of the world. In any international forum they can, their message has remained constant:

> Now we must all join together and know how strong we are. The Creator promised that if we followed the instructions then he would take care of us. He has proved that, because the people are still here. Mother Earth is still doing her duty, too. So we are still here and our children will be following us. Nobody can stop the generations. The important issue is how we will live. Will we live in fear and do as the authorities tell us and give us nothing in return? Or will we be strong enough to unite for the good of everybody? I say we will! We are now coming together, with all our brothers and sisters all over

---

136 Dennis 1993, 52. It is also possible that the "Little Ice Age" recorded in Europe beginning around AD 1300, which reduced crop yields and generally depressed people's minds, could have contributed to the violence.

137 Engelbrecht 2003, 7.

138 Toriwawakon Paul A.W. Wallace, in his introduction to Livingston 1956, 17.

139 Gibson 1912, 128–29.

the world. You may not be seeing it yet, but it is happening. None of us are going to be victims anymore.[140]

The *Basic Call to Consciousness* that accompanied the Haudenosaunee arrival at the United Nations in Geneva in the 1970s also extended the conversation about peace to the entire human family: "For centuries we have known that each individual's action creates conditions and situations that affect the world. For centuries we have been careful to avoid any action unless it carried a long-range prospect of promoting harmony and peace in the world. In that context, with our brothers and sisters of the Western Hemisphere, we have journeyed here to discuss these important matters with the Family of Man."[141]

The United Nations Declaration on the Rights of Indigenous Peoples reflects thirty years of effort by waves of Haudenosaunee delegates to the United Nations, and these people were fully aware that they were treading in the footsteps not only of Deskahe Levi General in Geneva in 1924 but of centuries of delegations to other nations in the name of peace and dignity.

Clans

The Haudenosaunee maintain that they have been visited by three great visionaries: the one who brought them the clans and the ceremonies;[142] the Peacemaker who brought the League together; and Skaniatariio (Handsome Lake),[143] who brought the societal reforms of the early 1800s.

One version of the way the clans were brought has the young fatherless man pointing out how the people found themselves on opposite sides of a river, and how this provided a natural way for them to accomplish their social tasks. That is, the society was two-sided, and the duality was an advantage. The clan system is a reflection of the natural world.

---

140   Thadadaho Leon Shenandoah, cited in Wall 2001, 55.

141   Mohawk 1977, 1.

142   Antone 1987.

143   Skaniatariio is the title of a Seneca royá:ner. The man with the visions lived in the late 1700s; John Arthur Gibson carried the same title at the Grand River Territory in the late 1800s and early 1900s; today the title is maintained by the Senecas at Tonawanda.

The clans existed, as institutions of social and ceremonial organization, before the coming of the Great Peace.[144] In Gibson's version of the Creation story, the young man who brought the clan system also made them cousins:

> Now we have seen that there are many different things in the world—the shrubs, the grasses, the trees. All have exclusive duties to perform, all are alive. There are different kinds of birds and animals. They differ among themselves, and we should emulate them. Now it is time that we should form clans. We have become numerous, and we should apportion the body of people. There should be a limited number of clans, and they should call themselves cousins in the future.[145]

> So then, do you consider in what manner exist all the things which he [the Creator] has completed; he thus made them to differ in kind and that causes everything to be good, and they are all charged with different duties to perform.[146]

Several consistent principles of Haudenosaunee law are set out in that statement. First, the components of the societal and legal system are deliberately patterned after elements or principles of the natural world. Second, as each animal has distinct attributes and duties, so each person and family is different, and has different gifts, and these ought to be acknowledged, fostered, and used effectively.[147] Third, this part of the Creation story provides for the "two sides of the stream" in the Condolence, which reflects the two-sidedness of government and decision-making processes and institutions. Fourth, there are not just distinct clans: they are all related, and they call one another *cousins*. Fifth, all living parts of creation have specific duties to fulfill in order to maintain life.

One aspect of the genius of the Peacemaker was to work with these existing institutions as elements of a new kind of society. Seeing that clans—especially the

---

144 Dennis 1993, 49: "Iroquoianists believe that clans originally formed about 1000 B.C. as a consequence of widespread Early and Middle Woodland patterns of trade and ritualism, not simply as an outgrowth of kinship groups. During the Owasco period clans probably developed further and assumed some of the new integrative functions characteristic of the Iroquois." Snow (1994, 57) asserts that the clans arose to "facilitate trade and exchange between residential groups."

145 Mohawk 2005a, 92. See also Hewitt 1928, 595–96 and Foster 1974, 72–73.

146 Hewitt 1928, 596. This belief was explained by the Haudenosaunee to colonial governors in September 1722: "it has pleased God to make you Christians and us Heathens, but we hope we shall both act according to our Capacities & be faithful to our respective Promises & Engagements. Some are placed in high Stations & some in Low; but there is One above Who rules & governs All & will judge us according to our Actions" (Wraxall [1754] 1915, 143). It is worth understanding the difference between "heathens" and "pagans" (heathens are not Christian, Jewish, or Muslim, but are monotheists).

147 Maybe this early recognition of individual attributes contributed not only to the individual freedoms in Haudenosaunee society, but also to resistance to assimilation into the kinds of European societies that value sameness.

Turtle, Wolf, and Bear Clans—crossed all the nations, he used them as another way to make everybody into relatives. The Peacemaker saw that the clan system could become a force for peace and understanding. Rather than seek to eliminate the clans, he extrapolated the clan system to the Confederacy level, so all the people would become a single family: "as clans are already established among the people, the several clans [shall] form relations as brothers and cousins."[148]

The clans also provide their members closer family relationships with the natural world. For Wolf Clan people, wolves are indeed relatives, and they share attributes. The relationship with the natural world extends well beyond clan animals, though: a people who refer to "Mother Earth," "our Elder Brother the Sun," and "Our Grandfathers the Thunderers" see all aspects of the natural world as part of the family, and that, too, affects their conduct.[149] John Mohawk observed that urban detachment from nature leads to a change in environmental values: "There was a time among Indians when the animals were perceived as people who live under the forest canopy and who run about on four legs. If you think of them as anything else, they ultimately become disposable. If you cling to the logic that the animals are less precious than us, then they get less and less precious, until they're not precious at all. We Indians thought of ourselves as animals. That's why we called ourselves turtles and wolves and bears and deer."[150]

It has been suggested that a person's clan is indicative of personality,[151] though in modern form this tends to resemble horoscopes. Of the Wolf Clan, the proper or formal name is Wakathahyón:ni, "they make paths": an old term descriptive of the habits of the wolf. Of Turtles (Wakenayáhten), it is said they are slow to anger, and thoughtful. Bears (Wakskare:wake), as the legends suggest, are hospitable. True or not, these stereotypes add a layer of expected conduct that contributes in its own way to social norms.

As one moves westward through the Longhouse of the Confederacy, one finds more clans in each nation. The Mohawks and Oneidas have only Turtle (or Tortoise), Wolf, and Bear, the three clans that cross the entire Confederacy. The Onondagas add Deer, Beaver, Ball, Snipe, and Eel. The Cayugas and Senecas have the same eight clans as the Onondagas, except that the Cayugas replace the Ball clan with the Hawk, and "among the Senecas both Ball and Eel disappear,

---

148   Parker 1916, 93.

149   Asked what clan he belongs to, a Mohawk will respond with the clan's formal name and niwaki'taro:ten—"I am made of that clay." Farmers are admonished not to plow too deeply, but only to "scratch our mother's face gently"; upon the first thunder of the year, people put out tobacco in respect for the Thunderers bringing the rain.

150   Mohawk 1996, 11. Several times in Gibson's 1912 version of the law, messengers transform themselves into animals so that they can move more quickly—hawks, wolves, and fish.

151   Porter 1993.

and are replaced by Hawk and Heron."[152] One explanation for the additional clans is the taking in of other peoples. Huron clans—Rock, Bear, Deer, and Potato[153]—might be reflected in modern Seneca clans. Little is known about the clans of the Wenro, Erie, and Attiwandaron peoples, whose survivors were absorbed by the Haudenosaunee—especially by the Senecas.[154] The absorption of these other nations in the seventeenth century would also explain why, though the Senecas have more clans than the other nations, they have only eight chiefs, and some of their clans have no direct representatives in the Grand Council.[155] Venables asserts that "the number of clans was severely reduced by an epidemic disease accidentally introduced by the Europeans, and it is therefore unknown if each clan once existed in every one of the nations within the confederacy."[156]

In the Haudenosaunee tradition, one belongs to, and is raised within, one's mother's ohwátsi're and clan. There are fifteen Haudenosaunee communities today, on both sides of the boundary between the United States and Canada, and when marriages take place between people from two different communities, a husband will often move to his wife's community, so the children may be raised in the midst of their own clan family (anthropologists would call this practice an indication of a "matrilocal" society).[157] As many people are not involved in issues of traditional government (Sotsisowah John Mohawk would say that only a few hundred people at a time would be engaged in "the Confederacy culture"), most Haudenosaunee would be conscious of their clan identity only at ceremonies (where seating in the longhouse is determined by clan) and in matters of marriage. Even non-traditional families take seriously the rules against marrying within one's own clan. Those rules have not only promoted genetic diversity: they have encouraged links between the components of community.

---

152 Hale (1883) 1989, 53.

153 The "Ball Clan": the name was explained by Jacob Thomas as originating with a kind of deer that hides by rolling itself into a ball and resembling a rock. The Ball may also have been derived from the Huron Potato Clan.

154 See Hale (1883) 1989, 55: "Almost all the captives were incorporated with the three western nations of the league." Hale believed that at the beginning of the Confederacy, there were only the three clans—Turtle, Wolf, and Bear. For basic histories of the absorbed nations, see Trigger 1976.

155 Morgan (1877, 70) suggests that the differences are the result of different events: "certain gentes in some of the tribes have become extinct through the vicissitudes of time, and…others have been formed by the segmentation of over-full gentes." In *Ancient Society*, Morgan uses the Roman *gens* as equivalent to a Haudenosaunee clan.

156 Venables 2010, 36.

157 The anthropologists say that following one's mother's clan or line is "matrilineal"; moving to live with one's wife's people is "matrilocal"; being ruled by women is "matriarchal."

As the members of a clan regarded themselves as brothers and sisters, marriages among them were not allowed.[158] This led, of course, to constant intermarriages between members of the different clans of which a nation was composed, thus binding the whole nation together. What the founders of the Iroquois League did was to extend this system of social alliances through the entire confederacy. . . . Mr. Morgan has well pointed out the wisdom shown by the Iroquois founders, in availing themselves of this powerful element of strength in the formation of their federal constitution.[159] Their government, though politically a league of nations, was socially a combination of clans. In this way Hiawatha and Dekanawidah may be deemed to have given to the system of clanship an extension and a force which it had not previously possessed.[160]

What if one does not have a clan? That does not seem to be an obstacle to coming within the circle of the law. Odatsehte, the leading Oneida chief, explained to the Peacemaker: "As to us, we no longer have clans, we have lost them, indeed, the reason is this: the things going on such as the habitual slaughter among the people, that is where we lost them. Moreover, this large crowd followed us for they want to observe it progressing, the doings pertaining to the League as it gets completed in all ways."[161]

The Peacemaker did not say that without clans they could not be Haudenosaunee. Instead, his response was to include them immediately by assigning them a clan:

> Thereupon Tekanawita said, "Now, next, as to you Ho'tatshehte, whom have you drafted[162] to help with the League?" Thereupon Ho'tatshehte said, "You two, come here, you drafted ones." Thereupon they stood up there in front of the chiefs. Thereafter Tekanawaita said, "As to you, in fact, you are the ones not having a

---

158 Fenton asserts (in his notes to Gibson 1899, para. 62) that "one cannot marry into one's father's maternal family or into one's mother's (one's own) maternal family, but other clans in the same moiety (as one's father's clan) are open. Can marry into one's father's clan but not into his lineage."

159 Morgan (1851) 1995, 81.

160 Hale (1883) 1989, 53.

161 Gibson 1912, 43.

162 "Drafted" seems inappropriate to describe what happened. In modern Haudenosaunee English, when a person of a different clan is placed in a position that a family does not have an appropriate representative to fill, the word used is "borrowed." "Drafted" implies a lack of consent, and that is not the case.

clan, and now they have chosen you. This, then, is what we shall call it: the Turtle clan, which will become their families' clan.[163]

There is an important principle here: reaching out generously and including people willing and able to join the League takes precedence over whether they can prove membership in a clan.[164] The Peacemaker acted spontaneously and deliberately, assuming the authority to name a group of people and give them identity within society. This was not only a means of healing and weaving society back together. It was a statement of intent, an example of more than tolerance. It was an act of immediate generosity, but also of pragmatism. To function within the society he was creating, families required a clan. Given a choice between inclusion and anomaly, the Peacemaker unerringly chose inclusion. It is the spirit of the law.

Within the clan system, there are further divisions. Thus, the Turtle Clan divides into Snapping Turtle, Painted Turtle, and Mud Turtle; the Bear Clan into large and small parts. For example, among the Mohawks, it has been said that Tekarihoken's family is the "Old Snapping Turtles," while Hiawatha's is the "Younger Snapping Turtle."[165] Among the Cayugas, there is an Old Bear Clan and a Suckling Bear Clan.

Many people today know their clans in a general, not subdivided, way. While in the Catholic communities of Kahnawake and Akwesasne, the Jesuits maintained clan identity within the church (in seating or in holiday processions, for example), and while in the Longhouse there are ceremonial reasons to remind one of one's clan, the clan subdivisions became less important to other people. Often an individual today will know that he is a Bear, or a Turtle, but not more than that. Genealogical research can connect the individuals with the titles of their chiefs, and through them to the parts of the clan.

Personal Names

At Midwinter and at Green Corn ceremonies each year, children are brought forward, and their names are formally announced in the longhouse. Their maternal uncle makes the announcement while carrying or walking with the

---

163 Gibson 1912, 45.

164 In 1999, the Grand River Council considered the question of the large number of people in that community who either had no clan or did not know their clans. The council concluded that those who could not identify a clan through their mothers should be able to take their fathers' clan. This would apply only to those who were living at the time of the decision.

165 Deborah Doxtator, personal communication through Teyawentathe Susan Hill, 2004.

child and then sings his atonwa, his personal chant of thanksgiving. The name is announced rather than given at this ceremony, because usually the name has been assigned to the child shortly after birth. The name is chosen by the women of the family, in consultation with the parents, from among the storehouse of names possessed by that ohwátsi're or clan family.

Lafitau, writing about Kahnawake in the early 1700s, described how names were preserved and kept alive:

> In each family a certain number of ancestral names, both men's and women's, are kept. These names are their own and known to be taken by such and such a family. Now it is the custom in each family to requicken and resuscitate, in some manner, those who, issuing from that family, have made it illustrious. They exalt thus, at the same time, the names of those who they make live again, and impose them on their grand nephews destined to represent them. The latter assume more or less importance according as those who had borne their names were more or less important themselves by their qualities, virtues and deeds. These names change with age. A child either has no name, or takes that of another child, a young man, that of a warrior and an old man, that of some elder. As soon as a person dies, the name that he bore is buried with him and it is only several years afterward that it is renewed.[166]

In this sense, a name belongs to a family as much as it does to an individual. The person bearing the name knows several important things: that the name is a link to a long line of ancestors; that he or she is the only person alive today carrying that name; that there will be people in the future who will be given that name; that the name is real and has reality on several levels. When a person is ill, and someone else goes to collect medicine for them, it is that person's real name (as distinct from his "English name") that is used to address the plants and their forces, as well as to seek help from the Creator. In ceremonies and in the longhouse in general, one's real name is the one the people and the Creator know. Names provide identity, connection, and continuity.

The custom of a person having several names in the course of a lifetime has waned but not disappeared. Sometimes, an individual is given a new name as a means of honouring him or her. Historically, there have been times when a Haudenosaunee individual will give their own name to an adoptee: the accounts do not clarify whether the giver of the name then has to return to their family to be given a new name.

In conversation, a person is asked "what are you called," and answers "they call me . . ." (yonkwats). In other words, the identity that accompanies a name

---

166 Lafitau (1724) 1974, 1:69–71.

comes from its use by other people. The name would be irrelevant if it were not used by others. In contrast, in some versions, when the Peacemaker announced himself, he tended to state "I *am* Tekanawita," possibly because he had grown up in isolation, so there were no people around (other than his mother and grandmother) to call him anything.

Ceremonies

The major ceremonies of traditional Haudenosaunee are said to have been brought by the same fatherless young man who brought the clans, long before the time of the Peacemaker.[167] The Great Law was not intended to affect the ceremonies; the Peacemaker left unchanged the aspects of the society that promoted or maintained peace: "The rites and festivals of each nation shall remain undisturbed and shall continue as before they were given by the people of old times as useful and necessary for the good of men."[168]

The chiefs were given a duty in the law to help maintain the ceremonies:

> It shall be the duty of the Lords of each brotherhood to confer at the approach of the time of the Midwinter Thanksgiving and to notify the people of the approaching festival. They shall hold a council over the matter and arrange its details and begin the Thanksgiving five days after the moon of Dis-ko-nah is new. The people shall assemble at the appointed place and the nephews shall notify the people of the time and place. From the beginning to the end the Lords shall preside over the Thanksgiving and address the people from time to time.
>
> The recognized festivals of thanksgiving shall be the Midwinter Thanksgiving, the Maple or Sugar-making Thanksgiving, the Raspberry Thanksgiving, the Strawberry Thanksgiving, the Corn-planting Thanksgiving, the Corn Hoeing Thanksgiving, the Little

---

167 There are also four beings who are said to be messengers from the Creator. They visited Handsome Lake, in his visions, bringing him the Good News. Robert Jamieson, the late Interpreter for the Grand River Council, used to call them "angels"—and that bothered me, because it mixed Judeo-Christian symbolism with something that was clearly a matter that came before contact between the Haudenosaunee and Europeans. That is, it bothered me until I realized that "angel" originates from the Greek *angelos*—meaning "messenger." Bob Jamieson had the spirit of the word right, and that is what an interpreter is supposed to do.

168 Parker (Newhouse and Cusick) 1916, 56.

Festival of Green Corn, the Great Festival of Ripe Corn, and the complete Thanksgiving for the Harvest.[169]

As for the ceremonies other than Midwinter, the faithkeepers are responsible for ensuring they are properly conducted. Each chief works with a male and a female faithkeeper,[170] part of the "cluster" of government that includes the chief, clan mother, faithkeepers, sub-chief, and "runner" for each title: "It shall be the duty of the appointed managers of the Thanksgiving festivals to do all that is needful for carrying out the duties of the occasions. . . . When the Thanksgiving for the Green Corn comes the special managers, both the men and the women, shall give it careful attention and do their duties properly."[171]

The ceremonies predate the visions of Skaniatariio in the 1790s. Some Haudenosaunee continue to maintain and participate in the ceremonies without following the Karihwí:iyo,[172] the Code of Handsome Lake.

The cycle of ceremonies is not unrelated to the principles of the law. Each of the thanksgiving ceremonies is a celebration that gives thanks for the food that Creation is providing and renews and acknowledges the forces that provide it. An underlying principle is *renewal,* keeping things fresh and alive in people's minds—the same principle that requires periodic renewal of the people's commitment to the law, and later would require periodic renewal of treaty relations, or "repolishing" the Silver Covenant Chain between the Haudenosaunee and the British Crown. What Wade Davis wrote of African ceremonies also applies to the Haudenosaunee: "The religion cannot be abstracted from the day-to-day lives of the believers . . . there is no separation between the sacred and the secular, between the holy and the profane, between the material and the spiritual. Every dance, every song, every action is but a particle of the whole, each gesture a prayer for the survival of the entire community."[173]

---

169 Parker (Newhouse and Cusick) 1916, 56. In some longhouses, there is also a Green Bean ceremony. Ohki:we, the "feast for the dead," was brought by someone else.

170 Fenton, perhaps to accentuate the similarity between the Longhouse religion and Christianity, called the faithkeepers "deacons."

171 Parker (Newhouse and Cusick) 1916, 56. The chiefs may be responsible for Midwinter because it is a ceremony of renewal and rebirth, and they are the living examples of how a title remains living, or is reborn.

172 Karihwí:iyo—Ka (it is; it is something which has been created); orihwa (word or matter); i:io (good)—"the Good Word," or "the Good Message."

173 Davis 1998, 54.

In several parts of the ceremonies, the people are split into two sides of the longhouse (the anthropologists call them "moieties").[174] Without the two sides, the ceremonies could not be put through: as in council, having two parts of the people creates harmony rather than division. They help each other.

Helping one another is part of every Haudenosaunee medicine society, as well. Usually, a person who has been healed by a particular medicine or medicine society becomes a member of that society,[175] with the responsibility of maintaining and renewing its medicine, and of curing or healing other people who need its help.[176]

As John Mohawk has pointed out, the ceremonies are the way Haudenosaunee society expresses its cooperation with the will of the sacred forces that have created life, as well as its gratitude. The ceremonies "recreate the conditions present when people first came to consciousness of these things."[177] By maintaining the ceremonies, society is maintaining, acknowledging, and renewing its relationship to its context within the natural world: "Our ceremonials acknowledge that in the time of the primeval universe there was a very remote chance that a place would be created which would support life and that, given a consciousness of this, expressions of gratitude are in order. Human beings who experience life should be grateful."[178]

Participation in the ceremonies reaffirms a person's understanding of their place in society, by reminding them where they sit in the longhouse, who they sit with, who speaks for them—and also of their place in the natural world and its cycles and inhabitants. If Haudenosaunee kinships have kept that society in

---

174 The Senecas, with their Hawk, Heron, and Snipe clans, have a "bird side" and an "animal side" in their ceremonies. Mohawks and Oneidas keep Wolves and Bears on one side, Turtles on the other. Some people note that the clan symbols cover water, land, and air life equally. Noting that in some nations the "moieties" are divided differently, Morgan supposed that "transfers of particular gentes from one phratry to the other must have occurred when the equilibrium in their respective numbers was disturbed." Morgan (1871) 1997, 91. Today, in Longhouse ceremonies, one "side" sometimes borrows speakers from the other.

175 In a sense, by joining the society that person has "crossed over" from being part of the people outside the society to the other side of the fire.

176 In a functioning tribal society, individuals are valued not for their economic activity so much as for what they do to help. Over time, most traditional Haudenosaunee become members of some medicine society, and that provides another layer that binds them within society, providing them with more helpers, more esteem, and, in a sense, more family.

177 Mohawk 2005a, xv. "At the time of the ceremonies, the longhouse becomes a reflection of the Sky World, the dances here those done there. Thus the ceremony not only celebrates the gifts of the creation, those who participate with their bodies in the music and the dance spend those moments recreating the Sky World on earth."

178 Mohawk 2005a, xiii.

place where others have been swept away, the ceremonies are an occasion for renewing the sense of "joined arms" among the people and with the natural world.

Not mentioned in most written versions of the law is the winter ceremony
of Ohki:we, or the Spirit Dance, in which the spirits of the people who have
passed away during the year are gathered together in one last farewell, and it is
said the spirits join with the living in the all-night women's dance. This may be
a descendant of the great Dead Feasts of four and five centuries ago.[179] Concern
for the dead, for their comfort and their journey, and for stilling their voices,
appears in the law through the ceremony of Condolence.[180]

Ohki:we is an aspect of the Haudenosaunee view of "the people." Unlike
societies that consider "the people" to be restricted to those alive at any given
time, the Haudenosaunee include both those who have lived before and those
who are yet unborn. From the ancestors, the living Haudenosaunee inherit
names, clans, traditions, laws, land, and obligations. To the "coming faces," the
living owe a similar inheritance. People are told that they must walk softly on
the earth, for the faces of the unborn generations are just below the surface of
the soil. Reverence and respect for the dead and reverence and concern for the
unborn are reflections of each other. These are further evinced in respect for elders, and a sense of respecting the independence and personhood of children.[181]
In a modern North American society that tends to concentrate its respect on
breadwinners, and its priority on the living, the Haudenosaunee value system
stands in stark contrast.

Repetition, or rather re-creation, of the ceremonies reflects a common human trait. If something has been done with power and effect, we seek to repeat
that, either to regain some of the original power, or to celebrate it. This is part
of how humans learn. It can be seen in something as complex as a Catholic
mass, which repeats the sequence of the Last Supper, and as simple as a baseball
player's wearing the same shirt or eating the same meal as the last time he hit

---

179 The Wendat (Hurons) would bury all the people who had died in the previous ten years
     or so in a large common grave, mixing the bones together and saying, "As we were one
     people in life, so we will be one people in death" (personal communication, Hayadaha
     Richard Wayne Hill, 2012). The Haudenosaunee themselves had less elaborate burial cer-
     emonies but still brought the dead together. Gathering the dead together, for the Wendat,
     was a preliminary to leaving one village site for the next.

180 Hewitt (1892b, 131) goes further: "The body of the rites and customs pertaining to the
     ancient decennial Dead Feast common to many, if not all, of the Iroquois tribes and
     peoples, was mainly the basis upon which the institutions of the Extended House were
     established."

181 In a child welfare case in an Ontario court, Oneida psychologist Kanakalut Roland
     Chrisjohn explained in an expert opinion that the Haudenosaunee consider children to be
     simple, small young people, so that their wishes as to whom they want to live with ought
     to be respected unless the result would harm them. In the "best interests of the child"
     analysis in that case, other psychologists argued that attachment, family ties, and culture
     were the most important factors.

a home run. Ceremonies and legal rituals remind us of continuity, but they also imbue us with power—the power of our predecessors, or of their actions.

As Haudenosaunee ceremonies are repeated each year, partly to keep them alive and partly to keep us alive, so the periodic reaffirmation of the law is conducted in the same way, and for the same purpose. The Canadian Royal Commission on Aboriginal Peoples recognized the connection between ceremony, law, and continuity: "The Great Law is infused with the same good mind that inspired the founders of the Great Peace and to which the children not yet born will also have access. The grandfathers and grandmothers who have gone to the spirit world and the generations not yet born are present in the ceremonies in a powerful way, and they are even visible to some with highly developed awareness."[182]

The cycle of ceremonies does more than renew and maintain the relationship between the Haudenosaunee and the natural world and the sacred forces that created it. The ceremonies also remind the people of their place in that world. Reminding is an essential element of the legal system, as well, and it is accomplished by some of the same paths as the ceremonies: public repetition, cooperative maintenance, individual reaffirmation. Since the ceremonies are so close in spirit to the law and its goals, it ought not to be surprising that they intersect, overlap, and complement each other. In Haudenosaunee society, church and state are not distinguishable concepts: both the spiritual practices and the governmental institutions have the same spirit and goals, and are maintained and conducted by many of the same people, so it is neither necessary nor possible to separate them.

The Date of the Creation of the League

Euro-American scholars have been fascinated with the question of the date of the creation of the Great Law and the League it brought together. The Haudenosaunee do not share that concern. For them, it has been enough that it existed long ago, before the arrival of the Europeans, and has continued to exist ever since.[183] Different peoples think about history (and time) in different ways, and it is likely that their understanding of the world affects their study of history

---

182   RCAP 1995, 640.

183   Euro-American scholars also discuss the span of seven generations, while for the Haudenosaunee the specific time is far less important than the knowledge that the coming faces seven generations downstream are ones that we will never see in our lifetimes.

and their concern about dates.[184] For Europeans, time (and therefore history, as time past) is linear, and important dates and events are temporal landmarks, worthy of recall and often legally significant.[185] For the Haudenosaunee, time is both linear (like a river)[186] and cyclical (in the sense that the annual cycle of ceremonies is repeated each year in the same way), so that what is being maintained and continuing is more important than what has occurred.[187]

The written records confirm that the Five Nations had already joined together by the early 1600s: the Jesuits among the Montagnais reported their existence in the 1630s, and Champlain mentioned them twenty years earlier. In the 1740s, the Moravian minister Christopher Pyrlaeus wrote: "The alliance or confederacy of the Five Nations was established, as near as can be conjectured, one age (or the length of a man's life) before the white people (the Dutch) came into the country."[188] This single statement became a focus of scholarly debate: what precise date did this suggest?[189] Later writers took Pyrlaeus's statement to indicate between 1460 and 1579.

Daniel Richter, pointing to archaeological evidence of "homogenization of material culture" between the original five nations, suggests the political

---

184 For Hindu scholars, the world is cyclical, so a particular event is less relevant. For Christians, history is linear, with a crucial period running from the time of Jesus to the apocalyptic last days. For Muslim scholars, space may be more important than time. See also Boorstin 1985.

185 To most lawyers, for example, the date something occurred immediately raises the important issue of limitation periods.

186 A river is part of a cycle, too: from condensation to the clouds and the Thunderers, to the rain and the runoff and streams, to the ocean and the dew and back to the condensation.

187 In political negotiations, Canadian federal negotiators request descriptions of specific treaty events, while their Haudenosaunee counterparts respond with descriptions of their ongoing relationship, often without reference to particular dates.

188 Fenton 1998, 53.

189 Schoolcraft (1894) took Henry Hudson's visit in 1609 as the date "the Dutch came into the country," and applied the "patriarchal and scriptural rule"—that the length of a man's life was seventy years—to arrive at 1539. Horatio Hale (1883, 177–180) suggested that Heckewelder had wrongly added the words "the Dutch," and that the arrival of white people had been Cartier's 1534 exploration of the St. Lawrence. With the "length of a man's life" at seventy-five years, he arrived at 1460. Beauchamp (1921) also wrestled with Pyrlaeus's dates, arguing that the League must have been founded after Cartier's St. Lawrence voyage (since Beauchamp thought that all the Mohawks were then living on that river). Turning "a man's lifetime" into a "generation," or thirty years, he decided the most likely date of the founding was 1579. Hewitt took Pyrlaeus's "one age" to be sixty years, which led him to 1559: he added that the war between the St. Lawrence Algonquins and the Iroquois had been going for over fifty years by 1622, when Champlain wrote about it, and this would have prompted the founding of a defensive league between 1550 and 1570 (see Schoolcraft 1894). Pyrlaeus had also observed that the Tuscaroras joined the League about 100 years after it was founded: since the Tuscaroras came in 1722, this would make the original date 1622.

changes that led to the founding of the League would have taken place in the late 1400s.[190]

Haudenosaunee accounts are also spread over time. Sagonaquade Albert Cusick stated grandly that the League was formed 1,000 years before Columbus. Grand River tradition places the founding three lifetimes before the arrival of Cartier, or about 1390. Morgan and Hale, working with chiefs and informants on both sides of the border,[191] separately concluded that the mid-1400s was a likely time. In 1895, the Council at the Grand River Territory issued a commemorative medal to celebrate the 500th anniversary of the founding of the Confederacy.

Schoolcraft was told by the Senecas that the League was founded about 1605, four years before Henry Hudson explored the river that bears his name today. Beauchamp reported that some Onondagas told him the date was about 1600.

Another approach to the date setting began with parts of collateral tradition. It was said that there was a total eclipse of the sun at the time the Senecas were considering joining the League, at a time when the grass was knee-high or the corn was ripening. In another version, the Mohawks were about to attack a Seneca village when the corn was receiving its last tilling. When the eclipse took place, it convinced them instead that war should end. Examining the times of total solar eclipses visible in upper New York State, Barbara Mann concluded that the Senecas had adopted the law on 31 August 1142, at a place that is now a football field in Victor, New York.[192]

Elisabeth Tooker, reviewing all these accounts, leans towards a later date because of the "lack of wampum in prehistoric sites" and "the statement in the traditional accounts that wampum was not used before the League was

---

190   Richter 1992, 31.

191   Skanawati John Buck told Hale in 1882 that he thought the League had been founded about 400 years earlier. The Onondaga chiefs in New York had told Hale that the founding was six generations before the arrival of white people. Hale chose 1459 as the appropriate date.

192   Mann and Fields 1997; Johansen 1995, 62–63. There had been another eclipse in 1451, but its shadow fell over Pennsylvania. Barbara Mann also cited Paula Underwood's calculations, based on family lineages—Underwood had arrived at a founding date of 1090. Mann averaged lifespans of European monarchs and popes and North American chief justices, adopting Tekaronieken Jake Swamp's figure of 145 Thadadahos, to conclude that a date between 1090 and 1142 was justifiable. See also Wallace 1948, 399–400. But see Henige 1999, in which he argues that Mann and Fields lacked the evidence to prove their theory.

founded." She suggests "an approximate date of 1600."[193] Her conclusion is part of "a line of thought which attributes the origins of all Indian confederacies to European influence. Confederacies are interpreted as tribal groupings formed to be better able to resist European intrusion. Alternatively, it is suggested that tribes living in the interior made alliances in order to break restrictive trading covenants between coastal tribes and the Europeans and to be able to participate in this trade themselves."[194]

Other hints concerning the possible date of the founding of the League come from archaeology. The cultivation of beans, then squash and then corn arrived from the south about AD 900, allowing seminomadic people living in small groups to become more sedentary. In the area south of Lake Ontario, they were living in unfortified hamlets of about 200 people. Around the mid-fifteenth century, there was a rather sudden change: while the total population of the territory remained more or less the same, the people moved into large towns of up to 3,000 people. There were still also small, unfortified hamlets, but they were clearly linked to these larger, protected places of refuge. It is as if the need for palisades came with a culture of war—the bloody Dark Times that preceded the coming of the Great Law[195]—as well as with larger settle-ments that required more structured forms of government. Since archaeology can be imprecise, it is also possible to link these Dark Times to the Dark Ages in Europe, times when a mini–ice age, a change in climate, affected crops, temperatures, sunlight, and attitudes.

The common traits that to archaeologists identify the Haudenosaunee—"the practice of horticulture, settlement in longhouses in villages, internecine warfare, burial of the dead in cemeteries, and distinctive ceramic assemblages"—coalesced in their homeland sometime between AD 1230 and 1375.[196]

Another possibility is that European diseases, which preceded the appearance of European humans, caused a breakdown in society. If people were dying of unknown causes, their relatives might tend to blame the death on malevolence

---

193   Tooker 1978, 418–22. In fact, there *was* wampum in prehistoric sites; there was just not much of it, nor is much of it shaped like later tubular "council" wampum. The accounts of the founding of the League don't require large amounts of wampum, though. Strings, not belts, were the order of the day before the arrival of metal tools—strings to conduct the Condolence, to create the "fire," and to make the circle. As well, the earliest records of the Confederacy are made of white wampum: this suggests that they could have been made of softer white shell from the Finger Lakes area, rather than the harder periwinkles and whelks of the Atlantic coast, and without the hard quahog clamshells required for purple wampum.

194   Trigger 1976, 163.

195   Snow 1994.

196   Atkins 2001, 27. Engelbrecht (2003, 88) points out that the fact that maize was "stor-able" made an important difference to the permanence and size of villages.

by others, and this could have precipitated the blood feuds.[197] Some aspects of the ceremony of Condolence seem designed to prevent revenge-taking against anyone who sent death through disease, and some Seneca trickster stories recall a time of great terror as new diseases arrived for which there was no cure. Jacques Cartier, wintering in Stadacona in 1534, mentioned that about one fifth of the Stadaconaronon died that season of disease—these were the same people who had enough knowledge of herbal medicine to cure his crew's scurvy. The Laurentian Iroquoians who had greeted Cartier were gone when the French returned two generations later. Epidemic disease certainly played a part in their disappearance.

In 1801, Thayendenega Joseph Brant wrote, simply: "We can say [no] farther respecting the date that it appears by the transaction to have been a considerable time before the arrival of the Europeans."[198]

There is no clinically provable date of the creation of the League. Nor does there need to be, for the purpose of the laws of the Haudenosaunee or the nations they work with. It is enough, for the purpose of Canadian and U.S. law, that the League predated European contact—and it does—and was an integral part of the people's distinctive society at the time of first contact.[199] In a world in which most nation-states and their constitutions have existed for less than a century, and in a North America where the United States of America was created in 1776 and the Dominion of Canada in 1867, a continuous government more than 500 years old is indeed a grandmother.[200]

---

197 Stannard 1992; Crosby 1986. For the tendency of humans to blame others for deaths by disease, see the accounts of Europeans blaming "Jews and Gypsies" for the Black Plague in Barbara Tuchman's *A Distant Mirror* (1978).

198 Boyce 1973, 290.

199 Sotsisowah John Mohawk simply says "around 500–1500 years ago." Others have stated that history is irrelevant to the Haudenosaunee, for whom the story of the founding of the League is a form of renewal of what exists now.

200 Nor are North American nation-states the only young ones. Modern Germany and Italy are products of the nineteenth century; the present forms, boundaries, and governments of most of central and eastern Europe were created in the twentieth century. Great Britain's United Kingdom, the product of waves of invasions by Celts, Romans, Saxons and Angles, Danes, and Normans, and of subsuming Scotland and Wales, cannot claim to have a constitution older than the Great Law.

PART II

The Nature of the Law: Principles and Processes

Principles, Not Details

To function effectively, a law preserved in memory rather than writing must place emphasis on principles rather than details.

This becomes apparent when one considers the variations in the four versions of the narrative of the lawmaking. The Cannibal can be Hiawatha in one version, Thadadaho in another, Tekarihoken in a third, and just a cannibal in a fourth. But the basic message, the principle that a person who has engaged in too much killing has something wrong with his mind and spirit, and that he can be healed and return to the Good Mind, remains constant.

The primacy of principle over detail is demonstrated at the opening and closing of every council and meeting: the Thanksgiving Address will be correct if it pays attention to each essential element in the proper order—it matters not how long or short it is.

Some people believe literally in every part of the Kayanerenkó:wa.[1] They believe that Thadadaho really had snakes in his hair and grotesque twists and turns in his body. Others believe that these are metaphors: that he had a powerfully twisted mind and the physical deformities make the story more forceful.[2] Those who believe literally can visualize the chief combing the snakes from his hair, rubbing the kinks from his body, making him normal in appearance. Those who feel the story is symbolic will still agree that Thadadaho was a real person whose evil stood in the way of the peace, and who had to be persuaded to come to the side of goodness and light, and that ceremony and spirit played an essential role in bringing Thadadaho's mind to the good.

Different versions of the law have Hiawatha losing two daughters, three daughters, or seven daughters. For the purposes of the law, the number of daughters is irrelevant. What matters is that his mind was clouded with grief at the loss of his family. Whether Thadadaho had real physical deformities is

---

1   Hewitt, providing Skanawati John Buck's 1888 version of the making of the Peace, suggested that "the greater part of the miraculous and mythic doings misapplied by the vulgar and uninitiated to Hai-on-hwat-ha, such as the story of the white canoe, the clearing of the rivers of obstructions and monsters, belong really to the sky god, Tharonhyawakon. Such confusion is not unusual among those who are uninitiated and unversed in the myths of their own people." Hewitt 1892b, 131. Hewitt, though, was usually more careful than to call the right-handed twin of the Creation Story "the Sky God." Haudenosaunee meta-narratives are not easily equated with European pantheons.

2   Horatio Hale maintained that the Haudenosaunee themselves did not believe the "fantastical parts" of the story of the making of the law (Vecsey 1988, 98).

irrelevant: what matters is how his powerfully twisted mind and spirit were made good again. People who take the story of the making of the law literally, and people who see parables and symbols in the story all agree that what is most important are the principles and the lessons that emerge from the law. Just as there is a spectrum of Biblical interpretation between literalists and symbolists, so are the Haudenosaunee divided about the story of the making of the law. Similarly, the people are united in recognizing that the principles and the message, not the details, are what count.

The Peacemaker said as much: "I will now leave all matters in the hands of your lords and you are to work and carry out the principles of all that I have just laid before you for the welfare of your people and others, and I now place the power in your hands and to add to the rules and regulations whenever necessary."[3]

Order

The law was born in a time of chaos. It sometimes seems as if it is designed to constantly pull people back from the brink of falling into that same chaos. When minds are scattered and tending towards anger in times of confusion or grief, the Condolence restores order. When people need to bring their minds together in council, the Thanksgiving (like the Condolence) reminds them of the basic order of the world, and then of how they fit into that order, with responsibilities mirrored by those of every other part of this great system. Haudenosaunee society seeks and recognizes order in dozens of things, insisting that speeches, ceremonies, and thinking be carried out in the appropriate sequences.[4]

Getting things in order often reflects pragmatism. The Condolence recognizes that one has to address and remove the physical obstacles to understanding—the ability to see, hear, and speak—before one can proceed to relieve the mental and spiritual burdens a person is carrying. The Covenant Chain recognizes that its three links have a logical order: one must respect a

---

3   Parker (Chiefs) 1916, 103.

4   It might be argued that just as the scientific method prescribes a deliberate, thoughtful approach to resolving questions, so does the Haudenosaunee method. Each facilitates resolution in its own way, the former by isolating the subject and reducing variables, the latter by taking matters one at a time and seeking balance.

person before one can trust him or her; one must have trust in place before one can have friendship.[5]

Especially for those whose introduction to Haudenosaunee culture is the Thanksgiving, there is a tendency to see hierarchy as well as order, particularly if those people are approaching the culture from a European perspective. The Thanksgiving does move gradually outward from the people and the earth to beyond the sky, and the temptation to find hierarchy in it is powerful. But the Thanksgiving is more a matter of space–time than authority. It describes how things are related and responsible to one another, rather than how some are more important than others.

English uses "order" to mean two quite different things. One is "orderliness," neatness. The other is sequence, getting things in the proper succession. In Haudenosaunee terms, getting matters in proper sequence helps restore the orderliness of peace.

Versions

Every Haudenosaunee gathering opens and closes in the same way. The "opening" is sometimes called the "opening thanksgiving," or "the words that come before all else," ohe'n:ton karihwatékwen:[6]

> Whenever the Confederate Lords shall assemble for the purpose of holding a council, the Onondaga Lords shall open it by expressing their gratitude to their cousin Lords and greeting them, and they shall make an address and offer thanks to the earth where men dwell, to the streams of water, the pools, the springs and the lakes, to the maize and fruits, to the medicinal herbs and trees, to the forest

---

5   The Silver Covenant Chain is often described as having three links, symbolizing respect, trust, and friendship. Each of these has to be maintained, kept free from tarnish. Peace is frequently mentioned, though I prefer to think of it as the context for the relationship rather than as one of its elements. In the Two Row Wampum, the three white rows between the two parallel dark ones are peace, trust, and friendship, and the white background in general, the River of Life, is also the peace. I consider the Two Row Wampum to be a depiction of the Covenant Chain relationship, moving through time.

6   Older texts say that "the words that come before all else" are the ones spoken at the woods' edge, as the Three Bare Words ("bare" because they are delivered by a speaker who is bare-handed, carrying no strings of wampum)—spoken before greeting the visitors who have come to the edge of the clearing, and are waiting to be welcomed. There are some references to them as the "Three Rare Words" (allegedly a reference to the "rare beauty" of the words, though "rare" is probably a misprint, the result of a Fenton mistranscription of Hewitt's notes). See Haudenosaunee Environmental Task Force 2001; Swamp 1997.

trees for their usefulness, to the animals that serve as food and give
their pelts as clothing, to the great winds and lesser winds, to the
Thunderers, to the Sun, the mighty warrior, to the moon, to the
messengers of the Creator who reveal his wishes, and to the Great
Creator who dwells in the heavens above, who gives all the things
useful to men, and who is the source and the ruler of health and life.[7]

Unlike the Lord's Prayer, which has words so well known to Christians that
entire congregations recite them together, the opening thanksgiving has no set
words. It is a series of ingredients, of concepts. As long as the speaker remembers
to include them all, in the right order, he has done his job. A "full" opening can
take about three-quarters of an hour, and most often a much shorter version is
delivered, either because time is also short or because the speaker may not have
the facility or gift to do the "full" opening. But each is complete and right.[8]
There is consistency of principle over time, in the opening as in the law: "When
Morgan published the Thanksgiving Address in the 1850s, he had heard the
Address given at Midwinter ceremonies and it was written down by Ely Parker
who said this was his grandfather's version, describing it as 'the ancient address
handed down from generation to generation. . . . Sose'ha'wa has delivered it
thus for the past twenty five years at Tonawanda.'"[9]

The *Iliad* and the *Odyssey* were 1,000 years old before they were reduced to
over 12,000 lines of writing. Scholars struggled with the issue of how, and how
well, they could be remembered over the centuries, before they learned that "oral

---

7   Parker (Newhouse and Cusick), 32. Note: Gawasowane Arthur Parker's 1916 *New
     York State Museum Bulletin* contains two very distinct versions of the law. The first is
     one of Dayodekane Seth Newhouse's versions, edited by Sagonaquande Albert Cusick;
     the second is the version produced by the Grand River Chiefs, but probably edited by
     Tahawennontye Duncan Campbell Scott.

8   Michael Foster found that traditional speakers considered their openings and closings to
     be "equivalent" versions, from the one-minute, seven-line version of Teyohtsiʔkrehkweh
     Howard Skye to the 48-minute, 419-line version of the opening by Tehanrahtihsokwa
     Enos Williams (Foster 1974, 177). Perhaps the longest published version is the one done
     by Shogʌdzowa Corbett Sundown in Chafe 1961.

9   Cornelius 1999, 71. It has been suggested that, in the days before the Karihwí:iyo, the
     Code of Handsome Lake, the words now used as the opening and closing thanksgiv-
     ing were the speech that was spoken at the White Dog Ceremony. The words would
     be spoken to the dog. It was of a special breed; its burning evoked the way the Creator
     could travel to the Sky World by stepping into the fire (recall how tobacco smoke travels
     as a message to the Sky World and to the Creator): the white dog, the Creator's favou-
     rite, would carry the message from the people to the Creator. If the ceremony is no
     longer performed today, its principles—communicating and in a sense reporting to the
     Creator—are still intact, and a basket of tobacco is burned in place of the dog (either
     because the breed died out or because of the distaste of the Victorian middle class for
     cruelty to animals). As for the modern opening thanksgiving, while similar sentiments
     are to be found in the records of the openings of historic councils ("we give thanks that
     we may meet here today"), the thanksgiving is not reproduced in lengthy detail, though
     the Condolence often is. That suggests the modern thanksgiving dates to the early 1800s.

bards"—"wisdomkeepers"—in many societies had sophisticated techniques of recall, but did not require exact reproduction of the knowledge each time. "The oral bard who uses such formulaic language is not, as scholars in the nineteenth century who struggled with the problem of illiterate bards all assumed, a poet reciting from memory a fixed text. He is improvising, along known lines, relying on a huge stock of formulaic phrases, lines and even whole scenes; but he *is* improvising. And every time he sings the poem, he may do it differently. The outline remains the same, but the text, the oral text, is flexible. The poem is new every time it is performed."[10]

The same speaker may not necessarily use the same words twice in a row, either. He is not reciting: he is "doing." As long as the ingredients are all there and in order, he is right. He has done the best he can, and that is all that is expected:

> Rather than "memorizing" speeches, good memories depended on recalling the structure of what was said and filling in with expected phrases and figures of speech. The speakers were relaying what the chiefs prompted them to say, but in their own words. They were accomplished and recognized virtuosos. This is what impressed colonial observers who were struck with the good memories of the speakers. "Verbatim recall" applies then to the structure if not to the identical words of the original.[11]

> Speeches are not memorized as wholes; at the same time the data demonstrate the relatively fixed nature of the formulaic phrases.... what is important is that the speaker preserve the three-fold division of the discourse and the rules governing section segments, for it is these things that the audience pays attention to, and give them the sense of sameness.[12]

"Formulaic language" and "expected phrases" provide structure to any speech; they maintain consistency of principle as well as form—and "they were of admirable service when a man was at a loss . . . this proves they are not wholly unacquainted with the art of Rhetoric."[13]

---

10   Knox 1996, 16.

11   William Fenton, in Jennings 1985, 34.

12   Foster 1974, 180–81.

13   NYSL MSS 13350-51: the manuscript, prepared in the late eighteenth century, was based on information obtained from Teyoninhokarawen John Norton, who made this remark. Cited in Johnston 1964, 28. Morgan ([1851] 1995, 107) suggested that "by the cultivation and exercise of [eloquence] ... was opened the pathway to distinction, and the chief or warrior gifted with its magical power could elevate himself as rapidly as he who gained renown upon the warpath." See also Bauman and Sherzer 1974.

In the different "versions" of the Kayanerenkó:wa, the details sometimes shift, while the principles remain consistent and constant. Teyoninhokarawen John Norton[14] noticed this in the early 1800s:

> In this tradition, there is also some variety in the manner it is related by the different nations; but all concur in substance: And whether they were induced to form this Confederacy, the more effectually to defend themselves, or to carry on hostillities against some neighbouring Nations, no traditions remain to inform us.[15]

> These traditions, for the most part, have become imperfect and confused from the failures of the memories of some; and perhaps from the invention of others. [Norton was writing about a version of the Creation related by "an Onondaga chief of near a hundred years old"].[16]

The Haudenosaunee pragmatically recognized that writing is also an efficient way of recording law. By the mid-1700s, while delivering the pro forma apology for possibly leaving something out, a speaker told Warraghyihagey William Johnson:

> If we are deficient in any manner of form, or should forget to answer in a particular manner any part of your speech, we hope you will excuse us. We only depend on our memories, and can not have recourse, as you may, to any written records.[17]

> You tell us you commit your affairs to Writing which we do not and so when you look to your Books you know what passed in former times but we keep our Treaties in our heads.[18]

Not long afterward, some Haudenosaunee did learn to write, and versions of the most important parts of the law were being transcribed onto paper.

---

14   John Norton was made a Mohawk Pine Tree Chief, and the name given to him means "an open door." It was carried before him by Theyanoguin, or "King Hendrick," but it is also close in meaning to the Seneca royá:ner title Donehogowa, the title held by Hasanonda Ely Parker.

15   Norton 1970, 105.

16   Norton 1970, 91.

17   Beauchamp 1907, 397. In contrast, Johnson several times displayed the "four great folio volumes" that constituted the records of the councils of New York and of British affairs with the Haudenosaunee.

18   NYCD 6:100–101, 1737, in council at Albany. Johnson, for his part, noted several times in council that the Indian Affairs records were kept in "four great folio volumes." Two of those volumes are at Library and Archives Canada, the base of the Indian Affairs collection; the other two were ruined by water damage when they were buried at Johnson Hall during the American Revolution (see LAC, MG27).

There are several written "versions" of the Kayanerenkó:wa. Hanni Woodbury, in her introduction to *Concerning the League,* divides them into three main groups of texts: narratives given in a European language by non-Indians; texts composed in English by native speakers of an Iroquoian language; and texts by the same people in their own languages.

Dayedokane Seth Newhouse, a Mohawk of the Grand River Territory, wrote several versions in English (and one in Mohawk) in the late nineteenth century[19]— including one that was edited by Sagonaquande Albert Cusick of Onondaga[20] and published by Gawasowane Arthur Parker of Tonawanda in 1916—as one of the two versions Parker included in *The Constitution of the Five Nations.*[21] He presented one version of his "rules and regulations" to the Council at the Grand River on 24 October 1899.[22] Newhouse and Hewitt translated some of Newhouse's English versions into Mohawk.[23] Partly as a reaction to problems they had with the sequence and some contents of the "Newhouse version,"[24] the Confederacy Council at the Grand River Territory appointed a committee of rotiyanershon,[25] who in 1900 produced a "Chiefs' Version." This was published

---

19   Fenton 1949; cf. Weaver 1984. In Canada, the Indian Advancement Act emerged in the 1880s, and traditional governments at Akwesasne, the Bay of Quinte, and Kahnawake were "replaced" by 1900. But the written versions came from places where the traditional governments were not being directly threatened at the time—the Grand River Territory, Onondaga, and Tonawanda.

20   Cusick had held the title of Thadadaho until he was removed, allegedly for becoming a Christian.

21   *The Constitution of the Five Nations, or The Iroquois Book of the Great Law*, by Arthur C. Parker; New York State Museum Bulletin No. 184, Albany, 1916. The Newhouse–Cusick version will be cited as Parker (Newhouse and Cusick) 1916; the version produced by the committee of Chiefs will be cited as Parker (Chiefs) 1916.

22   Six Nations Council Minutes, 24 October 1899. The minutes suggest that while he acknowledged that the information belonged to the Confederacy, he wanted to be paid for his work; and that rather than explain his stipulations, he left the council, prompting the chiefs to appoint their own committee to write down the constitution. Newhouse also offered one of his versions of the law to J.N.B. Hewitt—for a fee.

23   National Anthropological Archives (NAA), mss. 1361, 3504.

24   See Hewitt 1917, 430: the Council, he said, ultimately rejected Newhouse's version "as faulty in arrangement and erroneous or spurious in many of its statements." It seems they especially disliked the aspects of the Newhouse version that suggested that the Mohawks had some sort of primacy over the other nations, and the parts that gave the warriors the authority to execute errant chiefs.

25   The committee appointed on 24 October 1899 was comprised of John Frazer, John Arthur Gibson, David Sky, Thomas William Echo, William Wage, Nicodemus Porter, and Josiah Hill (according to the council minutes). According to the committee report, it consisted of Peter Powless (Mohawk); Nicodemus Porter (Oneida); William Wage (Cayuga); Abram Charles (Cayuga); John Arthur Gibson (Seneca); Thomas William Echo (Onondaga); and Josiah Hill (Tuscarora), with Josiah Hill (Delaware) and J.W.M. Elliott (Mohawk) as secretaries. The committee reflects a contemporary practice of including representatives of each of the nations in a joint endeavour. Gibson and Charles, as well as John Buck Sr., were J.N.B. Hewitt's principal collaborators in recording many Haudenosaunee texts.

(and probably adjusted) by Deputy Superintendent General of Indian Affairs Tahawennontye Duncan Campbell[26] Scott in 1912[27] and included in Parker's publication in 1916.[28]

One of the Newhouse versions is different from every other written version of the law in that it divides the law into numbered wampums ("Wampum XXVII," for example). This is an obvious attempt (possibly assisted by Cusick) to make the Kayanerenkó:wa look more like British or American laws, with section numbers, to make it resemble "a law" as white readers would understand that concept. Ordered wampums were not alien to Haudenosaunee thinking—the Condolence strings are arranged in strict sequence—but Newhouse's attempt at "legitimizing" the law by making it simulate the sections and subsections of the neighbours' laws was misguided and inauthentic, and the Chiefs' Version does not take that path. The path has tempted others: Cusick's history of the Confederacy seeks to increase the resemblance to European histories by making Thadadaho a monarch (or pope) with numbered successors ("Atotarho XI").[29] Less insecure keepers of the law are careful to maintain the structure and details unchanged, without trying to validate it in the eyes of people more used to the numbering of European systems.

Newhouse's Europeanized version was written after he had suffered a family tragedy, the death of his daughter, that he blamed on others, including the chiefs.[30] This version adopts a more mandatory tone, full of prohibitions and conditions, some of them difficult to fulfill. His bitterness shows through at times: this version fares poorly when compared to the expansive generosity,

---

26   Haudenosaunee history has been repeatedly and often injuriously affected by Campbells. Scott, the architect of Canada's "assimilation policies" of the late nineteenth and early twentieth centuries, was prominent among these.

27   Royal Society of Canada, Ottawa, 3rd series, vol. 5, section 2, 1912. Since the manuscript of the Chiefs' Version has not survived, it is impossible to know the extent, if any, to which Scott edited the original.

28   Ibid., 195–246; Parker (Chiefs) 1916, 61–113. Scott had been given the name Tahawennontye, which he translated as "Floating Voice," but is more like "disembodied voice" (Dragland 1994). He later became the Confederacy Council's worst enemy in Canada, and eventually was the prime mover behind its "replacement" by an elected system of government at the Grand River Territory (Titley 1986). He is better known as the architect of the genocidal residential school system.

29   In 1925, the anthropologist Frank Speck suggested to Deskahe Alexander General "a defense of the long house from critics by suggesting it is a form of Christianity." Deskahe would not agree. See *A Guide to Manuscripts Relating to the American Indian in the Library of the American Philosophical Society*, American Philosophical Society, Philadelphia, 1966, 94.

30   Six Nations Council Minutes, 14 February 1899: the council had found in favour of Dr. Secord with respect to Newhouse's charges that the doctor had not properly cared for his daughter. Ironically, Newhouse's withdrawal from his earlier versions of the law and his move towards the warriors and bloodshed—occasioned by the death of his daughter— echoes the life of Hiawatha.

Figure 1. Dayodekane Seth Newhouse with two family members, c. 1914. Canadian Museum of History, no. 17414. Photograph by Frederick Waugh.

vision, and courage of the more definitive 1912 Skaniatariio John Arthur Gibson version.

In 1801, Thayendenega Joseph Brant, a Mohawk Pine Tree chief (that is, a man chosen by the council as an adviser), wrote answers to a series of questions about the Haudenosaunee system of government.[31] Another English description came from Teyoninhokarawen John Norton, Thayendenega's secretary and adopted nephew, who also became a Mohawk Pine Tree chief.[32]

Possibly the richest source of recorded "versions" of the Kayanerenkó:wa are the ones written in their original language, since they have not suffered from the inconsistencies of translation. Hewitt, working with Skanawati John Buck[33] in the early 1890s, produced one such text.[34] Skaniatariio John Arthur Gibson, a Seneca chief who had been blinded in a lacrosse accident at the age of thirty-one, and who became a skilled rememberer,[35] also dictated a version to Hewitt in Onondaga[36] in 1899.[37] Toriwawakon Paul Wallace asserts that this version was "revised by Chiefs Abram Charles, John Buck Sr. and Joshua Buck, from 1900 to 1914."[38]

Two generations passed before efforts to write down the oral tradition resumed. The linguist Floyd Lounsbury worked with the Oneidas, and took down the recollections of Atsyatanunta Demas Elm, who by the 1970s was

---

31   Boyce 1973, 288–91. Brant also allegedly wrote a history of the Confederacy, but unless
      it is contained in Norton's published journal, it has not yet been found.

32   Norton 1970, 98–105. Teyoninhokarawen's mother was Scottish; his father was
      Cherokee. As an adopted Haudenosaunee, he is one of a distinguished line of natural-
      ized citizens that includes Warraghyihagey (Sir William Johnson), Thoregwi (the Duke
      of Northumberland), Sagoryos (Conrad Weiser), and Dehgewanus (Mary Jemison).
      Fenton, among others, sought to promote the idea that Norton had no "Indian blood,"
      though this would have been irrelevant to the Haudenosaunee in the eighteenth century,
      and Norton's journal of his journey to Cherokee country richly contradicts this attack.

33   Haudenosaunee tradition and law provides that when a person becomes a chief, he
      becomes known by his title rather than his personal name. Since there have been many
      people who carried the title of Skanawati, it is useful to combine the title with his
      English name, and as much as possible that approach will be followed in this work.
      Before the chiefs also had English names, one would be able to distinguish individuals
      only by the dates of the events, or by their use of their Haudenosaunee personal names.

34   NAA ms. 3130; Hewitt 1892b.

35   Goldenweiser 1912, 692: "Horatio Hale, David Boyle, M.R. Harrington, A.C. Parker,
      J.N.B. Hewitt, and a host of others drew a wealth of ethnological information from
      the ever polite, somewhat formal, marvelously omniscient chief. Notwithstanding his
      blindness, Gibson repeatedly represented his people in their dealings with the Canadian
      government, not uncommonly with signal success."

36   Hewitt, NAA ms. 2316 and ms. 1517-a; mss. 1517-b, 1517-c, 3478, and 3689.

37   After he had been blinded, he was tutored by an Onondaga Firekeeper, possibly John
      Buck. See Foster 1974, 23. This version was finished off by William Fenton and Simeon
      Gibson in 1941, with some editorial comment.

38   Wallace 1946, 27.

Figure 2. Skaniatariio John Arthur Gibson and his family, 1912. Canadian Museum of History, no. 21436.

over ninety years old. Michael Foster, an anthropologist and linguist, worked with Deyonwe'ton Jacob "Jake" Thomas,[39] a Snipe Clan Cayuga royá:ner, to record not only the law and the ceremonies but also aspects of council and treaty procedure. Thomas also did extensive recording—audiotape, videotape, and writing—on his own, and undertook several public recitations in Mohawk, Cayuga, and English. Some of these were recorded. In 2010, Tehahenteh Frank Miller taught a course based on one of these Mohawk versions, which provided me with additional insights into the relationship between language, thought, and law.

Toriwawakon Paul A. W. Wallace, working with the 1912 Gibson version—which he felt "tells a more coherent story than is found in the other versions and which at the same time points the allegory with greater insight."[40]—combined that and the 1899 Gibson version with the Newhouse and Chiefs' versions to produce his *White Roots of Peace* in 1946. Wallace maintained that "the only way to get an approximation of the original is to attempt a composite narrative," using his own "discretion in selecting the incidents or the words that best convey the central motif."[41] In effect, Wallace added a new version to the existing ones; his picking and choosing between those earlier versions produces a consistent narrative, though some of the spirit and detail of the majestic 1912 Gibson version is lost in translation and adaptation.

There are also versions of the law, or parts of it, in Haudenosaunee languages. In 1782, the Kahnawake Mohawk chief Ahsareko:wa (Big Knife) died. At that time, the Mohawks who had lived at Scoharie in the Mohawk Valley were living at Lachine, near Montreal, having been displaced by the American Revolution. John Deserontyon, one of their leaders, condoled the people of Kahnawake on behalf of the Mohawks. His written text of both the Condolence and the reply was transcribed and translated by Hewitt a century later.[42] Newhouse wrote in Mohawk as well as in English.[43]

---

39   Lounsbury 2000. Where oral tradition is used as evidence, it is always useful to cite the people who taught the carrier of the tradition, if they are known. Deyonwe'ton Jake Thomas learned from his grandfather, David Skye, and from Thadadaho David Thomas, both rotiyanershon. Like his contemporaries, though, he also learned from a crowd of other people, and learned by doing the speeches and ceremonies and by attending the longhouse and councils over many years.

40   Wallace 1946, 27.

41   The foreword of the 1994 edition is by Thadadaho Leon Shenandoah; the epilogue is by Sotsisowah John Mohawk.

42   The original document ended up in the Museum of the American Indian; the published version appeared in that museum's periodical, *Indian Notes*, in 1928 (Deserontyon [1928]).

43   *Onondagehakageh: Ji Kanonses*, 19 November 1880–22 March 1881, 126 pp., NAA ms. 3489.

Minutes of councils between the French, the British, the United States, and the Haudenosaunee frequently contain elements of, or references to, the Great Law. These appear in the greetings and Condolences that begin the councils (when they are not summarized by the recorder as "the usual ceremonies"), as well as in the occasional explanations by the Haudenosaunee of the legal reasons for their actions or positions. These council records are reproduced in a variety of collections, from the *Jesuit Relations* to the *New York Colonial Documents* to the *Papers of Sir William Johnson*. The council records run from the mid-1600s to the nineteenth century, with council minutes internal to Haudenosaunee communities often continuous to the present day. The treaty councils were run by the processes of the Great Law: they provide historic explanations for, or demonstration of, aspects of the law in action. However, one must always approach these records cautiously, since it is not always possible to separate original Haudenosaunee rules from European influence.

In the late 1700s, "David of Scoharie"[44] produced a Mohawk text of the parts of the law that deal with the Condolence. The text passed to a chief at the Grand River Territory who had Sakayengwaraton John Smoke Johnson copy it. The original was destroyed in a house fire in the 1830s. The copy became a central part of Horatio Hale's 1883 publication, *The Iroquois Book of Rites*. Hale also included a different copy of the Condolence, transcribed by John Green of the Grand River Territory in 1874, and kept by Skanawati John Buck.[45] Horatio Hale in 1875 and 1880 and then William Beauchamp used a mainly Mohawk version that had been kept by Ha-you-wehs Daniel LaFort at Onondaga.[46] Mrs. John A. Jones at Onondaga had a slightly different short version of part of the Condolence.[47] Kahynodoe George Key, a Grand River chief, had written another copy of the Mohawk songs, which he provided to another of the Elder Brothers, Ho-de-gweh Orris Farmer of Onondaga.[48] J.N.B. Hewitt transcribed several versions of the Condolence that remain among the unpublished materials in the Smithsonian American Museum of Natural History.

---

44 Scoharie, also known as Fort Hunter, was the Mohawk "castle" nearest Albany—that is, "lower" down the Mohawk River than Canajoharie, the "Upper Castle." David of Scoharie may be Karonghyontye David Hill, who may be depicted in Benjamin West's 1776 portrait of Guy Johnson.

45 Hale (1883) 1989, 43. Hewitt collected (his term) a thirty-nine-page version from Joshua Buck after his father's death (NAA ms. 3512).

46 Beauchamp (1907) 1975, 378; Hale (1883) 1989, 140–45; NAA ms. 3564.

47 Erminnie Smith, Report No. 6, Bureau of American Ethnology, Washington, 31.

48 Beauchamp (1907) 1975, 378, 381–85.

In 1883, Horatio Hale published *The Iroquois Book of Rites*. Its transcriptions of several of these earlier documents, written by Haudenosaunee, are still consulted when preparing for the Condolences today.[49]

Some differences between versions of the law are the result of time eroding memory. Other differences stem from the personal agendas and biases of the recorders. Seth Newhouse was involved in the political struggle at the Grand River Territory between the Confederacy Council and the "Warriors' Party." He supported Mohawk primacy (against the Onondagas)[50] and above all the Haudenosaunee against intrusion by the Canadian government. Other recorders also did more than record: "J.N.B. Hewitt, for instance, was not above 'revising' some of the legends in his search for a 'consistent historical background' to the founding of the League (1931:175). For their part, Goldenweiser, Parker and Fenton have all become embroiled in the debate about the possibility of aboriginal Iroquois constitutionality, and their disagreement has colored their work."[51]

In the early twentieth century, there were personal jealousies between the people who worked with the chiefs on the different versions. Hewitt attacked Parker's publication of the Newhouse and Chiefs' versions, Scott's publication of the Chiefs' Version, and Beauchamp's work on condoling councils: "These three publications . . . severally repeat old errors and so diffuse them broadcast under the patronage of learned institutions, and so the following strictures are made on the untrustworthy character of much of their contents, lest the unwary student be led into accepting misinformation for truth. . . . It is most unfortunate for the cause of historical truth that great institutions insist on publication at the expense of study and accuracy."[52]

---

49   William Fenton has written that "none of the books yet published satisfy the Iroquois
        ritualists. They rely on crib notes of their own, however, and the recordings that they
        made for me in 1945 follow the Book of Rites substantively if not precisely. . . . The
        Iroquois go on performing the rites nevertheless, and they have meanwhile become stu-
        dents of their own culture" (Hale [1883] 1989), xxiv). Fenton maintained in the 1950s
        that the Haudenosaunee were not sufficiently familiar with their culture, or practitioners
        (rather than students) of their culture enough, to deserve the return of their wampum
        belts from the New York State Museum (though he later tried to take some of the credit
        for the return of eleven wampum belts from the Museum of the American Indian in
        1988—when in fact he had tried to sell the same wampum, which he acknowledged
        had "left the Grand River in dubious circumstances," on an "as is" basis to the National
        Museum of Man in Ottawa, for $250,000).

50   "Wampum 6" of one Newhouse version states: "I begin by choosing you, the Mohawk
        Nation, to be the 'head and Leader' of the Confederate Government and Legislative
        Body and Council; therefore you are the foundation of the Government of the Great
        Peace now hereby established." Newhouse also stated that unless all nine Mohawk chiefs
        are present, Council shall not be opened, and cannot transact business except for "mat-
        ters of little importance."

51   Vecsey 1988, 97.

52   Hewitt 1917, 429.

Alexander Goldenweiser[53] also attacked Parker's publication, in a show of racism that would have shocked the Haudenosaunee whose company he kept: "[The Newhouse version] cannot justly be regarded as a genuine native product. It is, without doubt, based on a wide acquaintance, on the part of the compiler, with the beliefs, attitudes, and practices of the confederated Iroquois, but this native material has been welded into a highly formal and rationalized document, the product of a sophisticated mind, and, as such, conspicuously un-Indian in character."[54]

Goldenweiser was interested in compiling the law in as original a form as possible. While he was right in pointing out the "un-Indian" character of parts of Newhouse's text, the discrepancy was in form—Newhouse's attempt to imitate North American statutory structure—and not in content. As for sophistication, Goldenweiser, who transcribed but apparently did not analyze, seems himself to have completely missed the depth of the Great Law as a functioning legal system.

In a law text, it is tempting to "consolidate" or "standardize" the several versions, to seek consistency, to choose a "correct" version. To do so would mean going beyond interpretation and into the territory of judgement. As a matter of approach, I have generally chosen the structure of the 1912 John Arthur Gibson text as the most complete, but where other versions are different, I cite the differences. In some instances, other texts contain useful information or provisions missing in the Gibson version (Newhouse provides songs; David of Canajoharie provides a more detailed text of the Condolence; Jake Thomas provides cultural context; Hewitt's many fragments contain useful information from Gibson, Abram Charles, John Buck, and others).

In 2005, John Mohawk published his edited version of the *Iroquois Creation Story*, based on Gibson and Hewitt's late nineteenth-century version. In doing so, he explained an approach to "editing" Haudenosaunee narratives that set a number of important goals:

> [The editor] might consciously remove the various remnants of Victorian conventions and attitudes which sometimes surface in the original text along with some elements which clearly were added following contact with Europeans or people of European descent. . . .
>
> The job of editor, which could never be accomplished perfectly, was to preserve the elements of the narrative in language consistent with that used at the end of the twentieth century. It was my goal to

---

53 Wallis 1941, 250–55.

54 Goldenweiser (1916, 436) and a reply by Arthur C. Parker (1918). Parker quoted Kipling's *Neolithic Age*: "There are nine hundred and sixty ways of constructing tribal lays, and – every – single – one – of – them – is – right." Goldenweiser (1912, 693) held that John Arthur Gibson was "one of those wide-awake, keen-witted Indians, so rare nowadays. . . ."

eliminate repetitive language, preserve as much as possible the elements of the narrative such that the original authors might recognize it as their own, to avoid as much as possible changing the spirit or intent of the story, and to add very few of my own thoughts. Above all, I tried to preserve the thoughts of the ancients. Because the tradition lends itself to a contemporary interpretation, I anticipate some skepticism about possible alterations to lend it a modernist, or even postmodernist interpretation. I have tried to be transparent about my own interventions, albeit in subtle ways.[55]

John Mohawk was able to implement this approach because he had grown up within the culture, constantly interacting with the carriers of its knowledge, and was therefore able to distinguish between Hewitt's occasional quasi-European additions and the original, purer stream.

The Chiefs' Version of the law was an effort to produce a simple, authoritative, consistent, and de-Europeanized edition of the law, in the same spirit as John Mohawk's approach to the Creation story. It omits some of the details of the 1912 Gibson version and the Newhouse versions, but it contains all the essentials, in a coherent, cohesive sequence.

In approaching the Kayanerenkó:wa, I have adopted several of John Mohawk's methods. Since it is a living legal system, though, it is also important to cite how exposure to Europeans may have changed the law, or its interpretation. While I have eliminated some unnecessary repetition, and have added modern interpretation and commentary, I have also struggled with the challenge of reconciling several very distinct versions of the law. Where reconciliation is not possible, I point out the differences between the versions, and occasionally suggest which one is most consistent, either with the rest of the law, with historical reality, or with rational analysis.[56] Because this is a work about law, my personal comments are overt and declared rather than subtle.

---

55 Mohawk 2005a, ii. To believe that John Mohawk simply modernized and streamlined the Gibson–Hewitt text is to miss the significance of this work. The reconciliation also reflects his own work with contemporary Haudenosaunee leaders, thinkers, and modern keepers of tradition, and his own experience as a member of the society that lives within the principles of the tradition.

56 In a way, the Chiefs' committee that produced the Chiefs' Version of 1900 also did this work. The committee produced a sleek, tight version of the law that omitted much of the rich detail of the narrative but also improved the internal consistency of the story, as compared to the various existing versions. It would seem that their priority, though, was not the narrative but the actual functioning of the laws—because the Newhouse version, which had provoked their creation as a committee, had failed to describe accurately the way the council ought to operate.

Versions, Names, and Quotations

Though the first note in this book explained my approach to Haudenosaunee names, some additional complexities should also be addressed. Since the law has been recorded in several languages over two centuries, people's names and key concepts appear in different forms in different versions. They also differ from language to language. Especially for those who speak no Haudenosaunee language, this can be confusing. Thadadaho is the same person as Atotarho and Tatadahoh. Except where the names appear in quotations, I have deliberately used a single spelling for each such name. I have generally chosen to use modern Mohawk orthography, for several reasons. More people speak Mohawk than all the other Haudenosaunee languages combined. The spelling systems for modern Oneida, Cayuga, and Onondaga were developed by different linguists and all require special diacritical marks, inconvenient to use and difficult for occasional readers to learn. Mohawk uses a standard keyboard and simpler spelling. Mohawk is the language of council.[57] As a matter of convenience, and in the absence of a single standard Mohawk orthography, I use the spellings used by Kanatawakon David Maracle.[58]

My decision to put people's Haudenosaunee names before their English names also applies to nicknames, which I have decided to cite in parentheses only where the individual was best known by that nickname. Thus, I mention Sagoyewatha (Red Jacket) and Kayantwakha (Cornplanter). Some people have several names during their lifetime,[59] and I tend in such cases to use the name by which they were best known, with others sometimes cited in parentheses or footnotes. By the 1600s, Haudenosaunee often had European names as well as their "real names," and often they carried nicknames as well: the Onondaga chief Outrewati was also "Garangula" or "La Grande Gueule"; the Mohawk speaker Canaqueese Jan Smits also appears in history books as "the Flemish Bastard." Theyanoguin (Teianoken) was also known by his English name (Henry

---

57   Though none of the written versions of the law state this explicitly, there seems to be a consensus among the chiefs that this is the case, and the Chiefs' Version, where it uses non-English terms and names, uses Mohawk.

58   Kanatawakon David Maracle 2001. Kanatawakon uses "y" where standard (Eastern) Mohawk uses an "i." My hometown Grand River Mohawk uses the "y." The difference, trivial to outsiders, can become a linguist's battleground.

59   NYSL MSS 13350; cited in Johnston 1964, 29: "The same person at different periods of life is . . . commonly known by three different names the first belongs to the boy, 2d to the man, 3d to the old man."

Peters), his Dutch name (Hendrick Pieters), his nickname (King Hendrick), and his Mohawk chief's title, Tekarihoken. They would appear in this work as Outrewati, Canaqueese, and Teyanoken (later Tekarihoken).

It would be proper to refer to each of the nations in their own language. It would be a useful lesson in avoiding the imposition of foreign names. It would also be cumbersome, and make for difficult reading. It would be even more complex to refer to each nation by its council name, rather than its everyday name. But it is simply easier to refer to Mohawks rather than Kanienkehá:ka. On the principle of seeking the clearest communication possible, I use the usual English names for the nations, and not their names for themselves or their formal council designations.

The Haudenosaunee have always enjoyed puns and double meanings in their own language—the kind of stuff that simply does not survive translation into English. If the versions of the law are full of these double meanings,[60] that, too, says something about the attitudes of the people. English-speaking peoples also appreciate multiple meanings (although it has become common to groan at puns as a "lower form" of humour), but they take their law very seriously. In English law, and the common-law legal systems that have grown from it, and in most European law, every word has a specific, deliberate meaning, and the intent is that every word should have only one meaning, to the point that many statutes begin with pages of definitions.[61]

We are entitled to believe that the law contains a linguistic logic that also reflects its culture of origin.[62] If we work from English versions, and with twenty-first-century survivors, we can expect the law to suffer erosion of that logic. Maintaining the languages is therefore an important aspect of understanding and maintaining the law.

---

60   It is not just the spoken law that is full of multiple—but not inconsistent—meanings. The symbols of the law are also layered: the Hiawatha Belt, for example, depicts a Tree of Peace that, upside down, is a heart, for Onondaga also lies at the heart of the Confederacy; each square is a nation's fire, with the path of peace running from fire to fire; but the fires are also fires within the symbolic Longhouse, and the path is also the line that divides the Longhouse into its two sides. The three rows of beads that separate the dark rows of the Two Row Wampum are part of the river, but they are also the three elements of the Silver Covenant Chain.

61   It might be suggested that a legal system that aims at drafting unambiguously, so that each word has only one meaning, reflects a culture whose philosophy asserts that there is only one truth. European stories and fables have an explicit moral: Haudenosaunee stories, instead, are told in a way that different people can draw different conclusions, according to their ages, capacities, personal experiences, and talents.

62   The debate about whether a person's language inevitably colours their worldview began, in modern academic terms, with the work of Benjamin Lee Whorf, comparing the perspectives of Hopi-speakers and English-speakers. He arrived at the moderate conclusion that language (and, inevitably, culture) has some effect on perception. While linguists have debated the impact of language on worldview, lawyers and people engaged in thinking about law have given less thought to this issue. See Connelly 1999.

Language

Laws reflect aspects of the languages in which they are embedded, just as the languages reflect the cultures in which they live. Where it might be possible to make oneself understood in English with a succession of nouns and adverbs, Haudenosaunee languages require both action and relationship.[63] That is, a Haudenosaunee sentence, because of its structure and the language's grammar, will cause a person to consider not only the object but also its state or activity.

The difference between some European languages and English is instructive in explaining the differences. Latin languages require a person to consider the gender of the thing that is spoken of—and often provide few clues as to why things are assigned one gender or another.[64] In those languages, as well, there are different forms of address for people with whom one is familiar and for those whom one respects, or does not know well. In French or Spanish, crossing the line that separates *vosotros* or *vous* from *tu* is a conscious, often delicate move. In Haudenosaunee languages, a greater number of things are considered animate than in English (the difference, in a way, between *him* and *it*). People are frequently addressed according to their relationship with the speaker. There are more precise and selective ways of addressing groups.[65] Languages that encourage the speaker to consider his relationships with others are well suited to a legal system that is based on those relationships, and on maintaining them.

In Haudenosaunee languages, it is common to find interjections in speech that seek agreement or encourage consensus. Wahi, or "is it not so?" is a common interjection in everyday conversational Mohawk.[66]

---

63 This is true of other Indigenous languages of North America: "Aboriginal languages, and therefore the reality they describe and represent, are not made up of separate things with fixed characteristics. The focus is on relations between things or persons, and the nature of the thing or person can be defined by the relationship between the speaker and the object." RCAP 1995, 621.

64 In Spanish, a finger (*un dedo*) is masculine, but a hand (*una mano*) is feminine; in French, *la voiture* travels on *le chemin* or on *la route*. There is often no good explanation for the gender assigned to things.

65 Modern Haudenosaunee will sometimes use "yous" to speak to more than one person. This may not be poor grammar: it may be an unconscious reflection of the precision afforded by Indigenous languages that is absent in English. That is, they are speaking good Mohawk in English.

66 Modern Haudenosaunee, even those who do not speak a Haudenosaunee language, will often use terms like "innit?" or "ennit?" to seek the same agreement while they speak.

Duality, that persistent aspect of the Creation story and the Law, is also more frequent in Haudenosaunee languages than in modern European ones. Modern European languages distinguish between singular and plural, while Haudenosaunee languages have singular, dual, and plural forms (Arabic features dual forms, as did ancient Greek, and as do Gaelic, Slovenian, and some Polynesian languages).[67] On the one hand, this requires more specificity in normal conversation ("the two of us" rather than the more indefinite "us"). On the other, it promotes thinking about things in twos.[68]

Duality is accentuated by language structure, which adds useful prefixes to words and concepts. The prefix *te-* indicates that there are two of something involved—for example, tekká:nere, "me looking upon something," is a reminder that we have two eyes—or that the two-ness of the matter is a question of balance—tewáton, "it becomes," occurs in a balanced way.

Prefixes carefully distinguish between uncertainty (for example, things that have not yet happened, and may not) and fact. The prefix *wa-* indicates that the matter being spoken of is, in the words of Tehahenteh Frank Miller, "an incontrovertible fact." In conversations about law, this helps separate fact from opinion, and can be an indicator of which matters are firm or entrenched, a signal they are to be accommodated by the other side of the fire.[69]

The idea of a "matter" itself is quite different from the more precise English term. Orihwa can be translated as "matter," "business," "thing," "word," and as a component of "culture" (niionkwarihó:ten, our ways, or our business). The word allows a broad range of things to be considered. It also permits discussion—or, as John Mohawk would say, conversation—about matters before they must be described as disputes.

Haudenosaunee languages are descriptive. Where English provides the noun "deer," the Mohawk oskenonton can be interpreted as "it bears living bones," a reference to the stag's antlers. When the antlers are placed on a person—the metaphor for making a man a Confederacy chief—the thought is present that the person acquires the stag's antenna-like sensitivity. "Car," in English, becomes the Mohawk káse:re, "it (a created thing) drags itself." Not only are the languages descriptive: in many cases the words are metaphorical, and they condition a person to more easily understand and use a legal system

---

67   Some languages have dual forms of nouns; others have dual forms of pronouns; some
       have both. Some languages had them, but have shed them: Tagalog, Finnish, and
       Greenlandic Inuktitut, for example.

68   We know that the dual mode provides or reflects some of the crucial underpinnings of
       Haudenosaunee culture: balance, reciprocity, divisions between genders. But what is the
       purpose of duality in these other languages and cultures? And why does a language drop
       that mode?

69   In English, one contradicts a statement by simply saying that it did not happen. In
       Haudenosaunee languages, one cannot negate, for example, the definite past: one can
       only express doubt about it by shifting into the indefinite mode.

that is replete with symbol and metaphor. They are also active languages, and they encourage a person to think of the law as a living entity, one that is *being*, rather than as a passive or static concept. It is logical that a Mohawk would say that it is reconciling, not reconciliation, that is important.[70]

With such differences between Haudenosaunee languages and the English that surrounds the Haudenosaunee archipelago, it is not surprising that the leaders of the Confederacy want to sustain the languages and maintain their use in council. The Kayanerenkó:wa would be a poorer, weaker law if it existed for them only in English. Much would be lost in translation, including aspects of the spirit of the law:

> It has been argued, and has become almost a commonplace, that Native American languages are embedded in the local landscapes of First Nations; the verbs that speak exactly the voice of the west wind as it moves over the water, colors not generic browns and reds but the loam under pine needles and sumac buds when they are ready to eat. A worldview is lost, it has been said with greater and greater urgency, when an indigenous language is not spoken. Perhaps even more is lost when indigenous oral narrative is unspoken, when these stories lie quiet as truncated text, when they are gutted by the blades of academic discipline.[71]

Haudenosaunee languages are in dire trouble. The terms used by linguists to describe the state of languages are the same as those used by biologists to describe the state of species. Tuscarora is virtually extinct. Languages are "moribund" if they have fewer than 300 speakers, and most of the speakers are over fifty years old: Oneida, Onondaga, Cayuga, and Seneca fit into that category. Only Mohawk, with over 2,000 speakers, may have much chance of survival. Efforts are being made in many communities to revitalize the languages, but the power of English is difficult to resist, as that language gains vocabulary and technical specificity in ways that outdistance other languages, and as it becomes the tongue of commerce and international communication. At any

---

70 Amber Meadow Adams, in conversation about the evolution of "reconciliation" from a term that described how Crown responsibility and authority had to be reconciled, to reconciliation between nations, to a near-religious requirement of reconciliation from Canada's Truth and Reconciliation Commission, pointed out that "reconciling" is more compatible with Haudenosaunee thinking, and more descriptive of what is actually required—a process without definite end, rather than an event. As we had that conversation, a "reconciliation tour" was being arranged for the president of McMaster Children's Hospital to smooth over the hard feelings left from the hospital's unsuccessful attempt to force the Brant County Children's Aid Society to take custody of an eleven-year-old girl so the hospital could apply chemotherapy rather than traditional Haudenosaunee medicine. The family avoided the event: reconciling requires more.

71 Adams 2007, n.p.

given moment, nearly 20 percent of the conversations in English happening in the world are between two people neither of whom have English as their first language. English is omnivorous.

Haudenosaunee languages, like Haudenosaunee traditional governments, are endangered. For purposes of the law, the English versions provide information about the substance, but fail to deliver the entire bundle of knowledge and understanding that the law carries in its original languages.

Because several of the English versions are over a century old; because several of the translators were academics, with both broad vocabularies and a lack of concern for the intelligibility of their product to average readers; and because the original languages are very different from English, several of the translations of the law contain awkward or difficult English terms: "besom," "downfended," "condole," "verily," "whereupon," "thus," and "yonder."[72] Other terms, like "repent," "deacon," "righteous," and "sinful" carry powerful Christian baggage in English, and are explained quite differently by Haudenosaunee familiar with the meanings of the words used in their original languages. Using Christian terms has caused frustration and confusion, as Victorian speakers, either Anglo-American or Haudenosaunee, found no closer terms to translate essential parts of Haudenosaunee thought. Still other terms reflect the lack of colloquial English equivalents, and substitute obsolete or anthropological terms as a result: "moiety," "*gens*," and "matron." Yet others reflect inadequate or awkward translations of Haudenosaunee grammar into English: "continually," "repeatedly," "presently." When we read century-old translations of even older texts, we encounter linguistic difficulties not only across languages and cultures but across time.[73]

---

72   Was Hewitt trying to lend solemnity to the speeches, or was he trying to replicate the tone of what he was hearing—or was he Victorian enough to actually speak and write that way himself? Hewitt's account of his recording of the Creation story reflects a collegial and meticulous approach. John Arthur Gibson was the principal speaker, and Chiefs John Buck and Abram Charles would confirm and discuss five or six sentences at a time. When Gibson dictated the law to Goldenweiser, Hewitt had been confined to an office in the Smithsonian Institution in Washington due to political and financial changes—but the process had been established by the chiefs, not the anthropologists.

73   Sotsisowah John Mohawk's (2005) *Iroquois Creation Story* is an example of an effort to take an older text, remove the inappropriate or wrong effects of Victorian translation, restore cultural integrity, and deliver an intelligible, readable modern story. It is no coincidence that Russians who hear *Hamlet* translated into modern Russian connect quite differently with the story than do English-speaking people who continue to struggle with the majesty and difficulty of the sixteenth-century Elizabethan original.

Oral Tradition and the Rememberers

Don't forget the words he has spoken in front of us who
are the elders. This is where they should rest, his words,
in the bottom of our hearts, so that, whatever one's age,
one will keep remembering the story that he himself,
Tekanawita, has told. Thereafter the children repeated it,
reminding themselves of what he said in front of them.[74]

In the Longhouse today, there remains a prejudice against learning from tape recordings, especially recordings of sacred materials.[75] One is supposed to learn by listening, and by practising. This is not just technophobia.[76] There is a sound principle involved: "We don't want machines or paper to become our storage device. The human mind is where we keep important things."[77] It is portable, safe, flexible, reliable, and its information is easily transferred to other minds. Written materials, on the other hand, have often been misused, quoted out of context, or lost. A preference for memory as a storage device was supported, historically, by the presence of well-trained memories. As the Haudenosaunee described their ways: "We nevertheless have methods of transmitting from Father to Son an account of all these things, whereby you will find the rememberance of them is faithfully preserved, and our succeeding generations are made acquainted with what has passed, that it may not be forgot as long as the Earth remains."[78]

European observers confirmed that the Haudenosaunee had sophisticated, remarkable techniques for remembering the important things: "When any

---

74   Gibson 1912, 64.

75   Even so, the recordings made by various anthropologists in the first half of the twentieth century are now being transcribed and analyzed critically by people at the Grand River Territory seeking to assemble and recover the entire panoply of Haudenosaunee ceremonial life.

76   Antagonism to "white man's" technology does exist—and can be seen in the kerosene lights in the longhouse, the wood stoves, and the deliberate use of log rather than frame buildings.

77   Across the ocean and the millennia, ancient Egyptians told of how, when the god Thoth presented Pharaoh Thamus with the gift of hieroglyphic writing, the king was hesitant, concerned that writing would kill memory, or the need for it.

78   Minutes of the Provincial Council of Pennsylvania 1851, 4:84.

Foreign Ambassador comes to them & makes any proposal they contrive to remember every word he says: different people are appointed to learn by heart a separate sentence & no more; so when they come to put it together they know every word of it."[79]

Benjamin Franklin, who had attended Haudenosaunee councils with Pennsylvania and who as a printer had reproduced several of the treaties, asserted that the women were responsible for remembering council proceedings. Venables said that this was one more respect in which the Haudenosaunee maintained gender balance: "The old Men sit in the foremost Ranks, the Warriors in the next, and the Women and Children in the hindmost. The Business of the Women is to take exact notice of what passes, imprint it in their Memories, for they have no Writing, and communicate it to their Children. They are the Records of the Council, and they preserve Tradition of the Stipulations in Treaties a hundred Years back, which when we compare with our Writings we always find exact."[80]

Sakokwenonkwas Tom Porter explained: "They believed it should never die, that if it is put into a person's head and heart, it will truly live. In a book it will sit on a shelf where dust and dirt will cover it."[81]

Teaching a course in Haudenosaunee law at the Faculty of Law at the University of Toronto gave me an unusual opportunity. I asked the students whether any of them could recite, with some accuracy, three sections of the Constitution of Canada. None could. How about three sections of the Criminal Code? None could, either. How about the story of Goldilocks and the Three Bears? With the exception of a recent immigrant, they all knew the story, in detail. I pointed out that nobody eats porridge for supper today—that European peasants did, four centuries ago. This is an old story. And that they all knew that it was the middle-sized bowl that was "too cold," even though that defied the laws of physics, since the little bowl should have cooled sooner. The point, though, was that, especially for a people with low literacy rates, but even for a twenty-first-century modern nation-state, it makes sense to place one's basic values in a story everybody knows, rather than in a book nobody can remember. Sakokwenonkwas was right.

The oral tradition has its disadvantages. Not least of these is the fact that some of it is being lost, that fewer people are devoting their lives to learning the skills of memory and the vast materials involved, and that with the passing

---

79   Johnston 1964, 29. Today, Haudenosaunee working groups divide up responsibility
        between their members when they meet with outsiders, but the memorization has been
        replaced by note taking.

80   Franklin 1987, 970; see Venables 2010, 35.

81   Porter 1986, 52.

of some of the older people, valuable information that they kept only in their minds is gone forever. The written versions have never been complete.

This has always been the case, though: times change, and the things remembered pass down the generations in changing forms. Thus, every good speaker begins humbly, noting that we who are alive today do not possess the knowledge of our forefathers, and that we have forgotten much.[82]

For Indigenous peoples, who have a relatively short tradition of writing, memory passed down through the generations is an important aspect of knowledge. Literacy among Europeans—especially widespread literacy—is quite recent, and before literacy, there was Memory. As Daniel Boorstin observed:

> Before the printed book, Memory ruled daily life and the occult learning . . . The Memory of individuals and of communities carried knowledge through time and space. For millennia personal Memory reigned over entertainment and information, over the perpetuation and perfection of crafts, the practice of commerce, the conduct of professions. By Memory and in Memory the fruits of education were garnered, preserved and stored. Memory was an awesome faculty which everyone had to cultivate, in ways and for reasons we have long since forgotten. In these last five hundred years we see only pitiful relics of the empire and the power of Memory.[83]

The admission that we are not going to do this as well as our grandparents would, or as the men who first set these matters down, is probably true, but it is also a statement of modesty: "Now at present in some way, I may perform it improperly, compared to the way he used to do it, . . . my grandfather."[84] In the Haudenosaunee world, it is as normal as clearing one's throat before speaking. It is easily misunderstood. In *R. v. Taylor and Williams*,[85] the Ontario Supreme Court read the minutes of an 1818 treaty council with the Ojibways, in which they said: "Father: You see me here, I am to be pitied, I have no old men to instruct me; I am the Head Chief, but a young man. You must pity me, all the old people have gone to the other world. My hands are naked, I cannot speak as my ancestors were used to."

---

82 Even a very good speaker begins by saying that he will do his best, and that his efforts will not be perfect. It has long been so: in 1743, a Haudenosaunee speaker meeting with Pennsylvania officials "praised their Grandfathers' Wisdom in establishing the Union or Alliance, by which they became a formidable Body; that they (now living) were but fools to their wise Fathers." Beauchamp 1907, 428.

83 Boorstin 1985, 480.

84 Gibson 1912, 85.

85 [1981] 34 OR (2d) 360 at 363. Ojibway–British treaty council protocol had followed Haudenosaunee rules since the mid-1700s.

The court assumed that all the old chiefs had been killed in the War of 1812, and only young men were left. In fact, one would have heard chiefs in council—or, for that matter, in a ceremony of Condolence—200 years earlier making similar statements. Here are several examples:

> We who are now here are but children; the ancients being deceased.[86]

> Now hearken while your grandchildren cry mournfully to you, because the Great League which you established has grown old. We hope that they may hear.

> Hail, my grandsires! You have said that sad will be the fate of those who come in the latter times.

> Oh, my grandsires! Even now I may have failed to perform this ceremony in the order in which they were wont to perform it.[87]

> The Maquase sachems who spoke formerly with you are dead, and we have not so much knowledge as they had. Nevertheless, although they are buried, yet let the old Covenant that was made with our ancestors be kept firm.[88]

Modesty or humility in opening remarks should not be taken as an admission of either ignorance or incapacity. It is a polite, proper element of a good speaker's words. It is also a recognition of the human condition. We make mistakes. We do the best we can.[89] "The public stance of the speaker is one of humility. In his opening lines he should stress the fact that he has been appointed to the task; he has not taken it upon himself to rise and speak. It is also considered good form to make a formal apology for any errors of omission or commission. If he is especially confident he may invite the opposite speaker to 'correct' his errors in the response—an opportunity, however, usually declined."[90]

Memory has limits. Oral tradition has weaknesses. They show up in several distinct ways. People tend to remember recent events better than distant ones. People tend to remember important events better than insignificant ones. People tend to remember stories they have heard several times better than ones they have heard only once. They tend to recall the parts that affect them

---

86   Sagoyewatha Red Jacket at Canandaigua, 1794, cited in Ganter 2006, 63.

87   Hale (1883) 1989, 123.

88   NYCD 3:535–61. 18 September 1688.

89   "We are human beings. We do the best we can. When we make mistakes, we will work together to correct them." This paragraph has become standard in Haudenosaunee negotiations with Canadian entities: federal, provincial, and municipal lawyers initially express their discomfort about the wording, but soon acknowledge that it is all true, and generally accede to the use of the clause.

90   Foster 1974, 31.

directly rather than the parts that describe strangers or foreigners. For the Haudenosaunee, the creation of the Confederacy and the Law is a remarkable story, often repeated: it is what John Mohawk called a meta-narrative. It is not surprising that, as an oral tradition, it remains forceful and clear in comparison to other legal knowledge.

If modern institutions and practices reflect the traditions, they tend to corroborate the accuracy of the recall of the custodians of those traditions. Morgan approached the Haudenosaunee with the thinking of a lawyer as well as that of a proto-anthropologist.[91] He sought evidence and proof of what he was told, and he confirmed that modern practices tended to confirm the oral traditions—at least as far back as the time of the Peacemaker:

> Those traditions which reach beyond the formation of the League, are vague and unreliable, while all such as refer to its establishment assume a connected and distinctive form. It follows that confidence may be reposed in such inferences as are derived from these traditions, and corroborated by the internal structure of the government, and by the institutions of the League.[92]

> The present Iroquois are . . . perfectly familiar with the structure and principles of the ancient confederacy.[93]

> Tradition interposes its feeble light from the confusion which time has wrought on some of the leading events which preceded and marked that political organization.[94]

The Haudenosaunee designated "rememberers," not just for individual councils, but for specific ceremonies. An individual's gift of memory was acknowledged and cultivated: when Skaniatariio John Arthur Gibson was blinded in a lacrosse accident, the chiefs encouraged him to use and develop his powerful memory in the service of the people. In the twentieth century, the best-known Haudenosaunee ceremonial speakers were men who had avoided the Canadian education system, some to the point of illiteracy, and who had learned instead from their grandfathers.[95]

---

91   See Boorstin 1985, 636–46. "As a young lawyer without clients in the doldrums of the business depression that began in 1837, Morgan had ample time. . . ." By 1846 he was helping the Tonawanda Senecas fight for the return of their land.

92   Morgan (1851) 1995, 89.

93   Morgan (1871) 1997, 132.

94   Converse 1908, 128.

95   Deyonwe'ton Jake Thomas and Hononwirehton Peter Skye, crucial rememberers of the twentieth century, both walked out of school in grade three. Gordon Buck, a Grand River Seneca who often did the speaking at ceremonies, was apparently absolutely impractical and seemed to have limited intellectual ability—but had a memory that enabled him to reproduce any ceremonial speech impeccably after hearing it once.

Where Europeans supplemented memory with writing, the Haudenosaunee used wampum as a mnemonic device. Both sacred and permanent, the belts and strings of shell beads stood as symbols of the concepts of the law, and later as symbols and records of the promises and principles of the treaties. When wampum was not available, other objects were used to preserve words, even temporarily: history records councils in which sticks or furs were used in this way. Wampum—which was also more durable—made the commitments sacred.[96]

Haudenosaunee tradition states clearly that the use of wampum in connection with law dates to the time of the making of the Great Law of Peace.[97] The first legal use of wampum was the ceremony of Condolence, and other wampum records came afterward.[98] What is important to note at this stage of thinking about the Great Law is the fact that, for centuries, strings and belts of shell beads have been used to assist human memory. Wampum is not writing. Some suggest that each individual bead in a belt has its own secret meaning, capable of being interpreted by those who have received the esoteric training associated with that belt. This is not so. In the case of the strings and belts, it is the patterns and the colours that symbolically recall the concepts that were originally associated with them. Those concepts were stated in words, and the wampum acts as a device of recall. The symbols on the belts have standard meanings. For example, a diagonal line symbolizes a nation propping up the Longhouse from the outside, as an ally. Short lines at the end of a belt can indicate the number of nations or villages that support the proposition. A square or hexagon symbolizes a fire, the expression of a nation's existence. However, a wampum belt cannot be "read" like a book.

Patterns on belts and strings often recall physical phenomena. The alternating black and white beads on a Condolence string resemble the teardrops

---

96   Wampum comes in three main formats: individual beads, strings of beads, and woven "belts." The French referred to the belts as "colliers" or necklaces, and there are historic depictions of Wendat (Huron) chiefs wearing their wampum, which had a distinctive diagonal weave, around their necks. In contrast, there are no historic depictions of Haudenosaunee leaders wearing their important wampums at all. The British called them "belts," but modern Haudenosaunee tend to call them simply "wampums," and I will follow that practice. A "wampum," then, is a woven belt, and the other forms are "strings of wampum" and "wampum beads." There is no record of the chiefs wearing the belts around their waists.

97   Shell beads, including the cylindrical shell beads now known as wampum, existed well before the coming of the Great Law. Early shell beads were mostly discs, though—a limitation resulting from the stone and bone tools used to make the beads. Shell beads were used as ornaments, certainly. As for their uses in ceremonies, there is no record one way or another.

98   Hewitt stated that no Haudenosaunee ritual but the Condolence uses wampum in any form: 1928, 93. However, the Six Nations meetings to renew the Karihwí:iyo, the Code of Handsome Lake, involve a set of strings known as Katsistowá:nen, the Great Fire.

shed by grieving eyes. On another string, the dark area in the middle evokes a fire. The connection between wampum symbols and natural phenomena is a precursor to alphabetical literacy. The Phoenician letter "A" evoked an ox's head and horns, and only much later detached itself from the image and became linked in people's minds only to sound, and then to a sound as a component of a word made of several sounds, so that "A" today means only "A." Given time and isolation, wampum could have become a "literate" form of communication, in which its symbols would detach themselves from image.[99]

Wampum is "readable" in another sense, as well: it is a binary system, in which the two colours, white and dark, operate separately as symbols of the bright and dark sides of life, and combine to provide more subtle meanings: "This all white string is a sign of truth, peace and good will, this black string is a sign of hatred, of war and of a bad heart, the string with alternate beads, black and white, is a sign that peace should exist between the nations. The string with white on either end and black in the middle is a sign that wars must end and peace declared."[100]

Some say that the wampum records *are* the treaties. This is as erroneous as to say that the written documents are the treaties. Both the wampums and the documents are *evidence* of the agreements that were made. Each has its particular virtues and weaknesses—but the treaties themselves are the coming together of minds, not the physical objects that record or symbolize the agreements. For the Haudenosaunee, as well, the "treaty" is less the event at which the agreement was made, or the specific matter that was agreed upon, and more the relationship that flows from or is reaffirmed by the event.

Some wampums are notorious—they have become icons. That is, they are symbols known and understood by hundreds, sometimes thousands, of people (much as the colours and symbols on national flags are broadly known). People *know* that the five shapes on the Hiawatha Belt symbolize the original Five Nations. They *know* that the tree in the middle of the five is the Tree of Peace as well as the heart[101] of the Confederacy. They *know* that the two lines on the

---

99 See Coe 1999, and Abram 1996, 130–33. I do not mean to suggest that phonetic writing systems are necessarily more sophisticated, or reflect more sophisticated ways of thought or life; only that the dominant alphabets of the world originated from picture-symbols.

100 Soinowa Delos Big Kittle of Cattaraugus in 1905: cited in Parker (1923) 1989, 404. George Hamell of the New York State Museum developed a far more complex set of colour interpretations of wampum, including green, blue, and red (Hamell 1992). The problem with that approach is that, except for a few dark red pipestone Seneca belts (the Senecas, at the Western Door, would have better access to catlinite), and bright red war belts stained with the vermilion that symbolized blood, there are few records of wampum belts in any colours but natural white and dark purple.

101 This was described as such in the Grand Council at Cattaraugus in 1862 (Parker 1916, 145).

Figure 3. The Hiawatha Wampum. The pine tree in the middle symbolizes the Tree of Peace, and also the fact that Onondaga, as the central nation of the Confederacy, is also the location of the council fire. Each of the squares represents another of the original Five Nations, from east to west. The white paths between them are the paths of peace and communication. The paths go beyond the Five Nations, as the Great White Roots of the Tree of Peace go to the four directions.

Note: "A row of white wampum coming out of the white heart, right and left and which connects the four white square marks is the purest of all pure of the Great Peace and Charity of which compact is the Union of the Five Nations" (Newhouse 1898, 55). Jake Thomas suggested that the Oneida and Cayugas were symbolized by larger squares, since they are "adopting nations." The Oneidas took the Tuscaroras under their wing; the Cayugas the Tutelos and Conestogas. But history indicates that the Senecas were by far the most absorbent of the Haudenosaunee nations, taking in the Erie, Wenro, Attiwandaron, Tiionontate, Wendat, and others.

Two Row Wampum[102] symbolize the Indian canoe and the white man's ship, going side by side down the River of Life, neither interfering in the course of the other. They *know* that the thirteen men on the George Washington belt are the thirteen colonies, and that the two men on either side of a house on that belt are the doorkeepers of the Confederacy, the Mohawks and Senecas—and that the meaning of the belt is that the United States' arms will pass over the Longhouse without trying to get inside it. In the case of other wampums, the meaning is less well-known, but no less well recorded.

There are several kinds of wampum, from a Haudenosaunee legal perspective. The earliest, simplest, and most powerful are the strings associated with the ceremony of Condolence, the strings symbolizing the nations bringing their minds together in ronatennikonhraroron, collective thinking, and the Circle Wampum that is the symbol of the League's government. Then there are the wampum belts that record aspects of the Great Law of Peace. Following them, chronologically, are the wampums that record treaties and relations with other nations, both Indigenous and European. Other wampum also has legal significance: there are strings of adoption wampum;[103] there are wampums that are linked to specific ceremonies; and the rotiyanershon each carry a short string they refer to as their "horns."[104] Clan mothers each carry the counterparts of these short strings—longer strings symbolizing their responsibility for the chief's title.

British law—Saxon and Norman—was originally customary, and as such quite distinct from the written, codified Roman system. This customary law was allowed to develop through jurisprudence, to spread to meet additional circumstances, while keeping its principles intact. Unless replaced by statutes passed by the legislature, the "common law" of the people continued to apply and govern. The "common law" was not codified, nor reduced to writing except as revealed by court decisions. Modern British—and therefore American and Canadian—laws contain reflections of the customary and oral traditions

---

102 Modern usage suggests that the Two Row Wampum is called Kahswénhtha; yet in older speeches and usage, the term is applied to any wampum belt. It is a reference to the "flowing-ness" of the wampum. As such, it could be taken as a reference to the River of Life that is said to be the background for the sailing ship and the canoe in the Two Row Wampum—or to refer to the way the commitments and ideas preserved in any wampum are to flow through time.

103 Today's adoption strings are white and a handspan long. Perhaps, when they were "a name hung around the neck," they were actual necklaces (as the Tutelo adoption ceremony still uses a necklace), and the scarcity of wampum over the years caused their shrinkage.

104 "A bunch of white wampum strings, two spans of the hand in length (Deyoronhkarageh) being the symbol of a Lordship Title, be given to every one of the original forty-eight, now fifty, Awatchiras of the Five Confederate Nations." Newhouse 1897, w. 52. The string is left in the dead man's hands in the open coffin during his funeral, and then lifted before burial to pass on to his successor.

that lie at their roots. The laws of the United States and Canada are themselves a combination of custom, memory, and writing.[105] There are also instances in which objects and symbols rather than documents have legal significance: one has only to consider the importance of particular seals[106] to realize that Anglo-American law also goes beyond writing. The Euro-American legal system teems with meaningful symbolism: any courtroom contains a display of heraldry, flags, and judicial robes that confirm tradition and provide a graphic display of legal principles.

Haudenosaunee law is preserved in a different way. There has been more emphasis on memory, partly because literacy came later than for the settlers. It is also retained in memory because the law is a law of the mind—and if you keep your law in your mind, you will also keep it *in mind*, and it will influence your conduct. But the law is not kept only in memory. It is also preserved in action and in wampum, and for more than two centuries it has been finding its way into writing.

Because the relevant parts of the law would be recited or referred to at times when they were being applied, the thousands of pages of transcripts of "treaty councils" are actually a distinct source of recorded law. The people who put together the microfilmed *Iroquois Indians: A Documentary History* in the 1980s declared they were assembling the equivalent of the archives of the Iroquois Confederacy's Department of External Affairs.[107] The council records, though, also contain numerous references to specific parts of the law. Because the relationships that the Haudenosaunee built with the French, the Dutch, the British, and the United States are themselves reflections of provisions of the Kayanerenkó:wa, and are consistent with that law and its operation, the treaty councils illuminate the operations and principles of the law, as well.

---

105 The Canadian system is perhaps more custom oriented, because it is more closely linked to the British model: nothing in the written law speaks of political parties, for example, nor of the ceremonies and procedures that operate Parliament.

106 See, e.g., the Crown's courts' conclusion that the 1784 Haldimand Proclamation delivering the entire Grand River Valley to the Haudenosaunee was void because it bore his personal seal-at-arms rather than the Great Seal of the Province: *Doe dem. Jackson v. Wilkes* (1835), 4 UCKB (OS) 142. However, in the 1984 case of *Attorney General of Ontario v. Bear Island Foundation*, [1985] 1 CNLR 1, it was found that the absence of the seal, despite specific legislation requiring it for such a transaction to be valid, was no obstacle to the validity of a land surrender treaty.

107 Today's Confederacy has an External Relations Committee, as well as designated diplomats.

While oral tradition has been recognized in U.S. and Canadian courts as a means of bringing in "the Indian view" of history, it rarely travels alone.[108] It is a primary form of preservation of the law, but far from the only one. It is supplemented by writing, by scholars, by physical evidence, by wampum. All these flesh out the law, and make it more easily accepted and understood by the newcomer nations' courts.[109]

Some versions of the Great Law provide that the people should meet every five years to hear the entire law recited, and to reaffirm their commitment to it. This form of regular maintenance[110] applies not only to keeping the law fresh, but also to all other relationships that keep the peace. As Sir William Johnson wrote to Thomas Gage: "As it is the Way of keeping peace made use of by the Indians to meet frequently, so we can never expect a continuance of peace with them unless We have annual meetings with the Confederacies, or at least as often as may be for repeating past Transactions & renewing Treaties which is the way they preserve these things in rememberance."[111]

---

108 Williams 1996, 29–34. The validity of oral tradition as evidence has also been attacked: Alexander von Gernet, who had been hired as a consultant and expert witness for the Government of Canada in *Mitchell v. Minister of National Revenue* (and other governments, in other cases), produced *Oral Narratives and Aboriginal Pasts: An Interdisciplinary Review of the Literature on Oral Traditions and Oral Histories* (2 volumes, 1996), on contract with the Department of Indian Affairs' Research and Analysis Directorate. Von Gernet—a favourite expert witness for governments in cases against Indigenous peoples—generally does not claim expertise on the subject matter of his testimony, but rather on the literature (or "academic consensus," as he calls it) surrounding the subject matter.

109 See *Benoit v. Canada* (Federal Court of Appeal), leave to appeal to the Supreme Court of Canada denied 2003 FCA 236.

110 In *Benoit*, the Canadian Federal Court of Appeal suggested that oral tradition evidence would be acceptable if, like the ceremonial songs of the Git'ksan and Wetsuwelthen in *Delgam'uukw*, the oral tradition formed part of a system of public performances that left them open to challenge and scrutiny to maintain their correctness. However, recollections told repeatedly from a grandfather to a grandson, since they were private and unchallenged, were not admissible oral tradition.

111 SWJP 7:208, William Johnson to Thomas Gage, 7 October 1769. The metaphor used for the need to renew and refresh commitments was the removal of tarnish from the Silver Covenant Chain, and the removal of rust from the iron chain that preceded it.

Speakers

Haudenosaunee society tends to think of individuals according to their "gifts": the things they are good at doing. Some people have the gift of speaking, and they are asked to speak on behalf of others.[112] They are often speakers in the ceremonies, but they are also speakers in council, either internally or in meetings with other nations. "According to the Indian custom, the speaker regards himself as representing the whole party for whom he speaks, and he addresses the leader of the other party as the representative and embodiment of all who come with him. Throughout the speeches 'I' and 'thou' are used in the well-understood sense of 'we' and 'ye.' In like manner, tribes and nations are, as it were, personified."[113]

Talented speakers can be asked to speak, on occasion, for different groups. They are careful to state for whom they speak. Thus, Deyagolasera Thomas King was sometimes a speaker for the women, and sometimes for the warriors, and sometimes for the whole Confederacy in dealings with the British or other Indigenous nations.[114] Sakoyewatha (Red Jacket) spoke occasionally for each of those groups; he also had the opportunity to act as a "real" lawyer in the New York State murder trial of Soongise Tommy Jemmy, a Seneca who had executed a Seneca woman convicted of witchcraft.[115]

---

112 Deserontyon, in condoling Kahnawake over the death of Ahsare:kowa in 1784, also spoke on behalf of "Gorah" (or Corlaer), the local Superintendent of the Indian Department. In 1956, when the Haudenosaunee put through a "dead feast" at Tabor Hill in Scarborough, Ontario, the speaker, Thadadaho David Thomas, also spoke to the dead on behalf of the city council (as well as the chiefs). Sometimes a speaker will be "borrowed" to speak on behalf of a foreign people, or a visitor, who lack not only the standing but also the knowledge of how to speak properly.

113 Hale (1883) 1989, 146.

114 He spoke for the women at the Treaty of Lancaster in 1744; for the warriors at the council with the Cherokees at Johnson Hall in 1768; and for the entire Confederacy in 1770 during an effort to create a single Confederacy with the Cherokees, Creeks, Shawnees, and Catawbas—the precursor to the Ohio Valley confederacy of the 1790s and Tecumseh's efforts in the War of 1812.

115 John Mohawk said that Red Jacket may be most easily understood as a lawyer. In his speech on behalf of Soongise, Red Jacket argued that the execution of witches on behalf of the state was something that nations did—and that knocking the woman over the head was humane compared to what he had heard about the white people at Salem burning witches alive, a century before. His client was convicted, and pardoned. In 1830, New York State passed laws proclaiming its jurisdiction over all crimes committed by Indians in the state.

Anglo-Saxon law also has a tradition of designated speakers in a legal context. Every lawyer in court is essentially a hired speaker, presenting a spoken case in ways that the client wishes he or she could.

In the international political (rather than legal) context, Europeans had more difficulty with the Haudenosaunee concept of speakers. In council, speakers for the Europeans generally had executive authority, either as emissaries or negotiators or as governors themselves. They frequently had to be reminded that the person speaking to them was not a "chief," or was not speaking as a chief, but had only been chosen because of his talent for speaking:[116]

> You must not think that I am alone or that I speak for myself as I speak in the name of the whole, not only the Men, but the Women, who are here present. It seems as though you imagined that I spoke only for myself, and I assure you, I speak for the whole.[117]

> Onontio, lend me ear. I am the mouth for the whole of my country; thou listenest to all the Iroquois, in hearing my words.[118]

What constitutes a good speaker? Haudenosaunee rhetoric, like most human arts of speaking, recognizes a sonorous voice with rich tone and volume. It involves rhythm and tone, emotion and power.[119] A good Haudenosaunee speaker will also use meaningful and powerful phrases from the law.[120] His attitude is one of pride and dignity without arrogance. Where the speech is a reply to a matter raised across the fire, a good speaker has the recall to address each point in the order it was received, and to repeat entire parts of the original propositions. Where it is part of a ceremony, a good speaker will sound natural, rather than as if he is reciting something memorized, but will include every part of the speech in the proper order, often including formulaic words. Haudenosaunee orators had a distinct advantage over their Euro-American counterparts, because so many aspects of their speeches were already laid out for them, and this left them more time to concentrate on the original parts.

Michael Foster asserts that the Haudenosaunee distinguish between degrees of speaking talent. The distinctions range from hath'a:ha ("he speaks"), an ordinary speaker, to an exceptional speaker, kekyohkwaho' hath'aha ("he speaks

---

116 Fenton (1998, 7) suggests that the speakers and negotiators, who were "front men for the sachem chiefs," eventually "developed reputations as politicians who should be courted and heard."

117 Thomson 1759.

118 Thwaites 1901, 27:252.

119 Slobin 1991.

120 A Maori speaker would use proverbs; an effective British speaker might include quotes from Shakespeare; a common-law lawyer would cite the maxims of equity.

in crowds").[121] "Speakers were chosen for their ability to grasp principle and fact, for rhetorical gifts, and for retentive memory in a society in which most men and women were walking archives."[122]

A good speaker will be clear; his words will not be "sharp-edged" or injurious; they will reflect a desire to promote conciliation, reconciliation, and arriving at one mind about the subject at hand. He will sometimes use self-deprecating humour to soften his words.

In part to ensure that the speaker delivers the speech or puts through the ceremony properly, there is often someone designated to sit beside him and remind him of any missing elements. This is more common where the speaker was less experienced, or in training, or where the matter is especially difficult or delicate.[123]

Persuasion, rather than compulsion, drove decisions in Haudenosaunee society. This made rhetoric, and convincing speaking, far more important than the announcements delivered by colonial governors, federal ministers, or presidents. A talented speaker was doing far more than delivering a message in an entertaining way. He was hoping to bring about consensus through the power of words and logic.[124]

---

121 Foster 1974, 30–32. Today, the expression "he speaks in crowds" is still part of Grand River English.

122 Fenton, in Jennings 1985, 13.

123 The "reminder" or "helper" (Fenton calls this person a "prompter," a theatrical term used for a hidden person who provides lines to forgetful actors) often sits at the speaker's left elbow.

124 In this, as well, the analogy of the lawyer holds true. The lawyer seeks to convince the judge, or the jury, over neither of whom the lawyer has anything but the influence of words and logic.

The Power of Song: The Song of Peace

There was a time when a great speaker would "perk up the ears"[125] of his audience by "driving it into them with a song." This is rarer today.

"The hymn, or *karenna*, deserves a special notice. In every important council of the Iroquois a song or chant is considered a proper and almost essential part of the proceedings. Such official songs are mentioned in many reports of treaty councils held with them by the French and English authorities. In this greatest of all councils, a song must, of course, have a distinguished place."[126] Haudenosaunee reality is slightly more complex than Horatio Hale understood. Song may have come to humans before language. It is a distinct means of expression, and a powerful one. Virtually every religion delivers important parts of its ceremonies in song—often the *most* powerful parts. The cantor in the synagogue, the muezzin in the mosque, the chanting lama, the Christian congregation with its hymns and spirituals, all share the understanding that song is a separate and essential means of communication, both between humans and between humans and the spirit world. Modern North American society integrates song into weddings and funerals, political campaigns and advertising, but not into legislatures and courts.[127] Haudenosaunee diplomacy and law have taken this realization to a slightly different place: a speaker wishing to deliver a message with additional force or clarity may lapse into song. This is seldom done today, except in ceremonies—just as it is rare today to see a Haudenosaunee speaker walk about while he speaks—but songs in council would not only be official songs, they would be original expressions, additional ways of communicating the ideas in the speech. "To our astonishment an old Oneida began to sing the message which he had for the council, in a very high tenor voice. He continued for more than half an hour."[128]

---

125 The expression, poorly translated into English, refers to the way a dog's ears perk up when he is interested in something he hears.

126 Hale (1883) 1989, 62.

127 Is the absence of song from conversation a result of the way writing did not include notation? Dennis Tedlock (1983 and 1999) noted that transcription "takes the breath from the text." In Hawai'i, *mele oli,* or what in English is called "chant," became the record of historical events, genealogies, and relations with the land.

128 Onondaga, 19 June 1750, cited in Beauchamp (1907) 1975, 423.

On 15 September 1685, Canondondawe, the Mohawk speaker, used the power of song to drive the message of peace into the governors of New York and Virginia:

> Oh Brethren, Corlaer and Governor of Virginia, where will I look for the peace covenant, where else will I find it but on our path, and but where will this path lead but to this house, which is a house of peace and welfare, and started a song and sang completely the covenant song . . . Let us observe and keep to what has been commanded so sharply to us. Let me drive it into you with a song. Open now your ears, and he sang a song of admonishment, and gave one belt of wampum to the Governor and one belt to the Governor of Virginia, concluding all the proposals with a song and said that they were done for this time.[129]

An individual Haudenosaunee person often has his or her own song. Today, a man's personal song—his atonwa—is sung on occasion in the Longhouse.[130] It is ancient, one of the Four Sacred Ceremonies. An uncle sings his song before introducing his niece or nephew in a naming ceremony at Green Corn or Strawberries, and atonwa is sung by a person walking up and down with his arms linked with those of a person being adopted. A man may sing his song when renewing or joining the works of a medicine society. The song is a prayer, but also a statement of who a person is. An atonwa can be passed on from one person to another, as well,[131] so the song does not die.

Songs are not only individual. Sung together, they are an expression of the power of a group of people, and also of their unity.[132] For many peoples, voices

---

129 Livingston 1956, 89.

130 When there are references in historic documents to a man "singing his war song," it may be that man's atonwa—at the end of which the singer would sink the head of his axe into a post. Similarly, where men are described as "singing their death songs," these may also be atonwa (but see Thwaites 1901, 1:273). Yet in 1645, Kiotsaeton said in council: "I have only good songs in my mouth. We have a multitude of war songs in our country; we have cast them all on the ground; we have no longer anything but songs of rejoicing" (Jennings 1985, 139). War songs can also be personal and spontaneous: "when they come in sight of the enemy they advance each singing his war song; they are made in general *ex tempore*; they most commonly signify what they have before done against the people whom they are going to attack, or what they intend to do, or what number of scalps they will bring away" (Johnston 1964, 33). In this, the war songs would be similar to the tradition of the Maori *haka*.

131 While names are unique to an individual and belong, ultimately, to the family, an atonwa can be used by several men alive at the same time, and is not linked to families. Atonwa is one of the Four Sacred Ceremonies—the others being the Great Feather Dance, the Peach Stone Bowl Game, and the Drum Dance—that are done at the major ceremonies of the year, and which it is the duty of the rotiyanershon to maintain.

132 When Spain threatened to take over Gibraltar in the 1960s, 10,000 inhabitants of the British colony massed on the border and defiantly, together, sang "God Save the Queen" and then "We All Live in a Yellow Submarine."

joined together in hymn are thought to be a clearer message of praise to the Creator. Singing together creates solidarity, provides solace, and affirms companionship.

All these factors come together in the Song of Peace.[133] Composed by the Peacemaker, taught by Hiawatha,[134] learned by the people as they walked the path from Oneida to Onondaga, the Song of Peace is a song of power.[135] It is the song that pacified the fierce, scattered mind of Thadadaho. When people together sing a song, it is another layer of their unity of mind: "Long House used to sing when we were in power they went on in harmony."[136]

Most of the written versions of the Kayanerenkó:wa treat it as a prose text. Perhaps the most important exception to this is Horatio Hale's transcription of the two Condolence texts. Hale reproduced and translated the writing of Mohawks and Onondagas a century earlier, and the format appears as verse in short lines. The Condolence is intended to be recited, even chanted. There are pauses between the lines. The written versions came long after the words had been formed into a long song, a long poem—something that was oral, not written, and to be remembered, not read. The handwritten Newhouse versions are also clear about when the narrative switches into song: the lines become shortened, and stanzas appear. As with the research into how the *Iliad* and *Odyssey* were preserved over the centuries, if one examined the Kayanerenkó:wa, one would find that the entire law, and not just the Condolence, is intended to be recited. Today's annual recitals embrace an increasing comfort with vibrant chant rather than monotone. It is therefore not unreasonable that the format of written versions of the law is better adapted to be written with a break at the end of each spoken or chanted "line," the places where there would be real

---

133 Different nations had different peace songs, which they would sing along the path when approaching a foreign village. To the hosts, who might not understand the words, it would still be obvious that this was a peace delegation: they would come singing (instead of silently), along the broad path (instead of through the woods), carrying their sacred pipes before them.

134 Hale (1883) 1989, 62. Hale correctly points out that most of the Condolence songs were written after the founding of the League, for they "appeal to the wisdom of their forefathers . . . and lament the degeneracy of the later times. They expressly declare that those who established the 'great peace' were in their graves, and had taken their work with them and placed it as a pillow under them." Yet other parts of the songs are fresh, and express only the power of peace. Those parts, it is said, are the ones sung by the people as they went about the work of forming the peace.

135 Peace songs set the tone for treaty councils. In 1694, at a treaty at Albany, "ye [25] sachims were attended with many other Indians. When ye came to ye place where ye treaty was held, they came two in a rank, Rode, ye sachim of ye Maguase being ye leader, singing all ye way, songs of joy and peace. So, likewise, when ye were sat down, they sang two or three songs of peace before they began ye treaty." Mass. Hist. Soc. Coll. Ser. 4, 1:106, in Beauchamp (1907) 1975, 420–21.

136 Records of the December 1862 Council of the Six Nations at Cattaraugus (Parker 1916, 144).

pauses in the speech. The translated Thanksgiving at the beginning of this text is my conversion of Gibson's 1912 text into a more rhythmic, poetic format.

Having distinct lines leads to another element of long-remembered works: formulaic, repetitive strings of words that assist the reciter in recalling.[137] We can see those in the law in its frequent repetition of specific groups of words: "Now it will end, the bloodshed, the scalping, the killing"; "the smoke pierced the sky"; "peace, power, and righteousness." Why did transcribers such as Hewitt and Goldenweiser not write out the law in the "lines" in which it would be recited? Possibly because they were not hearing it in the way it would be done in public, but instead privately from a reciter in his home. Hewitt, in particular, would have an informant deliver two to six words at a time, write them down, check them again—and thus create a meticulous but not necessarily naturally flowing document.[138] Perhaps these recorders did not see the importance of the poetic format, not being performers or poets themselves.[139] They were transforming an oral text into a written one.

If one thinks of the Kayanerenkó:wa as a recited, oral epic matter rather than as transcribed prose, it can be more easily understood as also being a periodically performed event, part of the living cycle of the people, rather than something to be used for legal reference.[140]

---

137   In the *Odyssey*, we find repeated formulae, most memorably "the wine-dark sea," "the rosy fingers of dawn," and "the man of twists and turns."

138   "Owing to the great difficulty of putting on paper an unwritten language, and especially a long legend therein, Ska-na-wa-ti was compelled to dictate from two to six words and then wait until they could be transferred to paper by me; so that the whole was related disconnectedly, many passages being repeated several times. For this reason the legend is rather too concise and sentential rather than diffuse, and its periods are not so rounded and full as they would be were this legend spoken or related connectedly and without interruption." Hewitt 1892b, 131.

139   Hewitt did much of his recording in the 1880s, and he no doubt witnessed some of the ceremonies at that time, but it was not until he was invited to put through part of the Condolence at Oneida in 1917 that he would have had a participant's appreciation of how rhythmic and public the words were.

140   As a public event, in which the recitation is open to correction or discussion, the law becomes the kind of "oral tradition" that Canadian courts will accept. See the discussion of the acceptability of oral tradition in *Delgam'uukw* (SCC), *Mitchell* (Federal Court, Trial Division and SCC), and *Benoit* (Federal Court of Appeal). In the last case, the trial court accepted as oral tradition evidence Chief Francois Paulette's recollections of his grandfather's accounts of the treaty making, in which he had taken part. The Federal Court of Appeal rejected his evidence, adopting the standards proposed by the federal witness Alexander von Gernet, on the grounds that the accounts had not been delivered in a public manner.

One Family

"If you are one of us you are addressed as a relative"[141]—David Maybury-Lewis's summary of how tribal peoples view the issue of "membership"—is crucially important to any understanding of the Great Law. From the outset, the Peacemaker's approach was to create one family, to make everyone relatives. His predecessor, centuries earlier, had succeeded in the first step, by creating the clan system, the extended families. The Peacemaker accomplished two further steps: first, he wove the nations together by declaring that the clans were families that transcended national boundaries; second, he extrapolated the family metaphor upward, so that the nations and their leaders became a single longhouse, a single extended family.

As nations become known to the Haudenosaunee, the relationship is described in family terms: "our nephews" the Delawares; "our brothers" the Ojibways; "our brothers" the English; "our cousins" the Cherokees. Those terms have both social and legal meaning. They imply a structure of mutual respect and obligation. They imply obligations of deference (from a nephew to an uncle, for example) or equality (between brothers, though elder brothers have some privileges). They are not merely terms of affection. When one becomes a relative of the Haudenosaunee—by adoption, for example—one steps into a complex web of protection and duty, rights and obligations.[142] Kinship provides a person with a place to stay in a distant community;[143] with a place to sit in council or ceremonies; with providers, allies, and protectors; but also with

---

141   "It is common to address every one by some term of relationship, according to their age," wrote Teyoninhokarawen John Norton in 1816. Norton 1970, 10. Maybury-Lewis (1992) himself begins and ends his memorable book, *Millennium,* with his acquisition of a name and family among the Xavante of the Amazon, his initiation into the world of tribal peoples.

142   In the seventeenth century, there are accounts of captured Europeans adopted to replace men who were killed in battle. They told not only of receiving the dead man's name, but also his family and relationships, being treated as if the deceased had returned to life. Some historians suggest that the intertribal wars of those times were "mourning wars," in which women encouraged the warriors not to seek revenge so much as to capture adoptees, to replenish families.

143   "One of the prominent aims of their first lawgiver . . . was to bind the people together by family ties of relationship, and thus create among them an universal spirit of hospitality, and lasting desire of social intercourse." Morgan (1851) 1995, 165.

people to whom one bears obligations;[144] in whose presence one is ashamed if one has erred; whom one must protect and help provide for.

Before one wades into the complexities and technicalities of Haudenosaunee kinship, there is one important principle to keep in mind. In a tribal society, it is *belonging* that gives a person identity, an existence as part of a collective entity rather than primarily existing as an individual. It is the opposite of the loneliness an individual feels in a globalized, homogenized society. Belonging adds a layer of security as it adds more layers of complex social relationship.

Thayendenega wrote in 1801: "The conditions of the confederacy seem to be expressed by the titles given each other as that of brothers and sons, representing that brotherly and filial love which was to guide their conduct to each other—this was further cemented by friendships between individuals of the several nations which was held very sacred;[145] in consequence of this they considered themselves as mutually bound to partake in each others good or bad success."[146]

Every version of the Great Law of Peace makes frequent reference to family relationships. The rotiyanershon are "brothers" to one another,[147] and it is relevant which side of the fire are the "elder brothers" and which are the "younger," for the elder brothers are the "well," with the authority to introduce matters into council first. The clan mothers are the "sisters" to the rotiyanershon. People of the same clan are "cousins," no matter which nation they come from. All the people together are a family: they constitute one longhouse. The clans, which existed before the coming of the law, are an essential part of what weaves the Confederacy together. As Sakokwenionkwas Tom Porter said at the recital of the law in 2013, "we are relatives and family, and family does not hurt each other.

---

144 One explanation given for today's reluctance to adopt outsiders is a family's concern that it will be held accountable for the newcomer's actions.

145 He may also be referring to the special relationship now called "medicine friends," made famous in American cinema as "blood brothers." Brant's "special friend" was Lieutenant Augustine Prevost, who was transferred with his regiment to Jamaica in 1772. Brant was heartbroken, and became angry at a missionary who suggested he could take Prevost's place: there is no substitution. It is a lifetime relationship. In the eighteenth century, there seems to have been no requirement that such a friend be Haudenosaunee.

146 Boyce 1973, 291.

147 Professor Adriano Santiemma of the University of Rome took the terms literally, and assumed they were like European relationships: he maintains that the Peacemaker and Hiawatha were biological brothers, and that Thadadaho was literally their uncle (Vecsey [1988], 108, suggests that Thadadaho and Hiawatha may have been half-brothers). But then, Santiemma (1994) also maintains that the fifty chiefs represent the fifty moons in an eight-year cosmic journey, and that unanimity was a requirement because "one dissenting vote was enough for the chain of cosmic kinship to be interrupted." Santiemma concluded, on meeting modern Haudenosaunee, that their present mindset bears little resemblance to the cosmic governance of their forebears, as he sees it, since the people he met disagreed with his astrological/astronomical explanations of their history, culture, and laws.

They do not make blood shed." Gibson's 1912 version confirms: "I decree that a single family we shall become, our various nations. Furthermore, I decree that now it is at one house, from now on you shall all sit down together there, you of the five nations. Moreover, I decree, as to its name, that we shall say *Kanuhsyuni*, which means that now there is a single house and a single family, we having united."[148]

The use of kinship terms throughout the Great Law is not just a matter of respect. It is an integral, basic part of how the people view the world in which they live. It is impossible to understand the functioning of this legal system if one ignores or underestimates the fundamental role of kinship in shaping it and keeping it together. Morgan did not turn his back on law when he putatively invented modern anthropology by publishing his study of Haudenosaunee kinship.[149] His writing demonstrated one of the lenses through which the people were able to see and construct the world, including their legal system:

> Morgan pioneered the study of kinship systems, which became an important branch of anthropology. Anthropologists discovered that tribal peoples tend to see the world through the prism of kinship. Their mental world consists of various kinds of relatives, a view that sometimes extends to encompass all of society. In other words, if you are one of us you are addressed as a relative; if you are not addressed as a relative, you are not one of us. Kinship is then a kind of mental map, a map that differs sharply from one people to another. Morgan showed that you have to be able to read these maps in order to understand how other societies think and live.[150]

Kinship systems are part of the cultural scaffolding of Haudenosaunee society. They are part of the structure an outsider must understand in order to function within the society or appreciate its laws.

When Morgan set out to explain Haudenosaunee kinship systems, he was laying the foundation for a foreigner's understanding of the Great Law. It would be pointless for anyone to study the law and remain ignorant of the meaning of the kinship terms used throughout that law—because those terms contain

---

148 Gibson 1912, 309–10.

149 Morgan's first technical paper, sixteen pages long, delivered to the American Association for the Advancement of Science in 1856, was entitled *Laws of Descent of the Iroquois*. See Boorstin 1985, 636–46. Morgan eventually concluded that the human world consisted of two main modes of kinship systems: Indo-European and Semitic on the one hand, and everyone else on the other. He also concluded that different races had distinguishing characteristics: all Indians, he asserted, addressed each other by kinship, wore loincloths, and slept in the nude.

150 Maybury-Lewis 1992, 92.

so much of the law's meaning, as well as its fundamental assumptions about how society works. He wrote:

> Upon an extended examination of their institutions, it will become apparent, that the League was established upon the principles, and was designed to be but an elaboration, of the Family Relationships. These relationships are older than the notions of society or government, and are consistent alike with the hunter, the pastoral and the civilized state. The several nations of the Iroquois, united, constituted one Family, dwelling together in one Long House; and these ties of family relationship were carried throughout their civil and social system, from individuals to tribes, from tribes to nations, and from the nations to the League itself, and bound them together in one common, indissoluble brotherhood.[151]
>
> These relationships, so novel and original, did not exist simply in theory, but were actual, and of constant recognition, and lay at the foundation of their political as well as social organization.[152]
>
> The League was in effect established, and rested for its stability, upon the natural faith of kindred.[153]
>
> The cohesive principle of the confederacy did not spring exclusively from the benefits of an alliance for mutual protection, but had a deeper foundation in the bond of kin.[154]

Just as the Great Law of Peace was constructed by people who saw the world through the lens of kinship and family—and used that vision as a source of strength for the law itself—so treaty relationships with other nations reflect the law's basis in kinship, are consistent with the law's processes and assumptions, and must be seen through the same lens.

Europeans of the seventeenth and eighteenth centuries were not prepared for their encounter with a legal system that drew its metaphors and ideals from family terms. Some were not prepared to agree that this was a legal system at all: "From the time of first contact between Europeans and Indians the ideology

---

151 Morgan (1851) 1995, 57. Colleges in upstate New York, in the mid-1800s, were the birthplace of many of the extended fraternities that are part of the social fabric of post-secondary institutions in the United States. They drew their rituals and inspirations in part from Masonic rites, in part from would-be ancient Greek and Roman influence. When Morgan created and led his own Iroquois League, he was emulating the male brotherhoods that were springing up on college campuses, but trying to find North American roots for the organization. Donehogowa Ely Parker seems to have played along briefly, before returning to being a chief in a real Confederacy.

152 Morgan (1851) 1995, 82.

153 Morgan (1851) 1995, 86.

154 Morgan (1851) 1995, 133.

of Europeans has insisted that tribal Indians had no 'true' government because Indians ordered their communities by kin relationships instead of the impersonal, bureaucratic European state form. Only Europeans, in this view, had 'civil' government, so only Europeans were civilized. Because politics were assumed to be exclusively associated with the civil government that Indians supposedly lacked, Europeans assumed further that Indians had no political history."[155]

One of the first things Morgan noticed was that the Haudenosaunee have more terms for kinship than modern Europeans used.[156] Other, earlier writers had failed to understand the differences between specific kinship terms and used more general European near-equivalents,[157] leading to confusion at both personal and legal levels. Fenton stated: "Europeans never appreciated the widespread network of kinship that encompassed the Eastern Woodlands, and they misunderstood the values that Indians gave to the terms 'brothers,' 'cousins,' 'uncles/nephews,' 'fathers/sons,' assigning these terms the meanings conventional in Europe. The English and the Iroquois had little difficulty over the reciprocal term 'Brethren,' although they missed the nuances of 'elder/younger' siblings that were important in Iroquois society."[158]

What do the terms used in the law mean?

In Haudenosaunee languages, a word cannot stand on its own, as it does in English. A reference to a relative must include a reference to the person who is

---

155 Jennings 1985, xiv. Euro-Americans, though, dealt with the Indigenous nations pragmatically, recognizing their governments and entering into formal relations with them. The same Europeans who denied the legitimacy of clan-based societies had drawn many of their own institutions from ancient Rome—a society based on *gentes*, or clans. It was almost certainly helpful to the British that many of their representatives and settlers were Highland Scots, to whom the clans were not foreign at all.

156 Since Morgan's time, even more Euro-American terms of kinship, and their social and legal meanings, have fallen into disuse as North American society moves towards the nuclear family as its essential, mobile, interchangeable unit, leaving the "extended family" behind.

157 Bruce Trigger has noted that the Hurons "did not use kinship terms in the same way that Europeans use them and the failure of French writers to take note of this creates serious ambiguities in their accounts of Huron life" (1976, 46).

158 Fenton, in Jennings 1985, 11. The Europeans readily adopted the notion that the King was the "Great Father" without recognizing that, in Haudenosaunee society, fathers did not command obedience and were not the closest relatives.

speaking—and often to that person's gender.[159] It makes a difference whether the relative is aunt to a male or a female person: the words change. Thus, an older brother of a male person is rohtsi'a; an older brother to a female person is ronwahtsi'a. The requirement for precision is such that there is no equivalent for the vague English term "sibling." Many Haudenosaunee terms imply a sense of respect rather than power, a sense of care rather than authority.

Ihst'a, "mother," is another example of how Haudenosaunee society's different approach to relationships is reflected in the terms used in the languages. Kanatawakon David Maracle explains: "*Ihsta'a*: this term is similar to that given for 'aunt' as it is based on the matrilineal tradition that a woman's sisters were also considered to be a mother to her children. There is the variation *Istenha* used by some speakers to differentiate between the biological mother and her sisters . . . The term *Yethi'nihstenha* is often used in place of *Onkwa'nistenha* in situations of ceremonial reference or importance, such as in the designation *Yethi'nihstenha Onhwentsyakekha* . . . 'our mother earth' (lit.: 'she is to us mother of the earth')."[160]

Blurring the words used for "mother" and "aunt" means, even today, that there is a great deal more "co-mothering" in Haudenosaunee communities than in Anglo North America. It has meant an easy transfer from sister to sister of children when families get in trouble. Informal adoptions even today require neither ceremony nor legal formality. Babies get used to being passed from woman to woman and are comfortable in many arms. Children have many aunties and uncles, not all related by blood or clan.

In societies deeply involved with kinship, with metaphoric languages, the roles of relatives are sometimes explained by their synonyms. Thus, rakenahá:a, "he cares for your mind," is descriptive of the role of an uncle as mentor, teacher, and guide.

The language of Haudenosaunee diplomacy with other nations tends to be male, because it is the men who address one another across the fire. It uses terms based on kinship rather than "clan-ship," because the clans are internal

---

159 Just as English law often allows an individual to stand alone before a court without reference to his relationships with others, so the English language allows one to speak without reference to relationships, and to speak without deliberate reference to precise relationships. Haudenosaunee languages require one to specify relationships while speaking: they cannot be taken for granted, because one cannot communicate without thinking about them. Thus, in English, one might say, "Let's go to the store," without specifying whether the "us" is the speaker and one other person, or several, or which of the several. The difference between the languages lends different meaning to the old joke in which the Lone Ranger says: "Tonto, we're surrounded by hostile Indians," and Tonto replies: "What do you mean 'we'?"

160 Maracle 2001, 322. Similarly, one would use Yethisótha ceremonially referring to our grandmother the moon, and Onkenisótha ("she is a grandmother to us") in less formal references.

to the Haudenosaunee, while the international family relationships are both internal and external constructs.

In the Christian tradition, it is "Our Father Who Art in Heaven." Some feminists maintain that the patriarchal Judeo-Christian God has replaced the Goddess of earlier, matriarchal societies, paving the way for centuries of male aggression and paternalism. In Haudenosaunee tradition, a father is not irrelevant, but he is not considered to be one's closest male relative. He is not of one's own clan.[161] The child's closest male relative—the man who carries a child around the longhouse when the child gets a name, singing his own atonwa[162]—is the uncle, the child's mother's brother.

Seeking simplicity, some contemporary Haudenosaunee have concluded that one's father's family was irrelevant in "classical" times, and that only one's clan relatives were considered "real" relatives. The law does not support this view. While it is clear that paternal relatives were not considered as close as maternal ones, there was a real relationship with one's father's family, part of that wide web of relationships that protected and helped each individual.

The law makes explicit provision for the link between father and child. According to one of Newhouse's versions of the law, a father with great love for a child could give that child a name from his family and clan. Today, as familiarity with the law has decreased and a sense of strict matrilinearity has set in, there has been little discussion about a father giving a child a name.[163] Does this patrilinear name replace the child's original name, or is it intended to be an additional identifier, an additional layer of connection and protection? Is there a special naming ceremony—or is it the same process as any other naming? The possibility of patrilinear names creates opportunity to provide traditional identity to people who lack clans through their mothers, a means of reunifying communities divided by conflicts between Haudenosaunee law and Canadian federal legislation.[164]

---

161   In the days before DNA, one could always be certain of one's mother and her brothers and sisters, but one could not prove paternity. See, in British law, the 1592 *Case of Swans*, in which the cygnets were held to belong to the owner of the female swan.

162   If the child has no mother's brother, another man of the same family helps: in formal terms, all the older men of the family are the child's uncles.

163   Accentuation of matrilineal ways may be a way of pushing back against the patrilineal systems of the United States and Canada, a way of drawing the line between the societies. There is a constant tension between traditional societies entrenched in protecting the mother's line as a means of determining membership in the community, and the same societies' equally fundamental desire to respect the inclusiveness of families. Neither of these values has anything to do with the blood-quantum approach taken by the United States and Canada to determining "Indianness."

164   Stating that "it was not the children's fault," the Haudenosaunee Council at the Grand River in 1995 decided that a person could take their father's clan and family if they had none through his mother, but that this would not apply to people born after the date of the decision.

Most modern Haudenosaunee, while conscious of both extended family and clan relationships, live in single-family dwellings, in nuclear families in which the father is the main breadwinner. As a result, there has been change in Haudenosaunee perceptions of family; statements of relationships in the Kayanerenkó:wa reflect the intentions and realities of a time when the people were living in matrilocal bark longhouses. Some terms used in the law often carry legal baggage that is not reflected in the current society of the people who claim to follow the law.

Despite the erosion of Haudenosaunee languages, the rise of nuclear families, and economic change, there remains a strong sense of community and family. It manifests itself most strongly in times of trouble, when people pull together to help those who have suffered misfortune. *We help one another*.

Helping One Another

It is not only the human world that the Haudenosaunee see in kinship terms. Careful attention to the opening thanksgiving alerts the listener to the fact that we humans are related to the entire natural world. In acknowledging and thanking them, the earth is addressed as our mother, the moon as our grandmother, the sun as our elder brother, the animals as our brothers, and the Thunderers as our grandfathers. This social and legal web of protection and obligation acts as a prism for understanding our place, as humans and human societies, in the web of life.

When Haudenosaunee lawmakers say they follow "natural law," it is not in the sense that philosophers and ethicists understand—that there are constant laws of the universe reflected in nature. Rather, they are saying that the inspiration for principles of the laws of the Haudenosaunee is drawn from the structures and conduct the people see in the natural world around them.

In the fields, the Haudenosaunee planted corn, beans, and squash together in mounds. They are called "the Three Sisters," because they help one another. The corn supports the climbing beans. The squash spreads across the ground, and its leaves shelter the roots of the corn and beans and reduce weeds.[165] Each of the three takes a different set of nutrients from the soil, and each gives back what is needed by the other two.[166] They help one another.[167]

---

165 Perkl 1998, 280.

166 White and Cronon 1988, 419–20.

167 The help also extends to human nutrition: corn lacks the amino acids lysine and tryptophane, which are found in beans: a people who added bean protein to their corn staple would have more balanced, healthier diets (Engelbrecht 2003, 27).

In the forests, the wolves help the deer by culling the weak and the sick, but also by keeping populations down to prevent overgrazing; the deer help the wolves by providing them sustenance. The world abounds with complex symbiotic relationships, with plants and animals that depend upon one another in the web of life. Sotsisowah wrote:

> All the beings upon the Earth follow the Natural or Real ways—the ways of the Creation. And all of those beings are related in that they belong to the family of Creation. They support one another. The Oak Tree gives of its oxygen that the Rabbit may breathe, and the Rabbit gives of its flesh that the Fox may live. And the Fox, in death, returns to the Earth from which the Grasses feed, and the Grass gives of its flesh that the Rabbit may live. All things, in their real ways, support life. It is only when things leave their real ways that they cease to support Life—that they break away from the Life Cycle. It is the way of Creation that all things exist in real ways, and in the world of human beings, it is necessary that all things maintain real ways for all life to continue as we know it.[168]

In family relations with humans, in describing the way government should work, and in explaining the web of the natural world, the Haudenosaunee use several expressions to indicate that "they help one another." Among the most fundamental is tha'teioneniienawa'khontie,[169] which embodies the spirit of co-operation implicit in two people upholding something together. Other terms used include kaya'takehuháhtsera, to be helping someone's body (as in assisting with physical healing) and serihwawá:se, to be helping with an issue or speech (containing orihwa, a matter, issue, or speech).[170]

Mutual aid is part of Haudenosaunee society, not just a philosophy of its government. Carol Cornelius explained Haudenosaunee land use in similar terms:

> The Haudenosaunee system of land use was based on the philosophy that the land was given to the people for everyone to use and work together on the land. The cornfields were communal, but it was also allowable for individuals to plant their own individual fields, but they had to continue to do their share of work in the communal fields. A portion of the communal crops were reserved for ceremonial usage. Planting the cornfields was a community event. Parker describes how the women chose a woman leader who arranged the helpers and

---

168 Barreiro 2010, 9.

169 "You and I are helping each other, upholding something."

170 If Inuktitut has many words for snow, and this reflects the importance of snow to Inuit culture, then perhaps the many Haudenosaunee terms for helping indicate the cultural importance of assistance to Haudenosaunee culture.

supervised the planting. An ordinary planting day consisted of planting the field, with the woman leader, the owner of the field, providing
a feast of corn soup. All of this work was "accompanied by singing,
laughing, joking and inoffensive repartee, and the utmost humor prevails, topped off by a splash in the water to remove dust and fatigue."

Parker refers to this communal work as a "mutual aid society known
as *(in the) Good Rule they assist one another.*"[171]

"Helping one another" is a fundamental concept of the Kayanerenkó:wa, and
also a fundamental concept of Haudenosaunee society. In the bark longhouse, the
two families on either side of each hearth were to "help each other." It is a relationship that every person would see in operation almost every day. The relationship
is extrapolated to the council level: when an issue is brought into the council, the
two sets of brothers, across the symbolic fire from each other, help each another
deal with the matter. Together, they build a solution. This is in stark contrast to
British-style parliaments, where a matter introduced by the government is, by
definition, tested and assailed by the "Loyal Opposition."[172] In part, the spirit
of Parliament or Congress is adversarial because the opposition parties hope to
defeat the government, either in votes or in the next election, and to become the
next government. Their criticism is often constructive, but it remains adversarial
because it is always tinged with ambition. In the parliamentary system, cooperation is a by-product rather than a founding principle.[173] In the councils of the
Haudenosaunee, the chiefs are installed for life. The two sides have permanent
places, and there is no room for partisan ambition: the Mohawks and Senecas
have no desire to become the Cayugas and Oneidas, and could not do so if they
tried. There is therefore more room for the spirit of mutual aid.

Anthropologists and ethnohistorians have sometimes described this spirit of
mutual aid as "reciprocity,"[174] and indeed reciprocity is an important element of
how it works. But the term falls far short of describing the spirit of good will
that motivates and infuses helping each other at all levels of society and the law.

Charles Darwin argued in 1871 that "a selfish and contentious people will
not cohere, and without coherence nothing can be effected. A tribe rich in the

---

171   Cornelius 1999, 105.

172   The opposition was so real that, in the House of Commons, the government and opposi-
      tion are separated by green carpet "two swords' lengths apart," so that the members cannot
      physically harm one another.

173   Another indicator of the difference between the two systems appears when someone has
      made a powerful statement. In Haudenosaunee councils, there is an immediate sound of
      approbation (a deep, sonorous "moan," sometimes described in historical documents as a
      "guttural approval," sometimes as a "yo-hah"). In Parliament, the agreement is individual,
      not general, and appears in Hansard as: "Some Honourable Members: Hear, Hear," as they
      pound their desks, cheer, jeer, and insult one another.

174   Richter (1992, 21) affirms that "reciprocity works at all levels of Iroquois society."

above qualities ('reasoning . . . and foresight . . . the habit of aiding his fellows . . . the habit of performing benevolent actions . . . social virtues . . . and social instincts') would spread and be victorious over other tribes. . . . Thus the social and moral qualities would tend slowly to advance and be diffused throughout the world."[175] Traditional Haudenosaunee, hearing these words, would immediately think of their own symbols: the coherence of the five arrows bound together, the emblem of the unity of the Five Nations; and the Great White Roots of the Tree of Peace, advancing the social and moral qualities of the Great Law of Peace to the four directions, throughout the world. They might also consider the crucial difference between coherence and coercion.

Beyond government, traditional Haudenosaunee society is a web of relationships within and between families and clans, creating relations and obligations of mutual aid and support. The ceremony of Condolence is the culmination of this spirit: the clear-minded ones have the obligation and responsibility to help the downcast ones in their time of need. Mutual aid and support allow society and the entire world to continue to function. Condoling the afflicted and grieving is an obligation: "Wherever it might be that one whose mind is left fresh and untouched shall at once readjust the several things again."[176]

It was the families, and not the offender and the victims, who conducted the peacemaking that constituted Haudenosaunee restorative criminal law. The presentation of wampum to "cover the grave" has sometimes been called "compensation," especially since there is a tradition that a woman's death requires twice as much wampum as a man's,[177] but it is rather an element of pacification:

> As all quarrels were generally reconciled by the relatives of the parties, long-cherished animosities, and consequently homicides, were infrequent in ancient times. The present of white wampum was not in the nature of a compensation for the life of the deceased, but of a regretful confession of the crime, with a petition for forgiveness. It was a peace-offering, the acceptance of which was pressed by mutual friends, and under such influences that a reconciliation was usually effected, except, perhaps, in aggravated cases of premeditated murder.[178]

> . . . if as warrior kills people, or he rapes a woman, or he steals, as to that, this is what the chiefs should do; they should deliberate

---

175 Darwin (1871) 1989, 146–48.

176 Deserontyon 1784, in Hewitt, 1928, 96.

177 The explanation most often given for this today is that a woman represents not only one life, but also the potential to give birth to more life.

178 Morgan (1851) 1995.

carefully, and if they find him guilty,[179] then they will pick the matter up to consider sanctions, first trying to reach agreement for a
settlement in order to keep the peace; and if it is impossible to reach
agreement between the families—that is the people [lineage] of the
guilty one and the other side, that is the family of the person who
got killed—if it is impossible to agree, then the chiefs . . . will decide
if they will cover it by placing another person there who will replace
the one they have lost, the people of his family.[180]

Iroquoian societies also developed what anthropologists called "mutual aid
societies," more or less formal entities with a practical and economic spirit.
Among the Cherokees, they were called *gadugis* and were an open and integral
part of the way the towns functioned; when the Cherokees adopted some Euro-
American technologies, the *gadugis* also evolved.[181] Haudenosaunee mutual aid
societies tended to be more informal, and certainly less visible to outsiders.
Few written records of them remain, yet it is clear that they were part of what
helped society run smoothly.

For nearly a decade in the latter half of the seventeenth century, according
to Haudenosaunee oral tradition, the Mohawks and Oneidas concentrated on
fighting the French, and the Senecas and Cayugas provided the two eastern
nations with food. It would not be fifty elderly men in Onondaga who would
operate the sophisticated, extended network that would be required to accomplish this. It would be a complex but mostly informal system of determined
people, working together, in ways that would not have been obvious or even
visible to European observers. Vestiges of that system are still functioning in
Haudenosaunee longhouses and communities today: they appear most overtly
in crises, spontaneously and generously assisting individuals, families and communities in times of need.[182]

---

179   We should be careful with the concept of "guilt." When I was a court worker, in 1970,
      I found that Oneida people would translate "are you guilty" as "did you do it," rather
      than "can they prove you did it" or "do you feel responsibility or guilt for your actions."
      In this quote, what is intended is a factual inquiry: did he do it? Or rather, did his mind
      cause him to do it? Is he responsible?

180   Gibson 1912, 59. In 1764, the Haudenosaunee agreed to relinquish to the Crown
      jurisdiction over cases of murder and robbery where the victim was white (Sir William
      Johnson recognized this as a variance from the original Covenant). Later oral tradition
      added rape to create the "three matters" handed over to the Crown's courts.

181   Some Cherokee mutual aid societies served as credit unions for their members. The
      American Philosophical Society in Philadelphia has, in its collections, a financial record
      book of a *gadugi*.

182   In 1990, as the Sureté du Québec and then the Canadian Armed Forces began to tighten
      their ring around Kahnewake and Kanesatake, carloads of food and other supplies came
      in from every other Haudenosaunee community, their drivers taking risks in avoiding
      checkpoints, the spirit of mutual aid powerful and awake in that crisis.

The Structure of the Law

The Kayanerenkó:wa can be conveniently divided into two quite distinct parts. The first part is the narrative that describes how the Peacemaker brought his message of peace, power, and righteousness to the people of five nations and persuaded them to abandon bloodshed and adopt peace, order, and good government as their guiding principles. The second part, the "legislative" part of the law, was formulated once the chiefs met in the first council, and describes the form and rules of the government they created.

The two parts are inseparable as a description of the legal system. The narrative is not only a story: it describes how the Peacemaker achieved a rational and persuasive dialogue with people who stood in the way of peace, and his methods became living examples for later generations to use. The narrative describes the thinking behind the ceremony of Condolence, the ultimate, compassionate way to restore rationality and the threshold to any lawmaking. It sets out the principles of inclusiveness, mutual aid, generosity, and reciprocity. It confirms family as the foundation of the legal system. The narrative is also a template for the creation of consensus, unity of mind. It sets a path to be followed by Haudenosaunee government in every council and in all dealings with other nations.

Those who would seek something more legalistic and less legendary ought to recall that this is a *constitution*. That is, it "constitutes" a people and a way of living. As such, it ought not to be a dry recitation of processes and divisions of power between levels of government, but instead ought to embody the people's dreams and visions, songs and hopes. It ought to reflect the people, as they were at the time of its making, and as they hope[183] to become, within its framework.

The legislative, less narrative part of the law describes the structure and procedures of a system of government. It describes the way the fifty chiefs are divided among the five nations, and how the council functions. It provides rules for eligibility and appointment of chiefs, and the ratification of those appointments. It describes the checks and balances that protect the system against abuses of power. It sets limits to authority and provides for the removal

---

183   Until 2016 Canada characterized the United Nations Declaration of the Rights of Indigenous Peoples as an "aspirational" rather than binding document—which allows them to maintain that it does not affect existing domestic laws. Similarly, environmental protocols and treaties are later described as merely aspirational by nation-states that have no intention of meeting their commitments. The United States of America was also one of the last four nation-states to affirm the Declaration.

of those who violate the rules or cannot function properly. It provides for the amendment of the constitution, in ways consistent with its original architecture. It describes how foreigners will be dealt with—both foreign individuals and foreign nations, through foreign relations, war and peace, and immigration. The constitution is a real constitution, allocating authority in an organized, thoughtful manner and creating principled governmental structures that are designed to reflect the constant values of its framers while retaining the ability to evolve to meet changing needs. Like the best constitutions in the world, it expresses not only the legal and governmental systems of the people, but also their principles and visions. Unlike most current nation-state constitutions, but consistent with the culture of a people with a sense of the constant presence of the spirit world, it contains warnings about changes and challenges to come.

Both parts of the Kayanerenkó:wa reflect the powerful vision of the Peacemaker—the desire to create a society based on peace and reason that could provide for and protect the coming generations.

In some versions, once the Peacemaker and his allies establish peace, the chiefs take over finishing the law, responding to questions from the Peacemaker to create governmental structures. The dialogue reflects the process of consensus building that takes place in a Confederacy Council. In a sense, the chiefs create the protocols of council by performing them in their initial conversations. In other versions, the lawmaking around structures and processes is also the Peacemaker's work and his gift to the people.[184]

Without the legislative part of the Great Law, the narrative would be the history of a peacemaking without the stable institutions it needed to continue. It is rare that the person who inspires the revolution is also successful in establishing a secure system of government in the revolution's wake. It is rarer that such a person shows an aptitude for governing. The Peacemaker did not govern. He left when his work was done.

Certainty and Constancy

Just as not having a good relationship with one's neighbour might cause one to consider preparing for possible confrontation, having a legal system that contains uncertain elements leaves room for doubts that can blossom into precipitate action, or vacuums in which anger, ambition, or greed can seek lodging. The Kayanerenkó:wa guards against this by providing many constant

---

184 This is a significant difference between Skaniatariio John Arthur Gibson's 1899 and 1912 versions.

factors: known building blocks of the law. Constant and predictable factors remove risk and uncertainty.

There are a fixed number of core families[185] and a fixed number of rotiyan-ershon. These men have constant names (titles) and constant roles. Their clan mothers and helpers are known. Each of these people knows what is expected of them. The council fire is in a fixed location. There is a permanent firekeeper: the Onondagas have fulfilled that role for centuries and know what their duties are. The nations have set roles in the procedures of council.

Each time a matter is institutionalized in this way, it prevents potential problems. It removes ambition, from both individuals and nations, by limiting candidates and the pools from which they can be drawn.[186] It clarifies expectations—so that a person knows what they must do, and other people know what to expect or require from them.[187] It sets limits to authority.

While the possibility—even necessity—of change is built into the architecture of the Great Law, that architecture itself provides a framework, a set of constant principles to ensure that change is consistent, careful, and conducted so that the certainties are maintained.[188] The Longhouse can be extended, but only in ways consistent with its existing architecture. In this, the symbolic and legal Longhouse reflects the structures that the people would see every day: many of the longhouses that have been examined by archaeologists show evidence of having been extended during their short lifetimes.

Having a legal system brought by a messenger from the Creator, though, means that its modern practitioners are often reluctant to effect even consistent change. Traditionalists are often pessimists about the future and optimists about the past, said Mark Twain. The people who maintain the Kayanerenkó:wa are certainly traditionalists. A tendency to focus on details rather than principles,

---

185 Newhouse, seeking to make the rotiyanershon equivalent to British lords, would refer to "noble families."

186 The "downside" to this is that it can lead to the creation of oligarchies as the society expands beyond the original fifty families. It can prevent people of genuine merit from taking a role in leadership or decision making. One way to reduce the possibility of oligarchy, as we shall see, is the institution of Pine Tree Chiefs. Another is to ensure that there are many functions in the society in addition to those of chiefs and clan mothers. People can be kept busy with the work assigned to them.

187 Another example of Haudenosaunee provision for certainty is the way funerary matters are dealt with. For ten days after a death, the family is kept constantly busy with feasts and ceremonies, "letting go" of the one who has just died. The family is expected to perform these certain tasks, this business—and the result is not only that the people cannot dwell on their grief, but also, in the old days, that they could not turn their minds to revenge.

188 Having so many constants also means that radical change, when it occurs, results in total change, not adjustments to existing systems. The Seneca Nation's adoption of a party system of elections is deeply inconsistent with the consensus government of the Kayanerenkó:wa—as is the elective system imposed by Canada on Haudenosaunee communities beginning in the 1880s.

as an aspect of maintaining and protecting the law, and a great sense of conservative caution accentuate an unwillingness to risk change. Many would rather have it said of them that they were faithful to the Peacemaker's prescriptions than that the changes they made caused collapse. The very constancy and certainty that prevent controversy tend to heighten their reluctance to make necessary changes. Yet change was clearly an element of the Peacemaker's vision. After all, his greatest accomplishment was change, from a time of darkness and war to one of light and peace.

Confrontation Is a Last Resort

The Great Peace emerged from a time of bloodshed and feuding, in which vengeance and confrontation were often the first means of resolving any issue. The processes and structures of the Kayanerenkó:wa changed that. They make confrontation and violence a last resort, by placing deliberate, considered steps in the path of possible confrontations. As a matter of principle, in councils and negotiations, the easiest matters are dealt with first, and the most difficult (and therefore most potentially explosive) issues are approached last, though the commitment remains that what John Mohawk called "the rock hard things" must be dealt with.

The Peacemaker placed Thadadaho towards the end of his work, since he knew this would be the most difficult task and would require actual confrontation. He also made sure that, when the confrontation occurred, the forces of peace had become so overwhelming in their physical and spiritual power that there could be no effective response. Thadadaho was not killed: he was transformed.

Another example of slowing the path to anger is the three requests that are made before any extreme action is taken. An errant chief is asked formally to return to the proper path, and the requests escalate, becoming gradually more public and more urgent.[189] Only after repeated requests is the chief removed. In the same way, foreign nations are gently and repeatedly asked to join the Confederacy.[190]

---

189   In an Orthodox Jewish divorce, the husband repeats *gett* three times. While this is done in a single sequence today, it may be that the requirement of three repetitions was intended not only to impose deliberateness, but also to impose time for thinking—and rethinking—an important decision.

190   The final request could be accompanied by a visit in such force that the offer could not be refused.

The law requires not only a good mind and deliberate thought, but also the taking of specific steps in any situation that could result in confrontation or anger. These steps deliberately slow the people down,[191] compel careful thought, and prevent hasty or passionate actions. In assigning particular tasks or characteristics to each title holder, as well, the structure of the law makes sure that reflection and caution are imposed within the council by its own members. When, in council, one of the chiefs asks whether all sides of an issue have been considered, he may be cautious and rational, but he may also be fulfilling a role set for the man bearing his title five centuries ago. If an issue inflames passions, the council may decide to postpone a decision, putting the matter "under the pillow" until minds have cooled off. Confrontation in council can lead to the Onondagas "covering the fire," ending the council for the day. Deliberate avoidance of internal conflict cuts both ways: it creates a legal system that avoids internal aggression, but it also makes for a slow process that sometimes avoids difficult, divisive issues. One needs to be reminded of the commitment to deal with the rock-hard things.

---

191 In important councils, propositions would be answered the following day, allowing time for consideration, but also for the cooling of emotions. Visitors would be fed and given a chance to rest before council, so their minds and bodies would be healthy and not affected by fatigue. Another example is the long sequence of required tasks and ceremonies after a death—they keep people so busy they have no time for anger, no time to act while their minds are clouded, for a full ten days.

PART III

Bringing the Great Peace

Patterns and Principles in the Narrative

Most versions of the Kayanerenkó:wa can be divided into two parts, the "narrative" and the "legislative"—the first part telling the story of how the law was made, and the second describing how the details of the workings of the government were created. The narrative part of the law discloses a pattern, and the elements of the pattern are first set out in the story of the Peacemaker and the Cannibal. The Peacemaker's journey is recounted as a series of successful encounters with difficult, powerful, often irrational people. Only after overcoming those obstacles could the law be set in place. Both the narrative and legislative aspects of the story of the law reveal "one protracted effort of legislation."[1]

At each obstacle in the story of the making of the law, the Peacemaker met a person who was acting irrationally. He met the Cannibal who was killing and eating people; Tsikonsaseh who was encouraging destruction and war; Thadadaho who was ruling through fear; Hiawatha who had become a hermit with his mind clouded by grief. The narrative of the Great Law is a story of the Peacemaker meeting people whose minds are, for one reason or another, not working properly. Often these people are in places that block the path to peace: Tsikonsaseh on the Warriors' Path;[2] Thadadaho at Onondaga Lake. In each case, the Peacemaker does something to create an opening, a moment of rationality. For the Cannibal, who had lost contact with reality, the Peacemaker resorts to a trick to jolt him back to his senses. For Hiawatha, who had suffered great loss, it is the compassionate ceremony of Condolence. For Tsikonsaseh, the woman who promoted war, it is simple rational persuasion and conversation. For Thadadaho, the last great obstacle to the peace, it is the Song of Peace and all the spiritual power of the united people, while transforming Thadadaho's political opposition with an offer of political authority and responsibility. To the Seneca warriors, the Peacemaker offers the opportunity to become protectors of the peace rather than its destroyers. A different device is used every time. But the template is the same: to think and observe carefully; and then to approach the irrational or fearful person and do whatever it takes to create a moment or opportunity of sanity, an opening through which the rest of the message of peace,

---

1   Morgan (1871) 1997, 127.

2   While the Mohawk words used to describe the dark times are translated as "they were roaming about," the randomness involved was likely uncertainty about where and when violence would strike, rather than about what path the warriors might take. The uncertainty would increase the terror of the times.

power, and righteousness can enter and take root. In some cases, sweetness and reason are enough. In other cases, it takes trickery, demonstrations of courage, or displays of spiritual power. What is the name for a law with "whatever it takes" at its heart? Pragmatism, perhaps. The Haudenosaunee law of peace assumes that you will not achieve peace. But it assumes that you can reach enough of it to have something to work on so that you can "take the conflict from warfare to a place where, as they used to say, thinking can replace violence, and where the conversation about peace is ongoing."[3]

When the Peacemaker met people who were behaving rationally, they were often also lost, frightened, and desperate. They had covered their fires so the smoke would not reveal their location to their enemies. They yearned for peace, but did not know how to get there. The Peacemaker provided a way to deal with the ones who were the sources of the conflict, and enlisted the help and commitment of the right-thinking, clear-minded people: Odatsehte, Tekarihoken, and the other chiefs. He also enlisted the help of the people that he personally had caused to return to their right minds, converts like Hiawatha and Tsikonsaseh.

Some of the people he restored to rationality became leaders as well as walking examples of the power of the Good Message. Others, like the Cannibal, simply stopped killing, and went on their way.

The Great Law created both a technique and an obligation to expand the peace, using the same pragmatic, rational approach: making relatives out of strangers. It enabled and spread the structure of mutual obligation, "helping each other," that flows from being relatives.

Here is the other thing the Peacemaker did—and this is a little more complex. He came into a society in which the people already believed that they were related to everything. Their entire world was capable of functioning on the basis of kinship, and kinship was inextricably linked to mutual aid. This included their relations with the natural world—every part of it can be addressed as a relative. Our Mother the Earth, our Grandmother the Moon, our Elder Brother the Sun, our brothers and sisters the animals and birds, our Grandfathers the Thunderers. Within the village, every person could be addressed as a relative. Being related, to these people, meant a dynamic, two-way relationship. It meant reciprocity. It meant, for example, that tobacco and respect would be given to the Thunderers, but they would bring the rain for the crops. The concept that would link all the natural world to all the human world is that "they help one another"—like the Three Sisters, corn, beans, and squash, help one another. Within the village, the people also experienced kinship as not only the way to peace and stability but also as cooperation. Any individual, waking up in the morning, would see another family across the fire in the longhouse from his family. This other family would be relatives, and the relationship between the

---

3   Mohawk 2004, n.p.

two families would be that "they help one another." The Peacemaker politically knocked down the village palisades so that the family relations were extended across the nations, so that everyone became family, the people of a single longhouse. Then, using the same concept, he created a way to extend it even further through the Great White Roots of Peace, so that any person or nation the Haudenosaunee encountered in the world would have a way to become a relative and become part of the Great Peace.

In contrast to this is the uncertainty resulting from encountering people with whom one has no relationship at all. How does one relate to them? If one cannot address them as relatives, they are strangers. One does not have any way of knowing how they will behave. No rules apply to them. They are fellow humans, potential friends. They are also fair game for war, since no rules of kinship restrain either side. The edges of the landscape would always shimmer with the uncertainty and danger that came from the presence of unrelated peoples. But the Great Law, and its Great White Roots, provided the technique, the obligation, and the template for transforming unrelated peoples into relatives and for spreading the peace. It contained an explanation of the thinking, the logic, behind proceeding in this way. The narrative part of the Great Law also provided examples of the kinds of devices that would work.

In building a working legal system, the Peacemaker took the institutions that the people already had, and strengthened and expanded the ones that worked well. He spread the brotherhood of clans across all the nations. The chiefs were transformed from local and national figures into Confederacy leaders, and eventually into ambassadors to other nations. He ensured that each family had a voice in the council. He got rid of the things that were causing trouble, if he could. The hunting grounds became a shared bowl or dish instead of a source of friction or competition. He transformed other harmful things: the warriors became protectors of the Confederacy rather than a threat; Thadadaho became a guardian of the processes of peace rather than an obstacle to them. As for the harmful things he could not get rid of, he built safeguards against their influence. If gossip would never go away, he at least provided that the chiefs would have skins so thick it would not affect their thinking, and that they would be deaf to the twittering of the little birds of rumour in the branches overhead. If tempers would flare, he devised council processes to minimize their effect.

The Peacemaker also removed a major source of conflict by bringing a new way for people to deal with death. He had come into a society where the dead were revered and sorely missed, and where their voices called out for revenge against their killers. Mourning could lead to bloody retaliation. Death will never go away, so society needs to learn how to deal with it. With the ceremony of Condolence, he brought a way to put the dead away, out of mind, out of hearing, through a process that brings all the people together, compassionately and with an overlay of peace. Through the law, death was transformed from a source of conflict to an opportunity to reaffirm and re-enact the peacemaking.

The narrative of the making of the law also provides a template for solving social problems. The Peacemaker began by taking his message to people he believed would support it. He worked carefully to build support, and the people he had enlisted helped along the way. By the time of the confrontation with Thadadaho, he was able to call upon the political, moral, and spiritual support of all the people united. The procedure of council—building consensus by having a matter considered in a deliberate sequence, one nation at a time—reflects this approach. One meaning of "Haudenosaunee" is "they are people making a longhouse," and this recognizes that the work, like the conversation about peace, is always ongoing, never finished. The metaphor of building is reflected in the longhouse as the symbol of the people: it takes collaboration and effort to build it, and then to maintain it.

In the making of the law, the result of confrontation is not victory, in which the loser is relegated to an inferior status, but unity, in which there are no longer any losers. It is transformation from strangers and enemies to friends and relatives. Where the law describes the conversion of an individual, it may be reasonable to conclude that person brought with him or her relatives and followers.

The law contains its own maintenance mechanisms. It provides that it must be kept in mind in order for it to guide the people's minds, so it contains numerous opportunities for contemporary people and their leaders to re-enact and renew the original thoughts and actions that brought about the peace. Repeating the actions of the ancestors, refreshing the peacemaking, the law becomes not only theirs but ours. Symbols of the law—the fire, the longhouse, the pine tree, the eagle—were things the people would see or use every day, and these reminders would also serve as maintenance.

The Peacemaker

The Peacemaker was born on the north shore of Lake Ontario, "in the land which was called Tkahaa'nayg'n, where there are bottom lands, but which at the present time is called Ganyéngeh, at the flint place (i.e., Mohawk place), situated on the north side of the great lake, originally called Sganyadaiîyo [Ontario], "the beautiful great lake."[4] Most Haudenosaunee agree that the Peacemaker's birthplace was somewhere on the shores of the Bay of Quinte.[5]

He was either a Mohawk[6] or a Wendat (Huron).[7] His mother Kahetehsuk (She Walks Ahead)[8] and his grandmother Kaheto'ktha' (End of the Field) had gone to live apart from other people, for their own safety.[9] Killing and scalping had become commonplace. The cycle of war seemed endless. Oren Lyons and John Mohawk describe it:

> [It was] our darkest hour when the good message of how to live had been cast aside and naked power ruled, fueled by vengeance and blood lust. A great war of attrition engulfed the lands, and women and children cowered in fear of their own men.[10] The leaders were fierce and merciless. They were fighting in blind rage. Nations, homes and families were destroyed, and the people were scattered. It was a dismal world of dark disasters where there seemed to be no hope. It was a raging proof of what inhumanity man is capable of when the laws and principles of life are thrown away.[11]

---

4   Gibson 1899, para. 2. Fenton's footnote states that "the bottom lands lie around Bay of Quinte and in the vicinity of the present city of Kingston, Ontario."

5   Many people believe that the Peacemaker's birthplace is within the Tyendinaga Mohawk Territory, and that John Deserontyon and other Mohawks deliberately chose that location in order to be close to the Peacemaker's original home and to protect it.

6   Gibson 1912, 2: "This was happening where the Mohawks resided, at the lake shore, on the northerly side of the lake, Lake Ontario." Upon meeting Thoihwayei, the Mohawk, on the south shore of Lake Ontario, the Peacemaker tells him: "We are the same people" (Gibson 1912, 69).

7   Parker (Newhouse and Cusick) 1916, 14. "North of the beautiful lake (Ontario) in the land of the Crooked Tongues, was a long winding bay and at a certain spot was the Huron town, Ka-he-nah-yenh." Hewitt (1917) claimed that the idea that the Peacemaker was Huron originated in "misunderstanding certain information which the present writer many years ago gave to Mr. Newhouse concerning the early inhabitants of what is now Ontario, Canada." Later archaeological research indicates that the Wendat or Hurons did indeed live on the north shore of Lake Ontario before moving westward to the Penetanguishene area where they lived when they were first contacted by the French. Wright 1972, 75; Trigger 1976, 164–68.

8   Gibson 1912. In Gibson 1899, para. 16, she "indeed was named Djigohsaseeʔ (New Face)."

9   Rather than live on the shore of Lake Ontario, they found a hidden place on the Eagle River, according to Atahu'ta:yʌ Bob Brown in the 2013 recital of the law.

10   During the 2013 recital of the law, Odatsehte Howard Elijah pointed out that we have not come so far from the dark days: we ought to be ashamed that in every Haudenosaunee community, there is a shelter where abused women and children can seek refuge.

11   Joagquisho Oren Lyons, to the United States Senate Select Committee on Indian Affairs, December 2, 1987, Washington, DC; S. Hrg. 100–610, 7.

This was a time of great sorrow and terror for the Haudenosaunee. All order and safety had broken down completely and the rule of the headhunter dominated the culture. When a man or woman died, their relatives hired a soothsayer who then interpreted the death as the result of the magical charms of a specific other. The aggrieved family then sought vengeance and a member set forth with the purpose of finding the unsuspecting and arguably innocent offender and exacting revenge. That killing sparked a spiral of vengeance and reprisal which found assassins stalking the northeastern woodlands in a never-ending senseless bloodletting.[12]

The two women lived alone for several years.[13] For them, isolation meant safety.

Kahetesuk became pregnant. Kaheto'ktha' was angry, especially since her daughter would not name the father of the expected child. She began to mistreat her daughter, and the two women got along poorly until the old woman had a dream.

> Thereupon she questioned her daughter, saying "Who, then, is the father of the child you two are going to have?" Then Kahetehsuk said, "Mother, I do not know what happened nor how it is," but the old woman did not believe what she said, her daughter. Thereupon the old woman began to get angry, and said, "Probably, it is not true what she said, Kahetehsuk." That is how it was, every day and every night the old woman got angry, it seems, when she questioned her daughter . . . that is the way it was for quite some time: both the old woman and her daughter were unhappy.
>
> This, then, is what happened when it was night and they were asleep. The old woman dreamed[14] and she saw a man arrive where they had their house, and he said, "I have a message along which I shall tell you: you should stop the kinds of thoughts you are having. Indeed, your thinking is that it is probably not true what she says, your daughter. This, indeed, is the reason why it is not wholesome, your preoccupation with her confinement and her saying 'Indeed, I don't know where it came from nor how it is.' Now I will tell you what happened to your daughter's life, for it is true that she does not know what happened. This is the reason why you should now stop: don't

---

12   Mohawk 1989, 219.

13   Where Newhouse says that Ka-he-nah-yenh was a Huron town, Gibson (1912) gives it as the name of the "place where no one travels, a place where the river forks." Analysis of the meaning of the name is in Gibson 1912, 3.

14   In the 2013 recital of the law, the man arrived from the west, and not in a dream.

cause your daughter to worry. Moreover, you should ease her mind by apologizing to her.[15] Actually, a great thing has happened, for he is appointing your daughter to be the instrument of a male child's birth. He is sending him, the one you all believe is the Ruler,[16] and he is coming from the sky above the earth; and he will be born of Kahetehsuk herself. Moreover, when he is born, the boy, I will give him a name; you will say, Tekanawita.[17] And when you will see him, the two of you will be kind to him, and don't bother him when, in the course of time, he becomes a man.[18] In fact, he is going to be working here beneath and on the other side of the sun. Moreover, once he is born, Tekanawita, he will grow rapidly, and it will not be long before you two will see many unusual things. He will reveal his powers, and all of the people will acknowledge them when they see Tekanawita."[19]

   A boy without a known father is an important figure in several core narratives of the Haudenosaunee. The first of these children were the twins born of the daughter of Sky Woman (though some accounts state that Sky Woman's own pregnancy also occurred without apparent male participation).[20] The twins then proceeded to create many of the plants and animals that surround us on

---

15   "Easing her mind" through the apology, a directed and not spontaneous apology, is a precursor of the ceremony of Condolence.

16   Raya'takwe'ni:yo, according to Fenton's 1941 footnote in Gibson 1899, fn. 3, "means the master or ruler of things, the proprietor, or the Chief person in terms of rank or in terms of importance. It is used for head chief, and to designate the place or council as the chief or principal place of meeting where ambassadors and representatives foregather."

17   "And the reason that he shall have such a name is that he will travel about on the earth" (Gibson 1899, para. 6).

18   "Moreover when it shall happen that he travels about, don't either of you two interfere with the purposes of his mind (his intentions), for he is about to accomplish a most important work among mankind" (Gibson 1899, para. 7).

19   Gibson 1912, 9.

20   Gibson's 1912 version has the Comet—a traveller between worlds—become the father of Sky Woman's daughter. Later, the twins meet the Turtle, the ruler of the water world, who tells them he, too, is their father.

earth; the "right-handed twin" created human beings.[21] Centuries later, another fatherless child brought the clans and the ceremonies.

Though a child derives its clan from its mother, Haudenosaunee meta-narratives, the Creation story and the Great Law, suggest that a person's father was important, and that fatherlessness was unusual. It would be strange for a people so fascinated with balance (between light and dark, good and evil, male and female) not to seek the balance brought by the mother and father in a family.

While the spirit announced to the grandmother that the Creator had "appointed" her daughter to be the mother of his messenger, there is no suggestion that the Creator was the child's father. The Peacemaker is not a son of God.

The Peacemaker stands on a long, clear path of Haudenosaunee tradition: fatherless boys have a special connection with the Creator.[22] They are chosen to bring messages and teaching to the people.[23]

The grandmother consumed with doubt, shame, and anger is also an archetype: in the Creation story, Sky Woman was angry at her daughter for

21   Later accounts, influenced by Christianity, say there was a "Good Twin" and an "Evil Twin." The earlier versions explain only that one twin was better at making things than the other. With two creative forces, the Haudenosaunee refer to the right-handed twin as Sonkwaiatison, "He Completed Our Bodies," not as the creator of everything, but as the one who made *us*. Some historic missionary records have chiefs suggesting that white people were made by a "different God" than the one who made Indians—but there is no indication that the missionaries understood the implied insult in what they saw as quaint cosmological statements. The Creation story, as Amber Meadow Adams points out, actually describes several creators, not a single one. Sky Woman creates time, or at least brings it into order, and she dances the earth's surface into being. From her daughter's body grow corn, beans, squash, tobacco, and berries.

22   Daniel Richter wonders if the Peacemaker was "perhaps a reincarnation of the Good Twin," and was "a being of supernatural origins" (Richter 1992, 32). Vecsey suggests he is a "reincarnation of Tarenyawagon" (Vecsey 1988, 99). None of the Haudenosaunee versions state that the Peacemaker was anything other than an extraordinary human being, though Parker adds that "the animals loved him" (Parker 1916, 15). Some oral traditions suggest that three of the Four Beings who are messengers from the Creator have been sent to earth with messages, in human form. The first was the one who brought the Four Ceremonies; the second was the Peacemaker; the third was Skaniatariio. Yet Skaniatariio, in his visions, met with all four, and the Peacemaker makes reference to all four. A fourth messenger, with a final message, is yet to come. The four messengers also reflect the four winds, and the four directions.

23   The Haudenosaunee are not alone in according special powers to fatherless boys. In the Celtic tradition, Merlin was fatherless; in the Judeo-Christian tradition, Jesus himself had no earthly father. In their shared fatherlessness, some Haudenosaunee saw Jesus as the Peacemaker; others saw them as similar carriers of the same message of peace. In a matrilineal society, there would be less shame in not having an identifiable father, but one should never assume that fathers, in traditional Haudenosaunee society, were irrelevant.

becoming pregnant,[24] and pressed her to identify the man who had slept with her. Like Kahetehsuk, she was not able to say who he was, and this made her mother even angrier. Is the anger the result of the fact that the girl is pregnant, or the result of the woman's sense that her daughter is not telling the truth, and thus betraying her trust? If the issue is trust and not the pregnancy, the lesson involved is different. Gibson's 1899 version makes this clear: "Then at that time the old woman become depressed in her mind. She said, 'Certainly you do not love me, and the reason is that it is impossible for you to tell me the truth about what I have asked you.'"[25]

In Newhouse's account, the grandmother's anger at her daughter's unexplained pregnancy moved from attitude to action after the child was born:

> "You refuse to tell me the father of the child," she said, "and how do you know that great calamity will not befall us, and our nation? You must drown the child."
>
> So then the mother took the child to the bay and chopped a hole in the ice where she customarily drew water and thrust him in, but when night came the child was found at his mother's bosom. So then the mother took the child again and threw him in the bay but at night the child returned. Then the third time the grandmother herself took the child and drowned him but in the morning the child nestled as before on its mother's own bosom.[26]
>
> So the grandmother marveled that the child, her grandson, could not be drowned. Then she said to her daughter: "Mother, now nurse your child for he may become an important man. He can not be drowned, we know, and you have borne him without having marriage with any man. Now I have never heard of such an occurrence nor has the world known of it before."[27]

---

24   There is irony here: in some versions of the story, Sky Woman herself had become pregnant by the Comet, a non-human spirit force. The powerful roles of the grandmothers in both the Creation story and the early years of the Peacemaker's life reflect the authority of older women in Haudenosaunee society.

25   Gibson 1899, para. 4. In Gibson's 1912 version (1912, 1), "both the old woman and her daughter were unhappy": for the Haudenosaunee, feelings are contagious, so that it is important to raise up any troubled mind.

26   In the 2013 recital of the law, the grandmother tries to kill the baby by drowning him, then by burning him in a fire, then by burying him.

27   Parker (Newhouse and Cusick) 1916, 14. Some other versions have the grandmother making three attempts to kill the baby, including throwing him into the fire. The number three appears in the Great Law several times: the three warnings given to an erring royá:ner, for instance, or the three cries made on the death of a royá:ner, or the three calls of the Peacemaker's name in the bushes when things are dark and hopeless and it is time for him to return.

The grandmother does not try to kill the infant directly: she relies on the waters to do the job (and in other versions, the fire and the earth).[28] But the forces of the natural world refuse to harm him, just as later the Mohawks do not lay a hand on him but rely on gravity and the churning waters below Cohoes Falls to drown him, and once again nature does not injure him.

In the case of the twins in the Creation story, the grandmother, Sky Woman, continued to dislike Nikarondase, perhaps because Tawiskaron blamed his brother for his mother's death.[29] She sided with his brother Tawiskaron in many ways, including in the crucial bowl game that decided the question of whether life would continue to exist.

In the story of the Great Law, however, the grandmother repents of her hatred for the child—or of her distrust of her daughter—and begs forgiveness from her daughter. The daughter does forgive her, and harmony is restored.[30] The story is an important precedent for the thinking behind the Law. The Law requires collaboration between two sides; neither repentance without forgiveness, nor forgiveness without repentance, will restore peace.

In Gibson's versions, since the grandmother took no action against the baby, she regretted only her attitude of distrust: "Then when the old woman awakened again she at once told her daughter, saying, 'I am thankful that you told me the truth concerning the thing of which you did tell me. Indeed you do not know the source of the child that you are about to bring forth. So now it has been revealed to me in a dream as a certainty. So now I repent my former attitude. Now in truth a most important responsibility has been put on you.'"[31]

The Chiefs' Version confirms that it was the grandmother's feeling that she could not trust her daughter, and not the pregnancy itself, that was the source of the anger: "My daughter, I ask you to pardon me for all the ill-treatment I have given you, because I have now been satisfied that you told me the truth when you told me that you did not know how you got the child which you are about to deliver."

---

28 In ancient Greece, unwanted babies were left exposed on a mountainside to die of cold and neglect. They, too, were not put to death by clubbing, stabbing, or strangulation. It is as if the killers did not want blood on their hands too directly. Medieval Christian bishops carried maces into battle instead of swords, because they were prohibited from shedding blood.

29 One explanation is that she became confused about which twin had cut his way out of his mother's side, and so blamed Taharionwakon for her daughter's death.

30 In his account of the Peacemaker's childhood, Tekaronianenken Jake Swamp would say that he was "born to a woman and her mother," an interesting English expression of the Mohawk extended family. The expression is repeated in Gibson 1912, when the women visit their relatives.

31 Gibson 1899, para. 8. In the 2013 recital of the Law, the grandmother repented after being visited, not in a dream but in reality, by a man coming from the west.

"Repent" is the word used most frequently nowadays to describe an important concept in Haudenosaunee tradition: the action of a person whose mind
has caused him or her to do or think something profoundly wrong, and who is
now sincerely sorry. In the Christian tradition, one repents for sinful acts. "Sin"
is not an aspect of Haudenosaunee law. The grandmother's repentance is the
first step in an essential part of Haudenosaunee peacemaking; her daughter's
acceptance of that apology is the other side of it.[32]

The prediction of the Peacemaker's future life, in his grandmother's dream, is
not merely a counterpart of the Christian Annunciation.[33] Dreams have always
been important to the Haudenosaunee as a way of communicating with the
spirit world.[34]

---

32   This sequence of apology, repentance, and acceptance is the essence of much of tradition-
     al Haudenosaunee justice. Its modern manifestations include Akwesasne's Kanikonhrí:io
     Council, a Mohawk institutionalization of peacemaking that brings together the families
     to witness the acceptance of responsibility, the repentance, and the acceptance of the
     apology. That the participants sit in a circle rather than as two sides is a reflection, in
     part, of the sentencing circle tradition in Canadian law, and in part of the equality sym-
     bolized by the Circle Wampum.

33   The comparison is inevitable: in the Christian version, the angel (from the Greek *angelos*,
     "messenger") appears directly to the Virgin Mary, the mother of the apparently father-
     less boy, to calm her fears. Then at Jesus's birth, angels appear to tell the shepherds of
     the newborn's mission of "peace on earth, and good will among men." In his telling of
     the Creation story, John Norton notes that he asked an old Mohawk "who in his youth
     had much conversation with the Roman Catholic Priests, if he remembered the name of
     the Mother of Teharonghyawago. He answered, "not in our language, but in that of the
     Europeans, she is called Maria." Norton 1970, 91. Teharionhawakon is our Creator, the
     right-handed twin, "He holds up the Heavens."

34   Carl Jung drew upon Haudenosaunee treatment of dreams as part of the basis for
     his theories of psychoanalysis (he also believed that contact with Indians made Euro-
     Americans distinct in character from Europeans; see Jung 1928). Haudenosaunee believe
     the person's entire environment affects well-being. Where Western medicine might treat
     a broken arm, Haudenosaunee medicine would be more inclined to also consider the
     person's home life, work, activities, and other factors that could lead to the problem and
     might lead to its recurrence. "Health" includes physical, mental, and spiritual health,
     without clear dividing lines between them.

Why His Name Is Not Spoken

It may seem odd that a name that is known to everyone[35] is used so seldom.

Once the Peacemaker's work in forming the Confederacy and its government was finished, he said it was time for him to leave. According to some people, he went away to the east—and returned some years later with holes in his hands and feet, saying "look what they did to me over there."[36] Most accounts, though, say he went into the earth, covering himself with leaves and bark.[37] "I shall now, therefore, go home, conceal and cover myself with bark."[38]

---

35   What does the Peacemaker's name mean? Toriwawakon Paul Wallace (1946, 27) suggests
     that it means "Two water currents flowing together." He also says Dewaserage William
     Loft, a Mohawk Wolf Clan chief, interpreted it as "Double row of teeth," which would
     indicate that the Peacemaker had a speech impediment that forced him to use others
     (especially Hiawatha) as speakers, "like Moses used Aaron." However, Haudenosaunee
     names are not often literal descriptions of those who bear them during their lifetimes,
     and no version of the law suggests that the Peacemaker could not explain the message he
     bore.

36   Others say that it was not the Peacemaker but the man who brought the ceremonies:
     "I have been instructed by my father to go across the salt water because there are
     people living over there who need to hear how to be grateful for the good way to live.
     They need to hear a message that will bring them closer to their Creator." And then,
     when he returned, cut up and bloody, he said: "Don't touch me. On the [other] side,
     they think they have killed me." Native North American Travelling College 2000, 11
     (Kanentakeron). In traditional Haudenosaunee communities, one's father would have
     little authority: it is therefore very possible that this story of the Peacemaker being sent
     overseas has Christian roots, especially since most versions neither identify his father nor
     suggest that the father was divine. "Don't touch me"—*noli me tangere*—the words used
     by Jesus after his resurrection, seem to confirm the story's Christian origin.

37   When Sky Woman's daughter died in childbirth and was buried, her body gave forth
     useful plants: potatoes from her feet, tobacco from her head, corn from her heart, beans
     from her belly. Going into the earth can be a reaffirmation of life, not a denial.

38   Parker 1916, 105. Covering himself with bark has led some to suggest that he became or
     entered a tree. John Buck (Hewitt 1892b, 143) said he went to Sta:te, the home of his
     father's people, "there he lies buried, his grave being lined and his body being covered
     two spans deep with hemlock boughs."

He told the people that he would never be far away: should the darkest times come, when there seemed to be no hope, they should call his name in the bushes, and he would return:[39]

> If at any time through the negligence and carelessness of the lords, they fail to carry out the principles of the Good Tidings of Peace and Power and the rules and regulations of the Confederacy and the people are reduced to poverty and great suffering, I will return.[40]

> [Call on my name in the bushes] . . . if ever the law shall cease to function . . . then the law is nearing its end; and then again it is possible that I will stand there among your people here on earth.[41]

> "Let my name never be named (as an official of the League). No one shall be appointed to succeed me, as others can advise you; but having founded the Extended-House, a work which no other person could have done, I shall be seen no more of any man."[42]

That may be why many people tend not to use his name at all, while others use it only at particular times.[43] It is not yet time to call his name in the bushes. It would be wrong to bring him back inadvertently. It is also bad luck to misuse his name: "And it shall so happen that when you hear my name mentioned disrespectfully without reason or just cause, but spoken in levity, you shall then know that you are on the verge of trouble and sorrow. And it shall be that the only time when it shall be proper for my name to be mentioned is when the Condolence ceremonies are being performed or when the Good Tidings of

---

39 Winston Churchill suggested, in his *History of the English-Speaking Peoples*, that Britain got the leaders it needed at the time it needed them. The Haudenosaunee prophecy may reflect that thinking—that a new Peacemaker, perhaps bearing the name of the first, would come when he was needed most. It could also be literal: many nations have a "culture hero" who left them but never died, and who will return when things are darkest. King Arthur, sore wounded, sleeps in the Island of Avalon. Frederick Barbarossa sleeps under the mountain with his army. Nanabojo, to the Ojibways, is the Sleeping Giant in the harbour of Thunder Bay. Quetzalcoatl said he would return one day, and Cortez took advantage of this to suggest he was Quetzalcoatl himself. Millions await the return of Jesus—and others believe Elvis never died. In one version of the Creation Story, Taharionwakon returns from the Sky World to give people the Four Sacred Ceremonies (Mohawk 2005a, 75–76).

40 Parker (Chiefs) 1916, 105.

41 Gibson 1899, para. 128.

42 Hewitt 1892b, 143.

43 It is possible that in earlier days, the prohibition against using the Peacemaker's name was even stronger: this may explain why some second-hand writing about the Kayanerenkó:wa mentions only Hiawatha. Because the Peacemaker was not mentioned by name, the two men were blurred in the recounting of the story.

Peace and Power which I have established and organized are being discussed or rehearsed."[44]

This textbook is an instance in which the law is being discussed. According to the Chiefs' Version, therefore, it is probably proper to use his name in a legal text that discusses the Kayanerenkó:wa, especially when directly citing the law's various versions. Even so, I find myself reluctant to use his name, or to use it too often. . . . At the 2013 recital of the law, his name was used, and hearing the name used, in public, made it seem new and sparkling. The name had not been worn out with overuse.

Since the Peacemaker had not died, his name was not to be given to anyone else,[45] and his title in council was not to be given to anyone else. He had no successor, for he did not die.[46]

Deyonwe'ton Jake Thomas noted that there is "no Iroquois equivalent for the most often used English alias: "The Peacemaker."[47] Avoiding the use of the Peacemaker's name has led reciters of the law to the use of a number of substitutes: Hononhshonne:donh, "He constructed the house"; Tandaho'nehshan, "He has no father"; Honekho:wanenh, "He has a great mind."[48] They are descriptions, not euphemisms.

---

44   Parker (Chiefs) 1916, 103–5. Just as the authority to name something is a use of power, both spiritual and political, so is the ability to use the name. The Bible contains prohibitions against "using the name of the Lord in vain," and the Old Testament has several instances in which the Creator's name is announced with importance. While the Biblical Creator's name "YWH" is sometimes translated as "I am," the Peacemaker has a real name, another indication that he was indeed a real human historic figure.

45   Haudenosaunee practice and tradition is to avoid duplication of names: a name is to be held by only one living person at a time.

46   Morgan ([1871] 1997, 131) asserts that the Peacemaker and Hiawatha both "consented to take office among the Mohawk sachems, and to leave their names on the list upon condition that after their demise the two should remain thereafter vacant." Hiawatha remains an active Mohawk title, held today by a living person, and the Mohawks retain their full complement of nine chiefs. The Peacemaker's name is not among them.

47   Spittal, in Parker 1916, 118.

48   Modern American "Peacemakers": the Colt 1873 .45-calibre revolver and the Convair B-36 nuclear bomber.

The Peacemaker Meets His Own People First

The boy grew rapidly.[49] After a while he asked his mother and grandmother to introduce him to other people, "to see people of our own kind."[50] The two women moved back to the nearest village, where the grandmother announced the dream she had been given.[51]

> When the children began walking around, and more especially, when they played, some of the children repeatedly quarrelled, and they wanted to fight. Thereupon Tekanawita prevented them, saying, "You will stop it because it is sinful[52] for people to hurt one another; you especially, for you are all relatives, and so it is necessary for you to be kind to one another as well as to other people, those you know and those people you do not know; and you should respect them equally—all of the people—you should be kind to everyone."

---

49   Gibson 1899, para. 10. In other Haudenosaunee legends, people with special powers grow faster than others, as Sky Woman's daughter did. In Gibson's 1912 version, the women visit their relatives before the Peacemaker's birth. They are asked: "Who is the father of the child you two are going to have?" It is a question interestingly put: the child will belong to both women, not just its mother. And once again, though the society is matrilineal and matrilocal, the identity of the father is important, not only, as we have seen, to the grandmother, but also to the other relatives.

50   Gibson 1912, 25. Until then, suggests Tehahenteh Frank Miller, he had been "down-fended," sequestered, until he was able to think, speak, and travel for himself. The term "people of our own kind" suggests that there are other kinds of people as well. Gibson occasionally states that it is wrong to kill people of our own kind. Does this mean that it is permissible to kill people who are not of our own kind?

51   Gibson 1912, 15–28. She says: "It is of great importance, the message we are all bringing along." It is not just Tekanawita's message. The grandmother's dream, the mother's unusual pregnancy, and the young man's message are all part of the same powerful story and message, and it is brought by all three of them.

52   "Sinful" is probably an inappropriate translation for the kind of moral wrongness involved. While it is said that "sin" makes the Creator sad, the concept in the law does not involve the sense of personal guilt that the Christian, and especially Catholic, sense of the word implies. When the Old Testament God sees sin, it makes him angry. It has been said that "guilt" is what one feels oneself, while "shame" is what one feels around others; and that guilt is peculiarly European and Euro-American, while shame is more powerful in the rest of the world. Where the Old Testament God has the ability to punish sin drastically (with the great flood, or the destruction of Sodom and Gomorrah), the Haudenosaunee Creator does not punish. Not until the time of Skaniatariio in the 1790s does a Punisher appear, and he is distinct from the Creator. The Haudenosaunee Creator seeks to address the problem of sinful killing through his messenger. Is sending the Peacemaker as much as he is willing to do, or as much as he is able to do?

Thereupon the children were amazed at what Tekanawita was saying. When they got back to where they had their homes, they repeated what he had said, Tekanawita. Thereupon the elders said, "Now, indeed, they are beginning, the surprising events we heard about that he foretold, Tekanawita, for never, in fact, has it been the case that we might hear someone say, 'It is sinful for people to hurt one another,' nor has anyone ever said, 'You should all respect one another,' nor has someone said, 'You should be kind to the people you know as well as to those you don't know.' Now, indeed, it is coming true, this kind of thing we have heard about."[53]

He spoke to the children, saying: "Now you will listen well: now it is arriving, the Good Message, also the Power and the Peace. Moreover, now it will stop, the way in which matters are proceeding here on earth beneath the sky, such that they cause pools and streams of human blood to flow. Moreover, when it stops and when all the people are kind to one another, people of the same kind, then it will stop, human beings killing one another and also scalping one another, then all are relatives, they becoming brothers, the men, and all the women becoming sisters in future days to come, so that families will continue on."[54]

The elders of the village invited the Peacemaker to meet with them. The young man asked them to prepare a feast and to gather the people together to hear his message. The women would make cornbread and the men would bring game animals. The feast would therefore reflect the collaborative efforts of both male and female, the clearing and the forest, the plants and the animals. In the story of the making of the law, many of the important events are accompanied by people eating together, either as a prelude to bringing their minds together or as a way of confirming that consensus has been reached. In the modern Haudenosaunee world, a feast is an important part of any healing, and a meal an important part of the ceremonies in the Longhouse. Food is medicine.

The Peacemaker's message consisted of three "words" or "matters." First, the Good Message would stop the killing. Second, the Power would bind the nations together into one. Third, the Peace would make everyone into one related family. It was the same message that he would repeat during his travels—the three words, the Good Message, Peace, and Power. He explained to his own people:

First I will answer what it means to say, "Now it is arriving, the Good Message." This, indeed, is what it means: when it stops, the slaughter

---

53   Gibson 1912, 26–29.

54   Gibson 1912, 30–31.

of your own people who live here on earth, then everywhere peace will come about, by day and also by night, and it will come about that as one travels around,[55] everyone will be related . . .

. . . Secondly, I say "Now it is arriving, the power," and this means that the different nations, all of the nations, will become just a single one, and the Great Law will come into being, so that now all will be related to each other, and there will come to be just a single family, and in future, in days to come, this family will continue on.

Now in turn, my other, my third saying, "Now it is arriving, the peace"; this means that everyone will become related, men and also women, and also the young people and the children, and when all are relatives, every nation, then there will be peace as they roam about by day and also by night. Now, also, it will become possible for them to assemble in meetings. Then there will be truthfulness, and they will uphold hope and charity, so that it is peace that will unite all of the people, indeed it will be as though they have but one mind, and they are a single person with only one body and one head and one life, which means there will be unity. Moreover, and most importantly, one is going to assemble in meetings where it will be announced that all of mankind will repent of their sins, even evil people, and in the future, they will be kind to one another, one and all. When they are functioning, the Good Message and also the Power and the Peace, moreover, these will be the principal things everybody will live by; these will be the great values among the people.

Then Tekanawita said, "Now that I have finished my task, I will depart." Thereupon the older people said, "We are accepting the things that we have heard about the Good Message, and Power and also Peace."[56]

Haudenosaunee languages—reflections of Haudenosaunee thought—do not treat the future with the same precision as do European languages. The English distinction between "would," "could," and "should" exists as a result of the context of the statement rather than differences in wording. The future is more frequently indefinite, something that *may* happen.[57] As the Peacemaker delivered his message, his absolute certainty—"now it is arriving"—must have taken the people aback. Nobody would normally speak that way.

---

55   Travelling around in a landscape of peace would stand in stark contrast to the way things were before, when those roaming about were doing so with bloodshed in mind.

56   Gibson 1912, 36–41.

57   English reflects this, too: "hap" is a chance occurrence, the root of "happening," but also "mishap" and "happiness."

Newhouse asserts that the Peacemaker was abused by his people because of "his handsome face and his good mind. . . . [He] was a peculiar man and his people did not understand him." "Many things conspired to drive him away for the Crooked Tongues had no love for such a man. Their hearts were bitter against a man who loved not war better than all things."[58]

Barbara Graymont, without citing a source, adds details of her own: "Deganawida's ideas and actions were noticeably separating him from his people. The Wendots could not understand a man who loved peace more than war. They could not tolerate one whom they had known since childhood presenting himself to them as a prophet."[59]

In the Chiefs' Version, there is no mention of the Peacemaker having tried to bring his message to his own people first.

Were the Wendat (Hurons) part of the Great Peace? They did form their own confederacy of four nations, on the southern shore of Lake Huron. They had similar ceremonies and governmental structures. In some historic documents, the Haudenosaunee and the Wendat acknowledge a past relationship: in 1656, for example, the Wendat were being asked for the ominous third time to reunite with the Haudenosaunee, as a Mohawk speaker stated: "Thou knowest, thou Huron, that formerly we were but one cabin and one country. I know not by what accident we became separated. It is time to unite again."[60]

No matter what the version, the Peacemaker was soon done with his own people, either because they had accepted his message and would now be at peace, or because they had rejected it and he hoped to find a better reception elsewhere. He continued to live with his grandmother and mother for a while: if there had been a reliable peace, it is likely they would have moved back among their own people. That they continued to live apart suggests that the peace was not secure, and that they were safer where they had been.

---

58   Parker (Newhouse and Cusick) 1916, 14. "Crooked Tongues" is probably a translation of a Haudenosaunee name for a "people of a slightly different language," like the Attiwandarons.

59   Graymont 1988, 24. If the Peacemaker and his mother and grandmother had lived apart from the people, they would not have "known him since childhood."

60   Thwaites 1901, 42:253.

The White Stone Canoe

The Peacemaker saw that it was necessary that the peace should spread:

> It was not long before Deganawii'dah began to travel about. At that time then his grandmother said, "You alone must tell the two of us whether the time has arrived for you to depart." Then Deganawii'dah said: "in fact understand that I have now already begun to make my preparations. I am looking for something with which I may construct a canoe, and I intend to have myself a fine canoe. For understand that far on lakes and many rivers I will go seeking the (council) smoke of some people, holding my course steadily toward the sunrise."
>
> Then the old woman said, "How long will it be, perhaps, before you return?" Then Deganawii'dah replied saying, "I am not able to tell that. So then this shall take place when I shall depart, because then yonder[61] forked tree standing there on the hill top (edge of bluff?) shall be of assistance to us. And then when I shall have gone away, if it becomes necessary for you to know for certain what my fortune is where I have gone, then you will go to that standing tree, and when you will have arrived there you will chop into it; if the blood should flow from it, immediately you shall infer that already misfortune has befallen Deganawii'dah; but if blood should not flow from it, you shall then infer that Deganawii'dah's luck[62] has been favourable."[63]

---

61 "Yonder" is a word that has become obsolete in most English-speaking societies, but which indicates a distance that is intermediate between near and far. Often people in Haudenosaunee communities will use English terms that have become "archaic" among their neighbours but which reflect the precision or values of Haudenosaunee languages.

62 "Luck" is another word that is used by the Haudenosaunee differently than by their neighbours, though it is hard to define the difference. It is not unusual for people to express sympathy for a death in a family by referring to the "bad luck," and it is common to refer to a skilled hunter with a good relationship with the animals as having "good luck," though in neither case does the word indicate chance.

63 Gibson 1899, paras. 12–13. See also Parker (Chiefs) 1916, 67. Though the Peacemaker confidently announces that peace is on its way, his arranging this way of letting his relatives know his state indicates that he did not view it as a sure thing. In Gibson 1912, 49–50: "In the event that blood flows, it is a sign of this: that his luck will become bad and that they will not function, the Good Message, Power and Peace."

Then he began to build his canoe out of a white rock . . . [64]

Then the grandmother said, "How are you going to travel since your canoe is made out of stone? It will not float."

Then Dekanawideh said, "This will be the first sign of wonder that man will behold; a canoe made of stone will float."[65]

. . . they saw a stone boat and paddles of stone. Thereupon Tekanawita turned it right side up, the boat. Thereupon he said, "Examine it, and you will know what kind of a boat I have made here on earth." Thereupon Kahetoʔkthaʔ and Kahetehsuk examined it, and were surprised at the kind of boat that it was. Thereupon Kahetehsuk said "I love you, my child, but what are you doing in launching a stone boat, for surely, indeed, it will sink beneath the water's surface, the boat?" Thereupon Tekanawita said: "If it is true that it will sink, my boat, then I also may not survive nor can my work go forward here on earth ... Now, indeed, you two will help me as we drag the boat; then, into the water, we will launch it, and you will watch as I get in. You, moreover, will be the first to see this surprising accomplishment, and it is you who are to be witnesses as I take this step"...Thereupon his grandmother and his mother watched it depart, Tekanawita's boat, with him in it; he was in the boat, paddling swiftly when it left, and in a short time it actually disappeared as he was paddling along.[66]

The white stone canoe reappears (in Gibson's 1912 version) when the assembled chiefs are ready to confront Thadadaho. The Peacemaker, Hiawatha, and Tsikonsaseh travel across Onondaga Lake in it.[67]

What is the significance of the white stone canoe? Its whiteness symbolizes the purity and peace of the messenger it carried. Perhaps the stone symbolizes permanence and indestructibility. Perhaps it is a statement of spiritual power, because it is a floating contradiction: stones, almost by definition, are not boat-building material, because they sink. The majority of the discussion in the

---

64   Skanawati John Buck told J.N.B. Hewitt that the story of the white stone canoe was actually about Thaharionwakon, the right-handed twin in the Creation story, rather than about Hiawatha. Hewitt 1892b, 131.

65   Parker (Chiefs) 1916, 67. Newhouse makes no mention of the canoe being made of stone. In another version, the bark canoe was "amazing" in that it "skimmed so rapidly upon the water" (Gibson 1899, para. 21); it was indeed "swift."

66   Gibson 1912, 55–58.

67   There is no navigable water connection between Onondaga Lake and Lake Ontario, where the Peacemaker had left the canoe (probably near Oswego). The peace delegations were not coming to Onondaga from the north, in any event. And there is no record of the Peacemaker portaging a stone canoe.

versions of the law about this canoe, though, is simply that it is a remarkable thing, a memorable thing. Nobody had built a stone canoe, before or since.[68] The coming of the man in the white stone canoe would be remembered.

With the watercraft ready, the young man was prepared to leave. In Gibson's 1899 text, the canoe is of bark, and the leave-taking is emotional:

> Then Deganawii'dah said, "Now, then, both of you must assist me, you two must launch my canoe. So you both right this upturned canoe for me." Then at that time the mother and the grandmother of Deganawii'dah righted the canoe which was one of pure, white birch bark, and they dragged it and launched it on the water. Then Deganawii'dah said, "So now indeed we three must separate. Don't you two then let your minds mourn. We shall all meet again at some future time." Then again bidding them farewell he said, "Now!" (O:nénh).[69] Just then his mother who indeed was named Djigohsasee? (New Face) added, "Surely there where you will go, there too I will be." At that time he got into the canoe; so then he now departed, holding his course toward the sunrise.[70]

At the Bay of Quinte, near the place the Peacemaker is said to have been born, there is a strip of white rock near the water's edge that is said to be the underwater reminder of the place where the white stone canoe was launched. At that place, the water leaves small eddies, just like the short-lived trail that a canoe would leave.

---

68   After his beheading in AD 44, the body of Saint James was said to have been placed in a stone boat sailed by two disciples through the Mediterranean and the Straits of Gibraltar, to land in Galicia, where his relics were removed to the shrine in Compostela. In Mi'kmaq legend, the Creator, Glooskap, has a stone canoe (Paul 2007). In Anishinaabe legend, as recorded by Schoolcraft (1856, 223), a young man borrows a white stone canoe to travel to the land of souls.

69   As in many Indigenous languages, Mohawk has no word for "Goodbye." O:nenh ki wahi, or "Now (soon), indeed" is the usual form of leave-taking. In the 2013 recital of the law, Sakokwenionkwas Tom Porter translated the leave-taking movingly, as the mother said: "My son, I love you, because I raised you, and I will love you forever."

70   Gibson 1899, para. 15–16.

The Man Without a Nation, Without a Family

The Peacemaker grew up in isolation. He grew up without an extended family. The stories of the law do not mention his relatives, only his mother and his grandmother. Perhaps his lack of a set of cousins, the absence of uncles and aunts, had taught him how important a broad family is to survival. His plan for peace was based not on his own experience, but rather on what his own experience had shown him he lacked. Perhaps his seclusion allowed him time to think, pray, and prepare: "Without a tribe of his own, he was neutral. He had never been involved in any of the killing. Because no man's hand was against him, he could become a peace messenger among the tribes without disgrace or accusation of cowardice."[71]

The Peacemaker had no relatives among the peoples to whom he was bringing the word. He was not implicated in seeking revenge. He had no one to mourn. His family had not been involved in the killing, so no one would seek revenge against him. As a complete outsider, he was neither a threat nor a victim. His relatives were not around him, so he had no protection—but nor could it be said that he was acting in his family's interest. The outsider, with no political or family baggage, was the ideal peacemaker. John Mohawk described all peacemakers in the same terms as this man: "The people who are going to manage that, who are going to lead the way out of that jungle, those people can never lie. They have to be completely honorable, all the time. They can't take sides. They have to be neutral. They have to be peacemakers. Peacemakers aren't people with an agenda. They don't come to your country to take your forest. They don't come there to kill your buffaloes. They're there to end the violence. That's all. So they have to be completely honorable, completely honest."[72]

The outsider was also the most vulnerable person, the one whose death would result in the fewest consequences for the killers.[73] "[A stranger is an

---

71 Graymont 1988, 26.

72 Sotsisowah John Mohawk, "Peace Talks," KUNM radio, November 25, 2005.

73 There is no record of the Peacemaker's clan. When some elders are asked about this, they reply: he belongs to everyone. Similar thoughts were expressed in respect of the sons of Princess Diana after her death in 1999: they had become the children of the nation; they belonged to everyone. When someone is chosen as Thadadaho, it is said that he ceases to speak for or represent his own clan, but belongs to everyone.

enemy] Then the men said, 'Perhaps it would not result in good if they should see you, for possibly they would kill you on sight, because they do not know you?'"[74]

In a culture of revenge with no concept of forgiveness, there would have been a tendency for people to avoid travel,[75] to avoid the risk of being killed. For a stranger to appear alone in those days would have itself been remarkable. It would have aroused curiosity. It would have created an opportunity, an opening: "The word *stranger* denotes a living embodiment of that which is *strange*—from the Old French, *estrange*, extraordinary. Thus, the stranger functions as an unexpected messenger who can embody or mirror what is extraordinary within us, what is possible but yet unlived."[76]

Mindless Warfare

The Dark Times into which the Peacemaker was born involved cycles of war, bloodshed,[77] and revenge so dark and deep that nobody could remember how, or when, or why they had begun.

The Peacemaker, travelling swiftly, arrived at the mouth of the Oswego River, at the southeast end of Lake Ontario. There he found a timorous hunting party: people who had left their village because of the strife there,[78] but who were also engaged in the practical activity of gathering food. He told them to return to their settlement, to announce the good tidings.[79]

---

74   Gibson 1899, para. 22.

75   This, for example, had been the situation in Papua, where people avoided travel between valleys for fear of ambush, and where hundreds of languages developed in isolation from one another. In northeastern North America, the advent of agriculture and of this culture of fear and revenge was also marked by a radical change in trade; it seems there had been a more vigorous trade in earlier times.

76   Nepo 1995, 17.

77   Some versions blame the bloodshed on undisciplined young people, whose minds are restless—nithotiyén:sas ne tehonnatstikahwenhátye, "the young ones who are exploring about continually." The theme of curious young people uncovering matters that they should not, even graves, is echoed in the words of the Condolence. The young, whose minds are not seasoned, can be influenced to support peace, but are particularly susceptible to be drawn into anger and war. In the 2013 recital, Sakokwenionkwas Tom Porter said that the Peacemaker knew he was going to bring his message to a "merciless people."

78   In the 2013 recital of the law, Sakokwenionkwas Tom Porter said "they were too mean . . . they kill each other." A few Mohawk families leaving a town that has become violent or strife-torn is part of a pattern: Akwesasne was formed by families from Kahnawake in 1749; Wahta was created by families from Kanehsatake in the 1870s; Kanienkeh in the 1970s and Kanatsiohareke in the 1990s are further examples.

79   Parker (Chiefs) 1916, 67, 83.

Moreover he had journeyed some distance when suddenly at a distance he saw human beings moving about at the lake shore, so he directed his course there. Now in a very short time he beached his canoe there. Then he got out. Then he conversed with those men he had seen. Now then Deganawii'dah said, "Where do the people reside." The men replied saying, "Toward the sunrise (eastward)." Then Deganawii'dah said, "Indeed then it is a fact that no people lives here?" Then the men replied saying, "No" ["there are none."] Then Deganawii'dah said, "So then what is the reason that you are stirring about here?" The men replied saying, "Actually we are fugitives." Then Deganawii'dah asked saying "What is the reason that you are running away, for surely there is nothing amiss now?" The men said, "Understand that it so happened that where we lived our village was destroyed. So really we don't know the state of affairs there." Then Deganawii'dah inquired, "Who are these people who have destroyed your village?" The men answered, "It is indeed that person who continually harms us named Dehohsaheh'hwa, He whose house obstructs (the path).[80] Then Deganawii'dah said, "Now as for that, from now on that kind of work shall stop. Indeed understand that such an intention was not in the mind of the Creator of the earth and the sky-world. Moreover it is also my aim now to put a stop to the killing of one another, that too should cease. This is the reason that I am now traveling. So now you all must return home, go back there to the place where you all set out (which you abandoned)."[81]

This is not mere allegory. If the causes of the warfare had been known, a rational and powerful person like the Peacemaker would have sought to identify them, analyze them, and address them. Instead, he faced mindless warfare, without any discernible cause or origin. To stop the cycles of bloodshed, he could not go to their root. He had to address the symptoms first instead, to create the pause in the slaughter that would "allow the conversations to take place."[82]

---

80   Fenton (Gibson 1889, fn 13) suggests that a person whose house blocked communication within the symbolic Longhouse was "an obstructionist or saboteur of government."

81   Gibson 1899, paras. 17–20. The scattered people returning home is a recurring theme in the Kayanerenkó:wa, but it is also a theme in the eighteenth century, when the Haudenosaunee were spread from the Mohawk Valley to beyond the Ohio, and in the late seventeenth century, when the villages of the north shore of Lake Ontario were abandoned in a periodic strategic withdrawal. Consolidation and expansion seem to have been themes of Haudenosaunee history.

82   Sotsisowah John Mohawk saw peace as a process, and conversations as the medium by which the process worked. The conversation can begin only when there is a lull in the fighting, a pause in which the voice of reason can be heard.

In this time of bloodshed, the women and children were "made poor,"[83] because the men who bore the responsibility to protect them were instead threatening their safety. The poverty is not a lack of prosperity: it is a poverty of spirit, a sadness, a loss.

The Peacemaker and the Cannibal

The Peacemaker's first challenge, after landing on the southeast shore of Lake Ontario,[84] was his encounter with a monster—a man who had become an eater of human flesh.[85] "This man was a cannibal, and had left the settlement to which he belonged for a long time and lived by himself in an isolated place."[86]

Joseph Campbell wrote that a monster, in the mythology of most peoples on earth, is a creature that cannot distinguish what is real from what is not. Heroes, he says, do not attack the monster's strength—for monsters are endowed with great physical or spiritual power, too much for the hero to take on directly. Instead, heroes show their ingenuity and power by attacking the monster's weakness. Thus, Jack tricks the giant into falling down the beanstalk to his death. Hansel tricks the witch into thinking that the twig is his skinny finger; he tricks her again into looking into the oven, then kicks her in to her death. Rumpelstiltskin is tricked into saying his name. In Haudenosaunee myth, the Flying Head is tricked into eating hot coals, thinking they are roasted chestnuts, and the Stone Giant is tricked into drowning in the river.[87]

Human beings have no great speed, no fangs or claws or strength. They have a great mind as their most powerful weapon. The greatest heroes, in every culture, are the ones who demonstrate how that tool is used best.

In John Arthur Gibson's 1899 version, it is Hiawatha who is the Cannibal, and after his conversion to reason he becomes the Peacemaker's collaborator.

---

83   Odatsehte Howard Elijah, Great Law Recital, Oneida, 2013.

84   In Gibson's 1912 text, the Peacemaker deals with the Cannibal after he has persuaded the Mohawks to accept his message (72–95).

85   See Abler 1980, 309–16, Engelbrecht 2003, 44. What Abler sees as evidence of cannibalism is in part the archaeological evidence of the desiccated cadavers of the elevated winter graves being stripped of their flesh before being buried in a communal dead feast. But he also provides some convincing historical evidence.

86   Parker (Chiefs) 1916, 70.

87   Bruchac 1985, 161, 184.

In the Chiefs' Version, the Cannibal is Thadadaho,[88] though this does not really fit into a logical sequence. After all, if the Cannibal becomes a messenger for the Good Mind, then he should not backslide and become its greatest obstacle afterwards. More detailed versions tell of Thadadaho's slow descent into madness, at the same time as his ascent to Onondaga leadership. The latter is inconsistent with him becoming a hermit cannibal. In another version, the Cannibal is Tekarihoken, who not long afterwards is encountered again as a leader of the Mohawks, and later becomes their first sachem[89] (as, in the 1899 version, Hiawatha becomes a Mohawk leader along his path of bringing peace). This, too, is unlikely. The Cannibal may be more of a symbol than a person: unlike most other personages in the story of the peacemaking, his original name is never mentioned, and the Peacemaker does not give him a new name.

Perhaps the source of the confusion is that both Hiawatha and the Cannibal had left their communities and were living alone, in isolation. If the result of the Peacemaker's contact with the Cannibal is that the man's mind is completely changed for the good, then the Cannibal is not Hiawatha, who is found by the Peacemaker living alone, trying, in his grief, to raise up his mind again. The Peacemaker does not lift up the same person's mind twice. Hewitt suggested that Hiawatha was actually two different people, the Cannibal and the mourner.[90] Contrast this, though, with Gibson's 1899 version, in which the Cannibal is (or becomes) Hiawatha, and years later, as a Mohawk leader, suffers the tragedies that drive him alone into the forest. One problem with that is that it prolongs the Peacemaker's efforts, since in the interval between the conversion of the Cannibal and the Condolence of Hiawatha, the latter's daughters would have had to grow up.[91]

The point of this encounter is that the Cannibal's mind is *completely* changed. John Arthur Gibson's 1912 version avoids the controversy by not naming the Cannibal, and that is probably the cleanest approach. This is the first demonstration of the Peacemaker's ability and desire to cause people to abandon irrational behaviour. Hiawatha, Thadadaho, and Tekarihoken are each examples of other men converted to the Good Mind by the Peacemaker. He uses a different approach for each of them. The Cannibal, probably, is just a cannibal.

---

88   Parker (Chiefs) 1916, 69–70. Thadadaho appears early in some versions as the personification of all forms of obstacle and evil. In these versions, the changes in him take place in stages, and he is not completely transformed for the good until he is confronted directly, at his home, by all the chiefs and clan mothers together with the Peacemaker.

89   Native North American Travelling College 2000, 20. "The Peacemaker told Tekarihoken that because he was the first man who had accepted the 'Great Law of Peace' he would make him the first 'Sachem' in the Mohawk Nation."

90   Hewitt 1907b, 537–39.

91   In this narrative, many children seem to grow very quickly.

Skaniatariio John Arthur Gibson's 1912 version is detailed and structured:

> After Dekanawidah had departed in that direction [south] he came
> to a house belonging to a cannibal who had his house there. Then
> Dekanawidah went close to the house. Then, when he saw the man
> coming out,[92] departing, sliding down the hill to the river, and
> dipping water, thereupon Dekanawidah hurriedly climbed onto
> the house to the place where there was a chimney for the smoke
> to escape; he lay down on his stomach and looking into the house
> he saw that the task of breaking up meat and piling it up had been
> completed. Then the man returned, and he was carrying a drum with
> water in it. Thereupon he poured it into a vessel, put meat into the
> liquid, and hung the vessel up over the fire until it boiled. Moreover,
> the man watched it, and when it was done, he took down the ves-
> sel, placing it near the embers. Thereupon he said "Now indeed it is
> done. Moreover, now I will eat." Thereupon he set up a seat, a bench,
> thinking he will put it on there when he eats. Thereupon he went
> to where the vessel sat, intending to take the meat out of the liquid,
> when he saw, from inside the vessel, a man looking out. Thereupon
> he moved away without removing the meat, and sat down again on
> the long bench, for it was a surprise to him, seeing the man in the
> vessel. Thereupon he thought, "Let me look again." Thereupon he,
> Dekanawidah, looked again from above where the smoke hole was,
> again causing a reflection in the vessel, and then the man, standing
> up again, went to where the vessel sat, looked into the vessel again,
> saw the man looking out, and he was handsome, he having a nice
> face. Thereupon the man moved away again, and he sat down again
> on the long bench, and he bowed his head, pondering and thinking,
> "I am exceedingly handsome and I have a nice face; it is probably
> not right, my habit of eating humans. So I will now stop, from now
> on I ought not to kill humans anymore."[93] Thereupon he stood up
> again, went to where the vessel sat, picked up the vessel with the
> meat in it, and then he went out, sliding straight down the slope
> beside the river and near an uprooted tree he poured out the vessel

---

92 In the 1900 Chiefs' Version, the Peacemaker first sees the Cannibal carrying a human
body into the lodge.

93 In the Chiefs' Version, the wondrousness and greatness of the reflection, not the beauty
of the reflected face, causes the Cannibal to ponder: he says, "I did not know that I was
so strange a man. My mode of living must be wrong". . . . Then he arose, went to the
kettle and looked into it again, and he saw the same object—the face of a great man and
it was looking at him. Parker (Chiefs) 1916, 70.

full of meat.[94] Meanwhile Dekanawidah hurriedly climbed down again from on top of the house, and went to where he had gone, the man carrying the vessel containing human flesh. Just then, he having ascended the top of the hill, the one holding the vessel, the two met. Thereupon they both stopped, and the man said, "We two are meeting; where do you come from? We are strangers; what is your name?" Thereupon he began to speak, saying, "Really, it is true, we are strangers; it is the first time we have met. Now, moreover, I will tell you that the place I came from is the other side of the lake, and as to me, my name, indeed, is Dekanawidah."[95] Thereupon he said, "I will ask you what that is, that vessel you are holding?" and the man said, "It is surprising what happened: I was just about to take my meat out of the liquid to make a meal of it, when I examined it to see whether, indeed, it was done. And this: when I stood up next to the vessel, I looked into the vessel and I saw a man looking out. Now then, I went back to the long bench and sat down again and then I felt astonished at what was happening, for never had I looked and seen that kind of thing. Thereupon I thought 'I will repeat it and look again into the vessel.' Thereupon I stood up again and moved over next to the vessel, and I stood looking over where the meat was cooking in the vessel, and I saw the man looking out again; he was handsome, very handsome. Thereupon I unhooked the vessel, and placed it beside the fire. Then I sat down again on the bench, pondering, and thought, 'It is an amazing thing that I, indeed, am handsome, very handsome.' Thereupon I decided, 'Now I will stop eating humans, and now I will stop killing people.' Thereupon I again stood up, picked up the vessel, came out of the house and went near the hill to a tree that had uprooted itself; there I poured out the human flesh; so now I am stopping that work of mine. Only this, the vessel, that is what will remain, and I will use it for cooking meals."

Thereupon Dekanawidah said, "Now I understand everything; so now you will return, going to the village to tell your people, 'Now

---

94   Something that will not be seen again is placed in the hole left by an uprooted tree—like the weapons of war later in the story of the lawmaking. But, unlike the Peacemaker, the Cannibal cannot put the tree up again.

95   The Chiefs' Version repeats what may well be a reflection of Masonic ritual (many of the chiefs were Freemasons). The Cannibal asks the Peacemaker "who are you now speaking to me?" and the Peacemaker replies: "It is I who came from the west and am going eastward and am called Dekanawidah in the world." The Masonic recognition sequence involves one man remarking: "I see you have travelled," and the other responding, "Yes, from east to west." Parker (Chiefs) 1916, 68, 70, 71.

it is arriving, the Good Message, and also the Power, and also the Peace.' Now, indeed, you have ended your killing of humans."[96]

The Peacemaker observes the Cannibal from hiding for a while, before deciding what to do. This is prudent. Dealing with a deranged murderer is always dangerous, and the times themselves were black and perilous. In several other instances—notably later in his journeys when he eavesdrops on Hiawatha's efforts to create a way to raise up grieving people's minds—the Peacemaker also seems to sneak up on people. He watches and listens and then *thinks* before acting. A man alone, a stranger without family or friends, walking unannounced into any situation, would be vulnerable.

Observing before acting is not merely prudent; it is also a Haudenosaunee cultural trait.[97] As well, it is a sign of respect: repeatedly, in the story of the making of the Kayanerenkó:wa, the Peacemaker and Hiawatha do not rush to accept an invitation, but instead smoke or deliberate or think before doing so. To react in haste would be insulting, because it would imply that the proposition was not worthy of much thought.[98]

The encounter attests to the Peacemaker's ingenuity and power of mind (and extreme handsomeness and peacefulness of visage).[99] Mainly, though, the story of the Cannibal serves as a metaphor, a statement of a fundamental principle of the Kayanerenkó:wa. Sotsisowah explains:

> He began discussion in the bark hut of a man who was about to cut up a victim for the dinner pot. It was in that environment he offered the idea that all human beings possess the power of rational thought and that in the belief in rational thought is to be found the power to create peace.
>
> His words required considerable thought and understandably much discussion before his first student could take ownership of the ideas. He was not saying that human beings do not possess the potential for irrational thought. He was saying that *all* human beings possess the potential for rational thought.

---

96 Gibson 1912, 78–89.

97 In schools, Euro-Canadian teachers often express the wish that their Haudenosaunee students would be more "aggressive," answer questions more quickly, move faster. But the children have been taught to watch carefully before acting, and also that if an older person asks a question, it is impolite to answer quickly, because the questioner—and therefore the question—deserves respect and the benefit of thought.

98 Parker (Chiefs) 1916, 78.

99 There is a thread in the law, and in the culture, that appearance is linked to moral quality. The Peacemaker's handsomeness and goodness are linked, as are Thadadaho's twisted physical appearance and badness. In some versions of the law, physical deformities—lameness or blindness—disqualify a person being a chief.

Unless we believe that all human beings possess rational thought, we are powerless to act in any way that will bring peace short of the absolute destruction of the other. We cannot negotiate with irrational human beings. In order to negotiate with other human beings, we must believe in their rational nature. We must believe they are not suicidal or homicidal by nature, that we can reason with them. Thus the first principle that will bring us the power to act is the confidence in the belief that all people are rational human beings and that we can take measures to reach accord with them.[100]

There is no person, and no mind, that is so far gone that it cannot be changed by the power of the Good Message. If the person is acting irrationally, the tools that the law provides can bring reason back again.

When the Cannibal sees the Peacemaker's serene face and thinks: "That could be me," another fundamental principle of Haudenosaunee law and society is being enacted. The Peacemaker is, in effect, leading by example, showing the Cannibal that peace is possible, just as later generations of chiefs would set their own examples of conduct for the people.

The Peacemaker is also a risk taker. Other people would have avoided the Cannibal, for obvious reasons. He confronted Thadadahoh, whose ill will could have killed him. He faced Tsikonsaseh, who no doubt had her own armed guardians. To bring peace, again and again he acted with boldness. The Peacemaker's combination of personal courage and personal humility is especially admired among the Haudenosaunee.[101]

The Peacemaker and the Cannibal, in Skaniatariio's 1899 version, become collaborators and close friends. It happens thus: when the Cannibal has thrown out his stew of human flesh, he meets the Peacemaker:

> Now he who was standing there said, "It is true that just now I am seeking a congenial friend." Then he said, "Come, let's both go back inside."
>
> At that time they both went back inside the house and now the homeowner set the pot in its accustomed place. Then the homeowner said, "Be seated over there across the fire, here on this side I will sit down. You who visit my house (my guest) and I shall sit with the fire between us (occupy opposite sides of the fire); and the reason that this shall occur is that I have a new experience (message) to relate. Therefore I will relate it. So as owner of the house (host) I shall begin and I will tell it clear to the end. Then you in turn shall

---

100 Mohawk 1989, 220.

101 These are qualities that propel modern ironworkers, for example.

relate your message to the end. For surely, perhaps, you must bring some message."

At that time Deganawii'dah now said, "You and I entirely agree. Come, therefore, let it start."[102]

In this version, it is the Cannibal who describes some of the basic rules of procedure and seating of any council.[103] Either this process was already well-known to the people who became the Haudenosaunee before the Peacemaker brought the law, or this meeting of monster and lawbringer is another instance of collaborative lawmaking. Collaborative lawmaking, between the Peacemaker and Tsikonsaseh, between the Peacemaker and the chiefs, between the Peacemaker and Thadadaho, is the hallmark of Gibson's 1899 version.

The Cannibal describes the events that have led to his conversion. He then turns his mind to making things right:

"Then I thought I should see someone, that maybe one would visit my house and that he would tell me perhaps what I should do to make restitution to those minds I had offended by killing the people belonging to various bands (tribes), so that there might be a just peace again. Then I arose and took up the pot and went out from the house and descended the river bank, and there where there is an uprooted tree[104] I poured out the contents of the pot I carried, namely the flesh of a dead human being. Then I climbed the bank. I was surprised now, nearby you were walking along. At once my life rejoiced when I saw you. I thought 'That really fulfills my mind's desire, to meet a friend'. So now then I have finished. Now then in turn it rests with you. Moreover I in turn will listen to whatever message you bring."

Then Deganawii'dah stood up now and said, "Truly, what has happened this very day is indeed a wonderful story. Now you have changed the very pattern of your life. Now a new frame of mind has come to you, namely righteousness and peace. Right now you are seeking for someone to come tell you what you should do in order

---

102 Gibson 1899, paras. 41–43.

103 The host speaks first, and is uninterrupted; the visitor replies in full. They sit across the fire from each other.

104 Is this a fair description of a particular place—or a precursor of throwing the weapons of war into the pit created by the uprooted pine tree? Like the weapons, the meal of human flesh would never be seen again, like the covered bones of the dead after the Condolence. And in the Haudenosunee story of Creation, the uprooting of the Tree of Life is the precursor of the coming of death and the fall of Sky Woman to earth. Uprooting trees—and putting them back—is an essential image of Haudenosaunee meta-narrative and ceremony.

that peace shall prevail in the divers places in which you have done injury among mankind."[105]

The Peacemaker is replying in precisely the manner in which a skilled speaker moves matters along in council. He stands up—as speakers in council do, to be seen and heard, and out of respect—and he repeats the essence of what he has heard, to acknowledge it and to confirm that he has not misunderstood its import.[106] But, just as a speaker in council uses his reply to add another layer towards consensus, he adds to his account of what he has heard, in a way that presages his own message. In this way he links together his host's story and his own, "bridging" the thinking between them: in Hewitt's translation of Skaniatariio John Arthur Gibson, the key indicator of this is the word "moreover":

> "Now moreover I will tell you (what to do). This is the very message that I bring. I too am seeking a certain man (a friend) who would work with me, he and I would collaborate to advance the matter of Righteousness and Peace. Now indeed you and I have met, our two minds meet on the level (are quite agreed). Therefore this shall come to pass. So then you and I shall work together at preparing food. Accordingly you shall go for fresh water and you shall dip it from the river as it flows along.[107] As for me, I will go hunt for a game animal.[108] Moreover it is enough that when you will arrive back that you shall have the water hot by the time I shall return. Then at the same time you and I will work together at boiling the meat. At that time you and I will merge our two minds."

> At that time Deganawii'dah sat down again. Then the houseowner now stood up and said, "Exactly that is what I have in mind. Therefore it shall come about as you have outlined it."[109]

---

105 Gibson 1899, para. 44–46.

106 Since clear communication and understanding is essential to lawmaking and peacemaking, repeating the words back provides an opportunity to correct misunderstandings before they get worse. If there is an error in understanding a statement, it is gently corrected before the issue is fully considered and answered.

107 In making medicine, one always gathers water from the river in the direction of the flow. That is, one works with the water and its power, not against it. The Cannibal is assigned the task of bringing water partly as a means of purifying himself.

108 Kontírio, those animals that are destined to fall or give themselves to us, are a distinct kind of animal in Haudenosaunee languages.

109 "Outlined" is an unusual choice of words, but appropriate for Haudenosaunee councils, in which the matters agreed upon are not always decided with precision, nor do they need to be. What they decided together was clear enough, and detailed enough, that they could proceed.

Then Deganawii'dah arose and said, "So now in fact let us two depart. You shall go to fetch water, and I will go to hunt." At that time the two set out.[110]

The two men—all alone in the lodge—are nevertheless following the process of a formal council. Nor is it insignificant that the Peacemaker assigns separate tasks for each person: that is still a typical Haudenosaunee process for getting things done between meetings. The first thing they plan together as friends is a meal. Haudenosaunee tradition requires meals: "feasts" to mark transitions in life, as an integral part of ceremonies, including healing ceremonies, and as a prelude to councils.[111] Today, a feast shared by family and friends is an essential part of Haudenosaunee medicine, often used to assuage restless spirits, protect against those who send harm, and reconcile those who harbour hard feelings. Just as grief or fatigue are distractions to clear thinking, so is hunger. The meal is also a milestone: the Cannibal has changed what he eats.

Before the Dark Times, Haudenosaunee men lived by hunting. When times of war and revenge-taking came, they began to kill people; they became warriors. In that sense, the Cannibal was the ultimate warrior. When the Peacemaker taught him that he had to go back to eating venison,[112] he was also saying that the men had to turn from war back to hunting, their proper role. It was not just a change in what he ate: it was a fundamental change in how he led his life.

The Peacemaker and the (former) cannibal continue to work together: their collaboration in preparing the meal and the Cannibal's repentance lead to the creation of some of the fundamental symbols and ideas of Haudenosaunee law.

For example, the Peacemaker had killed a deer with quite large antlers. He then suggested to the former cannibal that "we two shall remove them and these antlers shall be placed here upon humans." This would have been the beginning of the idea of deer's antlers as the emblem of chieftainship.

Together, the two men clarified some of the principles by which Haudenosaunee society lives. The Cannibal had killed and killed. Now he shared responsibility for burying the dead. Today, funerals bring the people together. So does the annual ceremony for the dead. So do the many times the ancestors are invoked, mentioned in other ceremonies and speeches. In Haudenosaunee

---

110   Gibson 1899, paras. 47–49.

111   Kaientaronkwen Ernie Benedict suggests that Jacques Cartier's friends at the place he called Stadacona were really saying "Satekhón:ni"—"Let's eat." In the bleak uncertainty of the "Oka Crisis" of 1990, Sotsisowah John Mohawk set out as his fundamental rule of Haudenosaunee negotiations that "first, we eat: we don't know when we'll get another chance." The two men—Peacemaker and Cannibal—preparing a meal together is a beginning of their collaboration.

112   Hayadaha Richard Hill points out that diet has a profound effect on human behaviour, and that changing what we eat can change how we think and act. Again, as the Haudenosaunee are fond of saying, food is medicine.

thought, society is not only the people who are alive today, but also the dead and the unborn. By joining the Cannibal in burying the dead, the Peacemaker was providing another lesson in rejoining civil society.[113] Through their conversation and actions, the two helped develop the role of reason and "changing minds" in bringing peace:

> Then Deganawii'dah said: "Here in fact is the place where your wisdom (reasoning) lies." At that time he placed his two hands on the houseowner's head and then passed them down over his face, and Deganawii'dah said, One (the Master of Life) has brought you mind (reason). Now moreover you and I will look into the pot." At that time the two looked into the pot, and for a fact the two men saw that their two bodies appeared identical in the reflections from the depths of the pot.
>
> Then the owner of the house said, "It is wonderful that you and I have similar forms (appearances)." Then Deganawii'dah said, "In fact it is true that he (the Master of Life) has endowed us both with reason (mind)."[114]

As men's bodies are similar, so are they equal in their ability to reason, the Peacemaker was saying, and so are they equal in their potential to come within the peace that he was building. We are all human together, and therefore all potentially brothers and sisters. We have all been given minds.

The Peacemaker passing his hands over the former cannibal's face presages Hiawatha's combing out Thadadaho's hair and straightening out the kinks in his body. The Peacemaker may have been removing the physical manifestations of the twisted nature of the Cannibal's mind, "rubbing him down." By making the former cannibal look again at the reflections in the pot, the Peacemaker was both explaining the trick he had used and transforming that trick into a lesson about the nature of humanity.

The story of the Peacemaker and the Cannibal is the first in a series of demonstrations of a basic principle of the law: that all humans are capable of

---

113 The Peacemaker and the former cannibal went back to the place where the human remains had been dumped out of the pot, and they went to the edge of a high riverbank and dug a trench, and placed the body in it, and covered it with earth. The Peacemaker then said: "Now we two have finished it. So thus it shall continue to be in the future days to come that each individual shall be equally bound (responsible) to care for the body of a man." Gibson 1899, para. 57. At the 2013 recital of the law, at Oneida, it was stated that the Peacemaker told the Cannibal to clean up his house, and all the bones that had been strewn around the house—a precursor of the way the bones of the dead would be hidden as part of the Condolence. Just as seeing the positive symbols of the peace—the eagle, longhouse, and pine tree—would remind people of the law, so seeing human remains and disorder would place them in a dark frame of mind.

114 Gibson 1899, paras. 54–55.

rationality. They may be *behaving* irrationally, but if we are to have peace with them, we must find a way to address that behaviour and to restore the Good Mind in them. Otherwise, we will not have peace, since we will always have to be prepared to defend ourselves. We therefore have an obligation to help one another. When we find a person who is behaving irrationally, we have both an interest and an obligation to create peace through reason, for it is our peace as well as theirs. As Sotsisowah John Mohawk would say, we have to negotiate with their humanity. If there were any doubts that the lessons to be learned from the Peacemaker's conversion of a single demented individual could be extrapolated to address a whole people, the Peacemaker removed that doubt in their next conversation:

> Then the owner of the house said, "What do you mean when you say 'Justice and Peace'? What will occur when these shall be accomplished?"
>
> Then Deganawii'dah said: "By these I mean that this very day you have changed the disposition of your mind. And moreover it shall come about that all mankind shall change the disposition of their minds now prevalent. That means that this reformation shall begin at once, and Justice and Peace shall increase continually."[115]

Announcing Peace

Peace is coming, announces the Peacemaker. The bloodshed and the warfare and the revenge-taking are ending. Peace is inevitable. It is on its way. In most versions of the law, the Peacemaker is careful not to say that *he* is making or bringing peace, but rather that peace is arriving. He is only its herald, not its author. In later accounts, and especially Euro-American accounts, this crucial humility is missed.[116] Indeed, the word and idea of a "Peacemaker" is likely not Haudenosaunee, and not contemporaneous with the arrival of the Great Peace. Peace is coming as surely as the sunrise, Tekanawita assured the people. They had to believe it, and believe in it. Both culturally and linguistically, his use of terms of absolute certainty was part of the power of the message. To a people whose sense of the future is expressed grammatically in indefinite terms, the

---

115 Gibson 1899, paras. 59–60. The statement that "Justice and Peace shall increase continually" is a forerunner of the idea that the Great White Roots of Peace shall spread these principles to the four directions, across the earth.

116 Similar modesty appears in most of the New Testament, in which Jesus refers to himself most consistently only as the "son of man," rather than as the son of God.

clarity and confidence of the words were stunning. To accentuate this certitude, he linked it to another: that the sun comes up every day:

> Moreover, at present it is young as the day is when the sun is rising and lights up the earth; just as it causes warmth all over the earth and for all the people, we will help the people of every nation.[117] And just as all of the many things that grow on earth and sustain the people, the newly arriving Great Law will come to shed light on the minds of the people, the elders and the younger people, everybody, even the children, and this is what you will work at: everyone shall become related to one another, so that it will become a single family consisting of every tribe; and they will be kind to one another, all of the people; and this is what will unite them: the Good Message, and the Power, and the Peace.[118]

By staying focussed on the message of peace and the impending peace itself, rather than upon the messenger, the Haudenosaunee avoided becoming adherents to a messianic religion. Instead, the Kayanerenkó:wa, and not its bringer, became the Way.

The counterpoint to this message is not a denial, but an impatient, almost pestering question: in Gibson's 1899 version, Thadadaho repeatedly asks, Is it here yet?[119] His persistent question suggests that the people trapped in the cycle of bloodshed yearn to emerge, even as they maintain it. The question comes from the most unexpected source. The reply that it is still coming, still on its way, still being built, is part of the lesson that things take as long as they take;

---

117 The sun reappears in the ceremony of Condolence. The grieving people's faces are cast down, and their clear-minded friends remind them that they must believe that the sun will come up again tomorrow, and that their families and children still need them. The sun represents hope as well as constancy.

118 Gibson 1912, 127–29.

119 Why would Thadadaho keep asking this? Perhaps because the Peacemaker had met with him earlier, telling him that "I aim to prepare your mind (promise) for what shall happen so that you shall know that there shall come a day when I shall come with Hiawatha. And that will surely happen. We shall discuss together matters of Righteousness and Peace. At that time this man (stranger) replied, 'When will this be…?'" (Gibson 1899, paras. 30–31). By 1912, and in the Chiefs' Version, some of the contradictions and difficulties surrounding the role of Thadadaho are gone. The story is more cohesive if the killer is not Thadadaho, and if he is not both an obstacle to peace and impatient for it to arrive.

that one must have the patience to do things properly. It remains true that the peace is still, and will always be, being built.[120]

Skaniatariio John Arthur Gibson's 1899 Version

Skaniatariio John Arthur Gibson's 1899 narrative, dictated to J.N.B. Hewitt, follows a different pattern than others. The Peacemaker does not bring a complete message. He announces the Three Words, and then engages in a series of conversations and collaborations with the people he meets in his travels. His first collaboration is with Tsikonsaseh. His second and greatest is with the former cannibal Hiawatha. The constitutional aspects of the law result from later discussion among the chiefs, with the Peacemaker asking questions and the chiefs replying. It is almost like a bilateral Socratic conversation, with the Peacemaker each time guiding the flow of the discussion towards the structure he was seeking to build.

Hiawatha and the Peacemaker create parts of the law through a combination of prophecy—the Peacemaker explains things to Hiawatha that will take place[121] and then they happen—and suggestion and dialogue with the people they meet. This version reflects the back-and-forth nature of council proceedings, and also the way that Haudenosaunee decisions are not unilateral, and not one person's ideas, but rather the result of collaboration, cooperation, conversation, and thinking together. People are more likely to support and spread ideas if they believe they were among the originators of those ideas, the makers of the narrative. The Peacemaker acts as moderator as well as prophet. The Peacemaker is able to predict—but not prevent—misfortunes, and this is an indicator of his special powers. He is more of a catalyst, less of a lawbringer. He carries ideas, not stone tablets.

---

120 A theme of Haudenosaunee meta-narratives is the tension between impatience reflecting an immediate need, and the patience required to do things right. Amber Meadow Adams points out that tension in the Creation Story, a tension between the need to eat and survive right now, and the need to allow crops to mature, to store seed for the future, and to prepare foods carefully. It is the tension between the survival strategies of hunters and horticulturalists, and between Thaharionwakon, who is patiently preparing succulent corn, and his grandmother, who casts ashes on that corn because he will not share it immediately. "Is it here yet?" is properly answered with "Be patient. It is surely coming.".

121 The Peacemaker predicts that Hiawatha will join the Mohawks, will marry the Chief's daughter, and then will lose his family and exile himself in grief. The Peacemaker also makes predictions in dealing with Tsikonsaseh and Thadadaho; and generally, his vision of the law and the Longhouse can be called a prediction, as well. The ability to predict the future—to *see* the future—is supernatural (and is also a trait shared by other fatherless men of various cultures).

Tsikonsaseh: The Women's Side

The Peacemaker pursued a deliberate strategy of seeking out the very worst people, to show that even they could be converted to peace and goodness by the power of his message.[122] Again and again, he is told about a person who is feared, hated, or just dangerous, and he immediately finds that person and begins the conversation of peace. Sometimes it takes several meetings, spread over months and even years.

There are two sides to everything—night and day, old and young, good and bad—and so there are to all things a male and a female. Once he had dealt with a male monster—the Cannibal—and the grieving man—Hiawatha—the Peacemaker then turned to the female side.[123] A woman was keeping a house on the Warriors' Path[124] and was actively encouraging men to fight and kill one another. Her house lay along the path; just as later in the story, Thadadaho's location on the path made him an obstacle to the peace, so Tsikonsaseh's house permitted her to facilitate the conduct of war.[125] In some traditions, though, this woman was already an influence for peace, the Peacemaker's female counterpart, even as she lent sustenance to men along their path to make war:

> So then thereafter the nations of them that were Oweh[126] called the Great Woman, Yegowaneh, but through all the generations the Great Woman's name was Ji-kon-sa-she, the Lynx. Now in the territory of the Cultivators there was no war. Bands of warriors passed from east to west and from west to east through the paths of the Cultivators and delivered peace belts to Yegowaneh. So likewise, bands of warriors passed from south to north and from north to south through the territory of the Cultivators and delivered belts of peace because

---

122 Mohawk 1987, 10–17.

123 In Gibson's 1912 version, the Peacemaker deals with the Cannibal and Tsikonsaseh after bringing the Mohawks to support the message, but before condoling Hiawatha.

124 Sotsisowah John Mohawk, drawing on Seneca oral tradition, believed that Tsikonsaseh was a Neutral or Attiwandaron, with the Warriors' Path running between Haudenosaunee and Huron country.

125 In the Federal Court trial *Almrei v. Canada*, I learned of Afghan "guest houses," which the Government of Canada considered to be places that encouraged and fostered conflict because they would welcome all visitors, including active warriors. As places where fighters could congregate, they were suspected of being staging and planning areas. Some guest houses were well known as Al Qaeda quarters.

126 Ón:kwe—"original"; onkwehón—"original people."

the Great Woman was the Mother of Nations. She would provide food for the War Captains and then exhort them to follow the paths of peace since all men are brothers who are Oweh. It was therefore said, "the path of war runs through the House of Peace."[127]

A woman living alone in a time of warfare and bloodshed probably also had strong spiritual power,[128] perhaps even a reputation for witchcraft.[129] She had a great power of persuasion: the Peacemaker determined to transform that power for the good:

> Then Dekanawidah also said . . . I shall visit the west first. I shall visit there the house of this woman, Tsikonsaseh. The reason why I shall do this (go and visit this woman first) is because the path passes there which runs from the east to the west.
>
> Then after saying these words Dekanawidah went on his way and arrived at the house of Tsikonsaseh and said to her that he had come on this path which passed her home and which led from the east to the west, and on which traveled the men of blood-thirsty and destructive nature.
>
> Then he said unto her, "It is your custom to feed these men when they are traveling on this path on their war expeditions." He then told her that she must desist from practising this custom. He then told her that the reason she was to stop this custom was that the Kariwiio or Good Tidings of Peace and Power had come.[130]

Tsikonsaseh had been encouraging, supplying, and feeding the warriors. No good reason is provided for her doing so. As in the case of the Cannibal, one

---

127   Parker 1919, 45–46.

128   Though numerous early writings, and some of J.N.B. Hewitt's work, refer to spiritual power among the Haudenosaunee as orenda, and some of the explanations are complex, there is both little mention of orenda as a factor in the law and little discussion of it today in modern Haudenosaunee communities. It may usefully be compared to *mana* in Maori law, as a concept of spiritual power that has no European equivalent or clear translation.

129   Witchcraft, in the Haudenosaunee sense, is a term applied to the work of a person, male or female, intended to harm others through the misuse of spiritual or spirit power. While some people use the term "bad medicine," other thoughtful people say that the source is not potions or rituals, but rather the focused direction of ill will against another person. It implies the harmful use of the forces of the natural world. Generally, it is expected that this will return to harm the person practising the witchcraft. In Europe, the extended war of the Catholic Church against witchcraft was often directed against herbalists, practitioners of pre-Christian religions, and generally against those accused of using supernatural (rather than natural) powers. As well, in Europe, the majority of those accused of witchcraft were women.

130   Parker (Chiefs) 1916, 71.

issue to be addressed with the coming of the peace is that people must change what and how they eat, or what and why they feed others. There is a tradition that Tsikonsaseh tried to poison the Peacemaker. Tsikonsaseh offered the Peacemaker what appeared to be a delicious meal. What he saw in the bowl, though, was a mass of writhing worms. He refused to eat this, and asked her to prepare him a proper meal. She did so, as part of repenting her evil ways and converting to peace.[131]

Part of the transformation was of the path itself: with her acceptance of the Good Message, the great east–west path of the Longhouse[132] changed from being the Warriors' Path and became the path of peace depicted on the Hiawatha wampum, joining the nations together.

In Gibson's 1912 recollection, after the Peacemaker changes the mind of the unnamed cannibal, he proceeds to reason with Tsikonsaseh:

> Thereupon Dekanawidah departed and he arrived at the waterfalls on the easterly side of the river where she had her house, a lone female. Then Dekanawidah said, "As to you, I believe, this is your home." Thereupon the woman said, "Indeed, it is I who have this house." Thereupon Dekanawidah said, "What is your name?" and she said, "As to me, indeed, my name is Tsikonsaseh." Then Dekanawidah said, "you are indeed the person who has done a lot of work in relation to the warpath. Furthermore a path passes through here and this is how they cross over here, the warriors. As to these, repeatedly when they show up here, you share food with them; indeed, repeatedly, when they finish eating, they go on to kill people and also to scalp them. And when these warriors return, they stop here again, and again you feed them, doing so repeatedly, and you help both sides, those living to the west and to the east. So now you will stop; now, indeed, it is coming, the Good Message, also the Power, and also the Peace. Now, moreover, you will depart and towards the east that is where you will go. On the third day, indeed, you will become a peace chief and a leader for the Good Message, the Power and the Peace."[133]

---

131 Control over food is crucial to many societies. The women's role in providing food, as Tsikonsaseh did, can be seen as an exercise of authority rather than subservience.

132 The present route of the New York State Thruway follows the Great Path rather faithfully. See Morgan (1851) 1995, 44–45: "This route of travel was so judiciously selected that after the country was surveyed, the turnpikes were laid out upon the Indian highway, with slight variations, through the whole length of the State. This trail not only connected the principal village of the Iroquois, but established the route of travel into Canada on the west, and over the Hudson on the east."

133 Gibson 1912, 90–93.

The Peacemaker offered Tsikonsaseh political authority within the League (becoming "a peace chief and leader") in exchange for her support. It was pragmatic to do so, and consistent with the approach he later used with Thadadaho and with the Seneca warriors. In each case he recognized ability, talent, and possibility, and instead of seeking to destroy a threat, he succeeded in transforming it into a power for peace. He also used the power of logic and persuasion, the power of reason and the Good Mind. She was not naturally irrational: by promoting war, she was just *behaving* irrationally.

The crucial role played by Tsikonsaseh in the formation of the League illustrates the need to address both the male and the female side, and to keep them in balance.[134] She does not travel with the Peacemaker during his work with the nations, but she reappears towards the end of his work to add her powerful voice to the conversion of Thadadaho. Without her, without the women's voice, the work of peace would have failed.

In Gibson's 1899 version, Tsikonsaseh is the name of the Peacemaker's mother. But in that case it is likely that there is a second Tsikonsaseh, the great clan mother, Mother of the Nations,[135] with whom he discusses, and begins to formulate, the structure and laws that will bring peace. It is this Tsikonsaseh who helps him refine his ideas, and who suggests the women's role in the law—and the Peacemaker accepts that suggestion. By 1912, Gibson names Kahetehsuk as the Peacemaker's mother, but still refers at one point to Tsikonsaseh as his mother, as well:

> At that time Deganawii'dah said, "Now moreover I will go on [continue traveling][continue on my way]." The men replied saying, "Something which you might begin by doing is to visit the *goyaanehgoo'nah*,[136] the great matron whose house stands not far away." Then Deganawii'dah said, "Who is it? What is she

---

134 Barbara Graymont, without citing a source, states that once she was persuaded to become an advocate of the peace, the Peacemaker gave the woman the name "Jigonsasee, or New Face, because she reflected the New Mind," putting her past behind her (Graymont 1988, 25). Most other versions state that this was the woman's name before she met the Peacemaker. The name can also mean "Fat Cheeks," a term used to describe the lynx, which has led some to suggest that she was of the Erie or Cat Nation. Tom Hill says there is a legend that Thadadaho married Tsikonsaseh once he was transformed, the snakes combed from his hair, his limbs straightened, and his mind made good.

135 According to Seneca tradition, her name becomes a title, as her people become part of the Haudenosaunee (Parker 1919, 46). Thus, it was entirely possible for her to be of the Erie or "Cat Nation." Historically, the Eries lived west of Niagara. They were absorbed by the Senecas, and another Tiskonsaseh, generations later, was the leader of a peace village near the Genesee River in Seneca country.

136 "The great female title holder or chieftainess, or matron, or clan mother, is the head of a clan and household in Iroquois society." Fenton, in Gibson 1899, fn. 15.

named?" The men replied, "She is the one people call Djigohsa'hseh."
Deganawii'dah replied saying, "that is true, indeed" . . .

And so when he arrived at the place where her lodge stood he saw a
woman; then he said, who is the owner of the lodge standing there?
The woman responded saying, "I myself." Then he inquired further,
saying, "What then are you called?" She said, "Indeed, as for me,
Djigonhsah'seh is my name." Then he said, "She too is the one I am
looking for." Djigonhsah'seh now said, "Who then are you? From
what place do you come?"

Then he replied saying, "In this direction from the north side of
yonder beautiful lake[137] I have come. As for me, I am the one who
is named Deganawii'dah" (At once now she recognized him as her
own son. Truly now they both were satisfied).

Then at that time Djigonhsa'seh said, "Come, therefore, relate
then the nature of the message which you bring." Now then
Deganawii'dah said, "The message itself which I am bringing
is—*ga:iwi'yoh* (justice and righteousness); *ske:non* (peace), and
ga'shasdeen'shen (civil authority)."

Now the woman (his mother, *honoo'ha*) said, "That too shall come
to be, and first of all you shall stop (remain) here. And in the first
place I will prepare food. And when it is cooked (I have it cooked,
ready) then at that time you and I shall eat, indeed we two will eat
together, and the reason for this is because the nature of the message
which you bring is indeed very important and I am pleased with it."

Now then Deganawii'dah said, "I approve (accept – take hold of?
–) of the inclination of your mind (proposal). I also am pleasantly
surprised (pleased)."[138]

Why would the Peacemaker be pleasantly surprised that his mother would
accept his message and show him hospitality? Why did she not already know
the message he was carrying, since he had explained it to her before he left
home? This woman was not his biological mother, but rather someone who had
declared her kinship with him because of his mission. By adopting his message,
she had also adopted the man himself. "Mother" is not a term of biology, in this
context, but rather an address of respect. Their stay together is an opportunity
for dialogue, a two-sided, back-and-forth conversation in which the Mother of
Nations provides her own ideas and support, extending her protection to the
man with the message. Rather than provide food for the warriors, she is about

---

137 "Beautiful Lake" translates as "Oniatariio," now Lake Ontario.

138 Gibson 1899, paras. 24a–27.

to prepare a feast to welcome the message of peace. The good health that the good food provides reflects the spiritual health fostered by their discussions and agreements. The Peacemaker and the Mother of Nations bring their minds together to give names and form to the symbolic Longhouse:

> Then at that time Djigonhsa'seh prepared food. When she had finished then indeed the two did eat together.[139] When they two had finished (eating) the woman said, "Now surely this is fulfilled, both our minds are fully satisfied. So now I will ask you, what use will you make then of the propositions which you bring, that is, of Peace and Righteousness (justice) and the force of Law? The situation in the direction you are going is dangerous. There are dwelling in the direction you are going men who are really evil. They hunt people and kill them and they eat their flesh. A male person moreover whose house stands not far from here likewise eats humans."

> Then Deganawii'dah said, "In fact understand that I am trying to have this kind of business stopped. [This is, I understand, the kind of business I am trying to have stopped.] [Nay'ehseh.]" And then he asked, saying, "What then do you think (what is your opinion) of the propositions that I have brought with me? Do you yourself accept the (principles of) justice, and of peace and civil authority?"

> Djigonsah'seh said, "So what is the meaning of the message, the significance of the principles, which you bring?" Deganawii'dah said, "Indeed the meaning of Righteousness and of Peace and of Order is just this: that when the habitual killing of human beings shall have stopped, then peace shall prevail, and bands of people shall travel about from place to place where they reside, and also the individual maternal families (may come and go freely); all mankind shall continue peacefully to love one another."

> At that time Djigonhsa'seh said, "It is true indeed that the message which you bring is most important. So now I accept it; therefore I approve the work that you are advancing. What will you call it when it is completed?"

> Then Deganawiid'dah said, "I will call it *Ganonhsyo:ni*, the Extended House (the League), and also I will designate it *Gayenehsahgo:nah*,

---

139 Sharing a meal comes before doing business. In historic times, the visitors would be welcomed at the woods' edge; they would be fed; and then they would recover from their fatigue by delaying council until the next day. While the Peacemaker shares meals with his dangerous hosts, he does not risk falling asleep, but remains vigilant and moves directly to the business at hand after the meal.

the great law or commonwealth.[140] And the reason it shall have the name the Extended House is that in fact it shall come to resemble only a single household (*sganonh'sadah*) when it is finished; and furthermore the mind or reason will become the source of law (*Gayanenhseh*), or human welfare; thinking shall replace killing and welfare eventuate; and thus we shall all be peacefully disposed in the minds of the constituent maternal families; therefore it will unite the minds, and it shall be called *gayanehsa'goonah*, the great law or commonwealth. Moreover, this (institution) shall endure as long as there continues to be a single maternal family and until that time when the Holder of the Heavens will bring about a transformation of things on the earth."

At that time Djigonhsa'seh now said, "Now apparently I understand (comprehend) the whole affair (proposition), so now I accept it (I have taken hold of it)."[141] Deganawii'dah said, "Moreover this shall come about in the future that then the women shall possess the title to chieftainship (*gayaneh'dah*) [belonging to her maternal family]; and the reason for this is that you my mother were the first to approve (the principles) of Righteousness and Peace. So now then I shall move on."[142]

Barbara Mann believes that Tsikonsaseh is even more important than the existing versions of the Kayanerenkó:wa suggest: she blames the "European-centered and male-centered nature of existing history" for largely ignoring her role in insisting on gender balance in the law.[143] "It is only after the Peacemaker agrees to her terms that she throws her considerable political weight behind him. . . . She was, in short, invaluable as an ally, invincible as a foe. To succeed, the Peacemaker needed her."[144] Yet it is equally gender centred to suggest that

---

140 "Commonwealth" is not about common "wealth" but rather "weal": wellness, health, and goodness.

141 "Taking hold of it," as a token of accepting a proposition, becomes physical when the representative of a nation accepts wampum put forward across the council fire.

142 Gibson 1899, paras. 28–33.

143 "[Jingosaseh's] name has been obliterated from the white record because her story was a woman's story and nineteenth-century male ethnographers simply failed to ask women, whose story hers was, about the history of the League." Mann 1995; see also Mann 2000.

144 Mann 1995. For a more modern reminder of the authority of individual women in Haudenosaunee history, and of European recognition of this power, consider Konwatsionnwenni Mary Brant, who was said to have been able to command more men to fight than any other Mohawk, and who was the wife of Warraghyihagey William Johnson, Imperial Superintendent General of Indian Affairs. It is also unlikely that Europeans would have been ignorant of the role of Haudenosaunee women in the "mourning wars" of the seventeenth century.

the Peacemaker was incapable on his own to require and recognize the role of women in the constitution, and it is Tsikonsaseh's conversion to the Good Mind, rather than her "terms," that are important to the making of the law. Mann's interpretation might please some feminists, but there is no need to assume that "gender balance" was resisted by the Peacemaker—who designed balance into all other aspects of the law—or even that the balance was not his idea. Perhaps Tsikonsaseh is the only prominent woman named in the lawmaking and peacemaking process, yet for every chief there is a woman who selects and confirms him; for every male aspect of the law there is a corresponding female side. To an outsider, and especially one who sees only the Grand Council in operation as a government, the law does seem male dominated, with the female aspects not in evidence. To an insider, the influence of Haudenosaunee women is so powerful that it must trace its roots to before the founding of the law. The Peacemaker was raised by women, in isolation. The first Creator on earth was not the twins, but rather Sky Woman, who danced the earth into being on the turtle's back and planted the first seeds. To an insider, the equal presence of men and women at the civil ceremonies of the Haudenosaunee is a powerful indication of the vitality of the women's role in society.

The Peacemaker acknowledges Tsikonsaseh's power and creates a corresponding authority. He transforms her from a force for war to a force for peace. This is part of his approach to lawmaking: again and again, he recognizes the abilities and capacities of the people who challenge him, and once he has persuaded them to accept his vision, he explains to them how they will take part in bringing that vision to reality. From keeper of the house of war, Tsikonsaseh is changed by the Peacemaker into a keeper of the Good Message: "I shall, therefore, now change your disposition and practice. . . . I now charge you that you shall be the custodian of the Good Tidings of Peace and Power, so that the human race may live in peace in the future."[145]

He places a further burden upon her: to assist him in the final confrontation with Thadadaho: "You shall therefore now go east where I shall meet you at the place of danger (Onondaga) where all matters shall be finally settled and you must not fail to be there on the third day."[146]

---

145 Parker (Chiefs) 1916, 71. "Charge," in this context, means to place a burden upon someone.

146 This is one of the instances in the reciting of the law where it becomes clear that time is fluid. The Peacemaker could not have intended Tsikonsaseh to travel to Onondaga three days from then, because he still had not brought a single nation into agreement with his message, and Onondaga would have been three days' travel away from the western lands where Tsikonsaseh lived.

Tsikonsaseh is like the Peacemaker, in that her name does not become a title.[147] She becomes his female counterpart, a leader for peace (a "peace chief") in her own right. As an Erie she would not have had a family among the Five Nations. Like the Peacemaker, she is an outsider of influence; like him, she has no successor today.[148]

Hiawatha: The Man of Sorrows

Hiawatha,[149] it is generally agreed, was a great man among the Onondagas who had gone to live among the Mohawks.[150] In some versions of the Kayanerenkó:wa, the Peacemaker either does not appear at all, or is relegated to a minor role, while Hiawatha is given the credit for the idea of the League and for most of the work of bringing it together. Among the modern Haudenosaunee, though, the strongest, most consistent tradition is that the two men worked closely as partners, each drawing from the strengths and gifts of the other. In Gibson's 1899 version, Hiawatha is the reformed cannibal, who later becomes a Mohawk leader[151] and (as predicted by the Peacemaker) suffers the loss of his entire family. In the 1912 version, the Peacemaker and Hiawatha have already

---

147   There is, however, a Seneca tradition that the name did indeed become a title, and that in the mid-1800s Caroline Parker at Tonawanda carried it: see Morgan (1871) 1997.

148   In the case of the Peacemaker, though, there is a second reason for not giving his name to anyone else: he did not die, and no two people alive at the same time should have the same name.

149   To avoid confusion, I have spelled the name "Hiawatha" throughout. John Norton, using late seventeenth-century Mohawk–English orthography, spelled it "Hayouwaghtengh." More proper modern Mohawk spelling would be "Aionwat'ha"; others would spell it "Hayonwatha."

150   In Gibson's 1912 version of the Great Law, Hiawatha is a Mohawk chief who gathers his people together after the Peacemaker passes the "test" imposed by the Great Warrior. Only after the Mohawks accept the law does Hiawatha suffer the loss of his daughters and go off to live by himself. The other two Mohawk chiefs try to console him after the death of his first daughter, but the death of the second sends him into deep grief and withdrawal. Gibson 1912, 120, 134–35.

151   Hiawatha had rescued the Peacemaker from the gorge at Cohoes Falls, and the two had agreed that they would "exchange roles," so that Hiawatha would emerge from the test and work with the Mohawks, while the Peacemaker would travel to Cayuga country. Gibson 1899, paras. 79–82. He is then given the Mohawk chief's comeliest daughter in marriage (an unlikely scenario in a matrilineal society in which fathers had little influence over their daughters' choices). He then becomes one of the three head chiefs of the Mohawks, and the other two chiefs, Tekarihoken and Satekariwate, attend and participate in Hiawatha's wedding feast, at which he announces the coming league and law (Gibson 1899, paras. 94–105).

worked together, and Hiawatha has taken his place as a Mohawk chief (that nation having accepted the peace), when tragedy strikes.

Hiawatha, married to a Mohawk woman and living among the Mohawks[152] as a leader, is stricken by a series of calamities.[153] Upon the death of his last daughter, he is plunged into the deepest grief. He leaves his people and goes to live by himself in the forest:[154]

> Now his mind was stricken with grief and Hiawatha now said, "Of course I shall be unable perhaps to perform work of the mind because of the awful thing which has befallen me."
>
> Now, at that time, the people resident there thought of nothing that they could do to make Hiawatha have peaceful thoughts (be well disposed thereafter). It was Satekaríwate[155] who said, "It might be a good thing if we could divert the mind of our leader (great one)."
>
> Now the inhabitants assembled (got ready), and now indeed they attempted to divert his mind. But his mind refused to leave off grieving. They resorted to all those things which they thought would perhaps divert his mind . . .

Before he can recover from this first tragedy, Hiawatha suffers the loss of the rest of his family (in some versions, his fellow Mohawk chiefs seek to console him by arranging a lacrosse game, the very sport that led to more death in Hiawatha's family):

---

152 What is the thinking behind matrilocality—moving to live with one's wife's people and family? Snow expressed the belief that it promoted peace within the community by breaking up the natural fighting unit, a band of brothers. The true reason may be simpler: the land was women's business, because they worked together in groups, and therefore needed to get along together. Men, hunting and fishing, often alone, might be considered more interchangeable.

153 In Gibson's 1899 version, the Peacemaker had predicted this: "You shall know what will happen when Dehadodaaho becomes troubled in mind (impatient) and vengeful against you. It is such that your daughter will be carried away when there he raises his voice in shouting. Three times it will repeat and reverberate over the forests. So it is that as soon as you are bereft of all your daughters then at that time you shall go away (from home). And then moreover when you will leave then you shall say, 'Now my heart is filled with anger (I am angered), furthermore I will split the sky (go southward), and at some distant place, perhaps, one will have pity on me, one there will wipe away my tears for what has befallen me.' At that time you shall go away (depart). It is a fact of course that we two shall meet again at that place" (Gibson 1899, para. 84). Thus, in the 1899 version, the events that in other versions are meetings are actually reunions, predicted by the Peacemaker, as part of his power or gift.

154 Delos Big Kittle of Cattaraugus, in 1905, asserted that Hiawatha was living alone because "Thadahaho slew all my brothers and drove me away." Parker (1923) 1989, 404.

155 In the 1899 text, Shaʔdegaaihwaaʔdeʔ.

Then Hiawatha spoke, saying, "Awfully grave is the thing which has happened. Now, of course, the thing on which my mind depended has become extinct. Now, indeed, all my offspring have died out."

Now it was that he went forth from the lodge and he stood there out of doors. At this time the company of warriors was engaged in a ball game on the flats.[156] At this time the wife of Hiawatha too came out front and went down to the river bank there to fetch fresh water from the stream that flowed along there. So just as she turned about the crowd shouted saying "What kind of animal is it that is calling this way?"[157] At this moment everyone ran towards it and said, "Come, let's grab it." Then Hiawatha saw for a fact it came flying there. It fell right where she who had gone for water had been walking at the moment the men ran up.

They never noticed that the wife of Hiawatha was walking there as they were all looking up at what was flying there. They trampled her under foot crushing her and as a consequence she died there. For she was then about to have a child. Thereupon Hiawatha said, "Now indeed I am left utterly alone—a widower. So then I shall now go away. So then also I will split the sky (go directly south).[158] At some distant place someone may take pity on me and will wipe away my tears and also rub down my body."[159]

Sakokwenionkwas Tom Porter explained in 2013: "Hiawatha walked aimlessly. If he were to die in his wandering he would not care."

So it is that when the Peacemaker meets him, Hiawatha is living far to the south, alone in his grief:

> . . . Dekanawidah arose when Hiawatha had entered and he said: "My younger brother I perceive that you have suffered from some deep grief. You are a chief among your people and yet you are wandering about."

---

156 This earthly lacrosse game may be a reflection of the similar game in the Creation story that contributed to Sky Woman's fall to earth. In Gibson's 1912 version, it is not Hiawatha's wife but his last surviving daughter who is killed. It is a double tragedy: the girl was pregnant.

157 In another version, an eagle flies overhead, dropping a feather that everyone pursues.

158 In Gibson 1912, 138, "splitting the sky" accompanies travelling eastward.

159 Gibson 1899, paras. 114–16. "Rubbing down his body" presages Hiawatha rubbing down the body of Thadadaho, straightening out his limbs, just as Hiawatha wished to be reassured and made straight again.

Hiawatha answered: "That person skilled in sorcery, Osinoh, has destroyed my family of seven daughters.[160] It was truly a great calamity and I am now very miserable. My sorrow and my rage have been bitter. I can only rove about[161] since now I have cast myself away from my people. I am only a wanderer. I split the heavens when I went away from my house and my nation."

Dekanawidah replied: "Dwell here with me. I will represent your sorrow to the people here dwelling."

So Hiawatha had found some one who considered his distress and he did stay. Then Dekanawidah told of his suffering and the people listened.[162]

There are other descriptions of the events leading up to this meeting, and they are all tragic. All involve Hiawatha's loss of his family through the power of magic. In one version, the culprit is a sorcerer, Oghsinou:

Hiawatha had three beautiful granddaughters—a man of the name of Oghsinou desired to have the oldest, but she refused him. He is said to have possessed supernatural powers, and having transformed himself every night into an Owl, perched on a tree near the house, and intermixed with the notes of his new assumed species, dreadful to children, human speech, repeating, "The granddaughter of Hiawatha must admit the embraces of Oghsinou." In the day time, he repeated his addresses and entreaties; but notwithstanding these or his nocturnal visits, in a borrowed form, and mysterious commands, the lovely Maid persisted in refusing him. She was seized with sickness and died. Oghsinou continuing his visits, armed with Owlish dread, afflicting with the same notes, the disconsolate family, Hiawatha seized his bow and quiver, and going under the tree whence issued the disconsolate notes of the ill omened bird of night, he took aim, and down it came tumbling, resuming the natural form of Oghsinou as he expired . . . [163]

---

160 Thadadaho Leon Shenandoah stated that Hiawatha's seven daughters were found dead in a gully with Thadadaho, who might have clubbed them to death with his massive penis: Wall 2001, 5. Vecsey notes that the people who calmed Thadadaho "made his penis harmless" (Vecsey 1988, 104).

161 In the dark days, much of the roving about was done by bands of young men engaged in the constant killing. Hiawatha, though, withdraws from society for the opposite reason—as Christopher Vecsey says, not from killing too much, but from too much killing.

162 Parker (Newhouse and Cusick) 1916, 23.

163 Norton 1970, 100.

In another version, Thadadaho, angry and impatient, sends the deaths:

> The power of Tadadahoh yet followed them, and caused a high soar-
> ing Eagle to fall; it happened to reach the ground at the feet of the
> granddaughter of Hiawatha, who was far gone in pregnancy. The
> youth who crowded there to obtain the choice feathers, hurt her,
> that she died.
>
> The loss so affected Hiawatha, that he rejected all comfort and nour-
> ishment: he laid himself down in his Cabin; the principal people
> assembled there, but he could not look upon them. After some days,
> he began to sing; they listened, caught the air & joined in the chorus;
> the burden of the song was, "I am about to leave you; for the solace
> of my old age has been taken from me!"
>
> When he had finished his song, he took up his pouch, and bid them
> farewell, recommending his niece to fill his place: he rejected all their
> repeated entreaties to remain.[164]

In the oral recital of this part of the story of the law, the speaker's voice drops
sadly at the end of each sentence, and the speed of his speaking slows. There is
sorrow, loneliness, and hopelessness in each sigh.

Baptist Thomas, an Onondaga, provided this version, which Arthur Parker
edited and wrote:

> When a man's heart is heavy with sorrow because of death he
> wanders aimlessly. . . . That is why Hiawatha went away from the
> Mohawks. His only sister—he had only one sister—died. She was
> Da-si-yu and she died. She was not a comely woman but her brother
> loved her and so Hiawatha mourned and no one came to comfort
> him. Not one person came to him in his grief to comfort him,
> therefore his mind was clouded in darkness. His throat was dry and
> heavy and bitter. So he went away for he did not wish to stay among
> a people who had no hearts of sympathy for sorrow. The Mohawks
> had grown callous and so accustomed to troubled times that they
> did not care for the sorrows of others and even despised the tears
> of mourners. . . .
>
> After a time when another great sorrow came, some say it was be-
> cause his daughters died, he again continued his journey.[165]

---

164 Norton 1970, 100.

165 Parker 1916, 114–15. Barbara Graymont (1988, 15–18) maintains that it was
     Thadadaho's witchcraft that was responsible for the deaths of Hiawatha's daughters, and
     that this triggered "a contest of will and power between two great men, one evil and one
     good." Converse (1908, 117) says that Thadadaho killed three of Hiawatha's brothers.

Hiawatha was a beloved man, one who was able to resume leadership once he returned. But Baptist Thomas's observation that death had become so commonplace that the people had become hard-hearted and unmoved by tragedy is frightening. Living among people without empathy is an additional reason for self-exile. In the Creation story, Tawiskaron admits to his brother that he feels unable to bear any pity or empathy, and he is himself saddened by that loneliness. In both stories, there is a situation in which a person becomes aware of the reasons for his own sadness but cannot find a way out. They need help. That is part of the lesson in the design of every aspect of Haudenosaunee society. We all need help, at some point.

Thadadaho is in every case an obstacle to the creation of the law, and a man fascinated with evil, but it may be more consistent to conclude that the person responsible for the deaths of Hiawatha's family was not Thadadaho but some other sorcerer. There were certainly enough of them around in the dark days. Perhaps the most persuasive reason for this conclusion is that Thadadaho is never asked to account for, or repent for, the killings. Hiawatha is healed by the Condolence, but Thadadaho's actions would always stand between them unless repentance had taken place. Hiawatha, who would remain in council, could forgive but never forget.

If Thadadaho had been the killer, Hiawatha was setting the great example by not seeking revenge. It is Hiawatha, not the Peacemaker, who combs the snakes from Thadadaho's hair and straightens out the kinks in his body. To perform this act of compassion for a man who had killed one's family would be powerful, transcendent. Together, they would join in "putting the bodies away, so they may not be seen,"[166] through the ceremony of Condolence.

On the other hand, if another sorcerer had been responsible, this would leave unresolved murders, and evil at large in the world, a residual threat to peace. The law tends to tie up loose ends: Haudenosaunee belief recognizes that there is both good and evil in the world, and that evil never really leaves us. The continued existence of evil affirms to the historical rather than mythical side of the lawmaking's narrative.[167]

Regardless of the version of the law, Hiawatha had suffered deeply as a result of the deaths of his close female relatives, including the unborn child of one

---

166 Though the Haudenosaunee maintained a tradition of burying the dead, this was not always possible in winter, and sometimes the dead were kept on scaffolds (to keep them away from animals) or even inside the longhouse until it was possible to dig the graves.

167 As Amber Meadow Adams has pointed out, it is simplistic to look to the Creation story for this principle. The creator twins were not good and evil, but rather symbols of differing strategies for survival, perhaps eventually symbols for existence and non-existence. However, they are also symbols of duality, and of how entities in frequent conflict can coexist, in part by remaining at a safe distance from each other.

of his daughters.[168] He was suffering from not one death but a series of them. They were deaths in circumstances that strongly called out for revenge, but his reaction was not to urge or seek vengeance, but rather to withdraw in grief and pain. His first withdrawal was to leave his own people, the Onondagas,[169] and move eastward, to Mohawk country, to start over. His second withdrawal, after more family deaths, was away from all other people, to live by himself in the forest. He was alone in grief, and his behaviour had become odd: "Hayonwatha was 'noticed to be always talking about something, and constantly handling belts and strings made of curious white and purple shells.'"[170]

Hiawatha was moving towards the use of wampum, but in some versions, he was using substitutes, as did other people, as if they were groping towards the real thing but not achieving it. In these versions, purple sumac, white basswood, and the shafts of feathers were the precursors of shell wampum. True wampum, otkó:wa, the Great Shell, has a permanence that the substitutes do not offer.

> He cut off a sumac branch, cored it, cut it into short lengths, and then he strung up the sticks making several short strings. Thereupon he sat down next to the embers with his head bowed . . .[171]
>
> . . . they pondered the meaning of the short strands hung up in front of him, trying to understand the small basswood sticks which were cut into short lengths and cored, the sticks that were strung up.[172]

The chief of the nearby community, once he had heard what Hiawatha was doing, decided that he, too, would make short strands of beads, since he knew what the man needed: "The chief cut off the tips of feathers and strung them

---

168 Kayaneseh-oh (later Ya-ie-wa-noh) Harriet Maxwell Converse (1908, 118) preserved a legend in which Thadadaho was "bitterly opposed to Hiawatha and to defeat him put three of his brothers to death."

169 In Gibson's 1899 version, Hiawatha had already become a Mohawk leader when the tragedies struck, one after another.

170 Ely Parker, in Converse 1908, 187–88. Parker says that Hiawatha invented the use of wampum when his canoe paddle brought up white and purple shells from the bottom of Oneida Lake.

171 Gibson 1912, 139.

172 Gibson 1912, 145. In the Chiefs' Version (1916, 77), and in Gibson's 1899 version, the white wooden beads are cut from elderberry twigs.

up into short strands and said, 'Now I am finished, the short strands are my words, and these will lead the man.'"[173]

The act of putting beads in a string, for Hiawatha, was a physical manifestation of his desire to gather his scattered thoughts and feelings and to restore a sense of order. Stringing beads, as any beadworker knows, is a way to impose coherent order and direction upon chaos. It is an act of reunification.

In Gibson's 1899 version, typically, there is collaboration. Hiawatha's stringing of objects leads others to emulate him, and together, the mourner and the clear-minded ones who are seeking to help raise up his mind develop both the practice and the meaning of Condolence.

Delos Big Kittle of Cattaraugus, in 1905, has Hiawatha already collecting and stringing the shells as he develops the principles of the law: the Peacemaker, "from his hiding place," observes Hiawatha at work before approaching him. The first strings of wampum, in this account, are not those of the Condolence, but the beginning of the laws of peace, white for peace, black for war, black and white for the process of peacemaking. How can this be reconciled with other versions? By recognizing that the Condolence is indeed a beginning of the laws of peace:

> Presently, as [the Peacemaker] lay meditating, he heard the soft spattering of water sliding from a skillful paddle and peering out from his hiding place he saw in the red light of sunset a man leaning over his canoe and dipping into the shallow water with a basket. When he raised it up it was full of shells, the shells of the periwinkles that live in shallow pools. The man pushed his canoe toward the shore and sat down on the beach where he kindled a fire. Then he began to string his shells and finishing a string would touch the shells and talk. Then, as if satisfied, he would lay it down and make another until he had a large number. Dekanawida watched the strange proceeding with wonder . . .

---

173 Gibson 1912, 147 (in the Chiefs' Version, "quills" are used, this may also be feathers, or it may be porcupine quills: Parker [Chiefs] 1916, 78). This string of white wampum would have been the first "invitation wampum." In the Chiefs' Version, it is the Peacemaker who describes how the process of invitation is to work: "You must not go unless the invitation is official. A woman shall first come to you early tomorrow morning who will be the first to see you, then you shall cut and prepare some elderberry twigs. You shall cut them into pieces and remove the heart pulp and then you shall string them up. Then the Lord (Royaner) shall send a messenger to invite you, but you must not accept the invitation until he shall send to you a string of twigs similar to your own." Parker 1916, 77. Today, the invitation wampum is sent out with runners to call any Grand Council, and there have been numerous instances where invitations sent without wampum have not been accepted. See Foster 1974, 106 and n25, on invitation wampum.

After some deliberation he called out: "Kwe, I am a friend!" and stepping out upon the same stood before the man with the shells. "I am Dekanawida," he said, "and I come from the Mohawk."

"I am Haio'wentha of the Onondaga," came the reply.

Then Dekanawida inquired about the shell strings for he was very curious to know their import and Haio'wentha answered, "They are the rules of life and laws of good government. This all white string is a sign of truth, peace and good will, this black string is a sign of hatred, of war and of a bad heart, the string with the alternate beads, black and white, is a sign that peace should exist between the nations. This string with white on either end and black in the middle is a sign that wars must end and peace declared." And so Haio'wentha lifted his strings and read the laws.[174]

In Gibson's 1912 version, while the movement towards restoration of rationality and health is the same, the details are quite different. Hiawatha is invited by Tekarihoken to the Mohawk village, where Tekarihoken explains to him, in an assembly of the people, what the Peacemaker has done to date, and how peace is coming. Hiawatha replies, confirming this, reciting his own sadness and misfortunes. Hiawatha agrees to stay at Tekarihoken's house, and that night the Peacemaker returns.[175]

When the Peacemaker found him, Hiawatha was still in a state of deep depression,[176] mulling over how he—and so many others who had suffered, or were suffering—would come out of it. Where many others had sought revenge, Hiawatha was seeking only solace. Where others might cause trouble—up to and including vengeful murder—with their antisocial conduct, Hiawatha withdrew from society. His choices were peaceful, where others might be vengeful. Yet his mind was so troubled, so clouded by grief, that he could not see his way clear to raising it up again. His choice of peace was more stunned, catatonic, than active. The task of restoring Hiawatha's reason, and both mental

---

174 Parker (1923) 1989, 404.

175 Gibson 1912, 149–71.

176 Rather than accept Hiawatha as "the embodiment of the equable man, the ideal chief, who puts public concern above self and above family . . . [a] kind and generous man . . . the principal victim in the myth of the machinations of Atotarho," William Fenton maintains that "there is a better case that both characters were pathological personalities" (elsewhere, he calls Hiawatha "a disturbed chief . . . a recidivist cannibal and a victim of witchcraft" [Jennings 1985, 10]). If, in saying this, he means that each man was suffering from a disease of the mind, a suffering that could be healed, he is probably right. In denying Hiawatha's essential goodness, and suggesting that the source of his problems was innate "personality" rather than sorrow, Fenton was missing the whole point of the narrative (as he probably was about the "recidivist cannibal" accusation, which he gathered from the 1899 Gibson version).

and physical health, fell to the Peacemaker, in the first demonstration that it takes two sides to raise up minds again, through the ceremony of Condolence.

Sotsisowah John Mohawk explains:

> To bring this into contemporary thinking, if you say, "We don't negotiate with terrorists," you have taken away your own power. You have to negotiate with them; they are the people who are trying to kill you. But to negotiate with them, you have to acknowledge they're human. Acknowledging that they are human means acknowledging that they have failings, but you don't concentrate on the failings. You concentrate on their humanity. You have to address their humanity if you are going to have any hope of stopping the blood feud. Thus, the first meeting, and subsequent meetings, begin with an acknowledgment that people on all sides have suffered loss and that their losses are traumatic ones.[177]

The First Condolence

The Peacemaker observed Hiawatha for a while before meeting him directly. He crept close enough to hear the mourning man's words (just as he had crept up on the Cannibal to listen to his mutterings). Hiawatha was trying to console and condole himself. He had the essential idea, and understood the purpose, but he could not get past the first three "words," the need to clear one's senses so that the rest of the message would be understood.[178]

In his efforts to create wampum, Hiawatha had been experimenting, without success, with substitutes—small tubes of purple sumac and white basswood, dark and white porcupine quills, and feather shafts. It is as if he had the idea, but was not getting things quite right, and working with an ephemeral personal concept where the Peacemaker would make it permanent and universal. The feathers and softwood were drafts, predecessors of the enduring Great Shell. The symbiosis between the two men—one who could not get things quite

---

177 What John Mohawk (2004) is saying at the end of this explanation is different: instead of one grieving side and one clear-minded side, he says that in resolving the darkest times, *all sides* have suffered.

178 Delos Big Kittle's 1905 story sees Hiawatha completing both the wampum strings (of periwinkle shells) and the laws. The strings he describes—all white, all dark, alternating black and white and white on either end—are among the strings of the Condolence ceremony, though he does not say how many Hiawatha made: "then, as if satisfied, he would lay it down and make another until he had a large number." Parker (1923) 1989, 404.

right, the other who was near perfection—recalls the relationship between the twins in the Creation story, except that the Peacemaker and Hiawatha forge a partnership to help each other, while the twins are partners in creation despite themselves, and end up as antagonists.

> Late in the evening [Hiawatha, having gathered the wampum left by the ducks] came to a clearing and found a bark field hut. There he found a shelter and there he erected two poles, placed another across the tops and suspended three shell strings.[179] Looking at them he said: "Men boast what they would do in extremity but they do not do what they say. If I should see anyone in deep grief I would remove these shell strings from the pole and console them. The strings would become words and lift away the darkness with which they are covered. Moreover, what I say I would surely do." This he repeated.[180]

> The chiefs deliberated over the sad events and then decided to do as Dekanawidah should say. He then should remedy the trouble. Then Dekanawidah went in perplexity to his lodge and as he came to it he heard Hiawatha say, "It is useless, for the people only boast what they will do, saying 'I would do it this way', but they do nothing at all. If what has befallen me should happen to them I would take down the three shell strings from the upright pole and I would address them and I would console them because they would be covered by heavy darkness." Dekanawidah stood outside the door and heard all these words. So then Dekanawidah went forward into the house and he went up to the pole, then he said: "My younger brother, it has now become very plain to my eyes that your sorrow must be removed.

179 The wampum suspended from a horizontal pole stretched across two forked uprights reappears in numerous places. When Hermanus Van den Bogaert visited Onondaga in 1638, he saw this pole in the Confederacy's council house and noted that it was the way the agenda of councils was made apparent. In 1645, in the council area at Three Rivers, "the Iroquois caused two poles to be planted, and a cord to be stretched from one to the other on which to hang and tie the words they were to bring us . . . which consisted of seventeen collars of porcelain beads, a portion of which were on their bodies" (Jennings 1985, 139). At international treaty councils, the wampum belts and strings were suspended from the horizontal pole, near the fire, to be removed and answered in the order in which they were given. Today, the same horizontal pole is placed between the two groups in a Condolence. In a "Small Condolence," its role is taken by a cane stretched between two chairs, on which the twelve strings are placed. In modern council, the "fire" used to open the council is placed on pure white cloth, over a bench in the centre of the longhouse. While it is sometimes called "the Mace" (because it is a symbol that the House is in session), the way it is draped over the bench shows it is the direct descendant of the first wampum used by Hiawatha.

180 Parker (Newhouse and Cusick) 1916, 20. Baptist Thomas said Hiawatha "talked to himself about his sorrow. 'I would comfort others in sorrow,' he said, 'but no one comforts me'" (Parker 1916, 114).

Your griefs and your rage have been great. I shall now undertake to remove your sorrow so that your mind may be rested. Have you no more shell strings on your pole?"

Hiawatha replied. "I have no more strings but I have many shells in a tanned deer's skin." So he opened his bundle and a great quantity of shells fell out.[181]

The Peacemaker recognized in Hiawatha a kindred soul: from the very beginning of their relationship, he addressed him as "my younger brother."[182] He also recognized that Hiawatha could not condole himself: that he could not, in his grieving condition, clear his own mind. He needed another person's help.

Part of the power of the Peacemaker is his generosity of spirit: he assumes the obligations and authority of kinship towards complete strangers, spontaneously, as a means of helping them. So he does to Hiawatha.

Once again the Peacemaker meets a person who is behaving irrationally and brings him to the Good Mind. Each time he does so, in the narrative of the Great Law, the Peacemaker encounters a different kind of irrationality, stemming from a different source. In each case, the Peacemaker uses a different approach. In Hiawatha, the Peacemaker met an essentially good man whose mind was clouded by grief. This good man had already gone some distance towards restoring his own mind and reason, but he could not complete the task alone.

Hiawatha had conceived the idea of the Condolence ceremony. He had a great need to have his personal darkness lifted. In a way, he symbolized all the people, since each of them required the same attention, for they had all suffered.

The Peacemaker was bringing the Good Message, and now understood that a powerful spiritual act was needed as the threshold of the law. People would not be prepared to accept his message unless their minds were first made good again. Where it had been enough to trick the Cannibal into rationality and to persuade Tsikonsaseh through power and reason, with Hiawatha the process reached a more powerful level. The path to restoring the rational mind was a deliberate, structured, deeply caring and compassionate ceremony, a ritual of both a spiritual and a legal character. It was necessary to learn how to deal with death. In the dark days, death was still all around.

---

181 Parker 1916, 23–24.

182 A younger brother has certain obligations to an older brother: for example, when there is business to be transacted, generally the younger brother is expected to travel to the older brother's place. While generally younger people owe deference to their elders, between brothers—equals—this is less accentuated, since their obligations are nearly symmetrical in reciprocity. Since Hiawatha is probably older chronologically than the Peacemaker, it is clear that the relationship has less to do with age than with the kind of seniority that comes from wisdom and spirituality.

Compassion is indeed the threshold of the Great Law of Peace.

The two of them together—the clear-minded one and the grieving one whose mind was cast down on the ground—created the Condolence.[183] This is not merely a powerful partnership: it also shows how two-sidedness—helping each other—in building law and society can be effective and right.[184] There would be no structure without the Peacemaker's great compassion; there would be no restoration of the Good Mind without Hiawatha's decision to accept the Condolence rather than take up the path of vengeance.

The Peacemaker was already bringing peace by addressing the irrational behaviour of individuals. He was restoring the Good Mind. Hiawatha, in his grief, had understood that an individual cannot condole or console himself. Yet he had articulated not only the need for a Condolence, but also the beginning of a technique: the first three "words" or ideas, accompanied by the strings of the ceremony. The Peacemaker took up Hiawatha's invitation and provided not only the "words" that followed, but also the reciprocity and depth of caring that made the ceremony complete. The first Condolence raises up the mind. Later, after the government is created, the ceremony is extended to raising up a chief, in political terms, as well, by adding the last two "words." The Condolence is the product of a partnership, a brotherhood between the two remarkable men.

Together, they had also established the use of shell wampum as a lawmaking tool, a device for not only remembering, but also consecrating and ratifying the steps and decisions taken by the mind.[185] The first Condolence is the source of sacredness of wampum today, and using wampum is, every time, a way of recalling the beginning of law and peace. Every Condolence is a re-enactment of the first one.

---

183   Dean Snow (1994, 56) provides a darker, more limited view of the meaning of the Condolence: "The elaborate funeral rite ensured that everyone was either grieving or condoling, and that no one could be blamed for causing the death. The process effectively shifted blame outside the close-knit immediate community . . . [and] unified the rage of the survivors." Yet he can provide no examples of survivors' rage.

184   The Condolence, or some form of it, likely predated the coming of the Peacemaker. In the Creation story, once the people were divided into clans, the duty of condolence was also created: "The clans should become the chief means we will employ in the matters befalling us now because we are separating ourselves from one another. When a death occurs among a Sisterhood—a clan—the minds of the opposite sisterhood will be clear and they (the second sisterhood) will arise as one and go to the place where one has been lost. It shall be the duty of the unaffected sisterhood to utter words which will repeatedly cheer up and encourage those who have suffered loss and to comfort those who have become enshrouded in darkness. . . . It will be their duty to speak, and they will encourage the minds of those who remain alive, so that their minds will become settled again." Mohawk 2005a, 92–93.

185   In Delos Big Kittle's 1905 story, Hiawatha has devised both the laws and the use of wampum to preserve and transmit them—but the Peacemaker, a Mohawk, induces him to bring the laws to his people: "Then come with me . . . and together let us go back to my people and explain the rules and laws." Parker (1923) 1989, 405.

Once again, the Peacemaker has accomplished a transformation. Hiawatha's mind has been restored to health, and he has been changed from a mourning hermit to a partner in peacemaking. Compassion has brought Hiawatha back from the borderlands of death. Compassion looks at the man in sorrow, not at the chief in a time of incapacity. It is about rejoining life, not about resuming duty.

The Peacemaker says: "My junior brother,[186] your mind being cleared and you being competent to judge, we shall now make our laws."[187]

Christopher Vecsey recognizes that the transformation of the Cannibal and the raising up of Hiawatha's mind are two sides of the same coin:[188]

> The transformation of the outsider into the peacemaker and chief is matched by the three parallel transformations, boundary-crossings, that are the heart of the legend. First, the cannibal—whether it is Hiawatha or Tadadaho does not matter—is transformed into a messenger of peace and power. The figure moves from the most depraved form of human activity to the work of nation-building, from chaotic immorality to the moral project of making political order. Second, the transformation of Hiawatha from grieving wanderer to powerful lawgiver and chief is a replication of the first. In both cases Deganawida cures a sick person—sick from killing too much, sick from too much killing, sick as aggressor, sick as victim—and transforms him into an upholder of social order. Third, the straightening of Tadadaho's mind and body repeats once again the pattern of curing and transformation in order to create an orderly state. The message of peace is repeated in these episodes and underscores the point that the Iroquois Confederacy exists in order to stop wanton killing and the mourning that produces a desire for revenge and more killing.

> The myth replicates its message through these transformations. The person of Hiawatha (as cannibal and as mourner) is cured twice, but it is essentially the same cure for the same disease: the disease of killing. The person of Tadadaho is cured twice (as cannibal and as monster) for the same reason. In order to stop the cycle of killing

---

186 In Haudenosaunee law, "Senior" and "Junior" are poor English translations that refer to age (Older Brother and Younger Brother) and not to authority. In 1990, though, a reference in the report of the Haudenosaunee External Relations Committee to a group of older Oneida chiefs as "senior" sparked resentment by some Oneidas against the committee. It lasted a decade.

187 Parker (Newhouse and Cusick) 1916, 23.

188 What Vecsey may be missing is that every significant step along the Peacemaker's path is marked by a similar transformation. Dealing with Tsikonsaseh, Thadadaho, and the Seneca warriors are further instances of "transformational cures."

and mourning, and revenge and killing, Deganawida must cure those
caught in the cycle. He must cure the cannibal from his monstrously
excessive disregard for human life, and he must cure the mourner
of his disastrously excessive attachment to his lost family members.
The cannibal undervalues, the mourner overvalues, human life, and
Deganawida must cure them both. To the cannibal he says, stop killing and form a social order. To the mourner he says, stop mourning
and form a social order. The structure of the Confederacy is revealed
in these transformational cures. The league exists to stop killing and
to comfort the bereaved.[189]

Ray John, the Oneida chief, has explained the thinking of the Condolence in
more direct terms: sometimes, we feel there is nothing we can do but cry. Then,
more than at any other time, we have to believe that there will be a tomorrow.
We have to believe that our children still need us. It is up to our friends to help
us see this.[190] The obligation is not merely to perform the ceremony, but to truly
mean it. Another current translation of the way of the Condolence is to say
"We sit with you"—often in silent sympathy, for there is not much we can say.

To raise up Hiawatha's grieving mind and restore him to rationality, the
Peacemaker completes the process that Hiawatha has been trying to devise.
Hiawatha had been hanging the first three strings of the Condolence ceremony,
the same three "words" that are repeated at the woods' edge to welcome strangers. They are the first and most obvious steps to be taken to relieve grief. They
address the physical symptoms, the outward manifestations, and the things
that, if they continued to be obstructed, would block clear communication of
the rest of the Condolence: the senses. The Condolence is sometimes called
Teyonhonkwaráktha, "they pity them."[191] It would be more accurate in English
to say "they have compassion for them":

> Now then, we say, we wipe away the tears, so that in peace you may
> look around you.

> And further, we suppose there is an obstruction in your ears.[192] Now
> then, we remove the obstruction carefully from your hearing, so that
> we trust you will easily hear the words spoken.

---

189 Vecsey 1988, 112.

190 The Municipality of Thames Centre, in May 2005, had lost one of its staff members. In
     the middle of a mediation about a burial ground, Ray John felt the need to condole the
     municipal council, as part of a growing relationship.

191 Ray John, of Oneida, points out that the Oneida term for "to have pity" is gan:do, which
     sounds close enough to the English "condole" that it may have been the source of the use
     of the word.

192 In the 2013 recital of the law, Atahu'ta:yʌ Bob Brown and Sakokwenionkwas Tom Porter
     said: "The dust of death is in your ear . . . how strong it is. . . ."

And also we imagine there is an obstruction in your throat. Now, therefore, we say, we remove the obstruction, so that you may speak freely in our mutual greetings.[193]

The first wampum was all white: access to the purple quahog shells from the Atlantic would come later. The first three words of the Condolence are also white: the white deerskin to wipe the tears from the eyes, the white eagle feather to remove the dust from the ears, the white or clear water to remove the obstruction from the throat. The white beads reflect the whiteness and purity of the things that are used.

The Three Bare Words accomplish what John Mohawk explained: they recognize people's humanity; they acknowledge their losses, and that the losses have been traumatic; and they are the doorway to the conversation that is necessary to achieve peace. They are not simply the conversation that the Peacemaker had with Hiawatha: they are adaptable and useful in dozens of contemporary contexts. For example, in addressing the people suffering deeply damaging intergenerational effects of residential schools, Kanatiio Allan Gabriel began with the same words:

> It is said that, as we walk the path that is our life, there are times when the way is not clear. Things happen to make us lose our way. Perhaps a loved one is sick or has died—it could be something else that troubles us. When this happens we suddenly find ourselves stumbling through the brush.

> As we struggle to push our way through the underbrush, looking for the clear path, we pick up burrs and thorns which cling to our clothing, pricking our skin. We get dusty and scared. Our fear causes us to cry and our hearts pound.

> It is good to see that you have arrived here safely and that we may spend some time together. I know that you have come from far away and that many obstacles were placed in your way. And yet, despite these obstacles, you are able to be here. I take you by the hand as a brother or a sister. I offer you words of greeting and respect. I offer you food and drink.

> Because that which you carry may cause you grief, we have gathered here together. We know that as an individual you are very strong. But we also know there are times when one needs the strength of others.

---

193 Hale (1883) 1989, 121. This extremely short "three words" is a "woods' edge" version. For an even shorter version (omitting the ears, substituting the "bloody mat"), see Deserontyon 1928.

We understand that when one is in pain, the mind is distracted and one finds it difficult to use the power of a good mind.

I speak these words so that your mind may be put at ease and your load lightened. We come together in this way because you are grieving. We come to offer our thoughts and our support. We come to lift the weight of your burden from your shoulders and to share it among us.

First, I take the finest Eagle feather I can find, and with this Eagle feather, I sweep away the dust which clings to you. I remove any burrs or thorns or twigs which may be caught on your clothing. I remove these things because they surely cause you pain and discomfort. And so, I hope this makes you feel more comfortable and more at ease.

Your eyes may be filled with tears because of the grief you carry. These tears blur your vision and sting your eyes. There may be a sound like roaring in your ears because of the fear, pain and anger you may be feeling. And so, taking the finest and softest deer skin I can find, I gently wipe away your tears so that you may see the beauty that is all around you, and your friends and relations who have gathered here to support and help you.

Next, I wipe away any obstruction in your ears which may prevent you from hearing the good words that people speak to help ease your suffering. We offer you a place to sit so that you may rest your weary body.

Finally, your grief, your pain and your anger may cause an obstruction in your throat. It is important to remove that obstruction so that, when you speak, your words may come loudly and clearly so that all may understand what is troubling you. And so, I offer you a drink of pure, cool water. Water is indeed one of the most powerful medicines we have, for it has the ability to give and to sustain life.[194] The water will help to remove that which clogs your throat. It soothes your insides and quenches your thirst.

---

194 In the 2013 recital of the law, Atahu'ta:yʌ Bob Brown and Sakokwenionkwas Tom Porter referred to "medicine water" rather than pure water—but indeed pure water is medicine water.

Figure 4. The pole of the clear-minded ones at the woods' edge at Oneida, May 2010, when Odatsehte and Sonuhses were condoled. Photograph by author.

And so, with all this I hope you are now more comfortable and we
have helped to ease your burden. We hope these words have helped
to restore a sound mind, body and spirit.[195]

Kanatiio's Three Bare Words reflect the ones that are used to greet visitors
to a village—the greeting that was no doubt offered to Jacques Cartier at the
woods' edge at Hochelaga in 1534.[196] In that context, it is the visitors who may
be carrying grief, and the hosts who condole them. Where a chief has died in
the village, though, it is the visitors who come to console, and they are the ones
who deliver the words, without the greetings, the removal of dust and thorns,
and the offer of food and drink.

At a Condolence for raising up a chief, these three words are delivered outside the longhouse, with the grieving people lined up with their backs to the
longhouse and the clear-minded ones lined up facing them, having come singing the songs of peace along the road, and now waiting at a respectful distance,
but close enough to hear and see. The speaker for the grieving ones repeats and
acknowledges what has been said,[197] returning the first three wampum strings.
Then everyone goes into the longhouse for the rest of the Condolence ceremony,
to repeat and then complete the sequence.[198]

Inside the longhouse, the condolers will place the strings on a horizontal
rod. Their speaker will recite and recall the names of the original lords of the
Haudenosaunee (this has been called the "roll call of chiefs"[199]), walking back
and forth between the wood stoves. He carries a cane for cadence, and the
recitation is in a sonorous voice, with the last words of each stanza fading out,

---

195   Gabriel 2010. Kanatiio would often be called upon during his work with the Canadian
      Royal Commission on Aboriginal Peoples, which reported in 1994, to begin meet-
      ings with thanksgiving and Condolence. On September 30, 2016, he performed the
      three words at the reaffirmation of treaty relations between the Peskotomuhkatiq
      (Passamaquoddy) Nation and the Crown, for the Condolence is also part of their council
      rituals.

196   A century later, French Jesuits would note of the Haudenosaunee, that "if the condition
      of the dead permit, one of them makes a speech, in which he employs all those argu-
      ments that the most eloquent speakers are wont to use for the solace of grief" (Thwaites
      1901, 1:263).

197   In virtually every text on effective listening, this technique is recommended. At its core is
      respect: being able to assure the other person that you *have* been listening, that you have
      understood what was said.

198   The Three Bare Words are delivered "at the woods' edge," and in receiving them and
      acknowledging them, the grieving ones also greet their brothers and "rub them down,"
      symbolically removing the dust and thorns of the journey. "Rubbing down" also recalls
      the healing of Thadadaho, whose limbs were rubbed down as they were straightened out.

199   At one point, Hewitt mixed the names and functions of the chiefs: "This is the role of
      you who completed these rules of the Great Law." Hewitt 1892b, 144.

falling.[200] The clear-minded ones also sing the Six Songs, which are solemn, yearning reminders of the great days of the power and beauty of the League.

The following is a composite, but extremely short, Condolence speech in modern English words.[201] It contains the proper "elements," but not in the exact form delivered in either a Condolence to install chiefs or in full council with other nations.[202]

> Your eyes are constantly shedding tears for the ones who have departed, who have been gathered to the Creator's land. Because of these tears, you can no longer see your brothers clearly, and your ability to see the world around you has been affected. With this word we wipe the tears from your eyes, so that you may once again see clearly.[203]

> The grief and sorrow you are suffering have stopped up your ears, so that you can no longer hear clearly what is being said to you. Perhaps there is a ringing or rushing sound in your ears. We take a pure white deerskin [cloth], and with this we once again open your ears, so that you can hear clearly what is being said.[204]

> Your throats have been stopped up with grief, so that you are no longer able to speak. With this we once again open your throats, so that you will be able to say what you wish, without obstruction.[205]

---

200 The reciters of the *Iliad* and the *Odyssey*, the *rhapsodos*, would also mark their cadence with a staff, the *skeptron*, especially as they went through the "catalog" of the hundred ships that left Greece to fight on the sandy windswept plains of Troy. Williams 2007.

201 Christopher Vecsey (1988, 102) notes that the Peacemaker only used eight of the present thirteen strings of Condolence with Hiawatha, for he was not raising up a new royá:ner, but only raising up the man's mind again.

202 Slightly modified from Williams and Nelson 1994.

203 See Gibson 1912, 81: "Moreover, you will keep in mind that he passed his hand through his tears, they wiping your tears with this white, soft cloth they use when they wipe your tears. Then, moreover, you will look around calmly, and you will see them all about you, roaming around, your nephews and nieces, and you will see the land again. Thereupon you will begin to think calmly again, moreover for at least one day."

204 See Gibson 1912, 81: "My father's kinsmen, thus it happens and it is dreadful that it should happen to one, that repeatedly one's ears become plugged so that one cannot hear any more. . . . So now they are carefully reopening your ears. Now, moreover, they will be restored, and you will hear them speaking again, those moving about near you, your nephews and nieces. Now, also, you will hear again about how things are going at the settlement. Now, moreover, you will think calmly, and for at least one day you should continue thinking calmly."

205 Gibson 1912, 82: "It is dreadful for it to happen that one is overpowered by unhappiness. Thus it is repeatedly obstructing the throat, one's grief, so that it happens to you that your throat becomes clogged with grief. So now they free it from grief, your throat. Then, moreover, you will think calmly again, and then you will once more breathe peacefully, speaking out calmly, as we give thanks."

With the purest white deerskin I clean the insides of your bodies of any impurities that may have lodged there, so that you can go about your lives in comfort and peace.[206]

The memory of the people who have departed sometimes takes the form of the sight of blood on the space where you sit as Chiefs. With this we remove the bloodstains from your mat and once again prepare a safe and comfortable place for you to sit.[207]

In your sorrow and grief you sit in darkness in your mind. You cannot see your brothers who seek to raise your spirits once again. With this we remove the darkness you are seeing and feeling.[208]

When you have suffered a great loss, you sometimes cannot see the sky above you and around you; you are blind to the beauties of creation. With this word we restore the sight of the sky to your eyes, so that you can gaze about you in calm and beauty.[209]

In your sorrow and grief the sun is lost to you, and you can no longer feel his warmth and the light he casts about us. With this we

---

206 Gibson 1912, 89: "It happens . . . that repeatedly there is a great twisting around within one's body, there being much bile in addition to the displacement of the organs within the body, and eventually it will fail, one's spirit and one's strength … and just so, it twists around in circles, your mind, and there is a lot of bile, your organs are being displaced within your body. . . . Then moreover they will say, 'Now we are pouring in the liquid, the [?]. Moreover, when the liquid settles down, it will begin to work in your body, it will strengthen your mind, and it will wipe away the widespread jaundice and readjust the organs within your body.'"

207 Hale (1883) 1989, 123: "Every day you are losing your great men. They are being borne into the earth; also the warriors, and also your women, and also your grandchildren; so that in the midst of blood you are sitting. Now, therefore, we say, we wash the blood marks from your seat, so that it may be for a time that happily the place will be clean where you are seated and looking around you." Gibson 1912, 90: "Now we are wiping off the red marks from where you have your space. Moreover, they are using a handkerchief to wipe the red marks from your ceremonial seat. Moreover, now your space will be very fine again."

208 Gibson 1912, 90: "Now we are making it bright for you again. Then, moreover, you will see the daylight, you will notice them again, the ones wandering about in your vicinity, your nephews and nieces, and you will see the earth and you will be happy from then on."

209 Gibson 1912, 90: "Now we are clearing the sky for you. Moreover, you will see the sky. Thus when the sky is clear again, you can keep watching there. This, too: you will then think calmly."

restore the sun to the sky so that you can once again see the world around you.[210]

You have traveled far, and your path has been difficult. There are thorns in your feet, and you are in pain from your journey. With this we remove the thorns from your feet and once again make you comfortable.

The memory of the people who have passed away is refreshed in your minds whenever you pass their graves. With this we remove the sight of the graves and level the earth over them, so that their sight no longer disturbs your peace of mind.[211]

When grief and sorrow strike the people, their fires are sometimes scattered, as their thoughts are in disarray. With this we gather together the embers of your fire and rekindle the fire so that it can once again give you warmth and light.[212]

Not only a person's close family but all the people suffer when a respected person passes away. With this we once again raise up the minds of the women and the young men, that they may resume

---

210 Hale (1883) 1989, 142: "You are mourning in the deep darkness. I will make the sky clear for you, so that you will not see a cloud. And also I will give the sun to shine upon you, so that you can look upon it peacefully when it goes down. You shall see it when it is going. Yea! The sun shall seem to be hanging over you, and you shall look upon it peacefully as it goes down. Now I have hope that you will yet see the pleasant days." Hale 1883, 168: "The speaker reminds the mourners . . . that continued grief for the dead would not be consonant with the course of nature. Though all might seem dark to them now, the sky would be as clear, and the sun would shine as brightly for them, as if their friend had not died. Their loss had been inevitable, and equally sure would be the return of the "pleasant days." Gibson 1912, 90: "We are restoring the sun to you. Moreover the next day when the sun rises, when it moves up over the forest, you will keep watching the sun move along. Moreover, when it is in the centre of the sky, the sun, then it will shine all around you, and this, at the same time, will remind you, as it carries it here and there, your mind, you will remember your work for the people's welfare, and then you will think peacefully."

211 Hale (1883) 1989, 142: "And we will say that we will try to do you good. When the grave has been made, we will make it still better. We will adorn it, and cover it with moss." Gibson 1912, 91. "'Now we are stirring up the earth where his grave is,' and they reach out and grab all kinds of vegetation, and throw it there, and just there they put a piece of dressed lumber. Indeed, this is to accomplish two things: on the one hand great heat should not penetrate, and on the other hand great rains should not penetrate. Thus, peacefully, his bones will rest there, the one you used to depend on."

212 Hale (1883) 1989, 145: "We will now remake the fire, and cause it to burn again." Gibson 1912, 91: "And from the fire container [Death] caused the firebrands to scatter . . . we are gathering together firebrands again for your fire container. Moreover, we re-kindle it, smoke will rise again, beautiful smoke will rise again, and one will see again the number of fires we have rekindled in the vicinity. Moreover, we are raising your spirits again, you chiefs. We have repositioned you in ranks at the fires we rekindled for you."

their responsibility of supporting and advising the Rotiianeson in their deliberations.[213]

There are times when grief causes a person to behave in a way that is beyond reason, where they can injure or be injured by bad medicine. This can happen on earth, it is known to happen. With this we remove any shadow of insanity and all bad medicine from your minds, so that you can once again resume your place in our councils and our thoughts with a clear mind.

When a Roianer passes away, the deer horns that are the symbol of his title are said to fall from him, and fall apart. With this we put his horns back together again, so that the title may be passed on to another person who is worthy to carry that burden for the people.[214]

In the first Condolence, the Peacemaker may only have used eight strings of wampum. As time passed, the people who carried out the ceremony added others, to make the compassion more complete. Today, when the Haudenosaunee condole another people over a death, they will sometimes restrict themselves to the first three words, and occasionally go beyond to other aspects that make people's minds easy, but unless it is time to raise up a new chief, the fifteenth string or matter is not used.[215]

Hayadaha Richard Hill has pointed out that dispelling the darkness is not only metaphor. In some versions of the Great Law, it is said that as one moves west, towards the sunset, the sky becomes darker, in reference not only to the Senecas' ability to pile up the bones of those who approach without peace in their minds and hearts,[216] but also to the westward journey of the dead. Death itself is called a "thick darkness," in which the Faceless One acts as an accessory, a facilitator of Death. Dispelling the darkness, then, removes not only death but also the influence of death on our minds. That influence makes itself felt in numerous negative ways, from thoughts of revenge to thoughts of suicide.

---

213 Gibson 1912, 92: "The Creator . . . has given special importance to the women, decreeing that they will busy themselves around the fire, they being in charge of the foodstuffs . . . the source of newly born persons, they being the ones who will take care of raising the children."

214 Hale (1883) 1989, 145: "If any one should fall—it may be a principal chief will fall and descend into the grave—then the horns will be left on the grave, and as soon as possible another shall be put in his place."

215 In condoling the United States upon the death of General Israel Chapin, Sagoyewatha Red Jacket, apologizing for being "destitute of a belt," offered fourteen strings of black and white wampum (Ganter 2006, 69).

216 In the making of the Law, the Senecas retained war chiefs and warriors, because there were still enemy nations to the west. The two Seneca war chiefs were also rotiyanershon, but they had a special function as well: they were to check the sincerity of anyone trying to enter the longhouse from the west. They were allowed to kill those who meant harm.

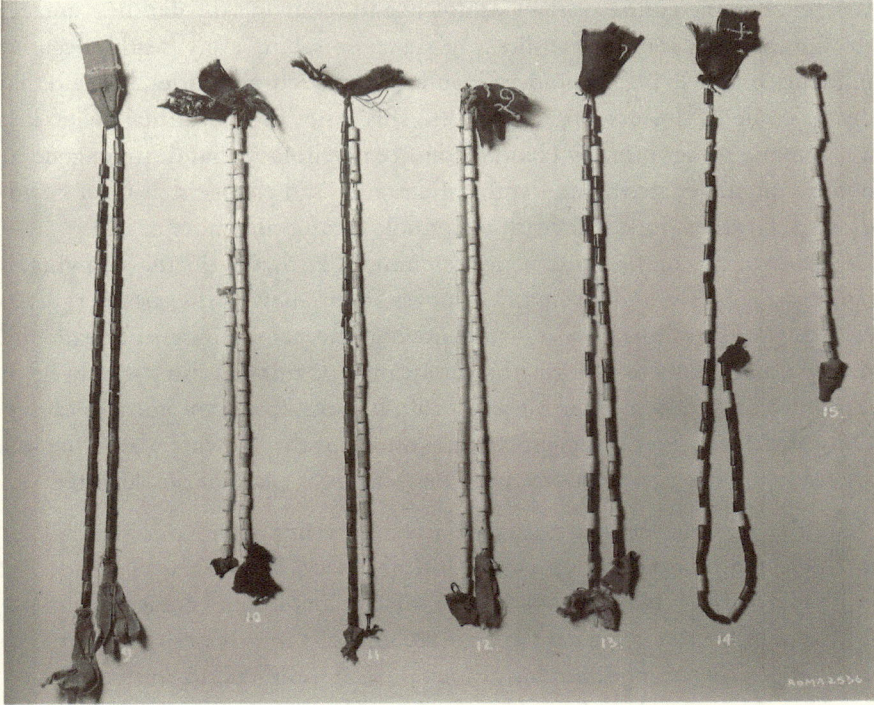

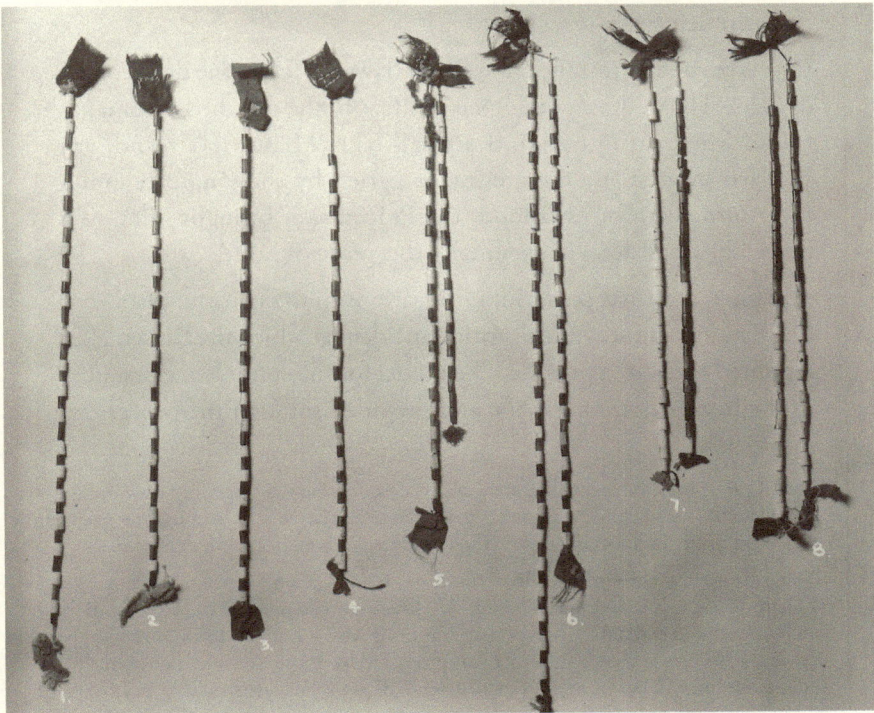

Figure 5. The fifteen strings of the Condolence.

Reference in the course of the Condolence to removing the darkness and restoring the light is therefore direct reference to taking away death's negative
influence on the living. In modern Haudenosaunee communities, it is said that
deaths come in clusters, often in threes. This is not just a spiritual belief: it is
a pragmatic recognition by Haudenosaunee psychology that death engenders
depression, anger, grief, and depths of emotion and change that must be addressed. Death suppressed, death uncondoled, can bring more death.

The structure of the Condolence ceremony, like that of the thanksgiving, is
deliberate, orderly, and layered.[217] It moves from relieving the simplest physical pain—of eyes, ears, throat—to removing external reminders of death and
revenge, and finally to restoring harmony, making things as they should be. It
moves from the easiest to the most difficult. It moves from symptoms to causes.
Only at the end does it suggest that the minds of the "downfended"[218] people
are ready to once again raise up a person to take the place of the departed:

> The message in this transaction is a very important one which
> needs attention in the area of political theory. The Peacemaker and
> Hiawatha seem both conscious of the fact that human beings reach
> places of psychological pain, or feelings of rage, or despairing of
> hope. They recognized that at such times it is difficult to reach clear
> thinking and they directed a considerable amount of attention to
> the pain being felt.
>
> In this particular instance, the pain Hiawatha felt at the death of his
> daughters has led him to despair of life. On the day the Peacemaker
> found him sitting beside the small lake, Hiawatha's mind was
> clouded in grief. By countering the grief, by showing care and a
> commitment to brotherhood, the Peacemaker brought Hiawatha
> from a place of despair, eventually to a place of hope.
>
> This encounter has powerful implications in the cultural history of
> the Haudenosaunee. The historical incident at which the Peacemaker
> recruited Hiawatha provided the model for the condolence practices
> in the installation of leaders, and provided some of the process by

---

217 Foster (1974) uses the term "hierarchical" to describe the thanksgiving: how the speaker
moves carefully and deliberately from the earth to the sky world, naming the parts of the
world and of life in a specific order. The Condolence, too, has its "hierarchy."

218 The term "downfended" is used in connection with the Condolence, especially by
William Fenton. It is an unusual word, and has given rise to unusual interpretations
(including the idea that the Peacemaker was born with a caul, and would require unusual
care and tutelage; or that his mother was protected by goose down and corn husks on
the ground around her home—"down-defended"—so that one would be able to see if
anyone had slipped in. I prefer to take the term to mean simply that the people's minds
are "downcast" by grief (see Gibson 1899, para. 131: Fenton's explanation of Hewitt's
notes on this issue).

which peace treaties were to be conducted in this part of the world for a long time.[219]

By converting the Cannibal, the Peacemaker had acquired a messenger: the man was a living demonstration of the power of the Good Message and would carry that demonstration among the people and nations he met. In Hiawatha, the Peacemaker had acquired a partner, someone who would carry the message with him. From this point on in the making of the law, most versions have the two men acting as a team, the man without a nation and the Mohawk/Onondaga; the messenger from the Creator and the reconstructed grieving hermit.

There are several possible translations for the name "Hiawatha." Each is linked to an aspect of the law. One says the name means "wampum seeker" or "wampum maker,"[220] recalling how he experimented with other kinds of beads and strings of beads in his attempts to construct ceremonies of Condolence before he and the Peacemaker agreed on shell wampum. Hewitt suggests that it means "River Seeker."[221] This could be a reference to wampum, again, since kahswénhtha, the old name given to wampum belts, can be a reference to how they flow through time like a river flows. Morgan calls him "He Who Combs," commemorating how he would comb the snakes out of Thadadaho's hair.[222] Skaniatariio John Arthur Gibson, in 1899, translated the name as "He rises early,"[223] and also as "He Sifts."[224]

Together, the two men devised a strategy for taking the message of peace to the five nations. They agreed that the Mohawks should receive the three words or principles of peace first. The Peacemaker approached them alone.

---

219   Mohawk 1989, 222.

220   Hale (1883) 1989, 21 and 154: "This name . . . is rendered 'He who seeks the wampum belt.' Chief George Johnson thought it was derived from *oyonwa*, wampum-belt, and *ratiewatha*, to look for something, or rather, to seem to seek something that we know where to find. M. Cuoq refers the latter part of the word to the verb *katha*, to make. . . . The name would then mean 'He who makes the wampum-belt'. . . . The Senecas . . . render [the name] 'he who combs.'"

221   Hewitt 1907b.

222   Tooker 1978, 424 (citing Hale 1883a, 154; Beauchamp 1891, 296; Fenton 1950, 59]; Morgan [1871] 1997, 130; [1851] 1995, 64.

223   Gibson 1899, para. 64—because when the Peacemaker arrived at his house, Hiawatha had already gone away to hunt. Assigning people new names is consistent with how the Peacemaker is creating a new peaceful world and giving people new lives. Power to name is power to define, and sometimes direct.

224   Gibson 1899, fn. 25.

The Three Words: Peace, Power, and Righteousness

The Peacemaker took his message to the Mohawk village[225] first. The people were assembled. They had to wait for three of their leaders, the chief, the Great Warrior, and his deputy.[226]

> For this plan to work the Peacemaker was required to convince a very skeptical audience that all human beings really did possess the potential for rational thought, that when encouraged to use rational thought they would inevitably seek peace, and that the belief in the principles would lead to the organized enactment of the vision . . .

> The Peacemaker spent considerable time moving from individual to individual among the leadership of the people who much later would come to be known as the Mohawk, the Oneida, the Onondaga, the Cayuga and the Seneca nations. His mission appears to have taken time. He was interested in reaching the thinking of each of these human beings as individuals. He seemed to go right at the intended target individual to offer his hope for the future of mankind, his definition of a way of coming to power, to peace, and to a better tomorrow for all his people, indeed for all mankind.[227]

In speaking to larger groups, the Peacemaker spoke more bluntly and simply. Where with Hiawatha he engaged in a long and caring Condolence, with the Mohawks he spoke of the three basic words:[228] those that have been translated as Peace, Power, and Righteousness.

---

225   In some versions of the Great Law, there is one village for each nation, it seems. By the time the Europeans arrived, it looks as if the Mohawks were living in clan villages—Bear, Turtle, and Wolf—and that some time afterward the villages became multi-clan. Archaeologically, it appears there would be a large palisaded or fortified village with several smaller hamlets up to four or five miles away. In wartime, the people of the outlying hamlets would retreat into the larger town.

226   This contains the shadow of the suggestion that civil and military affairs were already separated, with the chief dealing with peace and civil matters, and the Great Warrior dealing with war.

227   Mohawk 1989, 221.

228   In a culture without writing, it is understandable that the word for a "matter" and for a "word" would be the same: orihwa. But "word," the spoken part of speech, is also owenna.

While in the law and in councils, there is frequent reference to "words," in fact it would be better to think of these as "matters" or "ideas." Each is something to be considered separately and in the order it was given or proposed, but each one is also inextricably linked to the others. In council, the "words" are deliberately of a manageable, understandable size, so that once all the matters have been addressed and decided, one at a time, together they form a coherent policy. A "word" may be complex. It may be part of a sequence. But it is an idea, a whole unto itself:

> Then Tekanawita stood up, saying, "I, indeed, am arriving with the Good Message and the Power and the Peace; now it will cease, the warfare and the scalping and the shedding of human blood. This, actually, is how it is on earth: there are pools and streams of human blood. And this now will cease. This, too: you are the first whose village I am visiting with this message you are hearing now."

> Thereupon the chief and the Great Warrior and his deputy conversed in whispers, deciding that they would ask what was the meaning of the three words. Thereupon he stood up, the chief, saying, "We have heard you report the message you are bringing, and we want to ask you about the three words: first, what does "Good Message" mean? Secondly, what is "Power", and thirdly, what does it mean that "Peace is now arriving"?

> Then Tekanawita stood up in front of the whole group and said, "You shall listen well, for you wanted to ask questions so as to understand what it means, "Good Message"; this is what it means: people respect each other as though they are one person; also everybody is related among the various nations, so that now they will stop, the sins and activities of evil people; now everyone will repent, the old people and the young people; now everyone will respect one another among all of the nations; and just this is what will operate again, the good, and that is what the "Good Message" means.[229]

> Secondly, this is what "Power" means. All of the Nations will unite all their affairs, and the group of several nations will become just

---

229 Part of the procedure of a modern Haudenosaunee council, or a modern treaty council, is illustrated in this encounter. The speaker stands, while everyone else sits. When the speaker for one side of the fire has done speaking, the people on the other side talk softly about what they intend to reply, and then someone stands up to deliver the response. The two-sidedness, the gradual building of consensus, and the designated speaker are all things that would be typical of Haudenosaunee councils, at the clan, nation, Confederacy, and international levels.

a single one, and their power is that they shall join hands.[230] This, moreover, shall be the basis upon which they will survive as a group. Forming a single family, similar to being one person having one head and one life, surrounded by the Good Message. This is how peace will now come about among all of the Nations, and power will arise for families to continue from here on in.

Thirdly, this is what "Peace" means. Now it will stop, the massacre of humans and the scalping and bloodletting among themselves, specifically, among the people of the various nations. Now as to that, it will end, the human slaughter, because the Great Spirit never planned for humans to hurt one another nor to slaughter one another. So now it will end, the warpath, and everywhere it will become peaceful; the different nations' villages are as neighbours and as to the localized families and their children, what will happen is that they will all be very close relatives; and it will come to pass that they will become just like one family which will encompass every nation and every language. And this: when everyone can travel from village to village, then it will end, the danger and terror, and then everything will be peaceful, and they will rejoice by day and by night as the family continues on, there being no end to peace; that is what it means, the Great Law of Peace, that everyone will be united.[231]

An English translation does not accurately convey the actual meaning of the three ideas. They are more complex than the English words imply.

Ne'skén:nen means "peace," but it has different meanings when applied to a society or a people—where it means peace, tranquility, or rest (with its opposite being war, strife, or contention)—and to a living individual, where the same word also means health, soundness, and a normal functioning condition (with their opposites being disease, illness, and possession by witchcraft).[232] Good health—physical, mental, and spiritual—is thus an important aspect of the law. Haudenosaunee greetings carry this dual meaning, a wish for peace[233]

---

230 The joining of hands—tehatiatnetsha—is the symbolic way of becoming one family. It is repeated, later, in the making of peace with nations beyond the Longhouse, and in the making of the Covenant Chain with the British.

231 Gibson 1912, 101–8.

232 In his footnotes to the 1899 Gibson version of the law, William Fenton, writing Simeon Gibson's views, explains the multiple meanings of the three words. He translates them as "reason, righteousness and justice, peace and health, and authority or the force of law."

233 Shalom, salaam aleikum, pax vobiscum—greetings conveying the desire for peace are widespread. They are often interpreted as intended to wish personal peace, but they can be understood in the wider context, as well. Other concepts are also both societal and personal: *jihad* can mean holy war, but it is said that the great *jihad* is the one that is waged within each person.

in a social and a personal sense. The common Seneca greeting, "Kanien'ké:ha niyá:wen sken:nen," conveys the hope that the other person is grateful for his peace and good health. The Haudenosaunee perception of health does not stop at the boundary of the human body or human society. It extends to the world around us: environmental health means both that humans thrive in an environment that is free of things that cause disease, and that humans must avoid doing things that cause harm to the natural world. The mandate or responsibility of people in the world can be seen through the lens of health, in which "first, do no harm"[234] is a minimum standard, and restoration and maintenance of a healthy environment is an ongoing task.

Karihwí:iyo, which is translated as "righteousness," is more literally "the good word," but "word" and "way" are blurred. Fenton asserts: "Its first denotation is *gospel*, wholesome doctrine, what is good to be heard, ethical teaching, values, ethics—righteousness. As its second meaning, it denotes justice, right, as formulated in the customs, manners, religion and ritualistic summations of the past experiences of the people. The first is the teaching of good doctrine; the second is the establishment of the good doctrine in institutional forms."[235]

Sotsisowah John Mohawk warned of the implications of choosing the English word "righteousness" as a translation. It has taken on both a Christian religious aura and a negative tone (when someone is accused of being "self-righteous"). He explains the pragmatism that flows from the Haudenosaunee concept: "Righteousness . . . is a very dangerous word in English history. But let me just give a sense of how it was used. Righteousness means that almost all of us agree that some things are right, correct, positive, which is to say that they may not all agree that some things are obviously right and wrong. But there are some things they will agree on. So those are the things you start to build on. You have your conversation and your negotiations until you hit the rock hard things."[236]

Yoyanere, the root word of the law, Kayanerenkó:wa, can be translated into English as "good" or "goodness," but it has several other meanings.

Its broad spectrum ranges from "correct, proper, right" to "righteous, righteousness," to "a path, a way, a way of being," and "welfare."[237] The concept

---

234 In the Hippocratic oath taken by Western doctors, this is the preliminary thought, the equivalent of the Three Bare Words.

235 Gibson 1899, para. 133, fn. 5. Karihwí:iyo, today, is also used to describe the "Code of Handsome Lake," the summation of what the Seneca chief and teacher Skaniatariio taught in the late eighteenth century, codified at Tonawanda in the decades after his death. The Code represents "a good way of living" and is seen as an addition to the Kayanerenkó:wa.

236 Mohawk 2005b.

237 This last meaning is put forward in Fenton and Simeon Gibson's translation of Gibson 1899, para. 38.

encompasses all of these positive meanings. In its breadth, it has no English equivalent.

The lack of an English equivalent to yoyanere points out how ideas that are crucial in one culture can be seen, by the lack of similar words, to be less important in another culture, or to be understood with different emphasis. In Haudenosaunee terms, yoyanere is an important legal concept. In English, none of these ideas has a great deal of legal meaning. In criminal law, the ability to distinguish right and wrong is meaningful, but "rightness," as a moral concept, is not really what the legal system is about. Rather, it is about what is legal and illegal.[238] Yoyanere has no Anglo-American legal equivalent.

Other legal cultures in the world, though, do understand *law* as based on the same spectrum of meaning as yoyanere in Haudenosaunee law.[239]

One of those legal cultures is that of Hawai'i. *Law*, in the Hawai'ian language, is *kanawai*, a term translated as "responsibility for water." A fundamental concept of the legal system is *pono*, which has been translated as "righteousness," but which also carries the meanings of "good, proper, correct, righteous, a path, a way." The concept of *pono* is important enough to have been made a part of the motto of Hawai'i, created by its last king: *Ua mau ke ea o ha aina i ka pono,* the life of the land is perpetuated in righteousness. *Pono* is also a central concept in the criminal law system of traditional Hawai'ian law, *Ho'oponopono,* which centres on "prayer, discussion, repentance, and mutual restitution or forgiveness."[240]

Another legal culture that seems to have placed yoyanere at its core is that of ancient Rome. The *Lex Aquilia* governed loss wrongfully inflicted on property (*damnum iniuria datum*). For the first time in Roman history, a law provided a process for adjudicating disputes arising from property damage, and the most essential underlying element of this was the *wrongfulness* of the damage. *Iniuria,* "injury," does not mean "physical harm." It means a lack of *ius,* which is usually translated as "justice." An injury to property, then, is wrongful because it is unjust. *Ius* is defined in the *Encyclopedic Dictionary of Roman Law*[241] as embracing the whole of the law, "what is always just and fair," what is right.

---

238 There is an important exception: equity is a distinct stream of British and hence Canadian law, governed by principles or maxims of fairness rather than statutes and the common law. As such, it is closer to many Indigenous legal systems and to the fundamental questions those systems address.

239 The Highland Scots, too, carried a sense of righteousness. "The Gaelic word *náire* is usually translated into English as 'shame' or 'modesty', although it has a wider usage than this in Gaelic, referring to the sense of what is right, proper and honourable. It is a key concept in the operation of Gaelic society. 'Am fear a chaill a náire is a modh, chaill e na bh'aige' (The person who has lost his propriety and his manners lost all he had)." Newton 2009, 148.

240 Pukui and Elbert 1992.

241 Berger 1953, 525.

The fact that "law" is linked to following a proper path of conduct is demonstrated by the way the Romans dealt with dispute resolution and compensation. A person who has been sued, and who has denied liability and been found responsible by the court, is obliged to pay a double indemnity, twice the compensation claimed. By denying responsibility, he acted in a "non-Roman" way, unrighteously. The *Lex Aquilia* does not specify standards of conduct in detail. Roman society at the time was that of a city state, not an empire. It was coherent and cohesive enough that people *knew* what was right. The Code did not need to set out the principles of justice because they were already well-known: they were the fabric of society itself.

Halakha, traditional Jewish law, is derived from an archaic term that describes the path that leads directly to the water hole. So is *Sharia,* traditional Islamic law. In both cases, following the correct path is the key to maintaining life in the desert that both religions lived in.

In Asia, the Buddha taught the *Way* to release from sorrow, the doctrine of the Eightfold Path. He spoke of right views, right aspirations, right speech, right conduct, right meditation, and right rapture. Joseph Campbell points out that "right," in this context, is the "Sanskrit *samyak,* 'appropriate, whole, complete, correct, proper, true.'"[242]

Yoyanere. Ius. Pono. Halahka. Sharia. Samyak. They are essentially the same broad set of concepts. The idea is that people know what is right and will recognize and implement it. There is a moral dimension to law, and it is that dimension that makes it enforceable by society. It is what one feels viscerally, in one's guts (*na'au* in Hawai'i). There are times when this sense is manifested in modern North American society. When some of the financial firms the federal government had bailed out persisted in giving their executives generous bonuses, Congress's 2009 clawback of the bonuses was based on a groundswell of public opinion, based not on sentiment but on a sense of *injustice*. What they did, people said, was not *right*. The danger of translating yoyanere simply as "goodness" or "righteousness" is that those words do not imply the legality, in modern English, of the concepts. Having a law with yoyanere at its core presses towards a legal system based on principle rather than detail. The key questions, as John Mohawk insisted, are consistently: *What is the thinking? Is the thinking right?*

The third "word" or principle of the peace, Ka'satsténshsera, is often translated into English as either "power" or "righteousness." It is an imperfect translation. The concept can mean "the power of peace." It is the power to get things done. John Mohawk explained:

> He promised them power. Not military power, but the power of
> righteousness. Where would this power of righteousness come from?

---

242 Campbell 1972, 133.

In some societies this is a negative idea because righteousness is often presumptive, unthinking, and uncaring. He defined righteousness as the result of the best thinking of collective minds operating from principles which assume that a sane world requires that we provide a safe environment for our children seven generations into the future.[243]

Power, your power to act, depends upon your capacity to believe what it is that you set about doing can be done. In other words, you won't do what needs to be done if you think it is a futile gesture.[244]

Simeon Gibson explained to William Fenton that the term's first meaning is "force, authority based on force, as expressed in the war power of the people; and its second meaning is the power, force or authority of the orenda or magic potency of the institutions of the people." Both of these ideas are quite different from the thoughtful, pragmatic way John Mohawk explained the power to act.

The English word "power" derives part of its usefulness from its vagueness. It means two quite different concepts, ability and authority.[245] Thus, when one says *The Prime Minister has the power to chair cabinet meetings* (a matter of authority), one is referring to something very different from *Superman has the power to fly* (a matter of ability).[246] In the case of Thadadaho, the authority he ended up with in the law, as a result of the consent and consensus of the founders of the Confederacy, was quite different from the authority he had taken in his earlier form, which flowed from his "preternatural" ability to do harm.

The dual meanings in Haudenosaunee languages of the Peacemaker's three basic messages were generally complementary, each word implying a range of desirable consequences, whether the peace was social or personal, a matter of health or tranquility; whether the righteousness was about justice or about religion; whether the power was the physical or the spiritual force of the people. Translated into English, the three concepts have acquired the further baggage of the English words. "Peace" tends to lose the health connotations of ne'skén:nen; "power" tends to accentuate its military meaning; "righteousness" takes on its Christian connotations.

John Mohawk would translate the three concepts as "peace, righteousness and reason." Reason, he said, "means that you're going to do the rock hard things":

---

243 Mohawk 1989, 224.

244 Mohawk 2004, n.pag.

245 In French, *pouvoir* is verb as well as noun, and is much more linked to being able to do something.

246 The example comes from Dr. Kanakalût Roland Chrisjohn. In French, *pouvoir* is much closer to its root in ability: the verb means that one *can* do something.

You're not going to settle them, really, but you're going to do the best you can with them. You're going to move them as far forward on as many points as possible. The Iroquois law of peace assumes that you will not achieve peace. You will not achieve a perfect agreement between two warring sides about how the world ought to be in the future. But it also assumes that you can reach enough of it to have something to work on so that you can take the conflict from physical warfare over to a place where, as they used to say, thinking can replace violence.[247]

The ability to grasp the principles of Righteousness is a spark within the individual which society must fan and nurture that it may grow. Reason is seen as the skill which humans must be encouraged to acquire, in order that the objectives of justice may be attained and no one's rights abused. The Power to enact a true Peace is the product of a unified people on the path of Righteousness and Reason—the ability to enact the principles of Peace through education, public opinion and political and, when necessary, military unity.[248]

In explaining the three great ingredients of the law and the peace as a process, John Mohawk reflected on the difference between English, which would use statutes to establish standards, and Haudenosaunee languages, which look towards processes and relationships. Peace, he says, is permanently an objective rather than an achieved state.[249]

The Haudenosaunee Environmental Health Model, a modern manifestation of the three great matters of the law, breaks these three words down into additional components:

> *Kanikonhriio* is measured by assessing several areas:
>
> *Iakorihwenton* – Commitment
>
> *Karihwakwenienhtshera* – Respect
>
> *Kaiatakweniiotsera* – Responsibility
>
> *Skennenkowa* is measured by assessing several areas:
>
> *Enskarihwakwarihshion* – Ability to resolve issues

---

247 Mohawk 2004, n.pag.

248 Ibid.

249 Perhaps Canada and Australia applied this reasoning when they provided lukewarm endorsements of the United Nations Declaration on the Rights of Indigenous Peoples—which they had earlier voted against—as an "aspirational document." It is more likely, though, that they were worried about the implications of the Declaration concerning land and consent.

Kanoronhkwahthsera – Love

Atenonhwaratonhtserakon – Gratitude

Kasatstenhsera is measured by assessing several areas:

Iakotahsnienonhskon – Generosity

Ronatennikonhraroron – Collective thinking

Why three words? While they may be a reflection of the three words (eyes, ears, and throat) at the beginning of the Condolence, the words used without wampum in a greeting at the woods' edge, the number three is itself significant.[250] It recalls the three breaths that the Creator blew into the first human to give him life. Not all Haudenosaunee thinking involves duality: there are also triads.

Taiaiake Gerald Alfred explains:

> It starts with the rhetorical gestures that we call the "rare words":[251] wiping the eyes, cleansing the throat, and unblocking the ears. These are symbolic gestures to pacify grieving people, or the former adversary in a treaty process. The reason that you have to pacify these people is that they are in pain: they can't see properly, they can't hear, and they don't speak the truth. Something serious has happened to them, and the challenge for the strong-minded, the peacemakers, is to take them beyond the pain to a place of peace. What happened to bring them pain? In the ritual—and all your life, if you desire peace—you have to figure out a way of saying something to those people, doing something, or giving them something that will make them capable of seeing, hearing and speaking their way back to peace.[252]

The three concepts can also be understood as a sequence. A person hears and is persuaded by the word, the Good Message. He becomes good-minded, and this infuses him with the power of righteousness. In turn, this enables him to seek, create, and maintain the peace.[253] The three concepts are, in a way, a

---

250 A chief is warned three times before he is removed. There are three attempts to persuade Thadadaho, and the third succeeds.

251 Again, not "rare," but "bare": they are the words spoken at the edge of the woods without wampum in the speaker's hands.

252 Alfred 1999, xx–xxi. Taiaiake uses the structure of the Condolence to suggest political and social paths to "requickening" the sovereignty of Indigenous peoples.

253 A person who has joined the peace has the obligation to maintain and spread it. Similarly, a person who has been healed by a Haudenosaunee medicine society becomes a member of that society, who then takes part in maintaining its medicine and healing other people.

mirror of the three concepts contained in the silver links of the Covenant Chain treaty relationship, made with the British Crown in 1677 and with the United States more than a century later: respect, trust, and friendship. Respect must be achieved first. Based on respect, one may build trust, and friendship may grow from that. But one cannot trust someone one does not respect, and one cannot build a friendship with someone who cannot be trusted. In each case, the three concepts have an order to them, and must be implemented in sequence.

If the three factors that led to the breakdown of the society of the five nations were greed, hatred, and jealousy, the three new words are their counterparts and antidotes.

A constant element in the story of the making of the law is that the Cannibal, Hiawatha, and Tsikonsaseh are living alone—and the Peacemaker invites them not only to return to civil society, but also to learn to share again, for they were not only living but also eating alone. Refusing to share is selfishness, a denial of social responsibility. That is why these people share a meal with the Peacemaker once their minds accept the peace. It is a sign that they have once again accepted the proper way to live with other people. Restoring physical health, mental health, and social health are interwoven.

From Individuals to Nations

The building of the Great Law follows a deliberate strategy: to gather together individual minds first; to gather support and confidence; and to build from the conversion of individuals to the conversion of entire nations.

The Peacemaker tests his tactics on the Cannibal. He tests his reason with Tsikonsaseh. He develops his compassionate and spiritual authority with Hiawatha. He tests political pragmatism on Thadadahoh. Then he begins to bring the chiefs onside, and with them their families and communities. At each step, the momentum of peace builds, gaining both detail and weight.

This strategy is later reflected in the way consensus is built in council, and even later in the way the Haudenosaunee would deal with other nations. An idea is put forward. It is stated positively but gently, tentatively, to avoid convey-ing any sense of aggressive or confrontational intent. The people on the other side of the fire then agree with it and add to it, equally constructively, so that, as the matter goes back and forth across the council fire, it gathers energy as it becomes more precise and focussed. Along the way, the talents and gifts of each participant are added to make the movement more effective. In negotiations as in council, the Haudenosaunee will tend to address the easiest issues first, to develop a set of agreements that will carry the parties into a mood of harmony as they develop the momentum to deal with the rock-hard things. They know the hard things are there, and are not going away. Amassing agreement on the easier things makes it more difficult to walk away from the hard ones.

The process of peace is also structured, in the sense that it follows a pattern, from the smaller to the larger, from the least powerful to the most powerful, and from the easiest to the most difficult.

This flow is reflected in the discussion in the law about the nature of government. That conversation, like many Haudenosaunee matters, is about the process of authority rather than its specific events. It is also about the flow of authority from the people through the chiefs and clan mothers, rather than the vesting of authority in the chiefs to make executive decisions.

The Peacemaker's journey of bringing nations together is not simply an east-west path. Instead, he begins with the Mohawks, visits the Senecas, then moves across to the Oneidas and Cayugas, returns to the Mohawks and Senecas, and then faces the Onondagas.[254] He criss-crosses the Finger Lakes region. This geographical path of persuasion might also be said to reflect the path of an idea or proposal in council. The path flows from the Older Brothers across the fire to the Younger Brothers, then back again and at last to the firekeepers (that is, if one does not count overcoming the Seneca warriors' opposition at the very end).

Mohawk: Testing the Peacemaker

The Mohawks did not at first accept the Peacemaker's message. Naturally, it was the warriors who had the greatest hesitation, since they had the responsibility of protecting the village, but also because they had the heaviest personal stake in seeing the bloodshed continue. War was the source of their influence. They would not give it up easily.[255] The Great Warrior issued a challenge to the Peacemaker, as diplomatically and indirectly as possible under the circumstances:

> As to me, this is what I personally am questioning. What will happen
> if we accept the Good Message and the Power and the Peace, and

---

254   In the Gibson 1912 version, the Peacemaker goes to Seneca country after persuading the Mohawks and being rebuffed by Thadadaho (1912, 174–75).

255   An historic example of this occurred in Tahlequa, Oklahoma, in the summer of 1843. The Cherokees, recently arrived after the Trail of Tears, proposed to the seventeen nations gathered there that they should coexist under the principles of the Great Law, which the Haudenosaunee had brought to the Cherokees in 1770. According to one record, all the nations accepted the principles of peace, except the Choctaws, who stated that "we love our warriors too much to take their game away from them."

the other tribes do not accept it? Subsequently this could happen: perhaps they will come to massacre us. Hence this is what I personally would say to this man who has arrived, Tekanawita . . .

I might believe it if he were able to climb that tree growing over there beside the river, on the high bank, and if when he sits on the top of the tree, subsequently we were to cut down the tree, which would get knocked down in the direction of the river, now if this man . . . were to pass the test, surviving until dawn tomorrow, then I will immediately accept whatever message he has along.[256]

This test recalls the account of the Peacemaker's grandmother trying to kill him as an infant. In both cases, the actions involved near-certain death, but without anyone resorting to a weapon, or even using their hands. Burning, drowning, falling, burying, exposure: they relied on the forces of the natural world to do the killing. And the Peacemaker, like Taharonhiawakon before him, was allied with all the natural world.

The account of testing the Peacemaker shows that a good idea is often not enough: people want proof that the idea will work, that it has real, demonstrable power. Reluctance to join the peace is based on fear of what might happen if one community puts down its weapons and others do not. Their enemies may fall upon them. The fear is reasonable enough. People want peace. They just do not want to die as a result of accepting it. It is significant that, in all the versions of the law, nobody says that he rejects peace because he wants bloodshed to continue. Instead, they remain armed out of rational fear. They ask the Peacemaker for a demonstration of the power of his protection. If the power protected him, they reasoned, it would also protect them. In contrast to the Great Warrior and his deputy (for the deputy had issued the same challenge), the chief of the Mohawks fully and gladly accepted the Good Message, the Peace, and the Power on behalf of his family.[257] This is a precursor of the difference in attitude and function of the "peace chiefs" and the "warriors."[258] In token of this,

---

256 Gibson 1912, 108–10 (Native North American Travelling College 2000, 22; Parker [Newhouse and Cusick] 1916, 16; Parker [Chiefs] 1916, 72). Parker specifies that the tree is bitter hickory which stood at the doorway of a woman named Desiio, and that the Peacemaker, climbing the tree, sang six verses of the Pacification song (Parker [Chiefs] 1916, 73fn). Cutting down the tree is repeated in the Peacemaker's uprooting of a tree so that the weapons of war would be thrown into the pit beneath it.

257 Gibson 1912, 113. Jamie Jacobs of Tonawanada pointed out, in the 2013 recital of the law, that the chiefs of the eastern Seneca village were able to accept the peace without much hesitation, while the chiefs of the western town, which faced numerous enemies at the western door of the proposed longhouse, had to continue to act as war leaders as well as peace chiefs.

258 Tehahenteh uses Rotiskenrakéhte as a translation for "warrior." It describes a person carrying a burden of red ochre, to remind him that he is of the earth. –kehte describes both a burden and a duty.

the Peacemaker gave the chief a new name: "This is now your name and they will use it to address you: Hayewatha, and all of the people will live by it, your name, and it will help them in succeeding generations to say 'Hayewatha.'"[259]

Each time a leader accepts the peace, renouncing violence, repenting for his past conduct, the Peacemaker recognizes this by giving the man a new name, a name that will become a chiefly title. It is a watershed moment, marking a personal transformation.[260] In a way, it is as if the person who refused the peace no longer existed. He had become a new kind of person. The Peacemaker's authority is reflected in his power to rename people.

The Peacemaker submitted to the ordeal proposed by the warriors. He climbed the tree,[261] and the tree was cut down and fell into the gorge, disappearing into the turbulent waters. The next day, the people saw smoke rising from a fire downstream. They went to investigate.[262] The Peacemaker was alive and well.[263] The Mohawks then embraced the message of peace.[264]

Today, Cohoes Falls on the Mohawk River—which according to tradition is the scene of the test—is considered a sacred place by many Haudenosaunee, though its power and flow have been restrained by a hydroelectric dam.

To prove his power, the Peacemaker subjected himself to a test that was almost certain suicide. It is as if the legend of the making of the peace contains two streams: on the one hand, a rational path of teaching, preaching, and

---

259 Gibson 1912, 114–15.

260 If he gives a new name to the Cannibal, there is no record of it. But then, the Cannibal is not a leader nor part of government, and his name would not be passed on through the generations.

261 In climbing to the top of the white pine, is the Peacemaker emulating the eagle?

262 In Gibson's 1899 version, Hiawatha is waiting, hidden, below the falls. The two men meet, and agree that the Peacemaker will move on to persuade the Cayugas, while Hiawatha emerges to finish the work among the Mohawks. If the Peacemaker disappeared and Hiawatha took his place, though, the Mohawks would likely be unpersuaded of his power: by 1912, Gibson recounted how the Peacemaker showed himself, alive and well, to the Mohawks, before heading eastward to confront the Great Witch (1912, 125–32).

263 Other holy men, or men of power or divinity, across the world have been subjected to a similar test to prove their immortality or power. Odin was hung in a tree, then drowned, then burned. So, too, Merlin, when he came out of the forest, suffered the traditional Celtic "threefold death" by hanging, falling, and drowning (sometimes hanging, drowning, and clubbing on the head, which is often more final) and then lived as proof of his power. So, too, in a way, was Jesus: the cross has often been called a tree, and the proof of his power, just as in the case of the Peacemaker, was that he came back from what appeared to be certain death. In each case, another aspect of the man's power was fatherlessness.

264 At probably the same time as the Mohawks were testing the power and truth of the Peacemaker's message by having him risk his life, in many parts of Europe there was a practice of testing truthfulness by torture. The Inquisition in Catholic countries, and the war against witchcraft everywhere in Europe, reflected European reliance on torture in much the same spirit as the Mohawks' test.

persuasion, and on the other, a series of powerful, unusual, magical demonstrations of power.[265] In the latter path lie the white stone canoe, the test imposed by the Mohawks, and the physical "straightening out" of Thadadaho.[266] How can they be reconciled? Do they need to be reconciled? Perhaps one can acknowledge that the Peacemaker had a variety of tools he could use, and he selected the devices according to the nature of the challenge. He carried both "power" in the sense of the authority that stems from rationality and pragmatism and "power" in the sense of the ability to do wondrous things.[267]

In most accounts, the Mohawks had not debated whether the ideas proposed by the Peacemaker were correct, but rather whether he had sufficient power, ka'satsténshsera, both physically and spiritually. When he demonstrated that power, by his survival, he then explained to the Mohawks that, by the very process of their deciding to embrace his message, they had shown that the law he was proposing worked for them, and would continue to work. They had made their decision by talking the matter over as a single family—e'tho ní:yoht ne skahwá:tsire tsi ní:yoht tsi wa'tesewarihwayén:ta'ne.[268] They had taken hold of the law by spontaneously engaging in the process that would make the law work, and bringing themselves together as a people in the manner that the law required.[269]

By making a correct decision as a single family, the Mohawks had demonstrated ka'nikonhrí:yo, the Good Mind, in both its rational side and its moral side. By choosing peace over war, they had taken the second step, skén:nen,

---

265 According to Newhouse (Parker 1916, 16) the Peacemaker also asserted another difference between himself and ordinary humans: "I am able to demonstrate my power, for I am the messenger of the Creator, and he truly has given me my choice in the manner of my death." In Haudenosaunee belief, the number of the days of our lives is known only to the Creator and is preordained: the Peacemaker has been given an additional portion of free will.

266 John Mohawk points out that a fundamental difference between European and North American religions is the difference between "magic" and "miracles." "Magic" is something that is achieved as a result of the powers of the natural world—like the healing performed by the medicine societies. "Miracles," by definition, are unnatural. That is, if it can be shown that a "miracle" associated with a candidate for sainthood was actually a natural occurrence, then the event cannot be counted as a true miracle.

267 After the ordeal, a Mohawk chief asks Hiawatha to choose one of his seven daughters in marriage: Hiawatha selects the youngest, to which the father replies "that one indeed is the one I most dearly love" (Gibson 1899, para. 35). While there are suggestions of arranged marriages in early times, the idea of a man choosing among sisters, or of a father giving away that choice, is not consistent with what we know about the rights of women in Haudenosaunee society. While Hiawatha is married, the Peacemaker, in contrast, remains chaste and unmarried.

268 "They all began to speak with one another, the women, the children, even the old ones": Ta'ónen yakoya'terí:onh kentyohkwánen wa'thatihtarónnyon, konnónkwe, ratiksa'okón:a akwékon rotiksten'okón:'a nityotiyén:'a, nithotiyén:sa akwékon wa'thatihtharónnyon. Thomas 2010, 203.

269 Thomas 2010, 203–4.

bringing themselves both peace and health. These two steps, taken in order, would inevitably lead to ka'satsténshsera. By showing the people that he carried this power, the Peacemaker had caused them to enact the first step, accept the second, and bring about the third.

The Mohawks needed yet more reassurance. What if their enemies should continue to kill them "now that we are letting go of protecting ourselves to survive"? The Peacemaker reassured them, and told them not to worry: "It will stop now, the entire matter of the warpath, now that the door is closing, because now it will be in operation, the Good Message, where the several villages are distributed across the bush; it will be in operation, their Power, as they unite, the several nations; and there will be Peace from this Power."[270]

Tekarihoken, Hiawatha, and Satekariwate: The First Mohawk Chiefs

As the Peacemaker carried the message of the Three Words forward, he was constantly building the more detailed, internal structures of what would become the Haudenosaunee. The great message is constantly repeated in the various versions of the law, as the ingredients of what would become the council fall into place. With the Mohawks, the Peacemaker established the concept that a chief's title would become permanent, passed on to his successors. That is, the name of the first person to occupy a position would become the title conferred upon each person to hold that position in the future. In the case of the Mohawk chiefs, the Peacemaker gave them new names to recognize the importance of their commitment to peace.[271]

According to Teyoninhokarawen John Norton, writing in the early 1800s, the Mohawk chiefs were given their title-names as a direct result of their commitment to the peace and their will to confront Thadadaho: "Tekanawitagh laid down the wampum he appropriated for the occasion: another Chief laying down his proportion said, 'Sadekariwa-tegh, said, 'tekarigkogea wakerighwageron';

---

270   Gibson 1912, 129–30.

271   When the Europeans arrived, the Haudenosaunee imposed this practice upon them. The Sieur de Montmagny received the title of Onontiio, a rendering of his name, the Beautiful Mountain. Every governor of Pennsylvania became Onas, the Big Feather, after William Penn. The first Dutch commissioner, Arendt van Curler, lent his name—usually spelled Corlaer—to successive governors of New York and then governors general of Canada, as well as to the superintendent general of Indian affairs. For the sake of continuity, a title-name becomes a permanent reminder of historic relationships.

I put mine among the whole affair.' The first was called from this experience, Satekariwategh, the other Tekarihogea."[272]

Ely Parker stated that Hiawatha enlisted Tekarihoken as his speaker and brother, while he would work in the background.[273] In Gibson's 1899 version, Tekarihoken and Satekariwate are recruited at Hiawatha's wedding to the former's daughter.

> At that time the chief said, "So what kind of names shall you and I have?" Hiawatha replied, "You of course are the proprietor of this place. You moreover gave out the information that you and your collaborators had reached a common opinion (decision). And so then, as for you, your name (title) hereafter shall be Degaaihoo'geh, people shall continue to say, and now as to your particular co-worker, he is the one they shall continue to call Cha'degaaiwaa'de, 'Of the Same Opinion'[274] . . . these titles which I have bestowed upon you two shall then be confirmed by Deganawii'dah when he comes here."[275]

In Gibson's 1912 version, the Great Warrior of the Mohawks had been uncertain about the authenticity of the Peacemaker's message, and that was the origin of his title: "You were of two minds, with one you were thinking that it is not true what you have heard about the Good Message, and with the second you were thinking that to the extent that you will see an affirmation, it might be true. So now you accept the Good Message and the Power and the Peace. Now, moreover, I will tell you that this is your name, they will say Tekaihoke?, and the people of all nations will be sustained by your name in future days and nights as the families continue on."[276]

---

272 Norton 1970, 103. Thayendenega Joseph Brant, Norton's adoptive uncle, was known to have been writing a detailed history of the Haudenosaunee. That document has been lost. Norton's journal, which was published in England, probably contains elements of Brant's written document, but certainly contains elements of his knowledge.

273 Converse, 1908, 188–89. This is the reverse of Dewaserage William Loft's theory that Tekanawita would stay in the background while Hiawatha would do the speaking.

274 In Gibson 1912, the deputy to the Great Warrior, who had "accepted the entire Good Message," was named Satekariwade (Tshaʔtekaihwate) by the Peacemaker (1912, 126).

275 Gibson 1899, para. 91. The two chiefs are also chosen to give thanks after the wedding meal, another of the many feasts used to bind the people together. Confirmation of names by the Peacemaker is a precursor of today's confirmation of position through the Condolence.

276 Gibson 1912, 125–26. In Gibson's 1912 version, the Mohawks agree to join the peace before Hiawatha's last daughter is killed and he retreats into the woods.

These three men became the first decision-making committee[277] of the council of the Haudenosaunee: Tekarihoken, Satekariwate, and Hiawatha. The council of the League was being built, one piece at a time. All three titles are of the Turtle Clan. This is consistent with the historical record, in the sense that when Europeans first encountered the Mohawks, each of the three clans had a separate village.[278]

Westward

The Peacemaker's journey then took him to see the "Great Witch," probably Thadadaho, to prepare him for the coming of peace: "So this is what my errand was: we two should talk, so that he might change his habits. And this: shortly, he would work for and accept the Good Message and the Power and the Peace. This, moreover, is what happened: I promised that several tribes and I would come, and that we will all co-operate with him."[279]

The process of building the confederation was slow and deliberate. Visiting a reluctant chief involved planting seeds that might grow later, leaving ideas that could germinate, and slowly accumulating trust. If a person does not accept an idea immediately, one should avoid confrontation, and instead seek to return with more persuasive evidence at some later time. The Peacemaker does not retreat from his proposals, but he may move laterally, gathering strength and support, before coming forward again. "We two should talk" indicates the need for conversation. Conversation, communication, the process, is the beginning of peacemaking.[280]

---

277 "You will co-operate, you chiefs . . . now you will all work for the Good Message, and the Power, and the Peace." Gibson 1912, 127. The use of the term "committee" is uncomfortable: it is used in contemporary North America to describe a group of people with detailed authority, while in a Haudenosaunee context, in modern usage, there is a reluctance to establish "committees" for fear that they might usurp authority from the chiefs and therefore from the people. Delegations of tasks (and less frequently, authority) are generally made to individuals, or to ad hoc groups that will last as long as the task. "Committee" is the wrong word, but it is an English word that has been used to describe a group of people who are expected to work together.

278 By the late 1600s, the Turtle Clan villages were east of "Anthony's Nose," a peak on the Mohawk River near the present Westchester, New York. The Bears were a little west of there, and the Wolves several miles west. Bonaparte 2006; Sivertsen 1997. Since men would marry outside their clan and move to their wives' villages, each village would contain people of several clans, but a "Turtle Clan village" would have Turtle Clan women and Turtle Clan chiefs.

279 Gibson 1912, 173–74.

280 U.S. President Lyndon Johnson was fond of quoting the Bible: "Come, now, and let us reason together" (Isaiah 1:18).

Visiting the Great Witch alone, knowing that "he is the one who is able to kill; moreover, he has killed many people," was an act of courage and power.

From Onondaga territory, the Peacemaker went to see the Senecas. They, too, were reluctant to embrace the Good Message, though neither did they reject it:

> Thereupon I left again, going to where the Tionontowaneh live; I arrived at the Chief's house and talked to him, notifying him that they were arriving, the Good Message and the Great Law and the Peace, and then the chief said, "On the other side of the river is the house of my deputy," so then we crossed over and, arriving at the chief's house, we saw him and talked about all the matters and I reported everything.[281] Thereafter the two of them answered, saying we will consider it later. And then I said, "You two will be notified again when unanimity is reached."[282]

When the Peacemaker returned to Mohawk country and met with Hiawatha again, the Great Peace had become a movement. It was spreading with the help of many other people, and was not relying only on the efforts of the two leaders. The movement's spread was visible in the brave white columns of smoke rising to meet the sky:

> Tekanawita said, "look half way between the East and the South," and Hayewatha, looking there, saw smoke rising and piercing the sky. Thereupon Tekanawita said, "See the smoke rising, piercing the sky. Now as to that, they have heard about the Good Message. This also: they believe in the Power and the Peace."[283]

> The reason you see the smoke piercing the sky is because the Good Tidings of Peace and Power have come to the people of that settlement ... you will now see as you turn around in every direction the columns of smoke arising.[284]

As communities accepted the message, they would indicate their adherence with a column of white smoke, the colour of peace. In times of war and uncertainty, settlements would not advertise their presence: they would keep their

---

281 One aspect of the peacemaking process is ensuring that everyone has the same information. "I reported everything" implies that steps were being taken to reassure the chiefs that there were no secrets: that all was in the open, that nobody was being told things that the others did not know.

282 Gibson 1912, 175–76.

283 Gibson 1912, 176.

284 Parker (Chiefs) 1916, 79, 81.

fires low, smokeless, and unobtrusive.[285] As the message gained momentum, these columns of white smoke became visible all around: reassurance, power, and themselves a Good Message, gathering strength, piercing the sky, an impetus and invitation to their neighbours to join in the peace.

Oneida: Odatsehte

The Mohawks, at the eastern end of the geographic Longhouse, had embraced the message of peace and power first. East of the Mohawks lived Algonkian peoples—the Algonquins to the northeast; the Abenakis to the east; the Mahicans to the southeast. Between the Mohawks and these Algonkian peoples there were linguistic, geographic, and cultural barriers: it made more sense to work with people who were more open to the Mohawks. The Oneidas, living just west of the Mohawks, were linguistically, culturally, and geographically as close as possible.

> Tekanawitagh set off for Onondagui and ascending the rapid stream of the Mohawk River, he came to Tehikaghkwetsni, now called Utica: there he met an Onida, with a wolf skin quiver.[286] The Onida saluted him by the title of brother, cousin, friend. To all of which Tekanawitagh made no reply. He then said, "I salute you my father"—true, my son (returned Tekanawitagh) "for none of the trees of the forest are equal to me in age: the willows of the River's banks alone approach it." He then continued, "where are you going my father?" He replied, "I am going to soothe the angry feelings of Thatotarho; to reform his rugged appearance, and endeavour to make him like other men." He then named the Onida, Odatsheghte,

---

285 There is a tradition that one factor in choosing village sites was the presence of shagbark hickory trees. These trees would be girdled and would eventually fall over. The bark would be used in cooking fires, because it provides heat without smoke. In longhouses with overhead smokeholes, it would be important to avoid excessively smoky cooking fires. Conversely, one would boldly announce one's peaceful presence with a pillar of thick white smoke from an outdoor fire, an intentional signal fire.

286 That the law would recall unusual details—Odatsehte's wolf skin quiver, or Hiawatha's fawn-skin bag for the wampum—may be an indicator of its connection to historical reality. When modern historians examined the *Iliad*, they confirmed that the black-hulled ships described in the text would indeed have been the kind used at the time of the Trojan War, 1,000 years before the text was reduced to writing, and long after black-hulled ships had faded into disuse.

or the Quiver Carrier,[287] who replied. "Father, the day is now too far spent; let us remain at home this night. In the morning, if you will return, I shall throw a tree across the path to detain you a little while, and then we shall proceed together to the place where the smoke of Thadadarho's fires arise." This was spoken allegorically to the season.

Tekanawitagh returned home, and in the spring got ready for his embassy. They came to the abode of Odatsheghte, who entertained them kindly. The people of the Village assembled together, Odatsheghte rose and sung: "This is my father; he is my superior, and I will follow him." Tekanawitagh interrupting him said: "that will not do, you must sing: 'My father and I shall risk together—we are the same.'" Odatsheghte immediately complied, which satisfied him.[288]

The Peacemaker had met Odatsehte beside a cornfield. The Oneida chief had been guarding the corn. He told the Peacemaker: "They roam about, people we don't know, and they may spoil it, or perhaps wild animals might spoil the corn field, and this is what will impoverish the people, the old people and the infants and the children.[289] Actually, it is our sustenance, the corn."[290]

Thayendenega's 1801 version has the Peacemaker (the "Elder Brother" of two chiefs of the Mohawks) seek help from the Oneidas. He sought both their protection from Thadadaho's spiritual or magical power and their support in persuading Thadadaho to join in the peace. The story carries the flavour of the Peacemaker bringing the Oneidas into a protective alliance against the evil power of Thadadaho.[291]

The Elder Brother being grieved at the cruel disposition of the younger, resolved to go westerly and look for people, and form an

---

287 Gibson 1899, 53: "Then Deganawii'dah said, 'People to whom you are the great one (the Chief) shall call you Ho'datche'hde,' "He carries a quiver," and the reason for this is because indeed you are taking your quiver [on the way to see Thadadaho].'"

288 Norton 1970, 103–4. One of the techniques promoted by Fisher and Ury (1985) in *Getting to Yes* is sharing: not "I have a problem with you," but rather "we have a problem to address together." In this case, "we shall risk together."

289 In the 2013 recital of the law, Odatsehte Howard Elijah described the bloody days before the coming of the law, saying that the women and children "were made poor," literally and spiritually, by the warfare.

290 Gibson 1912, 192. It is ironic, linguistically, that the guardian of the corn should become a Confederate lord. The English word "lord" is derived from the Saxon *hlaford*, meaning "loaf-ward," the keeper or guardian of the bread and therefore the sustainer of his people. Equally ironic, the "corn" the loaf-ward would have guarded would be what in North America is called "wheat"—what is called corn in North America is still called "maize" in England; the keepers of very different crops were both guarding "corn."

291 The contrast between the peaceful and warlike brothers also recalls the twins in the Creation story.

alliance with them, he consequently went and met Odadseghte of the Onidas, by their conversation the Mohawk was found to be the elder, and therefore the Onida stiled him father, the Mohawk chief promised to come back the next day meaning the ensuing year and proceeded farther on the business of the confederacy. The next year he went to the Onidas according to the promise, he explained his intentions naming the nine divisions forming the Mohawk nation—it consisting of three tribes, the wolf, turtle and bear, and again were each divided into three subdivisions—the Onida got up and sang, mentioning that his father and him were united, and that his father would be the superior on this; the Mohawk stopped him, and rose, expressing by a song that it should not be so but that they both should be equal [at this the Onidas were satisfied]. Upon this being passed the Onida wished to stop him [to rest a little] saying that he would throw a tree in the way that he could not get over this the other stiled him the big tree and they are yet so called.[292]

Now that the Oneidas and Mohawks had committed themselves to the peace, the Peacemaker began to erect the structure that would sustain it. As the three Mohawk chiefs had formed a first brotherhood, so three Oneida chiefs—Odatsehte, Kanuhkwe'yotu, and Teyoha'kwete—would form a second. They would now cooperate in the manner of families on opposite sides of the council fire.[293]

The narrative of the making of the peace is also the narrative of the creation of the architecture of the symbolic Longhouse. With two nations committed, the Peacemaker was already able to begin describing how decision making would work, as matters would be considered by small committees first and then by the nations, and as matters would be passed across the council fire between the two groups of brothers.

292 Boyce 1973, 290; and Bonaparte 2006, 54.

293 In Gibson's 1912 version, Goldenweiser translates this as "from now on you are to be members of opposite moieties."

Removing Distractions: Opening the Path and Keeping It Open

In Haudenosaunee law and treaties, the need for open, unobstructed communication is a recurrent, persistent theme. It appears in the Condolence in the clearing of the eyes and ears and opening of the throat. It appears in treaty discussions as the removal of brambles and brush from the path of peace and communication between the nations. It appears in wampum belts that depict a straight line, the path between the nations' council fires.

Maintenance, keeping the paths open, renewing commitments, repeating Condolences, are all linked to the concept that the more a path of peace is used, the plainer and smoother it will become. Relationships are not assumed: they are actively maintained.

War is often the result of misunderstanding; misunderstanding flows from a failure to communicate; that failure results, at times, from obstacles and obstructions. The path of peace[294] is kept open through constant vigilance and renewal. The river is kept free of rapids and rocks. Neither should the path be obscured by darkness: one Delaware wampum had "sticks thrust through it, as torches to light the way."[295]

---

294 The path is a symbol, not a physical road. Yet even scholars like Horatio Hale seem at times to have taken the metaphor literally. After the founding of the League, says Hale, one tradition "which is in itself highly probable," has Hiawatha "devoting himself to the congenial work of clearing away the obstructions in the streams which intersect the country then inhabited by the confederate nations, and which formed the chief means of communication between them. That he thus, in some measure, anticipated the plans of DeWitt Clinton and his associates, on a smaller scale, but perhaps with a larger statesmanship, we may be willing enough to believe" (Hale [1883] 1989, 35). In fact, Hiawatha would have been continuing the work of peace by maintaining the openness of communication.

295 One of the seven wampum belts preserved by the Cherokees in Oklahoma also has sticks thrust through it.

Standing and Walking

In Haudenosaunee councils and ceremonies, the speaker stands while all the people he is speaking for remain seated. Standing is a mark of respect for the people being spoken to. It is not a suggestion that he stands "above" them. It is also a rhetorical and political act: it draws attention to the speaker. Today in the Condolence, and formerly in most political councils as well, the speaker does not stand in one place: "*Enyonghdentyonko kanoghsakonghson*—'to and fro in the house.' In councils and formal receptions, it is customary for the orator to walk slowly to and fro during the intervals of his speech. Sometimes, before beginning his address, he makes a circuit of the assembly with a meditative aspect, as if collecting his thoughts. All public acts of the Indians are marked with some sign of deliberation."[296]

Especially during long speeches, and more so in the past than the present, a speaker would walk up and down. Today, Western politicians tend to remain in one place, tethered to their prompters and microphones. Their Roman antecedents used a fixed rostrum, a pulpit adorned with the prows of defeated enemy warships, to address both the people in the Forum and the Senate. Occupying the rostrum was a sign of authority, a place of power. Different nations have their own reasons for having speakers stand in one specific location or move about as they speak. Architecture and acoustics affect the rhetorical cultures. As well, a speaker's location in council or in Parliament indicates his political identity and seniority. When a Haudenosaunee speaker would walk back and forth while speaking, he would do so on his side of the council fire.

Onondaga: Thadadaho

To the west of Oneida territory lies the land of the Onondagas, the People of the Mountain. Blocking the path to peace was the despotic leader of that nation, Thadadaho. He is presented in most accounts as the greatest obstacle to

---

296   Hale (1883) 1989, 151. "Some sign of deliberation" shows that the matter is worthy of respect and thought. To act quickly would indicate that the matter was of little import, or that the speaker was arrogant.

peace. It took the combined efforts of all the nations, all the people, both men and women, and both mental and spiritual power to overcome him.

There is no doubt that, by the time he was a mature man, Thadadaho's mind had become powerfully twisted.[297] One legend describes how he came to be this way:

> In his youth he had been gentle and mild, fond of innocent amusements and the chase, and he was beloved by his people who looked forward to the time when he would be chosen their chief and become their counsellor. But one day when hunting in the mountains he chanced to kill a strange bird which, though beautiful in plumage, was virulently poisonous. Unaware of its deadly nature, Ot-to-tar-ho, delighted with his prize, plucked its bright feathers to decorate his head and while handling them inhaled their poison which entering his brain maddened him and upon his return to the village in an insane rage, he sought to kill those whom he met. Amazed at the strange transformation the people were in great consternation and fled from him in fear. No more the gentle Ot-to-tar-ho; no more did he care for their games; no more did he care for the chase, but was sullen and morose and shunned all companionship with his people who also avoided him for he had developed a mania for killing human beings.

> The poisonous fire that had burned in his brain had so distorted his features that he became hideous to behold; his long glossy hair fell from his head and in its stead there grew serpents that writhed and hissed when he brushed them back from his face and coiled around his pipe in rage when he smoked.

> Many believed he had been witched, that some ferocious animal had taken possession of him; others that he was controlled by an evil spirit who was seeking to destroy the nation. Various were the surmises of the people but the mystery baffled them and their appeals to the medicine men were received by these wise men in silence; yet they sought by long fasting and dancing in various incantations to appease the wrath of the evil one, but their efforts were in vain for still the demon if demon it was, continued to dominate Ot-to-tar-ho, who only became more furious and violent and seemed to have endowed him with supernatural powers.

> His mind had become so powerful that it could project a thought many miles through the air and kill whomsoever he desired.

---

297 His name means "entangled," though Hewitt (1892b, 131) states that Skanawati John Buck translated it as "the Assassinator."

Developing clairvoyance of vision and prophecy, he could divine
other people's thoughts and through this power came to dominate
the councils, assuming a control that none dared oppose, and ruled
for many years with such insane and despotic sway that he broke their
hearts and the once powerful, proud and most courageous of all the
nations became abject and cowardly and weak.[298]

Other versions add details, almost joyously enhancing the physical and
spiritual distortions of Thadadaho:

South of the Onondaga town there lived an evil minded man. His
lodge was in a swale and his nest was made of bulrushes. His body
was distorted by seven crooks and his long tangled locks were adorned
by writhing living serpents.[299] Moreover, this monster was a devourer
of raw meat even of human flesh. He was also a master of wizardry
and by his magic he destroyed men but he could not be destroyed.
Adodarho was the name of the evil man.[300]

A thing—a shape—that was not human but rather supernatural and
deformed; for the hair of Tha-do-da-ho was composed of writhing,
hissing serpents, his hands were like unto the claws of a turtle, and
his feet like unto bear's claws in size and were awry like those of a
tortoise, and his body was cinctured with many folds of his *membrum
virile*—truly a misshapen monster.[301]

He was a person of a frightful deformed aspect, with hissing serpents
hanging from his head instead of hair.[302]

When they beheld him "A-do-dar-ho" they were so terrified that
they was going to run right out of the Long House. For he was such
Superhuman looking man, and of such preternatural of his humanity
which he exist, never was seen or heard off amongst the Nations. "His

---

298   Converse 1908, 118–19. Converse's source about the inhalation of the poison was
      Donehogowa Ely Parker.

299   Deyonwe'ton Jake Thomas used to say that the serpents were rattlesnakes that would
      strike at anyone coming close. Sakokwenionkwas Tom Porter has added that Thadadaho's
      skin was like fish scales, and his hair like Rastafarian dreadlocks.

300   Harriet M. Converse states that, becoming sullen and morose, he "developed a mania
      for killing people. His hair fell from his head." She says that with "his fingers and toes
      terminating with the hissing snakes, and by a glance of his eye, turning to stone anyone
      who dared deny his authority." The parallel with the snake-haired Medusa, whose glance
      turned ancient Greeks to stone, is too obvious (Converse 1908, 128, 129).

301   Hewitt 1892b, 136.

302   Norton 1970, 103.

hairs on his head was all full of living snakes. His finger ends were all snake heads, and little above both or his wrists was bent or crook."[303]

By the mid-1800s, the physical twistedness of Thadadaho was recognized as a matter of metaphor and legend, an extension of his entangled mind and spirit.[304]

Thadadaho drew his power—his ability—from the Dark Side, from spiritual and physical powers that complemented one another and that enabled him to threaten and injure people, both those near him and those at a distance. Through intimidation he ruled:[305] "Notwithstanding the evil character of Adodarho the people of Onondaga, the Nation of Many Hills, obeyed his commands and though it cost many lives they satisfied his insane whims, so much did they fear his sorcery."[306]

Though an element of the Dark Times was witchcraft—another contributor to the bloody revenge-taking, anger, and war—Thadadaho was exceptional, because his deformities of body and spirit, and consequent abilities, were so extreme that an entire nation was in thrall to them. To the peacemakers, he represented a true obstacle. If he could not be overcome, the peace would not be possible. As with the others that the Peacemaker met, the choice seemed to lie between changing him or removing him. In a time of uncertainty, the people working for peace recognized that there were many whose minds needed to be changed, but

> the craziest of whom was the chief of the Onondagas . . . they found him sitting on a pile of thorned mats,[307] with live snakes woven into his long hair. His eyes shook in horror and he could not focus them.

---

303 Newhouse 1885, 21.

304 Hale ([1883] 1989, 7) wrote that "the grave councillors of the Canadian Reservation, who recite his history as they have heard it from their fathers at every installation of a high chief, do not repeat these inventions of marvel-loving gossips, and only smile with good-humored derision when they are referred to." Even so, physical deformity must at some point have been considered to reflect mental deficiency or deformity, as well, or there would not have been a tradition that a royá:ner must be physically whole and wholesome. In 1870, at the General Council, John Smoke Johnson summarized the story: "the leader [of the Onondagas] was almost inhuman, not only in appearance but in mind, ungovernable in temper and fierce to all, until he was persuaded by them. His appearance in body, a crooked sort of man, with uneven crooks. Yet the brothers persuaded him and he became one" (General Council, 1870, 7).

305 Intimidation and imposition of authority stand in sharp contrast to the consent and affection that linked Thadadaho to the council and the people after his transformation. If a theme of the law is that individuals can be transformed and persuaded to stand for peace, the extreme spiritual, physical, and political transformation of Thadahaho is the most dramatic (but not the only) example.

306 Parker (Newhouse and Cusick) 1916, 17.

307 The thorned mats stand in contrast to the soft, down-lined mats prepared for the comfort of the chiefs, and in the Condolence. The physical discomfort caused by the thorny mats would contribute to the pain and anger in Thadadaho's mind.

He wanted to acquire power with murder. They offered him a chance to accept the good mind. Otherwise they would have to eliminate him. The only real threat to human survival is insanity—people unable to think clearly about other human beings. Clearly, he fit into that category.[308]

Over the Woods: Haii Haii

In Skaniatariio's 1912 version of the law, the Peacemaker and Hiawatha agree to meet in Oneida country. While Hiawatha conducts preliminary discussions with the Oneida chiefs, the Peacemaker has gone to see "the Great Witch," the one who has the power to kill people (Oneida territory is just east of Onondaga country, Thadadaho's home). Even before the Oneidas agree to join the peace, the Peacemaker appears to have persuaded the Great Witch that the nations would work with him if he abandoned his evil ways.[309]

The time had come to face Thadadaho. This is perhaps the only true, deliberate, face-to-face confrontation in the process of the making of the law.[310] It required planning, preparation, and courage. The Peacemaker took the time spent on the path from Oneida to Onondaga as an opportunity to teach the people the ideas and songs they would need and use in that confrontation. The songs would give them courage.

> And when Dekanawita's appointed time was due for them to go to Onondaga, the Mohawk chiefs and the people assemble together in their Long House. Dekanawida appointed a war chief to sing the Pacification [Confederating] Hymn [which Dekanawida did compose it] on their journey to Onondaga. So the [war] chief commence to sing thus "Haii Haii Haii haii" & so on as they went out of the Long House. And while [they were] journeying through the forest, and [were] passing by a certain tree, there was a very large knot in this tree, the tree spoke and said "Oh-ne-kenh, Ni-ya-wen-enh-ha-tyeh" (the meaning of this Mohawk words, "What's up"). Then

---

308 Mohawk 1987, 10–17. In the Condolence, one string is used to remove the insanity that is brought about by grief.

309 "Great Witch" is an unusual English equivalent for ho-otko-kowa, a person of great badness. Gibson 1912, 173. Gibson's 1899 version makes reference, as well, to Tehononsae'ehwan, "He whose house obstructs the path." It is suggested that the orientation of today's Onondaga longhouses—north-south where every other longhouse is east-west—echoes this blocking of the path (Gibson 1899, para. 145, fn. 82).

310 The later confrontation with the Seneca warriors does not seem to have been planned.

Dekanawida answered and said "We are on our way to Onondaga to
pacify and convert the [Great Sorcerer] monstrous [and] evil spirited
Thadodaho. To establish peace. In the hostile nations [that it may all
be done away]." The foregoing verses Dekanawida did compose in
"Confederating Hymn" which he used when he established the Five
Nations Confederacy he called "[ ] wa-di-nonh-senh-deh-thah." It
begins as follows Haii haii. Haii haii. & so on. And the writer of this
work succeeded in dividing it into thirty verses. And this is the hymn
that Dekanawida's singer was singing on their way to Onondaga.

From here below, while Dekanawida's messenger was exploring the
forests [where] to discover Thadadahoh's smoke ascending from the
earth to the sky. The reader will see the "Pacification Hymn" that
was sung all the way through the forest from the Mohawk River to
Onondaga in the State of New York. And the said Hymn was submitted to the Mohawk Chiefs after Dekanawita composed, and confirmed by them. With the ceremony to create (Rodiyaner) Lords.[311]

The people, led by the Peacemaker and Hiawatha, were walking the path
between Oneida and Onondaga.[312] It would not have been a terribly long path:
the distance from Oneida Lake to Onondaga Lake would take a man a day at its
shortest. The path may have been dangerous, and this would have been another
reason for the people to announce themselves by singing as they walked. The
song the Peacemaker taught them along the way is a song of dignity and power,
a song unlike others. It is a slow, dignified song, with a leader who carries the
main part and a response by the people as they walk. It is the song that the
people sing "along the road" as they walk today to the longhouse to condole a
grieving people and raise up a new chief.

As sung, it [Haii] is the most prominent feature, and is expressive of joy or
sorrow according to the tone, as with some of our ejaculations. Hennepin said:
"There was an Iroquese captain who, one day wanting his bowl, entered into
the town of Montreal in Canada, crying 'Hai! Hai!' which in their language is
the sign of peace; he was received with many caresses of kindness."[313]

While the songs themselves are probably unique to the Haudenosaunee, the
use of haii haii within the songs is probably not. The sound is one of pacification, for several nations: Onondaga sentinels in the woods would have known
that the walkers were coming in peace. Describing the Huron Feast of the

---

311 Newhouse 1885, 29. The song for the journey is called, in English, "Over the Woods."

312 The people involved were likely adults, male and female. The children would have been
     left at home, and the old people, who would have difficulty on long walks, would be
     looking after them.

313 Beauchamp (1907) 1975, 352–53.

Dead, Brebeuf wrote: "At the end of the feast, as a compliment to him who entertained them, they imitated, as they say, the cry of the souls, and issued from the cabin crying *haéé, haéé,* and reiterated this cry of the soul all the way. This cry, they say, comforts them greatly; otherwise this burden, though but of souls, would weigh heavily on the back, and cause them a pain in the side for the rest of their lives."[314]

The Haudenosaunee "cry of the soul," used in the original peacemaking, continued to be used in international councils. In 1723, meeting with representatives of Massachusetts, "The delegates made Three Moans, then their Speaker made a Procession thro' them, lamenting and bemoaning, which continued a long time, being now and then prompted by the Tribes; The Procession and Lamentation being at an end, their Speaker took his Seat, and after some time the Delegates made another heavy Moan."[315]

Haudenosaunee political discourse (like Haudenosaunee music)[316] is participatory. There are appropriate times for the entire delegation to express its agreement with or support for the speaker's words, and when a ceremony is being done, there are places in the speech where the delegation joins in with song. In dealing with Thadadaho, this participation sent two messages: it gave the speaker their support at a time when he might be intimidated, and it told Thadadaho that their minds were all one.

The Pacification of Thadadaho

The journey from Oneida country to Onondaga is different from all the earlier parts of the Peacemaker's journey: almost every other trip had been made by the Peacemaker or Hiawatha, either alone or the two of them together. Now, for the first time, all the people had gathered on a walk for peace. The song helped

---

314 Beauchamp (1907) 1975, 353. Hewitt asserted that "the body of rites and customs pertaining to the ancient decennial dead feast common to many, if not all, of the Iroquoian tribes and peoples, was mainly the basis upon which the institutions of the Extended House were established" (Hewitt 1892b, 131). I suggest that the Dead Feast exhibits many of the principles shared with the constitution—continuity and commitment of the people; gathering minds together and making them good again by removing grief and anger; gratitude; and the combination of spiritual and political leadership—but that sharing influenced rather than spawned the law.

315 *Journals of the House of Representatives of Massachusetts, 1723–24,* Massachusetts Historical Society, 198.

316 Though Dvorak used Seneca women's planting songs in his *New World Symphony,* there is little cross-fertilization between Haudenosaunee and Western music. Anton Kuerti told me this was because Western music tends to be audience-directed, where Indigenous music tends to be participatory.

their unity of mind, for it was something they would learn together and sing together. The walk helped bring them together as a shared experience. Facing a great danger together—and preparing together to face that danger—added to the practical unification they were experiencing.[317]

To get to the place where Thadadaho's fire burned,[318] the delegations had to face spiritual obstacles in the form of tangible dangers. They had to cross Onondaga Lake, and Thadadaho's evil mind controlled the waters and winds of the lake. This was an opportunity for the Peacemaker to show once again that he, too, carried spiritual power: the power of Peace.

> They then entered the boat and he (Dekanawideh) stood in front of the boat and Hahyonwatha sat in the stern and the rest of the lords then noticed that the boat was made of white marble. Then they embarked in this boat from the shore and they had not proceeded far on their journey when they heard a voice calling out, "A-soh-kek-ne—eh," and as soon as this voice had called out a strong wind arose and caused the lake to become very rough and troubled and great billows formed upon its surface and more especially around the boat.[319] Then those in the boat became frightened and said: "We are now going to die," but Dekanawideh spoke and said: "There is no danger because Peace has prevailed."
>
> Then Dekanawideh further said to the wind and lake, "Be thou quiet, Ga-ha, and rest." Then the wind and the roughness of the lake ceased. They had not gone much farther when the man across the lake called out "Asohkekne—eh," and then the wind and roughness of the lake became still more violent. Then again Dekanawideh said: "you, the wind and the lake, be still, for we have not crossed the water yet." Then again the lake became calm. Then Hahyonhwatha began to paddle hard and the boat went so swiftly that when they

---

317 A modern revival of the Peacemaker's journey by Deyonwe'ton Jake Thomas took on aspects of this yearning for new unity. With this knowledgeable chief as their guide, participants would be told about the making of the law in the places where the incidents occurred. Falling somewhere between a guided tour and a pilgrimage, these journeys ended at the place of the Peacemaker's departure.

318 Skanawati John Buck recalled instead that the chiefs lit the fire: "When we have reached our destination, the habitation of Tha-da-da-hoh, we shall make a fire for him 'at the woods' edge.' We shall speak to him and we shall hail him by congratulatory words" (Hewitt 1892b, 137).

319 Skanawati John Buck stated that Thadadaho had arrived at the peacemaking council place before anyone else, where "he seated himself facing the lake; there he sat with bowed head, silent but forbidding," and brought on the hurricane.

reached the shore, the boat plowed deeply into the dry land on the shore bank.[320]

Newhouse says that part of the pacification of Thadadaho was the recital by the Peacemaker of the Three Bare Words, the "first three out of the thirteen strings of wampum":

1st Wampum String

We now take the hand, and wipe the tears from off your eyes. So that you may see clearly.

2nd Wampum String

This it occurs when one of their number passes away by death. Then sorrowness and sadness is filled in their throat. Therefore we now take the sorrowness and sadness out of your throat, so you will now breathe more freely.

3rd Wampum String

This it occurs when one of their number is removed by death, it stops their ears from hearing. So now we unpluck [unplug] and clean out your ears, so you will now hear distinctly when any one address you.

Then and as the above three strings of wampums was read they was forwarded to the Onondaga chiefs one at a time. And was reread by them and were then brought back again to the Mohawk Chiefs. Dekanawita addresses to the chiefs of Thadadaho's attendants, and said we will finish the other part of the ceremony in your long house. The chiefs of Thadadaho's attendants left two warriors with Dekanawita, to lead him, the Mohawks and Oneidas, with their people into the Onondaga Long House.[321]

The Condolence that, for Hiawatha, was an act of compassion, transforming him from mourner to optimist, became for Thadadaho a physically, mentally, and spiritually transformative ceremony. After going through the entire

---

320 Parker (Chiefs) 1916, 88, 89. In the Newhouse version of the law, the dangerous passage of the lake is omitted: instead, there are three attempts to sing the peace song; the first two falter because the men are afraid and make an error in the singing—so the Peacemaker takes over, singing the song perfectly and proceeding to straighten out Thadadaho (Parker [Newhouse and Cusick] 1916, 28). When the boat was sent back to pick up Tsikonsaseh, she, too, stood up in front. Standing up in the bow of a canoe (as Kiatsaeton did in 1645) is a sign of authority, as well as of assumption of risk.

321 Newhouse 1885, 48–49. These are the same three words that Hiawatha managed to set out on his own before the Peacemaker helped him with the rest of the Condolence. They are also the three words that are delivered to visitors at the woods' edge. The greeting in treaty councils with other nations—the Three Words at the Woods' Edge—is a re-enactment of the Condolence of Hiawatha and Thadadaho.

Condolence ceremony, the Peacemaker suggested that the people who had come with him to Onondaga should go outside and sleep at the woods' edge, because it was after dark. The Onondaga chiefs had other ideas:

> And [it was now way] late in the night when this ceremony ended. Dakanawida [orator] then [announce] propose to his comrade Lords for them to depart out from the Long House and go to the edge of the bushes, and lay down to sleep. "Come let us go out," says Dekanawida, and as they were about to depart out of the House, then one of the Lords of the opposite side of the Council fire, spoke and said, "wait patiently for a few moments." And so it was [complied with and] in a very little time the Lords of the opposite side of the council fire spoke again and said it was decided by my lords, that we will "en-de-wen-na-ka-ra-nyeh." And be decided in your minds. But now we let our females go, [and be easy] [only don't be too much on them]. So they did enjoy themselves by their Indian dance. For the progress [and success] did made in creating and installing new lords to a satisfactory and with joy.[322]

Note: of the above part of the ceremony, it is always performed accordingly, afterwards when Dekanawida completely established the confederacy. But at time he omitted on account that he had to perform that peculiar and wonderful act with a superior power. The people that were eye witness at the time had never seen before. As you will see with the foregoing his acts.

Dekanawida said to the Chiefs we will commence on Thadadaho and convert him from sorcery, his ferocity and evil spirit, and remedy [transform] his preternatural humanity. If we will succeed, then we will say we have accomplished our undertakings [as anticipated]. And he said to the chiefs what will we say that we all lay down minds and spirit. The chiefs sanctioned his proposition.

Dekanawida then took one string of wampum in his hands and addressed Thadadaho in these words. "All the reptiles shall now be removed from under your hair, [it will now cease the malformation of your hair] and it shall become [clean like the hair of any other human being] like any other human hair." Then he laid the wampums down on the ground and he laid his hand on Thadadaho's head and rubbed it [stroke it] downwards and the reptiles immediately

---

322 Today, there are specific women's songs and dances towards the end of the installation of a royá:ner. Often, after the conclusion of important ceremonies or in the evenings after business meetings, there are social dances at the longhouse. People say: these were given to us because it pleases the Creator for us to enjoy ourselves.

disappeared [the malformation which was snakes before changed] and his hair became like any other human hair.

Dekanawida took another string of wampum in his hands and addressed Thadadaho in these words: "Your mind shall now be transformed . . . and shall become like any human mind" and the sorcery and evil spirit left him completely.[323]

He was seated at the further end of his house, without any clothing to cover the deformities of his body, his hair was frightful serpents. Tekanawitagh and the other chiefs approached him; they spoke, delivering wampum until they removed all his deformities; they then covered his body with a garment and put moccasins on his feet. After they thought that they had restored him to his natural state, and removed every deformity, they returned towards home . . .

Next summer [Tekanawitagh] again set out, taking his son Odatsehte by the hand as he passed his village. They came to the abode of Tadadahoh, who now made a more comely appearance than he did at the former meeting: he seemed to improve under their hands. The task which yet remained for them to perform was to rectify the concealed parts, to interest his heart in the welfare of the confederacy by inducing him to think, that his own interest and honour was linked to that of the public, to insinuate by this means into his mind, the seeds of brotherly love and affection.[324]

Thayendenega Joseph Brant has the Mohawks and Oneidas proceed together to Onondaga:

They went together to Onondaga, they found the chief there very obstinate, they with difficulty brought him to agree the Mohawk stiling him brother, and equal in the confederacy; when they went to return home, one of the young men had forgot his maukissins and went back to look for them, as he was by the side of the house he heard the Onondaga singing that what the father and son had proposed to him did not suit him and that he could not wear it— when he overtook them he told what he had heard—in consequence of which they agreed to return next year—they did and then the Mohawk proposed to the Onondaga, that he should keep the council fire of the confederacy, and that he should carry their title—these condescensions brought him to agree.[325]

---

323 Newhouse 1885, 63–65.

324 Norton 1970, 104.

325 Boyce 1973; Bonaparte 2006, 54.

John Buck described the chiefs meeting Thadadaho and going through the words at the woods' edge, and then doing the entire Condolence ceremony, much as it is today:

> Undaunted, De-ka-na-wi-da said: "We are now here. We came seeking Tha-da-da-ho. Now, chiefs, unwrap again your *matters*." Obedient to this command they took the wampum strings out of the pouch one by one, thirteen in number, representing as many matters of importance and moment, and they placed them in order on a horizontal rod. This done, De-ka-na-wi-da said, "Let us express our thanks, for this is now being competed." He then sang the Six Songs . . . When these Six Songs were being sung Tha-da-da-ho listened attentively to them and even manifested a feeling of pleasure. Lastly, he raised his horrid head, an act he had never been known to do. Whereupon De-ka-na-wi-da, elated by this propitious sign of mental regeneration, exclaimed, "So let it come to pass. What we have undertaken is being accomplished in the manifestation of returning reason and anthropic feelings." Then Tha-da-da-ho spoke and said, "It gave me great pleasure to hear the singing of the Six Songs."[326]

In John Buck's 1888 version, Thadadaho is returned gradually to humanity, by song and words, step by step. The Peacemaker explains each step to him before it is performed. After the Woods' Edge and the Condolence and the Six Songs, as he becomes increasingly rational, he is given his own song, which helps to "reconstruct and straighten out thy mind": "Hai-i, hai-i, hai-i, hai-i, hai-i, hai-i, hai-i, hai-i, a-kwe-wi'-yo e-kon-he-wa-tha (my beautiful thing, [it is a] besom)."[327]

The Chiefs' Version describes a gradual pacification, almost like a domestication of a wild animal:

> Then the man looked around and he saw these men (the lords) standing all around him, but he did not answer but kept silent. Then these lords looked at his head while he was sitting on the ground and they saw his hair moving as if it were all alive and they saw that the movements of the hair greatly resembled that of serpents, and they looked at his hands and saw that his fingers were twisting and contorting

---

326 Hewitt 1892b, 139. It is said that the Six Songs created an opening that gave the people the opportunity to persuade Thadadaho to change his mind.

327 Hewitt 1892b, 139. A besom is a broom made with a bundle of twigs. Thadadaho's duties included keeping the council house clean, both literally and figuratively. Symbolically, his broom would sweep away the snakes of discord and the dirt of discomfort. The beauty lies in what it does, not in what it looks like.

continually in all directions and in all manner of shapes, and they became impatient because he would not answer the message:

When Dekanawidah started to address this man, the man became troubled and after all of the lords finished addressing the man his sympathy was affected and he shed tears. Then Dekanawidah said: "We, the delegates of all the nations who have accepted the Good Tidings of Peace and Power, are now assembled here". . .

. . . Then the twisting movements of the fingers and the snakelike movements of the hair of Thadadaho ceased.

Then he spoke and said: "It is well. I will now answer the mission which brought you here. I now truly confirm and accept your message, the object of which brought you here."[328]

Most versions, written and oral, give Hiawatha the role of removing the snakes when Thadadaho's mind had been restored. Converse says Hiawatha combed the snakes from Thadadaho's hair with wampum.[329] Newhouse says that the Peacemaker did the combing, and put wampum down before Thadadaho first.

We have now accomplished our great work and completed everything that was required with the exception of shaping and transforming him (by rubbing him down), removing the snake-like hair from him and circumcising him.

The lords therefore all took part in doing this and Ohdahtshedeh was the first to rub down Thaddodahho and the others followed his example so that the appearance of Thaddodahho might be like that of other men.[330]

His hands we will mend and adjust, so that they will be like those of other men; his hair of living serpents we will change from its snakehood, so that his hair may be like that of other men; and his hands, awry and misshapen as they are, we will make like those of a human being; his feet, also, deformed and unnatural as they are, we will change to the shape common to those of other men, and lastly, that with which he is trussed, his *membrum virile*, we will reduce

---

328   Parker (Chiefs) 1916, 91.

329   Converse 1908, 117.

330   Parker (Chiefs) 1916, 91. "Rubbing down" is a transformative and comforting act. It also appears at the woods' edge, when the visitors are "rubbed down" by their hosts to remove any thorns or dust that they may have picked up on their path.

to its proper length and size—we will make it six thumb widths in length.[331]

There had been several steps. First, Thadadaho's opposition was checked. Second, he was pacified enough to be willing to be transformed. Third, he was physically transformed. Fourth, having been changed and comforted, his mind was also made good.

Combing Thadadaho's hair has another level of symbolic meaning. Ensnarled, matted hair indicated the ferment and confusion of the mind operating in the head that carried it. Just as Shonkwaiatíson straightened the rivers, smoothed the rapids, and opened the paths of communication, and just as, at the woods' edge, those paths are straightened again and the obstacles and brambles removed, so combing and straightening the powerful man's hair—and straightening his limbs, too—indicates straightening out his mind. Just as the best path to a place would be the most direct, so the best way for a mind to function is to address issues in a way that is straight, not twisted. Transforming his hair and his body meant transforming his mind.

If it is Hiawatha who combs the snakes from Thadadaho's hair and smooths out his body, this carries another layer of significance. Thadadaho had killed Hiawatha's family. Instead of seeking revenge, Hiawatha becomes a healer. It is an ultimate act of spiritual strength and reconciliation. He is both the most appropriate and the most unexpected person to heal Thadadaho.

Once Thadadaho had been physically transformed, and had become rational, he was ready for the pragmatic political conversation necessary to accommodate him within the structure of the law. His mind was now functioning properly: a good mind.

Tsikonsaseh and the Peacemaker placed the deer's antlers on Thadadaho's brow:[332] the slender antlers of a Confederacy chief replaced the waving snakes.[333] In doing so, she was acting as a clan mother would act. In placing the antlers on this crucial last chief, the chief responsible to all other chiefs, she was in effect acting as the clan mother for the entire Confederacy. Thadadaho became the keystone. "On this very day," said the Peacemaker, the peace had arrived.[334]

Once it had become clear that the power of the Song of Peace and the concepts that the Peacemaker had brought would transform even Thadadaho, the people became convinced that the power of peace would indeed spread, to

---

331 Hewitt 1892b, 139. Newhouse recounts the unsuccessful efforts of those who pacified Thadadaho to reduce the penis to a normal size (six thicknesses of the thumb). Gibson refers modestly to people seeing something hanging on Thadadaho.

332 Gibson 1912, 29.

333 The snakes would warn Thadadaho of anyone's approach; the antlers are also said to be sensitive like antennae, "living bones" on the stag.

334 Gibson 1912, 29.

other nations and later generations. As Newhouse states the Peacemaker said then: "For it matters not how ferocious a Nation we may come in contact with. We now know it to be certain that we can always succeed and establish this Government of Peace among the hostile Nations."[335]

Thadadaho had intimidated the entire Onondaga nation into supporting and obeying him. In this, the nation had taken part in the warfare and supported the evil. The Condolence of Thadadaho may have been directed at one powerful individual, but it was certainly also aimed at raising up and clearing the minds of the people around him.

The conversion of Thadadaho demonstrates several important principles of the law:

> The pursuit of peace is not merely the pursuit of the absence of violence, because peace is never achieved until justice is achieved. And justice is not achieved until everyone's interests are addressed. So you will never actually finish addressing everyone's issues. There will always be unfinished business. You can't achieve peace unless it's accompanied by constant striving to address the issues of justice. It means that your job will never end.[336]
>
> The Iroquois law of peace assumes that you will not achieve peace. You will not achieve a perfect agreement between two warring sides about how the world ought to be in the future.[337]

To deal with a difficult problem, the nations must remain committed to working together. Their unity of mind and purpose is their greatest strength.

The Peacemaker had tested his ways of dealing with irrational and dangerous people quite deliberately. He began with isolated individuals—the Cannibal and Tsikonsaseh. He did not shrink from testing, but he approached nations with caution and forethought. As a matter of tactics, it is often best to begin with the easiest and most obvious and to build towards the hardest challenges; to secure the agreement of the people most likely to support the proposition and to cause the holdouts to become increasingly more isolated as a means of persuading them that joining is their only viable option.

The process of securing peace had taken years, as the consensus built. The legend is a lesson in persistence and patience. Haudenosaunee teachers often explain that a thing worth doing can take years. They also say: "it takes as long

---

335 Newhouse 1885, 65.

336 John Mohawk, 2004, n.pag.

337 Ibid.

as it takes": better to do things right than to do them in haste.[338] The same idea of purposeful patience pervades the decision making of the councils, and that tends to frustrate deadline-governed business people and bureaucrats.

The power of men and women must be balanced and combined. The pacification of Thadadaho did not happen—it does not matter which version one looks to—until Tsikonsaseh joined in the ceremonial effort. She provided the "women's side." Gibson describes how Tsikonsaseh fulfilled the role of Thadadaho's clan mother: "Now she has arrived, our mother, the Great Matron whose name is Tsikonsaseh; now she has accepted the Good Message, and this, moreover, is what you should confirm and adopt, the Great Law, so that she may place antlers on you, our mother, and they together shall form a circle,[339] standing alongside your body."[340]

Thadadaho's Political Interests

Some analysts downplay the spiritual side of the pacification of Thadadaho and concentrate on the Peacemaker's astute political sense. He had offered the "powerful wizard" the "head chieftainship" of the new Confederacy. What, in fact, had been offered? And how did that translate into the practical functions of Thadadaho in the historic Confederacy?

When the Peacemaker met with "the Great Witch," early in the peacemaking efforts, he reported back to Hiawatha: "So this is what my errand was: we two should talk, that he may change his habits. And this: shortly, he would work for and accept the Good Message and the power and the Peace. This, moreover, is what happened: I promised that several tribes [nations] and I will come, and that we will all cooperate with him."[341]

The Chiefs' Version attributes the idea of granting Thadadaho special authority to Odatsehte of the Oneidas: "In my opinion this man may approve of our mission if we all lay our heads before him." (This means that the nations here represented would be submissive to this man Tha-do-dah-ho). Then

---

338 This thinking is reflected in sports, as well. Traditional Haudenosaunee sports and games are not time-limited: the game goes on until someone wins, by scoring, scoring a minimum number of points, or taking the opponent's markers. This may explain modern Haudenosaunee adoption of baseball and golf (today's organized lacrosse is time-controlled; lacrosse played traditionally, especially at ceremonies, is not).

339 The term translated as "to become a circle" also means "to become unified."

340 Gibson 1912, 232. In a modern Condolence, when the candidate is identified and accepted, his clan mother stands by his side (and his faithkeepers and sub-chief are also with him), "standing alongside his body."

341 Gibson 1912, 174.

Dekanawideh and Skanyadahriyo spoke and said: 'We acquiesce to all that Odatshedeh has said.'"[342]

Once the nations are committed to the peace, and the Onondagas, out of fear of Thadadaho, are seen as holdouts, the Peacemaker brings the delegation of chiefs to Thadadaho with their joint proposal to grant him special authority: "Moreover, everything reposes there, the minds of the several nations, and as to you, they place before you their proposition that it is you who are to be the title bearer, and Great Chief, and you are also to be fire keeper at the place where we will kindle the fire, whose rising smoke will pierce the sky."[343]

Becoming the firekeeper involved great prestige, but also great responsibility. Virtually every aspect of Haudenosaunee law seeks this balance of authority and obligation. The power given to Thadadaho was neither unchecked nor arbitrary. It was as much a burden as it was an honour. Furthermore, the exercise of the authority required considerate and careful stewardship, the qualities that the old, irrational Thadadaho lacked. In converting Thadadaho, the Peacemaker had employed interest-based negotiations,[344] understanding what Thadadaho and the Onondagas wanted and needed. This problem-solving technique is reflected in Haudenosaunee tactics and treaties over the following centuries.

Making the Onondagas the firekeepers was logical. Geographically, they were the central nation. Militarily, they were not numerous enough to be threatening or dominant. If their spiritual power was acknowledged, for good or evil, then their role as protectors of the council fire could become a powerful force for the good.

The combination of spiritual and political authority—and the understanding that these are separate concepts that gain further authority when they are combined—is not unique to the Haudenosaunee. The Queen of England opens Parliament as head of state[345] and as head of the Anglican Church, in a show

---

342 Parker (Chiefs) 1916, 90.

343 Gibson 1912, 232. When a contemporary council is convened, and the white wampum "fire" is placed on its clean white cloth on the bench in the middle of the longhouse, it is also said that symbolically this "fire" pierces the sky—so that the Creator can see and hear everything that is said, and each person's words and deeds are fully accountable.

344 For a modern explanation of the same approach to dispute resolution, see Fisher and Ury's *Getting to Yes*. They advocate listening intently; going "easy on the people and hard on the issues;" collaborating on tough questions through an agreed-upon process; and seeking to understand and fulfill one another's needs.

345 In a leftover from the days when the King and the Commons were at odds, the monarch enters the House of Commons only with the permission of the House, and escorted by the Gentleman Usher of the Black Rod. The head of state is not the head of the government.

of vestigial spiritual authority in a secular state.[346] However, different peoples define the separation differently, as the Maoris and *pakehas* have discovered in their differing interpretations of the effects of the Treaty of Waitangi.[347]

There are really two separate transactions with Thadahaho. Before a rational political conversation can take place, the spiritual and emotional obstacles must be removed.

The beginning of the pacification of Thadadaho is accomplished through the repeated singing of the Song of Peace. In contrast, the negative power of Thadadaho is manifested in his own songs and words, by which he daunts the Peacemaker's messengers, calling up the high winds, threatening to swamp their canoes on Onondaga Lake. His power is supernatural—or rather, it is power enlisted from aspects of the natural world—but if it is spiritual power, it comes from the dark aspects of the spirit.

The transformation of Thadadaho is symbolized in a number of different ways. When he is a force for harm, he has snakes in his hair: when he becomes a keeper of the council fire, one of his responsibilities is to remove any "crawling things" that might find their way near the fire. He himself becomes the remover of snakes.

Good-mindedness, health, and beauty are opposed to a twisted mind and body. Thus, the Peacemaker is able to call upon his own beautiful face to shock the Cannibal into right-mindedness; his opposite, Thadadaho, is twisted in limb and mind, but can be straightened out. Another contrast between the Peacemaker and Thadadaho is the former's association with the eagle, the highest flying of the animals of the air and sky world, while Thadadaho is linked with snakes, the messengers of bad news and the underworld[348] (once his mind is good again, he is also given a bird's wing to sweep the council area clean— usually said to be a white gull's wing for purity).[349]

---

346   In one example of the difference between Indigenous and settler thinking, a Cree delegation was prevented from opening its presentation to a Québec legislative committee with a prayer and sacred drumming. To the Crees, this was an insult. To the Québécois, who had until the 1950s chafed under the influence of the Catholic Church, allowing any religious practice in the legislature was seen as a possible opening of the floodgates.

347   Retaining their *mana,* or spiritual authority, the Maori leaders believed they had delivered only administrative governance to the British. The British believed they had acquired full sovereignty, the authority to make all laws. The modern Waitangi Tribunal has been working its way through the actual intent of the treaty.

348   There is no suggestion that "the underworld" is equivalent to the Christian hell. The Thunderers, the Grandfather protectors of humanity, drive snakes underground to prevent them from injuring the people. It is said that the dinosaurs were also driven underground (and will re-emerge one day). What is underground is out of our sight, and unable to harm us, we who walk about on the earth's surface.

349   It is not the council place alone that gets swept: "for by this the land will be preserved free from dirt and evil things." Hewitt 1892b, 138. There is also a reference to a "Great Black Wing" in a Newhouse version.

The process of condoling the other rotiyanershon is that their nation proposes a person to its brother nation (Cayugas to Oneidas, for example), and then that side of the fire proposes the person to the nations on the other side of the fire. That is not the way with Thadadaho: he is proposed only by the Onondagas, without being joined by the other Older Brothers, the Mohawks and Senecas. He is proposed to all four of the other nations together, and it is up to them together to accept him. He is thus to be a chief responsible to all other chiefs.[350] He has no clan mother. His uniqueness is accentuated by the other name he is called: Desenagehte, He Carries the Name.[351] It is possible to see this not only as a reflection of the idea that his "family" is the entire council, but also that his clan mother was Tsikonsaseh, a woman who, like the Peacemaker, had no successor.

The Fire

For human beings all around the world, the fire is a symbol of warmth and light and protection. In many languages, "hearth" and "home" are synonyms.[352] For the Haudenosaunee, a "fire" is also a symbol of a nation, and the symbol of the council.

Most North Americans have only intermittent contact with fire—as a campfire or bonfire, an ornamental fireplace, or perhaps a wood stove. They know of the fire's destructive power from television pictures of forest fires. They do not see a fire used for warmth and light and cooking every day. For the people who made the Kayanerenkó:wa, fire was a practical constant in their lives. There was always a fire burning near their sleeping place. The fire was the focus and the symbol of the family.

As Firekeepers, the Onondagas look after not merely a symbol or thing, but also a process. Anyone who tends a fire, and anyone who spends time with a fire, is aware that it is a process of consumption and combustion, with a modest beginning and a quiet, smouldering end. Tending a fire, looking after its appetite for wood, is a matter of patience. It takes as long as it takes.

Fire is also potentially dangerous. Especially in a woodland environment, and in wooden or bark houses, fire can easily get out of control. Being Firekeepers,

---

350   It occurs that, if a family does not have a man suitable to be its chief, it "borrows" from another family within that nation, or even from another nation. That has never been seriously considered for Thadadaho.

351   Hohahes Leroy Hill, recital of the Kayanerenkó:wa, 2013.

352   The beginning of architecture may have been the deliberate decision by a nomadic family about how to arrange their persons and possessions around a fire.

for the Onondagas, did not mean possessing control over the outcome of the councils, but rather control over the process of council. "Control" is probably the wrong word: the Onondagas carry the responsibility of ensuring that the council does not get out of control, in the sense that it should remain focussed on the work to be done, should not descend into anger or thoughtlessness, should not allow personalities or emotions to stand in the way of the good mind and its rational thought. As firekeepers, the Onondagas' "control" over the council fire means protecting both the fire against attack and the council against loss of reason. It is a procedural rather than substantive responsibility. Part of that procedural responsibility is to ensure that only one issue is considered at a time. Another is to ensure that the fire does not go out before the council is over. Being hosts of the Grand Council is an honour and a burden.

In the Great Law, fire is used for several purposes. It is mentioned briefly as the cooking fire. It is the fire by which one warms oneself. But it has three distinct purposes within the culture and eventually the law.

First, in a woodland environment, fire is a way of calling attention to oneself. One could not see a village from a distance, but one could see the smoke rising from its fires, "piercing the sky." An individual arriving at the edge of a clearing, and wanting to enter the village in peace, would probably have built a fire to announce himself. In the course of the making of the Great Law, the Peacemaker does this several times—for example, after he survives his test at Cohoes Falls. The smoke from fires to call attention to oneself always "pierce the sky." These fires were deliberately smoky. Newhouse states: "This was the custom, to make a smoke so that the town might know that visitors were approaching and send word that they might enter without danger to their lives."[353]

Second, a fire is a council fire. It has been said that the first step in all architecture was when nomadic hunter-gatherers would stop for the night and decide where to make the fire: the location of the fire determines where people cook, sleep, and eat. The council fire of the Haudenosaunee sets the places for the nations to sit: it provides the focus for the structure of the council. In the various versions of the Great Law, when the council fire is referred to, it is less frequent that it is referred to as piercing the sky. The council fire is a focus, not a distraction.[354] As council is to be a place of unobstructed communication, it would be counterproductive to have a smoky council fire, or one that distracted through its crackling and sparks.

---

353   Parker 1916, 22. At the 2013 recital of the law, it was stated that, at the woods' edge, there would often be a small hut for the visitors to rest in, and firewood piled for them to make the required signal fire.

354   Fire is a universal human concentrator—the candle flame is used in Buddhist meditation to focus attention and mindfulness, for example—and a means for many peoples to clear the mind of distraction. Fire burns away impurities, too.

During the making of the Great Law, the villages that supported the peace would show that support by sending brave white smoke to the sky.[355]

Third, the smoke rises, and in rising, connects to the Sky World, calling the Creator's attention to what is happening at the fire. If the source of the fire is sacred, the Creator's attention is attracted even more. Thus, tobacco burning is a ceremony deliberately used for the purpose of calling upon the Creator for attention and help: the white smoke rises, and as the tobacco originated as a sacred plant of the Sky World, so the Creator notices. In modern councils, while there is a fire in the wood stove in the longhouse, the "council fire" or katsistowá:nen is a bunch of wampum strings, the symbols of the fire as well as of the nations bringing their minds together. These strings are held by one of the firekeepers during the opening thanksgiving, but then they are placed on a bench, on a pure white cloth. They are a constant visual reminder that the council has drawn all the nations together for the purpose of peace. It is said that the Creator pays attention to the symbolic smoke from the wampum fire, and that in turn is sometimes used to admonish the participants to behave properly. Just as a sacred fire calls for notice, so does the sacred wampum that symbolizes the fire.

Thus, Sagoyewatha (Red Jacket) was able to say in council: "We consider ourselves in the presence of the Great Spirit, the Proprietor of us all."[356]

The Power of Unity

Thadadaho was persuaded and transformed partly by the unity of spirit and mind with which he was confronted. He also must have been persuaded by the quality of the people who had come together as chiefs to commit themselves to the peace: "Hiawatha and the Peacemaker also enlisted the pressure of public opinion to win over Thadadaho. They convinced him that he alone stood in the way of a goal that the overwhelming majority of other Iroquois leaders desired. By confronting Thadadaho with the combined support of chiefs from the Mohawk, Oneida and Cayuga Nations, as well as that of many Onondaga

---

355   Controlling the colour of the smoke is also a practice of the Catholic Church, which sends a plume of black smoke from Saint Peter's to indicate a failure to elect a pope, and a pure white plume to announce the election of a new pope.

356   Ganter 2006, 36.

leaders, Hiawatha and the Peacemaker severely limited Thadadaho's ability to go against public consensus."[357]

Thadadaho's conversion is also a lesson in what happens when there is a single holdout in a political or legal system that requires consensus and unanimity.[358] In any Haudenosaunee council, it is theoretically possible for a single chief to prevent a matter from being decided. In times past, this would not happen: if he could not persuade the others, or find some compromise, the individual would give in graciously. Another aspect of Haudenosaunee unanimity is that it did not require absolute agreement, nor agreement on every detail. The chiefs were trained to recognize times when they might not agree completely, but were close enough that the matter proposed was acceptable. In the interest of unanimity, then, they offered flexibility.[359]

The unanimity of the other nations helped persuade Thadadaho:

> Then Tyon-yonh-koh spoke and said to Thadodah-ho: "The Creator, the Great Ruler, created this day which is now shedding its light upon us; he also created man and he also created the earth and all things upon it. Now look up and see the delegates of the Four Nations sitting around you, you also see the chief warrior and this great woman our mother (Jikonsaseh), standing before you, all of whom have approved of this message. The lords and all the chief warriors and this great woman, our mother, have all agreed to submit the Good Tidings of Peace and Power to you, and thus if you approve and confirm the message, you will have the power to be the Fire-Keeper of our Confederate Council, and the smoke from it will arise and pierce the sky, and all the nations shall be subject to you."[360]

> Thereupon the man looked at Tekarioken and Hiawatha and Satekariwate [the Mohawks] and Hotatsehte [the Oneida] and Kanukweyotu [the Seneca] and Tiohaʔkwete and Hakaʔeyuk and Tsiʔnutawehe and Skanyataiyo and Tshaʔtekaehyes. Thereupon

---

357 Bonvillain 1992, 49. It may also be that, by being the single, most prominent, and most dangerous holdout, Thadadaho provided everyone else with a focus for their peacemaking efforts.

358 *Twelve Angry Men* is a demonstration of an opposite situation—in which the holdout was the only one whose mind was patient, calm, and observant.

359 Many Indigenous nations of the Americas have a similar state, with words that reflect the way a thing decided in council is not perfect but is agreed upon enough to proceed. In Choctaw, the word used in council is *Yakoke,* which has entered North American English as "okay" (though some dictionaries will attribute the origin of "okay" to "Oll Korrect" or the initials of George Washington's quartermaster, "Old Kinderhook." The concept of "okay" may be an important cultural division between North America and the more rigid requirements of European business and society.

360 Parker (Chiefs) 1916, 91.

Tekanawita said: "Now you are looking at all of the ones who will be standing with you." Thereupon the man bowed his head. Thereupon his hair stopped writhing and all of his fingers became quiet.[361]

The Peacemaker consistently speaks unconditionally.[362] Peace *will come*. These men *will be standing with you*. These announcements are not negotiable. It is his power and nature to persuade by the sacred force of his words.

Cayuga

In the minds of many modern Haudenosaunee, the pacification of Thadadaho is the climax of the making of the law, as he was the single terrifying remaining obstacle to the peace. Therefore, they would say, all the nations had already joined together, and this one Onondaga man was all that was left in the way. However, there are other versions. To the west of the Onondagas lay Cayuga country.

Thayendenega states that, after satisfying Thadadaho, the peacemakers "proceeded to Cayuga their chief had a big pipe, for which reason they give the nation that name [Shononenaweandwane], they stiled him their son, and brother to the Onidas."[363] This account would see the wave of peace sweeping from east to west, with one nation after another joining. It would explain how the wave did not stop with the Senecas, but continued—after the Seneca warriors joined—to absorb the nations westward to Niagara and beyond: Erie, Wenro, Attiwandaron, and eventually Tiionontate and Wendat. Today, the council name[364] for the Cayugas commemorates that role and that first pipe, and the Cayugas supplied the pipes and tobacco that the chiefs would smoke together after council opened and closed.

If the bringing of the Great Peace had been pure legend, it would have been likely that each nation would represent a separate obstacle to be overcome. This is not the case: the Cayugas and Oneidas welcomed the peace, contributed to it, and supported it. Like the Mohawks, they had rational questions: what if we lay down our weapons and the other nations do not? What if, by embracing

---

361 Gibson 1912, 233.

362 Once again, Haudenosaunee language provides tools for the creation of peace. The *wa*-prefix indicates certainty. In the mouth of a skilled orator, the people would be all the more persuaded that the peace was inevitable.

363 Boyce 1973; Bonaparte 2006, 55.

364 Each nation—like each clan—has both an informal or everyday name, and a name that is used formally, in council. Both names refer to characteristics of the people and their places.

peace, we only set ourselves up to become the victims of those who are still devoted to war? They needed to be convinced, not of the rationality of peace rather than war, but of its inevitability. The accounts of the making of the law do not suggest that the Cayugas set tests for the Peacemaker, or challenged his authenticity. Instead, once they were persuaded, they welcomed the law.

Seneca: The Doorkeepers

Thayendenega's 1801 version explains that after bringing the Cayugas into the Confederacy, "from there they went on to the Senecas, there was two principal chiefs of these, Kanyadariyoh and Shadekaroinyis, they also agreed to the confederacy; in consequence of their frontier situation they called them *ronin-hohhont*—or the doorkeeper."[365] He asserts that while bringing together the first four nations took four years, the Senecas joined "some time later." Though the names are different, this is consistent with the way the Seneca warrior chiefs were brought into the peace by being assigned the work of protecting the Great Black Doorway, escorting outsiders into the council longhouse and winnowing out those who meant harm to the League.[366]

The Senecas themselves explain their accession to the Confederacy more subtly. There were two Seneca towns at the time—as, historically in the eighteenth century, there were also two main towns, Kanedesaga (earlier Ganogaro), to the east, and Geneseo (on a bend on the Genesee River). While the chiefs of the eastern town were eager to join the peace, the western town faced a number of hostile nations, and its warriors were a bulwark against outside aggression. Making this town's chiefs into both rotiyanershon and war chiefs was pragmatic: it allowed the exercise of peace looking inward, while maintaining effective defence looking outward.

---

365 Boyce 1973; Bonaparte 2006, 55. Hayadaha Richard Hill says that these two chiefs joined the Peacemaker on the journey to straighten out Thadadaho. Each had expressed a personal desire to support the peace, even as he feared the warriors. Both said that they could not see what to do. The first said that it was as if he were on a mist-covered lake, and the Peacemaker renamed him Skaniatariio, Handsome Lake, because despite the mist he could still see the beauty of the lake. The other chief also received a new name, for he could see the sky, despite the fog. The Peacemaker constantly showed people the good that they could see and do.

366 The contrast between light and dark is repeated in connection with this doorway: just as emerging from the forest into the light of the clearing is marked by the meeting at the woods' edge, so passing through the dark doorway into the light of the council fire is marked by the doorkeepers' decision to admit or reject the visitors.

Dayodekane Seth Newhouse asserts that the two western Seneca leaders agreed to become lords in order to avoid a blood feud between their two villages, arising from a lacrosse game.[367]

The two Seneca doorkeepers were the leaders of the Seneca men. The law was born during a time of warfare, when to survive virtually every man had to be prepared to fight, to protect his family and his own life. They were also times of aggressive and vengeful warfare. Even so, the terms used by the Haudenosaunee today to describe the men and their duties are not terms of war. They refer instead to the obligation to protect the peace: "[The speaker of the Peace Hymn then] salutes the *oyenkondonh*, a term which has been rendered 'warriors.' This rendering, however, may have a misleading effect. The word has nothing to do with war, unless in the sense that every grown man in an Indian community is supposed to be a soldier. . . . The word comprises all the men (the 'manhood' or mankind) of the nation."[368]

There were "warriors." War and peace are one of the dualities reflected in the law: while its purpose was to create peace everywhere, the law is pragmatic enough to recognize that this is as impossible as creating universal goodness. There will always be war, and a rational government will be able to conduct it despite being designed to maintain and spread peace.[369] A rational peace-based government will also avoid allowing those who conduct war to become its leaders.

Yet the Peacemaker and the chiefs had to acknowledge that the warriors not only existed, but were the men who could decide whether the peace survived at all. Four nations had accepted the peace, and their leaders were beginning to discuss the internal structures and processes of their confederate government. The Peacemaker had brought about this state of affairs by facing personal risk to demonstrate the power of his message to the Mohawks; by persuading Hiawatha and Tsikonsaseh to become his clear-minded allies; and by·overcoming the evil and demanding Thadadaho. With four nations committed, the western Senecas remained outside the peace, both physically and politically. This became utterly, dramatically clear when the two Great Warriors arrived at the place where the

---

367 Newhouse 1885, 176.

368 Hale (1883) 1989, 64. Several modern interpreters of the law, Huron Miller most prominent among them, have stated that the coming of the Great Peace meant that there were no more warriors, because there was no more war. But we know from history that wars continued to occur. We know that Haudenosaunee men were proud of their ability to wage war, whether protectively or aggressively towards enemies from outside the Confederacy. Peace did several things: it prevented internal warfare; it institutionalized the role of the warriors as supporters of the peace and the chiefs. As for the relationship between the warriors and the women, that complex matter requires a separate examination.

369 Barack Obama's speech on accepting the Nobel Peace Prize refers to the difficulty of seeking peace while conducting necessary wars.

Great Law was coalescing. They came with a crowd of men who immediately surrounded the chiefs in a threatening manner:[370]

> Then they arrived, the two men walking together with a large crowd of warriors. Hiawatha said . . . so now we shall begin . . . so now you two shall listen well . . .

> Thereupon the Great Warrior said: "I meanwhile will first say that they who are with me, my force, they shall surround the place where they are seated, the chiefs, and not until they are ready, shall he [Tekanawita] begin to speak, so that they can hear everything, the warriors. Thereupon they encircled the place where they were seated, the chiefs. Thereupon the Great Warrior said: "Now we are ready."[371]

For the benefit of the warriors, the Peacemaker explained the making of the Great Peace, and how the people will all become as one family and henceforth respect one another. Offering this alternative, he appealed to the warriors' humanity. As Sotsisowah John Mohawk explains: "You have the power to make peace with an enemy only if you acknowledge that the enemy is human. To acknowledge that they are rational beings who want to live and who want their children to live enhances your power by giving you the capacity to speak to them. If you think they are not human, you won't have that capacity; you will have destroyed your own power to communicate with the very people you must communicate with if you are going to bring about peace."

There is a constant tension, historically, between the chiefs whose minds must yearn for peace, and the warriors whose bodies become the primary weapons of any war. The chiefs are slow to anger, slow to decide, while the young men are impatient. When the tension contributes to their collaboration, the young men stand behind the chiefs, sending a silent, muscular message to any other nation meeting with the Haudenosaunee: if you do not heed these wise old men, you will have to deal with us next. When the tension becomes too great, the warriors tend to act independently, often undermining the decisions of the chiefs.

Faced with the danger and opportunity provided by the Senecas, the Peacemaker chose opportunity. He offered the warriors and their leaders a crucial function within the new order:

> As to you and your deputy, you two Great Warriors, they the Chiefs chose you; it is you who shall guard the doors to the place of the

---

370   There is an oral tradition that the warriors arrived with their hair combed down over their foreheads. When Mohawk warriors of the late twentieth century came to threaten the chiefs in council, they also combed their hair forward: the effect was disturbing, menacing, inhuman.

371   Gibson 1912, 36–37.

Council Fire, of the Good Message and of the Power and the Peace. Moreover it is you who stand up in front, and the reason why it shall happen thus, is that you, as a matter of fact, shall have responsibility for the group; you shall control the warriors, that is to say all of them. And you shall be permanently in charge of the five nations' warriors; moreover it shall continue on as it is at present, with you two holding the power.[372]

Donehogowa and Kanuhkitawi, the two Seneca chiefs, had become the doorkeepers, responsible for determining the sincerity of other nations seeking to approach council, with responsibility as peace and war chiefs.[373] In the 2013 recital of the law, it was stated that Donehogowa was responsible for disarming the visitors, while Kanuhkitawi decided whether their minds were good.[374] One stood outside the door of the longhouse, while the other stood inside. Hayadaha Richard Hill sees the metaphor of the Great Black Door as meaning that if an individual refuses to be reconciled to the accepted behaviours of Haudenosaunee society, that individual relinquishes the right to live in that society. In some versions, some of the Senecas were added to the League as a result of the extension of the rafters, and that is when their roles were assigned: "And it came to pass in later times that they judged it necessary to add to the (roof) poles other great black (roof) poles:[375] Ka-no-ke-i-da'-wi and Tyo-nin-ho-ka'-we, who are cousins. These two are the doorkeepers."[376]

The tension must have been incredible. The warriors presented an immediate physical threat of violence to the chiefs. True to his earlier strategies, the Peacemaker drew them into the peace by acknowledging their abilities and authority—and then transforming them. The warriors had been a menacing and

---

372   Gibson 1912, 36–37.

373   Donehogowa Ely Parker almost certainly used his duality to argue that he should be permitted to join the Union army during the Civil War. As Ulysses Grant's adjutant, he administered one of the first technologically modern armies. As the possessor of the best handwriting among the Union staff, and, fittingly, as a peace chief, he wrote the terms of the peace at Appomattox. Was he Grant's doorkeeper, as he was a Seneca doorkeeper?

374   A purple Seneca wampum belt depicting two wolves is said to symbolize these two title holders.

375   The roof-poles or rafters become black with the soot of the fires. The darker the poles, the older the longhouse. The great black rafters indicate that the longhouse of the nations is old, and intended to be enduring.

376   Skanawati John Buck, in Hewitt 1892b, 144. The law provides that the two Seneca chiefs are the Confederacy chiefs who are also war leaders—leaders of all the warriors of all the nations. The versions that provide this also refer to only one Great Black Door to the Longhouse. Where did the tradition that the Mohawks were Keepers of the Eastern Door come from? And where did the additional "war chiefs" within the confederate structure come from?

encircling body: they were transformed into a protective circle, doorkeepers,[377] and guarantors of the safety of the chiefs and the council. By recognizing their ability and offering them a new kind of authority, the Peacemaker secured their cooperation—in much the same way he had acknowledged Thadadaho's power and given him special responsibilities within the circle of the law. The warriors had undergone a transformation even as they stood around the chiefs in their circle: "it is you who shall protect it," said the Peacemaker.[378]

Rather than reject or confront the warriors, the Peacemaker gave them a job to do. Nevertheless, in the centuries that followed, the tension between the chiefs and the warriors has been a constant factor in Haudenosaunee history and law. Newhouse's versions of the law encapsulate that tension: the warriors were always in a position to kill the chiefs and were sometimes angry or impatient enough to do so.

The four confederate nations had become five, with the Senecas accepting specific responsibility—and authority—to protect the institutions of government.

One Mind: Ska'níkon:ra

All along his path, the Peacemaker would show the power of the Good Mind as the first step towards peace. The concept of the Good Mind is made up of several components. A rational, right-thinking mind is not obstructed or twisted by emotions or thoughts of anger or grief. It is a mind that constantly tends towards goodness rather than evil. A mind that is rational and morally good will work towards peace. A good mind will seek to join with other good minds, for that is where the power lies.

People who join their minds together discover that, if they focus on an idea or on a state of mind together, they achieve synergy, a sum greater than the parts. Sagoyewatha (Red Jacket) spoke wistfully of how it used to be:

In ancient times, when we were called to a treaty of peace, our discourse was of nothing but peace. We did not repeat misfortunes,

---

377 Addressing Donehogowa and Kanuhkitawi, the Peacemaker said: "You two indeed for a long time argued to delay the completion of the work; you succeeded in causing them to engage in futile debate, you two caused them to be distracted, ensnarled, the minds of all those who have accepted Justice and Righteousness, also Order and Authority, as well as Peace and Health. . . . Now then, this affair has been settled, so consequently you two shall be the Doorkeepers, you two shall guard the doorway to the place where the Federal chiefs have kindled a council fire for Dehadodho, combining their minds in harmony at the main council fire of the Great Law (Commonwealth)." Gibson 1899, paras. 72–73.

378 Gibson 1912, 37.

when brightening the chain, because we put our minds on peace & friendship all in a heap. Now this was in old times. We not only made the chain of friendship very bright; but we locked arms, and took fast hold of each other's hands, and left the token of friendship.

Now, brother, I must tell you of some of our ancient rules: I believe you do not know our old customs: therefore make your mind easy. In ancient times, when we made peace, we cleared the path, and made it open both ways. Now I wish you would keep your mind easy & have no hard thoughts. You do not know our ancient ways, though you know the ways of the white people in doing business. When the two parties met together to make peace, we used to make it so bright that it was seen from the rising to the setting sun. Now you begin to see our way of doing business in the times of our forefathers. What we did, we did well. If any thing was bad, we did it afterwards.[379]

"Keep your mind easy and have no hard thoughts"? Sagoyewatha chose his words carefully, drawing them from a storehouse of formulaic expressions. An "easy" mind is one that is not distracted, one that is healthy, clear, and open. An "uneasy" mind would be carrying the baggage of grief, anger, or other distractions. Making one's mind easy—at ease—was not always something one could do oneself (and therefore one could call upon one's brothers for compassion and consolation), but it was an ideal, an intentional mindset to adopt before making difficult decisions.[380]

It is useful to consider the Kayanerenkó:wa not only as a law but also, as its name suggests, as a "path" or a "way," specifically a way of thinking about things and about doing them.[381] As Mohawk explained:

From what we know, the Indians had a tradition of law and the Iroquois are our surviving example of it. The Iroquois possessed a tradition of law, and that tradition of law is what has created them as a people. That part is definitely true, but the Iroquois tradition is not a tradition of law, exactly. The Iroquois tradition is a tradition of responsible thinking. It is not something written in paragraphs and lines because it doesn't matter whether the letter of the thing is

---

379 Ganter 2006, 29.

380 Before a difficult council or meeting, Haudenosaunee leaders will often burn tobacco together as a group. While they are imploring the Creator for direction and assistance, they are also bringing their minds together in a good way. The power of the tobacco burning, and the unity of their minds, sets them at ease.

381 In the same sense, the education provided in law school can be said to be less about the information provided and more about the *way* it teaches about thinking and solving issues.

right. The questions that have to be before the people are *What is the thinking? Is the thinking right?*[382]

The essence of the law is its confidence that good minds that are thinking right, using the right process, and working together will come up with the right decisions for the future generations.

Unity Is Power

There is a wampum that symbolizes the moment when all five nations have decided to bring their minds together as one, to form a single body. That it is made of strings, rather than woven into a belt, is testimony to its antiquity. Its simplicity is striking: it consists of five long strings, each the symbol of an individual nation. In 1722, a sixth string was added, as the Tuscaroras officially became the sixth nation of the Confederacy (the first five strings are white, the colour of peace: the sixth string is purple wampum, so that it can be distinguished from the original five). "We will begin now to use a single mind, and this we will do by being like a single person, working together to change the habits of the man."[383]

Today, at any Grand Council, the speaker who opens the council with the Thanksgiving holds these strings of wampum. They form a symbolic fire of the Haudenosaunee. Then, emulating the strings suspended from the pole in the Condolence, the strings are draped over a bench in the middle of the longhouse, a sign that the council is in session and the nations of the Haudenosaunee have brought their minds together.

> Upon the convening of the council a string of white wampum beads, about a foot in length, is passed from chief to chief, each holding it in his hands for a moment; it is then laid on a table in the form of a circle, the ends touching; this signifies that the council is "open" and harmony prevails. During the session, if a "condolence" is "called," by reason of death, a string of purple wampum is held by the side of the circled string, and so on. The "laying down of the wampum strings" one after another, each with its own significance, denotes the nature

---

382 Mohawk 1988, 16.

383 Gibson 1912, 221. In 1924, the Indian agent at the Grand River sought to paralyze the Confederacy Council, which he was seeking to replace, by seizing this wampum. He managed to take only the spare set. The original was sold to an anthropologist in 1930, and returned by the Canadian Museum of Civilization in 1990. The spare set was returned by William Montour, the chief of the elected council, in 1988.

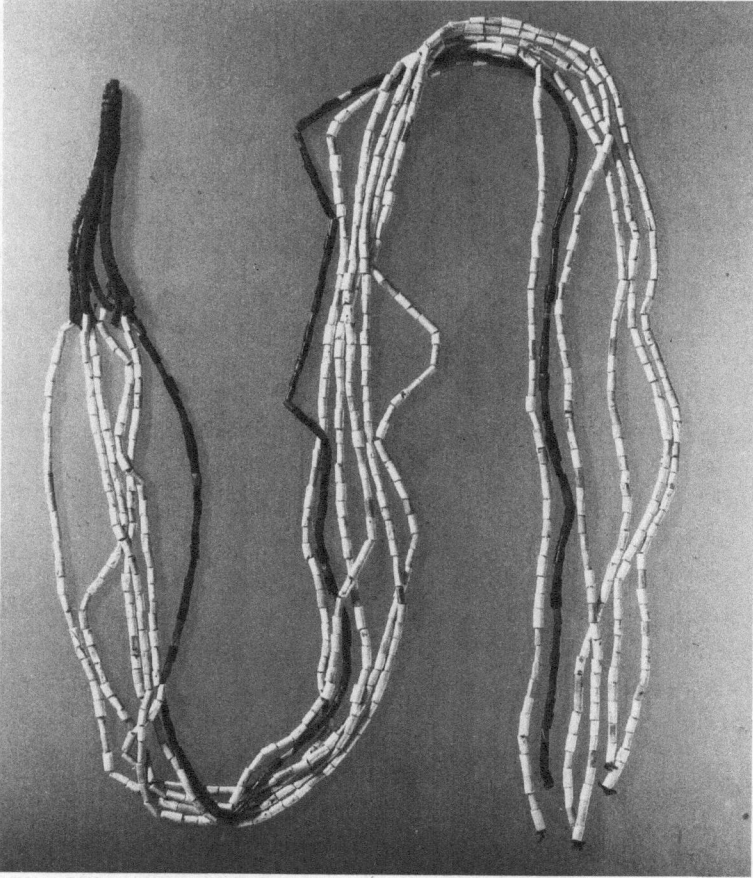

Figure 6. The Nations Bring Their Minds Together: Five strings of wampum, bound together at one end. The dark sixth string, added later, is for the Tuscaroras: This is "The Fire."

of the business or discussion of the council that is subject to consent, or rejection, by vote of the chiefs who are members thereof.[384]

In the chronology of the making of the law, the first wampum was made by the Peacemaker of strung freshwater snail shells, in the form of the strings used to condole Hiawatha. With the exception of the very short strings sent with the runners bringing word of an impending Grand Council, those short strings are also the simplest wampum that continues to be used. The first cylindrical wampum, found in "pre-contact" archaeological sites, was painstakingly made with bone and stone tools. It makes sense that the earliest, most basic wampum would be in the form of strings, because there would not be much wampum around. The five strings converging and joining into a single mind echo that simplicity. It stands to reason that they would also be among the earliest wampum symbols of the Haudenosaunee.

A similar symbol of the unity of the Haudenosaunee is a bundle of five arrows bound together.[385] The Peacemaker received one arrow from each of the five nations, showing that these could each be broken easily. He then took five more arrows and bound them tightly in a bundle, demonstrating that together they could not be broken:[386]

> So now I will warn you (shall have warned you): the number of your united nations (the five tribes) that it will ruin the confederacy (will be inappropriate, not right) for one of the member nations to pull out its arrow, for then consequently the number of them bound together (in the bundle) would be that much less. So it would be still worse if two were withdrawn (*dondwade'gwa*, less in number) (diminished by) (if the number were lessened by two), for then it might be possible for someone to bend it, perhaps even to break it.

---

384 Converse 1908, 142. This is a description of the Onondaga councils at Syracuse. The "circle" wampum of the Haudenosaunee at the time was kept by the Mohawks at the Grand River Territory, so the single string in a circle may have been a substitute for that. Today, the strings are not passed around first.

385 On September 10, 1784, Tehonwaghsloweaghte, or Black Cap, the Oneida speaker, spoke to the New York commissioners: "No evil Spirit shall be able to break the Covenant Chain which we have this Day completed; for Union begets Strength. An individual is like the single Stick which I hold in my Hand; how easy it is broke (then breaks the Stick in three Pieces and grasps them together); how weak when single and how strong when together" (Hough 1861, 205).

386 Gibson 1912, 306. The story is also told of the mother of the Mongol Nation, explaining the power of unity to her six sons. Five arrows bound together are on the coat of arms of the Scottish clan Cameron, symbolizing the unity of the clan's five families, and also on the Rothschild arms, for Mayer Rothschild's five sons. The thirteen arrows in the eagle's talons on the United States' coat of arms, symbolizing the original thirteen states, though, are probably derived from the Haudenosaunee rather than any European symbolism. See also Gibson 1899, para. 104: "and thus the power (strength) of the several nations (tribes, native lands) shall be now combined as one."

And so I shall warn (say unto) you, "Do not anyone of the several tribes attempt to draw out (withdraw) its arrow. It will be well if it will continue the way it is now as we have now completed (founded) it."[387]

Symbols of unity are another way to remind the people and their leaders of their obligations and commitments. As they take on the historic patina of sacredness, they increase the burden of keeping the commitments, maintaining the ideals. Though the Peacemaker and Hiawatha had taken several years to bring the five nations together, the story of their achievement has been compressed into a single seminal narrative,[388] becoming a single extended event—and a continuing process.

---

387   Gibson 1899, para. 105.

388   Depending on the version, the intervals between the incidents in the making of the law take days, weeks, or years—with the understanding that sometimes a symbolic "day" actually is a year. At this distance, time becomes relative. The peacemaking took a long time and a lot of effort.

PART IV

The Constitution

Overview

Horatio Hale identified three significant accomplishments of those who had devised the Great Law: the continuity of titles and government; preventing murder and revenge from becoming causes of further bloodshed;[1] and ending a fascination with death and the dead, replacing it with a ceremony of Condolence that raised up grieving minds. "In considering these remarkable laws, it becomes evident that the work which Hiawatha and Dekanawidah accomplished was really a Great Reformation, not merely political, but also social and religious. They desired not only to establish peace among the nations, but also to abolish or modify such usages and beliefs as in their opinion were injurious to their people."[2]

In any overview of the Kayanerenkó:wa, it is useful to consider the way the peace was accomplished and maintained. Institutions, usages, and beliefs that promoted peace and stability were kept, and extrapolated to the level of nation and Confederacy.[3] Injurious practices were abolished, and where this was not possible, their effects were mitigated. The laws reflected the best features of the people for whom they were designed, but they took into account and addressed their worst tendencies as well. If in any society the greatest strengths are also mirrors of the greatest weaknesses, the Peacemaker's work had been transformative, replacing anger with thought, fear with compassion, and the ring of angry warriors threatening the society's peace with a ring of protectors caring for that peace. The laws are pragmatic as well as symbolic: they indicate thought that considers the natural consequences and outcomes of any decision or strategy. The construction of the law shows the way for government to conduct itself in future.

The first phase of the Peacemaker's work had been accomplished: the people had made a commitment to peace, and the chiefs had been brought together at

---

1   Did the Great Law stop cycles of revenge? One school of thought says it did so within the Longhouse but left those thoughts richly alive with respect to nations beyond the Great White Roots. Thus, a Seneca speaker would tell the Hurons in 1704: "You know, my brothers, our customs which are to avenge, or perish in avenging our dead" (Papers of Cadillac, 33:191; cited in Brandão 1997, 37).

2   Hale (1883) 1989, 74.

3   Two and a half thousand years ago, in Athens, Cleisthenes reformed its political system in a somewhat similar way. "He did not tamper with existing social groups, with their cherished cults, or with their prestige. He had no need to: he merely created a new structure and gave it the authority." Boardman, Griffin, and Murray 1991, 33.

Onondaga. The three guiding principles had been accepted by all the nations. Thadadaho had been pacified and had accepted a major role in the new order. It remained to consolidate the accomplishments and to create the institutions that would perpetuate them. The Peacemaker set the tone with a dramatic announcement in council:

> I am Dekanawidah and with the Five Nations' Confederate Lords I plant the Tree of the Great Peace. I plant it in your territory, Adodarho, and the Onondaga Nation, in the territory of you who are Firekeepers.

> I name the tree the Tree of the Great Long Leaves. Under the shade of this Tree of the Great Peace we spread the soft white feathery down of the globe thistle as seats for you, Adodarhoh, and your cousin Lords.

> We place you upon those seats, spread soft with the feathery down of the globe thistle, there beneath the shade of the spreading branches of the Tree of Peace. There shall you sit and watch the Council Fire of the Confederacy of the Five Nations, and all the affairs of the Five Nations shall be transacted at this place before you, Adodarhoh, and your cousin Lords, by the Confederate Lords of the Five Nations.

> Roots have spread out from the Tree of the Great Peace, one to the north, one to the east, one to the south and one to the west. The name of these roots is the Great White Roots and their nature is Peace and Strength.[4]

The Longhouse of One Family

Today, in many Haudenosaunee communities, to speak of "the Longhouse" is to refer to a way of life that is sometimes called a religion, or to the building that the ceremonies of that traditional way of life are conducted in. This has led many people to think that "People of the Longhouse"—Haudenosaunee—includes only those people who follow that traditional way of life. That is, they have come to believe that it is a term that includes some people in the community and excludes others.

That was not the Peacemaker's intention.

The Peacemaker came upon a society with many institutions and a coherent way of life, but one that had become dysfunctional, its institutions struggling,

---

4   Parker (Newhouse and Cusick) 1916, 30.

its basic structure solid but its people having lost their way. He recognized that a society with internal peace and with war around its edges would still be a society at war. His plan, with the Great White Roots of the Tree of Peace gradually spreading to the four corners of the earth, was for universal peace, and that would mean that all the peoples of the world would eventually accept both the peace and the family relationships that would make it possible.

Morgan used the word "tribe" or *gens* to describe the clans. He recognized that the Confederacy had been built upon existing institutions:

> The founders of the Iroquois Confederacy did not seek to suspend the tribal divisions of the people, to introduce a different social organization; but on the contrary, they rested the League itself upon the tribes, and through them, sought to interweave the race into one political family.[5]

> . . . the Confederacy was in effect a League of Tribes. With the ties of kindred as its principle of union, the whole race was interwoven into one great family, composed of tribes in its first subdivision (for the nations were counterparts of each other); and the tribes themselves, in their subdivisions, composed of many households. Without these close inter-relations, resting, as many of them do, on the strong impulses of nature, a mere alliance between the Iroquois nations would have been feeble and transitory.[6]

Older and Younger Brothers

Kinship—knowing who you are by knowing who your people are—is crucial to understanding every part of the Great Law. The Peacemaker's achievement, in part, was to convince the Haudenosaunee that they were all one family, the people of a single longhouse. The same devotion to family that had fostered the desire for revenge in the dark days became the principle that brought and held the Confederacy together. The law provided the flexibility to bring in other nations as brothers, cousins, nephews, or other parts of the family. When the Europeans arrived, kinship worked in two distinct ways to protect the Haudenosaunee. One was that they were prepared to accept the Europeans as relations—to spread the roots of peace by greeting new relatives. But also the Great Law caused them to form a circle of people standing with their arms

---

5   Morgan (1851) 1995, 75.

6   Morgan (1851) 1995, 78.

joined in brotherhood, so firmly that they could not be broken apart. This protective circle is the comfort and empathy of family. James Bradley, writing that the Onondagas had survived "when so many other, comparable cultural groups did not," found kinship to be part of the explanation: "If locality served as the tangible focus for Onondaga culture, then kinship bonds were the glue that held it together. Kinship operated at several levels—family, clan, moiety, and village—and provided the definition of a person's roles and responsibilities. Taken together, these formed a social structure that was both flexible and resilient, one that was able to replenish itself through adoption and assimilation. As long as the structure of kinship was retained, Onondaga culture could (and did) accommodate a great deal of biological, ethnic, linguistic, and even material diversity and still remain coherent and functional."[7]

In every real, effective sense, the joined arms of brotherhood, or family, were the people's protection against being swept away: "This is what 'Power' means: all of the Nations will unite all their affairs,[8] and the group of several nations will become just a single one, and their power is that they shall join hands. This, moreover, will be the basis upon which they will survive as a group, forming a single family."[9]

In Haudenosaunee languages, it is difficult to simply say "Brother." One must be specific—younger brother or older brother. The specificity that the language requires encourages each person to think about relationships far more frequently than if they were speaking English, or even thinking in English. The practice of addressing many people, including those not related by blood, as "Auntie" or "Mother" or "Brother" further served to bind the people together.

Council diplomatic kinship terms are generally male: the chiefs are male, and male terms are usually used in respect of nations.[10]

---

7   Bradley 2001, 34.

8   "Affairs" is one of the most common translations of the root –orihwa, which is also translated as "matter," "word," "thing," and "substance." None of the English words picks up the broad purpose of the Haudenosaunee concept.

9   Gibson 1912, 104.

10   The exception: the Delawares, after attacking another nation within the Peace, had their weapons taken away from them and symbolically were said to wear aprons and be treated as women. How do we explain the apparent contempt in which these "women" were held, when Haudenosaunee culture and politics reserve such respect for women and their roles? Perhaps because the Delaware men were humiliated into (symbolically) behaving inappropriately for their gender, as the same thinking that respected the women also was very careful to separate men's and women's responsibilities. Teasing the Delawares about being made into women, then, is not misogyny but rather the equivalent of teasing a person for being made to wear a dunce cap.

Onondaga Longhouse

A Haudenosaunee longhouse, today, is multi-purpose. While it is clearly de-signed to put through the annual cycle of ceremonies, it is also a place of family meetings, weddings, and funerals. The same large, single-roomed log building is used for social dances.[11] Virtually all the longhouses are built along an east-west axis running from fire to fire (wood stove to wood stove), and each has a men's door and a women's door. The exceptions are the Onondaga longhouses.

There are two Onondaga longhouses in the world: one at Onondaga, near Syracuse, New York; the other in the Grand River Territory in Ontario. At these longhouses, councils of the Six Nations take place, and they have only one door,[12] in the middle of the building rather than at an end. It is said that this is so that the chiefs all go in together, so that they will more likely be of one mind. The entrance to the longhouse faces east, because the morning sun encourages clear thought. The shared doorway, at the heart of the Confederacy, confirms that this is "the Longhouse of All the Nations."

The Line Down the Middle of the Longhouse

If one enters one of the modern reconstructions of historic bark longhouses,[13] one can see immediately that a single line can be drawn from eastern to western door, passing through each firepit, each hearth.

A person living in such a longhouse would see that line every day. The line would serve as a reminder that many aspects of the world are divided in two parts: night and day, darkness and light, male and female, young and old. One family would live on each side of each fireplace, so that the people would be

11 A Maori *marae* offers the same multiplicity of purposes: social, ceremonial, political.

12 The "new" longhouse in Onondaga, built in the 1970s, has a back door that is used once a year, during Midwinter ceremonies; for all practical purposes, it has only one door.

13 Archaeologists know where the postholes of historic longhouses were; they do not know what the superstructures looked like. There are few accurate drawings of the roofs. Reconstructions range from rounded roofs to steep triangles. The Mohawk word kahnónsa strongly suggests rounded roofs, since it shares its roots with the words for the dome of a person's head and the dome of a turtle's back.

Figure 7. Reconstructed, aging longhouse at Ska-na-doht, near Oneida, 2010. Photograph by author.

used to the idea of pairs of families, facing each other across the fire, living in harmony, with each family constantly instructed to help the other.

Someone walking into a modern longhouse in Haudenosaunee territories would be able to see the same line—from the men's door to a wood stove (a "fire"), to another wood stove, to the women's door.[14]

The line down the middle of the longhouse becomes a real line in the ceremonies, when the two parts of the people ("moieties," in anthropological terms) sit on opposite sides of the longhouse.

The line is also a political line, between the two sides of the fire in council: "we shall now have two sets of lords, one on each side of the council fire."[15]

For modern Haudenosaunee, the two sides of the fire exist as visual realities in council and in ceremonies, and as conceptual principles in considering issues and strategies (that is, there are two sides to every matter—this being not a statement of inconsistency or confrontation but of a need to consider complexity and seek reconciliation). At the time the Great Law was being created, the two sides of the fire were part of every individual's daily family life. Duality and its companion, balance, were constant, physical presences. It seems it may have been persistent through changing technology and architecture, too: the people gave up bark longhouses for frame buildings in the late seventeenth and early eighteenth centuries, but in Seneca country and among the Onondagas at Oswegatchie, they were living in two-family log homes with shared hearths into the 1800s.[16]

---

14   In the two Onondaga longhouses, where there is only one door, the line still can be run between the wood stoves at each end of the longhouse. The wood stoves are indeed "fires," both for warmth and for burning tobacco when the occasion arises.

15   Parker 1916, 92. Morgan believed that "the phratric organization has existed since time immemorial. It is probably older than the confederacy." If he meant the clan system, and its use in the internal government of communities, this is in accord with Haudenosaunee tradition. The Peacemaker used the existing organization as a model, reflected in the League itself. Morgan (1871) 1997, 93.

16   Archaeologists examining these "transitional dwellings" between the bark longhouse and the single-family farmstead do not seem to have considered how many families were living in a structure, nor how the social arrangements were made. Nor has there been much contemporaneous writing on this point.

Calling Council

Unlike other lawmaking and governing bodies, the Grand Council of the
Haudenosaunee meets when necessary, without an appointed schedule or set
dates. It meets occasionally: there have been times when a year would go by
without a Grand Council. To outsiders and many insiders, both how a decision
is made that a Grand Council is necessary, and how a Grand Council is brought
together, can seem confusing, even mysterious.

Morgan asserts that any of the nations has the authority to "summon" the
Grand Council.[17] Newhouse explains that the request shall go to the Onondagas,
who, if they "find the case is worth the consideration of the Confederate
Council," will notify the rest of the chiefs to attend.[18]

The modern process for convening a Grand Council flows from any individual nation through Onondaga. The nation may request that a matter be
considered by the Grand Council, or Onondaga may decide to hold one of its
own initiative. Runners—today travelling by car—go from Onondaga to the
fireplaces of the other nations—Oneida (Ontario), Tuscarora, Akwesasne (for
the Mohawks), the Grand River and Tonawanda (for the Senecas)—carrying
strings of wampum and the message about the date of the council. Just as in
the days of the making of the law, there are usually two runners, travelling together.[19] The string of wampum is attached to a stick that has been notched to
indicate the number of days until the council will be held. The runners must
find specific chiefs, the firekeepers of their nations, to deliver the message. The
wampum delivered must be returned when the council convenes.

---

17   Morgan (1871) 1997, 135.

18   Newhouse 1885, 23.

19   One is the person who has actually been given the task of delivering the invitation and
     notice; the other is his companion, protector, backup. This resembles the times when
     someone is given the task of opening and closing a council or delivering a message to
     another nation. Part of the thinking may involve a vague distrust of what a person may
     do on his own and, in the case of messages to, or meetings with, other nations, a distrust
     of the people across the fire or table. You want a witness to confirm what you said and
     did.

Procedure in Council

Council is ready to begin when representatives of all the nations are present. It is also to begin at mid-morning, and given the distances that some chiefs have to travel, there is a convention that council can proceed, as a "meeting" that will discuss matters in a preliminary way, if only three nations are present. At the Grand River, there has historically been a practice of designating someone to represent an absent nation.[20] Since opening council requires a full Thanksgiving, which can last up to half an hour, there are times when council is started, in the knowledge that the people who are still on their way may arrive late, but not so late that a true council cannot proceed.

Though the basic process of nations speaking to one another across a council fire was not new to the nations, nor unique to the Haudenosaunee, the process of a Haudenosaunee council, carefully designed to promote consensus and avoid confrontation, was innovative. It is a complex, deliberate process, and as with many Haudenosaunee cultural processes, there is often concern about keeping things in the proper order and not omitting important steps. Council opens with everyone giving thanks together. The opening words of thanksgiving are delivered by an Onondaga chief. As the speaker completes each part of the speech, ending it with "and so our minds are one," all the men present indicate their agreement with "yoh!" or "tho!" The thanksgiving opening reminds the participants in council that they are all human beings in a complex, structured world in which each part has its own responsibilities and instructions. The opening creates an atmosphere of good will, commitment, humility, and unity of mind. In a modern Haudenosaunee council, the chief who opened the meeting does so holding the "fire" or "mace,"[21] the long strings of wampum symbolizing

---

20 Council at the Grand River requires the presence of all five nations, difficult since there are no local Oneida, Seneca, or Tuscarora Chiefs at the time of this writing. The council counts on chiefs from the other communities of those nations to attend.

21 In British-style parliaments, the mace is the symbol of the Speaker's authority, dating from the fifteenth century, when royal Serjeants at Arms would carry maces stamped with the royal arms as emblems of their authority to arrest without warrant. The House is not properly in session if the mace is not in the chamber. The mace sits on the clerk's table. Members who interfere with the mace are generally suspended. It is an interesting contrast that the symbols of British authority are weapons of war, while symbols of Haudenosaunee authority are reminders that the weapons have been put away.

the nations putting their minds together.[22] He holds it by the end at which the strings are joined, as if holding their minds together in his hand. When he has finished the opening, he places the "fire" on the bench[23] near the secretary, to symbolize that the council is now open.

It is useful to think of the council, in session, as actually consisting of five separate and simultaneous circles or councils. Once an issue has been placed before the chiefs, each nation becomes like a separate committee for the purpose of considering the matter. However, within each nation, the law provides for several permanent committees—chiefs who are to consider matters together. This process allows for multiple simultaneous discussions.[24]

The Peacemaker first chose the chiefs as individuals. Not long afterward, when he was describing the workings of the council, he organized them into groups or committees for the purpose of their deliberations. Most of the men were already village chiefs. The Confederacy Council was a new entity, and their roles in that council would reflect the workings of a village or nation council,[25] extrapolated to a new level. However, some aspects of the processes in the Grand Council were new: they were adjustments and designs made to take into account that many of the chiefs of this new body were strangers to one another, whose nations and communities were far apart geographically, and unfamiliar politically. The fifty rotiyanershon are also a larger body than most village councils, and needed new rules to maintain order and direction.

Part of the strategy of the council's process is to have matters discussed by small, manageable groups, in which each individual has the opportunity to

---

22   In 1924, the Indian Agent at the Grand River Territory, Colonel Cecil Morgan, tried to seize all the Confederacy Council's wampum as part of his efforts to install an elected system. Taking the "Fire," it is said, was his attempt to prevent the chiefs from opening council at all. But the wampum seized in the council house was the spare set, and the chiefs continued to meet. When the main wampum also disappeared (it was eventually returned from the Museum of the American Indian in 1988), the chiefs simply took whatever loose wampum they had and made a new "Fire." They showed that it is the principle, and not the artifact, that counts. If there had been no wampum, perhaps they would have reverted to sumac and basswood beads, or glass ones.

23   The bench is the same bench used in the longhouse for the ceremonies, generally the same one used for the sacred Great Feather Dance in the ceremonies of thanksgiving. The wampum is placed on a clean white cotton cloth, to signify that nothing im-pure should sully it. The cloth recalls the pure white deerskin of the first words of the Condolence.

24   In British parliamentary terms, being able to break into smaller groups for the purpose of discussing a matter is either accomplished by a "caucus," if the group is of one party, or by a "committee," if it is a multi-partite group.

25   Nation councils today seem to have two distinct decision-making structures. In formal meetings, in the longhouse, they will sit in their respective clans on their respective sides, with the issues being addressed back and forth as in a Grand Council. In informal work-ing meetings, they will sit around a table, in no particular order or structure. Generally, the more important the decision, the more people are involved, and the more formal the meeting.

speak and be heard. Generally, they consist of two to four of the chiefs. The English word "committee" is most often used to describe these smaller groups within the circle of the nation. Yet "committee" does not capture the nature of these groups, these slightly formalized clusters of thinkers—and no other English word comes close.

Thus, when a matter is considered, the first body to think about the issue is the "committee" within a nation. The Mohawk chiefs, for example, consist of three such groups, one for each of the three clans. The wampum symbolizing the Mohawk chiefs reflects this: instead of being a string with nine separate strings hanging from it, it has three clusters of three strings each.

The Peacemaker did not explain why he put specific individuals in particular committees. It may have been a matter of the unique capabilities of each member of the first group of chiefs. It may have been a desire to have the chiefs of each village discuss things first, before the matter was taken to the level of the nation. It may have been a way of weaving the clans closer together. Certainly the small committees were part of the larger design—the desire to promote agreement by creating political structures that were most likely to secure and devise consensus. At the committee level, this meant small groups of men who already knew and trusted each other, who could work compatibly, and who were likely to agree.

The momentum of agreement from a committee would then carry over into the nation council. The nation council would be able to discuss the matter in a microcosm of the Grand Council.

The council also consists of three distinct sides: most of the discussion will take place as the issue is passed back and forth between the Elder Brothers, the Mohawks and Senecas, and the Younger Brothers, the Oneidas and Cayugas (and Tuscaroras). The third side of the council, the Onondagas (who are actually Elder Brothers, too), becomes directly involved only after the first two sides have reached consensus, or if they ask for help, having failed to agree.

When an issue is brought forth in council, the path it must follow—from the Elder Brothers to the Younger Brothers and back, and then to the Firekeepers—is such that one might assume that the matter is discussed only after it reaches one's fire. In fact, each group continues to discuss the matter as it makes its way through the process. While each nation formally has one speaker on an issue, it is not uncommon to see the matter addressed more informally as individual chiefs cross the fire to talk things over, or go outside to "talk behind the bushes,"[26] or seek advice from their clan mothers or members of their families, or other advisers. The spirit of council is contribution and accommodation.

26　This term is not used much anymore. It reflects the geography of the old longhouses, where the edge of the woods was never far away. It reflects the privacy of these discussions, and also the fact that compromises are often worked out informally, between individuals, in quiet conversations away from the structure and formality of the council.

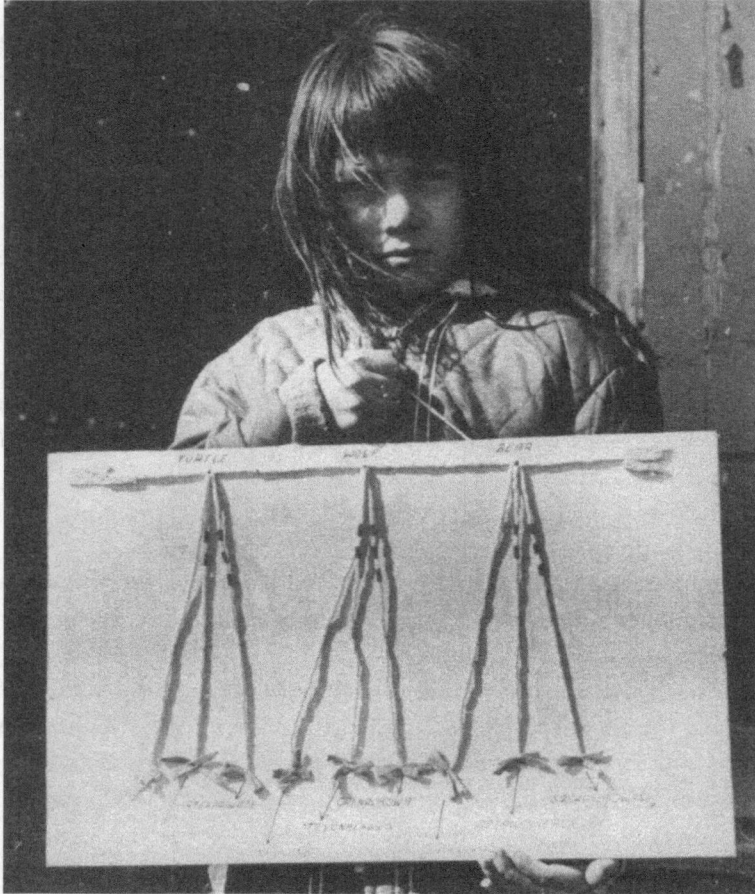

Figure 8. Mohawk Chiefs' Wampum. From *Wampum Belts of the Iroquois*, by
Tehanetorens Ray Fadden. Used with permission of Six Nations Indian Museum,
Onchiota, New York.

Opinions, when they are spoken openly, are not to be individual opinions but to reflect the thinking of groups of people: this prevents council from descending into personal attacks, and it prevents individuals from domineering by the force of their personalities.

A matter coming into the longhouse is generally brought in through the Eastern or Western Door. That is, it is introduced in council by the Senecas or the Mohawks, the doorkeepers (also known as "the Well"). Once the matter has been introduced, the five circles will consider it carefully. If the Mohawks and the Senecas have reached one mind on the matter separately, they will then confer together to seek an agreement. If they agree, then a speaker stands[27] to state the thoughts of the Elder Brothers and to "send it across the fire" to seek the views and thoughts of the Younger Brothers. Benjamin Franklin described council decorum: "He that would speak, rises. The rest observe a profound Silence. When he has finished and sits down, they leave him five or six Minutes to recollect, that if he has omitted any thing he intended to say, or has any thing to add, he may rise again and deliver it. To interrupt another, even in Common conversation, is reckoned highly indecent."[28]

The relationship between the Mohawks and Senecas, on one side of the fire, and the Oneidas and Cayugas, on the other side, is described in affectionate terms, terms of virtual equality. There is never any suggestion that, within this family, anyone is subordinate, lesser or inferior:[29] "This, moreover, is to be the relationship between the two sides, Tekarihoken and his [Mohawk and Seneca] colleagues [*siblings – brothers*] will raise issues, and when they address the other side of the fire they will say 'you are downstream from us,' which means this: it is like saying [*it means for one to say*] 'you, our children.'[30] Next, the other side of the fire, that is, Odatsehte and his [Oneida and Cayuga] tribal colleagues

---

27 Speakers stand—out of respect—and step forward. Anyone else standing in council is probably just getting up to leave to go to the bathroom.

28 Franklin 1987, 969–70. The pace of modern councils has increased, but the basic rules and courtesies remain.

29 It would seem that the title of Tekarihoken rested with the Scoharie or Lower Mohawks rather than the Canajoharie or Upper Mohawks. John Deserontyon used that title generically in his Condolence at Kahnawake on the death of Ahsarekowa. Sir John Johnson took matters a step further in 1790, when he explained that opposition to the leadership of Thayendenegea Joseph Brant (of Canajoharie) was opposed by the chiefs of the Lower Mohawks, "with a view to keep up their former consequence, having always been considered as the heads of the Six Nations Confederacy." Public Records Office, Colonial Office Records 42, 69:228.

30 Jacob Thomas rendered this as "my offspring"; Hewitt (1928, 93) as "my weanling." Hewitt explains that symbolically, the mother is on the side of the children. The term "offspring" also appears in condoling councils, "konyennetaghkwen" (Hale [1883] 1989, 60).

[*brothers*] they will address them, saying 'our father's kinsmen' [*yok-ni-sho*] which means this: it is like saying 'they are our fathers.'"[31]

The Oneidas and Cayugas then each consider the matter separately and then consult jointly. If they agree, their speaker explains their thoughts on the issue and sends it back to the Elder Brothers. In doing so, the speaker repeats the words of the Elder Brothers first and then either expresses agreement or adds the new elements for consideration. Repeating the words ensures that they have been understood. If in repeating the words it becomes clear there has been a misunderstanding, it is corrected gently in the reply.

In modern councils, the chiefs dress modestly and comfortably, wearing their everyday clothes. Generally, an outsider's only way to recognize a person as a chief is the fact that he is sitting on a front bench. Sub-chiefs, secretaries, and ordinary people sit on the two or three rows of benches behind the chiefs. Clan mothers and other women sit at the other end of the longhouse—partly a reflection of the separation between men's and women's roles, partly as a reminder that the clan mothers take no active part in council decisions but nevertheless must watch their chiefs, advise them when the opportunity arises, and report back to their families with the chiefs.

In modern councils, the Tuscarora chiefs sit with the Younger Brothers, and the speaker for that side speaks also for the Tuscaroras, who theoretically are "under the wing" of the Oneidas. In practice, the Tuscaroras are welcomed as equals and as an integral part of the decision making on the benches, but a Tuscarora chief will only speak to a matter to the entire council if there is agreement that he should. This is never denied:

> Thereupon they refer the matter across the fire to the other moiety's side, and they themselves will let go of it. Thereupon Shake?syone and his committee colleagues, now they will pick it up, consider it carefully, and when they reach consensus among themselves they will refer it back across the fire to the opposite moiety's side. Thereupon they will pick it up, placing it in front of the two firekeepers who will pick up the matter, consider it carefully, and confirm the matter; and it is this, their unanimous decision, this is what will become law where the people are.[32]

---

31   Gibson 1912, 431. When Governor Andros of New York addressed the Haudenosaunee as his "children," the Mohawks reminded him of the making of the Covenant Chain: "Then we were called Brethren, and that was also well kept; therefore let that of Brethren continue." Andros seemed to dismiss the difference: "You take notice of the words Brethren and Children, but leave it to mee: they are both words of relation and friendship, but Children the nearer." By the next council, everyone had reverted to "Brothers." New York Colonial Documents (NYCD) 3: 535; 557–61. See Jennings 1985, xv.

32   Gibson 1912, 426.

The "matter" is like a physical thing,[33] as well as something that has received thought: "letting go if it" means not only "delivering" it to the other side but also detaching oneself emotionally from the decision once it has been made.

Council procedure is structured to promote reason and prevent passion. Each side of the fire has a "speaker" on every issue so that one should not see many voices raised from a single bench.[34] A matter cannot be referred back and forth indefinitely: if there is a disagreement, the Onondagas can send it back, with their recommendations for consensus.[35] If passions are ignited—also rare—Thadadaho can close the council.[36] In modern councils, debate moves back and forth across the fire, as well as within the benches of each nation:

> First, the Mohawks, who will consider all of the issues, co-operating with their moiety colleagues, the Seneca, and reaching consensus with them. Thereupon their speaker, now he will move the issue across the fire to the other moiety where he will let go of it. Thereupon the Oneida and their moiety colleagues, the Cayuga, these will co-operate when they pick up the issue to consider it, and if they agree, they will confirm it unanimously. Thereupon their speaker, now he will move the issue back across the fire, letting it go again to where they are seated, the nation group initiating the issue. Thereupon their speaker will be the one to pick it up and he will direct his words to where their cousins, the firekeepers are seated, letting go of it in front of them, the decision of the two firesides. Thereupon their cousins, the namebearers, now they will pick it up, considering it until they decide. Thereupon their speaker, now he will give an answer for the firekeepers, and when they confirm, then the matter will be a rule of the Great Law for the various nations accepting the League. Moreover, they hold the power, the firekeepers, and if it should happen that they differ, the two moieties, if it should happen that they voice two opinions, both sides differing in the outcome of their discussions, then the firekeepers have the power

---

33   Where a responsibility is given to a specific group of people, it is described as a "bundle" that they are to carry. When they fulfill the responsibility and report back, it can be said that they are "unbundled."

34   Unfortunately, another reason there are designated individuals to do the talking is that many of the rotiyanershon are not fluent in Haudenosaunee languages.

35   Newhouse 1885, 22. They can also send it back if they feel it is "ruinous, injurious, or disadvantageous to the confederate people."

36   His authority to close the council is related to his being given the "Wing" or dust fan to keep the council house clean and clear and to remove any "crawling things." While closing any council is rare, especially considering the distances that the delegates have to travel, the decision to shut things down is made before matters get out of hand. Harsh words, anger, and deep disagreement can lead to closing council. In modern times, the decision is made by the Firekeepers together.

from among either of the two to choose one to support, or they can throw it back for them to reconsider on both sides of the fire—the Council as a whole, the two moieties—and if these reconsider, and if the same thing happens again, then again they will place both results together before the firekeepers, and whichever one they decide for they will support that outcome.[37]

... each of the opposing sides first takes up the proposition in a few words and sets forth all the reasons which have been alleged pro and con by those who first expressed their opinion. He [the speaker] then states his own opinion and concludes with these words: "That is my thought on the subject of this, our Council." After their deliberation on whatever subject it may be, there is almost no reason, for or against, which they have not seen or weighed.[38]

Any matter dealt with in council is addressed in the most positive manner possible: "they generally begin by some compliment to the last speaker, such as for instance they have listened attentively to the words he has uttered & maturely considered them that they are persuaded that they proceed from a sincere heart & desire for promoting the welfare of the 5 Nations; any sentence calling forth the glory of the nations or their antiquity is always well received & especially as they frequently use brethren of the same nation, friends to the same country, & similar expressions, they are always sure to obtain a favourable audience."[39]

The language of council is both decorous and indirect. It is considered deeply impolite to refer to anyone by name or to make an issue personal. Finger pointing is especially insulting (and may be associated with the ill will of medicine). Rather than present a complete position, anyone introducing a matter to council makes a point of designing it so that consensus can be built gradually and without disagreement.[40] Where there is disagreement, it is stated carefully but respectfully—often cloaked in statements like "we agree, and furthermore . . .":

---

37   Gibson 1912, 430–34.

38   Lafitau (1724) 1974, 2:296–97.

39   NYSL MSS 13350, cited in Johnston 1964, 28.

40   This is in stark contrast to the British parliamentary system, in which the government introduces a "Bill" in near-final form, and the "official opposition" then fulfills its function by challenging and attacking it, by proposing amendments, and eventually, often, by voting against the government's proposal. The parliamentary system "improves" a bill by having it pass through the fire of adversary opposition; the Haudenosaunee system builds the same solution through cooperation. The parliamentary system culminates in a vote, with winners and losers. The Haudenosaunee system culminates in consensus, one-mindedness, or at least accommodation (or deferral).

That People have however a Piece of Civility peculiar to themselves: for a Man would be accounted very impertinent, if he contradicted anything that was said in their Council, and if he does not approve even the greatest Absurdities therein proposed; and therefore they always answer, Niawa, that is to say, Thou art in the right, Brother; that is well.[41]

Notwithstanding this seeming approbation, they believe what they please and no more; and therefore 'tis impossible to know when they are really persuaded of those things you have mentioned unto them, which I take to be one of the greatest Obstructions to their Conversion; for their Civility hindering them from making any Objection, or contradicting what is said unto them, they seem to approve of it, though perhaps they laugh at it in private.[42]

To build towards agreement, a matter is sent back and forth across the fire, so that the approach to be taken by the Haudenosaunee to the matter is developed by the Mohawks and Senecas, on one hand, and by the Oneidas (and Tuscaroras) and Cayugas, on the other. If these four nations agree, the Mohawks and Senecas send the matter to the firekeepers, the Onondagas, who can either ratify the resolution or send it back for further discussion. In sending it back, the Onondagas will express the reasons for their hesitations.

Seth Newhouse stirred up a political storm when he produced a version of the law that gave the Mohawks primacy, putting these words into the Peacemaker's mouth:

It is provided thus: I begin by choosing you, the Mohawk Nation, to be the "Head and Leader" of the Confederate Government and Legislative Body, and Council. Therefore, you are the foundation of the Government of the "Great Peace" now hereby established. Therefore when in Council, if you disallow any proposition before the Council, or protest against any action of the Council, it shall not be lawful for the Legislative Body, or the Council to pass or the Firekeepers to confirm it.[43]

---

41   Though in some situations, niá:wen means "it is well," the word today is used as the equivalent of the English "thanks."

42   Hennepin (1688) 1974, 86. What happens when the council disagrees with a proposed course of action? Often it will indicate the disagreement by making positive statements about an alternative. For example, a 2010 proposal from an individual that his team should replace the council's negotiators was not met with a refusal, but instead the council asserted its confidence in the people it had appointed. Other decisions that amount to a refusal include putting the matter "under the pillow" for consideration and simply moving on to another matter.

43   Newhouse, 1885, "6th Wampum String."

It is provided thus: The Council of the Five Confederate Nations
Lords shall not be opened until all the "nine" of the Mohawk Lords
are present, and in case any of them are absent (it) is not lawful business can be transacted to Council; if all the three parties of Mohawk
Lords are represented by one or more Lords; such Council shall
not be legal except for matters of little importance; all the "nine"
Lords of the Mohawks must be present forming a full Council, for
transacting business or matters of importance.[44]

No other early version of the law makes the Mohawks so dominant. These
clauses, as well as Newhouse's statements that the warriors had the authority to
assassinate chiefs who disagreed with them, offended the council at the Grand
River so deeply that the chiefs decided to produce an authoritative version of
the law.[45]

In council, the Onondagas are the firekeepers, sitting by themselves at the
head of the longhouse, in an arrangement that clearly has three components.[46]
In Condolences, though, they are part of the Elder Brothers, the Three Brothers,
one of the two sides of the fire.

It is often said that decisions of the Confederacy Council must be unani-
mous, and that any nation or any individual chief can stop a matter in its tracks.
Potentially, this is true. It amounts to an individual and a national veto. Even
so, this is rarely used. A Confederacy born out of a desire to create unity of
mind maintains a deep aversion to disagreement. An individual who is alone
in his disagreement with a decision, and who cannot persuade the rest of the
chiefs to change their minds, would be ashamed to be the reason for the council's inability to decide—even where his position reflects the views of his clan
family. The Peacemaker instructed the chiefs to strive towards agreement in all
things: "I now charge each of you Lords that you must never seriously disagree
among yourselves. You are all of equal standing and of equal power, and if you
seriously disagree the consequences will be most serious and this disagreement

---

44   Newhouse 1885, "13th Wampum String." Newhouse also provided that the Mohawks
     (rather than the Onondagas) would have the authority to make "final" pronouncements.

45   Newhouse produced several versions of the law. Only after 1885—after his daughter
     had died and the council's investigation exonerated the doctor—did Newhouse begin to
     propose that the warriors could be justified in killing the chiefs. His anger at the Grand
     River Council may have led to his reorganization of the constitution.

46   Woodbury (Gibson 1912, 427) suggests that they are the "tie-breakers in consensus
     decisions," though in a consensus there can be no ties, but only one-mindedness. Other
     writers have suggested that the Onondaga chiefs have a deciding vote that they cast, but
     reluctantly. None of those writers was Haudenosaunee.

will cause you to disregard each other . . . then your grandchildren will suffer and be reduced to poverty and disgrace."[47]

One way to avoid disagreement is to concentrate on the principles of a matter rather than its details. Details can be delegated. Another common method is to secure agreement on the easy parts first and then build gradually, with a momentum of understanding, towards agreement on the more difficult parts of an issue.[48] One technique useful in doing this is to break a matter into components, and then to create strategies for resolving the parts about which there is certain agreement. The harder issues (John Mohawk called them "the rock hard parts") can be left for later, or they might be left for local or community decisions, which all the nations agree to respect.[49] If it is clear that the two sides—Mohawk and Seneca, Oneida, Cayuga and Tuscarora—disagree, it is not unusual for the Onondagas, who have been watching the matter progress, to suggest some areas for agreement, or to send the matter back to the Elder Brothers with both an idea for resolution and words of encouragement. The words of encouragement often include citing aspects of the Peacemaker's message.

If tempers begin to flare, or patience begins to fray, the Onondaga chiefs may call an end to the council, or a break, to allow minds to cool off. This also allows informal discussion—"speaking behind the bushes"—to seek resolution, often on a personal level. In some cases, a temporary adjournment is necessary to recover rationality. For example, in a council with the western nations in the Ohio country in 1792, the Shawnees bluntly accused the Haudenosaunee of making secret deals with the United States, and threw a string of wampum across the fire, into the dust. The measured Haudenosaunee response came from Honeyawus (Farmer's Brother), the Seneca chief:

Brothers;

We desire you all to sit still, we shall move to a little distance to consult on what answer to give you. You have talked to us a little too roughly, you have thrown us on our backs.

---

47 Parker (Chiefs) 1916, 103. Once again, the chiefs are urged to take the long view, considering the impact of decisions on future generations.

48 In doing this, they are repeating the strategy of the Peacemaker and Hiawatha in the making of the law, bringing those inclined towards peace onside before tackling those who would oppose the good message.

49 For example, in addressing the question of who would be entitled to receive a Haudenosaunee identification card—essentially, who is a citizen—the Grand Council concluded that each nation should be free to develop its own laws, within the principles of the Great Law, and that other nations would recognize the people accepted by each nation. This avoided the need to create a precise Haudenosaunee citizenship law.

The Farmer's Brother then put the String which had been thrown
down, over his head & hanging down his back they then moved
away & remained an hour.[50]

Exceptionally, blunt language from an ally is answered in kind: "You spoke
very fierce & roughly to us & we hope you'll give us the same liberty."[51]

"Sharp words" are capable of drawing blood, provoking violence, and breaking the peace. Just as the principle of shared hunting grounds allows no sharp
edges in the Dish with One Spoon, to prevent bloodshed, so sharp words are
not permitted in council. A speaker in a council between nations, after introducing himself, will often apologize in advance for anything he might say that
could be taken as sharp or injurious, and explain that this is not his intention.

Haudenosaunee councils refuse to be rushed. They are the product of a time
when there was always enough time to do things properly. Careful thought is
unhurried, uncluttered thought and deliberate, consistent work.[52] If a matter
is not agreed upon at one council, the chiefs can "put it under their pillow" to
consider it further and deal with it at a future council.

Another rule that promotes agreement is a determination to consider only
one issue at a time—to avoid confusion caused by a multiplicity of matters. In
theory, the Onondaga chief Hononwirehton has the responsibility of keeping
council's mind focussed.[53] In former times, this principle had a physical presence in council, in the form of a visible agenda of wampum strings and belts.

When Arendt van den Bogaert visited Onondaga in 1634—and he was
the first European to do so—he described an unusual feature of the council
house. There was a horizontal pole suspended upon two forked sticks. When
there was council, the wampum that symbolized each item on the agenda was

---

50   Cruikshank 1923, 1:224. The western nations had actually decided to assassinate all
      the Haudenosaunee chiefs at this council, and only the intervention of Egushaway, the
      Ottawa war chief from the Detroit area, saved their lives. Picking up the wampum but
      placing it on his head, Honeyawus indicated that it had not been rejected, and that it
      was being considered. In 1990, during the "Oka negotiations," when Mohawks from
      Kahnawake and Kanesatake began to accuse one another of bad faith, the Confederacy
      chiefs informed both groups that they would not take part in or listen to such disagree-
      ment, but instead would withdraw for an hour to permit them to sort matters out.
      Deskahe Harvey Longboat told them that "the only power we have is *enskat nikan-
      ikonhra*, one mind, and these sharp disagreements would injure and undermine that
      power." When the delegation returned, the disagreement continued, the chiefs with-
      drew—and the negotiations collapsed.

51   Wraxall (1754) 1915, 201. June 27, 1737, at Albany: the Six Nations to Lieutenant
      Governor Clarke.

52   Modern Haudenosaunee councils are hampered by a lack of time. Generally, they take
      place on weekends, rather than extending into as much time as required. Often, their
      agendas pile up, especially as many councils are cancelled as a result of deaths in the
      families that carry chiefs' titles, so that discussions and decisions are postponed.

53   Another name for Hononwirehton is Nkwahokó'wa, the Great Wolf.

hung on this pole, each item in the order in which it was to be addressed. No matter was to be spoken of until the matter before it had been fully dealt with and removed from the pole. The mind of the council was to focus on one issue at a time, without distractions. If people began to drift on to other issues, Hononwirehton would walk over to the pole and tap one of the uprights with his cane. That would be all it took to bring the mind of the council back on track. He might also use the wing or fan to keep the council house clean of dust and distraction. This is why, in the Circle Wampum that symbolizes the council of chiefs, with its fifty strings radiating towards the centre or fire, the longest string represents not Thadadaho but Hononwirehton, for he must sit closest to the fire, in order to have easiest access to the pole.

Just as the Thanksgiving and the Condolence are recalled in part because they are set out in a logical, particular order, so matters raised in council are considered one at a time, and answered in the order in which they are originally stated. Getting things in their right order is an important aspect of planning the process of council. An intentional structure to the agenda allows for the setting of priorities—so the important matters are dealt with first and the least important (or the hard ones everyone wants to avoid) might not be dealt with before the council ends. Often outsiders are dealt with first, so they can be invited to leave as the council moves on to its internal business. Maintaining an orderly progression also requires attention to detail—a matter that is raised and not addressed is pointed out, so that nothing is left undone. Father Hennepin, in the late seventeenth century, described council procedure:

> The next day the Iroquese answer'd our Discourse and Presents Article by Article, having laid on the Ground several little pieces of Wood, to put them in mind of what had been said the day before in Council; their Speaker, or President, held in his hand one of these Pieces of Wood, and when he had answer'd one Article of our Proposal, he laid it down, with some Presents of Black & White Porcelain, which they use to string upon the smallest Sinews of Beasts; and then he took up another Piece of Wood, and so all of the rest, till he had fully answer'd our Speech, of which those Pieces of Wood, and our Presents, put them in Mind. When his Discourse was ended, the oldest Man of their Assembly cry'd aloud for three times, Niaoua, that is to say, it is well, I thank thee; which was repeated with a full voice, and in a tuneful manner, by all the other Senators.[54]

The aversion to disagreement can result in the Confederacy Council failing to agree at all, leaving individual nations to take action as they choose, or even

---

54   Hennepin (1688) 1974, 86.

allowing individual people that choice.[55] This is accompanied by a sense of sorrow, especially since the Peacemaker warned against indecision by the chiefs at the time of the making of the law. Disagreement can result in the appointment by the council of individuals to work on the matter with the parties—for example, the Cayugas meeting with different Oneida groups—to report back to the next council. Even without a formal appointment, individual chiefs will continue to communicate and meet in small groups, seeking to resolve matters or to generate solutions that can be brought to the fire.

Thick Skins

For the council to function properly, its members needed enormous patience. They would become targets in a dozen ways. Their families would seek to influence them to make short-term decisions, to satisfy immediate needs, rather than to focus on the next seven generations. They would be provoked by insults and accusations. Their gossip-prone society would ensure that ugly rumours would spread about them. Even within the council, there could be hard feelings between individuals. Every version of the law repeats the Peacemaker's admonition to the chiefs that their skins must be so thick that no barbs will be able to penetrate them.

The Peacemaker understood that if communication and memory were strengths of Haudenosaunee society, they were also the sources of weakness: gossip was constant and rapid, and malicious gossip would never go away.[56] This was one of the matters that he recognized he could not change, so he had to develop ways of guarding against it. He fortified the chiefs against it, in the law itself:

> Chiefs skin must be thick & have patience.[57]

> I shall therefore charge each of your lords, that your skin be of the thickness of seven spreads of the hands (from the thumb to the end

---

55   In the American Revolution, the Mohawk and Oneida chiefs, in the Confederacy Council, initially urged neutrality, and argued that the Haudenosaunee should not get involved in the war. The Senecas and Onondagas felt that the Haudenosaunee had an obligation to help the King. In the absence of any agreement, individuals like Thayendenega Joseph Brant, Hanyery, and Atiatoharongwen Louis Cook were able to draw groups of Haudenosaunee into different sides of the war. See LAC, MG29.

56   In the 1970s, when the State of New York was intent on building Interstate 81 through Onondaga Territory, rumours were so quick and persistent that the chiefs installed a telephone line called "Rumor Central," which people could call about a rumour and find out whether it was true.

57   Parker 1916, 148; Council at Cattaraugus, December 1, 1862.

of the great finger) so that no matter how sharp a cutting instrument may be used it will not penetrate the thickness of your skin. (The meaning of the great thickness of your skins is patience and forbearance, so that no matter what nature of question or business may come before you, no matter how sharp or aggravating it may be, it will not penetrate to your skins, but you will forbear with great patience and good will in all your deliberations and never disgrace yourselves by becoming angry.)[58]

You will receive many scratches and the thickness of your skins shall be seven spans.[59] You must be patient and henceforth work in unity.[60]

. . . all of you yourselves shall be as standing trees[61] where the people will rest their eyes and minds. And so this will be the system (rule) amongst the persons (body) of your chiefs; and the thickness of your skins shall be seven times the first joint of the thumb (*oyonh'gaaʔ*), and the reason for this is that when you are all legislating . . . no matter if your public may employ a sharp point (shoot a magic dart) or perhaps (else) they might even stick you with it, it won't penetrate. This is what it means: thou shalt be of a strong mind, O chief! Don't carry feelings of anger (grudge) or of spite. Thus it shall come to pass when thou are considering (deliberating) the affairs of the people, always continually employ good will (*gaʔnigonii'yo*) and peace as well. Do not ever consider only thyself, O Chief! And always remember the future generations of our families, the grandchildren, and those yet unborn, and even those whose faces are coming beneath the earth.[62]

We're taught that you've got to have skin seven layers thick. You have to develop it. There's work to it. But when your skin is thick, nobody can get at you. They can't touch you. They can't hurt your feelings

---

58   Parker (Chiefs) 1916, 104.

59   A "span" means the length of a hand, from the tip of a little finger to the tip of the thumb. Short distances, to the Haudenosaunee, were measured in relation to parts of the human body (the wampum sent to the Cherokees in 1770 was "as long as a man is tall"). European measures of the time were no different: the inch is the length of a thumb knuckle (in French, *une pouce*); the foot *is* a foot. Gibson, 1899, 107: "the thickness of your skins shall be seven (inches) (times the first joint of thumb) (*oyon-gaah*)."

60   Parker (Newhouse and Cusick) 1916, 29.

61   In the inquiry into George Klock's fraudulent purchase of Canajoharie lands, it was asked who were the principal persons of that Mohawk community for public matters. The answer was: "Those who are here are the Chiefs for all such matters, being the Sachems for transacting everything of consequence, and as such are known to the whole Six Nations, being as Trees rising up amongst us." SWJP 4:56.

62   Gibson 1899, para. 310.

or cause you to have jealousy. Money won't tempt you. If somebody works bad medicine on you, it'll never find your weakness. It'll go right back on that person who sent it your way. That's why we say you've got to have skin seven layers thick. If something touches you a little, you'll always have another layer of skin for protection.[63]

Of course, by providing additional thickness for the skins of the chiefs, the law also provided a new metaphor for the people to keep in mind: a person who insisted on passing on rumours would be reminded that this kind of thing would not be allowed to penetrate anyone's skin. While some assume that the chiefs would build up the layers of their skin by toughening them from the outside, others maintain the layers are metaphors for internal character and fortitude.

The seven handspans recall other significant uses in the law of "seven"—the seven generations to look into the future when making decisions, for example.[64]

Mentors of the People

Europeans, emerging in the eighteenth century from a long tradition of absolute monarchies and executive authority, were often surprised at the lack of executive power that the chiefs of the Confederacy actually had. They led by example; they lived modestly and humbly. It was—and remains—a different kind of leadership: "Their Great Men, both Sachems and Captains, are generally poorer than the common People, for they affect to give away and distribute all the Presents or Plunder they get in their Treaties or War, so as to leave nothing to themselves.[65] If they should once be suspected of selfishness, they would grow mean in the opinion of their Countrymen, and would consequently lose their Authority."[66]

Today, it is no longer expected that the chiefs give away their property, in part because it is also no longer the case that their extended clan families look

---

63   Wall 2001, 34.

64   Wright (1999), who purports to examine how numbers are significant to Iroquoian peoples, drawing mainly from the Jesuit Relations, omits any mention of the number seven. Thadadaho had seven crooks in his body; the chiefs' skin is to be seven spans thick; the Seven Dancers of the Pleiades mark time for Midwinter; we are to think seven generations into the future.

65   Canadian law about equitable remedies assumes the highest and best use of the assets, and generally this is equated to investment. But in the 2016 *Huu-ay-aht* decision, the Specific Claims Tribunal pointed out that in Coast Salish culture, the highest and best use of assets can be to give them away in a potlatch, thereby creating social capital and prestige. Material poverty is only one measure of a person's worth.

66   Colden (1727) 1973, xx. After he is condoled, it is not unusual for a chief to say, "you have made me a poor man."

after all their needs. There is no chiefs' pension plan, and in most cases, beyond sometimes paying their travel expenses, there is no compensation for the time the chiefs put into their duties. "A free government for a free people," Joagquisho Oren Lyons has said. While it is vital that the chiefs should lack greed or a thirst for power, perhaps the best way in English to describe the manner that is proper for a chief is *sweetness*. The duties are a burden, an honour, but not a livelihood.

The Kayanerenkó:wa explains the attitude more elegantly:

> The Lords of the Confederacy shall be mentors of the people for all time. The thickness of their skin shall be seven spans—which is to say that they shall be proof against anger, offensive action and criticism. Their hearts shall be full of peace and good will and their minds filled with a yearning for the welfare of the people of the Confederacy. With endless patience they shall carry out their duty and their firmness shall be tempered with a tenderness for their people. Neither anger nor fury shall find lodgement in their minds and all their words and actions shall be marked with calm deliberation.[67]

In the Onondaga text cited in *The Iroquois Book of Rites*, care for the people was expressed in terms of both authority and obligation, the balance that runs like a current throughout the law:

> The chiefs must all be honest, that they must all love one another, and that they must have a regard for their people, including the women, and also our children, and also those children whom we have not yet seen; so much they must care for, that all may be in peace, even the whole nation. It is the duty of the chiefs to do this, and they have the power to govern their people. If there is anything to be done for the good of the people it is their duty to do it.[68]

> You shall be a good person, and especially you shall be kind to all people, not differentiating among them—the people who are wealthy and the poor ones, the good-natured ones and the evil ones who sin readily. All of you shall act kindly, and you shall not differentiate among them. And as to your own fireside, never consider only yourself; you must always remember them, the old people and the younger people and the children and those still in the earth, yet unborn, and you will always take into account everyone's well-being, that of the ongoing families, so that they may continue to survive, your grandchildren.[69]

---

67 Parker (Newhouse and Cusick) 1916, 37.

68 Hale (1883) 1989, 170.

69 Gibson 1912, 97.

Skanawati John Buck added: "Permit me to say to you, apply yourselves diligently to all the duties you have taken upon yourselves; faithfully perform every responsibility, because to you is entrusted the preservation and settlement of all things."[70]

Sayenqueraghta, of the Seneca Nation, explained the role of a royá:ner in 1765: "a wise dispassionate man [who] *thinks much* & thinks *slowly*, with great caution and deliberation, before he speaks his *whole mind.*"[71]

The settler expectation of executive authority might have proceeded from the use of the word "chief." Modern Haudenosaunee have often explained that the word is not appropriate, since it carries the wrong spirit:

> The word *chief* in our language means a position or office. We call it *royaner* and if there are many of them we call them *rotiyaneson.* If we take that word apart, what does it mean?
>
> It is coming from the root word *ioánere*, which means, in English, "nice" or "good." And then when you put *io* at the beginning of it, it means it is masculine, or a man who is of the "nice" or of the "good." And so that is literally, when translated into English, what Iroquois people think of their leaders—those men who are of the good.
>
> . . . Those leaders are the most humble ones and they are the poorest people of all of the nation because they are always giving, always giving, always giving, both materially, psychologically, spiritually and politically of themselves to all the people of the nation; they are always giving.[72]

Were the chiefs supposed to be like the fathers (or rather, uncles) to their families? The relationships within families were not the same as they were in European society. Children and wives were not property in any sense, and whereas in a European family of the eighteenth century the primary obligations were the child's obedience and the parent's providing, in a Haudenosaunee family that duty to obey was singularly lacking. Just as traditional Haudenosaunee government was not executive, and had no coercive power over the people, parents would not exercise authority over their children. John Long, in 1791, wrote: "From their infant state they endeavour to promote an independent spirit; they are never known either to beat or scold them lest the martial disposition which is to adorn their future life and character, should be weakened:

---

70   Hewitt 1892b, 143.

71   Samuel Kirkland, April 1765, in Pilkington 1980, 25. For a European view of the power-lessness of Indian leadership see Loudon (1808) 1971.

72   Porter 1988, 8–12.

on all occasions they avoid anything compulsive, that the freedom with which they wish them to think and act should not be controuled [*sic*]."[73]

Individual Haudenosaunee citizens carried a powerful sense of personal independence. It is no accident that the participants in the Boston Tea Party, defiantly sending a message about their own rebellious independence, dressed as Mohawks:[74] the Haudenosaunee image of individuality and freedom did inspire some aspects of the American Revolution. Balancing that independence, though, was an equally powerful sense of belonging—to family, clan, and nation. It left each individual with a need to contribute, to fulfill duties and responsibilities. While the individual was expected to make up his own mind,[75] that mind was expected to work for the good of the community.

One way that Haudenosaunee law avoids creating expectations of executive authority is by making people stewards rather than owners, "keepers" rather than bosses. Even early European documents describing functionaries within Haudenosaunee government use the term "keepers"—firekeepers, doorkeepers, wampum-keepers,[76] faithkeepers.[77] The term is not domestic;[78] it refers to

---

73   Long 1791. Father Hennepin quoted LaSalle saying that "the Children shew but small Respect to their Parents: sometimes they beat them without being chastised for it; for they think Correction would intimidate them, and make them bad souldiers." Hennepin (1688) 1974, 120–21.

74   In 1773, as the eighty costumed men threw imported tea into Boston harbour, a mob supporting them chanted "Rally, Mohawks, bring out your axes / And tell King George we'll pay no taxes / on his foreign tea." After that, patriots drank bergamot or Mohawk tea, while those loyal to the Crown drank the imported brew.

75   Haudenosaunee storytelling provides another example of that way of thinking. Unlike Aesop's fables, where the moral is explained baldly at the end of the tale, Sostsisowah John Mohawk points out that "it would be an Iroquois way of doing things to tell a story and to refuse to tell the listener what he should have learned from the story."

76   The authority of an individual wampum-keeper to dispose of the objects of which he holds the stewardship for the nation was examined by the United States Supreme Court in *Onondaga Nation v. Thacher*, 189 US 306 (1903): the court decided that the wampum-keeper had the lawful authority to dispose of the national wampum as he saw fit—including making the State University his successor—and the State University acquired apparently absolute authority to retain and use the wampum, regardless of the decisions of the council. The wampum was finally returned to the Onondaga Nation in 1989, ninety-one years after it had left.

77   Though Google is not a scientific method of determining the influence or prevalence of a term, it is interesting that a significant proportion of the "hits" for each of these terms are only Haudenosaunee—other peoples don't use the "-keeper" concept nearly as frequently.

78   Though Molly Brant's modern feminist biographers were offended that in Sir William Johnson's will he would describe a woman with whom he had shared a mansion and eight children as his "dear housekeeper," he was in fact merely providing the most direct English translation of the term used in Mohawk for a "wife": "she keeps the household."

stewardship and the peculiar mix of responsibility and authority that character-
izes Haudenosaunee government.[79]

The Chiefs: Permanence of Titles

Many of the fifty men who became the first rotiyanershon of the Haudenosaunee
were given new names by the Peacemaker. The new names were a sign of their
transformation, of their accession to a higher level of chieftainship. They were
no longer simply village chiefs. They were Confederacy chiefs, and in some cases,
their names reflected their roles in bringing the peace, or the state they were in
at the time of the peacemaking. Just as the Peacemaker's work was transformative, so the new names given to individuals reflected the way that individual
had accepted a new set of responsibilities.

The new names were also permanent. That is, if the Chief of the Small Bear
Clan of the Cayugas died, a new person would be chosen by that family to
take his place, and the new person would assume that title. Not only would
he assume the title: he would also be expected to carry on the special duties
and characteristics of his predecessor. "The principle that 'the chief dies but
the office survives'—the regular transmission of rank, title and authority, by a
method partly hereditary and partly elective, was the principle on which the
life and strength of the Iroquois constitution depended."[80]

When a title holder dies, his name is symbolically removed from him
and given to his successor. The Condolence ceremony, in that sense, is also a
"requickening" or making alive again. The death and rebirth of a leader is an
ancient human practice: the myths of Osiris or the Fisher King are examples of
the rebirth of the leader also restoring the spirit (and fertility) of the people and
the land, with the new incarnation carrying the same name as his predecessor.[81]

In a way, the new person carrying the name is also the old person in a new
body:

---

79   Another example of this "keeping" is the relationship between an individual and a hadu-
     wi or "false face mask." As a living being, it is not owned by the individual who looks
     after it—at least, not owned in the sense of the power to dispose of freely or destroy it.
     The medicine society has an interest in the mask, as does all of Haudenosaunee society,
     which it is intended to protect. The English language does not lend itself, especially in
     legal terms, to describing this kind of relationship. See Williams 2010.

80   Hale (1883) 1989, 68.

81   Though generally after Condolence a chief is known by his title while doing business,
     nowadays he also often retains his original personal name, at least for use within the fam-
     ily, and he retains his English name, since he has to continue to work with outsiders.

The savages have a custom of rescucitating or making their friends revive, particularly if they were men of distinction among them. They make some other bear the name of the deceased; and behold the dead man resuscitated and the grief of the relatives entirely gone. Observe that to the name given in a great assembly or feast, they add a present which is made on the part of the relatives or friends of the one whom they have revived, and he who accepts the name and the present is obliged to take care of the family of the deceased so well that the wards call him father.[82]

This is probably one of the reasons why the rotiyanershon were called "Confederate Lords," a designation possibly originated by Seth Newhouse, who sought to show how Haudenosaunee law ought to be respected by British law, since the two systems had such similarities. The British House of Lords functions the same way with respect to hereditary peers. If the Duke of Northumberland dies, the title does not die with him; instead, his heir immediately becomes "Northumberland."[83] The British system is truly hereditary: the succession is automatic, passing to the eldest child, and merit and choice play no part in it. The Haudenosaunee system is not strictly hereditary: each male member of the clan family has an equal potential for becoming the successor, and merit and the choice of the family play the key roles in choosing the new title holder. Or, as Morgan explained: "The office of sachem was hereditary in the gens [clan], in the sense that it was filled as often as a vacancy occurred."[84]

Sometimes the clan mother and women conclude that there is no man in the family who has the attributes needed to become its chief. In such situations, the family "borrows" a man from another family, and he is condoled into the title of the deceased chief. He holds that title for life, and once he has been condoled he is recognized by the entire Confederacy as that family's proper representative, carrying the duties within the Confederacy Council of that title. For the law to work, it is important that the family have the best representative possible, and also that his legitimacy should not be questioned.

---

82   Jesuit Relations of 1639, probably speaking of the Hurons; cited in Beauchamp (1907) 1975, 345.

83   The Duke of Northumberland, serving in the British Army in North America, became friendly with the Mohawks and was given the name Thoregwi, which he translated as "The Pine Break." He was especially fond of Thayendenega Joseph Brant. When Teyoninhokarawen John Norton went to England in 1807 as an emissary of the chiefs at the Grand River, the Duke of Northumberland supported him; when Ayonhwes John Brant went in 1821, another Duke of Northumberland welcomed him.

84   Morgan (1871) 1997, 71.

The Cluster: Chief, Clan Mother, Sub-Chief, Faithkeepers, Runner

Most Europeans engaged in political and legal dealings with the Haudenosaunee met with the chiefs and the warriors. While the women had authority, it was not their role to engage in negotiations with representatives of other nations.

The Europeans did not see that each Confederacy chief was actually the centre of a cluster of five people, often appointed and condoled at the same time. Each chief today has a clan mother, who is responsible to work with him on the women's side; a runner to carry his messages; a "sub-chief" to sit behind him in council, to learn from him, and to fill in for him when he is away; and a male and female faithkeeper to help with the ceremonies. This cluster of five people includes male and female, political and spiritual, young and old. It recognizes that the chief cannot carry the weight alone. As Morgan pointed out with Pine Tree chiefs, if authority is more widespread, it is more democratic.[85] Alone among all the chiefs, Thadadahoh has no sub-chief and no runner.

The sub-chief, according to Morgan, "was styled an 'aid.' It was his duty to stand behind his superior on all occasions of ceremony, to act as his messenger, and in general to be subject to his directions. It gave to the aid the office of chief, and rendered probable his election as the successor of his principal after the decease of the latter. In their figurative language these aids of the sachems were styled 'Braces of the Long House,' which symbolized the confederacy."[86]

Today, both in council and in ceremonies, a sub-chief often sits behind his chief, a visible support[87] as well as an apprentice or occasional substitute. While the chief has a "runner" or messenger, this person is more often used to carry word within the clan, and the sub-chief, often a younger man, is sometimes sent with messages to other nations. While satisfactory performance as a sub-chief can indeed "render probable" his selection as future chief, unenthusiastic

---

85   How these people fulfill their obligations provides the family with insight into their suitability for other functions. While often a sub-chief replaces the chief on the latter's death, this is not always the case.

86   Morgan (1871) 1997, 132; (1851) 1995, 65.

87   It is not unusual to see a sub-chief take physical care of the chief—getting him water in council, taking care of the driving to council and ceremonies. The time the two spend together, especially in travel, fosters a bond and ensures the transmission of knowledge and experience. Tehahenteh equates "sub-chief" with its more literal term: "protector." Sitting behind the chief, in the old days, also meant watching his back—as the Spanish term for "bodyguard" is *guardaespaldas*.

or mediocre performance as a sub-chief will generally ensure that the person will not become a chief at all.

Clan Mothers

Several versions of the law do not describe in detail the authority and duties of the clan mothers. Possibly this is because the institution of clans and their matrons was already in place before the coming of the law—having been brought by the fatherless young man of an earlier meta-narrative—and therefore did not need to have new provisions made for it. Less likely, it is because the versions that became public were kept and explained by men, who had a less generous view, and less knowledge, of the role of the women. Most likely, the provisions of the law about clan mothers were simply not transcribed by the anthropologists at the same time as the rest of the law. Skaniatari:io John Arthur Gibson was not hesitant in describing "the Law of the Woman Chief" to J.N.B. Hewitt in 1909, not long before he dictated the long, authoritative version of the Great Law.[88]

Since the position of clan mother was now linked inextricably with that of the chief, she became a visible participant in the Condolence ceremony that raised him up; her family would be condoled in the same way upon her death; and over time, things that were done to or for chiefs came to have their parallels with clan mothers.

To some outsiders, the decision about who should be a clan mother seemed simple: the position would pass to the oldest living female in the family. Chadwick described his understanding of the process at the end of the nineteenth century:

> The right of nomination vests in the oldest near female relative of the deceased chief, that is, the oldest of a class composed of his maternal grandmother and great aunts, if living, but if none of those are living, then the oldest of a class composed of his mother and her sisters (daughters of the mother's mother), or if none of these, then of his sisters, daughters of his mother, and if these are also wanting, then of his nieces, daughters of his mother's daughters; and if all these

---

88   Why, when Hewitt had been recording the Haudenosaunee meta-narratives with Gibson for twenty years, did Gibson dictate the Great Law to Goldenweiser instead? Because in 1912, there had been a change in management in the Smithsonian, and Hewitt found himself virtually chained to a desk in Washington, being paid by the line rather than a reasonable salary doing fieldwork. He survived by writing the massive *Seneca Fiction, Legends and Myths* with Jeremiah Curtin (1918), but he was not seen at Grand River for several years. Blind John Arthur Gibson forged on without him.

fail, then the right passes to collateral relatives of his mother's totem, and if there are none of these, no nomination can be made, and the chieftainship becomes extinct. The nominator consults with the two next senior women, ascertained by the same order, and classification of the family is thus made. It does not seem very clear what occurs if the three do not agree. . . . If a chiefship fails in consequence of the family to which it belongs becoming extinct, either in the person of a nominator, or of a qualified nominee, the Great Council has power to transfer the chiefship to another family (preferably one which is, or is considered to be akin to the extinct family), in which a chief is then nominated by the senior woman and her associates, and assumes the title in the usual manner, whereupon the succession goes in that family.[89]

Choosing a clan mother is more complex than simply finding the oldest woman in the family. Such a process would make little sense—no clan mother would last very long, and one of the key attributes of the system is its stability. In many families, it is the clan mother herself who names her successor, though often this is not necessary, because the choice will be obvious, since the clan mother will have been training someone—usually one of her daughters—in the duties and knowledge required. Different families have differing degrees of cohesiveness, adherence to tradition, and even their own internal traditions. Where no person has been designated before the death of a clan mother, and especially where there is some uncertainty about which families belong with that chief's title, there are situations in which the clan mother position remains vacant for years while rival claimants assert their entitlement. Since it is a family matter, and within a nation and a community, outsiders are reluctant to interfere: "On modern condolences one woman often has the sole nomination of a chief, but where several are to be consulted, the subject may be canvassed up to the last moment, and thus I have seen them running from house to house."[90]

Haudenosaunee society does not have a formalized group of "elders," but the clan mothers are often seen as people of wisdom and experience, whatever their ages.

While a chief represents his nation as well as his clan family, the same cannot be said for the clan mother. Her duties are to her family, and it is the family alone that chooses her. In contrast, because the chief needs to work with the other members of the council, his appointment must be confirmed first by the other clans of his nation; then by the other nations on his side of the fire; and finally, through the Condolence, by the nations on the other side of the fire. No similar

---

89   Chadwick, 36–38, cited in Beauchamp (1907) 1975, 349.

90   Beauchamp (1907) 1975, 347.

system of checks and balances exists for a clan mother. However, when a clan mother dies, there is a "Small Condolence" for her family, and the council does not sit for ten days after her death, because the mind of the entire community has been cast down and is clouded by sorrow.

The clan mother has a number of duties related to the law, and most of them are about maintaining continuity. Generally, she is responsible for keeping the clan family's personal names, so that she is consulted, along with other older women, about a choice of name for a new child. She also ensures that the new child does not take the name of a living person. If it is necessary to appoint a speaker to address women's issues, she will appoint that speaker—but she will also convene a meeting of the women to develop their position first. In consultation with the women of the clan family, she selects the successor to a deceased chief. While the chief can be removed by the women, in fact it is his clan mother to whom he remains most actively responsible.

Though today the situation varies from clan to clan, generally a clan mother is the custodian of three wampum strings: a white string representing her own office; a second white wampum as the "horns" or credentials of her chief;[91] and a purple string that is used to send notification of the death of her chief. While some clan mothers also hold strings of wampum associated with Pine Tree chiefs, those men are not appointed by or responsible to clan mothers but are appointed by and responsible to the condoled chiefs in council.[92]

Gibson describes the clan mother's responsibility to ensure that the chiefs in council are fed. The clan mothers do this today: in council at the Grand River, the responsibility for cooking for council rotates between several clan families, and the clan mothers and the women of their families both coordinate the cooking and take part in it. While to some this may seem menial, there are also good reasons for it.

After each instance in which the Peacemaker transforms someone, or a group, from being a threat to peace into being a mainstay of peace, they eat together. Eating together is a fundamental step in Haudenosaunee society towards creating, restoring, or maintaining peace. Feasts are connected to medicine, restoring harmony, and removing harm.

Food is medicine, in the Haudenosaunee understanding of the world. When the clan mother provides the meal for the chiefs in council, she is fulfilling an important role in maintaining their mental, physical, and spiritual health.

---

91   The chief generally carries a duplicate of this. It becomes visible in public only when it is placed in his hands at his funeral, when the "horns" are lifted so they may be passed on to someone else. It may also be seen when a chief is publicly dehorned, and hands the string back.

92   Hill 2009. In some instances, women who somehow acquired strings of wampum believed that they had become clan mothers as a result. It is not possession of wampum that makes you a clan mother, it is being a clan mother that entitles you to possession of the wampum.

Sken:nen is both health and peace. In the days when the women controlled the gardens, they were the economic mainstay of the community. Making the meals for the council was a reminder of the women's economic authority.

At council, after lunch, the chiefs always indicate their gratitude to the cooks: it is a public reaffirmation of their connection with, and debt to, the clan mothers. Yet it must be said that many people fail to understand the significance, the deep meaning, of providing the meal for the chiefs, and conclude that this practice today is a matter of subservience, a task that takes the clan mothers away from their true work of observing the chiefs in council and guiding them when they err. If some of the chiefs begin to forget why this work is important, they do begin to undervalue the role and responsibility of the clan mothers.

The clan mothers are mentors, just as the chiefs are. They are consulted by the people in times of personal crisis. They take special responsibility for counselling families and for ensuring that children are properly looked after. Today, the clan mothers together have taken up some of the responsibilities of provincial or state child welfare authorities: meeting with parents who fail to look after their children properly; helping to find homes for children in need; mediating family disputes. The children are their particular concern, and they easily find themselves acting as advocates and protectors in difficult family situations. Part of the power of the clan mother is discretion: her work is conducted quietly, behind the scenes, in times when people count on her advice but hesitate to make their issues public.

Just as the chief, when he is being condoled, appears with a cluster of helpers (including the clan mother), so the clan mother, too, has an assistant. Skaniatari:io John Arthur Gibson describes the role and nature of the clan mother's principal helper: "the young man with no title he is stronger, also he walked around, also he is able he outwitted the game, the wild walking around in the forest, he has the power of survival of the people, whatever he was able to provide, everything will go well, they will work together, he and the Clan Mother."[93]

Why would a woman chief have a strong young male helper, a man without a title? First of all, this is another example of gender balance in Haudenosaunee law. A chief has a clan mother. The clan mother has a male helper. Today, the chief has a male and female faithkeeper. Authority is balanced as between men and women, even as roles are differentiated. While the clan mother can count on the support and help of all the women of the clan family, her young male helper has specific duties as her spokesman, as her liaison with the men, and, in the worst case, as The Man Without Pity.

Why a young man? Partly to balance the clan mother's age, so that authority and communication span generations. Partly because the young man will be

---

93   Translation: 2013, Nora Carrier, Deyayohageh, Grand River Territory.

able to communicate with the hunters and warriors, and they are a crucial aspect of the family's social makeup. Beginning with the Jesuit Relations, Europeans observed that the women were the ones who would urge the young men to war or peace. Konwatsitsiaienni Mary ("Molly") Brant was said to have the ability, as a clan mother, to put hundreds of warriors into the field. Historians assert that the "Mourning Wars" of the 1600s were instigated by the women, and particularly the clan mothers, seeking to replace men who had been killed. While European observers seldom saw or knew what was happening in the councils of Haudenosaunee women, or in their dealings with the young men, the connection between the women and the warriors was functional, constant, and important. As well, a young man would have the energy to carry out many of the tasks that a clan mother needed to do, and at times he would provide the personal physical protection a clan mother might need.

Among the responsibilities of the clan mothers are ensuring that there are people in the family who can deliver all the speeches associated with the wampums and responsibilities that accompany them; ensuring that there are always qualified candidates for leadership positions; ensuring that the people of the family are given an opportunity to express their views at clan meetings; ensuring that the names within the family are properly bestowed and not duplicated; and ensuring the safety of children in the homes and stability of families.[94]

Removing a clan mother is a process that reflects the one used to remove a chief.

The young man without a title who is the clan mother's constant helper may also be the person who, after the required number of warnings, announces the removal of a chief. That is, this young man may fulfill the role that is described as The Man Without Pity.

There is not quite symmetry between the way a chief is removed and the way a clan mother is removed. Once again, the primary mover in this process is her family, not outsiders. If a clan mother is not thinking or acting right, "at that time now the sisters of the mother now one of them will have to speak, she will remind her where her duties are." If the clan mother does not agree and become remorseful for her actions, it falls to her assistant, the young man without a title, to speak with her and point out the error of her ways. If she does not listen to this, the matter passes to her entire family to discuss. If they decide to remove her, the matter is taken to the chief to be confirmed, and he will deliberate not only on the removal of the errant clan mother but also on the person the family has chosen as her replacement. If the chief agrees, "at that time the young man he will revoke her duties if she disregarded their word,

---

94   Hill 2009.

now he will remove her, he will take her authority away at that time, and then he will stand up a new person."[95]

The young man is placed in a complicated position: the person who selected him, and with whom he has been working closely, is now facing removal at his hands. The situation must be dire, and he would act not on his own initiative but impelled by the entire family.

Faithkeepers

Morgan suggests a less structured system of faithkeepers, with some clans appointing them more as a sign of greater devotion, and with an informal division of responsibility between women and men:

> They designated the days for holding the festivals, made the necessary arrangements for their celebration, and conducted the ceremonies in conjunction with the sachems and chiefs of the tribe, who were, ex officio, "Keepers of the Faith." With no official head, and none of the marks of a priesthood, their functions were equal. The female "Keepers of the Faith" were more especially charged with the preparation of the feast, which was provided at all councils at the close of each day for all persons in attendance

> The "Keepers of the Faith" were . . . selected by the wise men and matrons of each gens. After their selection they were raised up by a council of the tribe with ceremonies adapted to the occasion. Their names were taken away and new ones belonging to this class bestowed in their place. . . .

> It was the duty of the individuals selected to accept the office; but after a reasonable service each might relinquish it, which was done by dropping his name as a Keeper of the Faith and resuming his former name.[96]

Today, it is rare that a faithkeeper would drop his or her personal name and assume a faithkeeper name. Rather than raise up faithkeepers "at a council of

---

95   Gibson 1909, n.p.

96   Morgan (1871) 1997, 82.

the tribe," they are confirmed at the same time as their chief at a Condolence ceremony of the entire Confederacy.[97]

Faithkeepers, working together, have in practice become the managers of most longhouses, bringing together work crews for maintenance, arranging firewood, and keeping food in the cookhouses. In some anthropological works, they are referred to as "deacons,"[98] an indication of their civilian but religious roles.

With the advent of the message of Handsome Lake in the 1790s—as codified in the 1830s at Tonawanda—the faithkeepers were given new additional functions, political ones, and their titles became more permanent. Today, in some communities, faithkeepers are being installed without attachment to a chief's title, allegedly for life, and in some cases attached to longhouses rather than to the family titles. The Karihwí:iyo, the Code of Handsome Lake, is recited and renewed annually, just as commitment to the law was a periodic matter. The annual autumn recitals of the Code became known as Conventions, and over time they became increasingly political. Seating in Convention is strict, not quite a mirror of Confederacy seating, since the delegations are not quite a reflection of the confederate structure, but instead represent the different longhouses. Today, they are attended by a significant number of the chiefs, though many of those who attend (they are called "delegates") are not chiefs or faithkeepers. The creation of a process parallel to the Confederacy, one which includes the longhouses of Cattaraugus and Allegheny without their having a "fire," a traditional government, may serve to undermine the surviving government of the Confederacy. In theory, a discussion in a Convention is then taken to the communities, and then to the Confederacy Council for a decision: in practice, some people consider a decision binding if it was made at Convention.

---

97   There is some controversy over whether people cease to be faithkeepers when their chief dies, and need to be reappointed (or even can be reappointed). Generally, as a matter of practice, faithkeepers continue to do their work, and are reaffirmed, so there is no practical issue involved. One indicator of the permanence of the faithkeeper appointment is that faithkeepers are seldom appointed to be chiefs, because they already have a function to fulfill, and you cannot be both a chief and a faithkeeper responsible to the same chief to carry out your duties. At the Condolence, when the chief is stood up and told his duties, his cluster of faithkeepers, clan mother, sub-chief, and runner stand with him: if there are any vacancies, the family uses the opportunity to fill them.

98   Goldenweiser translated yeyakweni:yo (clan mothers) as "deaconesses," setting the stage for later anthropologists. The name diakonos means master or servant, but by the time of the New Testament it had acquired a religious meaning for Christians. St. Paul wrote Timothy (1 Timothy 3:8–9, 12) that "deacons must be chaste, not double tongued, not given to much wine, not greedy of filthy lucre, holding the mystery of faith in a pure conscience;" and that they should be married, "rule well their children and their own houses," and not be criminals. In the early Christian church, as in the Longhouse, a deacon or faithkeeper had an administrative as well as a ceremonial function.

Criteria for Becoming a Chief

The principle of choosing a chief is simple enough: they should be the best men, the most thoughtful and compassionate. They should be living examples of the way of life confirmed by the law: "When the Royaneh women, holders of a Lordship title, select one of their sons as a candidate, they shall select one who is trustworthy, of good character, one who manages his own affairs, supports his own family, if any, and who has proved a faithful man to his Nation. . . . Such a candidate shall not be the father of any Confederate Lord."[99]

The criteria have accumulated over the years (and people have become more imperfect over time, it seems) so that it is becoming increasingly difficult to find appropriate candidates.

Newhouse set out specific criteria that would disqualify a candidate, and would make a sitting chief ineligible to take part in council: "infancy, idiocy, blindness, deafness, dumbness and impotency, in such cases another man shall be appointed to act for him in Council meetings of the Confederacy. The above defects shall not deprive his right to be installed in case of necessity."[100]

Sakokwenionkwas Tom Porter says the right ones have been chosen by the Creator when they are born (a small step away from having their positions preordained before birth). He also says that the man must be married; should have at least three children; must speak his language fluently, or he will not be able to function in council; and must be "clean": that is, not married to someone of the same clan.[101]

While many Haudenosaunee today believe that choosing a new chief is a matter for the women of the clan to decide, Morgan described a Seneca system in the mid-1800s that involved elections:

> When the Indian system of consanguinity is considered, it will be found that all the male members of a gens were either brothers to each other, own or collateral, uncles or nephews, own or collateral, or collateral grandfathers and grandsons. This will explain the succession of the office of sachem which passed from brother to brother, or

---

99   Parker 1916, 44. At the Six Nations Grand River Territory, an exception was made in the late 1800s, when Onwanonsyshon George H.M. Johnson was allowed to sit as a Mohawk chief at the same time as his father, Sakayengwaraton John "Smoke" Johnson.

100 These "defects" did not prevent the installation of the blind John Arthur Gibson as Skaniatariio or blind David Thomas as Thadadaho at the Grand River. History records a number of instances of very young men being installed, but with older men as their guides and spokesmen.

101 This last criterion was used to block the Condolence of a Mohawk chief in Akwesasne in 2002. Some assert that the prohibition is not against sharing the same clan, but rather the same ohwátsi're.

from uncle to nephew, and very rarely from grandfather to grandson. The choice, which was by free suffrage of both males and females of adult age, usually fell upon a brother of the deceased sachem, or upon one of the sons of a sister; an own brother, or the son of an own sister being most likely to be preferred. As between several brothers, own and collateral, on the one hand, there was no priority of right, for the reason that all the male members of the gens were equally eligible. To make a choice between them was the function of the elective principle.

Upon the death of a sachem . . . among the Seneca-Iroquois, a council of his gentiles [clan members] was convened to name his successor. Two candidates, according to their usages, must be voted upon, both of them members of the gens. Each person of adult age was called upon to express his or her preference, and the one who received the highest number of affirmative declarations was nominated.[102]

One thing most Haudenosaunee do agree about: a person who demonstrates overt ambition for office is not likely to be chosen. It is not only that the ambitious one has shown a lack of humility: it is that if he wants a title for himself, he will probably want other things, as well, and will be selfish and prone to corruption.

---

102 Morgan (1871) 1997, 73. This was several years after the Senecas at Cattaraugus and Allegheny had moved to an elective system of government; Morgan's description may have been a reflection of the way things were done in some families at Tonawanda.

Raising Up Chiefs

Every ceremony of Condolence to raise up a new chief is itself a re-enactment of the time the Peacemaker condoled Hiawatha. It has been said that when a thing is re-enacted, myth and ritual become the same thing.[103] So, in every Condolence, all the people, in a way, become the Peacemaker.

Since the making of the Confederacy would also be explained, wrote Morgan, "the council to raise up sachems became a teaching council, which maintained in perpetual freshness in the minds of the Iroquois the structure and principles of the Confederacy as well as the history of its formation."[104]

The coronation of a European monarch is attended by the leadership of the nation, both political and spiritual, and by the heads of other states. It is a public legitimation of both the individual and the continuity of the state. The ceremony of Condolence, for the Haudenosaunee, fulfills some of the same functions: the presence of the leaders and the people confirms the legitimacy of the person who has been raised up. Until he is condoled, he has no security of title—he is called a "benchwarmer"—and does not receive the same respect. A "condoled chief" is a person whose identity and acceptability has been confirmed and is no longer open to question.[105] The fact that he is condoled enables him to conduct himself with the required humility but also the required authority. He has nothing to prove.

---

103   Throughout the Christian world, at Easter, there are re-enactments of the crucifixion of Jesus. Nikos Kazantzakis's *The Greek Passion* depicts an extreme example of re-enactment becoming real. Every time the Catholic Mass is celebrated, what is actually taking place is a re-enactment of a sequence of events that lies at the heart of the Church itself.

104   Morgan (1871) 1997, 143.

105   Canadian law applies this thinking to the acceptability of Indigenous oral tradition evidence in court; the courts have suggested that the fact that individuals can raise objections at public recital events is considered part of the checks and balances that make formal, regimented oral history reliable. See *Benoit v. Canada (Minister of National Revenue)*, (2003) FCA 236 at para. 110, citing *Delgam'uukw v. Attorney General of British Columbia*, (1997) 3 SCR 1010.

The Women: Landholders and Clanholders

The duality and balance between men and women is another theme that runs through the law. While there have been suggestions that the role of women has been downplayed over the years by a Haudenosaunee society that has come under the influence of Western patriarchal values and religions, constitutionally the women's role remains strong and well defined. Just as individuals are linked to the earth and clay from which they originate, the Creation Story began the connection between women and the earth, and the law continued it. European settlers, in contrast, endowed women with a far smaller bundle of rights. While nobody in Haudenosaunee society had ownership of the land in the way the common law of England had developed feudal fee simple, to the extent that anyone had authority over the land, it was the women. Virtually every version of the law confirms this:

> Women shall be considered the progenitors of the Nation. They shall own the land and the soil.[106]

> . . . our Mothers the Females . . . shall be the proprietors as well as the soil . . .[107]

> . . . and the soil of our land is all of our Mothers the Women of the Five Nations. They shall be the proprietors of the same.[108]

The Mohawks of Canajoharie told Sir William Johnson on March 11, 1763: "Being asked whether the Women were looked upon as having any right in the disposal of the lands, he answered 'that they were the properest owners, being the persons who laboured on the lands and therefore were esteemed in that light.'"[109]

To suggest, as William Fenton has, that the division of labour and law between men and women in Haudenosaunee society is a reflection of a duality that assigns life to women and death to men is too stark, too harsh. True, the men hunted and fished and made war, and these involve death; while the women gardened and bore children, and these involve life. But the women also gather and harvest living plants; they would join hunting expeditions; they would

---

106 Parker (Chiefs) 1916, 76.

107 Parker (Newhouse and Cusick) 1916, art. 30.

108 Newhouse 1885, 156.

109 LAC, RG10, vol. 1829, 273.

sometimes encourage warfare. The roles of women and men were, and remain, very different, and there are often good reasons for this, but they cannot always be boiled down to life and death. They are more often explained as reflections of the different gifts of men and women.

Though the women were the landholders, the men were responsible for dealing with other nations. Thus, it might be the men who met with the European representatives about land matters, but decisions concerning the land belonged to the women. On May 15, 1791, women of the Six Nations met with Thomas Procter, a representative of the United States, at Buffalo Creek. They told him: "You ought to hear and listen to what we women shall speak, as well as to the sachems, for we are the owners of this land—and it is ours; for it is we that plant it, for our and their use. Hear us, therefore, for we speak of things that concern us and our children, and you must not think hard of us, while our men shall say more to you; for we have told them."[110]

Seven years later, Thayendenegea Joseph Brant wrote to a British official that it would be legally wrong for the women to participate in a land surrender. But it is not clear from his writing whether he was saying that the women had no authority over the land, or just that the responsibility for such dealings with other peoples fell to the men: "Something further which I think of a very singular nature has been suggested to us by Mr. Stewart respecting a surrender to be made of the Land by our Women. Such a measure was however considered by them and the Chiefs as too singular and foreign from the known Customs of the Five Nations."[111]

Possibly it is because the women have the firmest connection with the clay or soil of a place that they also have authority to choose the male leaders. The life sustainers, the products of the gardens and fields, were raised by women working together, and cooperation between women, in the fields and in the longhouse, remained essential for the unity of the family. Women provided family stability, the memory of its names, and the guidance for its youngest children. To provide balance against an excess of authority being vested in the men, it made sense to have the power of nomination rest with the women: "This is how these matters shall continue on: these are to be the principal ones, the women controlling the title names, because it is by means of all their suffering that people are born here on earth, and it is they who raise them. . . . From now on the women shall confer antlers upon the men. Indeed, the women, our mothers, this is with whom we are co-operating. So that is how it shall be

---

110   American State Papers, Indian Affairs, vol. I, 155.

111   Brant to Russell, in Cruikshank and Hunter 1932, 85–90; Brant to Russell, February 19, 1798, cited in Johnston 1964, 101.

done in our several nations, this kind of matter, among our ongoing families and our grandchildren and those in earth, still unborn."[112]

Having authority without a means of expressing it would be frustrating. While generally the women, like the rest of the family, speak through their chief, there are numerous recorded instances when they made their feelings known collectively and directly. Sagoyewatha (Red Jacket) was a speaker for the women in several of his important speeches. So was Deyagorazera (Thomas King). Thus, the women of the Seneca town of Geneseo spoke through a male speaker when they intervened to reaffirm the legitimacy of the rotiyanershon (probably after the young men had attempted to take power):

> I speak now in the name of the Women of our Castle. They sincerely pity your late situation, and as they know their own power and influence, they now plant the Sachims Horns on their heads so they may be as powerful as ever, and be distinguished from all the rest.
>
> A Belt to the 5 Nations.[113]

To Europeans, the rights and influence of the women were surprising but not unnatural: "It is very remarkable that the Women are admitted to the Council fire & have the liberty of speaking, which is sometimes used; when the nature of the Education of this tribe [the Mohawks] is considered, the difference of the instruction of the girls & boys is so small, the sources of knowledge are so inconsiderable that I see no reason why a Woman with strong natural sense should not acquit herself in the Council with general Satisfaction."[114]

For the women to have to intervene at all was considered remarkable, for when the women did make their feelings known, the men paid attention: "We flatter ourselves you will look upon this our speech, and take the same notice of it as all our men do, who, when they are addressed by the women, and desired to desist from any rash enterprise, they immediately give way, when, before, every body else tried to dissuade them from it, and could not prevail."[115]

In some ways, the women stepping into a matter constituted a last step. It was a reminder that the key to bringing Thadadahoh to peace was Tsikonsaseh's intervention. It was a reminder that the women ultimately carried the authority to remove the chiefs when they failed to heed their duties.

When strangers or visitors came to the village, and waited at the woods' edge, it was the young men who went out to meet them. If necessary, it was the young

---

112 Gibson 1912, 419–20.

113 SWJP 11:323. This may be the "Women's Nominating Belt" that for many years was held in the Seneca Nation Museum.

114 NYSL MSS 13350, cited in Johnston 1964, 29.

115 The women of Onondaga speaking to Sir William Johnson, in May 1758. SWJP 13:111–13; 3:707–12.

men who would meet the enemies in combat at the woods' edge. They would bring the guests in after the preliminary greetings, to be properly welcomed in the village itself. The men took the responsibility and risk of meeting with strangers or foreigners. The women did not.

Even where a matter was the women's by right to deal with, like land, and where the decision inside the circle was made by the women, it was the men who carried that decision to outsiders. The women ordinarily did not speak in council with outsiders. However, one should not think that the women's world was sealed off from contact with foreigners just because their role in government was internal. Haudenosaunee women were not shy. They were protected by the men, but they were not prevented from having contact with outsiders. The first official interpreter for the Haudenosaunee with the Dutch was Hille van Olinde, the daughter of a Mohawk woman and a Dutchman. To the Europeans, there was probably no Haudenosaunee institution more surprising than that of the clan mothers, often mistakenly called a matriarchy. To be sure, the clan mothers had distinct roles, and influence well beyond that of their European contemporaries. The proper way to consider those roles is through the lens of balance, in providing the women's perspective as a counterpart to that of the men rather than exercising control. Like the chiefs, the clan mothers wear no special marks of office. They hold the wampum strings that indicate their positions (some clan mothers carry these in their purses). Like the chiefs, the clan mothers are mentors to the people.

Just as the chiefs in council were expected to build decisions by discussing the issues in small committees first, and then nation circles, and then discussions of a "side" of the fire, before seeking council unanimity, so the women had their own forms and forums of discussion. For anyone to be a speaker for the women, there would have had to be a decision made by the women. In turn, that would indicate that the women would have met, discussed the issue, and formulated that decision.

Women's institutions would probably have usually functioned without the men present—to some extent, they still do. Men would not know their structures and functions in detail, and would tend not to explain them to outsiders anyway. The separation between "men's things" and "women's business" would mean, among other things, that it could have taken a female anthropologist speaking with a female Haudenosaunee "informant" to gather the descriptions. When Morgan, Hewitt, and Goldenweiser were receiving accounts from the men, they had no female counterparts.[116] While this creates an imbalance of information, leaving a more complete record of the "men's version" of things, it is not deliberately sexist. The failure to fully gather and recount the women's side is indeed a failure, but it reflects the male domination of early anthropology, and

---

116 Frederick Waugh, on the other hand, some years later, included female informants.

probably the greater sense of privacy accorded Haudenosaunee women's work. Historically, it was the men who met and worked with outsiders and developed relationships with them, allowing the outsiders to learn about Haudenosaunee men's thinking and institutions. Haudenosaunee women had reduced contact with outsiders, and they could and did protect their knowledge and institutions, even from Haudenosaunee men.

The lack of documentation by anthropologists and writers has, ironically, had a double effect. On the one hand, it has left women's business relatively untouched by the opinions and speculation of outsiders. On the other hand, it has permitted the emergence of claims about women's authority, roles, and institutions that are not supported by established tradition or any historical or written record. The women have no visible equivalent of the Kayanerenkó:wa to document their doings. That protects them from the speculations of strangers while making them vulnerable to internal abuse.[117]

The Circle of Protection of the Law

The image of the chiefs standing in a circle with their arms joined is simple and striking: what is inside the circle is the people—past, present, and future—and the land. The Great Law and the Great Peace, intertwined and inseparable, are the perimeter of the circle, maintaining it, describing it. Skaniatariio John Gibson stated in 1899: "And quite possibly it will be appropriate to encircle the body of our people (the chiefs are going to join hands and surround the public of the Five Nations), and thus we shall roll up the minds of all our society. So now let us join hands and we the federal chiefs will encircle the crowd of our people."[118]

Encircling the people means protecting them. For the chiefs, as holders of the law, to encircle the people means that the Great Law and the Great Peace have also created that circle of protection. In this circle, there is a deliberate echo of the moment in the making of the law when the chiefs were surrounded by the Seneca warriors and the Peacemaker transformed the warriors from being a threat to the Confederacy and the peace into their protectors.

---

117 Since the Condolence is a very public ceremony, it leaves little doubt about whether a man is a Confederacy chief. There is little room for someone to claim falsely that he is a royá:ner. In contrast, a clan mother is chosen without an equivalent ceremony (though she is confirmed when she stands up with her chief in his Condolence). This leaves room for multiple claimants to hold the same clan mother position. It is harder to prove that a person is (or is not) a clan mother than it is to prove that a person is a chief.

118 Gibson 1899, para. 106.

Leaving the Circle

Just as creating the circle and joining the peace was a matter of a person's will, so remaining within the circle is a matter of choice. Any person has the right to leave the circle, to live elsewhere, and to live under another system of law. The Great Law of Peace is not coercive. It recognizes that to keep a free person against their will is to invite trouble, to foster hard feelings. Where a person's mind is not for peace and harmony, it is better for the community that they should be allowed to leave, either for a while or permanently.

If the person choosing to leave is a title holder, though, his family cannot be left without representation. His mind is no longer within the circle, so the family becomes free to choose another representative. The family cannot be deprived of a voice in council. The metaphor for this, with respect to a chief, is that the horns of his office will catch on the elbows of his fellow chiefs, who are standing in the circle of the law with their arms joined, as a stag's antlers catch in the bushes, and the "horns" of his title will thus fall within the circle, to be given by his family to someone else:

> If any one go through, his horns would fall off from his head.[119]

> . . . and if any of the Confederate Lords will go outside of the confederation, his crown of the deer's horns the emblem of his Lordship, together with his birthright, will lodge on the arms of the Confederate Lords, whose hands are joined. So that his crown of deer's horns falls off from his head, and forfeits his lordship title, together with his birthright, and they will remain inside of the confederation.[120]

> And so it shall surely happen in the days to come that some one person might escape beneath the circle of you chiefs around the crowd of our people. And his chiefly title shall catch its antlers there (on the arms of the chiefs) and his horns will lie there inside the circle that they surround (embrace); and so he will be stripped (*hoyaʔdo'goʔ*) when he passes the circle and goes out free; and there

---

119 Minutes of the Six Nations Council at Cattaraugus, December 1, 1862 (Parker 1916, 145).

120 Newhouse 1885, 151. John Buck, in Hewitt 1892b, 145, says that leaving the circle is a permanent move: "Naked-bodied shall he go out; never will it do to permit him to come back; his course shall not be changed." At the 2013 recital of the law, it was said that a chief who left the circle had his legs dangling over the edge of the earth.

his status (*hoiwaʔge*) will be reduced and becomes equal to that of the warriors, and he may never again hold any office.[121]

If an individual desires to leave, even a chief, he is free to do so. In other words, he leaves as an individual, so that the title can be picked up by his family and given to another individual to carry: "Thereupon the deaconess of the title, now she will take back the antlers. Thereupon she will choose a replacement, and this is the one on whom she will bestow the antlers, seating him instead on the former seat of the chief he is replacing."[122]

There is a tradition that a chief who chooses to go to war can "hang up his horns," or have his clan mother "lift his horns" while he is engaged in military activities. Newhouse confirms this: "If the Five Confederate Nations declare war and if any of the lords are desirous to take part in the war, he can do so by giving up the emblem of his Lordship Title which he has received from his women relatives, to whom the title reverts in such a case, for they are the proprietors of the Lordship title, until the war is over, when he may resume his title and seat in the Council."[123]

There is a logic to this: in times of war, the council often hands over its authority to the war chiefs, who are more able to move swiftly to protect the people.[124] With the council not sitting, the chief would have few duties, and his presence would not be missed.

The two last Seneca chiefs to come into the peace, Kanuhkitawi and Donehogowa, were to be both war chiefs and peace chiefs. In Dayodekane's version, the Onondaga chief Skanawati is also told that half of his body will be Lord and half will be war chief.[125]

What happens, though, when he engages in a war as part of someone else's army? Often, the Haudenosaunee will explain that they do so as allies, not as citizens or subjects. In the case of Donehogowa Ely Parker, according to Gawasowane Arthur Parker, there was celebration when he was granted an officer's commission in the American Civil War: "It was then that the Indians held a great council and asked their chief to remain to guide and protect them. A great feast was made in his honor and Do-ne-ho-ga-wa was commended to the care of the Great Spirit. A public thanksgiving was offered, thanking the

---

121 Gibson 1899, para. 309; see also Gibson 1912, 462.

122 Gibson 1912, 463.

123 Newhouse 1885, 32. The "emblem" would be the short string of white beads, his "horns."

124 A clear example of how the conduct of war was handed over to the peace chiefs, and how control was handed back at war's end, is in the transcript of the April 24, 1815, council at Burlington Bay at the end of the War of 1812 (LAC, RG8, vol. 258(1), 204–8).

125 Fenton 1949, 149.

Ruler of the Great-World-Above that the Keeper of the Western Door had indeed guarded it well. The 'Proclaimers of the Law' chanted the *Adoweh* ritual and the Keepers of the Faith invoked the spirits to guard the sachem who was to go to battle."[126]

Does a person so seated to replace a chief who has left the circle or been de-horned need to go through the ceremony of Condolence before he is recognized? There are two schools of thought: the first is that the Condolence is used only when someone has died and his family needs to be consoled, and a chief who has left the circle has not died. It would follow that even though the individual is no longer the holder of the title, his replacement would not be condoled, but would be acknowledged as sitting in that seat during the lifetime of the previous title holder. The second is that the Condolence is also necessary because it provides the necessary recognition and protection coming from the other nations of the Confederacy.

Individuals are always free to return.[127]

It appears that the same principle applies to holders of other offices: "A Canienga matron, becoming a Christian, left her country, with two of her children, to enjoy greater freedom in her devotions among the French. The act, writes the missionary, so offended her family that, in a public meeting of the town, 'they degraded her from the rank of the nobility, and took from her the title of Oyander, that is, honorable, (*considérable*)—a title which they esteem highly, and which she had inherited from her ancestors, and deserved by her good judgment, her prudence, and her excellent conduct and at the same time they installed another in her place.'"[128]

In its simplest form, the law states that a citizen who takes up citizenship in another nation, or who submits to its laws and acknowledges allegiance to that nation and those laws, ceases to be a citizen of the Haudenosaunee, and is no longer considered to be "within the circle" of the law's protection. "And if at any time any of the Confederate Lords will submit to laws and regulations made by other people he or they are no longer in, but outside of the confederation, and shall be called 'Gone Through.' And likewise if any of your people submit to the laws and regulations made by other people he or they shall forfeit his or

---

126 Parker 1919, 106. Donehogowa Ely Parker's title, as doorkeeper, in some versions, is that of both a peace and a war chief, so it would not be required to "lift" his horns for him to go to war. However, once he left, first for the war and then to a career in the United States civil service, it does not seem he ever resumed his duties as a Confederacy chief. There has been little discussion of whether his taking a position in the United States government constituted stepping outside the circle of the law.

127 The oral tradition is that such a returned person shall not be eligible for any special duties within the Confederacy but shall sit quietly on the back benches of the longhouse, against the wall of the building.

128 Hale (1883) 1989, 65; Thwaites 1901, 1671: 6.

their birthright, thereafter he or they shall have no interest or claim inside the Confederation."[129] An extreme interpretation of this would be that *any* obedience to other laws is an automatic loss of citizenship.[130]

In colonial times, European powers competed for sovereignty over North America, with France and Britain claiming both ownership of territory and overlordship over its peoples. The Europeans avoided explaining their ideas of empire to their allies, and this led to a strange dichotomy. Generally, the same British and French governors who treated Indigenous peoples as allies on the ground would report to their superiors across the Atlantic that they had secured obedient subjects. There were exceptions, though. Warraghiyageh Sir William Johnson wrote bluntly, after General Braddock had taken a "surrender" from several Indigenous nations:

> Altho' the words of the late Treaty [at Detroit, September 7–10, 1764] may at first appear extraordinary, yet, I am not at a loss to account for them, as I know it has been verry customary for many People to insinuate that the Indians call themselves Subjects, altho' I am thoroughly convinced they were never so called, nor would they approve of it. Tis true when a Nation find themselves pushed, their Alliances broken, and themselves tired of a War, they are verry apt to say many civil things, and make any Submissions which are not agreeable to their Intentions, but are said merely to please those with whom they transact Affairs as they know we cannot enforce the observance of them. But you may be assured that none of the Six Nations, Western Nations &ca. Ever declared themselves to be Subjects, or will ever consider themselves in that light whilst they have any Men, or Open Country to retire to, the very Idea of subjection would fill them with horror.
>
> Indeed I have been just looking into the Indian records, where I find in the Minutes of 1751 that those who made ye Entry say, that Nine different Nations acknowledged themselves to be His Majestys Subjects, altho' I sat at that Conference, made Entrys of all the Transactions, in which there was not a Word mentioned, which could imply a Subjection, however these Matters (notwithstanding all I have from time to time said on that subject) seem not to be well known at home, and therefore, it may prove of dangerous consequence to persuade them that the Indians have agreed to things which (had they even assented to) is so repugnant to their Principles

---

129 Newhouse 1885, 151.

130 This "thinking," no doubt, is what impelled Stewart Myiow of Kahnawake to refuse to stop for the flashing red lights of a Mohawk school bus, since the laws requiring him to stop were made by a government other than the Haudenosaunee.

that the attempting to enforce it, must lay the foundation of greater Calamities than ha[ve] yet been experienced in this Country.

It is necessary to observe that no Nation of Indians have any word which can express, or convey the Idea of Subjection, they often say, "We acknowledge the Great King to be our Father, we hold him fast by the hand, and we shall do what he desires"; many such like words of course, for which our people too readily adopt & insert a Word verry different in signification, and never intended by the Indians without explaining to them what is meant by a Subjection.

Imagine to yourself, Sir, how impossible it is to reduce a People to Subjection, who consider themselves Independent thereof by both Nature & Scituation.[131]

In the case of the Haudenosaunee, independent-minded nations reflect their independent-minded citizens. Loyalty to the law leads naturally to a refusal to submit to other laws and other sovereigns. At the Six Nations Grand River Territory, in the 1950s, Haudenosaunee teachers who refused to swear the oath of allegiance required of Canadian civil servants lost their jobs. Meanwhile, as if to accentuate the difference in allegiances between the elected and traditional councils there, a person taking office in the elected band council would swear an oath not only to perform his or her duties properly but also of allegiance to Canada—an oath not sworn in other places by elected councillors.

Calling People Home

As the people moved from their hunter-gatherer existence towards horticulture, they began to live in larger villages. A little more than 1,000 years ago, squash came first; then beans, corn, and sunflowers. It became possible to have towns of over 1,000 people. Archaeologists have concluded that the large towns had smaller satellite villages and hamlets, whose people would seek refuge behind the palisaded hubs in times of war and danger. At the same time, the people would often range farther from the towns in hunting season, for trapping, trading, or raiding, setting up temporary camps as they moved farther away from home.

With relatively small populations and vast territories, the people could spread out. As they became more distant from one another, communication between the groups became more difficult, and the risk of division and estrangement increased. When that distance became a problem, it would be

---

131 SWJP 11:395–96.

time to call the people home. This cycle of expansion and contraction—a cycle which might take generations—reflected the cyclical nature of other aspects of Haudenosaunee life.

"Calling people home" became an element of the law. As it was foreseen that the web of the League would be weakened as it was stretched, so the law provided a means of renewal and consolidation. Like other elements of the law, it is a way of healing things that have become injured or broken: "When any person or any of the people of the Five Nations emigrate and reside in a region distant from the territory of the Five Nations Confederacy, the Lords of the Five Nations at will may send a messenger carrying a broad belt of black shells and when the messenger arrives he shall call the people together or address them personally displaying the belt of shells and they shall know that this is an order for them to return to their original homes and to their council fires."[132]

Individuals left. Families left.[133] Entire clans and villages would move.[134] The arrival of European settlers and missionaries brought more disruptions and attractions. In historic times, in the east, at least half the Mohawks moved to the St. Lawrence, to the settlements of Kahnawake,[135] Kanehsatake,[136] and Akwesasne.[137] In the latter half of the seventeenth century, the north shore of Lake Ontario was home to numerous Seneca and Cayuga villages at its west

---

132 Parker (Newhouse and Cusick) 1916, 50. Newhouse 1885: "and when they understand the contents of the wampum belts, they then shall re-emigrate home with them again."

133 When there was conflict within a community that could not be resolved internally, one solution seems to have been the creation of a separate community by a group of families.

134 The earliest recorded European contact with Iroquoian people was with the "St. Lawrence Iroquians," the people of Stadacona and Hochelaga, in 1534–35. By the time the French returned, two generations later, these people had disappeared. European diseases no doubt affected them (a fifth of the people of Stadacona died the winter Cartier spent among them, of diseases for which they had no cure). War with their Algonkian neighbours diminished them. The archeological record provides evidence that some joined the Wendat and Onondaga. Mohawk tradition, recorded in the 1600s, asserts that some of the ancestors of the Mohawk Valley people came from the St. Lawrence and met the French there.

135 Kahnawake was established as a "reserve," an Indigenous community under the protection and supervision of the Jesuit Order, in 1640. A significant influx of Mohawk Valley people, including Tokwirowi, arrived in 1680. While the language and culture of the community was consistently Mohawk, it was in fact a composite community, incorporating people from all five Haudenosaunee nations as well as Ottawas, Algonquins, Nipissings, and others.

136 Where Kahnawake was under Jesuit influence, Kanehsatake, eventually settled on the shores of the Lake of Two Mountains, was influenced by the Sulpician Order. In 1791, there was a detailed description of its creation in 1727, including an explanation that, when the town was created, the Mohawks made a wampum belt with a dog at each end, to indicate that their territory would be protected.

137 Akwesasne itself was formed as a permanent community when, in 1750, fifty families from Kahnawake moved upstream to a place where they could be protected from the influences of the local French people and their liquor.

end and Onondaga settlements at its east and. Many Onondagas, in the mid-eighteenth century, had moved to Oswegatchie on the St. Lawrence,[138] and fifty years later were in Akwesasne.

"Calling people home" was a matter of law, but it was also pragmatic. There would be no point in calling people who would not come—or if there were no good reason to call them home. In the seventeenth and eighteenth centuries, the British would often state their desire for the Haudenosaunee—and especially the Mohawks—to call home their people on the St. Lawrence. While the British would give their reasons as wishing the Confederacy to remain strong, it was obviously in their interest to weaken the French alliance and to increase the numbers of British allies. The Haudenosaunee strategy, while unevenly implemented, remained one of either seeking balance between competing European interests or seeking to maintain an alliance with the winners. To British requests to call people home, the answers were sometimes blunt ("we can't persuade them"), sometimes ironic ("if you have the influence you say you have, why don't you call them home?"), sometimes suggestive that it was Haudenosaunee policy to have the people on both sides of the divide. "As to drawing home their Indians from Canada as they were Exhorted to do by the Gov'r yesterday they say, that as the Gov'r has a correspondence with those of Canada he can prevail more with them then they can do & desire he would do his Endeavour with those of Canada to draw their Indians home to their own Country."[139]

Consolidation was a natural reaction to attack: the Buffalo Creek reservation was such a refuge at the end of the American Revolutionary War; so was the Grand River Territory. There was strength not only in unity but in concentrated numbers. The nineteenth century was a turbulent time, with people moving under pressure from settler governments. By the 1830s, the United States had adopted an Indian Removal Policy, having concluded that moving Indian nations west of the Mississippi would provide both peace for the United States and land for the settlers. Following a series of disastrous land transactions, the Oneidas in New York bought land in Kansas but moved instead to Wisconsin. Internal differences led to a large group moving from Wisconsin to Ontario. Some Cayugas in New York had moved to Buffalo Creek. Another series of dubious land transactions left them landless, and many moved to the Grand River

---

138   In the 1790s, after the site of Oswegatchie was taken up by American settlers and re-named Ogdensburg, the Onondagas moved up the Black River to the vicinity of Lisbon, New York, and by 1800 had moved across the St. Lawrence to the present Johnstown, Ontario, and in 1807 most (but probably not all) the people moved to Akwesasne, settling in the District of Chenail or Snye. Akwesasne's present large Snipe and Deer clan population mainly owes its origin to the Onondaga people of Oswegatchie.

139   Richter 1982, 64.

Territory in 1840.[140] Others settled among the Senecas at Cattaraugus. Senecas from the Ohio country[141] moved to Oklahoma. In the early 1800s, Mohawks from Kahnawake who had sided with the United States in the Revolutionary War moved to the "American side" of Akwesasne. Mohawk families from Kanehsatake later moved to Wahta, on southern Georgian Bay.

These large-scale movements of families and communities were the result of outside pressures: wars, government policies, economic opportunities.

These movements on a larger scale were taking place while intermarriage and moving on a smaller scale continued as it always had. Intermarriage between communities was an important means of binding families and nations together, and remains so today. There are few people in any Haudenosaunee community who cannot point to ancestors from other communities. Individuals moved away, as emigration often matched immigration. The fur trade saw many men settle in trading locations—Mohawk communities in the Peace River country of northern Alberta; Michel Karihiio's community outside present-day Edmonton became "Michel's Band," recognized under the Indian Act of Canada and enfranchised in 1954.[142]

In 1954, Frank Thomas ("Standing Arrow"), moved "home" to the Mohawk Valley, partly in protest against the taking of Akwesasne land by the St. Lawrence Seaway. In 1974, after confrontations with the Quebec Provincial Police, some Mohawks in Kahnawake decided it was time for their people to return home. They circulated a broad belt of dark wampum to all Mohawk communities to announce their intention and invite the people to reassemble in traditional Mohawk territory. They had selected a former girls' camp at Moss Lake in the

---

140 At the same time as the United States was implementing its removal policies, the British were making adjustments in their approach to dealing with Indian affairs. The single greatest expense of the British Indian Department was the annual presents, promised at the 1764 Niagara Congress and delivered faithfully since then, though at a reduced rate after the War of 1812. The British wanted to devolve the Indian Department to the provinces, which were eager to take on the patronage and the possibility of gaining access to Indian lands but reluctant to take on the expense of the presents. This was partly resolved by announcing that Indians from the United States would cease to receive presents as of 1840, while those who moved to British soil would continue to receive them forever. Among the Haudenosaunee, the Cayugas and Oneidas came to Canada with promises that the presents would be continued to them. About two-thirds of the Potowatomis from Michigan and Wisconsin came to Canada, settling around Lake Huron, though the United States' attempt to place their people in malarial swamps in Iowa was also a strong reason for the removal to Canada. Ottawa, Ojibwa, and other communities also moved to Canada during the late 1830s.

141 The westernmost Seneca communities included many descendants of Huron, Tiionontate (Petun), Attiwandaron (Neutral), and Erie families. They had no great love for the British (as their destruction of the British forts south of Lake Erie demonstrated in 1763), and their ties with the other nations of the Haudenosaunee may have been looser than those of the core Seneca towns to the east.

142 Frisch 1978, 544.

Adirondacks and renamed the place Kanienekeh. While the Grand Council recognized the community—and it moved to a new site a few years later—the Mohawk council fire remained at Akwesasne. In 1980, Sakokwenionkwas Tom Porter announced his intention to return to the Mohawk Valley, to create a place of peace where Mohawk language and tradition would be maintained. This new community, Kanatsiohareke, has also been recognized as a Mohawk community by the Haudenosaunee.

Establishing new communities, then, does not seem remarkable to modern Haudenosaunee. It is something that has been done for centuries. It is provided for in the law—not so much in the creation of the new towns, which may have been taken for granted, as in provision for "calling people home" when those new towns become scattered too far afield, weakening communication and therefore weakening the Confederacy itself.

Returning

No matter how far away the people moved, physically or politically, they still remained, in the eyes of the Haudenosaunee, "our people." When, during the latter half of the seventeentth century, perhaps half the Mohawks moved to the St. Lawrence, and became linked to the French, it was still common for visitors from the Mohawk Valley to come and spend weeks with them (to the frustration of the French), or for people from Kahnawake or Kanehsatake to head south to visit their relatives. The trade between Montreal and Albany used Mohawk middlemen (one judge called them "traders rather than merchants"). Both the French and the British despaired of getting Haudenosaunee to fight one another: they would instead provide intelligence about British or French intentions and strategies, and would warn one another of impending attacks.

During the first half of the seventeenth century, the Haudenosaunee experienced a period of expansion. They took in nations from the east who were reeling from attacks by the colonists. They conquered and absorbed enemies, including the Andaste (Susquehannock) and Erie. They absorbed neighbours like the Wenro and Attiwandaronon. They absorbed many of the Hurons, decimated by war and disease. The north shore of Lake Ontario, from Niagara to the St. Lawrence, became settled with Haudenosaunee communities. By the early 1700s, though, there had come a sense that the Confederacy was stretched too thin. War with the Mississaugas, attacks from the French in the east, other pressure in the west, led to a decision to bring the people home, and by the 1720s there had been a consolidation back to the homelands. During the same period, there had been unsuccessful British pressure to bring home the people on the St. Lawrence, from the settlements of Kahnawake, Kanesatahke, Akwesasne, and Oswegatchie.

Perhaps it is fair to consider the retention of links between apparently estranged communities as something like chewing gum or mozzarella cheese: the strands that make people family seem to be able to stretch indefinitely without breaking. The law contemplates this, and indeed it provides the mechanisms for eventual reconciliation. The first of these mechanisms is the perception that it is always possible to become one people again.

> The Indians who live at Canada at least those of Cachnawage are part of the Five Nations and what ever Rough Treatment they receive will be resented by the Five Nations.[143]

> . . . the Six Nation Deputies & Cagnawagas spoke very smartly to the French Governor & told him it appeared to them that he wanted nothing more than to set them who were Friends & Relatives by the Ears & have them destroyed.[144]

> [In January, 1710] a Deputation from the 5 Nations to the Commissioners at Albany that they had sent some chosen Men to the Cagnawagas at Canada to endeavor to prevail upon those Indians to return to their Native Country to live.[145]

The most important procedural mechanism for reconciliation remains the Condolence. It is the way home: it reconciles after wars or separation, enabling people to forgive the most grievous offences. Historically, the Haudenosaunee had been split by several wars: the Seven Years' War; the American Revolutionary War; the War of 1812, had each seen Haudenosaunee fighting one another. In each case, the reunification of the Confederacy was accompanied by a Condolence that would put away the bones, cover the graves, prevent the blood of the dead from calling out for revenge, and remind everyone of the great dream of peace that they shared. No matter how estranged communities and individuals might be, the Great Law provided a hope that they could reunite, become one people again.

In September 1760, the British Army had taken Montreal. The Seven Nations of Canada had made a quiet arrangement with the Imperial Indian Department as early as 1757 that when the British attack came, they would remain neutral. Now, at a council in Kahnawake, the Haudenosaunee among the British forces met with the Seven Nations chiefs. Sir William Johnson confirmed

---

143 *Original Indian Records ii*, cited in Wraxall [1754] 1915, lii.

144 SWJP 9:606.

145 Wraxall (1754) 1915, 80.

earlier promises about land and peace. The Haudenosaunee proposed the re-unification of the Confederacy. The Speaker for the Eight Nations[146] replied:

> Brethren of the 5 Nat's.
>
> [You] In return to your Belt of Yesterday Whereby you told us that
> as your Br. W'y. [Sir William Johnson] had finished every thing with
> us, you on your part had something to say which was that as there
> had been during this war a division and disunion between us; and
> [thereby] desired us to reunite and be firm friends as heretofore, We
> hereby assure all present that we with pleasure agree to your friendly
> proposal and reunite as formerly.[147]

The reunification of the Confederacy at the end of August 1815 provides another example of reconciliation processes. The council was convened at the request of Deputy Superintendent General of Indian Affairs William Claus.[148] On one side were the representatives from the Grand River Territory, in Canada. On the other were representatives of the Senecas, Onondagas, and Cayugas from Buffalo Creek, Tonawanda, and Allegheny. Claus opened the council with a Condolence[149] and uncovered the fire by presenting a peace belt of white wampum. As in a normal Confederacy Council, the Mohawks put forward the matter for consideration. Significantly, the speaker was Tekarihoken: the matter was of great import. He said:

> Brothers and relations,
>
> We the several Nations residing at the Grand River salute you from
> the other side we are the same people with you, we are relations of
> the same colour, notwithstanding having been opposed to each other
> in the Field during the late Contest between our Father the King
> of England and the Americans. Our friend who has just uncovered
> the Council Fire has removed all obstructions, our minds are set
> at ease. The River which separates us is opened that we may have
> a free passage at all times.[150] The roads are cleared of all briars and

---

146 By this time the Seven Nations had become eight, with the addition either of Akwesasne
     (now distinct from Kahnawake) or Oswegatchie.

147 SWJP 13:162–64.

148 At the council at Burlington Bay in April 1815, the chiefs had asked Claus to assist them
     in convening a council with the nations on the American side of the Niagara River, since
     hard feelings had made it difficult for them to bring the council together themselves.
     Claus acted as intermediary.

149 Reference in the record to the "usual ceremony of condolence" indicates both that the
     recorder recognized the ceremony was a repetition of dozens of identical processes and
     that this recorder would tend to omit some details in the council.

150 At the April council at Burlington Bay, Claus had read Article III of the Treaty of Ghent,
     which restored the free border crossing rights provided for in the 1795 Jay Treaty.

rubbish, that we may again renew that friendly intercourse which formerly existed between us. I now speak to you in behalf of the Indians residing on the Grand River, and I am desired to assure you that all ill will is removed from their Hearts towards you from the [ ] American land.

Delivered a bunch of Strings of Wampum

Tekarihoken's words were followed by a speech by Echo, an Onondaga Chief:

Brothers

I salute you in the name of the Hurons, Shawnees and Six Nations at the King's Council Fire which has just been uncovered. I speak to the Senecas, Cayugas and Onondagas from Buffalo Creek, Tehaniwandi and Allegany who are now present at our Father's Council Fire. I also address those who are at their homes, before our Father the Deputy Supt. General, the King's Officers who are now present, and tell you that all ill blood has been removed from our hearts. What has been done, is now forgotten. We are all of the same colour and ought to be friendly towards each other.

To make our Friendship lasting, we put the Tomahawk the depth of a Pine Tree under ground; and that it may not be removed we place over it a Tree that the roots may so cover it that it cannot be found again. . . . We condole with you from the bottom of our hearts for the loss of your friends, and wipe the tears from your eyes, we open your throats so no obstruction shall remain, that you may speak your mind freely and with the same friendship which formerly existed between us, as we now in the name of the Nations already mentioned address you as friends. If you will stand up we will take you by the hands. Should an idle young Man make use of any improper Language we request that you will not take any notice of it.

A Large bunch of Strings of black and white wampum.

The American Indians stood up and the others took them by the hand repeating the assurances of friendship, after which the Old Eel, an Onondaga Chief spoke to the Deputy Supt. Genl. as follows:

Brothers

You have this day uncovered the King's Council Fire at this place where our forefathers were accustomed to assemble. I speak in behalf of the Indians who are now come here to meet our brethren from the Grand River. We salute you and wish you well. We have heard all that you have said now and last Spring, and are much pleased with it. We rejoice that the Great Spirit has brought us together to unite and be friends. Many have been the meetings at this place between the King and our Ancestors. I am an old man and have been present at many of these meetings when your Grand Father spoke to us.[151] We will always remember his words they are buried deep in our hearts. We look to you to be a friend to the Indians as he was. It is now late in the day, and as we are to answer you we will cover the fire and meet again tomorrow.

A few Strings wampum.

September 1st
Tekarihoga
Brothers

We thank the Great Spirit for giving us a new day, and permitting us to meet again. We wait to hear what you may have to say.

Red Jacket, Principal Seneca Speaker
Brothers

In the name of the Indians from the other side of the River. I now address myself to the King, the Commanding Officers, and Colonel Claus our head, and to the Six Nations, Wyandots and Shawanese.

Strings wampum.

Brothers

I am happy now to meet you in the usual friendly manner, and you may be assured that what has happened was not from any animosity towards our ancient Father and friends. We are a poor people. We cannot do as we would. We are as Prisoners. But the fetters are now off and we are at liberty to communicate freely with our friends. We are not of the same Nations only, but of the same Families also. We therefore ought to be united and become one Body.

Strings of Wampum.

---

151 William Claus's grandfather was Warraghyihagey Sir William Johnson, the first Imperial Superintendent General of Indian Affairs, appointed in 1755.

. . . The Road being now open, we will be glad to have a visit from you at Buffalo Creek. Eating and drinking together may be omitted at present, our time being so short, rising and shaking hands will do as well.[152]

Strings of wampum.

They then mixed with each other and spoke to the Deputy Supt. General as follows.

Tekarihoga, Speaker
Brothers

You have witnessed our proceedings which it has pleased the Ruler of the World to assist us in. It has finished as we could wish, and we desire that you will immediately acquaint our Western Brethren of the work we have been doing; and that we shall soon proceed to the west to meet them and perform the same ceremony there as was agreed upon last spring in Council. We now speak to you in One Body, and we hope that we shall be allowed to travel along the road peaceably and without being insulted by the inhabitants, and that you will give us provisions to enable us to travel homewards.[153]

The Haudenosaunee had again become "one body," in a council facilitated by the British. They had shaken hands and then literally "mixed together," becoming, in effect, one side of the council fire, with the British on the other side. Tekarihoken, by council's end, was speaking for the reunited Confederacy—and as speaker for the Mohawks, was once again properly addressing the British, who had originally arrived at the Eastern Door.

The Kayanerenkó:wa provides explicitly for the reunification of the Confederacy after a disruption. Estranged relatives are, after all, still family. A polity that is brought together by the yearning for peace in people's minds, and kept together by will rather than coercion, will tend to permit people to leave and to return. In anticipating this in the constitution itself, Haudenosaunee law differs deeply from that of its neighbours. Canada, threatened by Québec secession, has barely managed (through litigation) to set rules for the dismantling

---

152 Eating and drinking together cements the relationship, as the Peacemaker's feasts with the Cannibal, Tsikonsaseh, and Hiawatha recalled. Shaking hands is an act not only of peace (in many cultures, it is said that the handshake requires a warrior to drop his weapon) but of recognition. For example, it has been proposed that the way to recognize Tuscarora Chiefs would be for everyone to shake hands with them at a Condolence of Chiefs of another nation.

153 LAC, RG8, vol. 258, pt. 1, 204–8.

of the nation, and has no law concerning its reconciliation. The Civil War in the United States carved deep rifts, "testing whether that nation or any nation so conceived and so dedicated can long endure," in the words of Abraham Lincoln's Gettysburg Address. Historians have paid little attention to the way the Haudenosaunee heal their divisions: William Fenton ignored the reunification and declared the Confederacy finished after the American Revolution. Is the weakness of the law in its inability to hold the structure together the most important feature, or is the flexibility of the law, in providing a path for reconciliation, more remarkable and more noteworthy? In truth, they are another example of the system of balances contained within the entire legal system: the inability of the law to prevent people from leaving is balanced by the explicit ways within the law itself to bring them home.

Symbols of the Law

The Kayanerenkó:wa and the speeches and councils that accompany it are full of symbols and metaphors. The metaphors both explain and remind the people of the principles of the law.

While the metaphors are mostly visual, Haudenosaunee law uses several senses to convey meaning. Visual symbols include the longhouse and its extendable framework; the Tree of Peace, the eagle atop it and the Great White Roots spreading under it; and all the minor elements that assist with council.

Some symbols go underground. The weapons of war are buried deep underground, in the pit created by the uprooting of the great pine tree.[154] The blood and bones of the deceased are put away underground so that they, too, can never be seen again. In the Creation story, the terrible animals of an earlier age are also put underground, and kept there. Serpents, the companions of Thadadaho's bad-mindedness, venomous messengers, live underground. Underground means out of mind, the home of the negative.

Other symbols are kept above ground, and even aloft, to be kept firmly in mind. The eagle perches atop the white pine tree. The pine itself soars above all the other trees. When wampum belts are read, they are held up. The things the people need to remember are constantly before their eyes.

The Haudenosaunee use their other senses in the world that includes both law and ceremony. It is not only the smoke but the smell of tobacco that attracts the attention of the spirit world and the Creator. It is the sound of the songs

---

154 Of all the symbols of the Haudenosaunee, "burying the hatchet" seem to be the most acknowledged in modern North America, though the richness of the metaphor has been stripped away.

in the ceremonies—ceremonies of thanksgiving, the soothing sounds of the Condolence, the powerful sound of the Great Feather Dance—that carry the power to heal, to persuade, to express gratitude. Thadadaho is rubbed down as part of the effort to restore his good mind, as the legs of visitors are symbolically rubbed to remove the thorns and burrs of the road.

Yet, as with most legal systems, the symbolism is primarily visual, and the symbols themselves are things rather than concepts. Wisely, the Peacemaker chose things that the people would see often, so that in their daily lives they would be reminded of the law. What are modern Euro-American equivalents? Things that carry little practical meaning for the people themselves: eagles and crowns, coats of arms and flags. Their symbols are much more . . . well . . . symbolic. They are not part of the everyday lives of the people whose laws they represent.

The Tree of Peace

When the Peacemaker chose the great white pine as the symbol of the peace, he did so deliberately, for reasons that would have been obvious to the people of his time. The pine is the tallest tree of the forest, superdominant, towering over the surrounding mixed hardwoods, projecting upward past the oak canopy. It can be ancient, living four centuries. It is used as medicine, restoring health, its purifying smoke clearing the senses. The miracle of its growth from a tiny seed mirrors the birth of the Great Peace from the dream of a single man.[155]

Once the Peace and the Law were in place, the Peacemaker declared that the weapons of war should no longer be seen:

> The war clubs, the killers of humans, and the tomahawks and other weapons,[156] as to these, it will be better for us to hide them from them, so that they cannot see them again, our grandchildren.

> Thereupon Tekanawita said: There is only one way for it to get done, for us to be able to hide the weapons from them: we will pull up our great tree, Great Tall Tree, Great Long Leaf, and it will pass right through, making a hole through the earth. Thereupon we will pick everything up and throw it down where the earth is opened up, all

---

155 Parker 1912.

156 The weapons of war were made from other trees: maple for war clubs; hickory and ash for bows; cedar for arrows. The pine, with its soft wood, was never used as raw material for weapons, and was indeed a Tree of Peace. And unlike those of many other conifers, the cones of the white pine are thornless, and the needles are soft rather than stiff and sharp.

of the war clubs, and the strong current in the earth will carry these away. Thereupon we will replant the tree, and they will never see the war clubs again, our grandchildren. Thereupon we all will continue to think peacefully by day and by night as the families continue on.

Thereupon the chiefs, all of them, supported the matter unanimously, the several nations saying: We will bury them, the war clubs, and then we will never again see the people shedding each other's blood.[157]

As the tallest tree, the white pine also has strong roots, deep and widespread, rather than a single taproot. The deep, wide roots indicate stability, but they also become the carriers of the metaphor for the spreading of the peace. White pines are also relatively fire-resistant: they survive most surface fires due to their thick bark, branch-free trunks, and moderately deep roots. Metaphorically, they survive the fires of war.

Europeans had their metaphorical equivalent of the Haudenosaunee white pine: the May-Tree, around which the people of the villages of western Europe would gather in a spirit of reconciliation every spring. In February 1654, a Haudenosaunee delegation met with the Governor of New France. The third wampum they delivered, explained the speaker, "was a May-tree,[158] which he planted, he said, in the middle of the Great River St. Lawrence, opposite the fort of Quebec, the house of Onontio, the great Captain of the French . . . a May-tree which should rear its summit above the clouds, in order that all the Nations of the earth might be able to see it, and that it might be a rendez-vous where all the world could rest in peace under the shade of its leaves." The governor said that he accepted the proposal, but that he would "transplant the

---

157 Gibson 1912, 446–49. In Gibson 1899, para. 111, the weapons are tied in a bundle and wrapped in Thadadaho's shirt before being "cast into where the earth is upheaved . . . so the running waters shall carry these down under the earth." Water not only carries: it cleanses.

158 The pre-Christian European calendar had two days of reconciliation—May 1 and November 1 (and two days in which evil spirits were released—April 30 and October 31). May Day and Halloween are remnants of days that had legal significance, since grievances had to be resolved or abandoned by those dates. The "May Pole" that people dance around, with their hands joined in harmony, is the modern descendant of the "May-tree"—a happy convergence of French and Haudenosaunee symbolism. Replacing the May-tree with the May-pole is a retreat from an intimacy with nature that is paralleled in Greek temples, where the natural trees that were the first columns were replaced with Corinthian columns that retained the leaves at their tops, and then by Doric columns that allowed the symbols of the forest to fade into the past (Schama 1995).

May-tree to Montreal, in order that access to it might be easier, the latter place being on the frontier."[159]

"May-Tree" is a bad translation but a good interpretation, since it is the closest European equivalent to the most important aspects of the Tree of Peace. On May Day, throughout pre-Christian western Europe, a day of reconciliation and good will was celebrated. Wrongs that had not been adjusted by that date had to be forgotten (the equivalent of throwing them into the deep pit under the Tree of Peace), as the people joined hands (just as the brotherhood of chiefs would do around the Tree of Peace).

Just as Thadadaho was the keeper of the council house at Onondaga, so wherever a council place was appointed, a keeper was also named: "According to our ancient custom, whenever a council-fire was kindled up, and a Tree of Peace was planted, there was some person appointed to watch it."[160]

The Tree of Peace and the Tree of Council are two different trees, though. The Tree of Peace is the great white pine,[161] the tallest tree, closest to the Sky World. As such, it is the tree most likely to communicate with the Creator.[162] Alone among the pines of eastern North America, it has clusters of five needles, to remind us of the original Five Nations.[163] It is where the eagle perches, above the rest of the forest, to look out for danger coming from afar. The Tree of Council, on the other hand, is the oak. It has a canopy to shade the people meeting beneath it, and tends to shade flat, open areas.[164] The oak is also long-lived. It resists high winds.

Hiding the weapons from both the children and the warriors has a parallel: the admonition, as part of the Condolence, to hide the bones of the dead from the children, whose curious minds might be upset, and from the warriors, whose

---

159 Thwaites 1901, 1653–54: chap 2, 51–63. Here, the French were mixing the symbolism of two trees. The Tree of Peace, the pine tree, indicates that peace exists in that place. The tree of council, the oak, with its sheltering canopy, indicates that nations will come together in that place to bring their minds together to maintain and continue peace. The French were proposing to hold councils in Montreal. There was no need to move the Tree of Peace. Rather, it would be desirable to plant new peace trees in other places, including Montreal, as the peace spread. Today, Tekaronieken Jake Swamp, with the Tree of Peace Society, has maintained that tradition.

160 *Indian Affairs Papers*, 31, German Flats council with the twelve colonies, August 1776.

161 Newhouse 1885, 1. Newhouse translates "Jonerahdesegowah" as "Tree of Great Peace."

162 It is the maple, and not the white pine, that is named as the leader of the trees in the Thanksgiving. Each tree has its gifts and its purposes.

163 Tekaronianeken Jake Swamp would explain this when planting white pines for the Tree of Peace Society.

164 At Fort Johnson, New York (Warraghiyagey Sir William Johnson's first home on the Mohawk River), two large oaks in the front garden are said to have been grown from acorns shed by the great Council Oak tree at Albany). All through eastern North America, there were council oaks. The Creeks left their names behind—both Tallahassee, Florida, and Tulsa, Oklahoma, mean "council oak."

minds might then tend towards anger and revenge. Were the weapons actually hidden? The history of the Haudenosaunee for the past three centuries has been one of almost incessant warfare.[165] Putting them away, in pragmatic terms, may have come to mean reducing their visibility and their prominence.[166] Putting the weapons away in terms of their use within the community was paramount: that the Senecas guarded the Great Black Door indicated that the weapons could still be used against external enemies.

The Great White Wampum

The first wampum records of the Haudenosaunee are the simplest. They are the short strings of the ceremony of Condolence, the five strings that symbolize the coming together of the minds of the nations, and the circle that sets out the structure of the government. The originals would have been almost completely made of white beads.

Another of the first wampum records of the Haudenosaunee is the "great mat," a wampum belt of pure white beads. This wampum is associated with the Peacemaker just as other great wampums are linked to Hiawatha and Thadadaho. Perhaps the Peacemaker's wampum is a mat, connected to the earth, because he returned to the earth when his work was done. Certainly it is a "mat" because he would make people's minds comfortable by making their bodies comfortable first. The wampum recalls this:

> The lords have unanimously decided to spread before you [Thadadaho] on the ground this great white wampum belt Ska-no-dah-ken-rah-ko-wah and Ka-yah-ne-renh-ko-wah, which respect-fully signify purity and great peace. . . .[167]

> Article XIX:

> Thus it shall be. I and the confederate chiefs now plant a tree of Peace or shelter, at your residence A-do-dar-hoh of the Fire Keepers the Onondagas. And this Tree of Peace or shelter I called

---

165 When John Mohawk was being cross-examined during the *Mitchell* trial, in 1999, the lawyer for the Canadian government said: "I put it to you, sir, that the history of your people, the Seneca people, for the past three hundred years has been one of incessant warfare." And John Mohawk replied: "I put it to you, sir, that the history of the *world* for the past three hundred years has been one of incessant warfare. What's your point?"

166 At the beginning of Midwinter ceremonies, the first dance is the Standing Quiver Dance, in which the hunters symbolically put away their hunting equipment, for it is the end of deer hunting season.

167 Parker (Chiefs) 1916, 98.

"Jo-ne-rah-de-she-go-wah." And in the shade of this tree of peace or shelter we spread out this "Jo-no-da-ken-rah-ko-wah" (meaning belts of white wampum is spread under the shade of the spreading branches of this tree of peace or shelter). And on this place which we prepare it for you A-do-dar-hoh, your brothers, and your cousin Chiefs will be your seats, and we do now put you A-do-dar-hoh, your brothers and your cousin chiefs on the wampums spread out under the shade of its spreading branches of this tree of peace or shelter.[168]

It is said that part of this wampum was kept at the Grand River Territory. If so, part of it was returned in 1999 by the Royal Ontario Museum, where it had been since 1935.[169] Another fragment was later returned from the National Museum of the American Indian.

The Eagle

In Haudenosaunee legend, the eagle, flying higher than all other birds, has the best chance to see and visit the Sky World. It communicates between the worlds, like tobacco smoke. The eagle causes people to look up, to be inspired by its grace and strength:

Moreover, I decree that a large creature, a free one, which flies high and has long distance vision, and which is watching all over the world, that this is what we shall seat at the top of the tree, the tree we have growing, Skaetsi:kona [Great Tall Tree Trunk], as to that, it is there that we are seating it now, the one called Eagle. Moreover, it will be protecting [*holding*] our power, for it will be watching all over the world where they are settled, the many nations. And therefore it will notice things at once and it will observe when, possibly, someone will see a root growing along, of Tsyoktehhaekeaeto:kona[170] [the Great White Roots], and possibly someone will chop into the root enough so that it will be able to cause its blood to flow. . . .

Moreover this is what will happen in the future, in days and nights to come, and if it so happens in future days, that wherever the roots

---

168 Newhouse 1885, 24.

169 Hayadaha Richard Hill (personal communication) believes that the "mat" is both the very large wampum belt, and the actual mat that the chiefs would sit on in comfort in council, and the metaphor for the basis of the law. Is it a big mat, or just a big idea about the metaphorical mat?

170 Newhouse 1885, 1. Newhouse translates "Ohderakenragowah" as "Big White Root."

extend, the Great White Roots—all of the nations seeing where
those roots are—and if someone were to chop into them, at once it
will holler, the one perched at the top of the tree, Eagle, and that is
what everyone will hear, it notifying them.[171]

. . . So now at the very top of our standing tree, the Great Tall Pine,
have I perched the Eagle (great talons) [the symbol of foresight].
And so it shall have your collective power, and the reason for this is
that it shall occur that this Eagle aloft goes to and fro over the earth,
which means that your work for the Great Law and for Reason shall
prevail on the earth and even toward the skyworld. Both things are
reserved to you federal chiefs, and you shall regulate the minds of
the public, and also the individual families, and also the territories
and settlements of the people amid the forests.[172]

Eagles seek out nesting places at the tops of white pine trees that soar above
the oak canopies. They seek places with open areas, where they can take off and
land despite their broad wingspread. From their nesting places, they can see all
around them. They are unusually alert. In choosing the eagle as a symbol, the
Peacemaker was doing the same as he had done with the family, the fire and
the longhouse: he had chosen something with which the people were familiar;
something that would remind them of the law every time they saw it. In those
days before DDT, there were many eagles in the forest, and along the rivers.

Though no version of the Great Law says so, the eagle gradually became a
symbol of the Confederacy itself, a symbol of the way the nations had joined
together to become a single family or clan.[173] As Yankee Spring of Tonawanda
explained:

The Eagle is the symbol of the Confederacy.

The Iroquois, or the Five Nations, began as separate entities and
became known as such when they formed the League. When they
learned the great natural law (Gayaneshagowa) the Creator told the
people a way by which they might know each other. It should be by
wearing of an eagle feather, because that bird was a far-seeing bird,
and the Creator wanted his people to be far-seeing.

The great mutual law was designed for the future. It did not rest
upon the past. The Creator chose the eagle feather by which they
might recognize each other in the future. He chose the eagle as the

---

171   Gibson 1912, 311 and 319.

172   Gibson 1899, para. 110.

173   There is no Eagle Clan among the Haudenosaunee. The Senecas have a Hawk Clan,
       though.

totem of the Iroquois as a people, and he ordained that collectively the Five Nations should belong to one clan, that of the eagle, which is called variously, oswegadage'a, oshada'ge'a, "Dew Eagle,"[174] or do'nyonda, "Bald Eagle."

One feather he deemed enough for his people's headdress. In ceremonies they added to the single large whirling eagle feather by wearing a cap which had at the forehead a cluster of split feathers from which the quills had been removed.[175]

The Dish with One Spoon:
Sharing the Hunting Grounds

The Peacemaker had observed that one source of bloodshed had been disputes over hunting grounds. By this provision of the Kayanerenkó:wa he removed the idea of exclusive hunting grounds, replacing it with the concept of the Dish that would feed everyone: "Equally will we share the animals on which we will have to live (i.e. we shall have an equal right to hunt, etc.) as Haweni'yu, who dwells in the sky, has provided for us."[176]

In some renderings of the principle, it is stated that there is a single wooden spoon in the bowl—again, an implement that will assist in feeding the people, but without sharp edges, so that there will be no risk of bloodshed:[177]

> Thereupon Dekanawidah said: "it will turn out well for us to do this: we will say, "We promise to have only one dish among us; in it will be beaver tail and no knife will be there."" Thereupon the chiefs confirmed that so it shall happen. Thereupon Dekanawidah

---

174 The dew eagle flies in the western sky and helps put out forest fires.

175 Fenton 1953, 117. To this day, the Senecas can be recognized by the single eagle feather on the men's kahstó:was. Different nations carry different numbers of feathers in different arrangements: the Mohawks have three upright eagle feathers; the Oneidas two eagle feathers up and one down; the Onondagas have two feathers, one up and one down; the Cayugas a single angled feather; and the Senecas a single upright feather. At some point in the second half of the nineteenth century, some Haudenosaunee began to wear Plains-style eagle feather headdresses, and this continued, in public shows, until perhaps the mid-twentieth century. However, these headdresses were recognized as foreign to the Haudenosaunee, and in matters internal to the Confederacy, the men continued to wear their kahstó:was. Those who persisted in wearing Plains-style headdresses were subjected to prolonged teasing.

176 Hewitt 1892b, 145.

177 See, e.g., RCAP 1995, 656.

said, "Now we have completed the matter; we will have one dish, which means that we will all have equal shares of the game roaming about in the hunting grounds and fields, and then everything will become peaceful among all of the people, and there will be no knife near our dish, which means that if a knife were there, someone might presently get out, causing bloodshed, and this is troublesome, should it happen thus, and for this reason there should be no knife near the dish."[178]

The Lords of the Confederacy shall eat together from one bowl the feast of cooked beaver's tail. While they are eating they are to use no sharp utensils for if they should they might accidentally cut one another and bloodshed would follow. All measures must be taken to prevent the spilling of blood in any way.[179]

. . . I have decreed that all of you are federal chiefs; I have rolled up your publics (constituents) into one, as well as other tribes (at random) in neighbouring territories; so then there shall be only the common dish resting there for all of us, and this will contain beaver tail.

And surely this will come to pass. It will contain nothing that is sharp-edged. And this is what will happen if we should put any sharp-edged thing into that dish which we have set down, for surely it will cut somebody touching it. Then some one will surely bleed. This is what it means. When we have set down our dish of wild game, we shall all enjoy equal portions where the people have hunted (the hunting grounds amongst the several tribal territories of native lands), and all human beings shall now bear good will for one another in their travels.[180]

Then Dekanawideh continued and said: "We have still one matter left to be considered and that is with reference to the hunting grounds of our people from which they derive their living."

They, the lords, said with reference to this matter: "We shall now do this: We shall have only one dish (or bowl) in which will be placed one beaver's tail and we shall all have coequal right to it, and there shall be no knife in it, for if there be a knife in it, there would be danger that it might cut someone and blood would thereby be shed."

---

178 Gibson 1912, 458–60.

179 Parker (Newhouse and Cusick) 1916, 45.

180 Gibson 1899, para. 311.

(This one dish or bowl signified that they will make their hunting grounds one common tract and all have a coequal right to hunt within it.[181] The knife being prohibited from being placed into the dish or bowl signifies that all danger would be removed from shedding blood by the people of these different nations of the confederacy caused by differences of the right of the hunting grounds.)[182]

Recall that in the dark days before the coming of the law, it was not uncommon for people to live alone, in isolation from one another. Examples of this in the story of making the law include the Peacemaker, living with his mother and grandmother; the Cannibal; Tsikonsaseh; and Hiawatha. Bringing them to their good minds was followed by returning them to society. The threshold to that return was the sharing of a meal. They had to learn to eat with other people again, and they had to learn to share their meals. The meals and feasts the Peacemaker had with each of these people are microcosms of the transformation of attitudes implicit in the Dish with One Spoon. Again, the Peacemaker had taken his piecemeal accomplishments and extrapolated them to an entire society.

There is another aspect of the "no sharp edges" principle: it is that people will avoid using "cutting words" that might injure one another's feelings: "As the bowl circulated the Peacemaker said, 'We will drink from one common bowl. When we come here to the council, we will adopt civilized behavior. When people are here to put their minds to the problem of survival, we will be careful not to use words that cut anyone else. Our diplomacy is a version of our future as human beings.'"[183]

The wampum preserving this part of the Great Law is kept at the Grand River Territory,[184] and several documented readings of it have been by chiefs from that community. In 1862, at the council at Cattaraugus, the Grand River chiefs came to read the Great Law, to seek a reaffirmation of the Confederacy's commitment to it: "Canada nations presented the wampum with a dark spot in the middle represent a bowl or dish with beaver tail in it . . . represented with beaver meat in it. They should eat together—use no knife for fear they should cut and draw blood."[185]

Why beaver tail? Because, it is said, it is the chiefs' favourite dish. It is also extremely high in fats and nutrients, a delicacy in a society where meat was

---

181 Diondowe'ta, hunting ground.

182 Parker (Chiefs) 1916, 103.

183 Mohawk 1987, 10–17.

184 From 1931 to 1995, it was held by the Royal Ontario Museum in Toronto.

185 Minutes of Council of the Six Nations at Cattaraugus, December 1, 1862; Parker 1916, 145.

sometimes scarce. Another explanation is that the conflict over hunting grounds might have begun or revived with the fur trade, and the beaver was the prime object of that trade.

The idea spread as an element of the peace. That is, peace depended not only on the original Five Nations refraining from internal wars but also on removing sources of friction with other nations.[186] It is possible that the bloodshed of the Dark Times had its origins in conflicts over scarce resources—food. The source might have been a bad year, a starving year, and the bloodshed might have kept going, as blood feuds do. The Peacemaker, by addressing this conflict, went to the source of the problem rather than the symptoms. Sharing hunting grounds was an easy concept to grasp. The number of deer that visitors would take would have little effect on the overall population, and in any event shared hunting meant reciprocity.

Other readings of the wampum by Skanawati John Buck have been preserved, and they are consistent, both with one another and with the original terms of the Great Law. In 1887, Augusta Gilkison of Toronto recorded:

> The firekeeper told the first belt, all white except for a round purple patch in the centre. This represents all the Indians on the continent. They have entered into one great league and contract and they will all be one and have one heart. The pot in the centre is a dish of beaver, indicating that they will have one dish and what belongs to one will belong to all.[187]

> The new treaty, confirmed by the exchange of wampum-belts and by a peculiar interlocking of the right arms, which has ever since been the special sign of amity between the Iroquois and the Ojibways, was understood to make them not merely allies but brothers. As the symbol on one of the belts which is still preserved indicates, they were to be relatives who are so nearly akin that they eat from the same dish. This treaty, made two centuries ago, has ever since been religiously maintained.[188]

---

186 Lytwyn 1997.

187 Gilkison 1928, 48–50. When Skanawati John Buck died, his family sold the Confederacy wampum belts, including this one, which ended up with Dr. Boyle. The chiefs found out about this and secured their return, reimbursing the money. In 1935, this was one of the four wampums delivered secretly to the Royal Ontario Museum. They were returned to the Grand River Territory in 1999.

188 Hale (1883) 1989, 91. The "peculiar interlocking of the right arms" resembles the old Roman military handshake. It is considered to be stronger and more respectful than shaking hands. Strangers can greet and acknowledge each other properly in this way: wa'thyatenonhwerá:ton wa'tyatatenéntsha—"they greeted each other by the arm."

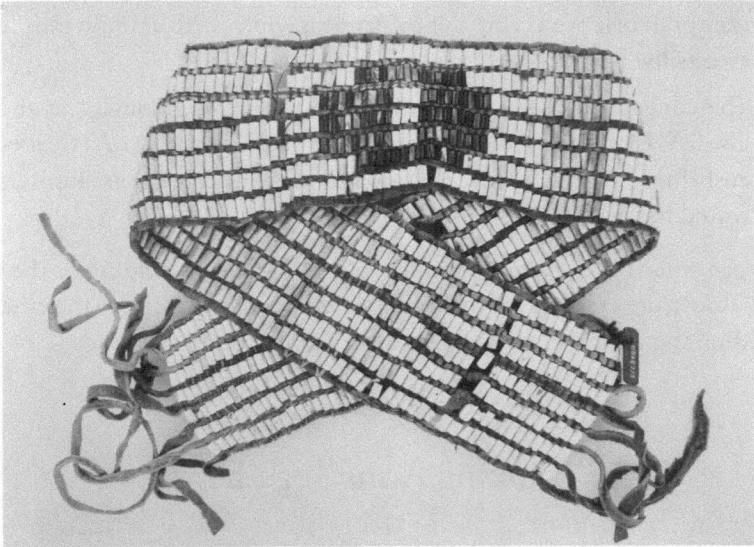

Figure 9. The Dish with One Spoon Wampum. Photograph by Richard W. Hill.

Like other elements of the Great Law, the sharing of hunting grounds was intended to expand, so that there would not be a territory of peace with conflict at all its edges:

> The dish with one spoon referred to in this provision of the Great Law appears often in councils between the Haudenosaunee and other indigenous nations, as well as in relations with Europeans. It refers to the hunting grounds. As the dish of beaver tail stew is shared between the chiefs, the land is like a bowl to feed all the people. The wampum belt preserving this principle is white, with a round purple area as the bowl.

> The concept of the dish with one spoon spread gradually, as the Great White Roots of Peace spread to other nations. . . . As treaties enshrining that principle were made with other nations, hunters would be able to use ever larger territories.[189]

Expansion of the hunting grounds, along with the spreading of the Great White Roots, are examples of the thinking reflected in "adding to the rafters"— expanding the Longhouse to take in other peoples and their lands.

Linking Arms Together

The Peacemaker had extrapolated the structure of village and nation government to a new confederate level.[190] He had used the complex terms of kinship that the people already knew as the glue to bind them together. Now he began to identify the metaphors and symbols that the people would use and recognize.

The terms of kinship did not just bind the people together—they also were the way the people related to the world around them. The thanksgiving address that begins any meeting or council has a careful structure[191] that sets out the organization of the natural world and the place (and obligations) of people within it. Everything is related, and everything is linked. Michael Foster wrote:

---

189 RCAP 1995, 657.

190 Morgan says that the council of the clan "was the germ of the higher council of the tribe, and of that still higher of the confederacy, each of which was composed exclusively of chiefs as representatives of the clans." Morgan (1871) 1997, 85.

191 See Foster 1974, for an analysis of a number of men's renditions of the Thanksgiving, noting that the versions varied greatly in length (from one minute to nearly three-quarters of an hour) but not in their basic content and structure.

"There is a certain symmetry in the Iroquois conception of the ritual process which is an interlocking chain of obligations between man and the Creator."[192]

If people knew who they were—as individuals, family members, clan members, citizens of nations—they felt that much more secure. If they also knew where they fit into the natural world, those links, as well, would help them avoid being swept away. The Peacemaker recognized the need for a web-like structure of obligations and relationships that reminded them of the kinship that lay at the heart of the peace. He sought consistent, uncomplicated symbols as reminders.

The Circle Wampum—a simple circle of two intertwined strings of white wampum, with forty-nine strings going from the circumference towards the middle, was such a symbol.[193] Each string represents a title holder, a chief. The two intertwined white strings around the circumference represent the Great Law and the Great Peace, which are so interwoven as to be inseparable. There are three white beads between each of the strings—and these are reminders of the Peacemaker's Three Words. As with King Arthur's Round Table, the circle reminds the chiefs that they are all equal, with none higher than any other. The circle is the circle of the law around the people: it is their protection. It evokes the palisade around the town. As with many other symbols of the Haudenosaunee—including the longhouse itself—maintaining the circle of the law requires constant effort. The chiefs have formed this circle by linking arms, holding each other's arms so firmly that even if a tree fell upon them, it would not break their hold, or their resolve: "We therefore bind ourselves together by taking hold of each other's hands firmly and forming a circle so strong that if a tree fall prostrate upon it, it could neither shake nor break it, and thus our people and our grandchildren shall remain in the circle of security, peace and happiness."[194]

The degrees of closeness between individuals and peoples are indicated by how they take hold of one another's arms: shaking hands in friendship; taking one another by the arm being closer;[195] linking arms reflecting brotherhood. This

---

192 Foster 1974, 125.

193 Niwadenraah Henry Lickers says his great-grandmother described to him two important occasions on which Thadadaho at Grand River picked up the Circle Wampum: he held it by the circle part, with the strings symbolizing the chiefs hanging down together—occasions when it was necessary for them to hold together tightly, for the strings representing the chiefs were closer together than ever. In the 1862 council in Cattaraugus, there may be a suggestion that there were two Circle Wampums, one kept at the Grand River on the Canadian side, the other at Onondaga: "this belt represents the circling of the Six Nations similar to the one at Onondaga" (Parker 1916, 145).

194 Parker (Chiefs) 1916, 102.

195 The Haudenosaunee and the Ojibways grasp each other's arms (not hands) in greeting and in brotherhood—as the Ojibways were reminded at the council at Willow Grove in 1870.

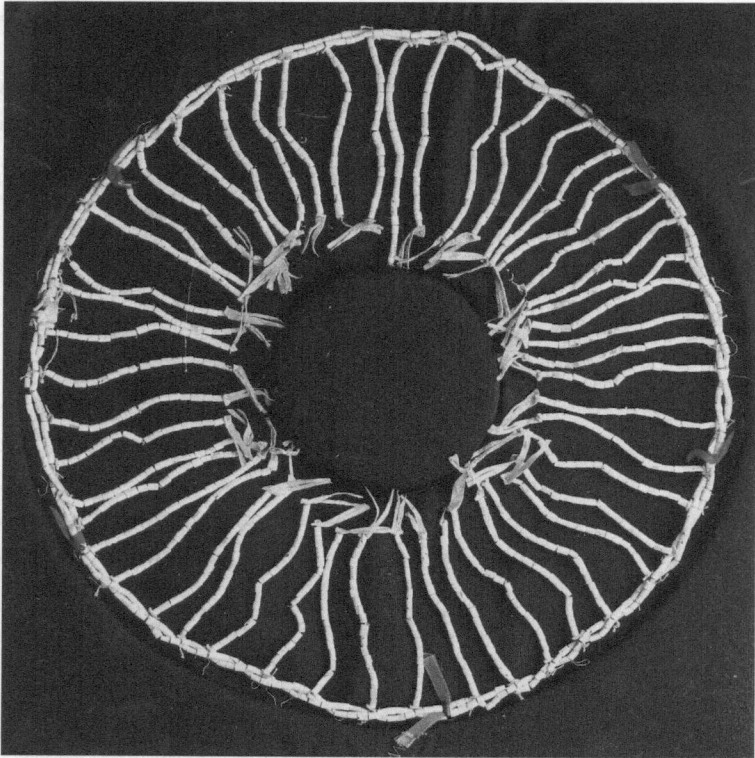

Figure 10. The Circle Wampum. Returned to the Grand River Territory by the Canadian Museum of Civilization, 1990. Photograph by Raymond Skye.

gradual rapprochement was often repeated in the symbolism of the evolution of relations between the Haudenosaunee and the British:

> We not only made the chain of friendship very bright; but we locked arms, and took fast hold of each other's hands, and left the token of friendship.[196]

> You, the Five Nations Confederate Lords, be firm so that if a tree falls upon your joined arms, it shall not separate you or weaken your hold. So shall the strength of the union be preserved.[197]

Holding hands, holding arms, and linking arms are three distinct acts of increasing closeness. The chiefs link their arms—the closest and firmest grasp, unbreakable.

Skanatariio John Arthur Gibson also described the circle of the peace and the law: "This is where it burns, the Great Fire, its smoke rising and piercing the sky; where the family is, the single family we have created; where they are forming a circle, the chiefs, linking arms. Moreover this is what encircles the group: the Good Message, and the Power, and the Peace, and the Great Law; even if the wind were to rise and the tree to topple where they hold each other by the arms, the circle cannot break."[198]

There is a difference in metaphor between "linked arms" and "joined hands." The linking of arms is a sign of brotherhood, whereas shaking or joining hands is a weaker matter of friendship. Careful translation is necessary to keep the two concepts separate. In the "Newhouse" version published by Parker, the ideas are mixed: "There are now the Five Nations Confederate Lords standing with joined hands in a circle. This signifies and provides that should any one of the Confederate Lords leave the council and this Confederacy, his crown of deer's horns, the emblem of his Lordship title, shall lodge on the arms of the Union Lords whose hands are so joined."[199]

The Chiefs' Version speaks only of joined hands: "And if any lord . . . shall break through this circle of unity, his horns shall become fastened in the circle, and if he persists after warning from the chief matron, he shall go through it without his horns and the horns shall remain in the circle."[200]

Gibson does not describe joined hands, only linked arms: "Moreover, if a chief of one of our several nations or clans, if a chief passes through the circle

---

196 Ganter 2006, 29.

197 Parker (Newhouse and Cusick) 1916, 45.

198 Gibson 1912, 462.

199 Parker (Newhouse and Cusick) 1916, 45.

200 Parker (Chiefs) 1916, 102.

Figure 11. The Chiefs Standing with Their Elbows Crooked. This wampum has been cut, with two of the figures removed. Returned to the Grand River Territory by the Royal Ontario Museum in 1999. Photograph by author, June 2019.

surrounding the crowd, his antlers will get caught where they are linking arms, and there, underneath, on the side of the encircled crowd, they will remain."[201]

This concept of joined arms in brotherhood was later used to describe the closeness or union of nations upon their joining in treaty relations with the Haudenosaunee. Perhaps the first such recorded description is the speech of Kitsaeton of the Mohawks at Three Rivers in 1645, when he described the new relationship between the Haudenosaunee, the Algonquins, and the French:

> The tenth [belt of wampum] was given to bind us all very closely together. He took hold of a Frenchman, placed his arm within his, and with his other arm he clasped that of an Algonquin. Having thus joined himself to them, "Here," he said, "is the knot that binds us inseparably; nothing can part us." This collar was extraordinarily beautiful. "Even if the lightning were to fall upon us, it could not separate us; for, if it cuts off the arm that holds you to us, we will at once seize each other by the other arm." And thereupon he turned around, and caught the Frenchman and the Algonquin by their two other arms—holding them so closely that he seemed unwilling ever to leave them.[202]

In another instance: "the Iroquois set himself to sing and dance; he took a Frenchman on one side, an Algonquin and a Huron on the other, and holding themselves all bound with his arms, they danced in cadence and sang with a strong voice a song of peace."[203]

When the proceedings of 1645 were completed, a Huron delegate declared the result: "It is done. We are brothers. The conclusion has been reached; now we are all relatives—Hiroquois, Huron, Algonquins and French; we are now but one and the same people."[204]

Linking arms together does more than recall the Kayanerenkó:wa and the circle of the rotiyanershon. It also reflects the Haudenosaunee ceremony of adoption. Today, in the Longhouse, when a person is adopted, they are walked up and down the length of the building, with their arms linked to another person on each side, while the people holding their arms sing their atonwa, and the men stamp their feet and women clap in unison,[205] in cadence, in approval

---

201 Gibson 1912, 462.

202 Jennings 1985, 141. See also Williams 1999, 53.

203 Thwaites 1901, 7:261.

204 Thwaites 1901, 7:289.

205 Since women should retain their connection with the earth, they do not stamp their feet. The Haudenosaunee do not applaud by clapping, they voice their approval.

and welcome.[206] "Of all the surviving Iroquois rites, the *Adonwa*, or Personal Chant ranks among the four most sacred. It is also pre-Columbian. When the Mohawk speaker took a Frenchman and a Huron on each arm, and marched them the length of the council space and return, to the accompaniment of his native auditors, he was dramatizing their adoption."[207]

It is not surprising that there is consistency between the linking arms in the Great Law, linking arms in a close treaty relationship, and linking arms in an adoption ceremony. They all deliver the same message: "Now we are one family. Now we are Brothers."

The Council Fire

The council fire, in historic times, burned in the centre of the council itself. The fire is not to be made from chestnut wood, because that wood crackles and throws sparks, and could distract the minds of the chiefs.[208] Since the council is held in daytime, the fire is not needed for light. In winter councils in today's longhouses, the fires in the wood stoves are necessary for heat. The fire is started well before the council begins, to warm the place and make it welcoming and comfortable. It is the responsibility of the Onondagas to start the fire and keep it going, and individual Onondaga men—not chiefs—add wood during council, both to the stove at the men's end of the longhouse and the one at the women's end. The fire, like the council, is a process, and as the Onondagas are stewards of the council, their care for the fire reflects their care for the council itself.

It is no coincidence that the root word for "family" is also the root word for "fire." In the old bark longhouses, where the central line from east to west would pass through several hearths, there would be one nuclear family on each side of each fire. They would care for and help the family on the other side of the fire in the same way the chiefs and nations would help and care for one another.

Fire is life, in the sense that it provides warmth and light. It is evidence of human presence. When the Onondagas informed the French Governor of Quebec that they were going to extirpate the military outpost at Cataraqui (present-day Kingston, Ontario), they said, "Onontiio, your fyre shall burn no more in this

---

206 See, e.g., the adoptions of F.H. Furniss and William Beauchamp, in Beauchamp (1907) 1975, 407 and 410. The same linking of arms takes place in the Longhouse today when a couple is married; they walk up and down before the people and the fire, arms linked.

207 Jennings 1985, 129.

208 Parker (Newhouse and Cusick) 1916, 31. Converse (1908, 139) says that Thadadaho's council fire was kindled from willow. Joyce King Mitchell says that willow is mentioned in the Gibson/Hewitt Creation Story as a fire whose smoke can be ascended to the Sky World by someone from that world.

place." On fundamental wampum belts, the squares depicted at each end—with the path of peace and open communication between them—are the fires of the nations depicted in friendship. Thus, when Canadian courts described the removal of Aboriginal rights as "extinguishment," they could not have chosen a more ominous word for many Indigenous nations, whose symbol of their very existence was the fire.

The Rod or Staff

Though Thadadaho had great personal power, the lawmakers gave him some emblems and implements of authority. In each case, authority came with responsibility. Just as the eagle atop the Tree of Peace was to watch for danger from afar, Thadadaho was to be vigilant against subtle dangers from within the council itself. Metaphorically, the danger was called a "creeping thing," both because of its subtle approach and because snakes were considered both danger-ous and evil, connected to the dark underground world:[209]

> He was to have a stick when he could not do it [remove the crawling thing with the stick] he was to whoop and in less than no time the chiefs [would come]. . . .[210]
>
> Then Dekanawideh said: "The lords of this confederacy have unanimously decided to lay by you this rod (Ska-nah-ka-res) and whenever you see any creeping thing which might have a tendency to harm our grandchildren or see a thing creeping toward the great white wampum belt (meaning the Great Peace), then you shall take this rod and pry it away with it, and if you and your colleagues fail to pry the creeping, evil thing out, you shall call out loudly that all

---

209   The Thunderers, protectors of the people, hated snakes and would kill them with light-ning when they could. The scales of particularly powerful snakes are part of the protec-tive medicine used by some societies.

210   Council of the Six Nations at Cattaraugus, December 1, 1862; Parker 1916, 145.

the Confederate Nations may hear and they will come immediately to your assistance."[211]

As a weapon against a crawling creature I lay a staff with you so that you may thrust it away from the Council Fire. If you fail to cast it out then call the rest of the United Lords to your aid.[212]

And if ye see any crawling creature approching toward the confederate council fire, and I now lay a stick by your side "A-do-dar-hoh" and you will take the stick and pitch the crawling creature away from the confederate council fire, and your brothers and cousin chiefs will act with you at time or times. Dust and the crawling creature signifies any case, to be brought before the confederate council fire which would be injurious to the confederate nations. And if ye will fail to reject, ye will call the rest of the confederate chiefs to aid ye.[213]

Thadadaho can call on the other chiefs for help.[214] This is one of the parts of the Great Law that vests him with the authority to call a Grand Council when

---

211 Parker (Chiefs) 1916, 98. Gibson 1899, paras. 97–98: "also we have provided a pole for you, the Great Black Pole . . . it possibly might happen that some kind of thing might crawl in and it will be unaware that only you see it; and right then you shall pick up the great black pole (the emergency pole) which you will insert beneath the creature (its body) and flick it out of the council, casting it far outside into the distance. If you cannot by yourself lift it body with the pole, then at that time shout and call your body guards among the federal chiefs (the five chiefs in his cabinet) who shall then assist you; at which time you shall all work together (co-laborate) to heave its body way outside."
  In international relations, as well, council fires are to be kept clean and clear:
  In 1698, the Mohawks met with Virginia. Before replying to the Virginians' speech, the Mohawk speaker said:
    But before we give an answer, we make the appointed House clean by giving this Fathom of Wampum [by cleaning the House, they mean putting away Hypocrisy and Deceit]. Colden (1727) 1973, 30.
  A British speaker, familiar with Haudenosaunee symbols and metaphor, stated in 1691:
    Brethren
    I am glad to see you in this house which is and hath always been the appointed place to speak with you and ought to be kept clean for the purpose. NYCD London Documents VII: 773, June 1, 1691.

212 Parker (Newhouse and Cusick) 1916, 31. In June 1755, the Haudenosaunee showed how this aspect of the Great Law had been extrapolated to relations with the British. In objection to the presence of Colonel Lydius, a participant in land frauds, one of the Oneida chiefs reminded Sir William Johnson about his home, Johnson Hall: "You promised us you would keep this place clean from all filth and that no snake should come into this Council Room. That man sitting there (pointing to Coll. Lydius) is a Devil and has stole our Lands." Wraxall (1754) 1915, cvii.

213 Newhouse 1885, 21. Is the staff also a physical symbol of power, like a mace?

214 There is also the suggestion that Thadadaho should call upon the two Seneca chiefs who are the doorkeepers to help him first.

he perceives the Confederacy is threatened—or when there is important business that must be attended to.

In June 1870, delegates from all the Haudenosaunee communities in Ontario and Quebec met at the Grand River with delegates from Ojibway communities. The purpose of this "general council" was to consider the new Canadian legislation about "Indians." Chief John Smoke Johnson said: "The position of the Confederacy of the Six Nations was the firekeeper in his proper place, the door-keeper in his proper place, and the door properly tiled, yet the fire-keeper has noticed that a great monster has crept in; he finds he cannot eject the monster or whip him alone; he calls the delegates together to assist him in ejecting the imp or monster."[215]

The crawling thing is sometimes said to be an external threat, warfare with outsiders. A close examination of the law suggests instead that it can also be internal. It is different from a confrontational disruptor: it can be subtly erosive.

The Wing

In the metaphors of the law and of council, "dust" has several meanings, all negative. The whiteness and purity of the peace must not be allowed to become stained or dirty. Dust must not be allowed to accumulate on the law: that is, the law must remain fresh and visible in people's minds, and must not be neglected. Dust swirling in the air gets in people's eyes and distracts them, and interferes with their ability to see clearly. For all these reasons, the place of council must be kept clear of dust—it is a place of purity and cleanliness, literally and symbolically. As firekeeper, this responsibility fell to Thadahaho, who was given a symbolic wing with which to take care of the area of council:

> The lords have laid before you this great wing, Ska-weh-yeh-seh-ko-wah,[216] and whenever any dust or stain of any description falls upon the great belt of white wampum, then you shall take this great wing and sweep it clean. (Dust or stain means evil of any description which might have a tendency to cause trouble in the Confederate Council.)
>
> You, Atotarho, and your thirteen cousin Lords, shall faithfully keep the space about the Council Fire clean and you shall allow neither

---

215 General Council, 1870, 7.

216 Newhouse 1885, 2: Shaweyesehko:wa Onerahóntsha, great seagull wing.

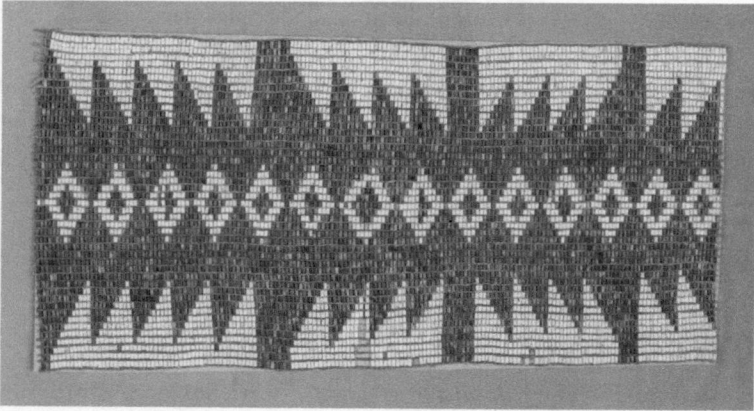

Figure 12. The Thadadaho Belt, also known as the Wing or Dust Fan of the Confederacy. Returned to Onondaga by the New York State Museum, 1989.

dust nor dirt to accumulate. I lay a Long Wing before you as a broom.[217]

. . . will allow no dust or dirt to be seen, around the council fire, and if there is any dust or dirt to be seen. I now lay it a sea gull wing by your side "A-do-dar-hoh." And you will take the wing and sweep the dust away from the confederate council fire. [218]

Dust or darkness can also mean violent disagreement: "and if the place where it is situated gets dark, then he shall pick up the Great Black Wing, the Great Chief, sweeping the place where it is spread out, which means that if the argument becomes too intense—causing minds to spoil—then he shall stop it at once."[219]

The symbol of the wing is one of the great wampums of the Haudenosaunee, the "Wing or Dust Fan" belt.[220] Though the law contemplates great tolerance, and sees the need to take time to find consensus, nevertheless "spoiled" minds have to be removed, rather than allow their disruptions to injure the great goodness.

No Council after Dark

*[And ye will] close the council before darkness sets in, for
ye will not council after dark.*[221]

If the people bringing their minds together are to work as well as possible, then they must guard against fatigue, because tired minds think more slowly and are quicker to anger. At sundown, the council is closed (the fire is covered). This does not mean an end to all business: often the participants will meet separately that evening to talk over the day's events. Perhaps there will be "talking in the bushes," informal discussions between the parties to the council. The basic principle, though, is that no decisions can be made after dark. Council resumes when people can see one another clearly and when their minds are rested: "and

---

217 Parker (Newhouse and Cusick), 1916, 31.

218 Newhouse 1885, 21.

219 Gibson 1912, 434. Though some versions describe the Wing as a gull's wing, with the whiteness of pure intentions, Gibson's black wing stands in contrast to the Great White Mat that it is intended to sweep clean.

220 A similar concern that the "Covenant House must be kept clean" appears in treaty councils with the British. See Colden (1727) 1973, 37.

221 Newhouse 1885, 22.

if the place where [the Council] is situated gets dark, then he shall pick up the Great Black Wing, the Great Chief [Thadadaho], sweeping the place where it is spread out [the Great White Mat], which means that if the argument becomes too intense, causing minds to spoil, then he shall stop it at once."[222]

If the light is the Creator's time, the night belongs to his brother. As light is life, so darkness is death and depression, but it is also rest and regeneration. To continue council into the night would be to invite the influence of the dark side, but also to interfere with the balance between work and rest.

The Birds in the Branches

One problem with a culture that passes on its knowledge by word of mouth is gossip. It is a problem that the Peacemaker was aware of and that persists to this day. Nor is it something the Peacemaker felt he could do away with. Instead, the law admonishes the chiefs in council to pay no attention to it. They are told not to listen to the birds twittering in the branches overhead.[223]

In July 1764, Sir William Johnson was able to use the same metaphor in his peacemaking with the Haudenosaunee and the Western nations at Niagara: "All that is wanting on your parts to attain this, is that you never more listen to Stories told you by People who have nothing to do with the Management of Indian Affairs, that you shut your ears against all bad Birds, and be no longer deluded by their Whistling."[224]

In 1799, rumours spread by New York State officials through Atiatoharongwen Louis Cook alleged that Thayendenega Joseph Brant and Odeserundiye John Deserontyon had sold to New York all the land claimed by the Seven Nations of Canada in that state.[225] A council in Kahnawake between the Haudenosaunee and the Seven Nations of Canada set matters straight. The Kahnawake speaker

---

222 Gibson 1912, 56.

223 The irony of the role of Twitter, the micro-message social medium of the Trump presidency, is not lost on Haudenosaunee constitutional scholars.

224 SWJP 11:280.

225 The accusations against Brant maintain hard feelings against him to this day among the eastern Mohawk communities. Brant maintained that he and Deserontyon had received compensation only for the lands they claimed, up to the boundary between the Mohawks of the Mohawk Valley and those of the Seven Nations of Canada, an east-west line drawn through a place on Lake Champlain. They had received fifteen hundred dollars, and felt shortchanged. The suggestion that Brant and Deserontyon had sold all the land allowed New York to reduce the offer it made to the Seven Nations, because Louis Cook believed the New York representatives—he had fought for the United States in the Revolutionary War.

said: "Brothers: On every turn along the road there is birds telling stories, our ancestors ordered that such things should not be listened to, but be cast behind our backs, let us Brethren do as our Forefathers commanded."[226]

Why birds? Because birds, like rumours, fly quickly, lack substance, and lack much brain.

The deliberate removal of distractions from council is part of the Peacemaker's strategy: people are not going to listen to one another, and not going to focus on the issues at hand, if they carry the burdens of grief and sorrow; if they carry anger; or if their attention is diluted by outside influences. Building a fire of quiet hardwood is a message about concentration rather than distraction. Paying no attention to the little birds constitutes recognition that there will be other voices in the chiefs' ears. The chiefs' thick skins prevent personal barbs from penetrating their thinking. Every step is aimed at promoting civil civic engagement and helpful, focussed thinking.

Considering the Coming Seven Generations

In weighing any decision, the rotiyanershon are instructed to consider the effects of their choices on the seven generations downstream from them. This long view is one of the arguments in favour of the stability of Haudenosaunee governments: men with a life term in office will be able to more confidently consider future generations, whereas leaders with a short election horizon will tend to be more eager to satisfy the short-term appetites and concerns of the voters:

> How shall we do that our chil[dren] shall have many days. Therefore you consider carefully in regard to this matter.[227]

> . . . they must have a regard . . . also for those children whom we have not yet seen. . . .[228]

> We must look to see how it's going to affect those future generations. How are we protecting? How are we safeguarding? You have to protect those future people. They don't have anyone else to protect them. When they stand there maybe sixty or a hundred years from now in a society which may be very hostile, when they stand there looking for a house or looking for a place to live, they are going to

---

226 Michigan Pioneer and Historical Society, vol. XX, 643–48.

227 Minutes of Council of the Six Nations at Cattaraugus, December 1, 1862 (Parker 1916, 148).

228 Hale (1883) 1989, 170.

look back at this time and say "Who was that who gave away my
land?" Everyone here will be gone but the names will be there.[229]

Why seven generations?[230] Even the oldest and most productive among us can
know and see only our great-grandchildren—four generations. We may know
the people who came before us, as well. Looking forward, looking back, our
perspective may span seven generations. But to consider unto the seventh generation is really to say that our thoughts must go beyond our physical capacity
to see; they must go downstream and around the bend in the river. It is not an
unreasonable period of time—but it is time beyond what we can see around us.

Life Terms

*Once they have antlers on [ka-wyen-eta-ih = completed
task] the length of time a man will hold the title is as long
as he lives here on earth and only death will remove it
from him.*[231]

It is often said that the best person to appoint as a chief is the one who does not
seek the title. Ambition is not a factor in the functioning of the Kayanerenkó:wa,
neither for individuals nor for parties. In Parliament or in Congress, the governing party introduces legislation to find it immediately opposed and tested by
parties whose ambition is to either defeat the government in the House, or to
replace the government in the next election. In Haudenosaunee lawmaking, the
people on the other side of the fire cannot seek to replace anyone, for they have
no influence over who is chosen (other than to potentially reject a candidate in
a Condolence), and there are no elections. The incentive to oppose the government is removed, and instead all the chiefs are part of the same government, and
their obligation, instinct, and tone are directed towards helping one another.

Having no elections—having leaders who need not seek periodic approval
from people whose self-interest is bound to be short-term—means that the
chiefs in council can consider the far horizon and the welfare of the coming

---

229 Joagquisho Oren Lyons 1982, v; speaking to lawyers: "When you talk about client rela-
     tionships, you are talking about the future of nations."

230 There have been attempts to analyze this scientifically—to try to state the length of a
     generation in the fifteenth century, and to multiply that by seven to set a fixed horizon.
     But this analysis misses the point. The point is that we must cast our minds to the com-
     ing faces, the ones that we cannot see, the ones we will never see.

231 Gibson 1912, 421.

seven generations. Elected politicians must always keep an eye on the next election, and their actions and decisions are often influenced by that election well in advance.

Head Chiefs?

Almost any written version of the Great Law will leave the reader with the impression that some chiefs are more important than others. Secondary sources carry this to another level: they ascribe executive authority to some of the chiefs, stating that Thadadaho became the "president" of the Confederacy; or that Tekarihoken was the "head chief" of the Mohawks. Morgan ascribes to Europeans a need to identify chief executives: "Thadadahoh was early seized upon by the inquisitive colonists to advance the person who held that title to the position of King of the Iroquois, but the misconception was refuted, and the institutions of the Iroquois were relieved of the burden of an impossible feature. In the general council he sat among his equals. The Confederacy had no chief magistrate."[232]

In any written version, there are words that suggest the primacy of some chiefs. Newhouse refers to the councils of nations as "Tekarihoken and his brother chiefs; Deskahe and his brother chiefs." Is this because they were named first by the Peacemaker, or do they have special functions and responsibilities? Today, messages to nations are passed through these particular individuals. Sometimes, they are the holders of their nations' fires.

They are: Tekarihoken for the Mohawks; Odatsehte for the Oneidas; Thadadaho for the Onondagas; Deskahe for the Cayugas; and Kanuhkitawi for the Senecas.

But did they have any form of executive authority? In the Thanksgiving, there is also hierarchy. The maple is head or chief of the trees;[233] the deer for the animals; the strawberry for the berries that crawl close to the earth; the raspberry for the bush berries; the eagle for the birds; the bee for the insects. The "leaders" of the animals are reflections of the rotiyanershon: they are more like speakers for their kind than like executives.[234]

---

232 Morgan 1877, 145.

233 Porter 1986, 11.

234 The hierarchy may be recent, even more recent than the layered Thanksgiving itself.

Specific Chiefs Have Specific Duties

Some of the chiefs have specific duties with respect to the process of the council or the maintenance of the law. Thadadaho's responsibility and authority was given to him as part of his pacification. The two Seneca doorkeepers were given the power to admit or reject visitors as part of what amounted to the transformation and pacification of the warriors. There are strong suggestions that each of the fifty lords has a specific bundle of responsibilities, though none of the written versions of the law mentions many of these. Individual chiefs can explain their particular understandings of their functions, passed down through oral tradition. Sometimes those functions are suggested by their title names. It is hard to tell, today, to what extent these personal functions are indeed part of the law and which have become added over the course of the past few centuries. **Hononwirehton** of the Onondaga Deer Clan is represented in the Circle Wampum by a string that is longer than the others. This is because (according to Shimony[235]) he has the deciding vote among the Onondagas, and thus in any decisions of the League:

> Honuwiyehti . . . he who is alone, he having two father's kinsmen [uncles on father's side] and two clans [according to Fenton] he of the Great Wolf Clan— everyone depends on him.[236]

> [The wampum belts of the Onondagas] are deposited as public records . . . and are held in safe-keeping by the guardianship sachem, Hononwenhto, the hereditary "keeper of wampum" whose office as expounder of the law, is to "read" or "talk" the wampum at all the councils.[237]

> All these national compacts were "talked into" strings of wampum, to use the Indian expression, after which these were delivered into the custody of *Ho-no-we-na-to*, the Onondaga sachem, who was made hereditary keeper of the wampum, at the institution of the League,

---

235 Shimony 1961, 110.

236 Gibson 1912, 427. Morgan ([1871] 1997, 143) states that Hononwirehto has two "aids" or sub-chiefs who were "required to be versed" in the interpretation of the wampums.

237 Converse 1908, 140. At the Grand River Territory, for the last half of the nineteenth century, Skanawati John Buck was the keeper of the wampums.

and from him and his successors, was to be sought their interpretation from generation to generation.[238]

It is his duty, as well, to bring the mind of the council back to the single matter that it is to focus upon at one time. He can do this by tapping the bench that the "fire" is resting on, with his cane.

Kanuhkitawi of the Snipe Clan of the Senecas had been a "Great Warrior." Once the League was formed, he and his "deputy" (in Skaniatariio's version, the translation is more accurately "body-guard") Deyoninhokarawen of the Wolf Clan, also formerly a great warrior, became the Keepers of the Western Door.[239] It became their duty, when a group of people approached with a message, following the Great White Roots, to decide whether to grant them access to council ("on the main bench where is spread the Great White Mat"), or to put them to death (in "the place where the elm bark is spread out and shove them inside the house where bones will come to pile up").

Deskahe of the Older Bear Clan of the Cayugas. During the making of the law, it is said that he deliberately stood off to the side. His name comes from the time the Peacemaker asked him how many families were with him, and he replied: "More than eleven."

Tekarihoken identifies consensus among the Mohawks. His clan is the old snapping turtle.[240]

Tehatkodons ("He is two-sighted," or "He looks both ways") sits at Thadadaho's left hand. He carries a special admonition to consider both sides of any question, and to urge consideration of alternatives. He is a "special aid and counsellor to Thadadaho." He is Beaver Clan.[241]

Enneserarenh is the other "special aid and counsellor to Thadadaho."

Skanawati, also, must carefully consider both sides of any issue.

Tehatkarine is a "watcher of the land." In conversations on the Mohawk bench, it is his duty to consider the impact of decisions on the land and environment, and to remind his fellow chiefs of that effect.

---

238 Morgan (1851) 1995, 336–37.

239 Gibson 1912, 315–18.

240 According to Teyawentathe Susan Hill, personal communication, 2010.

241 Hale (1883) 1989, 157. Modern holders of the title consider it their duty to think especially carefully about both sides of an issue: Dehatkodons (Irving Powless Jr.) and Dehatkodons (Arnold General).

When a Chief Dies

When a chief dies, the family meets immediately to begin the funeral process.

Within ten days,[242] the chiefs come together to perform the ceremony known as the "Small Condolence," at the house of the deceased chief (but in the absence of his body).[243] The chiefs sit in the living room, these days, on two sets of chairs, facing each other. The speaker for the clear-minded side delivers the first twelve parts or words of the Condolence, which are carried across the room by the "runner" and delivered to his opposite number. Each string is then strung across a cane that is lying across two chairs beside the speaker, for those whose minds are cast down, the grieving ones. This cane is today's equivalent of the pole van den Bogaert saw in the council house at Onondaga in 1638, and that pole is a direct descendant of the horizontal stick on which Hiawatha was stringing the first wampum, in his efforts to condole himself.

The chiefs, as brothers to the deceased chief, are not only responsible for condoling his family: they have their own role to play in part of the funeral. Their encircling the grave during the burial recalls the Circle Wampum; their three shovels of earth into the grave recall the three breaths that the Creator blows into people to give them life.

> After the body had been deposited in the grave the sachems and chiefs formed a circle around it for the purpose of filling it with earth. Each in turn, commencing with the senior in years, cast in three shovelfuls, a typical number in their religious system; of which the first had relation to the Great Spirit, the second to the Sun, and the third to Mother Earth. When the grave was filled the senior sachem, by a figure of speech, deposited the "horns" of the departed sachem, emblematical of his office, upon the top of the grave over his head, there to remain until his successor was installed.[244]

---

242   "It was a journey of ten days from earth to heaven for the departed spirit. . . . For ten days after the death of a departed person, mourners meet nightly to lament the deceased. . . . The dirge or wail was performed by women. It was an ancient custom to make a fire on the grave each night for the same period. On the eleventh day they held a feast; the spirit of the departed having reached heaven, the place of rest, there was no further cause for mourning. With the feast it terminated." Morgan (1871) 1997, 96.

243   Skaniatariio John Arthur Gibson text of this transcribed by J.N.B. Hewitt, in National Anthropological Archives (NAA), ms. 612 (21 pages).

244   Morgan (1871) 1997, 96.

At the Small Condolence, the grieving people sometimes announce, and install for the time being, some people to fill the seats[245] of the one who has died and the cluster of people who are with him.

The ten days following the death of any person are said to be the time when the person's spirit can remain on earth. The family is busy with many funeral duties, feasts, and songs, culminating in the Ten-Day Feast, in which all the mourners come together and the songs go all night long. One aspect of the thinking behind the funeral process is "letting go," convincing the spirit of the dead person that his family does not cling to his memory so tightly or miss him so much that he should stay around and postpone his trip along the strawberry-lined path, the Milky Way to the Creator's world. For the ten days following the death of a royá:ner, council cannot be held.[246]

When a relative of a title holder's family dies, in some communities, all political business is suspended for ten days. In some places, a Small Condolence[247] is held for the family. If the dead person held a function, the clan mother can announce the successor. This announcement—there is no succession ceremony—can be done at the Small Condolence, the Ten-Day Feast (at the end of the official mourning period), or at any Condolence for installing a chief.

There is no complete agreement on when things must happen: it is suggested that the clan mother should be ready within three days to name a successor, so that the announcement can be made at the Ten-Day Feast. However, the person so appointed must wait until the "other side of the fire" agrees to a time for a Condolence ceremony. The principle is that the family should always have a voice in council, though its permanent representative should be installed only after its minds have been cleared and raised up again:

> When it has become vacated, his chiefly space, thereupon the deaconesses [yeya:kweniyo = "body be most important"], the ones from the clans and the families, they are the ones who will repossess it [*grasp – hold*], they will decide, choosing again a new one to receive the antlers, and this new one will replace him, the one who has now passed back [*through again*], this one they shall rename with the title name, which she shall again give to the new one, conferring antlers

---

245 Colloquially, an uncondoled chief is called a "benchwarmer." In council, he sits in the place of that chief, but his influence is reduced by his informal status. His family has placed him there until they can name a permanent replacement for the deceased chief. Some families decide to honour the deceased by holding his seat completely vacant for a year.

246 Newhouse 1885, 22.

247 The Small Condolence, which uses all the wampums other than the ones used to raise up a chief, takes place in the home, and is aimed at raising up again the minds of the immediate family. This ceremony is not mentioned in any of the versions of the Great Law.

on him and seating him in the place that had become empty, for they shall always be occupied, the places where the chiefs are seated.[248]

The order of a discussion about a successor to the dead title holder follows a clear progression, from the immediate family, clan, and nation to the brother nations and then the entire Confederacy: "Hence at every occasion of filling vacancies, the character and merits of all the officers in the series and of all candidates, were liable to be passed upon: first, in the discussion of the families interested; secondly, in the convocation of the clans to which they belong; thirdly, in the meeting of the four clans, which occupied respectively the two ends of the council house; fourthly, by the assembled council of the particular nation; and fifthly, [by the] council at the Longhouse of the Six Nations."[249]

The clan mother can unilaterally name a candidate: the discussion about whether this person should become the permanent representative for the family then takes place among the women.[250] The discussion then moves to other members of the family and the nation, beyond the immediate family and the clan. Once the nation has agreed upon a candidate, it meets with the other nation or nations on its side of the fire: the Oneidas with the Cayugas; the Mohawks with the Senecas and Onondagas. In theory, the "other side of the fire" does not know who the candidate is until he is put forward in the Condolence itself.[251] Literally, a sheet is hung in the council house, so that the people on one side of the fire do not see the candidate until he is formally announced and put forward and the sheet is pulled aside. At the time of the Condolence of a chief, the clan mother can replace the entire cluster of people around him—sub-chief and faithkeepers.

There have been instances of very young men being raised up as rotiyanershon, and in those cases they also had mentors appointed to work with them, to help them. The following explanation of this process to Sir William Johnson in the 1750s also shows another phenomenon—that sometimes it was difficult to bring the nations together to install new Confederacy chiefs, so that the vacancies would accumulate, and then a group would be filled at one time. The original intention of the Kayanerenkó:wa was to have an empty seat filled at once, so that the family would not lose its voice in council, and so that the people's minds would not be burdened with a sense of absence.

---

248 Gibson 1912, 423.

249 Wright 1859, 310.

250 There are differences between versions of the law as to whether the clan mothers are to consult together or only work with their own families.

251 There have been cases in which a nation on one's side of the fire refuses to put a name across—saying that it wants to spare its brothers the humiliation of rejection.

Figure 13. The Women's Nominating Belt. Symbol of the authority of the women to select the rotiyanershon. From *Wampum Belts of the Iroquois*, by Tehanetorens Ray Fadden. Used with permission of Six Nations Indian Museum, Onchiota, New York.

Raising up very young men as rotiyanershon suggests another problem, perhaps specific to Onondaga at the time, but one that has persisted: some families may have dwindled to the point where they had very few candidates:[252]

> Then the Speaker Teyawarunte Spoke as follows:
>
> Brother before the General Meeting takes place we have Judged it proper to desire this Meeting with you in order to present to You those Young Men whom we appointed Sachims to assist us in our Councils as our Sachims are now too few to manage Matters properly, our place being ye proper Council fire for all the surrounding nations our Allies & Dependents them presented to Sir William Seven Young Men, whose names are as follows, viz't:

> Snipe: Amadagia, Bunt's Son   Beaver: Onessarakung

> Eel: Sagagare   Eel: Oyumanis
> Deer: Wahagheirong   Wolf: Ononwisaghti
> Turtle: Owigaiat   Turtle: Tawanasaroonda
> Turtle: Tayiatquari   Bear: Wathatodarho
> Turtle: Tawaskughta   Turtle: Tughhaghsi

> Deiaquande takes ye care of one of ye new made Sachims, Gingiaquasunt, & Kaghniagarodo also assist in ye same. Oroondisaghti an Old Man takes care of another of ye Young Sachims—Saristageghte, & Geghtahare two old Men take care of two of the Young Sachims, Inayenqueraghto takes charge of another of the Young Sachims— Brother having now finished so far, we have only to wish that these new Sachims now appointed may act agreable to the Rules laid down to us by our Ancestors, & follow what is good & agreable to our Brethren the English which would give us ye utmost pleasure. Brother as You are sensible of the trouble & great hardships We the few Sachims now present, have had since ye trouble began, we hope you will consider it in a proper light.[253]

Twelve young men are named, with seven older men "taking care" of them. What would "taking care" mean? That they were mentors and advisers? Or that

---

252 In 1750, about half the Onondagas were living at Oswegatchie, on the St. Lawrence River. It would seem that most of the Deer and Snipe clan people had moved there (and from there, by 1807, to Akwesasne). That would leave some families at Onondaga with few candidates for the vacant seats.

253 SWJP 11:709. While the Haudenosaunee are not asking Johnson for his consent to the putting up of these young men, they are presenting them across the council fire in a way that resembles some aspects of the Condolence ceremony.

they were more like regents, veterans from families who were not eligible to become sachems themselves, but who could wield power through their advisory positions? When would the young men emerge from the tutelage? Whether there were seven or twelve of these young sachems, the Onondagas had probably effectively doubled the size of their council (the law provides for fourteen Onondaga chiefs).

Condolence

The ceremony of Condolence to console a grieving family and raise up a new chief brings all the traditional Haudenosaunee together, even today. The ceremony is held at the community of the bereaved, so that all the downcast people can attend, and be heartened by the arrival of their clear-minded brothers and sisters.

Re-enacting the trip from Oneida to Onondaga undertaken by the Peacemaker and all the chiefs, to confront and heal Thadadaho, the condolers walk in a long line, generally two by two, led by a man known as the Great Hanging Tobacco Pouch (as the warriors were sometimes referred to as "Tobacco Pouches"), who also leads the singing. They sing the same song that the Peacemaker taught the people—"Along the Way"—to announce themselves. Today, the journey takes less than half an hour for the hundreds of visitors.

Today's Condolence procession re-enacts how the warriors would escort the chiefs from village to village, through the dangerous forest. In those days, the peace was internal, between the nations: it was not protection from external enemies. The escort stops at the woods' edge: the grieving people take over responsibility for their guests' safety once the condolers reach the village clearing. At the woods' edge, by the thorny brush, they welcome them. There is a real role for the warriors in the Condolence and therefore in the maintenance and renewal of the League. In historical reality, it is based in true need for protection and safety. Today's song leaders and escorts recall a pragmatic need for the warriors.

Today's Condolence ceremony fulfills a triple purpose of recall. First, it recalls the Peacemaker's raising up of Hiawatha's grieving mind—the use of the wampum strings re-enacts that first Condolence. Second, it evokes the transformation of Thadadaho—the use of the Six Songs does that. Third, it calls to mind the whole process of formation of the Great Peace, and the unity of the leaders—the "roll call" of the chiefs does that. Though the ceremony is seen by outsiders as the way to raise up and confirm new chiefs, and by insiders as that and as a means of expressing respect and consolation, it is also both a renewal of the Confederacy and a reminder to the people of the events that formed it.

The Condolence ceremony takes most of a day. People come from every community of the Confederacy to take part, to confirm and welcome the new leaders. The financial responsibility of the Condolence falls upon the family putting up the new chief, and it is not light. The visitors must not only be fed but feasted. Pipes must be made for all the chiefs. Sometimes, when there is more than one vacancy to be filled in a nation, two or more families will share the cost, and often the nation will contribute.

Unlike other rotiyanershon, Thadadaho is chosen not by a clan mother but by the Onondaga chiefs, and his confirmation comes not from the Younger Brothers but rather from all the chiefs of the Six Nations together.[254]

Removing a Chief

The primary authority to remove a chief has been said to rest with his clan, through his clan mother, if the chief is straying from his duties. That is, the people whom he represents and who selected him first ought to be the people with the first right to remove him. The process involves three formal warnings, each more stiff than its predecessor. The first comes from the clan mother's assistant or faithkeeper. The second comes from the clan mother herself. The third comes from the "Great Warrior," the young man without a title who assists the clan mother, or the chief's sub-chief, and it includes the removal of the chief—by removing his "horns." Sometimes the person carrying out this final task is called "The Man Without Pity."

"But if any should refuse to come back by three time, they should take them off."[255] Several parts of the Great Law involve three warnings or statements. They are, in a way, a means of remembering that the Creator blew three times into the mouth of the first man, to give him life.[256] Skaniatariio John Arthur Gibson describes how a chasm in the earth yawns open for the family if their chief disregards the second warning:

---

254 Wall 2001, 5. More recently, there has been insistence that Thadadaho must be chosen from the Eel Clan lineage.

255 Minutes of Council of the Six Nations at Cattaraugus, December 1, 1862 (Parker 1916, 145).

256 Sakokwenionkwas Tom Porter told me this. For the same reason, at the end of a sacred song, one calls out three times—"yo-ho-oooh." The three can also signify the Sun, the Earth, and the Great Spirit.

Then again, there is another matter: "You, my uncle and your two nepotic relatives should continue to listen to one another for, actually, it is a serious matter if it happens thus, that you leave your path from where it ought to lead you, you chief. If this happens, she will look at you, your niece, for, actually, it is a fact that he has given her wisdom. This one, you will notice with surprise, standing in front of you, she will speak up, saying, 'It is an amazing matter, my uncle, you who are chief, now you are straying from your path and you are not consulting with your colleagues; over there the people are left standing while you are alone, and now you are straying from your path; so I will ask you to return to your path, my uncle, you who are chief,'" and that is how she will do it, she will warn you and it is a dreadful thing to disregard her warning.

And this man, your nephew, he will see you, you who are chief, willingly working towards the extinction of the people. Thereupon you will notice with surprise that he is standing there in front of you; then he will speak up, saying, "My uncle, you who are chief, it is an amazing thing that you are working towards the extinction of the entire group, for you are the one who is alone, you are not consulting them or working together with them for the Great Law. Moreover, I ask you to return to your path, for it is your responsibility towards your colleagues." Thereupon he will turn back, for it is a dreadful thing if he once more disregards the warning, for then it will be there, over the earth's edge, that all of the people will come to hang their feet. As to that, no one is able to lift them up when it happens in this way, except just this one is able to lift them up, our Father, our Creator, our Ruler.

Moreover, when they see you—your nephew and niece—doing the same thing despite both of them having warned you to your face, you who are chief, they trying to cause you to return to your path, and you not having obeyed, thereupon they will summon the Great Warrior; they will all meet and you will notice them with surprise, standing up in front of you, he speaking up, the Great Warrior, saying, "it is amazing, my uncle, you who are chief, indeed you have not accepted their warning which was spoken by both the woman and the man, indeed, you have not accepted it. So now I am removing your antlers and hand them back to her, the deaconess of the title name. Moreover, you are free now and cannot wear antlers again; now you are an ordinary person. Now, moreover, you can go away, wherever you wish to go. Thereupon the people, the number of your followers, now they will notice that you no longer are wearing your antlers, and then they will let go of you."[257]

The version published by Tahawannontye Duncan C. Scott provides for three warnings as well, but the order is different: first the clan mother, then a warrior of the chief's clan, then the Great Warrior:

> If a Lord is guilty of unwarrantably opposing the object of the decisions of the Council and in that way showing disrespect for his brother Lords by urging that his own erroneous will in these matters be carried out, he shall be approached and admonished by the Chief Matron of his family and Clan to desist from such evil practices and urged to come back and act in harmony with his brother Lords.
>
> If the Lord refuses to comply with the request of the Chief Matron of his family and Clan and still persists in his evil practices of unwarrantably opposing his brother Lords, then a Warrior of his family and clan will also approach him and admonish him to desist from pursuing his evil course.
>
> If the Lord still refuses to listen and obey, then the Chief Matron and Warrior shall go together to the Chief Warrior and they inform him that they have admonished their Lord and he refused to obey. Then the Chief Warrior will arise and go there to the Lord and will say to him: Your nephew and niece have admonished you to desist from your evil course, and you have refused to obey. Then the Chief Warrior will say, I will now admonish you for the last time and if you continue to resist to accede to and obey this request, then your duties as Lord of our family and Clan will cease, and I shall take the deer's horns from off your head, and with a broad-edged stone axe I shall cut the tree down, (meaning that he shall be deposed from his position as Lord or Chief of the Confederacy). Then the Chief Warrior shall hand back the deer's horns (the emblem of power) of the deposed Lord to the Chief Matron of his family or Clan.[258]

Seth Newhouse's version provides a much shorter, though consistent, description of the removal of a chief:

> Article XXX
>
> We now finished all crowned ourselves with deer horns on our heads. We do now give this Honourable Noble and Sacred Titles and the

---

257 Gibson 1912, 672–78. "Let go of you," in this context, can also mean "throw you away, cast you off."

258 Parker (Chiefs) 1916, 106–7.

Soil, to our Mothers the Females. They shall be the Proprietors.
And if they see their Lords are gone out of the right course, and are
not counciling for the interests of the people in general, then the
females the relatives of the erroneous or erroneousness Lord shall
come, before their Council to warn him, to return again and council
for the interest of the people in general. Three times. If he disregard
their warnings on the third time. They will discharge him. They will
then notify the rest of the Lords of their own Nation, will sanction
it. The Females then will select another one, out of the number of
their sons, to fill the place of the expelled Lord, and will notify the
rest of the Lords of their select to be their future Lord, and their
Lords will only sanction it.[259]

The system of repeated and escalating warnings is consistent with the basic
assumption in the law that people are capable of reform—that they will take the
opportunity offered to them to return to the good path. Just as the Cannibal
and Thadadaho were brought back to the good mind, so an errant chief, with
these warnings, is given the chance to return to his proper ways.

The three attempts made by the Peacemaker to bring Thadadaho to accept
the Good Message may be a precursor of the three warnings—or opportunities—offered to a chief by his family.

The Haudenosaunee also offer other nations three formal opportunities to
come within the Great Peace. Refusal for a third time can be a signal for war.
In 1753, the Haudenosaunee gave the French three warnings to leave the Ohio
country because, as Scarooyady explained, "the great Being who lives above,
has ordered us to send Three Messages of Peace before we make War, and as
the Half King had before this time delivered the third and last Message, we had
nothing now to do but to strike the French."[260]

In certain circumstances, a chief can be removed immediately by the other
chiefs—for murder, rape, or theft: Gibson's 1912 version states:

Moreover, this is what I now decree concerning you chiefs: who-
ever of you irresponsibly sins by killing a person—if this is how he
performs his tasks, the chief—then his duties will get revoked, for
one will remove his antlers without adjudication;[261] the deaconess will take back the title, for it is in her power to appoint a new
man—replacing the offender by bestowing the antlers on the new
man—who will sit in the place of the one she removed, the former

---

259 Newhouse 1885, 103.

260 Beauchamp 1905, 299.

261 In cases of murder by a chief, it is the council that takes jurisdiction. Hale (1883) 1989,
     69.

chief; and now that it is finished, as to the former chief, it is the warriors that he rejoins. It is impossible for this same person ever to carry out chiefly duties again, and it will happen in the same way if a chief forces women; it will happen in the same way in that without adjudication they will at once remove him and take his antlers from him, returning to the deaconess the title and at once she will appoint another, a new man, bestowing antlers on him, and this one will sit where he used to be seated, the one whose antlers they took back; he rejoins the warriors, and then it can never happen again, his holding a chiefly status. And if a chief steals something, then the chiefs will deliberate with care concerning him, proving whatever is the truth, and if he was responsible, then, at the council of chiefs, they will judge his case, the chief's, they will find he is responsible.[262] Thereupon they will reach a decision to take his antlers from him, and these they will hand back to the deaconess with the title. Thereupon they will let him go again, the title will become vacated, and he will become a warrior again, it being impossible for him to assume chiefly duties again. Thereupon the matron will appoint another one, a new person, whom she will bestow antlers upon, and this is who will become chief. Thereupon he will sit in the seat, replacing the former chief.[263]

The Chiefs' Version states:

> If a lord is found guilty of wilful murder, he shall be deposed without the warning (as shall be provided for later on) by the lords of the confederacy, and his horns (emblem of power) shall be handed back to the chief matron of his family and clan.

> If a lord is guilty of rape, he shall be deposed without the usual warning by the lords of the confederacy, and his horns (the emblem of power) shall be handed back to the chief matron of his family and clan.

> If a lord is found guilty of theft, he shall be deposed without the usual warning by the lords of the confederacy, and his horns (the

---

262 While the English translation was "finding him guilty," the more literal translation is more accurate: there is no concept of "guilty" in Haudenosaunee law—either a person is responsible for an act or he is not. When I was a courtworker in 1971, one of my most difficult tasks was to convince an accused person that pleading guilty or not guilty was an issue of the prosecution's ability to prove the case, not of "did I do it."

263 Gibson 1912, 450–55.

emblem of power) shall be handed back to the chief matron of his family and clan.[264]

Newhouse, in his 1885 version, goes further: not only does the chief lose his title; so, too, does his family: it "forever forfeits the proprietorship of the title to the said Lordship to the other Lords of the Nation who shall transfer the proprietorship of the title of the aforesaid Lordship to a sister ahwatchira."[265]

Morgan asserts that "the council of the tribe also had the power to depose both sachems and chiefs without waiting for the action of a gens, and even against its wishes."[266]

Immediate removal of an offender prevents his continued presence from causing hard feelings or disunity. While the three warnings from a family may take days or weeks, a removal by the council—which would require a degree of unanimity—is, in effect, the removal of a kind of "crawling thing."

A removed chief is said to have been "dehorned." His wampum "horns" are taken away from him, to be placed with his successor. Generally, a dehorned chief leaves the community, in some disgrace. His ability to hold any office is finished. His reputation is shattered:[267] "it shall be that when a lord is deposed and the deer's horns . . . are taken from him, he shall no longer be allowed to sit in council or even hold an office again."[268]

Elaborate as the process for removing chiefs has been, there is no agreed-upon procedure for removing a clan mother. There have been instances where individual chiefs have claimed to remove clan mothers, and others in which the chiefs of a nation have removed clan mothers. In the case of a deep disagreement between a chief and clan mother, the family generally seeks to reconcile them, though it has happened that the clash can split the family itself. Once again, detailed provision in the law for the removal of a chief, and a lack of provision with respect to clan mothers, suggests that the position of royá:ner was created

---

264 Parker (Chiefs) 1916, 106. Jurisdiction over these three crimes is said to have been given by treaty to the British (see Noon 1949), but the only primary documentary evidence of this is the treaty in July 1764, in which the Geneseo Senecas agreed to hand over those guilty of robbery or murder "where the victims are white." Since the version of the law that mentions these crimes as a reason for removal is a Grand River version, it is possible that the thinking was that being placed under the jurisdiction of a Crown court would amount to "stepping outside the circle." It is equally possible, though, that these crimes were originally viewed as unthinkable and unacceptable conduct for a Confederacy Chief.

265 Newhouse 1885, 65.

266 Morgan 1877, 74.

267 There have been cases during the past twenty years when a chief who has been dehorned has maintained that the action was unfair or invalid, and has continued to come to council. This has caused consternation, since the good-mindedness of the council is disrupted, but the chiefs are reluctant to physically eject the man.

268 Parker (Chiefs) 1916, 107.

by the Kayanerenkó:wa, which could therefore also create the processes for appointment and removal, while the position of clan mother antedated the making of the law, so that the law left already known processes unchanged (and unexplained).

In modern times, chiefs have been dehorned for various infractions. These have generally involved doing things without the knowledge or sanction of the council, failure to perform obligations or attend council, submission to foreign governments, failure to account financially, disruption of council, and the commission of criminal offences.

The Right of Revolution

Alone among the versions of the Kayanerenkó:wa, Seth Newhouse's later tracts provide that the people have the right to remove—and kill—the chiefs as a body in certain circumstances. These versions appeared after the chiefs refused to support Newhouse's complaint against the doctor he alleged had contributed to his daughter's death, so they may reflect his growing animosity towards the council.

> This string of wampum vests the people with the right to correct their erring Lords. In case a part or all the Lords pursue a course not vouched for by the people and heed not the third warning of their women relatives, then the matter shall be taken to the General Council of the women of the Five Nations. If the Lords notified and warned three times fail to heed, then the case falls into the hands of the men of the Five Nations. The War Chiefs shall then, by right of such power and authority, enter the open council to warn the Lord or Lords to return from their wrong course. If the Lords heed the warning they will say: "we will reply tomorrow." If then an answer is returned in favour of justice and in accord with this Great Law, then the Lords shall individually pledge themselves again by again furnishing the necessary shells for the pledge. Then shall the War Chief or Chiefs exhort the Lords urging them to be just and true.

> Should it happen that the Lords refuse to heed the third warning, then two courses are open: either the men may decide in their council to depose the Lord or Lords or to club them to death with war clubs. Should they in their council decide to take the first course the War Chief shall address the Lord or Lords, saying: "Since you the Lords of the Five Nations have refused to return to the procedure of the Constitution, we now declare your seats vacant; we take off

your horns, the token of your Lordship, and others shall be chosen and installed in your seats, therefore vacate your seats."

Should the men in their council[269] adopt the second course, the War Chief shall order his men to enter the council, to take positions beside the Lords, sitting between them wherever possible. When this is accomplished the War Chief holding in his outstretched hand a bunch of black wampum strings shall say to the erring Lords: "so now, Lords of the Five United Nations, harken to these last words from your men. You have not heeded the warnings of the women relatives, you have not heeded the warnings of the General Council of women, and you have not heeded the warnings of the men of the nations, all urging you to return to the right course of action. Since you are determined to resist and to withhold justice from your people there is only one course for us to adopt." At this point the War Chief shall let drop the bunch of black wampum and the men shall spring to their feet and club the erring Lords to death. Any erring Lord may submit before the War Chief lets fall the black wampum. Then his execution is withheld.

The black wampum here used symbolizes that the power to execute is buried but that it may be raised up again by the men. It is buried but when the occasion arises they may pull it up and derive their power and authority to act as here described.[270]

Karonhjakte Louis Hall of Kahnawake decided that this right of the "warriors" to execute the Confederacy chiefs formed the basis of a separate source of power.[271] He advocated the summary execution of the present generation of chiefs in *The Warrior Manifesto*, a proposal for the revitalization of the Confederacy.[272] The *Manifesto* became a reference manual for the "Warrior" movement in Kahnawake and Akwesasne in 1990. Some people came to see the work as a companion to the Kayanerenkó:wa, a guide to its interpretation.

---

269 These references in Newhouse's versions to a "men's council" have given rise to new bodies, separate from the Council of Chiefs, at Oneida, New York, and more recently at the Grand River. They are not recognized by the Haudenosaunee as aspects of government.

270 Parker (Newhouse and Cusick) 1916, 46–47; Newhouse 1885, 56.

271 In 1762, Kindarunty, a Seneca chief, was assassinated by the warriors for having been "bullying." See SWJP 3:924, Thomas McKee to Johnson, November 2, 1762.

272 Hall 1983.

War and Peace

When warriors are leaders, then you will have war.
We must raise leaders of peace.[273]

The purpose of the Great Law of Peace was to stop cycles of bloodshed and to establish peace. The Peacemaker understood that a house at peace within itself would still be of troubled mind if there were continued bloodshed around it. Thus, the Great White Roots of the Tree of Peace were intended to spread the message of peace to the four corners of the world, creating what has been called "a landscape of peace." As Wallace put it:

> The minimum purpose of the League was to maintain unity, strength and good will among the Five Nations, so as to make them invulnerable to attack from without and to division from within. The native philosophers who rationalized the League in later years conceived also a maximum purpose: the conversion of all mankind, so that peace and happiness should be the lot of the peoples of the whole earth, and all nations should abide by the same law and be members of the same confederacy. "The white roots of the Great Tree of Peace shall continue to grow," the founder allegedly announced, "advancing the Good Mind and Righteousness and Peace, moving into territories of peoples scattered far through the forest. And when a nation, guided by the Great White Roots, shall approach the Tree, you shall welcome her here, and take her by the arm and seat her in the place of council. She will add a brace or leaning pole to the longhouse and will thus strengthen the edifice of Reason and Peace."[274]

There are some who maintain that the Great Law established internal peace within the Confederacy to enable the member nations to better defend themselves against their enemies—to wage war more effectively. Internal peace encouraged more external warfare. Indeed, Cayenderongue Cadwallader Colden stated that mutual self-defence was the main reason for the creation of the

---

273 Thadadaho Leon Shenandoah to the General Assembly of the United Nations, October 25, 1985.

274 Wallace 1969, 43.

League: some Algonquins (Adirondacks[275]) had killed some of the Five Nations out of jealousy over hunting: "[The Five Nations] conceiv'd a vast Indignation against the Adirondacks, who being advised of the secret movements of the Five Nations, Resolv'd to oblige them to submit to their Law, by force of Arms. The Five Nations apprehending their Power, retired to the Southward of Cadarackui Lake, where they now live, and defended themselves at first but faintly against the Vigorous Attacks of the Adirondacks. But afterwards becoming more expert, and more used to War, they not only made a brave Defence, but likewise made themselves masters of the great Lakes, and chased the Shawanons from thence."[276]

Without citing any authority for his statements, Allen Trelease goes beyond defence to an assertion that war was "a basic principle of the league": "In addition to self-defence the original motivation for forming the league may have included a sincere aspiration for universal peace. This ideal was, however, grounded in a tribal superiority complex. The Iroquois were convinced that they constituted a master race, and if universal peace were to be achieved, it must be done within their fold. As time passed, the eventual aim became less apparent than the actual process of reducing the gentiles to submission. One of the basic principles of the league was that its members were at war with all tribes not positively allied to it."[277]

In contrast, others suggest that the coming of the Great Peace was the end of all warfare, and that from the time it was established there were to be no more "warriors."[278] Skanawati John Buck asserted: "And when this matter will extend itself in all directions, there may be some who will not be willing to receive it, but we shall not be reprehensible, since we have offered it to them—to the Nations of Natural Men living alongside any Great White Root of the Great Law. We have likewise laid our heads upon these Roots for mutual protection."[279]

Newhouse proposed a coercive view of the expansion of the law: a foreign nation was to be made an offer it could not refuse (or rather, the customary three offers):

> A treaty was once impending between the Mohawks and one of the western nations, the Mohawks could not make them come to any moderate terms; and disliked the threats made against them, they sent at last this Laconic message: that if the western Nation would

---

275 Atíron:taks, "he eats bark," is a porcupine, but also possibly a reference to Algonquin birch-bark-biting.

276 Colden (1727) 1973, 6.

277 Trelease, 1960, 21.

278 One consistent exponent of this view in modern times was Huron Miller, an Onondaga sub-chief of the Grand River Territory and a frequent speaker in Karihwí:iyo events.

279 Hewitt 1892b, 142.

not enter into the Alliance, it was not their fault; they had conquered many enemies and driven them from their possessions & that if they would come they would fight them also.[280]

... when warriors are ready to go on the warpath against an opposing obstinate nation that has refused to accept the Great Peace ... one of the five War Chiefs shall be chosen by the Warriors of the Nation to lead the aforesaid war party on the war path and when that one is chosen, it shall be his duty and privilege to come forward and address a few words to the then ready and assembled Warriors and the whole tenor of his allocution to the warriors shall be to impress upon them the need and necessity of good behavior and strict obedience to all the commands of the war chiefs, enthusiastically exhorting them not to be cowards but to be brave and courageous.[281]

The Newhouse version does not fully reflect history. When the Haudenosaunee made war on other nations, they often did so for reasons other than that those nations had failed to agree to join the Great Peace. The reasons may have been economic, political, or social, and sometimes involved a struggle over territory, but they were complex and not based in the Great Law. Most frequently, other nations joined the Great Peace through persuasion, logic, diplomacy, and protection. The written record shows that the chiefs were constantly striving for peace, whatever the warriors did.

In the Creation story, the right-handed twin defeats his brother, but he does not kill him. He banishes him, but even that is a limited banishment, for he keeps him close by, because of his affection for him. The twins are not Good and Evil, but they are two sides of creation. Haudenosaunee government and law is full of things that have two sides: men and women, the clearing and the forest, the two sides of the council. Similarly, war and peace are two different states, neither of which will go away completely. Whether we need war or not, it will always be with us, always close by. That is why the law provides for war chiefs. Another two-sided phenomenon found its place in the law.

We should not presume that Haudenosaunee warfare, after the coming of the law, was the same as European warfare during that time. Champlain intervened in an arranged, mostly ritualized skirmish between his Algonquin, Wendat, and Innu allies and a Mohawk armed force. He killed people with his overloaded arquebus: before that, there had been no casualties, only teasing and insults, and everyone was preparing to go home. Joao Brandão noted, in *Your Fyre Shall Burn No More,* that during the ninety years of the most intense warfare between the Haudenosaunee and the French, more Frenchmen were taken for adoption than

---

280   NYSL MSS 13350, in Johnston 1964, 29.

281   Newhouse 1885, 60.

were killed.[282] The purposes, weapons, tactics, and strategy of Haudenosaunee warfare were not the same as those of their European neighbours. The warriors, standing behind the rotiyanershon in councils with other nations, sent a powerful, visual, unspoken message that there was an unpleasant alternative to the peaceful proposals coming from the Haudenosaunee.

Historical reality is a matter of shades of grey, not black and white. The Great Law did bring internal peace to the five warring nations. The result was that they were better able to defend themselves against their enemies. From the early 1600s to the late 1700s, the Haudenosaunee were engaged in constant warfare, against both European and Indigenous enemies. The warriors were real. The Haudenosaunee did absorb other nations, both by adopting refugees from other wars and by conquest. Without the warriors, the Haudenosaunee would surely have been destroyed. Yet the existence of war and warriors is not proof that a basic principle of the League was that its members were at war with everyone but their allies. That would be irrational and suicidal. Instead, as the conduct of the Haudenosaunee as recorded in their documentary history shows, the Confederacy was intent on spreading the Great Peace to all nations, through rational persuasion rather than war. The basic principle of the League was that nations who were not yet within the peace should be invited to join, so that the Great White Roots should spread. The League would defend itself vigorously against enemies but reasoned that its interests, the interests of the coming generations, were best served in a landscape of peace: "They employ all their industry to engage the other nations to give themselves to [the Iroquois]; they send them presents and the most able people of their nation to speak to them, and to let them know that if they do not give themselves to the Iroquois, they cannot avoid being destroyed . . . but on the other hand, if they want to give themselves up and disperse themselves among the longhouses, they will become masters of other men."[283]

The spreading of the Great White Roots gave other nations a number of options: they could seek to come within the Longhouse, becoming Haudenosaunee. They could choose to remain outside the Longhouse while grasping and adopting the principles of the Great Peace. In those cases, it would be said that they were supporting the Longhouse from the outside, as poles would be used to prop up a longhouse that had become unsteady with age.

---

282 Brandão 1997, 53. Brandão notes that between 1600 and 1701 the Haudenosaunee captured "well over 6,000 people," and that 55 percent of their raids on New France resulted in captives being taken.

283 Randot 1904, 184.

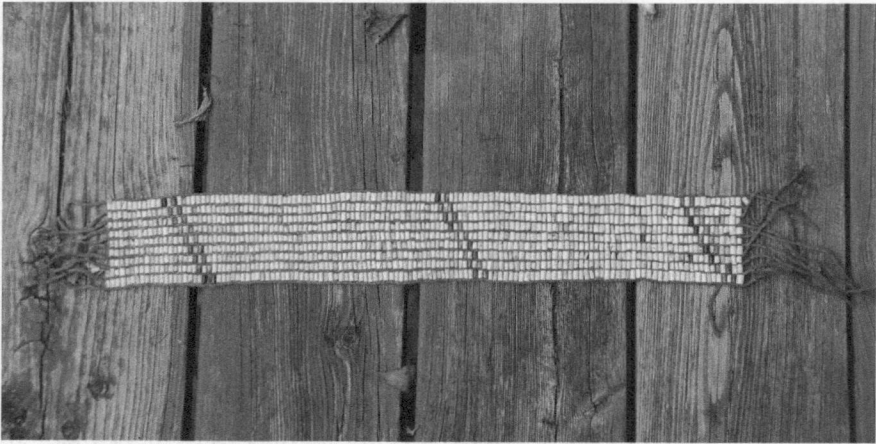

Figure 14. This is a pledge of alliance from a nation promising to support the Haudenosaunee from the outside: diagonal lines symbolize the poles set up as "props" or "braces" to the longhouse. Photograph by author, September 2018.

The Weakness of the Council

A system of government that depended upon unanimity, one-mindedness, was necessarily not agile. It was slow to react to threats and was often split into factions. The rotiyanershon led by example, by persuasion, and not by force or compulsion. All these factors made for a relatively weak Grand Council. Hurley, however, places this in a larger context:

> Accepting the imperfection of such authority is, however, different from denying it altogether. If limited, the jurisdiction of the general Council of the Confederacy was nonetheless real. This fact was particularly apparent in its control over the accession to office of national sachems and chiefs. Further, the very raison d'etre of the Iroquois Confederacy, the balanced distribution of power between the component nations and the General Council, dictated constraints upon the centralizing authority of the latter. Again, the absence of monopoly control over political power by the General Council does not equate with an absence of government in Iroquois society. Those jurisdictions not exercised by the General Council fell to other designated entities, of which the nation and clan councils were the most important.[284]

Part of the problem with seventeenth- and eighteenth-century descriptions of the relative weakness of Haudenosaunee central government originates from the experience of the European observers themselves—since they came from societies in which executive authority was powerful and centralized, they would consider anything looser to be excessively weak. Another problem with the descriptions is the fact that they were written by outsiders, not participants, in the society. Outsiders would not often see the exercise of authority by the women. Nor would they see (or understand, if they did see) the medicine societies healing the people and binding them together. Yet the observation that where the Grand Council did not govern, other entities picked up the torch, is essentially true:

> The sachems' job was to prevent "a disuniting of their minds." In a nutshell that was what the Great Peace was all about, for to Indians of seventeenth- and eighteenth-century eastern North America,

---

284 Hurley 1985, 47.

"peace" was primarily a matter of the mind. Headmen could not force anyone to forgo mourning-war raids; they could only advise, persuade, cajole and invoke the obligations of kinship. . . .

A League sachem, a man entrusted with preserving the Great Peace, had to be of a special breed. The chiefly virtues most prized in Iroquois folklore are those associated with peace and harmony: imperturbability, patience, good will, selflessness. "The thickness of their skin shall be seven spans—which is to say that they will be proof against anger, offensive actions and criticism," Deganawidah decreed of the League sachems. . . . A character of such restraint—even passivity—is almost by definition incapable of the kind of strong and innovative leadership that the Five Nations needed to survive the ordeals of the European invasion. Moreover, had a League sachem exercised such leadership and thus necessarily provoked political opposition, he would have ceased to be a peacemaker. . . . If the League sachems were to fulfil their traditional duties, they must remain aloof from everyday politics and diplomacy.[285]

During the seventeenth and eighteenth centuries, the names that appear in documents as speakers and leaders of the Haudenosaunee are mostly not "League sachem" titles. This led ethnohistorians like Richter, Fenton, and Jennings to conclude that there were actually two political entities, overlapping and parallel: the League and the Confederacy. The League's function was largely ceremonial, and consisted of maintaining the internal peace and the ceremonies, while the Confederacy was an active, aggressive, agile political body, whose business was conducted by chiefs who were not sachems.

Horatio Hale, working with John Smoke Johnson in the 1880s, provides a simple alternative explanation. In council, the chiefs did not address or refer to one another using their titles. They used their proper names, usually their Haudenosaunee names, but sometimes their English names. The title would have been the name of the person who first bore it, but not the name of successors—only their title. Rarely did the chiefs use their titles, though they were well known. In historic documents, some titles do appear, especially the Mohawk Turtle Clan title Tekarihoken and the Onondaga Turtle Clan title Skanawati. But the use by the chiefs of their proper names to sign documents is not evidence—as Fenton suggests it is—that the chiefs were not involved.[286]

My own conclusion, viewing the past through the lens of a Haudenosaunee present, is that things were more complex than this (as Richter admits, it is hard

---

285 Richter 1987, 19.

286 Hale's correspondence on the subject is to William C. Bryant, and is in the Bryant Papers (B00-13) in the Buffalo Historical Society.

to ascertain exactly what was happening from the European records: "Europeans *were* dense, and Indians *were* secretive"[287]). Rather than two separate political entities, I suggest that the Haudenosaunee were probably less united than they wanted to be during this period of cultural, microbial, military, and political battering—but that institutions developed like "props" for the Longhouse; people came forward to provide necessary leadership; and the rotiyanershon were never out of the picture, but retained influence in ways that kept them at the core of the people's stability. If treaty councils record only a few names of "sachems," that may be partly because the people present were using their personal names rather than their titles, and it must also be recalled that the councils were held with delegates, and that the rotiyanershon had probably directed the delegates' words and strategies—generally in the form of the wampum strings and belts carried to the council by the speakers. The question is not whether the people at the council were rotiyanershon but whether they were legitimate representatives of the Haudenosaunee. There was also a flux between chiefs and sachems. Someone appearing in the records as a village chief one year might be condoled as a Confederacy chief three years later. Thus, Theyanoguin was also known as Henry Peters, "King Hendrick," and by his Mohawk Turtle Clan title, Tekarihoken. The name he appears under in colonial records may not be his title; and the same can be said of the other forty-nine.

There *were* Haudenosaunee rotiyanershon at all times, and they had respect and authority and influence. There *were* other chiefs, local chiefs, and war chiefs, and they, too, wielded authority. When the Confederacy worked, it worked because all these people—and the clan mothers and the faithkeepers and others whose functions have faded over time—fulfilled their duties and did the best they could for the survival of the people. The Grand Council never was a European-style government, especially not in the age of absolute monarchies. But neither was it a government that failed the people through weakness or niceness.

The need for formal Condolences, and for the coming together of the nations to raise up the rotiyanershon, had created a cumbersome system that worked well in times of peace but often led to vacancies—empty seats in council—in more difficult times. Thus, when the Senecas in 1764 explained that "we have few or no old Sachims qualified to transact business of this importance," they were mentioning an extreme situation in what has been an ongoing problem.[288]

During the latter part of the seventeenth century, according to a strong Seneca oral tradition, the Mohawks and Oneidas, at the Eastern Door of the

---

287 Richter 1987, 17.

288 The Catholic Church faces the same problem, in a way: choosing an elderly Pope ensures that the nominee is experienced, proven, and wise—but also that he will not last very long, and the Church will soon have to go through another process of selection.

Confederacy, were forced to spend much of their time and energy fighting the French. As a result, the western nations of the Confederacy worked together to grow the crops needed to supplement whatever the Mohawks and Oneidas could grow. This required a complex logistical effort—the transportation of thousands of pounds of food over a distance of more than 500 kilometres, passing through the territories of several nations. It is impossible to believe that fifty mostly elderly men could have co-ordinated this effort. It is quite possible that the "mutual aid societies" had the complexity and concentration to pull this off—and these societies would have been almost invisible to European observers (as indeed they remain today).[289]

Dealing with the "Warriors"

One of the problems associated with the issue of "warriors" is the word itself. The word does not exist in the Kayanerenkó:wa. Instead, the word sometimes translated as "warriors," rotiskenrakéhte, is more properly translated as "they are upholding the House."[290] That is, they are the workers, the ones who implement the decisions of the chiefs, the rotiyanershon.

The relationship between the chiefs and the "warriors" was often confusing to the Europeans:

> Even in greatly agitated times, Iroquois chieftainship was two-headed. There was, on the one hand, a complex civil chieftainship, composed of male and female representatives of families, clans and nations and whose work consisted of creating a certain harmony within each social unit and between these social units. It could make decisions about war and peace, but its fundamental goal remained peace. It did not make war. Its operation rested upon discussion, consensus and the art of persuasion. It was a chieftainship founded on words that managed tranquility without coercion.
>
> There was, on the other hand, a military chieftainship, largely independent of the civil authority. It could agree with the civil authority, or dissociate itself from it. Its political role was to defend the honour

---

289   The theory and the oral tradition were kept by Sotsisowah John Mohawk.

290   Other translations: "they are carrying the mat"; "they are carrying the bones of the ancestors"; "they are holding up the house"; "they are holding up the peace"; "they carry ochre"; or that it contains a reference to the Sun, the Older Brother—the Great Warrior (so that the old war dance, now done at Midwinter, is a request to the Sun for help in war).

and respectability of the social units from which it emerged, as well as the inviolability of the living spaces and values tending toward accommodation with the other groups. It faced exclusively toward the outside, but its viability depended on the support it received from the inside. It captured the outside to direct it inward—whether it be a person or just his scalp. When the warrior marked his capture by leaving his war-club on the spot of capture, he was also committing a political act.

The civil chieftainship played in words. The military chieftainship played in muscle. When the two were in accord, the first seemed to dominate, but the second was always watching, extremely attentively, ready to appear and present the other solution. The Europeans had a great deal of difficulty in understanding this organization. They could not understand how the civil chiefs could be acting in good faith when they councilled with them at the same time as the military chiefs were in the field. Europeans often concluded that this apparently contradictory diplomacy was a matter of bad faith, when in reality it reflected internal dissensions, conflicts of interests, and complementary visions of the universe of relations.

Iroquoian warfare no longer exists, but the "warriors" are still here. Their existence raises questions: how do they attach themselves to tradition and ancient values? What is their role in modern societies? What do they represent? How to understand their evolution? What do they capture?[291]

This confusion remained, and was accentuated by two factors. First, the degree of individual freedom in Haudenosaunee society prevented the Confederacy Council from imposing a tight peace: there were always individuals who could be persuaded to join a fight. Second, if there was constant warfare, the men who took leadership in the wars became de facto decision makers for the people, especially since war required quick decisions and the Confederacy Council was not designed for agility. War provided an outlet for ambition: "there are two kinds of Chieftains, the war Chief & the Civil Chief; the War Chief is wholly elective any amiable man remarkable for his bravery & courage, who has lived quietly & conducted himself with propriety is chosen a Chief—his good qualities render him eligible not his rank or possessions; the civil chief is nearly hereditary; they are almost always chosen from particular families tho' not in what we would call regular succession; sometimes a Civil

---

291 Normand Clermont, introduction to Viau 1997, 12 (translated from French).

Chief [is] chosen a War Chief, & in this case supposing he has any talents for oratory, he has the greatest influence."[292]

The French and British in the seventeenth century were emerging from rigid feudalism, and were used to the exercise of coercive, decisive executive power. They assumed that their "savage" counterparts would have equal authority. In fact, Haudenosaunee chiefs had only the authority of persuasion and example, coupled with an extensive duty to consult and consider. Exchanges in council that reflect the difference between the societies were common:

> They said when all the sachems were convened together they would answer that Point, but a little After a Sachem rose up & said, as to that Matter, we desire to be excused from giving any positive Answer, because it is the Young Men that must do the Service[293] & they must be consulted about it.

> His Lordship replyed that he thought the Sachems had the sole Command of their Young Men without any controll.

> They answered, We have often proposed something to you & you have told us you would write to the King our Great Master about it, which gave us satisfaction and we never importuned you any more about it, therefore pray be satisfied with what we have now answered. . . .

> As to our Children to be sent to New York to be instructed to read & write, We answer, that we are not Masters or disposers of them that is a matter which relates to our Wives who are the sole disposers of our Children whilst they are under Age.[294]

There has always been tension between the young and the old, in every society. More so, no doubt, in societies without coercion, without complex hierarchies:

> We find divisions among us, the young men think to take the lead, who know nothing of our affairs, nor of what we suffered in the War.[295]

---

292 NYSL MSS 13350-51, cited in Johnston 1964, 27.

293 The young men would risk their lives, so they would have a say in the decisions. The women would till the soil, so they would have a say in decisions about land. There is no mystery to the idea that a democratic government should consult with the people most directly affected by the development of policies.

294 Wraxall 1754, 36–37. The chiefs were referring to the fact that the children were under the care of the women.

295 Thayendenega Joseph Brant to William Claus, July 28, 1906; cited in Johnston 1964, 108.

While we are indeed sachems we cannot simply turn our backs on our soldiers, for they are our protectors, and have to fight for us since we are old people.[296]

After generations of warfare, more and more of the conduct of the affairs of the nations was being taken by the "warriors." In 1762 the Geneseo Senecas explained to Sir William Johnson why the chiefs were not present at a Six Nations congress: "The reason you do not see many of our Sachems at present here is, that the weather and roads having been very bad, they were less able than we to travel, & therefore, we the Warriors were made choice of to attend you, and transact business; and I beg you will consider that we, are in fact the people of consequence for managing affairs, our Sachems being generally a parcell of old people who say much, but who mean or act very little, so that we have both the power and ability to settle matters."[297]

Alliances with the Europeans accentuated the imbalance. In "normal" times, the Great Law allowed a foreign nation to meet the Haudenosaunee in council and see the wise chiefs explaining the nature of the peace, while the foreigners could also see, standing behind the chiefs, the young men who represented the alternative to peace.

In times of war, the people dealing with foreigners, and especially with their foreign military counterparts, were the war chiefs. Sending warriors as speakers also sent a message about Haudenosaunee intentions. When the French occupied Cataraqui (the present Kingston, Ontario) to control access to the St. Lawrence River from Lake Ontario, the Haudenosaunee sent a delegation of warriors to express their views in no uncertain terms:

> Onontiio your fyre shall burn no more at Cataraqui it shall never be kindled again. You did steale that place from us & wee quenched the fyre with the blood of our children. You think your selfes the ancient inhabitants of this countrey & longest in possession yea all the Christian Inhabitants of New York & Cayenquiragoe thinke the same of themselves. Wee Warriours are the firste & the ancient people & greatest of you all, these parts and countrys were inhabited & trodd upon by us before any Christian (then stamping his foot upon the ground sayd) We shall not suffer Caderaqui to be inhabited

---

296 Livingston 1956, 40; June 4, 1677.

297 SWJP 3:698.

againe. Onontiio we Canonssoené[298] do say we will never suffer you
to kindle your fire at Cadaraqui. I repeat this again and again.[299]

European desires for military allies, first in wars between the British and
French, and then in the American Revolution and the War of 1812, meant a
constant stream of favour to the warriors coming from outside Haudenosaunee
society. European representatives would often speak with those who could help
them in war, regardless of the imbalance this created within the Haudenosaunee.
The tension between the chiefs and the warriors was probably constant throughout history—but the Euro-American influence turned the tension into an
imbalance. By 1776, as Britain and the United States vied for the alliance or
neutrality of the Haudenosaunee, reaching out to the warriors, the rotiyanershon began to despair of the changes: "Times are altered with us. Formerly the
Warriors were governed by the wisdom of their uncles the Sachems but now
they take their own way and dispose of themselves without consulting their
uncles the sachems. While we wish for peace they are for war. Brothers, they
must take the consequences."[300]

While the "warriors" saw themselves as the protectors of the League in a state
of extended emergency, the maintenance of a state of war was antithetical to the
Great Peace and in the long run would undermine the constitution and the law.

When the Oneidas in Wisconsin split, the people who moved to the
"Canadian side" were called the "Chiefs' Party," while those who stayed in
Wisconsin were the "Warriors' Party." When a group formed at the Grand River
Territory after the First World War, with the objective of installing a Canadian-
style democratic system of government, it called itself the "Warrior Society,"
partly because many of its members were war veterans. Yet at the Grand River
Territory in 1959, when the Confederacy resumed control of the territory,
however briefly, the "Warrior Society" of that time was an integral part of the
movement that supported the chiefs.

---

298   Kanonsionni—the People of The Longhouse.

299   NYCD, London Documents 91, 122. Cayenquirago was "Great Swift Arrow," the name
      given to Governor Fletcher of Maryland (but also later to Cadwallader Colden). The
      French forts at Cataraqui were destroyed several times by the Haudenosaunee.

300   Tenhoghskweaghta, an Onondaga chief, to delegates of the united colonies, March 10,
      1776. *Indian Affairs Papers*, 115. In contrast, the colonists (who were headed for war)
      could say: "We warriors cannot break the orders of our Great Chiefs. We must execute
      the advice of our Sachems. We always attend to their voice." Colonel Dayton, the
      speaker, was explaining in a conference with the Mohawks on May 20, 1776, why it was
      impossible to avoid the war. *Indian Affairs Papers*, 57.

The Ceremonies: Spiritual Authority and Obligation

The advent of Christianity no doubt complicated Haudenosaunee government. Some of the people of every nation moved to the St. Lawrence, to join the French mission villages that became Kahnawake, Kanehsatake, Akwesasne, and Oswegatchie. While the Jesuits and Sulpicians permitted and even maintained the continuity of the clans, they also set themselves up as spiritual authorities, leaders of the communities in ways for which the chiefs had until then been the guides. To the south, the British provided Anglican missionaries and churches, and Queen Anne provided the silverware and the names for Royal Chapels for the Mohawks. Methodists made inroads by employing Indigenous preachers. Those who continued to follow traditional Haudenosaunee religion became the custodians of both the law and the ceremonies:

> Everything is together—spiritual and political—because when the Creator . . . made this world, he touched the world all together, and it automatically became spiritual and everything that comes from the world is spiritual and so that's what leaders are, they are both the spiritual mentors and the political mentors of the people.[301]

> Everything is laid out for you. Your path is straight ahead of you. Sometimes it's invisible but it's there. You may not know where it's going, but you have to follow that path. It's the path to the Creator. It's the only path there is.[302]

To maintain continuity in the face of this erosion of authority, the Haudenosaunee adopted several different approaches. Some people were able to practise both Christian and traditional ways. For example, Thayendenegea Joseph Brant translated two books of the New Testament into Mohawk, as a good Anglican. But his haduwi, his medicine mask, is still in existence and use. Some people considered the good messages of Jesus and the Haudenosaunee way to be essentially the same message, so they could accept both. Some today

---

301 Porter 1988, 8–12.

302 Thadadaho Leon Shenandoah, in Wall 2001. When I was researching Australian national park co-ownership and co-management, especially at Uluru and Kakadu, I spoke with an official at the Australian High Commission in Ottawa. He told me (rather scornfully) that the Pitjanjaras believed that the world would end if they did not continue to put through their ceremonies at Uluru. It is intellectually arguable that *their* world—the world they had created through their beliefs—would die if the ceremonies ceased. But I asked the official: Would he be willing to take the chance that they are wrong?

assert that Jesus and the Peacemaker were the same person. Rather than have the community divided over religion, the Grand River Chiefs declared in the 1880s that they would hang their hats at the door of the council house, so that once they sat in council, "we are all wearing buckskins."

With every community, as well, there is a division between those who follow the Karihwi:yo, the message that Skaniatariio (Handsome Lake) brought in the 1790s, and those who maintain that the Kayanerenkó:wa is a sufficient guide for their way of life. In Kahnawake, this has resulted in there being separate longhouses for each path. In other places, there are separate medicine societies. Today, the majority of the rotiyanershon are Handsome Lake adherents, and some opposition to traditional governments comes from people who feel that religion and government should be kept separate. "That is why there are faithkeepers," reply some of the chiefs: while it is our responsibility to maintain the great ceremonies, and to set an example of spirituality, the faithkeepers are the ones who look after the details now. Even so, the traditional ceremonies, and respect for them, are part of the backbone of the legal system. Council is often postponed so that the major ceremonies, like Midwinter and Green Corn, can be completed (especially since the ceremonies and council take place in the same longhouses).

The Mother's Line

European and Euro-American legal systems made room for women's rights and women's equality during the twentieth century, removing aspects of laws that discriminated against women on the basis of gender. One of those laws was the Indian Act of Canada, which in 1869 was amended to strip Indian women of their status as Indians if they married non-Indian men. The Indian Act was amended in 1985, and women who had lost their status were reinstated and their children recognized as Indians. In 1870, the chiefs objected to the new provisions of Canadian law because they went against established Haudenosaunee customs. In 1924, Deskahe Levi General noted that the elected system Canada sought to impose in the Grand River Territory would remove women's political rights (women were not allowed to vote or hold political office under the Canadian system until 1951). The separation of the roles of men and women in government under the Kayanerenkó:wa is profound: it would be difficult to imagine male clan mothers or female chiefs, especially in the fulfillment of spiritual obligations. The principle of passing down identity, clan, and chiefs' titles through the mother's line is deeply ingrained in Haudenosaunee law:

Not the least remarkable among their institutions, was that which confined the transmission of all titles, rights and property in the female line to the exclusion of the male. It is strangely unlike the canons of descent adopted by civilized nations, but it secured several important objects. If the Deer tribe of the Cayugas, for example, received a sachemship at the original distribution of these offices, the descent of such title being limited to the female line, it could never pass out of the tribe. It thus became instrumental in giving to the tribe individuality. A still more marked result, and perhaps a leading object of this enactment, was the perpetual disinheritance of the son. Being of the tribe of his mother formed an impassable barrier against him; and he could neither succeed his father as a sachem, nor inherit from him even his medal, or his tomahawk. The inheritance, for the protection of tribal rights, was thus directed from the lineal descendants of the sachem, to his brothers, or his sisters' children, or, under certain circumstances, to some individual of the tribe at large; each and all of whom were in his tribe, while his children, being in another tribe . . . were placed out of the line of succession.[303]

This is how these matters will carry on, the women controlling the title names, because it is by means of all their suffering that people are here on earth, and it is they who raise them. Moreover, their blood, this is what we have, the people, for these are our mothers, the women, and this is why the families follow according to their bloodlines.[304]

As long as their neighbours' laws discriminated actively against women, the Haudenosaunee were able to maintain that their legal system was no more discriminatory than that of patriarchal, patrilocal Canada and the United States. At the beginning of the twenty-first century, most unequal treatment of women in the laws of those countries has been removed, and pressure on the Haudenosaunee to amend citizenship laws has increased.[305]

The difficulty, for the Haudenosaunee, lies in reconciling two fundamental principles in the law. The first is that the roles of men and women are distinct and separate, but equally respectable. The second is that families must be

---

303 Morgan (1851) 1995, 80.

304 Gibson 1912, 419–20.

305 The recommendations of the Truth and Reconciliation Commission of Canada include respect for Indigenous legal systems (the commission's report distinguishes between "Indigenous" laws, made by Indigenous nations for themselves, and "Aboriginal" law, made by Canada about Indigenous peoples). The commission's report significantly puts forward Haudenosaunee law as a distinct, powerful legal system. But the report also recommends that Indigenous legal systems remove gender discrimination.

respected. In theory, the inclusiveness and generosity of the law is the path to that reconciliation: family members excluded because their fathers rather than their mothers are their connection to the community would be brought in by adoption. However, the generosity and flexibility of the law has atrophied somewhat: adoptions, once common and often informal, have become rare.

Differing roles for men and women in traditional Indigenous societies are uncomfortable for neighbours who advocate for respect for Indigenous laws and governments. The most explicit recent statement of that discomfort is found in the report of Canada's Truth and Reconciliation Commission, which said:

> As with the common law and civil law systems, Indigenous law is learned through a lifetime of work. Applying Indigenous law requires an acknowledgment that it exists in the real world and has relevance today. It is most helpful when applied to humankind's most troubling behaviours. . . . Contemporary issues concerning gender and other inequalities must necessarily be part of these laws for them to be persuasively applicable in the present day.[306]

The Names: Continuity

Haudenosaunee names are not simply invented.[307] They are often ancient, and they belong to the clan and family. When a new person is born, the women of the family meet, observe the child, and choose a name that reflects the child's personality, or the people's hopes for the child:

> After the birth of a child a name was selected by its mother from those not in use belonging to the gens, with the concurrence of her nearest relatives, which was then bestowed upon the infant. But the child was not fully christened until its birth and name, together with the name and gens of its mother and the name of its father, had been announced at the next ensuing council of the tribe. Upon the death

---

306 Truth and Reconciliation Commission of Canada 2015, 6:46, 54.

307 There are ignorant jokes about "Indian names"—about how people are named after the weather or events on the day they were born. In western literature, "Indian names" are usually references to animals or things ("Big Bear," "Dull Knife," "Red Buffalo Woman"). Among the Haudenosaunee, names are more action-oriented, and less about things. "She Picks Sweetgrass," "He Cuts Off Business," "He Talks (Constantly)," "He Carries a Quiver" are all examples of Haudenosaunee names.

of a person his name could not be used again in the life-time of his oldest surviving son without the consent of the latter.[308]

The name may also recall a person who has died recently and left the name vacant—for a name does not simply disappear: it returns to the "storehouse" of names kept by the clan. The fundamental rule is that there should be only one person alive at any one time carrying a particular name.[309]

The Jesuit Relations described the Huron practice in 1644:

> No name is ever lost; so when some one of the family has died, all the relatives assemble and deliberate together which among them shall bear the name of the deceased, giving his own to some other relative. He who takes a new name enters also upon the burdens which belong to it, and so he is captain, if the deceased was so.[310]

> The names now in use among the Iroquois . . . are, in the main, ancient names handed down in the gentes from time immemorial.[311]

In 1724, Lafitau wrote that there was a practice of "requickening" or making alive again all the names belonging to a family. It is possible that he combined the practice of giving names from the family "storehouse" with the practice of "requickening" a chiefly title. However, it is also possible that, three centuries ago, every name brought with it the memory and honour of the people who had carried it before.[312] Lafitau wrote:

> In every family a certain number of ancestral names, both men's and women's, are kept. These names are their own and known to be taken by such and such a family. Now it is the custom in each family to requicken and resuscitate, in some manner, those who, issuing from

308 Morgan (1871) 1997, 78–79. The names of children today are confirmed in Longhouse ceremonies, in which there are specific days set apart for "names." While few would agree with Morgan's statement about a son having control over the use of a name, most people would agree that the name should be "given a rest" for a generation or so, before being brought back into use, though they would also agree that the name should eventually be kept alive.

309 The historic record shows that there were sometimes people in different villages with the same name. As traditions are eroded in modern times, there has been more duplication of names, as well as "borrowing" names from other clans or families. See Charles Cooke's 1950s collection of Iroquois names, available online in the American Philosophical Society Digital Library, http://diglib.amphilsoc.org/. See also Cooke 1952.

310 Cited in Beauchamp (1907) 1975, 346.

311 Morgan (1871) 1997, 80.

312 Until recently, Inuit naming involved giving a child the name of someone who had died recently, and the child, through the name, became related to all the deceased's relatives. This increased chances of survival by increasing the number of people upon whom the child could count for help. In Canadian law, the case of Kiviaq (formerly David C. Ward) stands for the right of Inuit to reclaim their original names.

that family, have made it illustrious. They exalt thus, at the same
time, the names of those whom they make live again, and impose
them on those of their grand nephews destined to represent them.
The latter assume more or less importance according as those who
had borne their names were more or less important themselves by
their qualities, virtues and deeds.[313]

Similarly, when Cadwallader Colden was adopted:

It is customary among them to make a Compliment of Naturalization
into the Five Nations; and considering how highly they value
themselves above all others, this must be no small Compliment.
This is not done by any general Act of the Nation, but every single
person has a right to it, by a Kind of Adoption. The first time I was
among the Mohawks, I had this Compliment from one of their old
Sachems, which he did, by giving me his own name, Cayenderongue.
He had been a notable Warrior; and he told me, that now I had a
Right to assume to myself all the Acts of Valour he had performed,
and that now my Name would echo from Hill to Hill all over the
Five Nations. . . . When about ten or twelve years afterwards, my
Business led me again among them, I directed the Interpreter to say
something from me to the Sachems; he was for some time at a loss to
understand their Answer, till he asked me whether I had any Name
among them: I found that I was really known to them by that Name,
and that the old Sachem, from the time he had given me his Name,
had assumed another to himself. I was adopted, at that time, into
the Tribe of the Bear, and for that reason, I often afterwards had the
kind Compliment of Brother Bear.[314]

People's names can change, or be changed. Morgan, paying attention to
names as well as families, explained:

Two classes of names were in use, one adapted to childhood, and the
other to adult life, which were exchanged at the proper period in the
same formal manner, one being taken away, to use their expression,
and the other bestowed in its place. . . .

At the age of sixteen or eighteen, the first name was taken away,
usually by a chief of the gens, and one of the second class bestowed
in its place. At the next council of the tribe the change of names was
publicly announced, after which the person, if a male, assumed the
duties of manhood. . . . After a severe illness it was not uncommon

---

313 Lafitau (1724) 1974, 71.
314 Colden (1727) 1973, 1, 28.

for a person, from superstitious considerations, to solicit and obtain a second change of name. It was sometimes done again in extreme old age.[315]

Lafitau adds: "These names change with age. A child either has no name, or takes that of another child, a young man, that of a warrior and an old man, that of some elder. As soon as a person dies, the name that he bore is buried with him and it is only several years afterward that it is renewed."[316]

When a child receives a name in the Longhouse, at the Midwinter or Green Corn Thanksgiving, it is usually his uncle who carries him, singing his atonwa, and introducing him to the people—explaining that this new person is to be known henceforth by this name.

The same ceremony takes place when an adult is adopted: "Another Chief led Mr. Furniss to the center, giving his Seneca name, To-an-do-ah, *One First to See*, afterward leading him up and down while he chanted the war song.[317] The Indians responded, the women keeping time by clapping hands.[318] He was then led to his new mother in the Turtle Clan and kissed her, the clan welcoming him. . . . In adopting women, the war song is not sung as when men are received."[319]

When William Beauchamp was adopted into the Onondaga Eel Clan in 1904, as Wah-kat-yu'-ten (Beautiful Rainbow), "Albert Cusick or Sa-go-na-qua-de . . . led the new brother up and down, singing the customary song of thanksgiving and then introducing him to those of his new relatives who were present. The song used was . . . one of the Adonwah or thanksgiving songs."[320]

The same ceremony, essentially, is used when a person becomes a royá:ner. His old name is no longer used for him, and he is introduced under his new title:

> The ceremony of induction consisted in the formal bestowal of the new name by which he was henceforth to be known. A chief placed himself on each side of the candidate, and, grasping his arms, marched him to and fro in the Council House, between the lines of the assembled senators. As they walked they proclaimed his new name and office, and recited, in a measured chant, the duties to

---

315   Morgan (1871) 1997, 79.

316   Lafitau (1724) 1974, 71.

317   There are suggestions that a man's atonwa, his "personal chant," used to be his personal war song. If this is true, it is no longer used or thought of in that way.

318   Women keep time by clapping hands, men by stamping their feet.

319   Beauchamp (1907) 1975, 407, describing an adoption by the Senecas in 1885. See also Akweks 1950, 6, 44–46; "A Seneca Adoption, *Masterkey* 26 (1952): 26, 94–96; Conover 1885; Keppler 1926, 3, 73–75.

320   Beauchamp 1885, 411.

which he was now called, the audience responding at every pause with the usual chorus of assent.[321]

In familiar intercourse and in formal salutation the American Indians address each other by the term of relationship the person spoken to sustains to the speaker. When related they salute by kin; when not related "my friend" is substituted. It would be esteemed an act of rudeness to address an Indian by his personal name, or to inquire his name directly from himself.[322]

Usually, however, the Indians do not willingly hear themselves called by the name given them and an inquiry as to what that is, is a kind of affront which causes them to blush. In addressing each other, they call each other by names of kinship, brother, sister, uncle, nephew, etc. observing exactly the degrees of subordination and all the proper age relationship unless there is a real relationship by blood or adoption.[323]

The use of names, or the reluctance to use names, is relevant to the law in several ways. A practice of salutation "by kin" is another constant reminder of the relationship between individuals, crucial in a legal system based on relationships. Using a person's name instead would be both a step back from the relationship (since one is using a non-relationship word instead of, for example, "my cousin") and an intrusion (since one's name is the name that the Creator knows one by, and the one that is used in ceremonies). Thus, while it is important to have a name, to link one to a clan and a family, the importance of the name lies not in its use but rather in the relations that it provides.

This point is apparent in the difference between English and Haudenosaunee languages. In English, it is easy to speak with someone, or about someone, without reference to the relationship between the two of you.[324] In Haudenosaunee languages, it is more difficult to do so. It is as if Mohawk *allows* one to speak without reference to relationship, while English *encourages* one to do so.

---

321 Hale (1883) 1989, 61. In one recent instance, a would-be Mohawk chief stated that an adoption was not valid because he had deliberately walked out of the longhouse before it was put through. It was pointed out to him that he had not openly objected; that the nation and clan involved was not his own; and eventually, when he persisted, that his own claim to a title was dubious.

322 Morgan (1871) 1997, 80.

323 Lafitau (1724) 1974, 72.

324 Haudenosaunee languages also require more precision in address: there is a difference between saying "You (singular) go for water," and "You (two) go for water," and "You (several of you) go for water," whereas in English the same four words could be used for all three situations.

Names are identifiers: they provide identity.[325] In Haudenosaunee society, they do so to identify the individual not only as an individual but also as a member of a family, clan, and nation. Even in the most mundane ways, the way a name is thought about can be different. An American will introduce himself by saying, "I'm Bill Smith," whereas a Mohawk, speaking Mohawk, will say "Teyanoken ne yonkyats"—"they call me Teyanoken." It is the difference between defining yourself by what you call yourself and defining yourself by your relationship with other people. It is true that in both societies, names are given to children by their parents; that names identify one in terms of family relations as well as individual identity; and that often there are public namings (including christenings and First Communion). The difference is subtle, but real.

Outsiders meeting the Haudenosaunee for the first time were often given names almost immediately. This was practical and legal. It gave them not only existence but also protection and obligation. Now they had a place to stay and relatives to stay with. Now they were related to the Haudenosaunee as members of the family, and it would not be legally possible for them to be enemies, to engage in war against the Confederacy, or to disturb the peace. Often those who were given names in this way understood the honour without grasping the reciprocity and obligation involved.

Citizenship and Immigration

The Haudenosaunee have been called a matrilineal, matrilocal[326] society. That means that people draw their identities from their mothers. They belong to their mother's clan. In the old days, it meant that upon marriage a man would move to live with his wife's people, in the longhouse of his wife and her clan.

---

325 The discussion about placement of Haudenosaunee names in Confederacy identity documents was instructive. The Documentation Committee concluded that the names, as "original names" or "real names," should go first in an IATA-format international travel document. Thus they would come before a person's *prenom*: "Deer, Teyowisonte Thomas Aaron."

326 "Matrilocal residence, wherein a young newly married couple takes up residence with the woman's family, was strongly developed among the Iroquoians. Matrilocality typically arises in dominant societies that expand into territories at the expense of hostile but subordinate societies already there. It is a form of social organization confined to societies operating at a tribal level of development. The matrilineage, a basic unit of Iroquois society five centuries ago, is a successful form of predatory organization in conflicts with other tribes." Snow 1994, 35. Engelbrecht (2003, 68) suggests that chiefs might remain among their mothers' people, basing this in part on Gibson's version of the Creation story. Certainly the chiefs would need to consult with their family constantly, but this would not become difficult unless they moved to other villages.

Traditionally, one's closest male relative is one's uncle: one's mother's broth-er.[327] He is the person who has the responsibility of walking the new baby up and down the longhouse to introduce the new person to the people, when names are given or confirmed at Strawberries and Midwinter.

Alone among the versions of the law, the Newhouse version edited by Gawasowane Arthur Parker provides for passing a name and clan through the father:

> The father of a child of great comeliness, learning ability or specially loved because of some circumstance may, at the will of the child's clan, select a name from his own (the father's) clan and bestow it by ceremony, such as provided. This naming is only temporary and shall be called "a name hung around the neck."[328]

David Maybury-Lewis's description of a principle of tribal peoples—that if you can be addressed as a relative you are one of us, and if you cannot be addressed as a relative you are not one of us[329]—could have led to a narrow, xenophobic view of the Haudenosaunee world and an increasingly inbred population. Instead, the Haudenosaunee used this principle in an empower-ing manner,[330] generous and open in defining how an outsider could become a relative.

The Right of Refuge

Choosing the longhouse as the symbol of the League was a deliberate message about how the peace would be expanded. Archaeologists say that about a third of the bark longhouse sites that have been excavated show that the houses had been extended after their original construction. Hale explained that, as a symbol, the longhouse was "a description and an invitation": "When the

---

327   The theory is that while paternity might be uncertain, one can always be certain about who one's mother is, and about one's mother's brother. The Anglo-Saxons had a similar tradition of maternal uncles having authority. There are vestiges of that today: the loser in a fight between children will "say uncle" to the winner; this is called "knuckling under," from the older English word "nuncle" (most famously used by the Fool in *King Lear*). One aspect of the resistance by tribal peoples in China to the "one child" policy of population control is that, within a generation, there would be no more uncles or aunts, and a child would be deprived of an important traditional support network.

328   Parker (Newhouse) 1916, 49. Richard Hill believes this was actually Parker's addition, adjusting Newhouse's writing to address his own clanlessness.

329   Maybury-Lewis 1992, 92.

330   Vecsey (1988, 111) also suggests that "adoption became a motive for war, as clan moth-ers demanded more sons and nephews."

number of families inhabiting these long dwellings was increased by marriage or adoption, and a new hearth was required, the end-wall . . . was removed, an addition of the required size was made to the edifice, and the closing wall was restored. It declared that the united nations were not distinct tribes, associated by a temporary league, but one great family, clustered for convenience around separate hearths in a common dwelling; and it proclaimed their readiness to receive new members into the general household."[331]

Historically, the Haudenosaunee increased their population by taking in people from other nations—as individuals, as families, and sometimes as entire nations. Deaths from the epidemics and from war were balanced by these immigrants. Archaeologists suggest that the surviving St. Lawrence Iroquoians were absorbed by the Hurons and Onondagas. As the British colonies pressed inland from the Atlantic, Indigenous peoples sought refuge among the Haudenosaunee. The law was already in place to permit this:

> And whosoever finds these roots and traces it up, and come to the "Tree of Peace and Shelter" he is welcome to take shelter under its spreading branches.[332]

> If any man or nation outside the Five Nations shall obey the laws of Great Peace and make known their disposition to the Lords of the Confederacy, they may trace the Roots to the Tree and if their minds are clean and they are obedient and promise to obey the wishes of the Confederate Council, they shall be welcomed to take shelter beneath the Tree of the Long Leaves.[333]

The welcome was not automatic, and it was not unconditional. The Peacemaker had installed the Seneca war chiefs as doorkeepers, and their function included verifying the intentions of those who arrived at the longhouse, seeking to be taken in:

> If the various nations' inhabitants—whichever direction they may come from, according to how the roots lead them, the Great White Roots, which will bring them—arrive where we have our house; and as to these beside the door they will meet the doorkeepers (Teyoninhokarawen and Kanuhkitawi). Thereupon the two will ask what messages they have along, and if what they bring along

---

331 Hale (1883) 1989, 76.

332 Newhouse 1885, 150. There were once "towns of refuge" or sanctuary, in which a fugitive could be safe from any pursuit. Is this the same in spirit? Note that American Indian Movement leader Dennis Banks, when he was being pursued by the FBI in 1984, sought refuge at Onondaga under this provision of the Great Law, and the Onondaga Chiefs informed the United States that they were obliged to provide him shelter and safety.

333 Parker (Newhouse and Cusick) 1916, 30.

is an evil thing; then they will consider it, the doorkeepers, and if
they see that it is bothersome and that they will use it to hurt them,
the people living here, they shall try to settle it peacefully to avoid
trouble, but if the others do not accept, then Kanuhkitawi will invite
them to the place where the elm bark is spread out and shove them
inside the house, where bones will come to pile up, and it is a serious
matter if it were to happen thus.[334]

Adoption

If other people—as individuals, families, or nations—had the right to seek
refuge under the Tree of Peace, and to ask to enter the Longhouse, then ways to
bring them in and include them had to be developed. The Haudenosaunee used
adoption as their means to give these immigrants a place within civil society.
Without a clan and a name, these people would not be accountable, and they
would not know who spoke for them, who carried responsibility for them, or
where to find their place in the ceremonies.

Morgan states that the right of adoption belonged to the clan, not to individuals, and that adoption into a clan conferred "the nationality of the tribe."[335]

Adoption meant that the adoptee became, in almost all respects, a member
of the family:

> The person adopting a captive placed him or her in the relation of a
> brother or sister; if a mother adopted, in that of a son or daughter;
> and ever afterwards treated the person in all respects as though born
> in that relation.[336]

> A prisoner, once adopted, was treated as if he had always been an
> Iroquois, and if he replaced someone who had died, he assumed all
> the rights and privileges of the deceased.[337]

---

334 Gibson 1912, 317–18.

335 Morgan (1871) 1997, 80. See also Parker 1940. Bloom (2001, 126) asserts that "new-
     comers to a Greek city [in ancient times] were often assigned a tribe at random—no
     matter who their forefathers might have been. But once you had your tribal label, it was
     unchangeable."

336 Morgan (1871) 1997, 80.

337 Boucher 1964, 125–26. See also Lafitau (1724) 1974, 2, 156.

In 1654, Father Simon le Moyne visited Onondaga. He remarked: "One calls me brother, another uncle, another a cousin: never have I had so many kinsfolk."[338]

Adoption was crucial to the survival of the Haudenosaunee: it was used to "replace" people who had died by war or disease, to expand or increase the population of communities that had been decreased.[339]

An adopted person is said to have his name "hung around his neck." That is, it is not completely a part of him, and it can be removed if he misbehaves.[340] This is not qualitatively different from the concept of a "landed immigrant" in Canadian law: it is a stage between being a foreigner and becoming a citizen.[341] The decision to remove a "name hung around the neck" is made by the family, clan, or nation that adopted the person.

Sometimes, historically, an adopted person was not "completely" adopted but was to be shared by both his adoptive people and his original nation. This was especially true of interpreters. It was also true of Warraghyhagey Sir William Johnson, the first Imperial Superintendent General of Indian Affairs—who had a Mohawk wife and children:

> The Six Nations answer'd. That the one half of Coll. Johnson belonged to His Excellency [the Governor of New York], and the other to them.[342]

> He is of our Nation, and a member of our Council, as well as of yours. When we adopted him, we divided him into two equal parts: One we kept for our selves, and one we left for you. He has had a great deal of Trouble with us, wore out his shoes in our Messages, and dirty'd his Cloaths by being amongst us, so that he is become as nasty as an Indian.[343]

---

338 Thwaites 1901, 41:75.

339 Lynch 1985. "The Iroquois Confederacy and the Adoption and Administration of Non-Iroquoian Individuals and Groups Priori to 1756." *Man in the Northeast* 30, 83–99.

340 When I was adopted, in 1990, Deskahe said to me "Now you are like us." He was referring to the Confederacy chiefs, and the fact that a chief can be "dehorned"—his name taken away—in the same way that an adoptee's name can be removed. He was also referring to the string of white wampum that both adoptees and chiefs are given. Though the expression and the principle are today well accepted, Hayadaha Richard Hill believes that Arthur Parker may have made this adjustment to one of Newhouse's versions of the law.

341 A "landed immigrant" in Canada cannot vote in national elections, and is liable to be deported back to his country of origin if convicted of a criminal offence, but otherwise has virtually all the rights of a citizen.

342 SWJP 1:342, Albany, July 3, 1751.

343 Canesatego, speaking of Conrad Weiser, in council in Philadelphia, 1742.

The adoption of Lewis Henry Morgan provides a clear picture of the process in 1846—the first part is a transcript by Donehogowa Ely Parker of a speech in Tonawanda Longhouse by Hasge-sa-h Jesse Spring:

"They no doubt knew the fact that, when anyone chooses to become a member of our nation by making an application to some of our leading and influential men, and providing for a feast which is always customary on such occasions as our inducement to bring the people together, [they ought not] to be scrupulous in adopting. The matter of adoption was referred to the managers[344] and prompters, and they concluded that there was no reason why we should not adopt them.[345] They accordingly stated to our brothers that they had agreed to grant their request, and so soon as the means wanted to be furnished for assembling the people, the arrangements would be completed. The managers at the same time referred the giving of names to the chiefs.[346] But in this we have been disappointed. The managers have this evening been informed that the chiefs have made no arrangements so far as this is concerned, and it now becomes the duty of the tribes [clans] to which they are to respectively belong to come forward and present their proper names. The people will observe into what tribe they are adopted by watching who it is that leads the initiate around the room. The managers desire to request the warriors to keep perfect order, and to lend their aid in making the evening performances interesting. The first dance in order will be the War dance, and the second the Grand Religious [Great Feather] dance as the proper accompaniments of the occasion. These will also be for the benefit of our brothers. When these are over, we shall have the privilege of having as many more as we choose. But whether we have any more or not we want all to behave with propriety and decency."

Donehogowa continued with his own description:

The dancers then withdrew to dress for the dance. But before they withdrew, the initiation ceremony was performed. L.H. Morgan was first led around the room by John Bigfire of the Hawk tribe.

---

344 The "managers" are probably the faithkeepers.

345 This approach to the issue mirrors the question the chiefs ask when faced with the Condolence of a chief of another nation: Is there some reason why he should not be accepted? It is a real question, not a matter of mostly ritual recitation like the declaration at a Christian wedding—"But first I am required to ask anyone present who knows a reason why these persons may not lawfully marry, to declare it now."

346 If the names being given were "real names" belonging to clans, it would seem that the assignment of them would have gone to the clan mothers. Referring the question to the chiefs might suggest that the names are honorific rather than real.

Morgan therefore became a Hawk. The leader sang a Thanksgiving song [Personal Chant] while the initiate went around the room,[347] the warriors keeping time to the song by a low guttural sound. The women also kept time by clapping together their hands. The name given to Morgan was Da-ya-da-o-wo-ko; it signifies lies across. Porter was then announced as the next person to be led around the room. The name was Da-ya-a-we; [it] signifies he is bringing or fetching. He was then also led around the room, the leader singing a Thanksgiving song. The leader was Isaac Shanks of the Wolf tribe. Consequently Porter became a Wolf de facto. The third and last person announced was Darling. The name given him was Ga-e-we-yo; [it signifies re-ligion, good news, or glad tidings]. The leader sang a Thanksgiving song while leading him around the room. He was led by William Kennedy of the Deer tribe. Darling therefore became a Deer man to us. This closed the mere ceremony of initiation.[348]

Giving names to groups of visitors is not just a Seneca practice of the nine-teenth century. When the Boundary Commission set the line between Canada and the United States through Kanatakon (St. Regis village in Akwesasne), the members of the commission were also given names: "The Chiefs of the village assemble at our lodgings to execute a lease. . . . They . . . christened us all with Indian names, Judge Atwater they called Ska ro ya te (Beyond the Sky), Col. Hawkins, Ga ron gon tia (the Flying Moon), myself, Ga ra give ne gen (the Rising Sun), R. C. Atwater, Ga ra giv a na (the Full Moon), Judge Richards, Ze ra go rus (the Split or Half Moon)."[349]

When Mary Jemison was adopted, the Seneca women took her to the river and washed her down, removing the "whiteness" from her. While this was a way of further removing her former identity, it also reflects the tradition, shared with the Cherokees, of "going to water" for purification. Water, after all, is recognized as the source of all life. Later Seneca adoptions also involved the adoptee having water poured over him.[350] Washing down also resembles

---

347 Morgan stated that the chiefs "taking the person by the arms then marched with him through the council house and back, chanting the song of adoption. To this the people responded in musical chorus at the end of each verse. The march continued until the verses were ended, which required three rounds." Morgan (1871) 1997, 81.

348 "Ely S. Parker's Report of the Adventures of Lewis H. Morgan, Charles T. Porter and Thomas Darling at Tonawanda on Saturday, the 31st of October 1846" in Tooker 2002, 38–39.

349 Delafield 1943, 145.

350 Recall, in the Creation story, how the Earth was first covered in water; how the Peacemaker had the Cannibal "go to water" to clear his body; and how, in the Condolence, pure clean water is used to clear the throat and then a person's insides, to restore harmony and balance.

the transformative rubbing down, of both Thadadaho and of visitors met at the woods' edge.

In more recent times, there has been unresolved discussion about the nature and consequences of adoption. One question is whether it is qualitatively different to bestow a made-up, honorary name as distinct from a name that belongs to a clan. Another discussion is whether the person who receives a name that belongs to a clan also receives all the legal rights and obligations that go with citizenship. William Fenton (Howan'eyo) describes the discussion at Tonawanda:

> The speaker of the longhouse, Henry Redeye, said that he opposed giving names belonging to clans to white people. In recent cases white adoptees had claimed hunting and fishing rights on the reservation by virtue of adoption as "Indians." The longhouse officers did not wish to confer the privilege on white men. Charles Butler, who interpreted for me that morning, said he disagreed that such conveyance of status was legally possible. . . .
>
> I inferred from Henry's statement that some Senecas regarded adoption, when done wholeheartedly, as conferring complete status as a member of the Seneca Nation. Still other Senecas opposed adoption on principle, in as much as they expected persons adopted to behave as Indians, which would imply rights to hunt and fish, privileges which they did not wish to convey. Other Senecas who regarded adoption as honorary did not expect full participation from those whom they honored, and they would confine the honor to an exclusive few persons who were genuinely interested.[351]

Nations Leave, Nations Return

One important difference between the Haudenosaunee and other confederate entities is the provision in the constitution for nations (as well as individuals) leaving and returning. No doubt the Peacemaker recognized that if the League were held together only by the desire of its members' minds to be together, then it would be possible for people and nations to drift away.

Against this possibility he made provision for the commitment to be renewed frequently.[352] It was not just a means of refreshing memory.

---

351 Fenton 2002, 94.

352 The same practice of frequent renewal is to be found in the Covenant Chain relationship, which requires "repolishing" on a regular basis to remove tarnish and reaffirm the desire of the participants to hold strongly to the Chain.

Even so, people left from time to time. A legal system without coercive force could not make them stay. Whereas the United States fought a bloody civil war upon the secession of the thirteen southern states, and Canada continues to wrestle with the spectre of Quebec secession, inventing difficult rules along a rocky path 130 years into Confederation,[353] the Haudenosaunee provided at their Confederacy's inception for what might happen if nations or people left, and concentrated on creating ways for them to return.

The individual who "leaves the circle" does so as an individual. If the individual is a chief or clan mother, the title stays within the circle, to be given to another member of the family. There are two schools of thought about whether there is a need for a Condolence in this situation. One is that nobody has died, so there are no grieving ones to be consoled. The other is that something is necessary in order that the other nations should have the same opportunity to exercise their right of approval and acceptance (or rejection) as they had when the original chief was put forward.

If a nation chooses to leave, it may do so as well.

In such a situation, the Condolence becomes the doorway back into the League. Once again, it serves as a means of putting sorrow, grief, anger, and hard feelings away where they cannot be brought out again. The Condolence serves as the agent of repair to seams in the Confederacy.

Thus, William Johnson would continually advise the chiefs to "gather the scattered people together."

No matter where they went, they were still "our people," connected by bonds of family. The kinship woven together through the clans was maintained no matter where people went. Mohawks from the Mohawk Valley would spend months in Kahnawake, to the confusion and frustration of the French. Kahnawake Mohawks would not fight other Mohawks in battles in which they were serving as allies to the French, and would warn other Haudenosaunee of the state of things.[354]

The chiefs in the 1750s would accuse the French and British of causing the dispersion of the people. They were frank in their assessment of European strategies:

353 The rules are both political and legal. The legal rules are to be found in the Supreme Court of Canada's decision in *Re Quebec Secession*, [1982] 2 SCR 17. The political rules, set out by the Government of Canada in 1999, would have included no shared currency or passports. Whereas the Canadian Confederation is brittle, as if held together by airplane glue, the Haudenosaunee have flexibility, as if the confederation were held together by mozzarella cheese or chewing gum.

354 That is why Oriskany, at the beginning of the American Revolution, was such a nightmare: the Mohawks and Senecas who had come to see the British regulars give the rebels a drubbing suddenly found themselves not only in the thick of the battle but actually engaged in hand-to-hand combat with their Oneida and Tuscarora brothers. It was a bad start to a bad war.

You are daily now making Disturbances & seem to forget the old Agreement. The Tree seems to be falling, let it now be put up, the Roots [——] and the leaves flourish as before. You formerly said, take this Bowl, & this piece of Meat, with this Spoon let us eat always friendly together out of one Dish; but now you forget & have separated the Indians very much as they can't well come together to eat out of this Dish, which is very hard as we have Children here & there scattered thro' the country by your means.

The English your Brothers & you are the common Disturbers of this Country I say you as white people together. We term the English your Brothers as you must have some. We Indians you call Children—You both want to put us Indians a Quarrelling but we the Six Nations know better, if we begin we see nothing but an entire Ruin of us, as we should not leave off till all was gone, so we are resolved to keep Friends on both sides as long as possible & not meddle with the white People. Our arms shall be between you endeavouring to keep you asunder.[355]

When the British took Montreal, there was a strong detachment of Haudenosaunee warriors with them. In September 1760, at Kahnawake, Sir William Johnson, the Imperial Superintendent General of Indian Affairs, invited the "Eight Nations," including the Iroquois communities of Kahnawake, Kanehsatake, Akwesasne, and Oswegatchie, to officially take up their place within the Covenant Chain with the British. At the same council, those communities were invited back into the Confederacy, and they accepted:

Brethren of the 5 Nat's.

[You] In return to your Belt of Yesterday Whereby you told us that as your Br. W'y.[356] [Sir William Johnson] had finished every thing with us, you on your part had something to say which was that as there had been during this war a division and disunion between us; and [thereby] desired us to reunite and be firm friends as heretofore, We hereby assure all present that we with pleasure agree to your friendly proposal and reunite as formerly.[357]

The American Revolution began with the Haudenosaunee determined to stay out of what they saw as a fratricidal war between their European brothers. As the war progressed, though, the Haudenosaunee were drawn in. Mohawks

---

355 SWJP 9:669.

356 Johnson's Mohawk name, Warraghyhagey, is most properly translated as "He Cuts Matters Short."

357 SWJP 13:162–64.

close to the Johnson family were impelled to defend them, encouraged by Mary Brant. Oneidas close to Samuel Kirkland joined the rebels, and the survival of the Continental Army at Valley Forge is attributed to Oneida food supplies. Senecas, Onondagas, and Cayugas who had mostly remained neutral joined the British with a vengeance after the 1779 Sullivan-Clinton campaign laid waste to their towns and countries. William Fenton has argued that "by the eighteenth century, the League of the Longhouse was a convenient fiction, and the Iroquois Confederacy had become the effective political institution." The Haudenosaunee, today and historically, have never distinguished between the two. Fenton followed this with the conclusion that the council fire of the Confederacy itself had been extinguished with the exception of token remnants, and that "when a pattern of culture is shattered, a people loses its vital spark."[358] Joagquisho Oren Lyons disagrees: "people who argue that the Confederacy ceased to exist fail to understand the non-coercive nature of the Confederacy vis-a-vis its members and the fact that disruption is not the equivalent of cessation."[359]

In the War of 1812, the British once again called upon their allies for help. This time, the help came at first more reluctantly than ever, and ended again with the Haudenosaunee on both sides of the Niagara frontier, fighting on opposite sides, shedding their brothers' blood. The Seneca chief Little Billy explained: "We know that neither of these powers have any regard for us. . . . Why then should we endanger our families, to enjoy their smiles only for the Day in which they need us?"[360]

Another Seneca chief told John Norton: "We find ourselves in the hands of two powerful Nations, who can crush us when they please. They are the same in every respect, although they are now preparing to contend. We are ignorant of the real motives which urge them to arm,[361] but we are well assured that we have no interest therein, and that neither one nor the other have any real affection

---

358 Fenton 1998, 5, 16.

359 Lyons 1992, 39.

360 Norton 1970, 289–91. John Norton, Joseph Brant's adopted nephew, a Scots-Cherokee Mohawk Pine Tree Chief, was interested in becoming an officer in the British Regular Army. Despite his personal commanding roles in the battles of Queenston Heights and Beaver Dams, he was ignored. Was it his age or was it racism? A little of both—but his hard work on behalf of the British was as overlooked after the war as the welfare of the Six Nations. After the war, Norton tried farming, but fled the Grand River country after a duel in which he killed a Mohawk chief who had been flirting with Norton's wife. He may have been spotted in Laredo, Mexico, some years later, when he would have been in his sixties, but he had disappeared from the Mohawk scene.

361 Most of the British and Americans were also ignorant of these motives, and historians today wonder whether the war ever made any sense in the first place.

towards us. We know that our Blood shed in their battles will not even ensure their compassion to our Widows and Orphans."[362]

After the war, when Deputy Superintendent General of Indian Affairs William Claus met with the Crown's Indigenous allies at Burlington Bay on April 24, 1815, he explained the "Indian clauses" of the Treaty of Ghent, which restored to the Indian nations their rights as they had been before the hostilities. The war chiefs handed the conduct of the council over to the rotiyanershon, and Tekarihoken then requested British assistance in reconciliation with their brothers on the other side of the boundary line: "It is the sincere wish of the Six Nations and your Children of the other nations[363] that you uncover the Council Fire and request the attendance of the Americans and the Indians attached to them."[364]

At the end of August 1815, the council of reconciliation took place at Niagara. On the "American side" of the fire were Senecas, Onondagas, and Cayugas from Buffalo Creek, Tonawanda, and Allegheny. On the "Canadian side" were people from the Grand River Territory. The council began with "the usual ceremonies of Condolence" by the Crown's representative, but the Haudenosaunee immediately took over the work of peacemaking. By the end of the process, the Haudenosaunee had "mixed together" and become "one people" once again. While the council was lengthy and officially at the "King's Council Fire," it was a good example of internal Haudenosaunee reconciliation processes. While the British opened the council, the first day consisted of the propositions of the Grand River chiefs, and the "American side" chiefs replied the next day:

> The Deputy Superintendent addressed all the nations present, per-forming the usual ceremonies of Condolence and uncovering the King's Council Fire by presenting a Belt of White Wampum.
>
> Tekarihoga, Principal Mohawk Chief, Speaker:
>
> Brothers and relations,
>
> Our Father has performed the Ceremonies which were customary with our Ancestors, and which we endeavour to continue. Our meeting is at our Father the King's Council Fire which has just been uncovered that we may proceed to deliberate upon the good work for which we are now assembled. We the several Nations residing

---

362 Norton 1970, 290.

363 It is bad etiquette in council to contradict a speaker directly. By distinguishing between the Six Nations and the "Children" of the other nations, Tekarihoken was reminding Claus, in an indirect way, of the "brothers" relationship between the Haudenosaunee and the Crown.

364 LAC, RG8, C Series, vol. 258, pt. 1, 60–70a. See also Benn 1999.

at the Grand River salute you from the other side we are the same people with you, we are relations of the same colour, notwithstanding having been opposed to each other in the Field during the late Contest between our Father the King of England and the Americans. Our friend who has just uncovered the Council Fire has removed all obstructions, our minds are set at ease. The River which separates us is opened that we may have a free passage at all times. The roads are cleared of all briars and rubbish, that we may again renew that friendly intercourse which formerly existed between us. I now speak to you in behalf of the Indians residing on the Grand River, and I am desired to assure you that all ill will is removed from their Hearts towards you from the [illegible] American land.

Delivered a bunch of Strings of Wampum.

Echo, an Onondaga Chief:

Brothers

I salute you in the name of the Hurons, Shawnees and Six Nations at the King's Council Fire which has just been uncovered. I speak to the Senecas, Cayugas and Onondagas from Buffalo Creek, Tehaniwandi and Allegany who are now present at our Father's Council Fire. I also address those who are at their homes, before our Father the Deputy Supt. General, the King's Officers who are now present, and tell you that all ill blood has been removed from our hearts. What has been done, is now forgotten. We are all of the same colour and ought to be friendly towards each other.

To make our Friendship lasting, we put the Tomahawk the depth of a Pine Tree under ground; and that it may not be removed we place over it a Tree that the roots may so cover it that it cannot be found again. This ceremony was performed by our Father at Burlington last Spring in presence of the Western Nations and I will now repeat to you the speech which our Father delivered to us when he informed us of the Pacification with the Americans, and our Answer (here the proceeding of the Council at Burlington last Spring on the 24th, 26th and 27th April last was repeated). We condole with you from the bottom of our hearts for the loss of your friends, and wipe the tears from your eyes, we open your throats so no obstruction shall remain, that you may speak your mind freely and with the same friendship which formerly existed between us, as we now in the name of the Nations already mentioned address you as friends. If you will stand up we will take you by the hands. Should an idle young Man make use of any improper Language we request that you will not take any notice of it.

A Large bunch of Strings of black and white wampum.

The American Indians stood up and the others took them by the hand repeating the assurances of friendship, after which the Old Eel, an Onondaga Chief spoke to the Deputy Supt. Genl. as follows:

Brothers

You have this day uncovered the King's Council Fire at this place where our forefathers were accustomed to assemble. I speak in behalf of the Indians who are now come here to meet our brethren from the Grand River. We salute you and wish you well. We have heard all that you have said now and last Spring, and are much pleased with it. We rejoice that the Great Spirit has brought us together to unite and be friends. Many have been the meetings at this place between the King and our Ancestors. I am an old man and have been present at many of these meetings when your Grand Father spoke to us.[365] We will always remember his words they are buried deep in our hearts. We look to you to be a friend to the Indians as he was. It is now late in the day, and as we are to answer you we will cover the fire and meet again tomorrow.

A few Strings wampum.

September 1st

Tekarihoga

Brothers

We thank the Great Spirit for giving us a new day, and permitting us to meet again. We wait to hear what you may have to say.

Red Jacket, Principal Seneca Speaker

Brothers

In the name of the Indians from the other side of the River. I now address myself to the King, the Commg. Officers, and Colonel Claus our head, and to the Six Nations, Wyandots and Shawanese.

Strings wampum.

---

365 Deputy Superintendent General William Claus was the grandson of Sir William Johnson, the first Imperial Superintendent General of Indian Affairs. The Imperial Indian Department remained under Johnson family control from 1755 to 1830: their strong Mohawk connections meant that British councils with the Haudenosaunee followed clear Haudenosaunee protocol, mindful of a long continuum of relations.

Brothers

I am happy now to meet you in the usual friendly manner, and you may be assured that what has happened was not from any animosity towards our ancient Father and friends. We are a poor people. We cannot do as we would. We are as Prisoners. But the fetters are now off and we are at liberty to communicate freely with our friends. We are not of the same Nations only, but of the same Families also. We therefore ought to be united and become one Body.

Strings of Wampum.

Brother

You have informed us that the King's Council Fire is again uncovered. We are also informed that the United States have done the same. We seriously recommend that your people will now attend to your usual occupations of hunting and agriculture and that you pay due attention to your Women, who by our ancient customs have a voice in bringing up our Young people to the practice of truth and industry.

Strings of Wampum. . . .

The Road being now open, we will be glad to have a visit from you at Buffalo Creek. Eating and drinking together may be omitted at present, our time being so short, rising and shaking hands will do as well.

Strings of wampum.

They then mixed with each other and spoke to the Deputy Supt. General as follows.

Tekarihoga, Speaker

Brothers

You have witnessed our proceedings which it has pleased the Ruler of the World to assist us in. It has finished as we could wish, and we desire that you will immediately acquaint our Western Brethren of the work we have been doing; and that we shall soon proceed to the west to meet them and perform the same ceremony there as was agreed upon last spring in Council. We now speak to you in One Body, and we hope that we shall be allowed to travel along the road peaceably and without being insulted by the inhabitants, and that you will give us provisions to enable us to travel homewards.

The Deputy Superintendent General

Brothers

In compliance with your particular request expressed in your Speech of 26th April last, your Father General Drummond ordered that I should be present at this meeting, and I have now to express how much I am satisfied with the whole of your proceedings which I very earnestly recommend you to keep in remembrance. The Road has been open'd and made smooth for you all. When the King of England made peace with the Americans he was particular in stipulating that no difficulties should be thrown in the road to interrupt a free intercourse between his Indian Children. I am sorry to understand that the Inhabitants have in some cases behaved improperly towards you but your young men have provoked the resentment by their own misconduct. You are all under the protection of your Great Father the King, and if you conduct yourselves peaceably towards his white children, they will not be permitted to ill treat you. Provisions will be provided for you on your return homewards. I now cover the Council Fire and wish you a safe return home.[366]

The Haudenosaunee had required the assistance of the British to create the opportunity for reconciliation—to kindle the council fire at which this would take place—but by the end of the council (and unaccountably omitting the feast that would have firmly brought them together) they spoke across the fire to William Claus as "one people" again.

Perhaps the Haudenosaunee are always at the edge of division: the bonds that link the nations, despite their strong description, are voluntary, not the result of compulsion. Recognizing the possibility of these splits, the Peacemaker built into the law the means of reconciliation. In contrast, there is no constitutional provision for secession—or rejoining—by states or provinces in the Euro-American nations. Instead, there have been Quebec referenda and court decisions, and an American Civil War.

---

366 Transcript of a council at Niagara, August 31–September 1, 1890. LAC, RG 8, vol. 258, pt. 1, 204–8.

Pine Tree Chiefs

From the beginning, it was clear that there would be able leaders who were not members of the lineages of the rotiyanershon. This would be especially true of a League that was designed to bring in people of all nations, extending the longhouse. The Great Peace would require their participation and support. The Peacemaker created a new institution, the Pine Tree Chief:

> Thereupon Dekanawidah said, "Now, again, I decree another thing: you chiefs of the several nations of our League, if something should happen, if ever a disruptive idea were to enter where the Great Pine is located, where the power is situated, if the chiefs are unable to agree, thereupon someone among the warriors or the people—just whoever in the crowd is able—that one shall help, assisting them at the Council, the League chiefs. This is also the one who will help the crowd, for he is able, this one, to climb their tree, Skaehetsi:kowa, Great Tall Tree, and he is able to perch on top of the tree. There upon he will look around for a place having an opening, a space for them to escape, the entire crowd, so that they may survive and also our grandchildren. Thereupon he will descend again and stand up there in front of the chiefs. Thereafter he will place in front of them his own opinion, he having observed where they can escape in order for the entire group to survive, so that the day will dawn for generations of our grandchildren.
>
> Thereupon the chiefs will take it up, considering whether they can see that it will be correct, the warrior's information, that this is what will help them. After the chiefs accept it, the suggestion of the one not holding office, they will confirm it, and if it turns out well—the warrior's information concerning the great matter with which he is helping all of the people—then the chiefs will think carefully about the man, the warrior holding no office, thinking about his ability to save them, the ongoing families. Thereupon they will decide to include him where they are seated to counsel together, the chiefs of the five nations. And there they will stand him up, in front of the chiefs who will then give him a title which they will call Pine Tree Chief,[367] the self-made

---

367 Newhouse 1885, 154, calls these people Yoh-neh-doh-da onh, "a chief by merit," and says "the chiefs will proclaim in their assembly '*O-ka-yon-don-tshe-rah*' that such a one has now become what is called '*Wa-ho-di-neh-dot-hah-she*' (it means a Pine Tree has grown out from the ground for them)."

chief, and this is because he helped the chiefs and the entire group. Moreover, actually, he has as much power as the antlered chiefs of our various nations, all of the trees being of equal height.

If it should happen that a Pine Tree Chief, a self-made one, if ever he spoils certain matters between the chiefs and the people, the chiefs will pick up the matter of the Pine Tree Chief, and if they find that he is not truthful in his dealings, then the chiefs will decide to take back his title,[368] and he will come back out from where the chiefs are located. Then it will come to happen again that he will be like the public, he no longer having a title, and we will call this they knocked the tree down again; but if the one who becomes a Pine Tree Chief is righteous, and works conscientiously—he not causing trouble for the chiefs and the people—then they will be permanent, his duties with his colleagues, which means that he will help the whole group—including the coming generations of our grandchildren—and that he should not spoil matters within the League. In fact, his duties as a chief will last as long as he lives, and when he dies, then it will end, the title, which he will take with him, so that never another should be given that title. That is how it will continue to be done among the several nations and clans of our League.[369]

The Pine Tree Chief, then, is an adviser to the council.[370] His advice is of such consistently good quality that the chiefs in council may decide to raise him up themselves. As he is a "pine tree," it is said, his roots are in the council, not in his family, so that he can be removed by the chiefs without any reference to a clan or clan mothers. At the same time, because he has been raised up by the chiefs, he is protected by them against the ill will of the people. He sits in council as an equal, in the sense that he has a right to be heard equal to other chiefs: "Whenever we discover a warrior who is wise and trustworthy and who will render his services for the benefit of the people and thus aid the lords of the confederacy, we will claim him into our midst and confer upon him the title 'He has sprung up as a Pine Tree' (Eh-ka-neh-do-deh) and his title shall

---

368 Newhouse 1885, 154, says that "no one is able to put him out of the council when he does anything contrary to the Constitution of the Confederate Nations or other mischief, but his mouth can be closed."

369 Gibson 1912, 464–72.

370 Snow 1994, 65: "The office of Pine Tree Chief was defined to accommodate men of ability who did not happen to come from clan segments that held League titles." This is not quite accurate, since it was also designed to include men of merit whose families already had a representative (for example, in the first part of the twentieth century, William Loft held the Mohawk title Dewaserage; his brother Anadahes Frederick Loft was a Pine Tree Chief).

last only during his lifetime and shall not be hereditary and at his death it shall die with him."[371]

A Pine Tree Chief sits in council with the chiefs of his nation.

His title lasts only as long as his lifetime: the name is then retired, in the sense that he does not have any successor. While there is no official limit to the number of Pine Tree Chiefs, they never crowd out the rotiyanershon. They are men of exceptional ability, and there are not many of them.

Teianoken (Deyanoga) was a Pine Tree Chief before he became a Mohawk title holder. When he went to England in 1710 he was known as Teyoninhokarawen. It is said that Sir William Johnson, Warraghyihagey, became a Pine Tree Chief in 1746–47 under the "sponsorship" of Theyanoguin. It is also said that Thayendenegea Joseph Brant became a Pine Tree Chief under the sponsorship of Warraghyihagey. And it is said that another Teyoninhokarawen, John Norton, Thayendenegea's adopted nephew, became a Pine Tree Chief, put forward by Thayendenegea. Through this succession of Pine Tree Chiefs, one can see the bones of a multi-generational Mohawk strategy for survival in turbulent times.

At Tonawanda, it is said that Sagoyewatha (Red Jacket) was appointed chief of the Beaver Clan, but because of his actions, the title was removed not only from him but also from the clan. A gifted orator, he was speaker for the council fire at Buffalo Creek, and also occasionally for the women,[372] but there are few references to him as a chief.[373] Instead, he is often referred to as a speaker, and occasionally as a Pine Tree Chief.

Lately, the Confederacy has been reluctant to appoint Pine Tree Chiefs.[374]

---

371   Parker (Chiefs) 1916, 108.

372   Sagoyewatha spoke for the Women at the Canandaigua Treaty in 1794 (Ganter 2006, 62).

373   Morgan says that "it would have been unwise to raise up a man of his intellectual power and extended influence to the office of sachem; as it would have concentrated in his hands too much authority" ([1851] 1995, 98). See also Stone 1841. Toriwawakon Paul Wallace, basing his statement on Seneca oral tradition, says that Red Jacket was removed as speaker and Handsome Lake was installed as a supreme chief at Buffalo Creek. The history of the Buffalo Creek council fire—the interim measure before the split between Grand River and Onondaga—has not been fully written.

374   Possibly the split at Tonawanda in the 1980s between the condoled chiefs and the men they had appointed as Pine Trees has contributed to the reluctance. Another reason, more commonly given, is that they are waiting to restore the full complement of the council before moving on to the other institutions of the Confederacy. Sometimes it is suggested that the problem of duplication of titles between communities could be resolved by the appointment of Pine Tree Chiefs to fill the needs of local councils. While this would satisfy leadership needs, it would mean using an institution for a purpose for which it was never intended, a sometimes dangerous proposition. Appointing temporary local "representatives" has been tried, with difficult results, since the representatives often later refuse to step aside, as in the Oneida and Cayuga communities in New York.

Local or Village Chiefs

When the Peacemaker arrived, the leaders he met were all local or village chiefs. In creating the League, he "raised them up" to be leaders not only of their own village or nation but of all the nations together. However, it is clear that the villages were administered not as dictatorships but as democracies, with councils held among families, clans, and all the people, and also among men and women, to make necessary decisions. Each town or village had "chiefs" for specific purposes: there would be people who would be "chiefs" of certain ceremonies or societies; "war chiefs" and probably "chiefs" for fishing or hunting. Though the fifty men whose names became permanent titles of the Haudenosaunee were often called "the chiefs," in fact the institution of "village chief" for local purposes continued.

The use of the English word "chief" to describe several quite different kinds of Haudenosaunee leaders had added a layer to the confusion. To distinguish the rotiyanershon from others, the Algonkian word "sachem"[375] began to be used in the seventeenth century. Confederacy chiefs, Pine Tree Chiefs, local chiefs, including local "life chiefs"—the actual authority of the individuals led to confusion, at first among the Europeans who met them, and eventually among the Haudenosaunee themselves.

It appears that, historically, when a new village was created (as distinct from an existing village moving to a new location), a local council was created that reflected the clan and family makeup of the community. That way, every part of the community would have a voice in its council. Thus, the mainly Mohawk community of Akwesasne had nine chiefs for the three Mohawk clans (Turtle, Bear, and Wolf) from its founding in 1749 to the arrival of the Onondagas from Oswegatchie, when three more chiefs were added to reflect the Snipe and Deer clans.

Morgan suggested that the local chiefs originated later than the formation of the Confederacy, but that local chiefs and Pine Tree Chiefs were similar:

> When the power of the Ho-de-no-sau-nee began to develop, under the new system of oligarchies within an oligarchy, there sprang up around the sachems a class of warriors, distinguished for enterprise upon the war-path and eloquence in council, who demanded some participation in the administration of public affairs. The serious

---

375 Delaware *sagamo*, Ojibway *ogima*, Passamaquoddy *sakima* or *sakokum*.

objection to the enlargement of the number of rulers, involving, as it did, changes in the framework of the government, for a long period enabled the sachems to resist the encroachment. In the progress of events, this class became too powerful to be withstood, and the sachems were compelled to raise them up in the subordinate station of chiefs. The title was purely elective, and the reward of merit. Unlike the sachemships, the name was not hereditary in the tribe or family of the individual, but terminated with the chief himself; unless subsequently bestowed by the tribe upon some other person, to preserve it as one of their illustrious names. These chiefs were originally invested with very limited powers, their principal office being that of advisers and counsellors of the sachems. Having thus obtained a foothold in the government, this class, to the number of which there was no limit, gradually enlarged their influence, and from generation to generation drew nearer to an equality with the sachems themselves. By this innovation the government was liberalized, to the sensible diminution of the power of the sachems, which, at the institution of the League, was extremely arbitrary.[376]

By the institution of this office, the stability of the government was increased rather than diminished. In their own figurative enunciation of the idea, the chiefs served as braces in the Long House—an apt expression of the place they occupied in their political structure. It furnished a position and a reward for the ambitious, and the means of allaying discontent, without changing the ruling body. In this particular, the oligarchy of the Iroquois appears to have enjoyed some superiority over those of antiquity.[377]

The chiefs in each gens were usually proportioned to the number of its members. Among the Seneca-Iroquois there is one chief for about every fifty persons. They now number in New York some three thousand, and have eight sachems and about sixty chiefs. There are

376   Morgan (1851) 1995, 95.

377   Morgan (1851) 1995, 96–97.

reasons for supposing that the proportionate number is now greater than in former times.[378]

The same method of election and confirmation [as for a sachem] existed with respect to the office of chief, and for the same reasons. But a general council was never convened to raise up chiefs below the grade of a sachem. They awaited the time when sachems were invested.[379]

Other famous Pine Tree Chiefs include Anadahes Frederick Ogilvie Loft, a Wolf Clan Mohawk from the Grand River Territory who in 1920 founded the League of Indians of Canada and became its first president. The league was the direct ancestor of the National Indian Brotherhood and the Assembly of First Nations.

---

378 Morgan (1871) 1997, 73. In the days when the Senecas numbered above 20,000, they still had only eight rotiyanershon. Morgan included sub-chiefs and possibly faithkeepers as "chiefs." In some communities today, local councils include faithkeepers, who are sometimes called "chiefs," though this raises some controversy in the communities that reserve that title for rotiyanershon. Two thoughts emerge from this discussion. First, it may be the lack of representation of all the clans and families that made the Seneca Nation especially susceptible to the pressures of government by election. Second, the small number of chiefs was probably a reflection of the many foreign nations the Senecas had adopted, none of whom would find representation in the Confederacy Council.

379 Morgan (1871) 1997, 73. In the early twenty-first century, there has been a debate about whether Tuscarora chiefs can be condoled by the other nations. In an argument parallel to how Morgan described recognition of local chiefs, it has been suggested that the Tuscaroras should wait for a Condolence of the rotiyanershon of another nation, and then introduce their new chiefs at that ceremony, where the rest of the Confederacy will then recognize them by lining up to shake their hands.

Maintenance and Renewal

A bark longhouse had a life span similar to a human generation. Towards the end of that time, it would become necessary to prop it up from the outside with poles. That was taken as a sign that it was time to begin to look for a new site for the village, and to begin clearing the land there.[380] Bark houses required maintenance and renewal: water, wind, insects, ice, and time would wear away their sturdiness and comfort.

Similarly, the League and the law required periodic renewal, to keep them fresh in the minds of the people. Newhouse made it a precise obligation: "Every five years the Five Nations Confederate Lords and the people shall assemble together and shall ask one another if their minds are still in the same spirit of unity for the Great Binding Law and if any of the Five Nations shall not pledge continuance and steadfastness to the pledge of unity then the Great Binding Law shall dissolve."[381]

Maintaining the longhouse, architecturally, did not mean replacing any part of its framework: the posts that formed its core remained in place throughout the life of the building. Cedar posts did not rot. The bark shingles would be replaced regularly. This made it easy for people to understand that the trappings of the constitution could be changed, while its core architecture must remain constant.

Propping up the longhouse from the outside[382] became the metaphor for those nations that would "support the League" without coming inside it for shelter. On wampum belts, the commitment of these nations was symbolized by diagonal lines, leaning like supporting poles. Once the Tuscaroras were brought into the house, it was said that they had propped up the house from the inside—just as adding rafters would strengthen the structure.

---

380 Two other factors made a move desirable: the soil of the fields and gardens could be getting tired after a generation of planting, and the people would have greater distances to walk for firewood. See Engelbrecht (2003, 102–3), who also suggests that the longer walks for firewood would also be unsafe for women venturing farther from the safety of the palisades, but argues that the intercropping of maize and beans may have mitigated exhaustion of the soil.

381 Parker (Newhouse and Cusick) 1916, 45. Another Newhouse version states maintenance more positively, omitting the dissolution, and merely saying that "all of the Five Nations shall declare continuance and steadfastness in the unity of the pledge of the Confederacy of the Great Peace" (14th Wampum). Counter to this "dissolution theory" runs the tradition that as long as there remain three nations committed to the Great Law, the councils and government can continue.

382 Hayadaha Richard Hill, personal communication.

Amendment: Adding to the Rafters

When the Confederacy was formed, the Senecas were the westernmost nation; the Mohawks were at the Eastern Door; the communities of each nation were not far from one another, in clusters. The population was small enough that each citizen had direct contact with the people who spoke in council.

Today, the Mohawks are still at the Eastern Door—at least, those of Kahnawake, Kanehsatake, and Akwesasne are. But there are also Mohawk communities at the Bay of Quinte, the Grand River, and Wahta. The Oneidas in New York are west of the three eastern Mohawk communities—but there are also Oneidas at the Grand River, on the Thames River, and in Wisconsin. The Onondagas are evenly split between those who remain at Onondaga and those on the Grand River. The Cayugas are in New York but also on the Grand River and in Oklahoma. The Senecas are in New York, on the Grand River, and in Oklahoma.

Nor are the chiefs' titles spread around evenly or equitably. Some communities claim all the titles belonging to a nation; some have none.

If the principle of the law is that everyone should have a voice in council, then there is room for constitutional adjustment. The Peacemaker recognized that change should be possible within the structures he had created: he called it "adding to the rafters"—indeed, amendment would be necessary as the peace expanded: "This is then just what should happen: namely that we should afterward join additional roof poles to the framework (*hosedwawanahsdahso'den*), 'great sooty black rafters' (by amendment to the structure of our government)."[383]

The basic principles would remain as constant as the architecture, though the size of the house might evolve.[384]

---

383 Gibson 1899, para. 70.

384 About 30 percent of the historic longhouses that have been excavated by archaeologists show signs of having been expanded or added to (Engelbrecht 2003, 72; Warrick 1996, 21). Because the posts at the ends of longhouses were not load bearing, they were not sunk as deeply as the side posts, and the archaeological record of adding to and subtracting from longhouses seasonally is incomplete. There are very few reliable eyewitness drawings of the exteriors of longhouses, and even fewer of the interiors.

Few versions of the Kayanerenkó:wa explain how "adding to the rafters" shall take place, but each version confirms that change is possible and contemplated.[385] Amending a constitution is difficult enough in most nations, whether it is to be accomplished by a referendum, by high levels of approval in the legislature, or by approval from the legislature of another nation. The Peacemaker brought a message from the Creator: even while acknowledging the intention to allow change consistent with the architecture of the law, many are reluctant, as mere humans, to tamper with the details of the law. Whereas the Peacemaker had the self-confidence of an artist, modern generations of Haudenosaunee have the hesitancy and reluctance of restorers—the reticence of those who are following in the path of the great. As a result, the evolution of the Kayanerenkó:wa tends to be more organic than deliberate.

Furthermore, modern Haudenosaunee lawmakers tend to be conservatives. That is, they are conservative in their adherence to tradition and their resistance to change. Not only do they see Haudenosaunee principles and values as constant—they are also concerned that any change at all is likely to be a step towards assimilation into the Euro-American societies of the United States and Canada. As a result, instead of seeing change—adding to the rafters—as a vehicle for adaptation, they see maintaining tradition as a vehicle of resistance to assimilation.

There are those who would insist that, since the Peacemaker was a messenger from the Creator, it would take another messenger from the Creator to bring any significant constitutional change. These people are supported in their position by a view that Skanaiatariio, Handsome Lake, was just such a messenger, bringing visions and prescriptions for Haudenosaunee conduct in a time of rapid social, economic, and technological change. Since new messages are possible— indeed, many believe that a fourth and final message is due soon—tinkering with the constitution by mere humans should not be permitted.

Any constitution that is a "fixed canon" created in a "constitutional moment" rather than organically, over time (like the British constitution, which, while mostly written, is not contained in a single document) creates a tendency

---

385 In Canadian law, the courts have said that "the British North America Act planted in Canada a living tree capable of growth and expansion within its natural limits" (*Edwards v. A.G. Canada*, [1930] A.C. 124). Chief Justice Dickson wrote that "A statute . . . is easily enacted and as easily repealed. A constitution, by contrast, is drafted with an eye to the future. Its function is to provide a continuing framework for the legitimate exercise of governmental power. . . . Once enacted, its provisions cannot be easily repealed or amended. It must, therefore, be capable of growth and development over time to meet new social, political and historical realities often unimagined to its framers" (*Hunter v. Southam Inc.*, [1984] 2 S.C.R. 145 at 155). While deliberate change is one way for a constitution to evolve, Canadian law also recognizes that there is a "doctrine of progressive interpretation" through which the courts and legislators can also help the constitution adapt to social change (Hogg 1997, 15–43 to 15–44; *Halpern v. Canada* (2003), 65 O.R. (3d) 161 at 175).

towards "ancestor worship," a retrospective view that attributes wisdom and prescience to the founders.

This resistance to change by "traditionalists" manifests itself most obviously in terms of a resistance rather than an adaptation to new technology.

Four kinds of constitutional or governmental changes have swept the Haudenosaunee in the past century and a half.

One kind of change, exemplified best by the "Seneca Nation of Indians," involves a movement within the people themselves to adopt a constitution that abandons the Kayanerenkó:wa and adopts the forms and values of the governments of the United States or Canada.[386] In each case, though, there are people in the community who recognize and sustain the Confederacy and its laws.

A second kind of change, exemplified best by the experience at the Six Nations Grand River Territory, involves the imposition of a system of local government chosen by elections and created and authorized by external laws.

A third kind of change, reflected in the operations of the Oneida Nation of New York, maintains aspects of traditional structures (a "Men's Council," for example) while breaking away from the Kayanerenkó:wa itself.[387]

The fourth kind of change—apparently the hardest to accomplish—is within the law, maintaining its spirit and intent, and adapting it to reflect the needs of modern Haudenosaunee communities. The best example of this is the determination of the Grand Council in 1998 that there should be only fifty rotiyanershon in all the Confederacy, and that negotiations should occur within each of the nations to ensure that the benches were filled and that each of the communities had a clear voice in the government of the Haudenosaunee. This decision was clearly conservative: it marked a return to the original terms of the law rather than a recognition of "duplication of titles" that was leading to the existence of "two confederacies"—one in Canada, one in the United States. There had been a belief, especially among some on the American side, that a royá:ner's "horns got caught in the bushes at the border," so that he would only be a chief in the country in which his own community was located, and this would justify duplications of titles. The Grand Council decision refuted this. As a statement of intended unity, it was consistent with the values that the Peacemaker expressed. Implementation has been more difficult than anticipated: no individual nation has resolved its issues, and allocation of titles has become a new source of friction.

---

386 Not all traditional values have been abandoned by the Seneca Nation of Indians. Its judiciary, for example, is still called a "Peacemaker's Court."

387 Without land recognized as "Indian reserve" land, the Mohawk community of Kanehsatake vacillates between an Indian Act–style elected council and a council that reflects aspects of the Kayanerenkó:wa, although there is also a separate presence of traditional Haudenosaunee government in the community. Litigation between rival groups brings Canadian courts to consider what constitutes Kanehsatake Mohawk government, but not very well.

Prophecy: Things Will Go Wrong

The great Haudenosaunee narratives contain predictions that may be warnings or may simply be explanations of how things will end. In the Creation story, the end of days is dire:

> Long before the end, you will see that the things upon which you live will gradually decrease in quantity, all the things on earth that grow will become weaker, and finally it will happen that nothing more can grow.
>
> The same will happen to the animals and the birds. They will also grow fewer in number until at some future time you will see no more of them. And at that time awe-inspiring things will happen. There will be earthquakes and things which have great power which now abide in the earth will come forth and they will be more powerful than human beings.[388]

Compared to those calamities, the future difficulties of the Confederacy, as predicted by the Peacemaker, seem benign:

> Thereafter Tekanawita said: This is what else I ordain. It may happen in future that something is going to impoverish them, it wasting their land; or it may happen that perhaps someone will roll their heads somewhere, and he, walking along, a man, will observe, their heads rolling along, and thereupon the man may say, "Indeed, now it serves them right, they of the League," and kick the heads. Thereupon he may say, "In the past, in our former days, they used to have power and they used to be proud of their strength." Thereupon the man will pass through and he will not have gone far, before he will vomit

---

388 Mohawk 2005a, 88–89.

blood, for it is still possible for it to punish him for kicking his League's head.[389]

Thereupon Tekanawita said, "This is what it means, 'their heads will roll, they of the League.' If the Five Nations make a mistake where they have their families, then they will disperse, some going towards the east, some going towards the west, some going towards the south, some going towards the north; thus, the families will scatter, and the several nations will live all over the Island, and nowhere can one find space to live and multiply, for they won't make space for them and give them shelter, the individual families. If it happens that they do shelter them, it won't be long before those living there will begin to abuse them, eventually forcing them to leave their settlement, and the reason why they will do this is that they have never accepted the League's Great Law and Peace; this is what they will see, our grandchildren, should it happen that they don't watch out, the chiefs of the League."

Thereupon, Tekanawita said, "Moreover, I decree that if this is what will happen to the coming generations, if they are going to be impoverished, our grandchildren, then these chiefs are to look for the very biggest tree, the large elm, which is tall and has huge branches and roots, all of them extending equally into the depths, and if they find such a large tree with long branches and roots extending equally deep, they will have good luck in generations to come, our grandchildren; in that place they will collect their heads, all of the nations of our League, all of us will place our heads there, and there we will hide our heads as long as it will last, the earth which is beneath the sun. This is where it will again be possible for them to be happy for they will continue to hold on to that which protects the group, that is, the Good Message and the Power and the Peace and the Great Law; there the fire will be rekindled, our fire of our League which will keep burning and the smoke that will keep rising, piercing the sky, and again it will be able to help them at our various smoking fireplaces whose smoke is piercing the sky, where all of us share our beliefs."

---

389 "It will be hard and your grandchildren will suffer hardship. And if it may so occur that the heads of the people of the confederacy shall roll and wander away westward, if such a thing should come to pass, other nations shall see your heads rolling and wandering away and they shall say to you 'You belong to the confederacy, you were a proud and haughty people once,' and they shall kick the heads with scorn, and they shall go on their way, but before they shall have gone far they shall vomit up blood (Meaning that the Confederacy shall still have power enough to avenge their people)." Parker (Chiefs) 1916, 105. See also Gibson 1899, para. 124.

Thereupon Tekanawita said: "Now we have completed our task. This, again, will help them, the families of our League."[390]

The chiefs' heads rolling around is a symbol of their inability to make decisions or to bring their minds together. Another symbol used in this part of the law, with the same meaning, is that the chiefs will shuffle their feet in indecision under their benches.

It is said that during the time of the American Revolution, the settlers had so crowded the Haudenosaunee, especially in the east, and had abused them so much, that the Grand River Territory was the fulfillment of the Peacemaker's prophecy—and so the fire of the League was rekindled there, with all the titles and all the families settling along the banks of the river. There they had found the Great Swamp Elm to which the Peacemaker had referred.

Reality is more complex, and a crucial period of Haudenosaunee history has been poorly studied and often misinterpreted. William Fenton concluded that the council fire at Onondaga was extinguished—permanently put out—and that marked the end of the Confederacy. He viewed subsequent Haudenosaunee governments as illegitimate, and maintained that the League and Confederacy came to an end.[391] James Deane, an enemy of the Haudenosaunee, whose instructions to negotiators at Fort Stanwix in 1784 were to intimidate and insult the chiefs, declared the Confederacy dead: "But as the heads of the Confederacy had now declared themselves so fully upon the subject, they now let go their Hold of peace; extinguished the Council Fire, sunk the Tree of Peace into the Earth and caused a total Darkness to overspread the Confederacy."[392]

However, Haudenosaunee tradition and action point to a different conclusion, based on resilience, pragmatism, and necessity. Samuel Kirkland, a missionary to the Oneidas, refuted this premature death: he wrote on January 19, 1776: "The dissolving their Body-politic, or extinguishing the Council Fire at Onondaga, is only a pretext by which they will repair to Niagara and then to renew their ancient Covenant with the British King. I apprehend it will be wise

---

390 Gibson 1912, 478–85.

391 Fenton 1998, 710–723. Fenton's great antipathy towards the Confederacy chiefs arose mainly from his dogged war against the repatriation of the Confederacy's wampum belts from the New York State Museum, of which he was a trustee. He declared the wampum to be "the Elgin Marbles of New York State," and argued that the modern Haudenosaunee were not legitimate successors to the Confederacy; that the Museum was trustee of these important artifacts for all the people of New York; and that the "young Indians" like Sostsisowah John Mohawk, Joagquisho Oren Lyons, and Hayadaha Rick Hill were disrespectful of his knowledge, which was superior to theirs, and ignorant of the meaning of the wampum. To Fenton, who had made his reputation as a scholar of Haudenosaunee history and culture, a living Confederacy was a constant challenge to his authority.

392 James Deane to General Schuyler, January 18, 1779, *Indian Affairs Papers*, 181.

and politic for you to perform the ceremony of condolence and replace those sachems and thereby rekindle the capital fire of the Six Nations."[393]

The fire at Onondaga was "covered over," not extinguished.[394] The council fire of the Confederacy was rekindled for a while—from 1784 to 1838—at Buffalo Creek. Buffalo Creek—halfway between the new Grand River Territory in Upper Canada and the remaining unsurrendered Seneca territory—was also large enough to be a central council fire. However, there was internal dissension, including an ugly confrontation between Handsome Lake on one hand and Farmer's Brother, Cornplanter, and Red Jacket on the other—and eventually the fire at Onondaga was rekindled, and an arrangement was made for what seemed to be a "two-headed" confederacy, with one part dealing with the British and one dealing with the United States. The wampums were divided according to how they would be most useful (some minor individual belts may have been "split" into two), with the belts recording agreements with the United States remaining at Onondaga, and the belts with the British at the Grand River.

The Condolence has given the Haudenosaunee a means of healing rifts and hard feelings. The split in the Confederacy has occurred several times in the past two centuries, usually when the neighbours are at war and draw the warriors into the conflict. After the French capitulation at Montreal in 1760, there was a separate council at Kahnawake, in which the Mohawks who had accompanied the British Army invited the people of Kahnawake, Kanehsatake, Akwesasne, and Oswegatchie to reunite as formerly, and become one people again. The invitation was accepted, and the one Confederacy restored. The American Revolutionary War saw Oneidas side with the rebels and Mohawks side with the Tories, and eventually Seneca, Onondaga, and Cayuga communities, seeking neutrality, were attacked in the Sullivan-Clinton campaign of 1779 and sided with the British. After the war, though, there was reconciliation and reunification. In the War of 1812, there were Oneida and Tuscarora fighters on the American side, and people from the Grand River (at Queenston Heights, Chippewa, and Beaver Dams) and the eastern Mohawk communities (at Chateauguay, Chrysler's Farm, and Beaver Dams) fighting for the British. In 1815, when peace was announced, the two sides came together, condoled,

---

393 *Indian Affairs Papers*, 70. Kirkland may have been referring to the part of the ceremony of Condolence that rekindles the council fire—he would use the ceremony to reactivate the fire at Onondaga.

394 The word "extinguishment" was chosen by United States and Canadian courts to describe transactions and laws that put an end to Aboriginal title and rights. For a people whose symbol was the fire, "extinguishment" and "genocide" are not far apart. And in Canadian law, since to establish an Aboriginal right, one must show that the practice is "an integral part of the distinctive society," so important that "they would not be the same people without it"—the taking ("infringement") of an Aboriginal right—after "consultation" and compensation—could meet elements of the international definition of "genocide."

and reunited. The Condolence serves as the formal record of that accord, as it serves as formal evidence that a person is indeed a royá:ner.

It is useful to think of Haudenosaunee communities as an archipelago, their people navigating between these islands of culture, history, ecology, language, and law. There is constant communication. As the Government of Canada learned the hard way in 1990, in a crisis, the people come together without regard to boundaries or political leanings. In dealings with other Indigenous nations and with the nation-states of the world, there is no doubt that the Haudenosaunee still exist, and that the institutions created by their laws still function. Nevertheless, there is also erosion of culture, values, institutions, and law. The Peacemaker's warnings are never far from people's minds.

Most of what the Peacemaker did in designing the law was immediate and remedial, and dealt with the challenges of his times—yet the reference to the chiefs' heads rolling around, and the people seeking the great swamp elm, is prophecy. It is also a warning: anyone who shows disrespect for the League will suffer. More literally, anyone who kicks the chiefs when they are down will vomit blood and die:

> It may be that after the lapse of time, some person may come and will see this Root (or, one of these Roots) extending along, and seeing that it is a Root beautiful beyond measure, will raise his hatchet and will strike it into the Root—blood will flow from the Root, we all shall feel it. Whenever we have felt this, we shall know that he who has struck his hatchet into the Root does not desire to receive the Great Law. Then we will look and we shall see the lack of the retreating culprit, and before he has gone far something occult and supernatural will happen to him, for blood shall come forth from his mouth, and there will be yet power to repeat this mystic stroke upon him.[395]

At the very end, when the chiefs in council can no longer agree, when the League's affairs diminish, and when the chiefs are constantly making mistakes, a white meteor will descend and remove the Great Law as a source of dispute. The earth will open up and "their feet will dangle over the edge."[396] At that time, "the chiefs of the League no longer control their Power and Peace and it is impossible for them to save the people, and really the only one who will be able to save the people, the only one able to do it, will be the Creator, the one who has created all things on earth."[397]

---

395 Hewitt 1892b, 143.

396 This phrase is also used to describe the fate of a chief who leaves the circle of the law (Hohahes Leroy Hill, Oneida, August 2013).

397 Gibson 1912, 61.

Is this dire warning a certainty? No: the Peacemaker follows it with another prediction—that the League will last as long as the matters of the natural world:

> These shall last as long as the earth exists, and as long as they are going to grow, the grasses and also the various weeds, and as long as the shrubs keep growing wild, the various shrubs, and as long as they keep growing wild, the trees, all kinds of trees, and as long as springs emerge the water of the rivers will keep flowing, also the large rivers and the various lakes; and as long as the sun keeps rising and setting and the moon keeps up its phases, and in the sky the stars do the same, and the wind is stirring on the land, and heavenly bodies continue to provide light by day and by night; thus, it shall last, the task we are completing, the Great Law, and these two shall co-operate, the earthly land and the other one, the heavenly land.[398]

Nevertheless, the earth is warming. Its climate is becoming more extreme. Many of the people on the move today are not economic migrants: they are climate refugees. Their homes are being eaten by droughts and floods, and by wars that were spawned by droughts and floods. The anger and sorrow of the people of the earth are intensifying. The trees are dying from the tops down, as Haudenosaunee prophecies have warned. We all need condoling and compassion, for we are one family.

And in the End . . .

As a legal system, the Kayanerenkó:wa is too complex to be described in a single volume. Its principles are distinctive and pragmatic enough that they deserve study and can withstand careful scrutiny. They are not a historical curiosity: above all, they are *alive*.

John Ralston Saul has suggested that the Canadian tendency to seek consensus rather than confrontation originates in an extensive colonial and Canadian experience with Indigenous peoples and processes.[399] The United States Congress

---

398 Gibson 1912, 62. These words evoke two related addresses. In their order and completeness, they echo the Thanksgiving. They are clearly precursors of the words spoken of treaties between the Crown and the Haudenosaunee, and later other Indigenous nations. This is unsurprising: the speakers for the Crown, in the treaties from the 1750s to the 1830s, were often members of the Johnson family, who had been immersed in council procedure by the Haudenosaunee. "As long as the sun shall shine, the grasses grow and the waters flow" (see Denning, J. in *Secretary of State (Indian Association of Alberta)*, [1982] 2 All ER 118).

399 Saul 2008.

acknowledges a debt to the Haudenosaunee in the thinking behind its own constitution, the system of checks and balances that, it is hoped, will prevent any single branch of the government from gaining abusive power over the others. These would be significant contributions, but there are other aspects of Haudenosaunee constitutional thought that are also worth emulating. Protection for the environment; respect for women; consideration of impacts on future generations; maintaining peace through long-term relationships; a system for resolving concerns before they become disputes—all contribute to a viable alternative to short-term political confrontations. Against fierce odds, the Haudenosaunee way of thought and law has survived. Its contemporary challenges, from within and without, come in the form of individualism (David Newhouse spoke glowingly of "the Borg of capitalism") and a desire for prosperity that tumbles into greed; of cultural, linguistic and institutional loss, the legacy of generations of deliberate and collateral assimilation policies; of simple human weaknesses. Indeed, the world is a cruel place for small peoples. Nevertheless, the "Confederacy culture" that Sotsisowah John Mohawk spoke of is more than an ember. Its carriers are convinced that their stewardship is worthwhile.

On May 6, 1993, speaking to the Canadian Royal Commission on Aboriginal Peoples, Otsitsaken:ra Charles Patton of Kahnawa:ke explained: "We are the ones that are living on the earth today; right at this time. We are the ones that are carrying the responsibility of our nations, of our spirituality, of our relationship with the Creator, on our shoulders. We have the mandate to carry that today, at this moment in time. Our languages, our spirituality and everything that we are was given to us and was carried before us by our ancestors, our grandparents who have passed on. When they couldn't carry it any longer and they went to join that spirit world, they handed it to us and they said: 'Now you are the real ones. You have to carry it.' Now they are in the spirit world. They are our past. Now we have a responsibility to carry that because we hear seven generations in the future. They are our future. They are ones that are not yet born."[400]

By the 1990s, the councils began to permit my colleagues and me to use the principles of the law in our negotiations with other governments. We were dealing with municipalities, provincial bodies, state and federal agencies. Many were unfamiliar with Haudenosaunee ways, and we often found that they were the most eager to learn, and the most open.

We would give thanks together, at the beginning and end of each meeting. That would reaffirm our common humanity, and remind us of our humble place in this provident world.

---

400 RCAP 1995, 620.

When we sometimes opened our first meetings with the compassion of the Three Bare Words, more often than not those words would cause our counterparts to shed tears.

We insisted on equality and reciprocity as integral to respect. Respect, we understood, was the first element of any effective relationship. The Covenant Chain consists of three links—respect, trust, and friendship—and like any Haudenosaunee concept, there is an order to them.

Across the negotiating fire, as in council, we would sincerely ask: How can we help you?

We insisted that we eat together.

We would not meet when we were tired, or after dark, or when our minds were burdened by sorrow.

We sincerely sought to transform adversaries into allies, enemies into friends.[401]

We understood that lasting good would come from establishing relationships, not from single transactions. We would keep our eyes on the long term, and sincerely consider the impact of our work on future generations.

We took care to explain the thinking that accompanies the customs, and sometimes we were able to bring out the original wampum belts that preserve the principles and commitments, to strengthen our explanations.

With growing confidence, we were uplifted by the power and certainty of the law, exhilarated that it works, powerfully, as it always has, and by the knowledge that we were part of a continuum, a tradition of skén:nen, ka'nikonhrí:yo, ka'satsténshsera that originated centuries ago and, with care, will endure into the future.

Closing

. . . we have completed all matters that follow in the family through the generations,

and these shall last as long as the earth exists,

and as long as they are going to grow,

the grasses and also the various weeds,

and as long as the shrubs keep growing wild, the various shrubs,

and as long as they keep growing wild, the trees, all kinds of trees,

---

401 Both Nelson Mandela and Abraham Lincoln had said that "if I make my enemy my friend, have I not conquered?"

and as long as springs emerge the waters of rivers will keep flowing;

also the large rivers and the various lakes;

and as long as the sun keeps rising and setting;

and the moon keeps up its phases,

and in the sky the stars do the same,

and the wind is stirring on the land,

and heavenly bodies continue to provide light by day and by night,

thus, it shall last.[402]

---

402 Gibson 1912, 476–77.

Bibliography

Abler, Thomas S. 1980. "Iroquois Cannibalism: Fact not Fiction." *Ethnohistory* 27, no. 4 (Fall): 309–16.

———. 2004. "Seneca Moieties and Hereditary Chieftainship: The Early Nineteenth Century Political Organization of a Multi-reservation Community." *Ethnohistory* 51, no. 3: 459–88.

Abram, David. 1996. *The Spell of the Sensuous.* New York: Vintage.

Adams, Amber Meadow. 2007. "Yellow Woman's River and the Integrity of Story." Keynote Speech, Third Annual Storytellers of the Americas Conference, State University of New York at Buffalo, March 30.

———. 2014. "Teyotsi'tsiahsonhatye: Medicine and Meaning in the Haudenosaunee Story of Life's Renewal." PhD diss., State University of New York at Buffalo.

Akweks, Aren. 1950. "A Mohawk Adoption." *New York Folklore Quarterly* 6, no. 1: 44–46.

Alfred, Taiaiake Gerald. 1999. *Peace, Power and Righteousness: A Mohawk Manifesto.* Toronto: Oxford University Press.

Antone, Robert A. 1987. *The Longhouse of One Family: A Kinship Model of the Iroquoian Clan System.* Brantford, ON: Woodland Indian Cultural Education Centre.

Apio, Alani. 2003. "New Hopes Arise for Ancestral Culture." *Honolulu Advertiser*, January 19.

Armstrong, William H. 1978. *Warrior in Two Camps: Ely S. Parker, Union General and Seneca Chief.* Syracuse, NY: Syracuse University Press.

Asch, Michael, ed. 1997. *Aboriginal Rights in Canada: Essays in Law, Equity and Respect for Difference.* Vancouver: University of British Columbia Press.

Asimov, Isaac. 1994. *I, Asimov: A Memoir.* New York: Doubleday.

Atkins, Sandra Erin. 2001. "The Formation of the League of the Haudenosaunee (Iroquois): Interpreting the Archaeological Record Through the Oral Narrative Gayaneshagowa." MA thesis, Trent University, Peterborough.

Bakker, P. 1990. "A Basque Etymology for the Word 'Iroquois.'" *Man in the Northeast* 40: 89–93.

Barber, Benjamin. 1995. *Jihad vs. McWorld: How Globalism and Tribalism are Reshaping Our World.* New York: Times Books.

Barreiro, Jose. 2010. *Thinking in Indian: A John Mohawk Reader.* Golden, CO: Fulcrum.

Bauman, Richard, and Joel Sherzer. 1974. *Explorations in the Ethnography of Speaking.* New York: Cambridge University Press.

Bell, Catherine, and Michael Asch. 1997. "Challenging Assumptions: the impact of precedent in Aboriginal Rights Litigation." In Asch 1997, 38–74.

Beauchamp, William. 1895. "Onondaga Tales of the Pleiades." *Journal of American Folklore* 13: 281–82.

———. 1907. *Civil, Religious and Mourning Concils and Ceremonies of Adoption of the New York Indians.* Albany: New York State Education Department.

———. 1921. "The Founders of the New York Iroquois League and Its Probable Date." *Researches and Transactions of the New York State Archaeological Association* 3, no. 1. Rochester, New York.

Beauchamp, William (Wah-kat-yu'-ten). (1907) 1975. *Civil, Religious and Mourning Councils and Ceremonies of Adoption of the New York Indians*. New York State Museum Bulletin 113. Reprinted 1975. Albany: University of the State of New York.

Benn, Carl. 1999. *The Iroquois in the War of 1812*. Toronto: University of Toronto Press.

Berger, Adolf. 1953. *Encyclopedic Dictionary of Roman Law*. Philadelphia: American Philosophical Society.

Biggar, H.P., ed. 1924. *The Voyages of Jacques Cartier*. Ottawa: Public Archives of Canada.

Blair, Emma Helen, ed. 1911. *The Indian Tribes of the Upper Mississippi Valley and Region of the Great Lakes*, 2 vol. Cleveland, OH: Arthur H. Clark.

Blau, Harold. 1967. "Notes on the Onondaga Bowl Game." In *Iroquois Culture, History and Prehistory: Proceedings of the 1965 Conference on Iroquois Research*, edited by Elisabeth Tooker, 35–49. Albany: University of the State of New York.

Bloom, Howard. 2001. *Global Brain: The Evolution of Mass Mind from the Big Bang to the 21st Century*. New York: John Wiley and Sons.

Boardman, John, Jasper Griffin, and Oswyn Murray, eds. 1991. *The Oxford History of Greece and the Hellenistic World*. New York: Oxford University Press.

Bodner, Connie Cox. 1999. "Sunflower in the Senecas Iroquois Region of Western New York." In *Current Northeast Paleoethnobotany*, edited by John P. Hart, 27–45. New York State Museum Bulletin 494. Albany: University of the State of New York.

Bogdanor, Vernon. 2009. *The New British Constitution*. Oxford: Hart.

Bonaparte, Darren Akiatonharonkwen. 2006. *Creation and Confederation: The Living History of the Iroquois*. Akwesasne: Wampum Chronicles.

Bonvillain, Nancy. 1992. *Hiawatha: Founder of the Iroquois Confederacy*. New York: Chelsea House.

Boorstin, Daniel. 1985. *The Discoverers: A History of Man's Search to Know His World and Himself*. New York: Vintage.

Boucher, Pierre. 1964. *Histoire veritable et naturelle des moeurs et productions du pays de la Nouvelle France, vulgairement dit le Canada, Paris 1664*. Boucherville, QC: Société Historique de Boucherville.

Boyce, D.W. 1973 . "A Glimpse of Iroquois Culture History Through the Eyes of Joseph Brant and John Norton." *Proceedings of the American Philosophical Society* 117, no. 4: 286–94.

Bradley, James W. 2001. "Change and Survival Among the Onondaga Iroquois since 1500." In *Societies in Eclipse: Archaeology of the Eastern Woodlands Indians, A.D. 1400–1700*, 27–36. Tuscaloosa: University of Alabama Press.

Brandão, José António. 1997. *"Your Fyre Shall Burn No More": Iroquois Policy Toward New France and Its Native Allies to 1701*. Lincoln: University of Nebraska Press.

Brown, Dee. 1970. *Bury My Heart at Wounded Knee*. New York: Henry Holt.

Bruchac, Joseph. 1985. *Iroquois Stories: Heroes and Heroines, Monsters and Magic*. New York: The Crossing Press.

———. 1989. *New Voices from the Longhouse*. Greenfield Center, NY: Greenfield Review Press.

Byrne, Dennis R. 2003. "Nervous Landscapes: Race and Space in Australia." *Journal of Social Archaeology* 3, no. 2: 169–93.

Campbell, Joseph. 1972. *Myths to Live By*. New York: Viking Press.

Canfield, W.W. 1902. *The Legends of the Iroquois*. New York: A. Wessels Co.

Chafe, Wallace. 1961. *Seneca Thanksgiving Rituals*. Washington, DC: U.S. Government Printing Office.

Coe, Michael D. 1999. *Breaking the Maya Code*. London: Thames and Hudson.

Colden, Cadwallader. (1727) 1973. *History of the Five Indian Nations*. New York: AMS Press.

Connelly, Kevin. 1999. "The Textual Function of Onondaga Aspect, Mood and Tense: a Journey Into Onondaga Conceptual Space." PhD diss., Cornell University, Ithaca, NY.

Conover, George S. 1885. *The Naming Ceremonies and Rites of Adoption by the Seneca Indians.* Geneva, NY: n.p.

Converse, Harriet Ga-ya-nes-ha-o. 1908. *Myths and Legends of the New York Iroquois,* edited by Arthur C. Parker. New York State Museum Bulletin 125. Reprinted 1981. Albany: University of the State of New York.

Cooke, Charles. 1952. "Iroquois Personal Names—Their Classification." *Proceedings of the American Philosophical Society* 96: 427–38.

Cornelius, Carol. 1999. *Iroquois Corn in a Culture-Based Curriculum.* Albany: State University of New York Press.

Cornplanter, Jesse. 2007. *Legends of the Longhouse.* Ohsweken, ON: Iroqrafts.

Crosby, Alfred. 1986. *Ecological Imperialism: The Biological Expansion of Europe, 900–1900.* New York: Cambridge University Press.

Cruikshank, Ernest Alexander, ed. 1923. *The Correspondence of Lieut. Governor John Graves Simcoe (Simcoe Papers).* Toronto: Ontario Historical Society.

Cruikshank, E.A., and A.F. Hunter, eds. 1932. *The Correspondence of the Honourable Peter Russell.* Toronto: Ontario Historical Society.

Cuoq, J.A. 1882. *Lexique de la Langue Iroquoise avec notes et appendices.* Montreal: J. Chapleau.

Curtin, Jeremiah, and J.N.B. Hewitt. 1918. *Seneca Fiction, Legends and Myths.* 32nd Annual Report of the Bureau of American Ethnology. Washington, DC: Smithsonian Institution.

Darwin, Charles. (1871) 1989. *The Descent of Man, and Selection in Relation to Sex.* New York: D. Appleton.

Davis, Wade. 1998. *Shadows in the Sun: Travels to Landscapes of Spirit and Desire.* New York: Broadway Books.

Day, Gordon M. 1953. "The Indian as an Ecological Factor in the Northeast Forest." *Ecology* 34: 329–46.

———. 1968. "Iroquois, an Etymology." *Ethnohistory* 15, no. 4: 389–402.

Delafield, Major Joseph. 1943. *The Unfortified Boundary: A Diary of the First Survey of the Canadian Boundary Line from St. Regis to the Lake of the Woods,* edited by Robert McElroy and Thomas Riggs. New York: Privately printed.

Delage, Denys. 1993. *Bitter Feast: Amerindians and Europeans in Northeastern North America, 1600–64.* Translated by Jane Brierley. Vancouver: University of British Columbia Press.

Demos, John. 1995. *The Unredeemed Captive: A Family Story from Early America.* New York: Vintage Books.

Dennis, Matthew. 1993. *Cultivating a Landscape of Peace: Iroquois-European Encounters in Seventeenth Century America.* Ithaca, NY: Cornell University Press.

Deserontyon, John. 1928. *A Mohawk Form of Ritual of Condolence, 1782.* Translated by J.N.B. Hewitt. *Indian Notes* 10, no. 8. New York: Museum of the American Indian.

Dragland, Stan. 1994. *Floating Voice: Duncan Campbell Scott and the Literature of Treaty 9.* Toronto: Anansi.

Drake, Samuel G. 1834. *The Book of the Indians of North America.* Boston: Josiah Drake.

Ehrlich, Paul. 2002. *Human Natures: Genes, Cultures, and the Human Prospect.* New York: Penguin Books.

Engelbrecht, William. 2003. *Iroquoia; The Development of a Native World.* Syracuse, NY: Syracuse University Press.

Fenton, William N. 1949. "Seth Newhouse's Traditional History and Constitution of the Iroquois Confederacy." *Proceedings of the American Philosophical Society* 93, no. 2: 141–58.

————. 1953. *The Iroquois Eagle Dance: An Offshoot of the Calumet Dance*. Bureau of American Ethnology Bulletin 156.

————. 1978. "Northern Iroquoian Culture Patterns." In *Handbook of North American Indians*, vol. 15 (Northeast), edited by Bruce Trigger, 296–321. Washington, DC: Smithsonian Institution.

————. 1998. *The Great Law and the Longhouse: A Political History of the Iroquois Confederacy*. Norman: University of Oklahoma Press.

————. 2002. "He-Lost-A-Bet (Howanɂneyao) of the Seneca Hawk Clan." *Strangers to Relatives: The Adoption and Naming of Anthropologists in Native North America*, edited by Sergei Kan, 81–98. Lincoln: University of Nebraska Press.

Ferris, Neal. 2006. "In Their Time: Archaeological Histories of Native Lived Contacts and Colonialisms in Southwestern Ontario AD 1400–1900." PhD diss., McMaster University, Hamilton, ON.

Fisher, Roger, and Steven Ury. 1985. *Getting to Yes*. New York: Penguin.

Foster, Michael. 1974. *From the Earth to Beyond the Sky: An Ethnographic Approach to Four Longhouse Iroquois Speech Events*. Ottawa: National Museums of Canada.

Fox, Everett. 2000. *The Five Books of Moses*. New York: Schocken Books.

Francis (Pope). 2015. *Laudato Si': On Care for Our Common Home*. Encyclical Letter. Washington, DC: U.S. Conference of Catholic Bishops.

Franklin, Benjamin. 1987. "Remarks Concerning the Savages of North America." In *Benjamin Franklin: Writings*, edited by J.A. LeMay. New York: Library of America.

Frisch, Jack. 1978. "Iroquois in the West." *Handbook of North American Indians*, vol. 15 (Northeast), edited by Bruce Trigger, 544–46. Washington: Smithsonian Institution.

Fritz, Gayle G. 2002. "Levels of Native Biodiversity in Eastern North America." In Paul E. Minnis and Wayne J. Elisens, *Biodioversity and Native America*. Norman: University of Oklahoma Press, 223–47.

Fry, Douglas. 2006. *Beyond War: The Human Potential for Peace*. New York: Oxford University Press.

Gabriel, Allen Kanatiio. 2010. Intergenerational Survivors in British Columbia: Options in the light of the Residential School Settlement Agreement. March.

Ganter, Granville, ed. 2006. *The Collected Speeches of Sagoyewatha, or Red Jacket*. Syracuse, NY: Syracuse University Press.

Gibson, John Arthur (Skaniatariio). 1899. "Founding of the League." NAA ms. 3569.

————. 1909. "The Law of the Woman Chief." NAA ms. 1586.

————. 1912. *Concerning the League: The Iroquois League Tradition as Dictated in Onondaga by John Arthur Gibson*, edited by Hanni Woodbury. Winnipeg: Algonquian and Iroquoian Linguistics, 1992 (cited in the text as Gibson 1912, because it is Skaniatariio John Arthur Gibson's 1912 version of the Great Law, translated by Woodbury and Reg Henry).

Gilkison, Augusta I. Grant. 1928. "What is Wampum? Explained by John Buck, Firekeeper, July 20, 1887." *Annual Archaeological Report* 36: 48–50. Toronto: Minister of Education, Ontario.

Gipson, L.H. 1939. *Zones of International Friction*, vol. 5. New York: Knopf.

Goldenweiser, Alexander A. 1912. "The Death of Chief John A. Gibson." *American Anthropologist* 14: 692–94.

————. 1915. "Functions of Women in Iroquois Society." In *American Anthropologist* 16: 376–77; reprinted in *Iroquois Women: An Anthology*, edited by W.G. Spittal Ohsweken, ON: Iroqrafts, 1996.

————. 1916. "Review: The Constitution of the Five Nations." *American Anthropologist* 18(3): 431–36.

Graymont, Barbara. 1988. *The Iroquois*. New York: Chelsea House.

Hale, Horatio. 1882. "A Lawgiver of the Stone Age." *Proceedings of the American Association for the Advancement of Science* 30: 324–41.

———. (1883) 1989. *The Iroquois Book of Rites*. Ohsweken, ON: Iroqrafts.

Hall, Louis Karoniaktajeh. 1983. "Warrior Manifesto." Indian Survival Crisis Bulletin No. 2. *Warrior Society Newsletter* (October).

Haudenosaunee Environmental Task Force. 2001. *Words That Come Before All Else: Environmental Philosophies of the Haudenosaunee*. Akwesasne: Native North American Traveling College.

Hauptman, Laurence M., ed. 1995. *A Seneca Indian in the Union Army: The Civil War Letters of Sergeant Isaac Newton Parker, 1861–1865*. Shippensburg, PA: Burd Street Press.

Henige, David. 1999. "Can a Myth Be Astronomically Dated?" *American Indian Culture and Research Journal* 23, no. 4: 127–57.

Hennepin, Louis. (1688) 1974. *A New Discovery of a Vast Country in America*. Toronto: Coles. First published 1688.

Hewitt, J.N.B. 1892a. "Raising and Falling of the Sky in Iroquois Legends." *American Anthropologist* 5: 344.

———. 1892b. "The Legend of the Founding of the League." *American Anthropologist* 5: 131–48.

———. 1898. *Constitution of the Confederacy by Dekanawidah*, collected and translated from the Mohawk text by Chief Seth Newhouse, NAA ms. 1343.

———. n.d. "The Requickening or Fifteen Matters." NAA ms. 3588.

———. 1907a. "Means Used in the Settlement of Murder." NAA Ms. 3563.

———. 1907b. "Hiawatha." *Handbook of American Indians North of Mexico*, vol. 1, edited by F.W. Hodge. Bureau of American Ethnology Bulletin 30. Washington, DC: Smithsonian Institution.

———. 1907c. "Iroquois." *Handbook of American Indians North of Mexico*, vol. 2, ed. F.W. Hodge. Bureau of American Ethnology Bulletin 30. Washington, DC: Smithsonian Institution.

———. 1917. Three Book Reviews. *American Anthropologist* 19, no. 3: 429–38.

———. 1926. "Some Laws of the Ancient Iroquois League: The Iroquois Law of Atonement." NAA ms. 663-b.

———. 1928. *The Myth of the Earth-Grasper*. Bureau of American Ethnology, Annual Report, Washington.

———. 1929. "The Laws of Adoption: Of Persons, Families, Clans and Tribes." NAA Ms. 496.

Hill, Richard W. Sr. (Hayadaha). 2009. *The Seven Areas of Responsibility for Clan Mothers*. Ohsweken, ON: Iroqrafts.

Hill, Susan M. 2017. *The Clay We Are Made Of: Haudenosaunee Land Tenure on the Grand River*. Winnipeg: University of Manitoba Press.

Hinderaker, Eric. 2011. *The Two Hendricks: Unraveling a Mohawk Mystery*. Cambridge, MA: Harvard University Press.

Hobbes, Thomas. (1651) 1997. *Leviathan*. New York: W.W. Norton.

Hogg, Peter W. 1997. *Constitutional Law of Canada*. Toronto: Carswell.

Hough, Franklin B. 1861. *Proceedings of the Commissioners of Indian Affairs*. Albany, NY: Joel Munsell.

Hunt, George T. 1940. *The Wars of the Iroquois: A Study of Intertribal Trade Relations*. Madison: University of Wisconsin Press.

Hurley, John. 1985. *Children or Brethren: Aboriginal Rights in Colonial Iroquoia*. Saskatoon, SK: University of Saskatchewan Native Law Centre, 1985.

Ignatieff, Michael. 1994. *Blood and Belonging: Journeys into the New Nationalism*. Toronto: Penguin.

Jacobs, Carol. 1995. "Presentation to the United Nations, July 18, 1995." *Akwesasne Notes* (Fall): 116–17.

Jemison, G. Peter. 1995. "Sovereignty and Treaty Rights: We Remember." *St. Thomas Law Review* 7 (Summer): 631–43.

Jennings, Francis. 1990. *The Ambiguous Iroquois Empire*. New York: W.W. Norton.

Jennings, Francis, ed. 1985. *The History and Culture of Iroquois Diplomacy: An Interdisciplinary Guide to the Treaties of the Six Nations and Their League*. Syracuse, NY: Syracuse University Press.

Johansen, Bruce. 1982. *Forgotten Founders: How the American Indian Helped Shape Democracy*. Boston: Harvard Common Press.

———. 1995. "Dating the Iroquois Confederacy." *Akwesasne Notes*, n.s. 1, no. 3–4: 62–63.

———. 1998. *Debating Democracy: Native American Legacy of Freedom*. Santa Fe, NM: Clear Light.

Johnson, William. 1921. *The Papers of Sir William Johnson*. Albany: University of the State of New York.

Johnston, Charles M. 1964. *The Valley of the Six Nations: A Collection of Documents on the Indian Lands of the Grand River*. Toronto: University of Toronto Press.

Jung, C.G. 1928. *Contributions to Analytical Psychology*, translated by H.G. and G.F. Baynes. New York: Harcourt Brace.

Keener, Craig, and Erica Kuhns. 1997. "The Impact of Iroquoian Populations on the Northern Distribution of Pawpaws in the Northeast." *North American Archaeologist* 18, no. 4: 327–42.

Keppler, Joseph. 1926. "Cayuga Adoption Custom." *Indian Notes* 3: 73–75.

Knox, Bernard. 1996. Introduction to *The Iliad*, by Homer. Translated by Robert Fagles. New York: Penguin.

Lafitau, Joseph Francois. (1724) 1974. *Customs of the American Indians*, edited by W.N. Fenton and Elizabeth Moore. Toronto: Champlain Society.

Largent, Floyd B. 1996. "Iroquois Chief and Union Officer." *America's Civil War* 9 (September): 54–60.

LeBlanc, Steven, and Katherine Register. 2003. *Constant Battles: Why We Fight, the Myth of the Peaceful, Noble Savage*. New York: St. Martin's Press.

Livingston, Robert. 1956. *The Livingston Indian Records, 1666–1723*. Gettysburg, PA: Pennsylvania Historical Association.

Lightall, W.D. 1899. *Hochelagans and Mohawks: A Link In Iroquois History*. Toronto: Copp-Clark.

Long, John. 1791. *Voyages and Travels of an Indian Interpreter and Trader*. London: n.p.

Longboat, Daniel (Rohoronhiakewen). 2007. "Owenna'shona: the Haudenosaunee Archipelago." PhD diss., York University, Toronto.

Loudon, Archibald. (1808) 1971. *A Selection of Some of the Most Interesting Narratives of Outrages Committed by the Indians in their Wars with the White People*. New York: Arno Press.

Lounsbury, Floyd. 2000. *The Oneida Creation Story, from Demas Elm and Harvey Antone*. Lincoln: University of Nebraska Press.

Lowrie, Walter, and Matthew Clarke, eds. 1832–34. American State Papers: Indian Affairs, 1789–1827. 2 vols. Washington: Gales and Seaton.

Lynch, James. 1985. "The Iroquois Confederacy and the Adoption and Administration of Non-Iroquoian Individuals and Groups Prior to 1756." *Man in the Northeast* 30: 83–99.

Lyons, Oren (Joagquisho). 1981. "Our Mother Earth." *Parabola* 6, no. 1: 91–93.

———. 1982. "When You Talk about Client Relationships, You Are Talking about the Future of Nations." In National Lawyers Guild, Committee on Native American Struggles, *Rethinking Indian Law*, iv–vii. New York: National Lawyers Guild.

————. 1992. "The American Indian in the Past." In *Exiled in the Land of the Free: Democracy, Indian Nations, and the U.S. Constitution*, edited by Chief Oren Lyons and John Mohawk, 13–42. Santa Fe: Clear Light, 1992. Santa Fe, NM: Clear Light.

Lytwyn, Victor P. 1997. "A Dish with One Spoon: The Shared Hunting Grounds Agreement Between First Nations in the St. Lawrence Valley and Great Lakes Region." *Papers of the 28th Algonquian Conference*, edited by David H. Pentland, 210–27. Winnipeg: University of Manitoba.

Mann, Barbara. 1995. "The Beloved Daughters of Jingosaseh." Paper Presented at 3rd Annual Meeting of the Group for Early Modern Cultural Studies, Dallas.

————. 2000. *Iroquoian Women: The Gantowisas*. New York: Peter Lang.

Mann, Barbara, and Jerry Fields. 1997. "A Sign in the Sky: Dating the Haudenosaunee." *American Indian Culture and Research Journal* 21, no. 2: 105–63.

Mann, Charles C. 2005. *1491: New Revelations of the Americas Before Columbus*. New York: Knopf.

————. 2007. "America, Found and Lost." *National Geographic* 212: 32–55.

Maracle, Kanatawakhon David. 2001. *Karoron Ne Owennahshonha: Mohawk Language Thematic Dictionary*. London, ON: Kenyen'keha Books.

Maybury-Lewis, David. 1992. *Millennium: Tribal Wisdom and the Modern World*. New York: Viking.

Mohawk, John C. (Sotsisowah). 1977. *Basic Call to Consciousness*. Akwesasne, NY: Akwesasne Notes.

————. 1987. "Cultural Encounter: Europe Meets the Indian Mind." *Northeast Indian Quarterly* 4, nos. 1–2: 10–17.

————. 1988. "The Indian Way Is a Thinking Tradition." *Northeast Indian Quarterly* 4, no. 4 and 5, no. 1.

————. 1989. "Origins of Iroquois Political Thought." In *New Voices from the Longhouse*, edited by Joseph Bruchac, 218–28. Greenfield Center, NY: Greenfield Review Press.

————. 1996. "A Native View of Nature." *Resurgence* 178 (Sept.–Oct.): 10–11.

————. 1999. *Utopian Legacies: A History of Conquest and Oppression in the Western World*. Santa Fe, NM: Clear Light.

————. 2004. "The Warriors Who Turned to Peace." *Yes! Magazine*. November. http:www.yes-magazine.org/issues/healing-resistance/the-warriors-who-turned-to-peace.

————. 2005a. *Iroquois Creation Story: John Arthur Gibson and J.N.B. Hewitt's "Myth of the Earth Grasper."* Buffalo, NY: Mohawk Publications.

————. 2005b. "What Can We Learn from Native America About War and Peace?: The Progressive Pragmatism of the Iroquois Confederacy." *Lapis Magazine Online*, n.d. http://arnieegel.blogspot.ca/2006/12/john-mohawk-what-can-we-learn-from.html.

Momaday, N. Scott. 1997. *Man Made of Words*. New York: St. Martin's Press.

Morgan, Lewis Henry. (1851) 1995. *League of the Ho-de-no-sau-nee or Iroquois*. North Dighton, MA: JG Press.

————. (1871) 1997. *Systems of Consanguinity and Affinity of the Human Family*. Lincoln: University of Nebraska Press.

————. 1877. *Ancient Society: Researches in the Lines of Human Progress from Savagery through Barbarism to Civilization*. London: MacMillan.

Murray, Louise W., ed. 1931. *Selected Manuscripts Relating to the Aboriginal History of the Susquehanna*. Publications of the Society for Pennsylvania Archaeology, vol. 1. Wilkes-Barre, PA: Society for Pennsylvania Archaeology.

Nabhan, Gary Paul. 1997. *Cultures of Habitat: On Nature, Culture, and Story*. Washington, DC: Counterpoint.

Native North American Travelling College. 2000. *Traditional Teachings*. Akwesasne, ON: Native North American Travelling College.

Nepo, Mark. 1995. "The Bridge of Well-Being: The Stranger, the Fellow, the Completing Other." *Parabola* 22, no. 2: 17–20.

Newhouse, Seth. 1885. "Cosmogony of Dekanawida's Government of the Iroquois Confederacy: The Original Literal Historical Narratives of the Iroquois Confederacy." LAC R7954-0-2-E.

———. 1898. "Constitution of the Confederacy by Dekanawidah." NAA ms 1343.

Newton, Michael. 2009. *Warriors of the Word: The World of the Scottish Highlanders*. Edinburgh: Birlinn.

Noon, John A. 1949. *Law and Government of the Grand River Iroquois*. Viking Fund Publications in Anthropology 12. New York: Viking Fund.

Norton, John. 1970. *The Journal of Major John Norton*, edited by Carl F. Klinck and James Talman. Toronto: Champlain Society.

Parker, Arthur C. Gawasowane. 1912. "Certain Iroquois Tree Myths and Symbols." *American Anthropologist* 14, no. 4: 608–20.

———. 1916. *The Constitution of the Five Nations*. New York State Museum Bulletin 184. Albany: University of the State of New York. https:babel.hathitrust.orgcgipt?id=coo1.ark:1 3960t5k93s71t;view=1up;seq=5.

———. 1918. "The Constitution of the Five Nations: A Reply." *American Anthropologist*, n.s. 20, no. 1: 120–24.

———. 1919. *The Life of General Ely S. Parker, Last Grand Sachem of the Iroquois and General Grant's Military Secretary*. Buffalo, NY: Buffalo Historical Society.

———. (1923) 1989. *Seneca Myths and Folk Tales*. Buffalo, NY: Buffalo Historical Society. Reprint, Lincoln: University of Nebraska Press.

———. 1940. *The Longhouse of the Iroquois and Its Rite of Adoption*. Typescript on birch paper. Arthur Caswell Parker Papers. University of Rochester Library, A.P23, Box 12.

———. 1968. *Iroquois Uses of Maize and other Food Plants*. Book 1 of *Parker on the Iroquois*, edited by W.N. Fenton. Syracuse, NY: Syracuse University Press.

Parker (Chiefs) 1916. See Parker 1916.

Parker (Newhouse and Cusick) 1916. See Parker 1916.

Parmenter, John. 2013. "The Meaning of Kaswentha and Two Row Wampum Belt in Haudenosaunee (Iroquois) History: Can Indigenous Oral Tradition Be Reconciled with the Historical Record?" *Journal of Early American History* 3: 82–109.

Pattison, Eliot. 2007. *Bone Rattler*. Berkeley, CA: Counterpoint.

Paul, Elizabeth. 2007. *The Stone Canoe: Two Lost Mi'kmaq Texts*. Kentville, NS: Gaspereau Press.

Perkl, Bradley. 1998. "Cucurbita Pepo from King Coulee, Southeastern Minnesota." *American Antiquity* 63, no. 2: 279–88.

Pilkington, Walter, ed. 1980. *Journals of Samuel Kirkland*. Clinton, NY: Hamilton College Press.

Pollan, Michael. 2008. *A Place of My Own: The Architecture of Daydreams*. New York: Penguin.

Porter, Tom Sakokwenonkwas. 1986. *Ceremonies*. Akwesasne: Akwesasne Communication Society.

———. 1988. "Men Who Are of the Good Mind." *Northeast Indian Quarterly* 4, no. 4 and 5, no. 1.

———. 1993. *Clanology*. Akwesasne: Native North American Travelling College.

Potier, Pierre. 1920. *Huron Manuscripts*. 15th Report of the Bureau of Archives for the Province of Ontario, 1918–1919. Toronto: Clarkson James.

Pukui, Mary Kawena, and Samuel H. Elbert. 1992. *Hawaiian Dictionary*. Honolulu: University Press of Hawaii.

Quammen, David. 1996. *The Song of the Dodo: Island Biogeography in an Age of Extinction*. New York: Simon and Schuster.

Randot, Antoine. 1904. *Relation par lettres de l'Amerique septentrionale*, edited by Camille de Rochmontie. Paris: Letouzay et Ainé.

Richter, Daniel K. 1982. *Rediscovered Links in the Covenant Chain: Previously Unpublished Transcripts of New York Indian Treaty Minutes, 1677–1691*, vol. 92, pt. 1 (April). Worcester MA: American Antiquarian Society.

———. 1987. "Ordeals of the Longhouse: The Five Nations in Early American History." In *Beyond the Covenant Chain: the Iroquois and Their Neighbors in Indian North America, 1600–1800*, edited by Daniel K. Richter and James H. Merrell, 11–27. Syracuse, NY: Syracuse University Press.

———. 1992. *The Ordeal of the Longhouse: the Peoples of the Iroquois League in the Era of European Colonization*. Chapel Hill: University of North Carolina Press.

RCAP (Royal Commission on Aboriginal Peoples). 1995. Ottawa: Queen's Printer.

Rudes, Blair. 1994. "J.N.B. Hewitt, Tuscarora Linguist." *Anthropological Linguistics* 36, no. 4: 467–83.

Russell, Emily. 1983. "Indian-Set Fires in the Forests of the Northeastern United States." *Ecology* 64, no. 1: 78–88.

Santiemma, Adriano. 1994. *L'Unione dei Cinquanta Cieli di Iroquoia*. Rome: Bulzoni Editore.

———. 1998. *In Viaggio Sul Sentero Irochese*. Rome: Bulzoni Editore.

Saul, John Ralston. 2008. *A Fair Country: Telling Truths about Canada*. Toronto: Penguin.

Schama, Simon. 1995. *Landscape and Memory*. Toronto: Random House.

Schimer, M. Rosarii. 1964. "Growth-Inhibiting Agents from Mercenaria Extracts: Chemical and Biological Properties." *Science* 144, no. 3617: 413–14.

Schoolcraft, Henry. 1856. *The Myth of Hiawatha and Other Mythological and Allegorical Tales of the North American Indians*. Philadelphia: Lipincott.

———. 1894. "Era of the Formation of the Historic League of the Iroquois." *American Anthropologist* 7: 61–67.

Shannon, Timothy J. 2000. *Indians and Colonists at the Crossroads of Empire: the Albany Congress of 1754*. Ithaca, NY: Cornell University Press.

Shenandoah, Audrey (Gonwaiannih). 2006. In *Wisdomkeepers: Meetings with Native American Spiritual Elders*, edited by Harvey Arden and Steve Wall, 24–27. New York: Simon and Schuster.

Shimony, Annemarie Anrod. 1961. *Conservatism Among the Iroquois at the Six Nations Reserve*. Yale University Publications in Anthropology 65. New Haven, CT: Department of Anthropology, Yale University.

Shoemaker, Nancy. 2010. *A Strange Likeness : Becoming Red and White in Eighteenth-Century North America*. New York: Oxford University Press.

Sivertsen, Barbara. 1997. *Turtles, Wolves and Bears: A Mohawk Family History*. Westminster, MD: Heritage Books.

Slobin, D. 1991. "Learning to Think for Speaking: Native Language, Cognition and Rhetorical Style." *Pragmatics* 1, no. 7: 26.

Snow, Dean. 1994. *The Iroquois*. Cambridge, MA: Blackwell.

Snow, Dean, Charles T. Gehring, and William Starna, eds. 1996. In *Mohawk Country: Early Narratives About a Native People*. Syracuse, NY: Syracuse University Press.

Snyderman, George. 1951. "Concepts of Land Ownership among the Iroquois and their Neighbours." *Bureau of American Ethnology Bulletin* 149: 13–34.

Stannard, David. 1992. *American Holocaust: The Conquest of the New World*. New York: Oxford University Press.

Stiles, Sara Henry. 1905. *Economics of the Iroquois*. Lancaster, PA: New Era Printing.

Stone, William L. 1841. *The Life and Times of Red Jacket*. New York: Wiley and Putnam.

Sturm, Circe. 2002. *Blood Politics: Race, Culture, and Identity in the Cherokee Nation of Oklahoma*. Berkeley: University of California Press.

Swamp, Jake (Tekaronianeken). 1997. *Giving Thanks: A Native Good Morning Message*. New York: Turtleback Books.

Taylor, Alan. 2006. *The Divided Ground: Indians, Settlers and the Northern Borderland of the American Revolution*. New York: Knopf.

Tedlock, Dennis. 1983. *The Spoken Word and the Work of Interpretation*. Philadelphia: University of Pennsylvania Press.

———. 1999. *Finding the Center: The Art of the Zuni Storyteller*, 2nd ed. Lincoln: University of Nebraska Press.

Thomas, Jacob. 2010. *Reading of the Great Law in Mohawk*. Transcribed by Tehahente Frank Miller.

Thomson, Charles. 1759. *An Enquiry into the Causes of the Alienation of the Delawares and Shawanese from the British Interest*. Philadelphia, PA: J. Campbell.

Thwaites, Reuben Gold, ed. 1901. *The Jesuit Relations and Allied Documents: Travels and Explorations of the Jesuit Missionaries in North America, 1610–1791*. Cleveland: Burrows Brothers.

Time-Life, eds. 1993. *Realm of the Iroquois*. Alexandria, VA: Time-Life Books.

Titley, E. Brian. 1986. *A Narrow Vision: Duncan Campbell Scott and the Administration of Indian Affairs in Canada*. Vancouver: University of British Columbia Press.

Tooker, Elisabeth. 1978. "The League of the Iroquois: Its History, Politics and Ritual." *Handbook of North American Indians*, vol. 15 (Northeast), edited by Bruce Trigger, 418–41. Washington, DC: Smithsonian Institution.

———. 2002. "Lewis H. Morgan and the Senecas." In *Strangers to Relatives: The Adoption and Naming of Anthropologists in Native North America*, edited by Sergei Kan, 29–56. Lincoln: University of Nebraska Press.

Trelease, Allen W. 1960. *Indian Affairs in Colonial New York*. Ithaca, NY: Cornell University Press.

Trigger, Bruce. 1976. *Children of Aataentsic*. Montreal: McGill-Queen's University Press.

Trigger, Bruce, ed. 1988. *Handbook of North American Indians*, vol. 15 (Northeast), Washington, DC: Smithsonian Institution.

Truth and Reconciliation Commission of Canada. 2015. "Canada's Residential Schools: Reconciliation." *Final Report*, vol. 6.

Tuchman, Barbara. 1978. *A Distant Mirror: The Calamitous 14th Century*. New York: Knopf.

Vachon, Robert. 1992. "The Mohawk Nation and its Communities." *Interculture* 25 (Winter): 14–20.

van den Bogaert, Harmen Meydertsz. 1991. *Narrative of a Journey into the Mohawk and Oneida Country, 1634–1635*, edited by William Starna. Syracuse, NY: Syracuse University Press.

Vecsey, Christopher. 1988. *Imagine Ourselves Richly*. New York: Crossroads.

Venables, Robert W. 2010. "The Clearings and the Woods: The Haudenosaunee (Iroquois) Landscape – Gendered and Balanced." In *Archaeology and Preservation of Gendered Landscapes*, edited by Sherene Baugher and Suzanne M. Spencer-Wood, 21–55. New York: Springer.

Viau, Roland. 1997. *Enfants du néant et mangeurs d'âmes: Guerre, culture et société en Iroquoisie ancienne*. Montreal: Editions Boreal.

———. 2000. *Femmes de Personne: Sexes, genres et Pouvoirs in Iroquoisie Ancienne*. Montreal: Editions Boreal.

Von Gernet, Alexander. 1996. *Oral Narratives and Aboriginal Pasts: An Interdisciplinary Review of the Literature on Oral Traditions and Oral Histories*. 2 vols. Ottawa: Department of Indian Affairs and Northern Development.

Wall, Steven. 2001. *To Become a Human Being: The Message of Tadodaho Chief Leon Shenandoah*. Charlottesville, VA: Hampton Roads.

Wallace, Anthony F.C. 1969. *The Death and Rebirth of the Seneca*. New York: Knopf.

Wallace, Paul A.W. (Toriwawakon). 1946. *The White Roots of Peace: The Iroquois Book of Life*. Port Washington, NY: Ira J. Friedman.

———. 1948. "The Return of Hiawatha." *New York History* 29, no. 4.

———. 1971. *Indian Paths of Pennsylvania*. Harrisburg: Pennsylvania Historical and Museum Commission.

Wallis, Wilson D. 1941. "Alexander A. Goldenweiser." *American Anthropologist* 43: 250–55.

Warrick, Gary. 1996. "Evolution of the Iroquoian Longhouse." In *People Who Lived in Big Houses: Archaeological Perspectives on Large Domestic Structures*, edited by G. Coupland and E.B. Banning, 11–26. Madison, WI: Prehistory Press

Weaver, Sally. 1984. "Seth Newhouse and the Grand River." In *Extending the Rafters: Interdisciplinary Approaches to Iroquoian Studies*, edited by M.K. Foster et al., 165–82. Albany, State University of New York Press.

White, Leslie A. 1957. "How Morgan Came to Write Systems of Consanguinity and Affinity." *Papers of the Michigan Academy of Science, Arts and Letters* 42: 257–68.

White, Richard, and William Cronon. 1988. "Ecological Change and Indian-White Relations." *Handbook of North American Indians*, vol. 4 (History of Indian-White Relations), edited by William C Sturtevant, 417–29. Washington, DC: Smithsonian Institution.

Williams, Gayoh:no Karenna. 2010. "Hadu:wis: Repatriation Efforts of the Haudenosaunee in the United States and Canada." *Indigenous Law Bulletin* 7, no. 17: 17–20.

Williams, Kaseneyohsta Lauren. 2007. "Oral Tradition and Memory: The Catalogue of Ships in the *Iliad* and the Haudenosaunee Condolence Speech." MA thesis, University of Bristol.

Williams, Paul. 1996. "Oral Tradition on Trial." In *Gin Das Winan: Documenting Aboriginal History in Ontario*, edited by Dale Standen and David McNab, 29–34. Occasional Papers 2. Toronto: Champlain Society.

Williams, Paul Kayanesenh, and Arihote Curtis Nelson. 1994. *Kaswentha*. Ottawa: Royal Commission on Aboriginal Peoples.

Williams, Robert A. 1999. *Linking Arms Together: American Indian Treaty Visions of Law and Peace, 1600–1800*. New York: Routledge.

Wilson, Gilbert L. (1917) 1987. *Buffalo Bird Woman's Garden: Agriculture of the Hidatsa Indians*. St. Paul: Minnesota Historical Society Press.

Wrangham, Richard. 1997. *Demonic Males: Apes and the Origin of Human Violence*. London: Bloomsbury.

Wraxall, Peter. (1754) 1915. *Wraxall's Abridgment of the New York Indian Records, 1678–1751*. Edited by C.H. McIlwain. Cambridge, MA: Harvard University Press.

Wright, Asher. 1859. "Seneca Indians." *Ethnohistory* 4, no. 3: 302–21.

Wright, James V. 1972. *Ontario Prehistory: An Eleven-Thousand-Year Archaeological Outline*, Ottawa: National Museum of Man.

Wright, Joyce M. 1999. *Numbers: A Message From the Past*. London, ON: London Museum of Archaeology.

Wright, Ronald. 2011. *A Short History of Progress*. Toronto: House of Anansi.

Wykoff, William M. 1991. "Black Walnut on Iroquoian Landscapes." *Northeast Indian Quarterly* 8, no. 2: 4–17.

York, Geoffrey, and Loreen Pindera. 1991. *People of the Pines: The People and the Legacy of Oka*. Toronto: Little, Brown.

Court Decisions

Almrei v. Canada (MCI), DES-5-01 (F.C.T.D.).

Attorney General of Ontario v. Bear Island Foundation, [1985] 1 CNLR 1.

Benoit v. Canada (Minister of National Revenue), 2003 FCA 236.

Blueberry River Band v. The Queen, [1995] 4 SCR 344.

Daniels v. Canada (Indian Affairs and Northern Development)], [2016] 1 SCR 99.

Delgamuukw v. Attorney General of British Columbia, [1997] 3 SCR 1010.

Doe v. Kamehameha Schools, US Court of Appeals, 9th Circuit 8921 (2005).

Doe dem. Jackson v. Wilkes (1835), 4 UCKB (OS) 142.

Edwards v. Attorney General of Canada, [1930] AC 124.

Guerin v. The Queen, [1985] 2 SCR 387.

Halpern v. Canada (2003), 65 OR (3d) 161.

Hamlet of Baker Lake v. The Queen (1980) 107 DLR (3rd) 513.

Hunter v. Southam, Inc., [1984] 2 SCR 145.

Isaac v. Davey, [1977] 2 SCR 897.

Jones v. Meehan, 175 US 1 (1899).

Mabo v. Queensland (1992), 175 CLR 1 (Australian High Court).

Mikisew Cree First Nation v. Canada, [2005] 3 SCR 388.

Mitchell (Kanentakeron) v. Minister of National Revenue, [2001] 1 SCR 911.

Onondaga Nation v. Thacher, 189 US 306 (1903).

People v. Neil Patterson Jr. (New York Court of Appeals, June 14, 2005).

Re Quebec Secession, [1982] 2 SCR 17.

R. v. Adams, [1996] 3 SCR 101.

R. v. Badger, [1996] 1 SCR 771.

R. v. Gladstone, [1996] 2 SCR 723.

R. v. Ireland, [1991] 1 OR 3d 577.

R. v. Marshall, [1999] 3 SCR 456.

R. v. Marshall; R. v. Bernard, [2005] 2 SCR 220.

R. v. NTC Smokehouse, [1996] 2 SCR 672.

R. v. Powley, [2003] 2 SCR 207.

R. v. Sioui, [1990] 2 SCR 1025.

R. v. Sparrow, [1990] 1 SCR 1075.

R. v. Syliboy, [1929] 1 DLR 307 (Nova Scotia County Court).

R. v. Taylor and Williams, [1981] 34 OR (2d) 360.

R. v. Van der Peet, [1996] 2 SCR 507.

Rice v. Cayetano, 528 US 495 (2000).

Secretary of State (Indian Association of Alberta), [1982] 2 All ER 118.

Seneca Nation v. Charles E. Appleby. Rochester Democrat & Chronicle, 1907. Rochester, NY: Buffalo Historical Society.

Southern Rhodesia, Re, [1919] AC 211 (JC).
Swans (The Case of), Court of King's Bench, Trinity Term, 1592.
Worcester v. Georgia, 6 Pet. (31 US) 515 (1832).

Index